Wynar's
Introduction to
Cataloging and
Classification

Library and Information Science Text Series

The School Library Media Center. 5th ed. By Emanuel T. Prostano and Joyce S. Prostano

Library and Information Center Management. 5th ed. By Robert D. Stueart and Barbara B. Moran

The Academic Library: Its Context, Its Purpose, and Its Operation. By John M. Budd

The Social Sciences: A Cross-Disciplinary Guide to Selected Sources. 2d ed. Nancy L. Herron, General Editor

Introduction to United States Government Information Sources. 6th ed. By Joseph Morehead

The Economics of Information: A Guide to Economic and Cost-Benefit Analysis for Information Professionals. By Bruce R. Kingma

Reference and Information Services: An Introduction. 2d ed. Richard E. Bopp and Linda C. Smith, General Editors

Developing Library and Information Center Collections. 4th ed. By G. Edward Evans with the assistance of Margaret R. Zarnosky

The Collection Program in Schools: Concepts, Practices, and Information Sources. 2d ed. By Phyllis J. Van Orden

Information Sources in Science and Technology. 3d ed. By C.D. Hurt

Introduction to Technical Services. 6th ed. By G. Edward Evans and Sandra M. Heft

The School Library Media Manager. 2d ed. By Blanche Woolls

The Humanities: A Selective Guide to Information Sources. 5th ed. By Ron Blazek and Elizabeth Aversa

Introduction to Library Public Services. 6th ed. By G. Edward Evans, Anthony J. Amodeo, and Thomas L. Carter

A Guide to the Library of Congress Classification 5th ed. By Lois Mai Chan

The Organization of Information. By Arlene G. Taylor

Systems Analysis for Librarians and Information Professionals. 2d ed. By Larry N. Osborne and Margaret Nakamura

Wynar's Introduction to Cataloging and Classification. 9th ed. By Arlene G. Taylor

Arlene G. Taylor

Wynar's Introduction to Cataloging and Classification

NINTH EDITION

with the assistance of
David P. Miller

2000
LIBRARIES UNLIMITED, INC.
Englewood, Colorado

LIBRARIES UNLIMITED, INC.
P.O. Box 6633
Englewood, CO 80155-6633
1-800-237-6124
www.lu.com

Library of Congress Cataloging-in-Publication Data

Taylor, Arlene G., 1941-
  Wynar's introduction to cataloging and classification-- 9th ed. / Arlene G. Taylor ; with the assistance of David P. Miller.
    p. cm. -- (Library and information science text series)
  Includes bibliographical references and index.
  ISBN 1-56308-494-5 -- ISBN 1-56308-857-6 (pbk.)
    1. Cataloging. 2. Anglo-American cataloguing rules. 3. Classification--Books. I. Title: Introduction to cataloging and classification. II. Miller, David P. III. Wynar, Bohdan S. Introduction to cataloging and classification. IV. Title. V. Series.

Z693.W94 2000
025.3--dc21

                                                                        00-030932

Contents

Part IV
SUBJECT ANALYSIS

Part V
AUTHORITY CONTROL

Part VI
ADMINISTRATIVE ISSUES

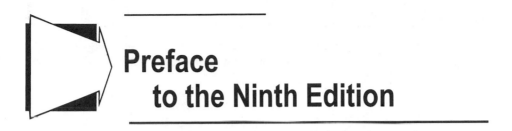

Preface
to the Ninth Edition

Since the publication of the eighth edition of this text in 1992 there have been changes in almost all areas of the organization of information, both in general and in cataloging and classification in particular. The world of information has changed radically with the advent of the World Wide Web. Not only are cataloging tools now much more readily available, but completely new ways of thinking about organizing information are the subjects of experimentation. Catalogs, still with a majority in card format in 1992, are now available internationally on the World Wide Web. These and other changes have made the task of revision formidable; nevertheless, the revision is now as up-to-date as possible given the constraints of human understanding and the passage of time between writing and publication.

There are a number of changes in this edition in addition to updating. Chapter 3, "Encoding," is a new chapter in this text, having been treated only in an appendix in the eighth edition. With emphasis on encoding with *MARC 21*, the chapter is an introduction to the area of encoding data for the purpose of being read by computer so that the data can be displayed online.

A major conceptual shift in description of resources occurs in the discussion of the rules for description in chapter 4, "Description." It is now divided according to the eight areas of the International Standard Bibliographic Description (ISBD), rather than according to type of material being cataloged. There is such a proliferation in ways in which information can be presented that it seems appropriate to concentrate on presentation in a catalog record of the identifying data that will clearly describe information packages and aid in the provision of access to information packages, rather than to concentrate upon the physical manifestations of the information packages. The work of combining the former chapters on description in general, description of books, description of nonbook materials, and description of serials, and, at the same time, of updating information about the rules and including cataloging of Internet resources, has been ably accomplished by my colleague, David P. Miller, Levin Library, Curry College. Mr. Miller also updated the chapters covering analytic materials, choice of access points, and form of headings for names and titles.

The subject analysis chapters have also been thoroughly revised. New discussion of natural language processing and ontologies has been added, and discussion of classification of Internet resources is included. The chapter for Dewey Decimal Classification has been updated for the 21st edition, and the section on Universal

Decimal Classification has been completely rewritten to reflect the changes in the 1990s in administration of that scheme. Most of the Library of Congress Classification schedules have been revised since the eighth edition, and the current chapter reflects the new revisions. In the area of verbal subject access the chapters on *Library of Congress Subject Headings* and *Sears List of Subject Headings* have been completely revised to reflect the changes in terminology, attitudes, and approaches manifested in the most recent editions of those lists. Discussion of the *Art and Architecture Thesaurus* was added to the chapter on other types of verbal access, along with updating to the newest editions of the other thesauri described there.

Considerations of authority control have been updated to reflect current concerns with international access control, where thought must be given to various cultural and verbal traditions that differ from each other. None can be considered to be superior, and ways must be found to integrate these different approaches into one means of access to all the world's information.

The chapters entitled "Processing Centers, Networking, and Cooperative Programs" and "Catalog Management" have been completely rewritten. The changes in these areas have been very dramatic indeed, and the new chapters reflect much new work at the Library of Congress and by bibliographic utilities along with completely new ways of accomplishing the control of catalogs. New sections on outsourcing, online catalogs, workstations, and arrangement issues have been added.

The old discussion on filing rules was relegated to an appendix, but was kept because issues of arrangement of the order in which catalog records are displayed to users can be a major concern in the use of online catalogs. The glossary includes many new terms, reflecting the major changes in the world of information since 1992. Other definitions in the glossary have been updated.

Examples of MARC records used in this edition are shown in the format that is displayed in OCLC's PRISM system. I am grateful to OCLC for permission to use its format in this book.

There are a number of people whose assistance I wish to acknowledge. Again, I acknowledge the work of David P. Miller in updating and consolidating the chapters related to *AACR2R*. The project would have taken much longer without his assistance.

Two of the chapters were largely rewritten by others whom I wish to acknowledge. Chapter 19, "Processing Centers, Networking, and Cooperative Programs," was revised and updated, with new material added, by Barbara B. Tillett, Library of Congress. She had some assistance from Sally McCallum and Kathryn Mendenhall, both of the Library of Congress, to whom I am also very grateful. Chapter 20, "Catalog Management" (with the exception of the section on "Outsourcing"), was revised and updated, and new material added, by Susan Hayes, Bobst Library, New York University. The section on outsourcing was written by Katherine Ryner, Library, Dowling College. Ms. Ryner was also of great assistance in updating the suggested readings for many of the chapters. For all the assistance from Dr. Tillett, Ms. Hayes, and Ms. Ryner, I am deeply grateful.

I was assisted in the completion of chapter 11, "Library of Congress Classification (LCC)," by Patricia Beam, Pittsburgh Theological Seminary Library. Ms. Beam allowed me access to the updated LCC schedules that are published by The Gale Group, and I would like to acknowledge her assistance in use of these schedules.

Chapter 16, *Sears List of Subject Headings*, could not have been completed without the assistance of Joseph Miller, current editor of *Sears*, who works for the H. W. Wilson Co. Mr. Miller went over my chapter with its new revisions very carefully and made many suggestions for improvements.

Two current users of the text were kind enough to send me suggestions for improvements to the text, and I appreciate their thoughtfulness. They are Alva Stone, Florida State University Library, and David Weisbrod, School of Information and Library Science, Pratt Institute. Their suggestions were quite helpful. Two other people who assisted with answering my many questions were Lynn El-Hoshy, Cataloging Policy and Support Office, Library of Congress, and Ammon Ripple, Information Sciences Library, University of Pittsburgh. I appreciate their assistance immensely.

I am most grateful to my husband, A. Wayne Benson, for his ability to understand and accept that projects such as this one can totally consume my time and energy. His patience, encouragement, and "wordsmithing" are acknowledged and deeply appreciated.

I continue to appreciate the opportunity afforded me by Bohdan S. Wynar to work on this text. Finally, I wish to thank Carmel Huestis, Kay Minnis, and other members of the editorial/production staff of Libraries Unlimited for their major contributions to this work.

—Arlene G. Taylor

Part I
INTRODUCTION

1 Cataloging in Context

INTRODUCTION

The purposes of this chapter are to set the context in which cataloging takes place and to introduce the basic concepts of cataloging. The discussion begins with an introduction to the whole realm of bibliographic control and where catalogs fit into that realm. Catalogs are discussed, with attention given to their functions, their forms, arrangements of their entries, and their component parts. An overview of the entire process of cataloging is then given—descriptive cataloging, subject analysis, and authority control—followed by a look at cooperative and copy cataloging that makes original cataloging of all materials for every collection unnecessary. Finally, there is an introduction to the formats of bibliographic records in catalogs.

BIBLIOGRAPHIC CONTROL

Definitions

Cataloging is a subset of the larger field that is sometimes called bibliographic control, or organization of information, and it is helpful to view it in that context. Bibliographic control has been defined by Elaine Svenonius as "the skill or art . . . of organizing knowledge (information) for retrieval."[1] Richard P. Smiraglia defines it as "encompassing the creation, storage, manipulation, and retrieval of bibliographic data."[2] Arlene G. Taylor, in *The Organization of Information*, points out that "retrieval of information is dependent upon its having been organized." She goes on to say that "organization of information also allows us to keep a usable record of human endeavors for posterity."[3]

Anyone who has attempted to maintain a file of references to articles, books, and other types of materials containing information on a particular subject, or perhaps by a particular artist or author, has practiced bibliographic control over a very small part of the universe of information/knowledge. For such a project to succeed it is necessary to decide what pieces of data to record about each article, book, or other container of information/knowledge, referred to hereinafter as *information package*. Taylor defines information package as "an instance of recorded information (e.g., book, article, videocassette, Internet document or set of 'pages,' sound recording, electronic journal, etc.)."[4] It may be decided to record author(s), title, keywords, abstract, and location of the information package. These become the bibliographic data to be created, stored, manipulated, and retrieved. As the file grows, storing, manipulating, and retrieving become more and more complex. Then, art and skill become necessary for successful maintenance and use of the file.

In the universe of all knowledge (including knowledge that cannot necessarily be expressed verbally—e.g., music, art) there is a certain amount of that knowledge that has been recorded in some way—e.g., written down, printed, digitized, taped, painted. This subset is often referred to as the bibliographic universe. Only the bibliographic universe can be controlled. Such control is performed by means of bibliographic tools in which each discrete item of knowledge is represented by a bibliographic record (also sometimes called an *entry* or *surrogate record* or *metadata*). Bibliographic tools (which are also *retrieval tools*) include bibliographies, indexes, catalogs, finding aids, registers, and bibliographic databases. We have been told by futurists that someday when all recorded information/knowledge is digitized and available online, it will be possible to gain access to needed information directly online without the intermediate step of using bibliographic tools. More and more, though, experts have realized that there must be some kind of control and some way to have preliminary information (e.g., title, author, date, subject keywords, etc.) before one tries to sort through thousands of information packages. The creation of a number of metadata standards is a result. Taylor defines *metadata* as "an encoded description of an information package (e.g., an *AACR2* [*Anglo-American Cataloguing Rules, Second Edition*] record encoded with MARC [MAchine-Readable Cataloging], a Dublin Core record, a GILS [Government Information Locator Service] record, etc.)."[5]

Component Parts of Bibliographic Control

Librarians and library users have traditionally been taught that bibliographies, indexes, catalogs, etc., are quite different tools. In fact they are all parts of the same realm of bibliographic control, but they have developed separately and in somewhat different formats for various reasons. Economic factors have been pervasive in the development of catalogs in libraries. Because libraries are generally not-for-profit agencies, there have seldom been enough resources to allow library catalogs to provide access deeper than what might be called "macrolevel indexing"—i.e., access to a whole book, entire serial, etc. Other agencies have stepped in to create indexes with what might be called "microlevel indexing"—i.e., access to articles in serials, poetry in collections, chapters in books, etc. These are sold for profit, while access to library catalogs generally has not been sold. (There are also indexes that analyze the contents of a single item—e.g., "back-of-the-book" indexes—but these are usually published at the same time as the item rather than being prepared separately for the purposes of bibliographic control.)

Economic constraints have also dictated generally that library catalogs could index only materials owned and housed in that particular library, and in this sense each one has been a microcosm of the entire bibliographic universe. On the other hand, periodical indexes have covered items owned and not owned by the library, or a larger portion of the bibliographic universe. Bibliographies typically cover much smaller parts of the universe than either catalogs or indexes. That is, each bibliography usually has one subject or theme—e.g., works of an author, works on a particular subject, items published during a particular time or in a particular place. (Subsets of this category include discographies and art catalogs.) Because of their limited scope, bibliographies can easily include entries at both macro- and microlevels.

In the recent past technology has enabled bibliographic databases to be developed without the earlier economic constraints that limited the level of indexing. Many online bibliographic databases are enhanced indexes. That is, they provide microlevel indexing of bibliographic entities and provide more bibliographic data for each item indexed—e.g., more keywords, abstracts. There are also a number of bibliographic databases that provide primarily macrolevel indexing and function as extended catalogs.

Finding aids have been developed in archives as lengthy surrogate records for whole collections housed by an archive. In archives a catalog record is often made for each finding aid. Registers have been developed in museums and provide the means for maintaining control over the artifacts housed in a museum. The Internet now has retrieval tools called "search engines." Most of these so far do not create surrogate records ahead of time, but create them "on-the-fly" as requests are made by users. *Yahoo!* is an exception to this.

An important feature of catalogs is that they typically have some kind of authority control, while the other tools typically have little or no such control over names and titles, although they often have some control over subject terms used. Authority control is, in part, the process of maintaining consistency in the form of the headings in a bibliographic tool. A heading is the character string provided at the beginning of an entry in a bibliographic tool and provides one means for finding that entry. In some printed tools and in most computer systems the heading is provided at the top of a column, page, or screen on which several entries for the heading may appear. In a tool with authority control the heading is given in the "official" form representing a name, title, or subject. Authority control is defined and discussed in more detail later in this chapter.

One difficulty with the fragmentation of bibliographic control into different bibliographic tools is that users are expected to know about the existence of all of them and to be able to use them effectively. This is a somewhat unreasonable expectation since the tools overlap in their coverage of the bibliographic universe but provide their coverage in different ways. Approaches to searching the tools differ, as do the vocabularies used for searching. Once desired entries are found, conventions for displaying bibliographic data differ. In tools where there is no authority control, one cannot know whether all possible forms of a name, title, or term have been found. In an ideal bibliographic control environment a user could start with any tool and be led to other tools as needed without having to know ahead of time which tool would be appropriate.

Functions of Bibliographic Tools

Bibliographic tools have three basic functions. The first is the identifying or finding function. All tools aim at allowing a user, who has a citation or has a particular bibliographic item in mind, to match that known item with an entry in the tool—limited, of course, by the scope of the tool. The scope of a library catalog, for example, is often the items owned by the institution; therefore, the user should be able to match or identify or find an entry for a known item that the library owns, but not for one that the library does not own.

The second function is the collocating or gathering function. Collocation is a means for bringing together in one place in a bibliographic tool all entries for like and closely related materials; for example, items about dinosaurs are grouped together. In many cases a particular work is shown in its relationship to a larger group of works—e.g., the bibliographic record for a play based upon *Huckleberry Finn* should be found with records for editions of *Huckleberry Finn*, which are in turn found with records for other works of Mark Twain. One of the best ways of accomplishing collocation is through the process of authority control. If entries for *Huckleberry Finn* are sometimes found in the H's (under *Huckleberry Finn*) and sometimes in the A's (under *Adventures of Huckleberry Finn*) with no connecting references, collocation has not been accomplished.

The third function of bibliographic tools is the evaluating or selecting function. This function allows a user to choose from among many records or entries the one that best seems to represent the knowledge/information or specific physical item desired. For example, a user looking for a particular edition of *Huckleberry Finn* should be able to select it from among several, if it is one of those listed in the tool; or, given a choice between a spoken recording on tape or disc, a user could choose the one appropriate for the equipment available. It can be seen that the three functions are somewhat interdependent.

Uses of Bibliographic Control

Catalogers, indexers, abstractors, bibliographers, and information scientists establish bibliographic control over portions of the bibliographic universe. Reference librarians, readers' advisers, and information specialists create a bridge between the user and the many bibliographic tools available. The institutional library is a major focus of these activities, but not the only one. Archives, museums, the Internet, individual freelance efforts, and commercial enterprises also play a role.[6]

The bibliographic tool *created* in the institutional library is the catalog, although extensive *use* is made of all the bibliographic tools in that setting. *Groups* of libraries work together to create some of the online databases—those that are essentially extended catalogs for the holdings of more than one library. The remainder of this book concentrates on the processes involved in creating, maintaining, and providing access to catalogs and catalog-like databases.

CATALOGS

Definition and Functions

A catalog is an organized set of bibliographic records that represent the holdings of a particular collection. A collection may consist of any of several types of materials—e.g., books, periodicals, maps, coins, sound recordings, paintings, musical scores, to name a few. Traditionally the collection represented by a catalog has been located in one place or at least in different parts of the same institution. Increasingly, however, catalogs represent the holdings of more than one library, as libraries form consortiums and otherwise link their catalogs for the purposes of interlibrary sharing. (Such catalogs are sometimes called union catalogs.) In addition catalogs increasingly include Internet resources that are not owned, but to which the library can provide access.

Why prepare catalogs? Catalogs are necessary whenever a collection grows too large to be remembered item for item. A small private library or a classroom library has little need for a formal catalog; the user can recall each book, sound recording, map, or other such item by author, title, subject, the item's shape, its color, or its position on a particular shelf. When such a collection becomes a little larger, an informal arrangement, such as grouping the items by subject categories, provides access to them. When a collection becomes too large for such a simple approach, a formal record is necessary. There are two major reasons to make such a formal record in larger collections: for retrieval and for inventory purposes. In addition to being unable to remember what is in a large collection for access purposes, it also becomes impossible for the owner to remember what has been acquired, lost, replaced, etc. A catalog can serve as a record of what is owned.

The functions of bibliographic control identified earlier—identifying, collocating, evaluating—are functions of every bibliographic tool, including catalogs. These functions for catalogs were first stated by Charles A. Cutter in his *Rules for a Dictionary Catalog* in 1904. His statement serves as the basis for today's understanding of the functions of a catalog, although in modern practice the statement is somewhat incomplete:

Objects
1. To enable a person to find a book of which either
   (A) the author
   (B) the title   } is known.
   (C) the subject

2. To show what the library has
   (D) by a given author
   (E) on a given subject
   (F) in a given kind of literature.

3. To assist in the choice of a book
   (G) as to the edition (bibliographically).
   (H) as to its character (literary or topical).

Means
1. Author-entry with the necessary references (for A and D).
2. Title-entry or title-reference (for B).
3. Subject-entry, cross-references, and classed subject-table (for C and E).
4. Form-entry and language-entry (for F).
5. Giving edition and imprint, with notes when necessary (for G).
6. Notes (for H).[7]

To conform to modern practice, the first objective needs to be rephrased as follows: To enable a person to find any intellectual creation whether issued in a print, nonprint, or electronic format. Cutter's first object is inadequate even for printed materials inasmuch as "book" does not unambiguously encompass "periodical," "serial," or "pamphlet."

Cutter's object "e" also does not go far enough for our current understanding. Rephrased, it should read "on given and related subjects." It is clearly a prime function of a catalog to guide patrons in using the system of subject headings that any particular library may have adopted. Cutter's apparent assumption that the user always has a clearly formulated "given" subject in mind is contrary to all observation of catalog users.

Cutter's objectives remained the primary statement of catalog principles until 1961, when the International Federation of Library Associations (IFLA) at the Paris

Conference approved a statement about the purpose of an author/title catalog. It stated that the catalog should be an efficient instrument for ascertaining:

1) whether the library contains a particular book specified by:
   a) its author and title, *or*
   b) if no author is named in the book, its title alone, *or*
   c) if author and title are inappropriate or insufficient for identification, a suitable substitute for the title,

and 2) a) which works by a particular author *and*
   b) which editions of a particular work are in the library.[8]

These principles, often called the "Paris Principles," were purposely restricted to an author/title catalog, and so no mention is made of subject access; but they, as well as Cutter's rules, bring out the three functions already mentioned of identifying (1.a–1.c), collocating (2.a–2.b), and evaluating (2.b). In both Cutter's statement and the Paris Principles, the evaluating function is limited to choice of edition and to Cutter's "choice of a book . . . as to its character." With time and the advent of multiple ways of presenting the same work, both intellectually and physically, it has become more important to make certain that the catalog can assist in making choices. This continues a long history of evolution of functions of the catalog.

A fourth function served by a catalog is that of locating, a function not often served by other bibliographic tools. One can tell from a library catalog whether the library contains a certain information package and, if so, where it is physically located. This is true even of expanded interlibrary union catalogs in the sense that the catalog identifies which libraries house particular items, although one may need more detail to know where in a particular library to find an item. Recently, it became possible for catalogs to give the virtual locations of Internet information packages through their uniform resource locators (URLs).

Forms of Catalogs

Presently, the library catalog exists in one of several physical formats: book catalog, card catalog, microform catalog, or online computer catalog. Online computer catalogs may take the form of text-based interface or graphical user interface (GUI). The printed book catalog is the oldest type known in the United States; it was used by many American libraries as the most common form of catalog until the late 1800s. The report of the Bureau of Education in 1876 gives a list of 1,010 printed book catalogs, 382 of them published from 1870 to 1876. Because the book catalogs were rather expensive to produce and quickly became outdated, they were gradually replaced by card catalogs. In a survey of 58 typical American libraries undertaken in 1893, 43 libraries had complete card catalogs and 13 had printed book catalogs with card supplements.[9] Thus, for many years book catalogs were out of favor in American libraries.

It was only with more modern, cheaper methods of printing and with the advent of automation for quicker cumulation that book catalogs again became popular with certain types of libraries. An example of a book catalog produced by more modern production techniques was the Library of Congress's (LC) *Catalog of Books Represented by Library of Congress Printed Cards*, known since 1956 as the *National Union Catalog*. It is now published only in microform. As its earlier title indicates, it was, for many years, produced by photographic reduction of pre-existing catalog cards; hence, it was a by-product of a card catalog. A similar technique has been used by a number of commercial publishers (e.g., G. K. Hall), which have reproduced card catalogs of certain libraries in a book catalog format.

Beginning in the 1950s, a new type of book catalog appeared, based on the use of computers. These computer-produced catalogs, using machine-readable cataloging records, varied widely in format, typography, extent of bibliographic detail, and pattern of updating. LC began publishing its book catalog series via computer in the 1970s.

At the beginning of the 1990s the card catalog was still the library catalog most often found in the United States. It is still found in libraries that have not been able to afford the software and equipment necessary for an online catalog, and it is also found in libraries that have not been able to complete the retrospective conversion of records from card format to machine-readable format. Each entry was prepared on a standard 7.5 cm x 12.5 cm card (roughly 3"x 5"), although the size was not always standard. In the first card catalogs a variety of sizes was used from library to library, including 1½" x 5", 1½" x 10", and 4" x 6". Entries on cards were at first handwritten before the typewriter came into standard use. Typeset cards were available from LC beginning in 1901. Later, cards were often prepared by photoreproduction of a printed or typed original. Cards are now most often computer-produced from machine-readable catalog records.

Microform catalogs became much more popular with the development of computer output microform (COM). COM catalogs are produced in either microfilm or microfiche. It is feasible with this form of catalog to provide a completely integrated new catalog every three months or so, rather than providing supplements to be used with a main catalog.

The online computer catalog, often referred to as an online public access catalog (or OPAC), has rapidly become the catalog of choice. Bibliographic records stored in the computer memory are displayed on a video screen in response to a request from a user. Entries may comprise the full bibliographic record or only parts of it, depending on the system and/or the desires of the user. Until the 1990s such systems were costly, and only very large libraries were able to afford them.

Now systems have been developed for use on every size computer from mainframes to personal computers and have become quite affordable. There are so many choices of systems with operations and retrievals configured so differently that many librarians are finding it difficult to choose among them. Our current era resembles the time before the standardization of the card catalog, when sizes of cards and order of elements of bibliographic data differed from library to library. As we learn what works best, OPACs will eventually become standardized as did card catalogs.

An effective catalog in any format should possess certain qualities that will allow it to be easily consulted and maintained. If it is too difficult, too cumbersome, or too expensive, it is virtually useless. Hence the following comparative criteria exist for judging a catalog:

- **A catalog should be flexible and up-to-date.** A library's collection is constantly changing. Since the catalog is a record of what is available in that library, entries should be added or removed as items are added to or discarded from the collection. The card catalog and the OPAC are totally flexible. Records can be easily added to or removed from the files whenever necessary. However, backlogs of records to be entered can develop, especially with card catalogs.

Book, COM, and compact disk-read only memory (CD-ROM) catalogs are inflexible in that once they have been printed, they cannot admit additions or deletions except in supplements or new editions of the catalog. On the other hand, because they are computer-produced, they can provide flexibility in making changes in existing entries. For example, a single command can change many entries, while with a card catalog, each change must be made individually. OPACs can be considered the most flexible and current of all catalog formats if bibliographic records are stored on read/write disks quickly accessible to the memory. Additions, deletions, and changes can be made at any time, and the results are often instantly available to the user, or at least are available by the next day.

- **A catalog should be constructed so that all entries can be quickly and easily found.** This is a matter of labeling, filing, and, in the case of online catalogs, simple and clear screen instructions. So far as the card catalog is concerned, the contents of each tray must be identified to the extent that a patron who wants to locate, for example, the works of Charles Dickens can find the Dickens entries easily. The patron must know exactly what part of the alphabet each tray contains. Within the trays themselves, arrangement of entries must be such that items are not overlooked because the filing is not alphabetical, and guide cards should be sufficiently plentiful to identify coverage. Book catalogs are usually labeled on the spine, like encyclopedias. Often they have guides at the top of each page, indicating what entries are covered there.

Microfilm catalogs typically are stored in readers that are equipped with alphabetic index strips designed to get the user to the desired part of the alphabet. Microfiche catalogs have at the top of each sheet of fiche eye-readable labels that indicate the part of the alphabet covered. Typically, each sheet of fiche has a microimage index in one corner that tells in which cross section of the fiche particular parts of the alphabet are found. Such systems are time-consuming to use, and reading the magnified fiche is often difficult. Many patrons will do almost anything to avoid using a microfiche catalog.

Filing arrangement in computer-produced catalogs is not the same as in traditionally filed card catalogs because of the difficulty of programming computers to arrange according to traditional library filing rules. As a result, traditional rules have been re-evaluated, and new filing rules closely resemble computer filing rules.

Entries are located in online catalogs in a variety of ways. In some the computer must be told whether an author, title, or subject search is desired. A few systems, still require the user to construct "search keys" made up of combinations of letters and/or words. For example, a title search key may consist of the first three letters of the first word that is not an article plus the first letter of each of the next three words. In other systems one can enter as much of the title, author, or subject as seems useful, starting at the left of the entry as it would appear in a card catalog. Still other systems allow users to input only the words they remember in any order (called *keyword* searching), and the system searches for all records containing all the words input. The most recently created systems allow sophisticated combinations of searching certain words from an author field, other words from a title field, words from a subject field, etc., all at the same time.

Responses to searches in online catalogs also vary by system. In some of the first systems, display of multiple responses (e.g., a listing of works by Charles Dickens) was in the order of "last in, first out"—the last record cataloged or worked on in some way was the first one displayed—and there was no alphabetical collocation. Ironically, the first Web-based catalogs returned to this order of display. Many systems alphabetize displays, but are not consistent in the way that the arrangement is accomplished.

- **A catalog should be economically prepared and maintained.** The catalog that can be prepared most inexpensively and with greatest attention to currency has obvious advantages.

In summary, the following observations can be made about the major types of catalog:

The online catalog, with the exception of that using CD-ROM technology, is the most flexible and current. Online catalogs, including the CD-ROM versions, are compact and entries can be found quickly. Searching methods and retrieval displays, however, are not standardized, and collocation is not as reliable as in other types of catalogs. It is the most expensive type of catalog; however, expense is offset by such things as the ability to offer the catalog for searching from distant sites and the great potential for new and innovative ways of searching.

Cards for the card catalog are easy to prepare and relatively inexpensive. The chief virtue of the card catalog is its flexibility. Although it is not compact and trays cannot ordinarily be removed for long intensive study, it should be remembered that many people can use it at the same time, as long as they do not need the same drawer.

The book catalog is expensive to prepare unless numerous copies of the catalog are required; library systems that need multiple copies will find the book catalog less costly than the card catalog. Entries can be found quickly in the book catalog, and it is compact, easy to store, and easy to handle; however, it lacks flexibility.

The microform catalog is much less expensive than the book catalog, and there is evidence that its maintenance is less expensive than for the card catalog, although the initial investment in catalog conversion to machine-readable form is high. It is compact and easy to store. It can be flexible if the library can afford to run new cumulations often. However, many patrons find the microfiche versions particularly unpleasant to use.

Arrangement of Entries in a Catalog

A printed catalog (unlike an online catalog) requires multiple copies of each bibliographic record so that the record can be found under any of several access points. Traditionally there is an access point for each author and any other person or corporate body associated with the work and deemed important enough that someone might search for them. There are also access points for titles, variant titles, and subject headings assigned to the record. A copy of the bibliographic record appears under each access point. In some book and microform catalogs a full copy of the record appears only at the "main" access point (a concept discussed in more detail later in this chapter and in chapter 6), and abbreviated versions appear at all other access points. In all printed catalogs each access point with its associated version of the bibliographic record is called an entry.

Online catalogs do not have "entries" in the same sense. One master copy of each bibliographic record is stored by the system. Indexes are made that link each name, title, subject heading, or other entity decided upon as an access point to any associated bibliographic record. In response to a search request, selected data elements from each relevant bibliographic record are copied to the user's screen in the display format chosen for that system.

A printed catalog (unlike an online catalog) must be arranged according to some definite plan. Depending on the subject and scope of the collection, many arrangements are possible. But no matter which one is used, it should cover the contents of the collection and guide the person who consults it to these contents.

Online catalogs must arrange the results of a search on the user's screen. In some instances the user is allowed to choose to have the display presented by main author, by date, by classification number, or by title, to name a few. The choice having been made, however, the user does not have control over any further subarrangement. Most online catalogs still do not allow any choice of display order at all.

Public access catalogs are traditionally arranged according to one of two systems: classified or alphabetical. The differences between them lie in the arrangement of the entries, or in the display of responses to queries.[10]

Classified Catalogs

The classified catalog has the longest history. Many American libraries used this form before they changed to the more popular alphabetical form. It is based upon some special system of classification. The shelflist, a record of the holdings of a library arranged by classification notation, is a classified catalog of a kind. But in a true classified catalog, a bibliographic record may be entered under as many classification notations as apply to its contents, not under just one notation as in a shelflist. In addition, the shelflist lacks an alphabetical subject index, which a true classified catalog has.

The major advantage of a classified catalog is that because it uses symbols, letters, and/or numbers, it can keep up with changing terminology and thus be up-to-date. It is also useful for in-depth study of a subject. Closely related classes are brought together in sequence—often hierarchically. This is good for scanning or for moving from general to specific. In addition this arrangement permits easy compilation of subject bibliographies. Perhaps its greatest disadvantage is that it is constructed on a particular classification scheme (even though this was an advantage as noted above). Since many patrons are not familiar with classification notations, they might need special assistance when consulting the classified catalog. Numerous Internet sites are organized by classification schemes. The notations are not used without verbal equivalents; so the user is not required to understand the meanings of notations. This approach is quite popular for browsing purposes. Perhaps Web-based catalogs will eventually offer such an option for display.

Some fields—particularly the sciences—can make good use of such a catalog, since the classified catalog is flexible and can be easily updated—e.g., only the index entries would have to be changed when terminology for a concept changes, rather than having to revise all records using the concept. Classified catalogs are also of value in locations where the patrons may speak one or two or more languages. In such a case, an alphabetical subject index may be made in each language. In Quebec, for example, where both English and French are spoken, there would be one major classified catalog with French and English indexes. There are only a few classified catalogs in use in the United States today. They are more widely used in Europe, Canada, and a few other countries. There are some predictions that international cooperation will encourage the use of classification for subject exchange, since classification symbols transcend language.

Classified catalogs are actually only the subject part of a divided catalog (*see* discussion below). They must be accompanied by a name/title catalog. Figure 1.1 (*see* page 14) shows a complete set of cards for a classified card catalog.

Alphabetical Catalogs

Alphabetical catalogs came into use because of their ease of arrangement and use. The alphabet is commonly understood. A user is likely to find information under direct terms—those consulted first by choice. Verbal headings are more easily understood than classification symbols. On the other hand, some terminology is quickly dated, and many terms have multiple meanings. In very large catalogs alphabetic arrangement becomes quite complex. There are two traditional arrangements of alphabetical catalogs: dictionary and divided.

Dictionary Catalogs

In the dictionary arrangement of card catalog entries, widely used in American libraries until the 1990s, all the entries—name, title, and subject—were combined, word by word, into one alphabetical file. This arrangement was said to be simple; undoubtedly it was, in the sense that only one file needed to be consulted. As libraries grew, however, the dictionary arrangement became cumbersome and complex, because all entries were interfiled. The problem became partly one of filing (are books by Charles Dickens, for example, filed before those about him?) and partly one of dispersion. The subject of "industrial relations" has many aspects. How can all these aspects be located if they are entered under headings from "A" for "arbitration" to "W" for "wages"? Two primary justifications have been offered in favor of the dictionary arrangement: most patrons seek material on one aspect of a subject rather than upon the broad subject itself, and patrons are provided with ample *see* and *see also* references, which direct them to other aspects of their subjects. Ironically, as card catalogs and cataloging backlogs grew, many libraries stopped making references for subjects in the early 1980s, saying that they would be converting to online catalogs "soon," and, therefore, inconvenience to users would not last long. However, online catalogs began to provide subject references with regularity only in the mid to late 1990s. Figure 1.2 (*see* page 15) shows a complete set of cards for a dictionary catalog.

(Text continues on page 16.)

Fig. 1.1. Card set for a classified catalog.

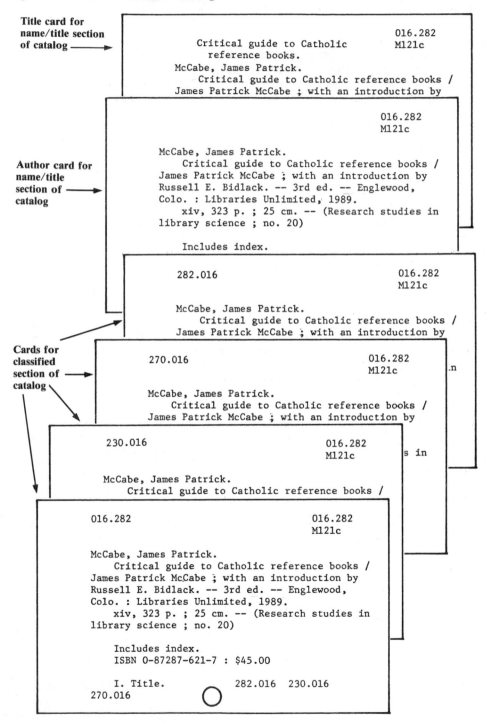

Title card for
name/title section
of catalog ——————>

```
                                                      016.282
              Critical guide to Catholic              M121c
                 reference books.
           McCabe, James Patrick.
                Critical guide to Catholic reference books /
           James Patrick McCabe ; with an introduction by
```

Author card for
name/title
section of ——————>
catalog

```
                                                      016.282
                                                      M121c

           McCabe, James Patrick.
                Critical guide to Catholic reference books /
           James Patrick McCabe ; with an introduction by
           Russell E. Bidlack. -- 3rd ed. -- Englewood,
           Colo. : Libraries Unlimited, 1989.
                xiv, 323 p. ; 25 cm. -- (Research studies in
           library science ; no. 20)

                Includes index.
```

Cards for
classified
section of ——————>
catalog

```
           282.016                                    016.282
                                                      M121c

               McCabe, James Patrick.
                    Critical guide to Catholic reference books /
               James Patrick McCabe ; with an introduction by
```

```
               270.016                         016.282
                                               M121c              .n

                   McCabe, James Patrick.
                        Critical guide to Catholic reference books /
                   James Patrick McCabe ; with an introduction by
```

```
               230.016                         016.282
                                               M121c          s in

                   McCabe, James Patrick.
                        Critical guide to Catholic reference books /
```

```
           016.282                            016.282
                                              M121c

           McCabe, James Patrick.
                Critical guide to Catholic reference books /
           James Patrick McCabe ; with an introduction by
           Russell E. Bidlack. -- 3rd ed. -- Englewood,
           Colo. : Libraries Unlimited, 1989.
                xiv, 323 p. ; 25 cm. -- (Research studies in
           library science ; no. 20)

                Includes index.
                ISBN 0-87287-621-7 : $45.00

                I. Title.          282.016   230.016
           270.016
```

Fig. 1.2. Card set for an alphabetical catalog.

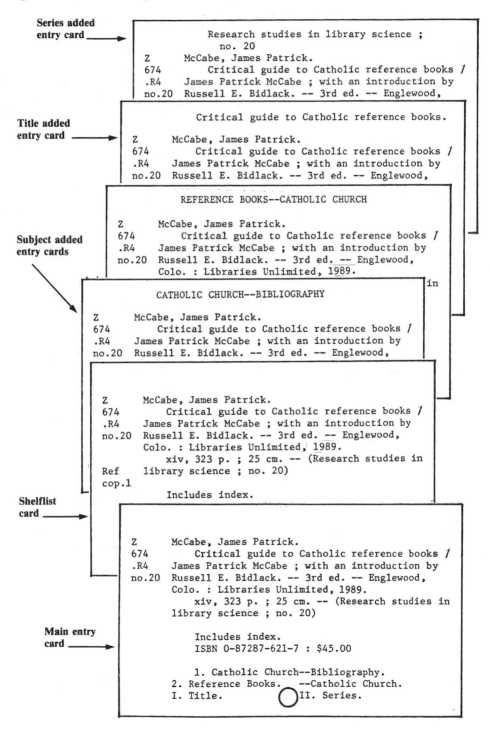

Series added
entry card

```
                    Research studies in library science ;
                         no. 20
        Z       McCabe, James Patrick.
        674         Critical guide to Catholic reference books /
        .R4     James Patrick McCabe ; with an introduction by
        no.20   Russell E. Bidlack. -- 3rd ed. -- Englewood,
```

Title added
entry card

```
                 Critical guide to Catholic reference books.

        Z       McCabe, James Patrick.
        674         Critical guide to Catholic reference books /
        .R4     James Patrick McCabe ; with an introduction by
        no.20   Russell E. Bidlack. -- 3rd ed. -- Englewood,
```

Subject added
entry cards

```
               REFERENCE BOOKS--CATHOLIC CHURCH

        Z       McCabe, James Patrick.
        674         Critical guide to Catholic reference books /
        .R4     James Patrick McCabe ; with an introduction by
        no.20   Russell E. Bidlack. -- 3rd ed. -- Englewood,
                Colo. : Libraries Unlimited, 1989.
```

```
               CATHOLIC CHURCH--BIBLIOGRAPHY

        Z       McCabe, James Patrick.
        674         Critical guide to Catholic reference books /
        .R4     James Patrick McCabe ; with an introduction by
        no.20   Russell E. Bidlack. -- 3rd ed. -- Englewood,
```

```
        Z       McCabe, James Patrick.
        674         Critical guide to Catholic reference books /
        .R4     James Patrick McCabe ; with an introduction by
        no.20   Russell E. Bidlack. -- 3rd ed. -- Englewood,
                Colo. : Libraries Unlimited, 1989.
                     xiv, 323 p. ; 25 cm. -- (Research studies in
        Ref     library science ; no. 20)
        cop.1
                     Includes index.
```

Shelflist
card

Main entry
card

```
        Z       McCabe, James Patrick.
        674         Critical guide to Catholic reference books /
        .R4     James Patrick McCabe ; with an introduction by
        no.20   Russell E. Bidlack. -- 3rd ed. -- Englewood,
                Colo. : Libraries Unlimited, 1989.
                     xiv, 323 p. ; 25 cm. -- (Research studies in
                library science ; no. 20)

                     Includes index.
                     ISBN 0-87287-621-7 : $45.00

                     1. Catholic Church--Bibliography.
                2. Reference Books.     --Catholic Church.
                I. Title.            II. Series.
```

Divided Catalogs

In the 1930s the realization that dictionary catalogs were becoming more and more complex led to a modification of the dictionary arrangement. The result was the divided catalog, which, in its most common form, is in reality two catalogs: one for entries other than subject; the other for subject entries only. The divided catalog permits a simpler filing scheme than does the dictionary catalog. Thus it is easier to consult, although the problem of scattered subjects still exists. There is a further complication implicit in this arrangement. The patron must determine whether an author or title entry or a subject entry is wanted before knowing which part of the catalog must be checked. When this divided approach is used, books about Dickens and books by Dickens are not filed together in the catalog. Patrons need some guidance and education in this matter. OPACs have perpetuated this problem.

There were some libraries that used other types of divided catalogs, such as the three-way divided catalog consisting of separate sections for author, title, and subject entries. Although this system may have simplified the filing of cards, it can be even more confusing for a patron than the two-way divided catalog. In this arrangement, entries for books by Dickens are filed under Dickens' name in the author catalog, the titles of his individual novels are filed in the title catalog, and books about Dickens are filed in the subject catalog.

Another type of two-way divided catalog is a name/title catalog and a topical subject catalog. In such a divided catalog, names and titles that are used even as subject headings are filed in the name/title section. This type of divided catalog allows all the material by and about an author or a title to be filed together. To continue our previous example, books by and books about Dickens would be filed together in the same catalog. This system is potentially less confusing to the patron than any other form of divided catalog.

Arrangements of Online Catalogs

Because entries do not have to be arranged in a linear fashion, online catalogs do not fit easily in the earlier mentioned categories. The internal arrangements of records in the computer vary greatly from system to system and make little difference to a user. What does matter to the user is the way in which entries are displayed in response to a search request. Most online catalogs are in effect divided catalogs because a user must choose to search through one of the indexes: author, title, subject, and sometimes classification and other notations. In this kind of system, a name as subject is almost always searched through the subject index, separating any records about a person from those representing works by that person. An increasing number of systems allow searching of two indexes at once using the words *and*, *or*, and *not* or their equivalents (a form of what is called Boolean searching). These systems do, of course, allow a sophisticated user to find works by and about a person in a single search, but experience has shown that few library patrons are this capable of manipulating the system when the user must create a command. Fortunately, catalogs with GUI interfaces are offering forms to fill in that automatically create the Boolean search, *if* the user understands that a person's name must be typed in *both* the author field *and* the subject field. Virtually all systems also allow for keyword searching of almost any words in any record. In such a system, a keyword search for a name brings together for display all records for works by and about the person, but the display is most often arranged by date and is not collocated in any logical fashion.

In online catalogs that provide for searching by classification notation, there is a semblance of a classified catalog except that in United States cataloging practice each work is limited to one place in a classification scheme. In this respect it is more like a shelflist (*see* discussion below). Research has been done on using classification to enhance subject retrieval in online catalogs.[11] In time there may be ways to gain access to bibliographic records through the hierarchy of the classification scheme used to classify the works they represent.

Components of Catalog Systems

Basically there are three components making up a whole catalog: a public access catalog, a shelflist, and an authority file or files. In printed catalogs these are separate physical components. In online catalogs the OPAC and shelflist are really different ways to search the same file; the authority file is actually a separate file. The preceding sections on form and arrangements of catalogs have, for the most part, covered public access catalogs. These are the catalogs readily available for the use of library patrons.

A shelflist is a record of the holdings of a library; entries are arranged in the order of the items on the shelf—hence the name "shelflist." With the cataloging of computer files, programs, and Internet resources, for which there is often not a physical item to be placed on a shelf, the name is less descriptive. Records of a library's holdings for such entities may be placed in order by classification notation, acquisition number, or some other device. This pattern will increase as libraries provide access to more materials of this sort in the future. The shelflist record usually contains a record of ownership of numbers of copies and/or volumes held, as well as information about locations of copies, especially when a library is made up of several collections.

Shelflists in print form have traditionally been kept in an area not accessible to the public. There have been notable exceptions to this, however, especially in situations where the areas in which materials are shelved (called stacks) are not open to the public. In these situations, browsing the shelflist can substitute for browsing in the stacks. Another change in availability of shelflists has occurred with online catalogs. When classification is an access point in the catalog, the results of classification notation searches are displayed in shelflist (i.e., classification) order, essentially making the shelflist available to everyone. In addition most online catalogs provide copy and location information at all access points.

Authority files contain records of the forms of names, uniform titles, series, and subject headings that have been chosen as the authorized forms to use as headings in a particular catalog. The authority records also contain lists of references made in the public catalog from unauthorized forms to those used for headings so that users do not have to know authorized forms to use the catalog. Traditionally, these files also have been kept in areas inaccessible to the public. Again, online catalogs have changed this. In some systems authority records serve as an index to the catalog.

Online catalogs contain these three components, but not always as distinctly separate as they are in printed catalogs. Authority files still are nonexistent in some online catalogs, and in some they are unlinked files; but increasingly they are linked to the bibliographic files so that they may serve as the index(es) to the headings used in the system, and in some cases they serve to alert catalogers automatically to inconsistencies in headings. In addition a number of other components have been added to online catalogs. For example, acquisitions and in-process records are available to the public in many systems, and circulation information—e.g., whether an item is charged out and, if so, when it is due back—is available in virtually every system.

CATALOGING

The means by which catalogs are prepared is through the process called cataloging. This process usually begins with descriptive cataloging and continues with subject analysis, and throughout both phases is intertwined the process of authority control.

Encoding

Encoding permeates the entire cataloging process. The results of each of the descriptive, subject, and authority processes are entered into a machine-readable form that is compatible with the online system in which the catalog record will be used.

Descriptive Cataloging

Descriptive cataloging is that phase of the cataloging process that is concerned with the identification and description of an information package, the recording of this information in the form of a cataloging record, the selection of access points (except for subject access points), the formation of headings, and the encoding of the entire surrogate record so that it will be machine-readable. Descriptive cataloging describes the make-up of an information package and identifies the responsibility for intellectual contents, without reference to its classification by subject or to the assignment of subject headings, both of which are the province of subject cataloging.

Description

Identification and description are interrelated processes in descriptive cataloging. Identification consists of the choice of conventional elements, guided by a set of rules. When the cataloger has properly identified the conventional elements, they are described in a catalog record in such a fashion that the description is unique and can be applied to no other entity in the collection. In other words, each information package should be distinguished from everything with which it could be confused. Elements considered essential for this purpose in describing physical information packages are title, statement of responsibility, edition information, and publication, distribution, or production information. Physical description—extent and size of item—and series data are often essential to this purpose as well. Components essential for describing virtual information packages (e.g., Internet documents) are title, statement of responsibility, edition information (if present), date information, and location information (e.g., URL). In addition the cataloger gives elements of description that may be helpful to a user in evaluating potential use of the information package, such as whether it is illustrated, what equipment is needed to use it, or that its mode of access is the World Wide Web.

Access

After describing an information package the cataloger selects access points. Names of persons and corporate bodies associated with a work are chosen according to the cataloging rules used. Title access points also are chosen—in addition to the obvious main title (called title proper) there may be alternative titles, variant titles, series titles, and titles of other works related in some way with the work being cataloged.

In traditional practice one of the access points is chosen as the main one. This is called the main entry, but it should not be confused with the use of the word *entry* as defined earlier, meaning an access point with its associated version of a bibliographic record that appears as a unit in a catalog. The remaining access points are called added entries. Identification of the main entry is usually essential for identification of the work (or intellectual content) that is embodied in an information package being cataloged. A combination of main entry and title—uniform title if the work has appeared with variant titles—is the most common way of referring to a work in the realm of cataloging. Of course many works appear only once in one form and are not referred to again, so there is some controversy in the cataloging world about the necessity for choosing a main entry in all cases.[12]

The access points chosen are formatted as headings, constructed in a form that will make them readily accessible in the catalog and will enhance collocation. This is done following cataloging rules and through reference to the authority file, thus continuing the process of authority control.

Subject Analysis

Subject analysis involves determining what subject concept or concepts are covered by the intellectual content of a work. Once this has been determined, as many subject headings as are appropriate are chosen from a standard list. Again, an authority file must be consulted if the subject headings are to be properly collocated into the catalog with other works covering the same or related subject concepts.

The final step in the subject analysis process usually is to choose a classification notation from whatever classification scheme is used by the library. Traditionally in the United States the classification serves both as a means for bringing an item in close proximity with other items on the same or related subjects and, in the case of tangible information packages, as the first element of the call number, a device used to identify and locate a particular item on the shelves. The cataloger therefore must choose only the one best place in the classification scheme for the item.

Authority Control

Authority control is the process of maintaining consistency in the verbal form (heading) used to represent an access point and the further process of showing the relationships among names, works, and subjects. It is accomplished through use of rules (in the case of names and titles), use of a controlled vocabulary, and reference to an authority file to create an authorized character string called a heading. An authority file is a grouping of records of the forms of names, titles, or subjects chosen for use in a catalog. Each authority record in an authority file may contain, in addition to the form chosen for use as the heading, a list of variant forms or terms that may be used as references. A very carefully prepared authority record also contains a list of sources consulted in the process of deciding upon the heading and the variant forms to use as references. It is possible to practice authority control by letting the catalog itself serve as the authority file—i.e., by assuming that the form of heading used in the catalog is correct. In large files this has proved to be difficult, and it is very difficult to keep track of references made in any size file without an authority file.

It is authority control that makes cataloging more than a process of creating a series of bibliographic records to represent discrete works without apparent relationship to any other. The process of cataloging can be defined as "creation of a catalog using bibliographic records" because authority control allows the cataloger to create headings for names, titles, and subjects that show the relationships among the works cataloged. It means that the heading for the same name in different records is always the same so that bibliographic records for all works by and about the same person or emanating from the same corporate body can be displayed together. The heading for a work (called a uniform title, but often consisting of the name of the author, or other main entry, followed by standardized title, as mentioned earlier) can be consistently presented so that bibliographic records for all editions, translations, sound or video recordings, adaptations, abridgements, or any other kind of manifestation of a work can be displayed together. The heading used to represent the same subject concept in different works can be used always in one form (called controlled vocabulary) so that, to the extent that works are identified as being about the same subject concept, all such works can be displayed together. Authority control of controlled vocabulary also makes it possible to refer users from terms not used to those used and from terms used to other related terms.

As we move more and more into the international arena, authority control is becoming known as *access control* because of the need to allow the creators of catalogs in various countries using various languages to designate their own "authorized" forms of names. They should not be required to use the English language "authorized" forms, but we all should be able to use the same authority records.

Cooperative and Copy Cataloging

The process of cataloging described above is often referred to as original cataloging. Fortunately it is not necessary for every information package in every library to be cataloged originally in that library. Because libraries acquire copies of many of the same items, or decide to catalog the same Internet resources, their catalogers can share cataloging by adapting for their own catalogs a copy of the original cataloging created by another library, a process commonly called copy cataloging.[13]

LC began to sell its standard printed catalog cards to libraries in 1901. H. W. Wilson entered the field in the 1930s with simplified catalog cards for sale. A number of other companies created and sold catalog cards from the 1950s into the 1970s. In addition LC book catalogs were available in large libraries, and methods were devised for photocopying entries from them for adaptation and use in local catalogs.

With the development of the MARC format in the late 1960s, cooperative cataloging took a new turn. At first the companies selling cards simply loaded LC's MARC tapes into their computers and printed cards from them. But the beginning of bibliographic networks based on MARC not only changed the availability of cards but also introduced the truly cooperative availability of cataloging data. The first network was OCLC—at first the Ohio College Library Center, but now the Online Computer Library Center. Libraries can become member libraries (usually through regional networks) and then contribute original cataloging to the system. Any member library can use records found in the system contributed by LC, several other national libraries, or any other member library.

At first the OCLC cataloging system was used only for the production of cards, and cards continue to be a product (although now only a very small part) of the system. Adaptations are easier online than changing photocopies or pre-printed cards. Now, however, most libraries download MARC records directly into their local online systems. Other major networks in use in the United States include Research Libraries Information Network (RLIN) and A-G Canada Ltd. (formerly ISM/LIS [Information Systems Management/Library Information Services]). WLN (Western Library Network) merged with OCLC in January 1999. Smaller regional and local networks exist in large numbers.

The amount of original cataloging remaining after use of cooperative cataloging depends upon the type and size of library. The more specialized the library, the more original cataloging it has, so specialized collections can require a high percentage of original cataloging, even though they may be quite small. In public, academic, and research libraries the percentage runs from around 5 percent to 35 percent depending upon size—in general, the larger the collection, the higher the percentage.

In the mid-1990s there was a movement toward outsourcing both original and copy cataloging in some libraries. Outsourcing involves contracting with vendors outside the library to do some of the cataloging (or occasionally all the cataloging) for the library. The move has both advantages and disadvantages, and much has been written on this subject.[14]

FORMATS OF BIBLIOGRAPHIC
RECORDS IN CATALOGS

The records created in the cataloging process must be displayed in some format. Uniformity of display is very desirable so that patrons can know how to read a record and where to expect to see certain elements of data. In printed catalogs the display of data elements has been quite standard. Most libraries and card production sources followed the LC pattern, because LC printed cards were so extensively used and because the order of elements devised by LC made a logical presentation of data. That order was codified by the various versions of the *Anglo-American Cataloguing Rules* (discussed in greater detail in the following chapters).

Today, the vast majority of catalog records are created using one of the MARC formats. The first MARC format was developed at LC around 1965. The version used in the United States was, for many years, referred to as USMARC to distinguish it from the versions used in other countries (e.g., CAN/MARC, UKMARC, etc.). The latest version, published in 1999, is called *MARC 21*. It is a "harmonization" of CAN/MARC and USMARC, and the name is meant to show that it is ready for the 21st century.

The structure of *MARC 21* and its various formats is discussed in more detail in chapter 3. A general discussion of MARC and several other encoding standards can be found in Taylor's *The Organization of Information*.[15]

Display of MARC-formatted records is far from uniform. There have been numerous calls for standards for OPAC displays so that users may once again move from catalog to catalog (now most often while sitting at the same terminal screen),

and see displays that make sense because they are predictable. IFLA has been working on a set of guidelines for display in OPACs.[16] Figure 1.3 shows the record from
figures 1.1–1.2 as displayed by OCLC's cataloging subsystem.

Fig. 1.3. Identification of information included in a MARC record.

```
OCLC: 19124014            Rec stat:    p
Entered: 19890119         Replaced: 19900317        Used: 19980615
> Type:   a      ELvl:    Srce:     Audn:       Ctrl:      Lang: eng
  BLvl:   m      Form:    Conf: 0   Biog:       MRec:      Ctry: cou
                 Cont: b  GPub:     Fict: 0     Indx: 1
  Desc:   a      Ills:    Fest: 0   DtSt: s     Dates:1989,   <
>  1  010      89-2835 <  ◄——————————— 18
>  2  040      DLC $c DLC <  ◄—— 12
            16
>  3  020  ↘  0872876217 : $c |$|45.00 <
>  4  050 00 {Z674 $b .R4 no. 20} $a Z7837 $a BX1751.2 <
>  5  082 00 020 s $a 016.282 $2 19 <
>  6  090      $b <
                    ↑
                    17    ┌1
>  7  049      DD0A <        ╱
>14 8  100 1   McCabe, James Patrick. <        ╱2              3
>  9  245 ⑩    Critical guide to Catholic reference books / $c James  ╱
Patrick McCabe ; with an introduction by Russell E. Bidlack. <
> 10  250      3rd ed. <◄—4  ╱6      ╱7        8
> 11  260   5 { Englewood, Colo. : $b Libraries Unlimited, $c 1989. <}5
> 12  300   9{xiv, 323 p. ; $c 25 cm. < }9      ╱10
> 13  ⑷⑷⑨ 0  Research studies in library science ; $v no. 20 <
15 ▸
> 14  500      Includes indexes. < ◄——11
> 15  610 20 ┌Catholic Church $x Bibliography. <     ┐13
> 16  650   0 {Reference books ⑸ Catholic Church. <   ╱
                    ↑
                    13              ↑
                                    19
```

Key for Fig. 1.3:

1. Heading: author's name
2. Title proper
3. Statement of responsibility
4. Edition statement
5. Publication, distribution, etc., area
6. Place of publication
7. Publisher
8. Date of publication
9. Physical description area
10. Series statement
11. Notes

12. Standard number (ISBN)
13. Subject headings
14. MARC indicator that tells computer that title will be added entry
15. MARC tag that indicates that series will be added entry
16. Library of Congress call number
17. Dewey classification number
18. Library of Congress control (card) number
19. MARC subfield code

CONCLUSION

This chapter has presented an overview of the entire cataloging process. Greater detail about the content of description is discussed in chapters 4–5. Choice and form of headings are covered in chapters 6–7. Subject analysis is given thorough treatment in part IV, with chapters 9–13 devoted to classification and chapters 14–17 devoted to subject headings. Part V covers authority control, and the final part deals in more detail with networking, computer cataloging, and management issues.

NOTES

1.   Elaine Svenonius, "Directions for Research in Indexing, Classification, and Cataloging," *Library Resources & Technical Services* 25 (January/March 1981): 88.

2.   Richard P. Smiraglia, "Bibliographic Control Theory and Nonbook Materials," in *Policy and Practice in Bibliographic Control of Nonbook Media*, ed. by Sheila S. Intner and Richard P. Smiraglia (Chicago: American Library Association, 1987), p. 15.

3.   Arlene G. Taylor, *The Organization of Information* (Englewood, Colo.: Libraries Unlimited, 1999), p. 2.

4.   Ibid., p. 244.

5.   Ibid., p. 246.

6.   These ideas are discussed in greater detail by Ronald Hagler in *The Bibliographic Record and Information Technology*, 3rd ed. (Chicago: American Library Association, 1997), pp. 17–18.

7.   Charles A. Cutter, *Rules for a Dictionary Catalog*, 4th ed. (Washington, D.C.: GPO, 1904), p. 12.

8.   International Conference on Cataloguing Principles. Paris, 9th–18th October, 1961, *Report* (London: International Federation of Library Associations, 1963), p. 26.

9.   A good discussion of the historical development of cataloging practices is presented in an article written by Charles Martel, "Cataloging: 1876–1926," reprinted in *The Catalog and Cataloging*, ed. by A. R. Rowland (Hamden, Conn.: Shoe String Press, 1969), pp. 40–50.

10.   *See also* discussion in: Taylor, *The Organization of Information*, pp. 25–27.

11.   Karen Markey and Anh N. Demeyer, "Findings of the Dewey Decimal Classification Online Project," *International Cataloguing* 15 (April/June 1986): 15–19.

12.   *See* further discussion of main entry in: Taylor, *The Organization of Information*, pp. 105–114.

13.   For an in-depth discussion of the decisions and adaptations necessary in the process of copy cataloging *see* Arlene G. Taylor, with the assistance of Rosanna M. O'Neil *Cataloging with Copy: A Decision-Maker's Handbook*, 2nd ed. (Englewood, Colo.: Libraries Unlimited, 1988).

14.   For example, *see* Claire-Lise Benaud and Sever Bordeianu, *Outsourcing Library Operations in Academic Libraries: An Overview of Issues and Outcomes* (Englewood, Colo.: Libraries Unlimited, 1998), and Marylou Colver and Karen Wilson, eds., *Outsourcing Technical Services Operations* (Chicago: American Library Association, 1997). *See also* discussion on pp. 462–463 of this text.

15.   Taylor, *The Organization of Information*, pp. 57–76.

16.   Martha Yee, *Guidelines for OPAC Displays*, prepared for the 65th IFLA Council and General Conference, Bangkok, Thailand, August 20–August 28, 1999 (available: http://www.ifla.org/IV/ifla65/papers/098-131e.htm [accessed 3/5/00]).

SUGGESTED READING

Byrne, Deborah J. *MARC Manual: Understanding and Using MARC Records*. 2nd ed. Englewood, Colo.: Libraries Unlimited, 1998.

Carpenter, Michael, and Elaine Svenonius. *Foundations of Cataloging: A Sourcebook*. Littleton, Colo.: Libraries Unlimited, 1985.

Dunkin, Paul S. *Cataloging U.S.A.* Chicago: American Library Association, 1969.

Hagler, Ronald. *The Bibliographic Record and Information Technology*. 3rd ed. Chicago: American Library Association, 1997.

Oder, Norman. "Cataloging the Net: Can We Do It?" *Library Journal* 123, no. 16 (October 1, 1998): 47–51.

Taylor, Arlene G., with the assistance of Rosanna M. O'Neil. *Cataloging with Copy: A Decision-Maker's Handbook*, 2nd ed.   Englewood, Colo.: Libraries Unlimited, 1988.

Taylor, Arlene G. "The Information Universe: Will We Have Chaos or Control?" *American Libraries* 25, no. 7 (July/August 1994): 629–632.

Taylor, Arlene G. *The Organization of Information*. Englewood, Colo.: Libraries Unlimited, 1999.

Development of Cataloging Codes

INTRODUCTION

In current United States cataloging practice there is no comprehensive code of rules that tells a cataloger how to create bibliographic records that provide descriptive cataloging and subject access or how to create a catalog with those records. There is a widely accepted set of rules that covers description and name and title access and addresses authority work to some extent, but provision of subject access, authority control, and creation of catalogs are depending upon following conventions—to a great extent, those established by the Library of Congress (LC). The rules for description and name and title access, the *Anglo-American Cataloguing Rules, Second Edition, 1998 Revision (AACR2R98)*,[1] is the result of a progression of ideas about how to approach the cataloging process to prepare catalogs that provide the best possible access to library collections. *AACR2R98* represents in print form the current agreements that have been reached to standardize descriptive cataloging practice and thereby facilitate cooperation among libraries. It expands on the agreements presented in earlier codes and forms the basis for further agreements that will be added to future codes.

The first cataloging rules were prepared by individuals. Anthony Panizzi, Keeper of the Printed Books at the British Museum, constructed a set of rules for that institution that was published in 1841.[2] This set of rules, often referred to as Panizzi's "91 Rules," was the first major modern statement of principles underlying cataloging rules; as such it has exerted an influence on every Western world code that has been created since its publication. Panizzi believed that anyone looking for a particular work should be able to find it through the catalog, and he wrote rules with that goal in mind—e.g., he insisted on entering pseudonymous works under pseudonym rather than under the author's real name. One characteristic of Panizzi's code was his occasional use of form headings as main entry—e.g., universities and learned societies were entered under the general heading "Academies," and missals, prayer-books, and liturgies were entered under "Liturgies." The concept of subject access as we know it had not yet been separated from that of main entry, and there were no provisions for subject headings as such. Clearly, though, he thought there were some kinds of publications that ought to be gathered together.

Charles A. Cutter, Librarian at the Boston Athenaeum, also created an important set of rules. His *Rules for a Dictionary Catalog*,[3] in its fourth edition at his death in 1903, gave voice to the concept that catalogs not only should point the way to an individual publication but also should assemble and organize literary units. These rules were also the first complete set of rules for a dictionary catalog. Cutter's rules were truly comprehensive, incorporating rules for subject access and filing as well as for description and name and title access. From the beginning of the twentieth century, codes have been drawn up by committees, but the influence of these early farsighted individuals has been apparent.

As mentioned earlier, the rules we have are for description and name and title access. After Cutter's rules for subject headings, two major American lists of subject headings were developed—each containing introductions explaining conventions for use.[4] Haykin enumerated principles for creating subject lists in 1951,[5] and LC issued its *Manual* for applying its headings in 1984 (5th ed., 1996),[6] but there is no comprehensive code for subject access. Some librarians began calling for such a code in the late 1980s. The history related to subjects is discussed in more detail in chapters 14 and 15.

Rules for descriptive cataloging have progressed through a number of different manifestations in the twentieth century: LC's *Rules on Printed Cards* (1899 through the 1930s),[7] American Library Association (ALA) and the (British) Library Association's *Catalog Rules* (1908),[8] *A.L.A. Cataloging Rules* (1941),[9] *A.L.A. Cataloging Rules for Author and Title Entries* (1949),[10] LC's *Rules for Descriptive Cataloging* (1949),[11] *Anglo-American Cataloging Rules* (1967) (*AACR*),[12] *Anglo-American Cataloguing Rules*, second edition (1978) (*AACR2*),[13] *Anglo-American Cataloguing Rules, Second Edition, 1988 Revision (AACR2R)*[14] and the present *AACR2R98*.

The Anglo-American *Rules* of 1908 were the result of a seven-year study by a committee of ALA and the (British) Library Association. In 1901 LC had begun its printed card service, with the result that libraries became interested in ways to use LC cards with their own cards. One of the important responsibilities of the committee was to formulate rules to encourage incorporation of LC printed cards into catalogs of other libraries. The committee attempted to reconcile the cataloging practices of LC with those of other research and scholarly libraries. The use of LC cards increased dramatically between 1908 and 1941; standardization of library catalogs progressed. However, the 1908 *Rules* were not expanded during this 33-year period, drastically curtailing attempts of cataloging practice to stay in touch with cataloging done at LC. In 1930 a subcommittee was appointed by ALA to begin work on a revision of cataloging rules, and the problems were outlined. Dissatisfaction with the 1908 code was expressed on the grounds of "omissions"; the basic rules were not in question. Expansion was required to meet the needs of large scholarly libraries or specialized collections:

> The preliminary edition, published in 1941, expanded the rules of 1908 to make more provision for special classes of material: serial publications, government documents, publications of religious bodies, anonymous classics, music and maps; to amplify existing rules to cover specific cases of frequent occurrence.[15]

The revised edition of 1949 states that in the 1949 edition:

> the chief changes from the preliminary edition are a rearrangement of the material to emphasize the basic rules and subordinate their amplifications, and to make the sequence of rules logical as far as possible; reduction of the number of alternate rules; omission of rules for description; rewording to avoid repetition or to make the meaning clearer; and revision, where possible, of rules inconsistent with the general principles.[16]

The 1941 and 1949 rules were sharply criticized for being too elaborate and often arbitrary; emphasis had shifted from clearly defined principles to a collection of rules developed to fit specific cases rather than the conditions that the cases illustrated. Seymour Lubetzky, then a specialist in cataloging policy at LC, commented that any logical approach to cataloging problems was blocked by the maze of arbitrary and repetitious rules and exceptions to rules.[17]

Because of the omission of rules for description from the 1949 ALA *Rules*, LC published its *Rules for Descriptive Cataloging in the Library of Congress*,[18] also in 1949. This set of rules was much more simplified than had been the rules in Part II of the 1941 ALA preliminary edition. Therefore, these were not criticized, as were the rules for entry and heading, and were incorporated virtually intact into the next edition of rules published by ALA in 1967.

Because the 1949 rules were not satisfactory, ALA invited Lubetzky in 1951 to prepare a critical study of cataloging rules. Early drafts of Lubetzky's principles came out against complete enumeration of "cases" in rules and pointed toward a less complex code based upon well-defined principles. At the International Conference on Cataloging Principles held in Paris in 1961, a draft statement of cataloging principles based upon Lubetzky's *Code of Cataloging Rules* was used as the basis for consideration. The final version of the "Statement of Principles" (often called the "Paris Principles")[19] was adopted and the participants from 53 countries agreed to work in their various countries for revised rules that would be in agreement with the accepted principles.

ANGLO-AMERICAN CATALOGING RULES **1967** *(AACR)*

The Catalog Code Revision Committee that prepared the *Anglo-American Cataloging Rules (AACR)* realized that revision must be a complete reexamination of the principles and objectives of cataloging, not merely a revision of specific rules. First, the objectives of the catalog were agreed upon; it was further decided that the Paris Principles should be the basis for rules of entry and heading. This was an important step toward international bibliographic standardization. International standardization was not accepted overnight, however. The British and Americans were attempting to produce a joint code, but American conservatives were worried about the probable costs of full implementation of the Paris Principles. When the code was finally published it was published in two texts—one British and one North American.[20]

AACR was oriented toward large research libraries, although in a few instances of obvious conflict, alternate rules were provided for use by non-research libraries. Unlike the 1949 ALA code, which was only for entry and heading, *AACR* incorporated rules for entry and heading, description, and cataloging of nonbook material. An important shift occurred in the philosophy underlying the rules for entry: "The entry for a work is normally based on the statements that appear on the title page or any part of the work that is used as its substitute."[21] This meant that information appearing only in the preface, introduction, or text was not to be considered unless title page information was vague or incomplete. Another basic shift in point of view was to that of cataloging by types of authorship rather than by types of works and by classes of names rather than by classes of people.

Unlike earlier codes, *AACR* emphasized that choice of entry was a completely separate activity from construction of the heading used for the entry chosen. General principles became the basis for the rules for choice of entry:

1.   Entry should be under author or principal author when one can be determined

2.   Entry should be under title in the case of works whose authorship is diffuse, indeterminate, or unknown

Application of rules based on these principles continued the practice of choosing a main entry, with other names and/or titles becoming added entries. However, the choice was no longer a result of first determining the type of work involved and then finding the specific rule for that type.

The construction of the headings for names that were to be main or added entries centered on two problems: choice of a particular name, including both choice among different names (e.g., Jacqueline Onassis or Jacqueline Kennedy) and choice among different forms of the same name (e.g., Morris West or Morris L. West), and the form in which that name is presented in the heading (e.g., Seuss, Dr., or Dr. Seuss; Von Braun, Wernher, or Braun, Wernher von). Rules for form of name became based on a general principle of using the form of name used by a person or corporate body rather than the full name or official name as the 1949 ALA *Rules* directed. Thus a person could be entered under an assumed name, nickname, changed name, etc. A person who used both his or her real name and an assumed name, however, was still entered under the real name, and a person who used a full form of a forename or used a forename initial, even though rarely, was entered under the fullest form ever used. Another change was to use a firmly established English form of name rather than the vernacular form for many well-known names (e.g., Horace, not Horatius Flaccus, Quintus).

Another important area of change was in the form of entry for corporate bodies. The general rule followed the principle of using the form of name the body itself uses. Entry was usually under that form of name except when the rules provided for entry under a higher body or under the name of the government. However, the North American text gave exceptions exempting specified bodies of an institutional nature from the principle of entry under name; these were to be entered under place as in the old rules. These exceptions were contrary to the Paris Principles and to the British text of *AACR*, but they had been requested by the Association of Research Libraries, whose member libraries feared being overburdened with the necessity for changing thousands of entries already in catalogs.

The fear of the research libraries was also eased by LC's January 1967 announcement of the policy of superimposition:

> This means that the rules for choice of entry will be applied only to works that are new to the Library and that the rules for headings will be applied only to persons and corporate bodies that are being established for the first time. New editions, etc., of works previously cataloged will be entered in the same way as the earlier editions (except for revised editions in which change of authorship is indicated). New works by previously established authors will appear under the same headings.[22]

This policy continued throughout the duration of the application of *AACR*. As a result, thousands of headings were made between 1967 and 1981 in a form created under the 1949 ALA *Rules* or earlier rules on bibliographic records that were otherwise *AACR* records. The abandonment of the policy of superimposition with the implementation of *AACR2* was a major step toward ultimate user convenience in finding entries and improved international cooperation; but for many large libraries, thousands of entries in pre-*AACR* form already in catalogs had to be dealt with after January 1981.

In 1974 the rule in *AACR* for corporate entry under place was dropped. Because of superimposition, only new corporate bodies were established and entered under their own names. Besides this change, some 40 other rules were changed, and three chapters were totally revised in the years following publication of *AACR*. Perhaps the most significant change was the application of standards of bibliographic description, based on International Standard Bibliographic Description (ISBD), to descriptive cataloging of monographs, audiovisual media, and special instructional materials. ISBD facilitates the international exchange of bibliographic information by standardizing the elements to be used in the bibliographic description, assigning an order to these elements in the entry, and specifying a system of symbols to be used in punctuating these elements. (These symbols are discussed and illustrated in Appendix B of the 8th ed. of *Introduction to Cataloging and Classification*.) In addition:

> ISBD requires that a publication be totally identified by the description. It is independent of the provisions for headings, main or added, and of the provisions for the use of uniform titles; these were internationally standardized by the Paris Principles.[23]

ANGLO-AMERICAN CATALOGUING RULES, SECOND EDITION (AACR2), THE 1988 REVISION *(AACR2R),* AND THE 1998 REVISION *(AACR2R98)*

The numerous changes to rules in *AACR* and the progress toward an international standard for description not only of monographs, but also of serials and all media, were two of the reasons for the meeting in 1974 of representatives of the national library associations and national libraries of Canada, the United Kingdom, and the United States to plan for the preparation of *AACR2*. Two other reasons were a proliferation of other rules for nonbook materials that reflected dissatisfaction with *AACR* treatment of these materials and LC's announcement of intention to abandon the policy of superimposition.[24] The objectives established at that meeting were:

1) to reconcile in a single text the North American and British texts of 1967

2) to incorporate in the single text all amendments and changes already agreed and implemented under the previous mechanisms

3) to consider for inclusion in AACR all proposals for amendment currently under discussion between the American Library Association, the Library Association, the Library of Congress, and the Canadian Library

Association; any new proposals put forward by these bodies and the British Library; and any proposals of national committees of other countries in which AACR is in use

4)   to provide for international interest in AACR by facilitating its use in countries other than the United States, Canada, and the United Kingdom[25]

The representatives at the 1974 meeting also agreed to establish a Joint Steering Committee for Revision of *AACR* (JSC) made up of one voting and one nonvoting representative of each author organization. The JSC was to appoint an editor from each side of the Atlantic and was generally to oversee the process of revision through to publication.

The result of the revision process was what the preface to *AACR2* calls a continuation of the first edition: "for, in spite of the changes in presentation and content which it introduces, these are still the *Anglo-American Cataloguing Rules*, having the same principles and underlying objectives as the first edition, and being firmly based on the achievement of those who created the work, first published in 1967."[26] However, *AACR2*, published in late 1978 but not implemented by the major national libraries until January 1981, had some significant differences that are worth noting here.

Before discussing these differences, we should note that *AACR2* has undergone a process of continuous revision. Participating countries have committees that work continually on recommendations for revisions. Approved recommendations are passed to the JSC, which then acts to accept or reject the proposals. Before such recommendations can be accepted, they often have to be revised, and differences of opinion must be reconciled among the countries involved. The countries currently represented on the JSC are Australia, Canada, Great Britain, and the United States. Approved revisions were published three times, in 1982, 1984, and 1986.[27] Rather than publish a fourth set of revisions, it was decided to consolidate *AACR2* and all its revisions, including the ones approved since 1986, into a single volume. The result was *AACR2R*. Over the next decade the revisions accumulated again, and another cumulation was called for, resulting in the current *AACR2R98*. The following discussion applies to *AACR2* and all its revisions unless otherwise noted.

In the process of reconciling the North American and British texts, it was decided to use British spelling of words if the British spelling appears as an alternative in *Webster's Third New International Dictionary of the English Language, Unabridged*. In cases where terminology differs, British usages were chosen in some cases (e.g., *full stop* instead of *period*), while American usages appear in other cases (e.g., *parentheses* instead of the British *brackets*).

One significant change is in the presentation of rules for description: one general chapter presents broad provisions that can be applied in many different situations. This chapter is followed by specific chapters for different types of materials and for different conditions and patterns of publication. The rules for description are deliberately less specific in legislating ways to handle certain phenomena. The cataloger is thereby encouraged to exercise judgment in interpreting the rules in light of the needs of the user being served. One possibility for such interpretation is that *AACR2* provides three "levels" of description with increasing amounts of detail at each level. The cataloger may choose the level that provides the amount of detail relevant to the particular library's users and, at the same time, meets the standards called for in a set of international cataloging rules.

In the rules for choice of access points, it is significant that less emphasis has been placed on "main" entry, although the concept is still present. Many people have expressed the opinion that when multiple access points are readily available, and when the bibliographic description is complete by itself, there is no need to designate one of the access points as the "main" one. The original main entry concept, which remained basically unchanged from Panizzi's rules through *AACR*, was based on the idea that the purpose of the catalog is to identify works and that once the work is identified, sufficient bibliographic detail is added to facilitate finding the item that contains the work. This was based on the assumption that there is a one-to-one correspondence between work and item. This assumption worked fairly well until the latter part of the twentieth century, when the tremendous growth of literatures and formats of all kinds rendered the assumption obsolete. Now, as noted in chapter 1, use of a main entry combined with title or uniform title is the only way we have to identify the same work in several containers. It is also the most common way to identify in a note a work that is related to the work being described by the bibliographic record. As long as this is true the concept of main entry cannot be abandoned.

A significant consideration in choice of main entry is that a corporate body is not considered to be an "author." Instead, there are specified categories of works that are entered under corporate body. This concept greatly reduces the number of corporate main entries made, although those corporate bodies that would have had main entry under earlier rules are given added entry under *AACR2*, and thus there is not a reduction in number of corporate entries.

Rules for form of headings for personal names now emphasize using the form of name most often used by an author (e.g., Benjamin Disraeli instead of Earl of Beaconsfield; Bernard Shaw instead of George Bernard Shaw). If a person, other than one using a pseudonym, uses more than one name, again the predominant one is chosen. Rules for pseudonyms have evolved more than other rules for choice of personal name since *AACR*, in which only one form—the real name, if used—was chosen to represent a person who used more than one pseudonym or a real name and one or more pseudonyms. In the 1978 *AACR2* a predominant name was chosen; only if there was no predominant name could multiple headings be made for that author. This placed the mathematical works of Charles L. Dodgson under Lewis Carroll. *AACR2R* introduced the concept of "separate bibliographic identities," which allows separate headings in such cases as the Dodgson/Carroll example. It also called for multiple headings for all contemporary authors who use more than one pseudonym or a real name and one or more pseudonyms. This practice continues in *AACR2R98*.

For corporate names, too, there is more emphasis on using the name as it is used by the body, removing provisions for inverting, amplifying, etc., that appeared in *AACR* (e.g., W. K. Kellogg Arabian Horse Center instead of Kellogg (W. K.) Arabian Horse Center). Geographic names are treated more internationally (e.g., states of Australia are treated like states of the United States). In the 1978 *AACR2*, counties of England, Scotland, and Wales were also treated like states of the United States, but this has been revised so that places in the British Isles now are qualified by the constituent parts of the British Isles rather than by counties.

At the time of publication of *AACR2* there were some general hopes for advantageous results from use of the new code. First, *AACR2* laid the groundwork for much more international and national cooperative cataloging, which was expected to improve greatly library service of a bibliographic nature and to result in considerable cost savings. Second, by providing the framework for standard description of all library materials, it made possible an integrated, multimedia catalog. Third, it was expected to reduce user search time by providing headings that conform more often to the forms found in works and citations. Fourth, personal name headings were expected to be more stable than formerly, thus reducing catalog maintenance costs.[28] The first two of these expected advantages have been widely accepted as having come to pass. As to the third, Elizabeth Tate demonstrated that headings do indeed conform more often to the forms found in citations.[29] In order to know if the last one has been realized, studies would have to be completed, and this has not been done.

When *AACR2* was published in 1978, a period of time was set before implementation in order to allow libraries to prepare for the change. The date for implementation was postponed twice, but implementation finally occurred January 2, 1981, after much angst and a flurry of local *AACR2* studies to determine impact.[30] The problem was exacerbated by the fact that most libraries had card catalogs, and changes had to be accomplished by erasing and retyping or by marking through headings and writing new forms above them. By the mid-1990s most libraries had online catalogs, in which changed headings can be changed by "global search and replace" methods, and new rule changes can be accommodated with more ease.

Rule interpretations made by LC in their process of applying *AACR2* are published regularly in *Cataloging Service Bulletin*. Official changes made to the rules are also published there. There are also occasionally official publications of rule changes such as the publication of the group of revisions that was published as "Amendments 1993."[31] These and subsequent revisions were incorporated into *AACR2R98*, which was published in two formats: in print and in electronic form. The work has been translated into several languages, as its influence continues to grow.

It is hoped that chapters 4 through 7 of this text will prove helpful in illustrating the basic rules. The complete *AACR2R98* should be consulted for additional rules covering aspects of problems too detailed for inclusion in this text and for further explanations, definitions, and references.

NOTES

1.   *Anglo-American Cataloguing Rules, Second Edition, 1998 Revisions*, prepared under the direction of the Joint Steering Committee for Revision of AACR (Chicago: American Library Association, 1998). Also available on CD-ROM: *AACR2-e, Anglo-American Cataloguing Rules, 2nd Edition, 1998 Revision.*

2.   Antonio Panizzi, "Rules for the Compilation of the Catalogue," in British Museum, *The Catalogue of Printed Books in the British Museum* (London, 1841), 1: v–ix.

3.   Charles A. Cutter, *Rules for a Dictionary Catalog*, 4th ed., rewritten (Washington, D.C.: GPO, 1904).

4.   Library of Congress, Catalog Division, *Subject Headings Used in the Dictionary Catalogues of the Library of Congress* (Washington, D.C.: Library Branch, GPO, 1910–1914); Minnie Earl Sears, *List of Subject Headings for Small Libraries* (New York: H. W. Wilson, 1923).

5.   David Judson Haykin, *Subject Headings: A Practical Guide* (Washington, D.C.: GPO, 1951).

6.   Library of Congress, Subject Cataloging Division, *Subject Cataloging Manual: Subject Headings* (Washington, D.C.: Library of Congress, 1984).

7.   Library of Congress, *Rules on Printed Cards* (Washington, D.C.: Library of Congress, 1899–194?).

8.   *Catalog Rules, Author and Title Entries*, compiled by Committees of the American Library Association and the (British) Library Association, American ed. (Chicago: American Library Association, 1908).

9.   *A.L.A. Cataloging Rules, Author and Title Entries*, prepared by the Catalog Code Revision Committee of the American Library Association, with the collaboration of a Committee of the (British) Library Association, Preliminary American 2nd ed. (Chicago: American Library Association, 1941).

10.   *A.L.A. Cataloging Rules for Author and Title Entries*, prepared by the Division of Cataloging and Classification of the American Library Association, 2nd ed. (Chicago: American Library Association, 1949).

11.   Library of Congress, Descriptive Cataloging Division, *Rules for Descriptive Cataloging in the Library of Congress* (Washington, D.C.: Library of Congress, 1949).

12.   *Anglo-American Cataloging Rules, North American Text*, prepared by the American Library Association, the Library of Congress, the (British) Library Association, and the Canadian Library Association (Chicago: American Library Association, 1967).

13.   *Anglo-American Cataloguing Rules*, 2nd ed., prepared by the American Library Association, the British Library, the Canadian Library Committee on Cataloguing, the (British) Library Association, and the Library of Congress, ed. by Michael Gorman and Paul W. Winkler (Chicago: American Library Association, 1978).

14.   *Anglo-American Cataloguing Rules, Second Edition, 1988 Revisions*, prepared by the Joint Steering Committee for Revision of AACR, ed. by Michael Gorman and Paul W. Winkler (Chicago: American Library Association, 1988).

15.   *A.L.A. Cataloging Rules*, 1949, p. viii.

16.   *A.L.A. Cataloging Rules*, 1949, p. ix.

17.   Seymour Lubetzky, *Cataloging Rules and Principles: A Critique of the A.L.A. Rules for Entry and a Proposed Design for Their Revision* (Washington, D.C.: Processing Dept., Library of Congress, 1953); also by the same author, *Code of Cataloging Rules, Author and Title: An Unfinished Draft . . . with an Explanatory Commentary by Paul Dunkin* (Chicago: American Library Association, 1960).

18.   L.C., *Rules for Descriptive Cataloging*, 1949.

19.   International Conference on Cataloging Principles, Paris, 9th–18th October, 1961, *Report* (London: International Federation of Library Associations, 1963).

20.   *Anglo-American Cataloging Rules, North American Text* (Chicago: American Library Association, 1967); *Anglo-American Cataloguing Rules, British Text* (London: Library Association, 1967).

21.   *AACR, North American Text*, p. 9.

22.   *Cataloging Service*, bulletin 79 (January 1967): 1.

23.   "International Standard Bibliographic Description," *Cataloging Service*, bulletin 105 (November 1972): 2.

24.   "AACR 2: Background and Summary," *Library of Congress Information Bulletin* 37 (October 20, 1978): 640.

25.   *AACR2*, pp. vi–vii.

26.   *AACR2*, p. v.

27.   *Anglo-American Cataloguing Rules, Second Edition, Revisions*, prepared by the Joint Steering Committee for Revision of AACR (Chicago: American Library Association, 1982); *Anglo-American Cataloguing Rules, Second Edition, Revisions 1983*, prepared by the Joint Steering Committee for Revision of AACR (Chicago: American Library Association, 1984); *Anglo-American Cataloguing Rules, Second Edition, Revisions 1985*, prepared by the Joint Steering Committee for Revision of AACR (Chicago: American Library Association, 1986).

28.   "AACR 2: Background and Summary," p. 652.

29.   Elizabeth L. Tate, "Access Points and Citations: A Comparison of Four Cataloging Codes," *Library Research* 1 (Winter 1979): 347–359.

30.   Arlene Taylor Dowell, *AACR 2 Headings: A Five-Year Projection of Their Impact on Catalogs* (Littleton, Colo.: Libraries Unlimited, 1982), pp. 22–35.

31.   *Anglo-American Cataloguing Rules, Second Edition, 1988 Revision: Amendments 1993* (Chicago: American Library Association, 1993).

SUGGESTED READING

Baker, Nicholson, "Discards." *New Yorker* 70, no. 7 (April 4, 1994): 64–86.

Cutter, Charles Ammi. *Rules for a Dictionary Catalog*. 4th ed., rewritten. Washington, D.C.: GPO, 1904.

Dowell, Arlene Taylor. *AACR 2 Headings: A Five-Year Projection of Their Impact on Catalogs*. Littleton, Colo.: Libraries Unlimited, 1982.

International Conference on AACR2, Florida State University, 1979. *The Making of a Code: The Issues Underlying AACR 2*. Chicago: American Library Association, 1980.

Lubetzky, Seymour. *Cataloging Rules and Principles: A Critique of the ALA Rules for Entry and a Proposed Design for Their Revision*. Washington, D.C.: Processing Dept., Library of Congress, 1953.

Osborn, Andrew. "The Crisis in Cataloging." *Library Quarterly* 11 (October 1941): 393–411.

Russell, Beth M. "Hidden Wisdom and Unseen Treasure: Revisiting Cataloging in Medieval Libraries." *Cataloging & Classification Quarterly* 26, no. 3 (1998): 21–30.

Taylor, Arlene G. "Development of the Organization of Recorded Information in Western Civilization." Chapter 3 in *The Organization of Information*. Englewood, Colo.: Libraries Unlimited, 1999.

Part II
ELECTRONIC FORMATTING

3 ⟩ Encoding

In the age of online catalogs the content of catalog records must use some kind of electronic encoding scheme in order to be machine-manipulable for searching and display. Encoding allows each part of a record to be set off from every other part. Then computer programs can be written so that each part will be displayed in a certain position according to the wishes of the programmer. Encoding also allows for access to a catalog record through the creation of search programs that provide for the searching of certain parts of a record (e.g., the author, the title, a subject, etc.).

Since the mid-1960s an encoding system called MARC (MAchine-Readable Cataloging) has been used to create electronic catalog records. An excellent history of its development may be found in Deborah Byrne's *MARC Manual*.[1] The most current version for use in the United States is MARC 21, a harmonized version of USMARC and CAN/MARC, published in 1999.[2]

Other encoding systems have been developed recently in response to the desire to make catalog records available on the Web. Standard Generalized Markup Language (SGML) is an international standard for document markup. It is a set of rules for designing markup languages that describe the structure of a document. The markup languages thus designed are SGML applications called Document Type Definitions (DTDs). DTDs often used for bibliographic data include Text Encoding Initiative (TEI), HyperText Markup Language (HTML), and Encoded Archival Description (EAD). A DTD for MARC records has been developed, and at this writing is in experimental stages. Extensible Markup Language (XML), a subset of SGML that adds some features that solve earlier problems with SGML and HTML, is gaining in use. A description of these encoding systems may be found in Arlene G. Taylor's *The Organization of Information*.[3]

Currently, the MARC encoding system holds the position of being the one used for bibliographic records in the vast majority of the world's online catalogs. The remainder of this chapter contains an introduction to this system.

INTRODUCTION TO
MACHINE-READABLE CATALOGING (MARC)

Formats

There are *MARC 21* formats for five types of data. The following formats are currently defined:

- Bibliographic format—for encoding bibliographic data in records that are surrogates for information packages

- Authority format—for encoding authority data collected in authority records created to help control the content of those surrogate record fields that are subject to authority control

- Holdings format—for encoding data elements in holdings records that show the holdings and location data for information packages described in surrogate records

- Community information format—for encoding data in records that contain information about events, programs, services, etc., so that these records can be integrated with bibliographic records

- Classification data format—for encoding data elements related to classification numbers, the captions associated with them, their hierarchies, and the subject headings with which they correlate[4]

This introduction is to the *MARC 21* bibliographic format.

Components of the Record

A record is a collection of fields. A field contains a unit of information within a record. A field may consist of one or more subfields. Tags, that is, three-digit numerical codes, identify each field. Every field ends with a field terminator (in OCLC, for example, the field terminator may appear as a backwards paragraph sign or as a left angle bracket). Each subfield is preceded by a delimiter sign (often represented by a $ or | or ‡) followed by a single character code (usually alphabetical, but can also be numerical).

Each record has the same components:

1. Leader
2. Record directory
3. Control fields
   a. Fixed fields
4. Variable fields

Leader—The leader is like the leader on a roll of film. It identifies the beginning of a new record and provides information for the processing of the record. The leader is fixed in length and contains 24 characters.

Record directory—The record directory contains a series of fixed length entries that identify the tag, length, and starting position of each field in the record.

Control fields—Control fields carry alphanumeric (often encoded) data elements. Control field tags always begin with the digit 0. Many control fields are fixed in length, that is, each fixed-length field must consist of a set number of characters (*see* also "Fixed field" below). Common control fields are:

001 – Control number

005 – Date and time of latest transaction

006 – Fixed-length data elements—coding information about special aspects of the item being cataloged that cannot be coded in field 008 (separate character descriptions for books, computer files, maps, music, serials, visual materials, and mixed materials)

007 – Physical description fixed field—physical characteristics of an item, usually derived from explicit information in other fields of the record, but expressed here in coded form (separate character descriptions for map, computer file, globe, tactile material, projected graphic, microform, nonprojected graphic, motion picture, kit, notated music, remote-sensing image, sound recording, text, videorecording, and one for "unspecified")

008 – Fixed-length data elements—positionally defined data elements that provide coded information about the record as a whole or about special bibliographic aspects of the item being cataloged

010 – Library of Congress Control Number (LCCN)

016 – National Bibliographic Agency Control Number

020 – International Standard Book Number (ISBN)

022 – International Standard Serial Number (ISSN)

033 – Date/time and place of an event

034 – Coded cartographic mathematical data

040 – Cataloging source

041 – Language code

043 – Geographic area code

047 – Form of musical composition code

048 – Number of musical instruments or voices code

Fixed field—There is one fixed length control field that is commonly referred to as "*the* fixed field." Field 008 carries general information about the content of the bibliographic record. This field is often displayed in a single paragraph at the top of the screen and is usually displayed with mnemonic tags. The field has 40 character positions. The data stored in this field are used to manipulate records for retrieval, filing, indexing, etc.

A fixed field from the record for a book as it is displayed in OCLC:

Type:	a	Elvl:		Srce:		Audn:		Ctrl:		Lang:	eng
Blvl:	m	Form:		Conf:	0	Biog:		Mrec:		Ctry:	ilu
		Cont:	b	Gpub:		Fict:	0	Indx:	1		
Desc:	a	Ills:	a	Fest:	0	DtSt:	s	Dates:	1997,	<	

Sometimes fill characters (displayed as ■ or _ or |) are used to indicate elements of the fixed field that were not in use when the record was created or were not provided by the inputting library. A blank space (when written represented as a letter b with a forward slash through it) is meaningful. That is, a blank is input to represent a coded value. In "Srce:" above, the blank means "Library of Congress."

Variable fields—Variable fields carry alphanumeric data of variable length. The variable fields carry traditional cataloging data elements. Three-digit numeric tags (100–999) identify variable fields. In order to talk about these tags in groups, a convention is followed in which all fields beginning with "1" are identified as 1XX fields; those beginning with "2," as 2XX fields; etc. Variable fields consist of heading fields and descriptive fields. Although classification fields may be considered to be control fields because they begin with 0, they are placed here with other elements that make up the "surrogate record" or the "bibliographic data" of a completed MARC record. Among the most used variable fields are:

CLASSIFICATION NOTATIONS AND/OR CALL NUMBERS (05X–08X)

    050 — Library of Congress (LC) Call Number

    060 — National Library of Medicine Call Number

    082 — Dewey Decimal Classification Number

    etc.

MAIN ENTRY FIELDS (1XX)

    100 — Main entry—personal name

    110 — Main entry—corporate name

    111 — Main entry—meeting name

    130 — Main entry—uniform title

TITLE AND TITLE-RELATED FIELDS (20X—24X)

    240 — Uniform title

    245 — Title proper, general material designation, remainder of title, statement of responsibility

    246 — Varying form of title

    etc.

EDITION, IMPRINT, ETC., FIELDS (25X—28X)

    250 — Edition statement

    254 — Musical presentation statement

    255 — Cartographic mathematical data

    256 — Computer file characteristics

    260 — Publication, distribution, etc. (Imprint: place, publisher, etc., date)

    etc.

PHYSICAL DESCRIPTION, ETC., FIELDS (3XX)

    300 — Physical description (extent of item, other details, size, accompanying material)

    310 — Current publication frequency

    362 — Dates of publication and/or volume designation (serials)

    etc.

SERIES STATEMENT FIELDS (4XX)

    [title proper of series, remaining title information, statement of responsibility relating to series, ISSN of series, numbering, etc.]

    440 — Series statement / added entry—title

    490 — Series statement (not an added entry)

NOTE FIELDS (5XX)

    500 — General note

    502 — Dissertation note

    504 — Bibliography, etc., note

    505 — Formatted contents note

    506 — Restrictions on access note

    508 — Creation/production credits note

    510 — Citation/References note

    511 — Participant or performer note

    516 — Type of computer file or data note

    520 — Summary, etc., note

    533 — Reproduction note

    534 — Original version note

    538 — System details note

    546 — Language note

    547 — Former title complexity note

    580 — Linking entry complexity note

    etc.

SUBJECT ACCESS FIELDS (6XX)

600 — Subject added entry—personal name

610 — Subject added entry—corporate name

611 — Subject added entry—meeting name

630 — Subject added entry—uniform title

650 — Subject added entry—topical term

651 — Subject added entry—geographic name

653 — Index term—uncontrolled

655 — Index term—genre/form

etc.

ADDED ENTRY FIELDS (70X—75X)

700 — Added entry—personal name

710 — Added entry—corporate name

711 — Added entry—meeting name

720 — Added entry—uncontrolled name

730 — Added entry—uniform title

740 — Added entry—uncontrolled related/analytical title

etc.

LINKING ENTRY FIELDS (76X—78X)

770 — Supplement/special issue entry

772 — Parent record entry

776 — Additional physical form entry

780 — Preceding entry

785 — Succeeding entry

787 — Nonspecific relationship entry

etc.

SERIES ADDED ENTRY FIELDS (80X—840)

800 — Series added entry—personal name

810 — Series added entry—corporate name

811 — Series added entry—meeting name

830 — Series added entry—uniform title

HOLDINGS, LOCATION, ALTERNATE GRAPHICS, ETC., FIELDS

852 — Location/call number

856 — Electronic location and access

880 — Alternate graphic representation

etc.

Subfields—All·subfields are distinct elements within fields. Subfield definitions vary from field to field. Some of the most commonly encountered ones are:

050   LC call number
   $a   classification number
   $b   item number and date

082   Dewey Decimal Classification number
   $a   classification number
   $b   item number
   $2   edition number [edition of DDC used]

X00   Personal name
   (X00 means that these subfields apply in fields 100, 600, 700, and 800.)
   $a   name
   $q   qualification of name [e.g., Lewis, C. S. $q (Clive Staples)]
   $b   numeration
   $c   titles (e.g., Mrs., Sir, Bishop)
   $d   dates
   $e   relator (e.g., ill. [for illustrator])

X10   Corporate name
   $a   name
   $b   subordinate unit
   $e   relator
   $k   form subheading

X11   Meeting name
   $a   name
   $n   number
   $c   place
   $d   date

245   Title and statement of responsibility
   $a   title proper
   $b   other title information
   $c   statement of responsibility or remainder of area

260   Publication, distribution, etc.
   $a   place
   $b   publisher, distributor, etc.
   $c   date

300   Physical description
    $a   extent of item
    $b   other physical details
    $c   dimensions

4XX and 8XX   Series
    $a   name of series
    $x   ISSN (4XX fields only)
    $v   numbering of series

6XX   Subject access point
    $a   main subject (name, topic, etc.)
    $x   subject subdivision
    $y   time period subdivision
    $z   geographic subdivision
    $v   form/genre subdivision

856   Electronic location and access
    $a   Host name
    $b   Access number
    $d   Path
    $h   Processor of request
    $u   Uniform Resource Locator
    etc.

Indicators—The two digits that follow after the tags in a MARC field are called indicators. Each digit position has a certain meaning relating to its particular field and provides computer instructions for processing the data contained in the field. For example, in the OCLC-formatted 245 field shown below, the first indicator, "1," tells the system that there should be an access point for the title, and the second indicator, "4," tells the system that four nonfiling characters (i.e., T, h, e, and [space]) precede the first significant word of the title:

    245   14   The dictionary of misinformation   / $c   Tom Burnam.

DISPLAY OF MARC RECORDS

MARC records are distributed in the MARC Communications Format.[5] Each record consists of one long character string beginning with the leader, followed by the record directory, followed by the fields one after another, with no breaks, to the end of the record (at which point there is a character to represent a record terminator). Such a record is practically unreadable if printed as transmitted, and so each system has a program that will display the record in a form that is more easily read. Figures 3.1, 3.2, 3.3 (*see* pages 45–46), and 3.4 (*see* pages 46–47) show the same MARC record as it is displayed in four different systems.

Fig. 3.1. MARC record as displayed in OCLC.

```
OCLC:  19124014              Rec stat:   p   Entered:    19890119
Replaced:       19900317      Used: 19990309
Type:  a     Elvl:       Srce:       Audn:       Ctrl:       Lang: eng
BLvl:  m     Form:       Conf:  0    Biog:       MRec:       Ctry: cou
Cont:  b     Gpub:       Fict:  0    Indx:  1 Desc: a    Ills:
Fest:  0     DtSt:  s    Dates: 1989,
     1 010       89-2835
     2 040       DLC $c DLC
     3 020       0872876217 : $c  |$|45.00
     4 050 00    Z674 $b .R4 no. 20 $a Z7837 $a BX1751.2
     5 082 00    020 s $a 016.282 $2 19
     6 090       $b
     7 049       DD0A
     8 100 1     McCabe, James Patrick.
     9 245 10    Critical guide to Catholic reference books / $c James
Patrick McCabe ; with an introduction by Russell E. Bidlack.
    10 250       3rd ed.
    11 260       Englewood, Colo. : $b Libraries Unlimited, $c 1989.
    12 300       xiv, 323 p. ; $c 25 cm.
    13 440  0    Research studies in library science ; $v no.  20
    14 500       Includes indexes.
    15 610 20    Catholic Church $x Bibliography.
    16 650  0    Reference books $x Catholic Church.
```

Fig. 3.2. MARC record as displayed through the Z39.50 system of LC.

```
001     89002835
003 DLC
005 19900227083313.4
008 890119s1989   cou    b    001 0 eng
010     $a  89002835
020     $a0872876217 :$c$45.00
040     $aDLC$cDLC$dDLC
050 00$aZ674$b.R4 no. 20$aZ7837$aBX1751.2
082 00$a020 s$a016.282$219100 10$aMcCabe, James Patrick.
245 10$aCritical guide to Catholic reference books /$cJames Patrick
McCabe ; with an introduction by Russell E. Bidlack.
250     $a3rd ed.
260 0 $aEnglewood, Colo. :$bLibraries Unlimited, $c1989.
300     $axiv, 323 p. ;$c25 cm.
440  0$aResearch studies in library science ;$vno. 20
500     $aIncludes indexes.
610 20$aCatholic Church$xBibliography.
650  0$aReference books$xCatholic Church.
```

Fig. 3.3. MARC record as displayed in RLIN.

```
ID:DCLC892835-B              RTYP:c      ST:p   FRN:  MS:p EL:   AD:01-19-89
CC:9110 BLT:am    DCF:a    CSC:       MOD:   SNR:   ATC:     UD:03-18-90
CP:cou    L:eng   INT:     GPC:       BIO:   FIC:0  CON:b    TOC:
PC:s      PD:1989/         REP:       CPI:0  FSI:0  ILC:     II:1
010       892835
020       0872876217 :$c$45.00
040       DLC$cDLC$dDLC
050 00    Z674$b.R4 no. 20$aZ7837$aBX1751.2
082 00    020 s$a016.282$219
100 10    McCabe, James Patrick.
245 10    Critical guide to Catholic reference books /$cJames Patrick
McCabe ; with an introduction by Russell E. Bidlack.
250       3rd ed.
260    0  Englewood, Colo. :$bLibraries Unlimited, $c1989.
300       xiv, 323 p. ;$c25 cm.
440    0  Research studies in library science ;$vno. 20
500       Includes indexes.
610 20    Catholic Church$xBibliography.
650    0  Reference books$xCatholic Church.
```

Fig. 3.4. MARC record as displayed in the GEAC system of New York University.

```
Local Control #   : 10258080  Transaction type   : Reserved for LC Marc
Last updated      : 13 JUL 1994 Leader            : pam0 2
Cataloguer        : System

008       890501s1989    cou            00110 eng
010 BB a    80016209
020 BB a  0872872033 :
        c 22.50 035 BB a GLIS002580801
035 BB a  (CStRLIN)NYUG6357361B
040 BB a  DLC
        c DLC
        d NNU
050 B4 a  Z674
        b .R4 no. 20, 1989
082 BB a  016/.282
        2 19
100 1B a  McCabe, James Patrick.
245 10 a  Critical guide to Catholic reference books /
        c by James Patrick McCabe ; with an introd. by Russell E. Bidlack.
250 BB a  3rd ed.
260 BB a  Englewood, Co :
        b Libraries Unlimited,
        c 1989.
300 BB a  xiv, 323 p. ;
        c 25 cm.
440 B0 a  Research studies in library science ;
        v no. 20
500 BB a  Includes indexes.
```

Fig. 3.4.—*Continued*

```
610 20 a  Catholic Church
       x  Bibliography.
650 B0 a  Reference books
       x  Catholic Church.
950 BB l  BRef1
       a  Z674
       b  .R4 no. 20, 1989
       i  01/01/01 N
       x  5
```

Format	: BK Book & monographs
Local Control Number	: 10258080
Transaction type	: Reserved for LC Marc
Date record created	: 01 MAY 1989
Date of last record update	: 13 JUL 1994 18:18:53

```
 1. Record status           : p
 2. Type of record          : a
 3. Bibliographic level     : m
 4. Type of control         :
 5. Encoding level          : 0
 6. Descriptive cat. Form   :
 7. Indicator Length        : 2
```

Format	: BK Book & monographs
Local Control Number	: 10258080
Transaction type	: Reserved for LC Marc
Date record created	: 01 MAY 1989
Date of last record update	: 13 JUL 1994 18:18:53

```
 1. Date entered on file    : 890119    12. Festschrift          : 0
 2. Type of date code       : s         13. Index                : 1
 3. Date 1                  : 1989      14. Literary form        : 0
 4. Date 2                  :           15. Biography            :
 5. Place of publication    : cou       16. Language             : eng
 6. Illustrations           :           17. Modified record      :
 7. Target audience         :           18. Cataloguing source   :
 8. Form of item            :
 9. Nature of contents      :
10. Government publication  :
11. Conference publication  : 0
```

NOTES

1.   Deborah J. Byrne, *MARC Manual: Understanding and Using MARC Records*, 2nd ed. (Englewood, Colo.: Libraries Unlimited, 1998), pp. 1–15.

2.   *MARC 21 Format for Bibliographic Data: Including Guidelines for Content Designation* (Washington, D.C.: Cataloging Distribution Service, Library of Congress, 1999), 2 v.; *MARC 21 Concise Format for Bibliographic Data* (available: http://lcweb.loc.gov/marc/bibliographic/ecbdhome.html [accessed 8/25/99]).

3.   Arlene G. Taylor, *The Organization of Information* (Englewood, Colo.: Libraries Unlimited, 1999), pp. 63–73.

4.   Ibid., p. 64.

5.   For an example of a record in the communications format, *see* Taylor, *The Organization of Information*, p. 60.

SUGGESTED READING

Avram, Henriette D. *MARC, Its History and Implications*. Washington, D.C.: Library of Congress, 1975.

Byrne, Deborah J. *MARC Manual: Understanding and Using MARC Records*. 2nd ed. Englewood, Colo.: Libraries Unlimited, 1998.

Ferguson, Bobby. *MARC/AACR2/Authority Control Tagging: Blitz Cataloging Workbook*. Englewood, Colo.: Libraries Unlimited, 1998.

Understanding MARC: Bibliographic. Washington, D.C.: Cataloging Distribution Service, Library of Congress, 1998. Also available: http://lcweb.loc.gov/marc/umb (accessed 11/20/99).

Part III

DESCRIPTION AND ACCESS

Description

INTRODUCTION

Description as a cataloging process was briefly defined in chapter 1. This chapter discusses the process in more detail, and then introduces the rules for description in *AACR2R*. Although this work is referred to as *AACR2R98* elsewhere in this text, in this chapter and chapters 5–7, all of which cover description and access, the work that includes the additions and changes from 1993 and 1998 is referred to as *AACR2R* unless specific quotations and/or specific pages from the 1998 print version are being cited. This is because in the Anglo-American cataloging community, the concept for *AACR2* has been that after its revision in 1988, any subsequent additions and changes have been equivalent to loose-leaf publications, whatever their physical form may be. The work is still *AACR2R* even though additions and changes were issued in 1993 and 1998.

Description is that part of the cataloging process concerned with identification of an information package, and with recording information about it in a bibliographic record in such a way that it will be identified exactly and cannot be confused with any other. Many elements contribute to the identification of an information package. A title is almost always the first identifying element, followed by the name(s) of a person or persons responsible for the contents of the work. Next, one looks for information identifying an edition; the name of the edition; the name of an editor, reviser, illustrator, translator, performer, producer and/or publisher; the date of publication or copyright date; and a series of which the edition may be a part. Even the size, the type or number of illustrations, or the extent of the item (e.g., number of pages for a book or number of cassettes for a videorecording) may be helpful information for a patron seeking a particular edition of a work. When found, all these elements are useful in the description of the information package.

TECHNICAL READING OF AN
INFORMATION PACKAGE TO BE CATALOGED

In order to identify conventional elements of an information package so that they can be described on a catalog record, it is necessary to know not only what to look for, but also how to look. Technical reading in this manner is scarcely the same as reading for information or for entertainment, when the entire item may be read, seen, or heard. Obviously, the cataloger will have no time for "reading" of this sort, and therefore must learn to read technically. Reading technically involves recognizing quickly certain devices peculiar to the particular type of information package being cataloged. In this way, the cataloger can quickly determine its contents and how it can be described uniquely in such a way that this information can be passed on to potential users. The following discussion contains definitions useful to the cataloger in both descriptive cataloging and subject cataloging.

The first part of an information package that the cataloger examines in detail is the chief source of information. This source varies according to the type of material. In books, manuscripts, printed music, and printed serials, it is the title page. In microforms, films and videotapes it is the title frame(s). For sound recordings, it is the label and sometimes a container that is affixed to the item (e.g., cassette of a tape cassette). For cartographic and graphic materials, and for three-dimensional artifacts and realia, the chief source of information is the object itself, including permanently affixed labels or unifying containers. If computer files have title screens, these are used as the chief source; otherwise formally presented evidence or accompanying documentation is used. The home pages of World Wide Web sites, a type of computer file, are title screens by nature. In all these cases, the chief source of information may be absent for some reason, in which case cataloging rules prescribe alternate sources. Usually, however, the chief source of information provides the most complete bibliographic information about the information package: the author or other person responsible for the intellectual contents, the fullest form of the title, the name and/or number of the edition, the name of the publisher, distributor, etc., and the place and date of publication, distribution, etc. Figure 4.1 shows half the chief source of information for a sound recording. (The chief source for an audiocassette consists of all labels taken together. The side 2 label in this case differs only in the listing of contents.)

Fig. 4.1. Label from side 1 of an audiocassette.

The first element that the cataloger ordinarily notices is the title. The title from the chief source of information (minus any subtitle or other title information) is called the *title proper*; as such, it is used in all library records, in trade catalogs, and in bibliographies. It may or may not adequately describe the contents of the item. The book title, *Short History of the United States*, is self-evident, but the title of the serial, *Toward Freedom*, needs an explanation. A glance through an issue will reveal that the serial discusses the development of new nations; this will be indicated as a subject heading on the catalog record.

In addition to the major part of the title, some items have secondary parts. The *alternative title* is introduced by *or* and was widely used in books published before the twentieth century. As in Gilbert and Sullivan's *Patience, or, Bunthorne's Bride*, it amplifies the title by telling the reader that "Patience," in this case, is a woman's name rather than the name of a specific virtue. The *parallel title* is the title proper written in another language or in another script. For instance, a bilingual book on snowmobiles in the Province of Quebec has its title proper in French, *La motoneige au Québec*, and its parallel title in English, *Snowmobiling in Quebec*. *Other title information* is often used to qualify the title proper. Such qualifications are often called *subtitles*. For example, the complete title of a tape cassette is *Behavior Control: The Psychologist as Manipulator*. "The Psychologist as Manipulator" is the subtitle. It explains the aspect of behavior control covered in the tape. There is also other title information that is not "subtitle" but does give further explanatory information. In the title, *Barbara Morgan Photography: Trisolini Gallery of Ohio University, Athens, Ohio, January 9–February 3, 1979*, the "other title" information tells where and when the show was held.

The title proper and other titles in the chief source of information, however, are not the only possible ones. Other titles exist, and the cataloger must note those that vary significantly from the title proper. When such titles are noted, the patron who knows a work only by a variant title can be directed to it. For example, Haydn's *Symphony 94 in G Major* is also known as the "Surprise Symphony"; many patrons would look for this popular form of the title instead of the title proper. Books may carry a cover title (i.e., title printed on the cover), binder's title (i.e., title lettered on the original spine of the book), or running title (i.e., title repeated at the top of each page or each alternate page of the book) that differs from the title proper. Sound recordings, videotapes, graphic materials, or computer software may have titles on their containers that differ. World Wide Web sites may display different titles on the main body of the home page and in the title bar. Serials may have title variations on the cover or on an added title page.

The series title, however, is not a title variation, but indicates the series, if any, to which the information package belongs. A series may be the work of one author or several authors as in Will and Ariel Durant's *The Story of Civilization*, which consists of several uniform volumes. This is called an author's series. A series may also be issued by a publisher who commissions several authors to write one or more volumes on a specified subject. Such is the case with the Rinehart *Rivers of America* series of many volumes. Or perhaps an author is not commissioned but submits a work that happens to fit into a category established by the publisher. An example is Dodd, Mead's *Red Badge* series of mystery novels. Such series are called publishers' series.

The monographic series is a series that is usually issued with some regularity; each title in a monographic series ordinarily is given a number, usually in chronological order. For many patrons, the name of the series and the number of a title in it are the important identifying elements. Patrons may not remember individual authors and titles but look for these under the series name. Thus, although author and title of an individual item are major identifying elements, the series title in a monographic series assumes a significant role.

The second element to be identified by the cataloger is the statement of responsibility. This is also found in the chief source of information and is usually the author, whose name usually becomes the main entry. According to *AACR2R*, a personal author is "the person chiefly responsible for the creation of the intellectual or artistic content of a work."[1] In addition to writers of books and composers of music, this includes cartographers, artists, photographers, performers, etc. It may be necessary to locate some information about an unfamiliar author. For example, if the work is imaginative in nature, the author's nationality must be known since most classification schemes use the device of nationality to classify novels, drama, and poetry. This is discussed in the chapters on classification in this text. It is also sometimes necessary to know an author's nationality to know how to form the heading for the name. This is discussed further in the chapter on form of headings for persons.

An author is not the only possibility for inclusion in a statement of responsibility. Any person or persons responsible for intellectual or artistic content or for performance, or any corporate body from which the content is issued, may need to be included in the catalog record.

The edition, if named, is usually found in the chief source of information, but may also be found in other places. In a book, a piece of printed music, or a serial it may appear in the preliminaries (i.e., title page, verso [or back] of the title page, any pages preceding the title page, and the cover), in the preface to the work, or in a colophon (i.e., a statement at the end of the work). In cartographic or graphic material, sound recordings, motion pictures and videorecordings, machine-readable data files, and three-dimensional artifacts, the edition may appear in accompanying printed material. For those items with a container, the edition may be found there.

The edition is distinguished from a printing or issue in that a new edition indicates that certain specific changes—additions, deletions, modifications—have been made from earlier versions of the item. On the other hand, a new printing (or reprinting) or issue, means that more copies of the work were manufactured in order to keep up with demand. In the case of books and book-like materials, printings may have minor corrections or revisions, usually incorporated into the original type image. For other materials, a new issue may have slight variations from the original.

Editions may be named (e.g., "revised and enlarged," "abridged," "expurgated") or numbered (e.g., "5th edition"). Any of these edition statements indicates to the cataloger and the patron that some change in content or in form has been made. This information is very important to a scholar. To study the development of a poet, the literary scholar must have early and late editions of the poet's work. A physicist might want only the latest edition of a book on thermodynamics.

Because the name of the publisher or distributor, etc., might indicate the type or quality of a work, this information might be important to the patron who must choose one item from several on a specific subject. If the publisher or distributor, etc., is noted for excellence in a certain area (e.g., Skira in art; McGraw-Hill in technology), publisher/distributor information has some value to the patron. This information, including place and date, is usually found in the chief source of information, but may also be found in the same other locations as the edition statement. If the item is copyrighted, the copyright date and the holders of the copyright must be listed in or on it. This information is important when the publication date and the copyright date differ. In such a case, both dates are given in the catalog record.

The cataloger must learn to assess quickly the details of physical description. These include the extent of the item (e.g., number of pages or volumes, number of pieces, length of playing time), dimensions (e.g., height), and physical data other than extent or dimensions (e.g., presence of illustrations, playing speed, material of which made).

The cataloger must also be quick to identify other important and useful pieces of information about an item. Such information as variant titles of the same work (e.g., original title of a translation), other related versions of the work, language, edition history, accompanying materials, intended audience, contents of multi-volume items, and presence of bibliographies should often be noted in the catalog record. The standard number (e.g., International Standard Book Number [ISBN] or International Standard Serial Number [ISSN]) has become of major importance as a means of unique international identification. It is also given in the catalog record.

If there is a preface, the cataloger should read it as an aid to determination of the author's plan or objective and as an aid in identifying the edition. It also provides a key to subject matter. Similar aids are introductions, forewords, accompanying printed materials, and containers. The table of contents, with its listing of topics, is a valuable indication of the scope of a work. An index is a good source for determining subject content and special emphases. Bibliographies may also serve as an aid by indicating the author's point of view.

During the process of the technical reading the cataloger takes note of relevant elements of information as they are found, so that they can be formed into a coherent description for the bibliographic record that will represent the information package in the catalog. Figure 4.2 shows the *AACR2R* description for the sound recording whose partial chief source of information is shown in figure 4.1. The description was completed after a technical reading of the item. In the examples of description in this chapter, the choice of main entry is not taken into consideration in the formatting. That is, a "hanging indention" is not used when title would be chosen as main entry. Choice of main entry is discussed in chapter 6 of this text. In addition, the formatting of examples is given as prescribed by *AACR2R*; online catalogs often display bibliographic information quite differently.

Fig. 4.2. Description of the item whose partial chief source of information is shown in Fig. 4.1.

Altamont [sound recording] : Black stringband music from the Library of Congress. — Cambridge, Mass. : Rounder, p1989.
1 sound cassette : analog, Dolby processed.

Credits: Nathan Frazier, vocals and banjo, Frank Patterson, fiddle (1st–7th works) ; Murph Gribble, banjo, John Lusk, fiddle, Albert York, guitar (8th–14th works).
Recorded Mar. 1942 in Nashville, Tenn. (1st–7th works), Sept. (?) 1946 (8th–13th works), and spring 1949 (14th work) in Rocky Island, Tenn.
Contents: Dan Tucker — Old cow died — Bile them cabbage down — Po black sheep — Eighth of January — Corrinne — Texas traveler — Rolling river — Old sage friend — Apple blossom — Pateroller'll catch you — Across the sea — Cincinnati — Altamont.

If the record is to be entered into an online system, it is usually coded with the tags, indicators, and subfield codes of the MAchine-Readable Cataloging (MARC) format and is formatted with the spacing required by the system into which it will be entered. Figure 4.3 shows the description from figure 4.2 with MARC coding, formatted as it would be in the OCLC system.

Fig. 4.3. Description coded according to the MARC format and spaced and formatted as it would be for the OCLC system.

```
  OCLC:   23949490        Rec stat:     c
  Entered:    19910618    Replaced:     19960403      Used: 19960305
> Type: j        Elvl: I   Srce:  d    Audn:      Ctrl:        Lang: eng
  BLvl: m        Form:     Comp:  fm   AccM:      MRec:        Ctry: mau
  Desc: a        FMus: n   LTxt:       DtSt: s    Dates: 1989,    <
>    1 040       CLE $c CLE <
>    2 007       s $b s $d l $e u $f n $g j $h l $i c <
>    3 028  00   C-0238 $b Rounder  <
>    4 033  0    194203-- $b 3964 $c N2 <
>    5 033  2    194609-- $a 1949---- $b 3960 <
>    6 043       n-us--- $a n-us-tn <
>    7 047       fm $a cy <
>    8 090       M1630.18 $b .A48 1989 <
>    9 049       CUMM <
>   10 245  00   Altamont $h [sound recording] : $b Black stringband music
from the Library of Congress. <
>   11 260       Cambridge, Mass. : $b Rounder, $c p1989. <
>   12 300       1 sound cassette : $b analog, Dolby processed. <
>   13 511  0    Nathan Frazier, vocals and banjo, Frank Patterson, fiddle
(1st-7th works) ; Murph Gribble, banjo, John Lusk, fiddle, Albert York,
guitar (8th-14th works). <
>   14 518       Recorded Mar. 1942 in Nashville, Tenn. (1st-7th works),
Sept.(?) 1946 (8th-13th works), and spring 1949 (14th work) in Rocky
Island, Tenn. <
>   15 505  0    Dan Tucker -- Old cow died -- Bile them cabbage down --
Po black sheep -- Eighth of January -- Corrinne -- Texas traveler --
Rolling river -- Old sage friend -- Apple blossom -- Pateroller'll catch
you -- Across the sea -- Cincinnati -- Altamont. <
>   16 650  0    Afro-Americans $z Tennessee $x Music. <
>   17 655  7    Country music $z Tennessee $y 1941-1950. $2 lcsh <
>   18 655  7    Folk music $z Tennessee. $2 lcsh <
>   19 655  7    Square dance music. $2 lcsh <
>   20 655  7    Fiddle tunes. $2 lcsh <
>   21 700  1    Frazier, Nathan. $4 prf <
>   22 700  1    Patterson, Frank, $c fiddler. $4 prf <
>   23 700  1    Gribble, Murph. $4 prf <
>   24 700  1    Lusk, John. $4 prf <
>   25 700  1    York, Albert. $4 prf <
>   26 710  2    Archive of Folk Song (U.S.) <
```

DESCRIPTION OF MATERIALS
USING *AACR2R*

The rest of this chapter covers in some detail the *AACR2R* rules for descriptive cataloging of materials in all formats. Not all rules are discussed, and the reader should examine the appropriate chapters of the code for more complex problems.

AACR2R does not contain instructions for MARC coding (discussed in chapter 3). The Library of Congress (LC) issues a general outline of the MARC 21 format that includes definitions of all tags, indicators, and subfield codes and dictates the contents of each field and subfield, but does not indicate spacing or layout.[2] Each system that uses a MARC format creates its own spacing and layout, and it issues system documentation demonstrating how MARC records will be formatted in that system. Only *AACR2R* content, spacing, and punctuation are discussed in this chapter, although MARC 21 field numbers and subfield codes are identified beside many of the *AACR2R* rules.

The first chapter of *AACR2R* covers description in general and is applicable to all types of materials (e.g., print, sound recordings, etc.) in all conditions (e.g., microform) and patterns (e.g., serial) of publication. Chapters 2 through 12 of *AACR2R* cover in detail various types of material and conditions and patterns of publication. These chapters often refer back to chapter 1 for rules that are generally applicable, but they also give specific guidance for situations that are peculiar to the type of material or condition of publication under discussion. Chapters 2 through 12 of *AACR2R* cover:

2   Books, Pamphlets, and Printed Sheets
3   Cartographic Materials
4   Manuscripts (including Manuscript Collections)
5   Music
6   Sound Recordings
7   Motion Pictures and Videorecordings
8   Graphic Materials
9   Computer Files
10 Three-Dimensional Artifacts and Realia
11 Microforms
12 Serials

Special considerations pertaining to the cataloging of many of these materials are discussed below. *AACR2R* Chapter 13, rather than dealing with a type of material or condition of publication, covers a special problem in cataloging: analysis. There are purposely no chapters numbered 14 through 20 in *AACR2R*. These numbers were left vacant for later construction of rules for new types of material, as it becomes necessary to develop rules for cataloging them.

THE STRUCTURE OF
ANGLO-AMERICAN CATALOGUING RULES, SECOND EDITION (AACR2R) CHAPTERS 1 THROUGH 12

An important concept in using chapters 1 through 12 of *AACR2R* is that the rule numbers are mnemonic. In International Standard Bibliographic Description (ISBD), upon which *AACR2R* is based, there are eight "areas" of description as follows:

1. Title and statement of responsibility area
2. Edition area
3. Material (or type of publication) specific details area
4. Publication, distribution, etc., area
5. Physical description area
6. Series area
7. Note area
8. Standard number and terms of availability area

Not all areas are used in describing all library materials, but in chapters 1 to 12 of *AACR2R* all are mentioned, if only to say that the area in question is not used to describe the particular material (e.g., rule 2.3, Material [or Type of Publication] Specific Details Area: "This area is not used for printed monographs."). The rules are numbered in such a way that the number preceding the period is the chapter number and the number following the period is the rule number. Rules 1 through 8 in each chapter represent the eight "areas" named above. Thus, rule 1.2 deals with the edition area in general, while rule 5.2 covers the edition area for music, and rule 8.2 covers the edition area for graphic materials. Further, the rule numbers are subdivided by letters sometimes followed by numerals which are also mnemonic. In the general chapter, rule 1.1D is the rule for parallel titles; for books, the comparable rule is rule 2.1D, and for serials it is rule 12.1D. In addition to the rules for "areas," all the chapters have general rules assigned the numeral "0." Chapters 1–3 and 5–12 also have rules 9, "Supplementary items," and 10, "Items made up of several types of materials." These rules do not all have exactly the same heading, but address the same concept (e.g., rule 10 for serials is entitled "Sections of Serials"). Chapters 1–3, 5, and 8 have a rule 11, "Facsimiles, Photocopies, and Other Reproductions." Chapter 2 has, in addition, rules 12 through 18 that deal specifically with early printed monographs.

Throughout *AACR2R* there are "optional" rules that allow for adding or deleting information in certain instances or that allow alternative methods of handling certain situations. Each cataloging agency must decide whether and how these options will be applied. Because so many libraries rely on LC for cataloging data, this text includes, in this chapter and the ones on *AACR2R* that follow, a discussion of LC's decision about application of each option that occurs in the rule sequences discussed in this text.

LC has issued rule interpretations that affect LC's implementation of rules in addition to the decisions about optional rules. LC rule interpretations for *AACR2R* have been published separately and are available from LC's Cataloging Distribution Service.[3] They also have been published in issues of *Cataloging Service Bulletin.*[4] These have been cumulated by individuals outside of LC and are available at modest cost.[5] It is assumed that the version in the *Cataloging Service Bulletin* is available most widely, and so when LC's rule interpretations are referred to in this text, they are cited as *CSB* followed by the issue number and page(s) (e.g., *CSB* 45: 13–15 means *Cataloging Service Bulletin*, number 45, pages 13–15).

SPECIAL CONSIDERATIONS FOR NONBOOK MATERIALS

Chapters 3 through 10 in *AACR2R* cover materials that have been variously called "nonbook," "nonprint," "audiovisual," or "media"—the last term often including monographic materials, as in "School Media Center." Often these special materials are not handled in the same way as monographs are handled. An administrative decision within each library determines whether to catalog and/or classify each of these special materials; because of their dimensions, many cannot be shelved with corresponding monographic materials. The dimensions of such materials, then, become quite significant in bibliographic descriptions because this directly influences their location in a given collection, a consideration that often makes classification relatively insignificant and description of greater importance.

If the librarian cannot easily remember the contents of the collection, then cataloging control is needed. If the library has only six maps, for instance, there is little need to catalog them. Sixty maps, however, or even 16, may well need to be cataloged. The disadvantage of failing to catalog descriptively any special materials is that the patron must look somewhere other than in the main catalog for the record of the material. It is strongly recommended that as many special materials as possible be cataloged descriptively and thus recorded in the main catalog. Past problems in doing this were greatly eased by the publication of *AACR2*, followed by its revisions, with its integrated approach to the description of special materials. In *AACR2R* all materials are described according to the same set of principles.

Manuscripts. Collections of manuscripts can be cataloged at different levels. The collection can be described as a whole (collection-level cataloging), or individual manuscripts can be described separately (item-level cataloging). The challenge of cataloging manuscripts is that each is unique. The manuscript or the manuscript collection does not exist in another library, except perhaps in reproduction. It is not the kind of material for which catalogers can find cataloging copy already in existence. In addition, such materials often do not have any clearly defined chief source of information, and, indeed, they often do not have clearly defined titles. There may be difficulty even reading the handwriting in which a manuscript is written. It may be difficult to know whether one is dealing with an original or with a handwritten copy and, if a copy, the date it was copied and by whom. The manuscript cataloger is often dealing with events and names of persons not recorded elsewhere.

Music. One challenge in cataloging this material is that a musical composition in printed form normally appears as a series of staves upon which notes are printed, but increasingly other systems of notation are used. The description of music written for a solo instrument, such as the piano, is relatively straightforward. The description of music written for several instrumental or vocal parts (i.e., scores) presents some special problems, especially in the title and statement of responsibility area, in the physical description area, and in the notes area.

Sound recordings. Both classification and description of sound recordings are affected by the fact that extremely disparate materials often appear on a single physical piece. This problem is addressed for description in *AACR2R*, rule 6.1G, described below.

Motion pictures and videorecordings. Two of the complications involved in describing these materials involve the source of information and the large numbers of people responsible for them. Titles and other information, as they appear in the item itself, in accompanying materials, or on containers, often vary considerably. The large number of people involved presents problems for deciding how many "credits" will provide useful description of an item. Another problem is concerned with the ease with which videorecordings may be made, thus complicating the concepts of "copy" and "edition." These and other problems are addressed in the rules that follow, but ultimately the cataloger must use some judgment based on general principles.[6]

Graphic materials. These include, among other forms: art originals, art prints, art reproductions, charts, filmstrips, flash cards, photographs, pictures, postcards, posters, slides, study prints, technical drawings and wall charts. Many of these materials are not cataloged and/or classified in many libraries. An administrative decision within each library determines whether to catalog and/or classify these materials. Because most of them cannot be physically shelved with the corresponding monographic materials, standard classifications such as *Library of Congress Classification* (*LCC*) or *Dewey Decimal Classification* (*DDC*) often are not used. Rather, use is made of a simple accession or serial number to determine shelf order. On the other hand, catalog records of these materials are easily integrated in a database with records for monographic or serial material, because, in *AACR2R*, all materials are described according to the same standard—ISBD(G).

Computer files. The cataloging of computer files is a more recent addition to the cataloging field, and poses some of the greatest challenges to established practice at present. The need for standards for cataloging these materials was recognized in 1970 when the American Library Association's (ALA's) Cataloging and Classification Section established a subcommittee to develop rules for cataloging computer files (then referred to as "machine-readable data files," or "MRDFs"). Since then, steady progress has been made, but the form in which bibliographic information for computer files can be found varies so greatly that cataloging them is somewhat more of a challenge than for most other materials. The state of the art of production of computer files is comparable to that of books in the early days of printing. At first there was no source of data comparable to a title page. Program files and World Wide Web sites now usually have such a source, with non-standard and varying amounts of information, but data files still usually have no such source. As with videorecordings there is the problem of ease of duplication, complicating the ideas of "copy" and "edition."

Microcomputer software developed after the publication of *AACR2* in 1978. As a result it was necessary to develop some supplementary interpretations for the rules in Chapter 9. These guidelines were published as a separate booklet.[7] In 1986, Chapter 9 of *AACR2* was completely revised and published as a separate publication.[8] The revision was expanded to include all types of computer files then existing. This revised Chapter 9 was incorporated into *AACR2R* with a number of revisions and editions. Since then, as computer hardware has increased in speed and sophistication, a popular form of software, known as "multimedia," has been produced for both the home and educational markets. These software packages are characterized by the integration of many media, including text, digital video, sound and still images, and often include multiple physical pieces. In 1994, ALA published a set of guidelines which may be used to supplement *AACR2R* in the description of these materials.[9]

In similar fashion to the development of microcomputer software, widespread use of the Internet came about after the publication of *AACR2R*. In particular, the explosive growth of resources now available on the World Wide Web was enabled to a great extent by the release of Mosaic browser software in 1993–94. As a result, remotely-accessed computer files, intangible and easily modified without warning, have become resources of major importance in many libraries. These materials present their own set of challenges for description, classification, and management. While *AACR2R* does not address the description of Internet materials explicitly, there is a standard guidebook edited by Nancy B. Olson which may easily be consulted to address problems faced by the cataloger.[10]

Three-dimensional artifacts and realia. Prior to the advent of *AACR2*, three-dimensional artifacts and realia were not cataloged or classified except in a few museum libraries. With a method of description consistent with that of describing other materials, however, we are seeing more cataloging of these materials— especially in media centers where emphasis is no longer on the "book" as the principal means of transmitting information.

A number of manuals have been written that supplement *AACR2R* in the area of nonbook materials. They are listed in the "Suggested Reading" section at the end of this chapter. They should be consulted for more detailed discussion of the problems of cataloging these materials, for definitions of terms unique to these types, and for in-depth examples of cataloging.

SPECIAL CONSIDERATIONS FOR MICROFORMS

The cataloging of microforms requires knowledge of a number of different types of material. Books, manuscripts, maps, music, and graphic materials all can be reproduced in microform. In addition, microform can be the original means of publication of some kinds of content. According to *AACR2R*, all microforms, whether original publications or reproductions, are described in terms of the microform format with details of the original, when applicable, given in a note. As mentioned below under the discussion of rule 1.5A3, this is a controversial method for handling microforms. Those who oppose it say that the user is misled by being given a modern date in the publication, distribution, etc., area when the intellectual content of the work is much older. They are also concerned about short-entry catalogs in which the notes are not printed. Publishers that specialize in reproducing older printed material in microform say that the purpose of the reproduction is to make older materials available for scholarly study and research, not to create a new edition of it as a printed reprint of the text would do.

Earlier rules called for description of the original in the major part of the record with microform details in a note. Those opposed to this method point out that the physical form of the information package is important. A user who comes into the library wanting to borrow an item to take elsewhere to read needs to know whether it is in book form or microform. There are also potential problems for the cataloger in determining what the original was and what its physical description should be. A microform of a dissertation, for example, may be a positive copy of a negative master that is a copy of a photocopy of a printout of text originally held in a computer file. Two articles that discuss the issues involved should be read for further information.[11] Americans have tended to prefer the method of describing the original, with details about the microform in a note, but Europeans have espoused describing the original in a note. In 1980 and 1981 ALA's Committee on Cataloging: Description and Access examined this question again and put forth a recommendation; its recommendation was that the original be described in the body of the entry, with details of the microform given in a note. The rules were not revised, but LC issued a policy decision to this effect.[12] Both methods are illustrated in this text.

In December 1989 an Airlie House conference sponsored by the Council on Library Resources was held during which a solution was sought to the problem of "multiple versions." "Multiple versions" is the name given to the concept of two or more formats of the same work (e.g., a book, a negative microfilm of the book, and a positive microfilm of it; or, a published research paper and a photocopy of it). At the conference a decision was made to pursue a possible two-tiered hierarchical solution in which the top level of the hierarchy would be a bibliographic record containing a description of the common elements of the various versions of the work, while the next level would contain the elements of description unique to each version. Although the Airlie House conference recommendations were not implemented, the relationship(s) between a work and its manifestations remains an important subject of current discussion. As with so many other questions in cataloging and classification, the "multiple versions" issue is further highlighted by the increasing reliance on remote-access computer files, which may reproduce print materials to a greater or lesser extent, or be produced in different digital formats simultaneously.

In October 1997, the "International Conference on the Principles and Future Development of AACR" was held. The conference, which sought and received extensive comment online on a range of issues in advance, produced a number of recommendations. Among them was the charge to re-examine *AACR2R* rule 0.24, which states in part: "It is a cardinal principle of the use of part I [of the code] that the description of a physical item should be based in the first instance on the chapter dealing with the class of materials to which that item belongs." This is often paraphrased as "Catalog the item in hand." Any significant change in this rule will have important implications for cataloging microforms, as well as computer files and information packages in many media. The conference proceedings have been published,[13] and the reader should watch for developments on this issue.

SPECIAL CONSIDERATIONS FOR SERIALS

As defined in *AACR2R*, a serial is a publication in any medium issued in successive parts at regular or irregular intervals and intended to continue indefinitely. Serials include both periodicals and non-periodicals. A periodical may be defined as a serial that has a distinctive title and that is issued more frequently than once a year and at regular intervals, with each issue containing articles by several contributors. Non-periodicals are all other forms of serials, such as yearbooks, annuals, memoirs, transactions and proceedings of societies, and any series cataloged together instead of separately.

A clear distinction should be made between serials and monographs. A monograph represents a complete bibliographic unit; it may be issued in successive parts at regular or irregular intervals, but it is *not* intended to continue indefinitely. In most cases, of course, a monographic publication is completed in one volume. There are certain types of monographs, though, that are often treated as serials by libraries because they are not complete in one volume. These include continuations of sets, provisional serials, and pseudo-serials. A continuation of a set is a nonserial—i.e., monographic—set in process of publication. The *Oxford History of English Literature* and the *Dictionary of Literary Biography* are examples of continuations of sets. Neither publication is presently complete although many individual volumes have been issued. Such publications require a special order record—i.e., a standing order—for follow-up purposes; if such works are cataloged as sets, this creates problems for maintaining accurate records in the library's holdings record for the set. Provisional sets are those publications that are treated as serials while in the process of publication and as nonserials when complete. The justification for such treatment is often a particularly lengthy period of publication and/or a complicated numbering of individual issues. Either of the two previous examples of continuations of sets could be treated by individual libraries as provisional serials.

A pseudo-serial is a frequently reissued and revised publication that is generally treated as a monographic work at first publication but that is often treated as a serial after numerous successive editions have appeared. Serial numbering may be taken from the edition number or from the date of publication. Examples of pseudo-serials are Sir John Bernard Burke's *Genealogical and Heraldic History of the Peerage* (commonly called *Burke's Peerage*) or the *Guide to Reference Books* edited successively by Alice Bertha Kroeger, Isadore Mudge, Constance Winchell, Eugene P. Sheehy, Robert Balay, and others. Monographic treatment of a pseudo-serial requires individual descriptive cataloging for each new edition as well as additional added entries for previous editors or compilers. If a pseudo-serial is treated as a serial, the main entry is made under the title instead of the author and will require only one set of catalog entries.

The distinction between monographic and serial publications has, however, been put to the test by the recent proliferation of experiments in electronic journal publishing, primarily via the World Wide Web. While some electronic journals mimic print publications in enumeration, chronology, and visual appearance (including pagination), others dispense with any or all of these features. It is difficult to reconcile the *AACR2R* definition of "serial" with the reality of online scholarly journals which store articles in a single cumulating database, without partitioning them into separate volumes or issues. Although opinion is divided on this question, some catalogers maintain that these resources are monographic in nature, with the result that an online version of a print serial might be an electronic monograph.

The October 1997 conference in Toronto examined the nature of seriality in the light of difficulties such as these. It produced the charge to redefine "serial" to take into account these new publication patterns (and, in addition, bring the description of traditional looseleaf services into the fold). A report to the Joint Steering Committee for Revision of *AACR* that has been prepared by Jean Hirons makes a number of recommendations, that, if adopted, will have far-reaching implications for *AACR2*.[14]

The principles for cataloging serials are generally the same as those for cataloging monographic publications. On the other hand, certain physical characteristics of serial publications (e.g., numerous changes in bibliographic descriptions, including changes of titles) necessitate some special rules. The aim of these special rules is to prepare an entry that will stand the longest time and will allow necessary changes to be made with a minimum of modification. If the serial is still being published or if the library has only part of the set and hopes to complete it, an open entry is prepared according to the rules that are presented in this chapter.

The descriptive cataloging of serials is generally more complex than that of monographs because of their greatly varied and possibly intricate bibliographic structure. On the other hand, classification and subject headings are likely to be somewhat more general, and therefore simpler. Indeed, in many libraries, periodicals are not classified at all but are shelved alphabetically by main entry. The detail with which serials are described may vary widely from library to library. Some consider a highly analytic description essential, while others reduce serials cataloging to the title and statement of responsibility area and a holdings note.

The serials cataloger is likely to be faced with the problem of describing a full set completely although all that may be at hand are a few volumes or current issues. The most important sources of additional information are the *Union List of Serials*, *New Serial Titles*, *British Union Catalogue of Periodicals*, *Standard Periodical Directory*, *Ulrich's International Periodical Directory* (which now incorporates the formerly separate *Irregular Serials and Annuals: An International Directory*), and *Ulrich's Update*.[15] Other important sources are the LC catalogs and national and trade bibliographies, as well as publishers' catalogs. *Titles in Series* is useful for its lists of titles in monographic series, especially those published by university presses, and Bowker's *Books in Series in the United States 1966–1975* lists monographs distributed in popular, scholarly, and professional series.[16] In addition, the LC publication, *Monographic Series*, lists all monographs cataloged by LC that appeared as parts of series between 1974 and 1983, as well as all revised records, regardless of the date of publication.[17] Series access has been incorporated in the *National Union Catalog* since 1982. OCLC and other databases are sources of additional information, as are published state union lists of serials.

SELECTED RULES AND EXAMPLES

The balance of this chapter is devoted to the *AACR2R* rules for description, covering *AACR2R* Chapters 1 through 12. The aim in this edition has been to integrate the parallel or analogous rules for description in each medium. Thus, for example, the rules and subrules for Area 1, Title and statement of responsibility, are discussed integrally across all media. To the greatest extent practicable, general principles applying to the greatest number of media are described first, followed by selected variations in specific *AACR2R* chapters. This organizational plan cannot always be carried out at the most detailed level, however. Despite *AACR2R*'s general parallelism across Chapters 1 through 12, analogous rule numbers in different chapters do not always discuss the same subjects. These exceptional situations are noted as they arise. Section headings for rules and subrules which have general application are designated with an X (e.g., X.5C) in place of a specific chapter number.

For each type of material, one or more examples has been chosen to demonstrate a bibliographic record for that type. In each case, the chief source of information is illustrated. At the end of this chapter, complete bibliographic records, presented both in ISBD ("card") format and MARC format, are given. Because no one example can demonstrate every eventuality, other examples of particular instances are also given throughout each chapter.

RULE X.0.   GENERAL RULES

1.0A.   Sources of information
A chief source of information is specified for each type of material or condition or pattern of publication. Information in the chief source is to be preferred to information found elsewhere. Some parts of the description may be taken from "prescribed" sources rather than the chief source. In either case information that is not from the chief source, where required, or from prescribed sources in the other instances, must be enclosed in square brackets.

Lack of a chief source of information may be a problem with such items as locally produced sound recordings. If the item cannot be used as a basis for description, the information is taken from any available source and is given a note explaining the source of the supplied data.

This rule in chapters 2–12 identifies the kinds of materials covered in that chapter. It also sometimes points out certain kinds of information packages *not* covered, or not covered completely, and suggests the chapter that should be consulted instead or in addition. For example, rule 4.0A directs that for the cataloging of manuscript cartographic items, one should also consult chapter 3 of *AACR2R*.

12.0A Serials: A rule interpretation from LC gives guidelines for distinguishing between monographic and serial publications. (*CSB* 76: 20–24)

X.0B1. Chief source of information

TYPE OF MATERIAL	CHIEF SOURCE OF INFORMATION
2.0B1. Printed monographs ("Books"): i.e., all printed texts except serials (covered in *AACR2R* chapter 12) and microform reproductions of printed texts (covered in *AACR2R* chapter 11)	The title page. If there is not a title page, then the part of the item that gives the most complete information is used as a substitute. In this case, the part used as a substitute is given in a note. The information from the substitute is treated as if it were from a title page, i.e., brackets are not used. If the item has no part that can substitute, information may be taken from any available source.
	If information that would ordinarily appear on a title page is given on facing pages, both pages are treated as "the title page."
3.0B1. Atlases	Title page (same as for books).
Other cartographic items	a) cartographic item itself, or, if a) is inappropriate, b) container or case, or the cradle and stand of a globe.
4.0B1. Manuscript*	The manuscript itself.
	If information is scattered the order of preference is: title page if there is one and it was originally part of the manuscript, colophon, caption, heading, text itself.
	If information cannot be taken from the manuscript, use, in this order: another manuscript copy of the item, a published edition of the item, reference sources, and other sources.
5.0B1. Published music	a) List title page, cover, or caption – whichever furnishes the fullest information.
	b) If information cannot be taken from a), use, in this order: caption, cover, colophon, other preliminaries, other sources.

---

*The cataloging manual *Archives, Personal Papers, and Manuscripts* (*APPM*) has been accepted by LC, the Research Libraries Group (RLG), and OCLC as the standard for cataloging this type of material. One significant difference between this manual and chapter 4 of *AACR2R* is that for manuscript collections *APPM* allows the finding aid to serve as the chief source of information.

6.0B1.   Sound recordings:

Disc	Disc and label
Tape (open reel-to-reel)	Reel and label
Tape cassette	Cassette and label
Tape cartridge	Cartridge and label
Roll	Label
Sound recording on film	Container and label

For all: two or more labels are treated as one chief source.

If textual material has a collective title while the chief sources above do not, then the source of the collective title may be treated as a chief source.

If information cannot be taken from a chief source above, use, in this order: accompanying textual material, a container, other sources. Prefer printed data to sound data.

7.0B1.   Motion pictures and videorecordings

Item itself (e.g., title frames) and, if in a permanent container (e.g., a cartridge), the container and its label.

If information cannot be taken from the chief source, use, in this order: accompanying textual material, container that is not an integral part of the piece, other sources.

8.0B1.   Graphic materials

Item itself, including permanently affixed labels or containers. For an item consisting of two or more parts (e.g., slide set), use a container that provides a collective title if the items do not.

If information cannot be taken from the chief source, use, in this order: non-integral container, accompanying textual material, other sources.

9.0B1.   Computer files

Title screen(s). If there is no title screen, other internal sources, such as main menus, program statements and file headers may be used. The source with the most complete information is preferred.

In the case of files that cannot be read without processing (e.g. compressed files), information should be taken after the file has been processed for use.

If the information cannot be gained from internal sources (either because it is not there or because the cataloger does not have the right equipment), use, in this order: the physical carrier or any permanently attached publisher-produced labels, documentation issued by the publisher or creator with the file, information printed on the container issued by the publisher or distributor.

If the container has a collective title and the sources above do not, the source of the collective title should be treated as the chief source. If information is not available from any of these sources, use, in this order: other published descriptions of the file, other sources.

10.0B1. Three-dimensional artifacts and realia	The object itself, along with any accompanying textual material and container issued with the item. Information on the item or permanently affixed to it is preferred.

11.0B1. Microforms	
Microfilm	The title frame, usually at the beginning of the item giving full title and publication details.
Aperture cards:	
set of cards	Title card
single card	Card itself
Microfiches and microopaques	Title frame

If there is no title frame for a microfiche or a microopaque, the "header" (i.e., eye-readable data at the top of the fiche or opaque) is used unless the title there is in shortened form, while it appears in fuller form on the accompanying eye-readable materials or container. In the latter case the source of the fuller form is used as the chief source of information, and a note is made to indicate the source of the title proper. Information that is usually presented on one title frame or card may be presented on successive frames or cards. In this case, the successive frames or cards are treated as one chief source.

Information not available in the chief source is taken from other sources. The order of preference is:

> the remainder of the item
>
> container
>
> accompanying material
>
> other sources

12.0B. Serials	
12.0B1 Printed serials	The title page (or title page substitute) of the first issue of a serial is used as its chief source of information. If the first issue is not available, the first issue that is available is used.**

If a printed serial lacks a title page, the following substitutes are to be used in this order: analytical title page, cover, caption, masthead, editorial pages, colophon, other pages. The source of title page substitute is given in a note. LC gives a rule interpretation that makes the following exception: if an item has two or more different titles and the title on the preferred source is known to be less stable than another title, then the source with the stable title is to be used as the title page substitute. (*CSB* 76: 24-25)

12.0B2. Nonprint serials	Rule .0B of the relevant chapter is used.

** This is a change from pre-*AACR2* practice that called for using the latest issue. While there is some objection to using the first issue because of all the changes that can occur in such areas as the publication area, the former practice could not, in fact, be followed because of the extreme difficulty of examining every new issue. As is the case with many other issues in cataloging, the great variety in publication patterns displayed by electronic serials is calling the present practice into question. What, for example, is the "first issue" of an electronic journal with no numeric or chronological designation?

X.0B2.   Prescribed sources of information

Each area of the description has a prescribed source or sources from which information should be taken. These prescribed sources are fairly standard from medium to medium, although there are variations. If information in an area is from a

MATERIAL	TITLE AND STATEMENT OF RESPONSIBILITY	EDITION	[AREA 3]	PUBLICATION, DISTRIBUTION, ETC.
2.0B2 Books	Title page	Title page, other preliminaries, and colophon	[Not used]	Title page, other preliminaries, and colophon
3.0B2 Cartographic materials	Chief source of information	Chief source of information, accompanying printed material	Chief source of information, accompanying printed material	Chief source of information, accompanying printed material
4.0B2 Manuscripts	Chief source of information, published copies of the item	Chief source of information, published copies of the item	[Not used]	Chief source of information, published copies of the item (Only the date is given.)
5.0B2 Music	Chief source of information	Chief source of information, caption, cover, or colophon, other preliminaries	Chief source of information	Chief source of information, caption, cover, or colophon, other preliminaries, first page of music
6.0B2 Sound recordings	Chief source of information	Chief source of information, accompanying textual material, container	[Not used]	Chief source of information, accompanying textual material, container
7.0B2 Motion pictures and video-recordings	Chief source of information	Chief source of information, accompanying material	[Not used]	Chief source of information, accompanying material
8.0B2 Graphics	Chief source of information	Chief source of information, container, accompanying material	[Not used]	Chief source of information, container, accompanying material
9.0B2 Computer files	Chief source of information, carrier or its labels, information issued by publisher or creator, container	Chief source of information, carrier or its labels, information issued by publisher or creator, container	Any source	Chief source of information, carrier or its labels, information issued by publisher or creator, container
10.B2 Three-dimensional artifacts and realia	Chief source of information	Chief source of information	[Not used]	Chief source of information
11.0B2 Microforms	Chief source of information	Chief source of information, rest of the item, container	Chief source of information, rest of the item, container	Chief source of information, rest of the item, container
12.0B Serials 12.0B1 Printed serials	Chief source of information	Chief source of information, other preliminaries, colophon	The whole publication	The whole publication
12.0B2 Nonprint serials: see the chapters for the type of material, e.g., Chapter 9 for computer file serials. The first issue of a nonprint serial should be used.				

non-prescribed source, it should be enclosed in square brackets. A table of the most common prescribed sources is given below (pages 68–69), with the variations noted.

PHYSICAL DESCRIPTION	SERIES	NOTES	STANDARD NUMBER AND TERMS OF AVAILABILITY
The whole publication	Series title page, monograph title page, cover, rest of the publication	Any source	Any source
Any source	Chief source of information, accompanying printed material	Any source	Any source
Any source	[Not used]	Any source	[Not used]
Any source	Series title page, caption, cover, title, colophon, other preliminaries	Any source	Any source
Any source	Chief source of information, accompanying textual material, container	Any source	Any source
Any source	Chief source of information, accompanying material	Any source	Any source
Any source	Chief source of information, container, accompanying material	Any source	Any source
Any source	Chief source of information, carrier or its labels, information issued by publisher or creator, container	Any source	Any source
Any source	Chief source of information	Any source	Any source
Any source	Chief source of information, rest of the item, container	Any source	Any source
The whole publication	The whole publication*	Any source	Any source

---

* A rule interpretation from LC clarifies the prescribed source for this area. (*CSB* 76: 25)

1.0C. Punctuation

An extended discussion of punctuation in *AACR2R* is given in the 8th edition of this text.[18] Most areas in most chapters of *AACR2R* have a rule numbered .A1 (1.1A1, 1.2A1, 1.4A1, etc.) in which detailed guidance for punctuation of specific areas of the description is given.

1.0D. Levels of detail in the description

AACR2R provides three recommended levels of description. The minimum requirements for each level are specified in this rule. The rules in chapters 1–12 of *AACR2R* provide guidance for every element of level 3. The examples in this text, for the most part, follow LC practice in cataloging at level 2. Figures 4.4 and 4.5 illustrate the first and second levels for the same item. The third level includes every possible element set out in the rules and is likely to be used only in cataloging such things as rare items.

Fig. 4.4. Rule 1.0D1. First level of description.

Scottish crofters. — Holt, Rinehart and Winston, c1990.
xii, 175 p.

Bibliography: p. 167-169.
Includes index.
ISBN 0-030-03754-6

Note: Cataloging to the first level of description requires use of only rules 1.1B, 1.1F, 1.2B, 1.3, 1.4D, 1.4F, 1.5B, 1.7, and 1.8B. In the use of rule 1.7, all notes are optional.

Fig. 4.5. Rule 1.0D2. Second level of description.

Scottish crofters : a historical ethnography of a Celtic village / Susan Parman. — Fort Worth : Holt, Rinehart and Winston, c1990.
xii, 175 p. : ill. ; 24 cm. — (Case studies in cultural anthropology)

Bibliography: p. 167-169.
Includes index.
ISBN 0-030-30754-6

1.0H. Items with several chief sources of information

Single part items. An information package that has more than one chief source of information should generally be described from the first one, with a few major exceptions outlined in this rule. For example, in cataloging sound recordings, two or more chief sources of information (e.g., labels on both sides of a disc) should be treated as a single source. Also, the chief source with the latest date of publication, distribution, etc., should be preferred. In addition, *AACR2R* prescribes preferences to follow by language, if there are different languages in the chief source. (*See AACR2R98*, pp. 16–17.)

Multipart items. The chief source of information for the first part of a multipart information package should be used for the basic description, with variations in later parts shown in notes. If the first part is missing, the first part that is available is used. If there is no "first" part, the part that gives the most information or the unifying container is used.

Illustrative Examples

What follows are examples of chief and prescribed sources of information for many of the types of materials covered in *AACR2R*. These examples will be used to build descriptions throughout this chapter. Complete descriptions and MARC records for these examples are given on pages 147–160.

Chapter 2, Books

Figures 4.6–4.8 illustrate the title page and "other preliminaries" for the book that is used in this text to illustrate building a description. *Preliminaries* is defined in *AACR2R98* as "the title page(s) of an item, the verso of the title page(s), any pages preceding the title page(s), and the cover."[19] *Colophon* is defined as "a statement at the end of an item giving information about one or more of the following: the title, author(s), publisher, printer, date of publication or printing...."[20] The book used here has the title, author, and edition statement on the front cover, with the information on the spine duplicating that on the title page. It has no colophon. Colophons are not common in English-language books but are found more often in books in other languages.

Fig. 4.6. Title page of book.

A Guide to the Library of
Congress Classification

Fifth Edition

Based on the Fourth Edition of
*Immroth's Guide to the
Library of Congress Classification*

Lois Mai Chan

1999
LIBRARIES UNLIMITED, INC.
Englewood, Colorado

Fig. 4.7. Verso of title page.

Based on *Immroth's Guide to the Library of Congress Classification*,
1st and 2d Editions,
© Barbara F. Immroth 1968, 1971
All Rights Reserved

3d Edition,
© Libraries Unlimited, Inc. 1980
All Rights Reserved

4th Edition,
© Lois Mai Chan 1990
All Rights Reserved

A Guide to the Library of Congress Classification
5th Edition,
© Lois Mai Chan 1999
All Rights Reserved
Printed in the United States of America

No part of this publication may be reproduced, stored in a retrieval system, or transmitted, in any form or by any means, electronic, mechanical, photocopying, recording, or otherwise, without the prior written permission of the publisher.

LIBRARIES UNLIMITED, INC.
P.O. Box 6633
Englewood, CO 80155-6633
1-800-237-6124
www.lu.com

Library of Congress Cataloging-in-Publication Data

Chan, Lois Mai.
    A guide to the Library of Congress classification / by Lois Mai
Chan. -- 5th ed.
    xviii, 551 p. 17x25 cm. -- (Library and information science text series)
    "Based on the fourth edition of Immroth's Guide to the Library
of Congress classification."
    Includes bibliographical references and index.
    ISBN 1-56308-499-6 (cloth)
    ISBN 1-56308-500-3 (pbk.)
    1. Classification, Library of Congress.   I. Chan, Lois Mai.
Immroth's Guide to the Library of Congress classification.   4th ed.
II. Series.
    Z696.U4 C47 1999
    025.4'33--dc21   99-15279
                                                 CIP

Fig. 4.8. Recto of leaf preceding title page (series title page).

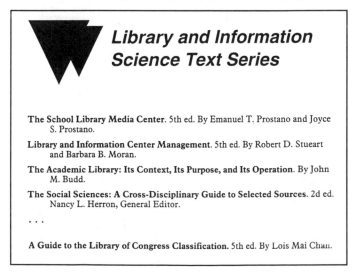

Library and Information Science Text Series

The School Library Media Center. 5th ed. By Emanuel T. Prostano and Joyce S. Prostano.

Library and Information Center Management. 5th ed. By Robert D. Stueart and Barbara B. Moran.

The Academic Library: Its Context, Its Purpose, and Its Operation. By John M. Budd.

The Social Sciences: A Cross-Disciplinary Guide to Selected Sources. 2d ed. Nancy L. Herron, General Editor.

. . .

A Guide to the Library of Congress Classification. 5th ed. By Lois Mai Chan.

Chapter 3, Cartographic Materials

Figures 4.9-4.12 show sources of information for a map.

Fig. 4.9. Upper right corner of map.

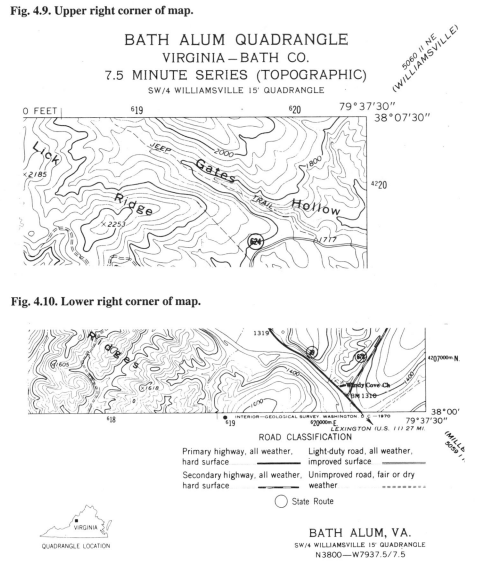

Fig. 4.10. Lower right corner of map.

Fig. 4.11. Lower left corner of map.

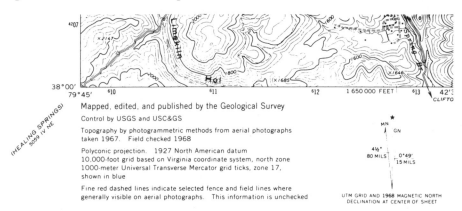

Fig. 4.12. Lower center of map.

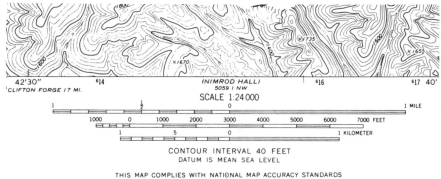

Chapter 4, Manuscripts

Figures 4.13–4.15 show sources of information for a manuscript.

Fig. 4.13. Outside of letter shown in Fig. 4.14.

Fig. 4.14. Letter from George III to Henry Dundas. [Reproduced by permission of the Manuscript Department, William R. Perkins Library, Duke University.]

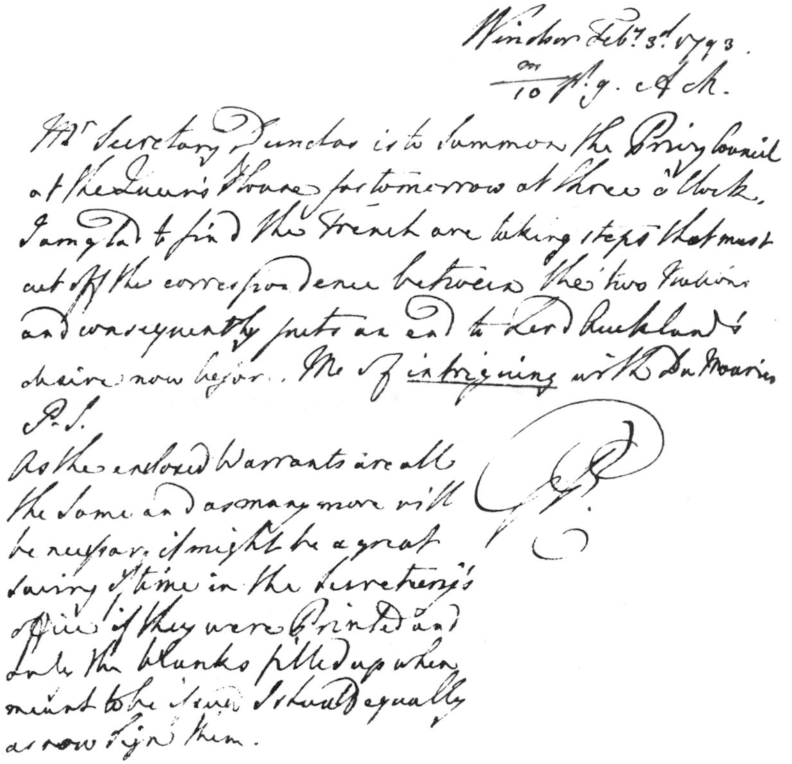

Windsor Feb.y 3d 1793.
10 m. p. 9. a.m.
Mr Secretary Dundas is to summon the Privy Council
at the Queen's House for tomorrow at three o'Clock.
I am glad to find the French are taking steps that must
cut off the correspondence between the two Nations
and consequently puts an end to Lord Auckland's
desire now before Me of intriguing with Du Mourier.
GR
P.S.
As the enclosed Warrants are all
the Same and as many more will
be necessary it might be a great
saving of time in the Secretary's
office if they were Printed and
only the blanks filled up when
meant to be issued I should equally
as now Sign them.

Fig. 4.15. Transcription of letter shown in Fig. 4.14.

[*Windsor, 3 Feb. 1793, 9:10 a.m.*] Mr. Secretary Dundas is to summon the Privy Council at the Queen's House for tomorrow at three o'Clock. I am glad to find the French are taking steps that must cut off the correspondence between the two Nations, and consequently puts an end to Lord Auckland's desire now before Me of intriguing with Du Mourier.

GR.

P.S. As the enclosed Warrants are all the Same and as many more will be necessary it might be a great saving of time in the Secretary's office if they were Printed and only the blanks filled up when meant to be issued I should equally as now Sign them.

Chapter 5, Music

Figure 4.16 shows the chief source of information for a piece of music.

Fig. 4.16. Chief source of information for a score.

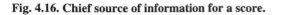

TOMMASO ALBINONI

TRIOSONATE H-MOLL
für zwei Violinen und Basso continuo

TRIO SONATA IN B MINOR
for two Violins and Basso continuo

op. I/8

Herausgegeben von / Edited by
STEFAN ALTNER

BÄRENREITER KASSEL • BASEL • LONDON • NEW YORK
HORTUS MUSICUS 240

Chapter 6, Sound Recordings

Figures 4.17–4.18 show sources of information for a sound recording.

**Fig. 4.17. Chief source of
information from disc.**

Fig. 4.18. Information from accompanying booklet.

INSTRUMENTARIUM

Violin:
Cornelius Kleyman, Amsterdam c. 1680
Bow:
W. Baumann, Amsterdam

Recording Data: 1984-06-07, 09/11 in the Petrus Church, Stock-
   sund, Sweden
Recording Engineer & Digital Editor: Robert von Bahr
Sony PCM F1 Digital Recording Equipment, 4 Neumann U-87
   Microphones, SAM 82 Mixer, Sony Tape
Producer: Robert von Bahr
Cover Text: Stig Jacobsson
English Translation: John Skinner
German Translation: Per Skans
French Translation: Arlète Chené-Wiklander
Front Cover Picture: Conny Asberg
Back Cover Photos: Robert von Bahr
Album Design: Robert von Bahr
Type Setting: Marianne von Bahr
Lay-Out: William Jewson
Repro: KåPe Grafiska, Stockholm
Print: Offizin Paul Hartung, Hamburg, West Germany 1985

Also available as LP and MC: BIS-LP-275 & BIS-MC-275
© & ℗ : 1984/85, Grammofon AB BIS

This record can be ordered from
Grammofon AB BIS
Väringavägen 6 S-182 63 Djursholm Sweden
Phone: Stockholm (08)*(Int.: + 468)* - 755 41 00
Telex: 13880 bis s
or from BIS' agents all over the world

Chapter 7, Motion Pictures and Videorecordings

Figures 4.19–4.21 show sources of information for a videotape.

Fig. 4.19. Videotape label.

Fig. 4.20. Transcription of title frames at beginning of videotape.

The Firesign Theatre presents

The Martian Space Party © 1972 TFT

Fig. 4.21. Transcription of credit frames at end of videotape.

Produced and edited by
The Firesign Theatre
and Stephen Gillmor

Production Assistants: Mike Rozsa
Kurt Hahn
Edina Gillmor
Alan McKay

Camera: Stephen Winsten
Robert Guralnick
Stephen Gillmor

Special thanks to dear friends:
Bill McIntyre, Rick Bralver,
Edgar Bullington and
the Grassroots and
KPFK-FM Los Angeles

Sound: Peter Pilafian
Bill Driml
Phil Cross

Written and Performed by
The Firesign Theatre
Phil Austin   Peter Bergman
David Ossman   Philip Proctor
with Annalee and Tiny, the Firebelles

Titles: Dr. W. Deadjellie
Bass: Cyrus Faryar
Lights: Ken Tosic

Directed by Stephen Gillmor

Chapter 8, Graphics

Figures 4.22–4.24 show sources of information for a set of stereograph reels.

Fig. 4.22. Chief source of information for set of stereograph reels.

Fig. 4.23. Unifying container for stereograph reel set.

Fig. 4.24. First page of accompanying booklet.

Chapter 9, Computer Files

Figures 4.25–4.26 show sources of information for computer software.

Fig. 4.25. Compact disc's chief source of information.

Fig. 4.26. Title screen print.

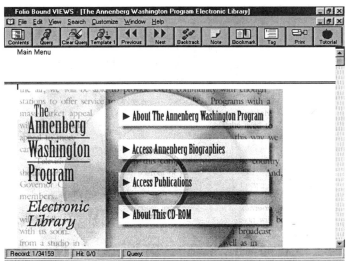

Figure 4.27 shows the chief source of information for a World Wide Web home page.

Fig. 4.27. World Wide Web home page.

Home Page: American Memory from the Library of Congress   http://memory.loc.gov/ammem/amhome.html

The Library of Congress

Over 70 Collections Now Online

Collection Finder
Select a collection or group of collections to search

Search
Search for items across all collections

Learning Page
Organized help for students, teachers, and life-long learners

Today in History
April 13, 2000

What's New!

Frequently Asked Questions

How To View | Copyright & Restrictions | Technical Information | Future Collections

Meeting of Frontiers
A multimedia English-Russian digital library

Sponsors
See who is helping to bring a virtual library to all Americans for the 21st Century

LC/Ameritech Competition

National Science Foundation Digital Libraries Initiative
Co-sponsored by the Library of Congress

Library of Congress Home | Using the Library | Thomas | Copyright Office | Exhibitions
The Library Today | Bicentennial | Help & FAQs | Search the Catalog | Search LC Site | LC Site Map

am Dec-15-99

Library of Congress
URL: www.loc.gov
Questions: American Memory Help Desk

NOTICE

Chapter 10, Three-dimensional Artifacts and Realia

Figures 4.28–4.29 show sources of information for a game.

Fig. 4.28. Top of box for dominoes game.

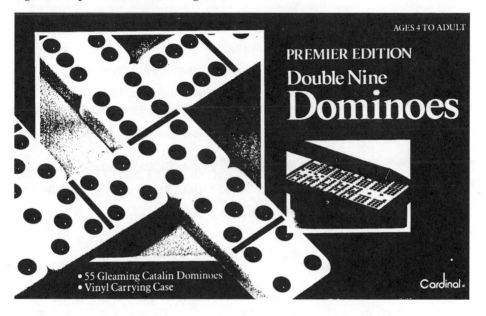

Fig. 4.29. Side of box for dominoes game.

Chapter 11, Microforms

Two items, one in microfilm format and the other in microfiche format, are used in this text to illustrate the building of description for microforms. The item illustrated in figures 4.30–4.31 is one that was assembled and filmed specifically for the purpose of bringing out an original edition in microform. The item illustrated in figures 4.32–4.34 is a microform of a previously existing work.

Fig. 4.30. Transcription of the first five frames of a microfilm.

Frame 1   WOMEN AND/IN HEALTH
                 filmed by the
                 WOMEN'S HISTORY RESEARCH CENTER
                 JULY 1974

Frame 2   WOMEN'S HISTORY RESEARCH CENTER
                 2325 Oak Street
                 Berkeley, California 94707

Frame 3   © Women's History Research Center, Inc. 1974

                 Reproduction of the material contained herein may not
                 be reproduced in any form except by express permission
                 from Women's History Research Center, Inc. and the
                 Publisher(s).

Frame 4   THIS FILM WAS MADE POSSIBLE BY A
                 REVENUE SHARING GRANT FROM THE
                 ALAMEDA COUNTY BOARD OF SUPERVISORS.

Frame 5   Filmed at a reduction ratio of 15:1

**Fig. 4.31. Transcription of label on container of first
reel of microfilm.**

WOMEN AND HEALTH/MENTAL HEALTH
Reel No. 1   Positive
Section 1
Women's History Research Center

Fig. 4.32. Transcription of title frame of microfiche.

                                                      87-15914
BAUM, Christina Diane
    THE IMPACT OF FEMINIST THOUGHT ON AMERICAN
LIBRARIANSHIP, 1965-1985.

University of Kentucky   Ed.D. 1987

University
   Microfilms
International 300 N. Zeeb Road, Ann Arbor, MI 48106

                      Copyright 1987
                           by
                  BAUM, Christina Diane
                   All Rights Reserved

Fig. 4.33. Transcription of eye-readable data at top of fiche.

87-15914   c 1987   BAUM, Christina Diane   THE IMPACT OF FEMINIST   1 of 03
                       THOUGHT ON AMERICAN LIBRARIANSHIP, 1965-1985

Ann Arbor, Mi.; University Microfilms International 1987

Fig. 4.34. Copy of title page of original dissertation (seventh frame of microfiche).

THE IMPACT OF FEMINIST THOUGHT ON
AMERICAN LIBRARIANSHIP 1965-1985

DISSERTATION

A dissertation submitted in partial fulfillment of the
requirements for the degree of Doctor of Education
at the University of Kentucky

By
Christina D. Baum
Lexington, Kentucky

Director: Dr. Leonard L. Baird, Professor of
Educational Policy Studies

Lexington, Kentucky

1987

Chapter 12, Serials

Figures 4.35–4.36, page 86, show the chief source for the first issue of a printed serial.

Figures 4.37–4.38, pages 87–88, show the chief source of information for an electronic journal.

Fig. 4.35. Front cover of printed serial.

Fig. 4.36. Contents page of printed serial.

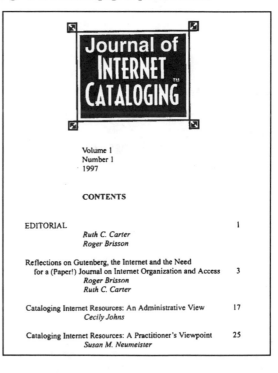

Fig. 4.37. Home Page of electronic serial.

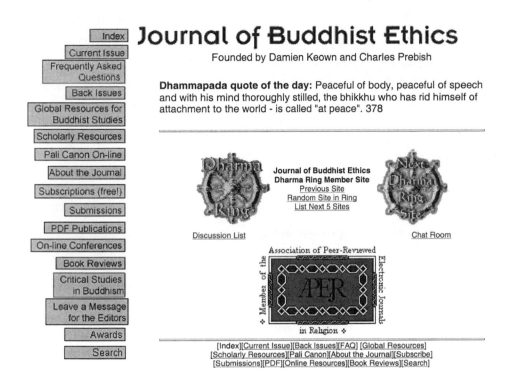

You are visitor number **0250625** since December 1, 1995

Fig. 4.38. Contents page of electronic serial.

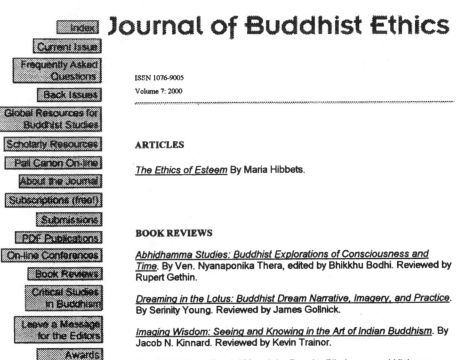

Journal of Buddhist Ethics

Index
Current Issue
Frequently Asked Questions
Back Issues
Global Resources for Buddhist Studies
Scholarly Resources
Pali Canon On-line
About the Journal
Subscriptions (free!)
Submissions
PDF Publications
On-line Conferences
Book Reviews
Critical Studies in Buddhism
Leave a Message for the Editors
Awards
Search

ISSN 1076-9005
Volume 7: 2000

ARTICLES

The Ethics of Esteem By Maria Hibbets.

BOOK REVIEWS

Abhidhamma Studies: Buddhist Explorations of Consciousness and Time. By Ven. Nyanaponika Thera, edited by Bhikkhu Bodhi. Reviewed by Rupert Gethin.

Dreaming in the Lotus: Buddhist Dream Narrative, Imagery, and Practice. By Serinity Young. Reviewed by James Gollnick.

Imaging Wisdom: Seeing and Knowing in the Art of Indian Buddhism. By Jacob N. Kinnard. Reviewed by Kevin Trainor.

The Cult of Pure Crystal Mountain: Popular Pilgrimage and Visionary Landscape in Southeast Tibet. By Toni Huber. Reviewed by Alex McKay.

AREA 1. TITLE AND STATEMENT OF RESPONSIBILITY AREA
   (MARC 21 field 245)

1.1A2. Sources of information
Title and statement of responsibility information is to be taken from the chief source of information. There is a prescribed order for data, regardless of their order in the chief source. The prescribed order should be followed except when grammatical construction does not allow it.

X.1B.   Title proper (subfield a, MARC 21 field 245)

1.1B1.   The exact wording, order, and spelling of the title proper should be followed in the transcription, but punctuation and capitalization may be changed. Example:

> **Chief source of information:**   Feeling Mad
> Feeling Sad
> Feeling Bad
> Feeling Glad
> **Transcription:**   Feeling mad, feeling sad, feeling bad, feeling glad.

Three dots or square brackets in the title are replaced by a dash or by parentheses, respectively. Also, if the source of information uses a colon, slash, or equals sign, LC replaces it with other punctuation unless the space may be closed up on both sides. (*CSB* 44: 9-10)

1.1B2.   A statement of responsibility that is connected to the title proper with a grammatical construction (such as a case ending) is transcribed as part of the title proper. Example:

> Bill Collins' Book of movies.

1.1B4.   Very long titles may be abridged if this can be done without giving up important information. The first five words may not be abridged, however. The mark of omission (i.e., ". . .") shows where omissions have been made. Example:

> Hearings before the Subcommittee on the Rules and Organization of the House of the Committee on Rules, House of Representatives, Ninety-fifth Congress, second session . . .

1.1B7.   If the chief source of information (or its substitute) lacks a title proper, one may be supplied from some other source, or may be constructed by the cataloger, if none can be found. Square brackets are used in such a case. Example:

> [Map of Kerr Lake Recreation Area, North Carolina]

1.1B10.   When a chief source includes a collective title and also the titles of the separate works of the collection, the collective title is transcribed as the title proper. The separate individual titles are given in a contents note. (For transcription of titles when there is no collective title, *see* rule 1.1G.) Example:

The great stone face & other tales [sound recording] / by
Nathaniel Hawthorne. — Charlotte, Md. : Recorded Books,
p1986.
    2 sound cassettes (120 min.) : analog, mono.

    Narrated by Nelson Runger.
    "Unabridged."
    In container.
    Contents: The great stone face — The ambitious guest — The
great carbuncle — Sketches from memory.

X.1B for AACR2R Chapters 3–10 and 12:
    Because the numbering of subrules of X.1B in these chapters does not clearly
parallel the general rules in Chapter 1, those subrules are discussed separately here.

5.1B1   Music: If a title consists of the name(s) of one or more type(s) of composition with or without the medium of performance, key, date, and/or number, those
elements are all treated as the title proper. Examples:

        Concerto in B-flat for cembalo and strings
        Triosonate H-moll für zwei Violinen und Basso Continuo

If, however, the medium, key, date, and/or number are present with a title other than
type of composition, those elements are treated as other title information. Example:

        Short meditations : for string trio and harp

6.1B1   Sound recordings: An LC rule interpretation instructs the cataloger that if
the name of an author or performer is given before the titles of individual works and
if it is possible that the name was meant to serve as a collective title proper, it should
be treated as a title proper, unless the works are musical compositions and the name
is the composer of the works, in which case the name would be given as statement of
responsibility. (*CSB* 44: 25)

7.1B1   Motion pictures and videorecordings: An LC rule interpretation states that
credits for performer, director, etc., that precede the title in the chief source are not
considered part of the title proper unless they are within the title or represented by a
possessive immediately preceding the title. (*CSB* 13: 15) Example:

    Chief source:
        Twentieth Century Fox presents Star Wars

    Title proper:
        Star wars

This applies only to Chapter 7 and thus could not be applied to a title on a sound recording reading, for example, "Armstrong presents Lerner & Loewe's Brigadoon."

X.1B2-B3.   Rule X.1B2, and sometimes X.1B3 and following, in each chapter presents
special instructions for titles proper for that type of material. In most cases rule
X.1B2 gives instructions for supplying a title when the item lacks one. Examples:

[Letter] 1793 Feb. 3, Windsor [to Henry] Dundas
[Public library advertisement]
[Harris 1967 public opinion survey, no. 1702]

3.1B2.   Cartographic materials: The rules instruct one to include statement of scale if it is part of the title proper. Example:

Arabian peninsula 1:500,000 / prepared by . . .

3.1B3.   There are also directions to the cataloger on how to choose from more than one title in the chief source for cartographic materials. Choice is made on the basis of language, sequence, or layout, and if these are insufficient, then the most comprehensive title is chosen. Thus, the title proper for the map whose chief source is illustrated in figures 4.9–4.12 would be:

Bath Alum quadrangle, Virginia–Bath company

12.1B2   Serials: If a serial title in the chief source of information includes both an acronym or initialism and the words represented by the initials, the full form is recorded as the title proper unless the initials are used alone in other places in the serial. Examples:

Transnational data report
[Chief source and other sources read: TDR Transnational Data Report]

RSR
[Chief source reads: RSR Reference Services Review. Elsewhere the title is given as: RSR]

12.1B3.   A corporate body's name is considered to be part of the title proper only when it consistently appears as part of the title in various locations in the serial. LC applies this criterion to any word, phrase, etc., that may or may not be part of the title proper. (*CSB* 71: 18)

12.1B4-12.1B6.   These rules cover transcription of titles that are sections of, or supplements to, other serials. In general if the title common to all sections appears with the section or supplement title, both are transcribed as title proper. An LC rule interpretation should be consulted when using rule 12.1B4. (*CSB* 71: 19) Examples:

Solar energy.   Cumulative index

Major studies of the Congressional Research Service.   Supplement

If the common title is not present with the section or supplement title, the section or supplement title is treated as title proper. Example:

Bibliography of Utah geology
Note reads:
Supplement to: Utah geology.

12.1B7.   When the title proper of a serial includes a date or numbering that changes from issue to issue, the date or numbering is omitted. It is replaced by the mark of omission unless it is at the beginning. LC uses the mark of omission at the end of the title proper only if there is a grammatical reason to do so. (*CSB* 44: 31) Example:

> Proceedings of the ... annual meeting

12.1B8.   A change in title proper of a serial (as defined by rule 21.2) means that a new description must be made for the new title.

X.1C.   *Optional addition.* **General material designation** (subfield h, MARC 21 field 245)

1.1C1.   *AACR2R* gives two lists of general material designations (GMDs). List 1 is for British use and list 2 is for North American and Australian use.

List 1	List 2	
braille	activity card	microform
cartographic material	art original	microscope slide
computer file	art reproduction	model
graphic	braille	motion picture
manuscript	chart	music
microform	computer file	picture
motion picture	diorama	realia
multimedia	filmstrip	slide
music	flash card	sound recording
object	game	technical drawing
sound recording	globe	text
text	kit	toy
videorecording	manuscript	transparency
	map	videorecording

Users of list 2 are instructed to add "(large print)" or "(tactile)" to any term in the list when cataloging material for the visually impaired.

LC uses list 2. The examples given in this text will do likewise. The only GMDs currently supplied by LC are:

> computer file
> filmstrip
> kit
> microform
> motion picture
> slide
> sound recording
> transparency
> videorecording (*CSB* 84: 11)

Some of the others would be used if LC were to begin cataloging those kinds of materials; however, the decision was made *not* to use the GMDs for maps, manuscripts, music, and text.[21]

A footnote to list 2 should be consulted for interpretation of particular terms. *See AACR2R98*, p. 20.

1.1C2. When the GMD is used, it is added to the description in square brackets immediately after the title proper. It precedes any other title information that may be added using rule 1.1E. Examples:

> Scared straight! [motion picture]

> Basic concepts of humanistic psychology [sound recording]

> Gargoyles [videorecording] : guardians of the gate

When an item has no collective title (see X.1G), the GMD is given immediately after the first title. This is taken to include part titles and alternative titles, but to exclude parallel titles and other title information.

1.1C3. When an item is a reproduction of a work that originally appeared in a different form (e.g., microform of a map, or sound tape of an original sound disc), the GMD for the reproduction, not the original, is given. For example, the videorecording with the following title, although originally issued as a 16mm motion picture, would be entered as:

> The Americans, 1776 [videorecording]

The set of slides with the following title, which was originally issued as a filmstrip, would be entered as:

> Blood pressure [slide]

1.1C4. Some items consist of parts that fall into more than one category of the list of GMDs chosen. If one of these is predominant, that form is given as the GMD. If none is predominant, the GMD used is "kit." (*See also* rule 1.10.) For example, the following item contains one book, one sound cassette, one poster, two puppets, and an activity guide, and would be entered as:

> Why mosquitoes buzz in people's ears [kit]

12.1C Serials: The GMDs appropriate to serials are governed by the type of material being cataloged. For example, the discussion of rule 2.1C indicates that "[text]" is not used for printed serials, and the application of rule 9.1C indicates that "[computer file]" should be used for cataloging serial computer files.

X.1D.   Parallel titles (subfield b, MARC 21 field 245)

1.1D1. Parallel titles are recorded in the order found in the chief source of information. Examples:

La motoneige au Québec = Snowmobiling in Quebec

Canadian journal of psychiatry = Revue canadienne de psychiatrie

[A space-equal sign-space precedes a parallel title.]

X.1E.   Other title information (subfield b, MARC 21 field 245)

1.1E1.   Other title information is transcribed using the same rules as for the title proper. Other title information includes, but is not limited to, subtitles. If there is more than one kind of other title information, each follows its own space-colon-space. Examples:

> The midnight patrol : the story of a Salvation Army lass who patrolled the dark streets of London's West End on a midnight mission of mercy

> From Poussin to Matisse : the Russian taste for French painting : a loan exhibition from the U.S.S.R.

> The scales of justice [filmstrip] : our court system

12.1E1 Serials: In cases where both an acronym or initialism and the words represented by the initials appear in the chief source of information, the form that was not chosen as the title proper according to the rule 12.1B2 is given as other title information. Examples:

> DNR : daily news record

> Transnational Data Report : TDR

LC has decided to catalog serials using an augmented first-level description, rather than the second-level description used for other materials. The first-level description is augmented with: GMD (when appropriate); parallel title(s); first statement of responsibility; first place of publication, etc., with first publisher, etc.; other physical details and dimensions; series. Therefore, other title information is usually omitted. However, a rule interpretation gives three instances in which other title information for serials must be given: when the title consists of both an initialism and a full form of the name, when a statement of responsibility is inseparable from the other title information, and when it is needed to explain the title proper as called for in rule 1.1E6. LC catalogers also are permitted to give other title information in other instances where it is judged to be useful. (*CSB* 44: 31)

3.1E2 Cartographic materials: In the case of maps, if the title does not indicate the geographic area, this is added as other title information. Example:

> Land use and industry : [in East Germany]

4.1E2 Manuscripts: For manuscripts, there are extensive directions (in rule 4.1B2) for creating supplied titles. If a manuscript item has a title and it lacks information required for a supplied title for that type of document, the information is added as other title information. Example:

> The duty of communicating in the Lord's Supper enforced : [sermon]

1.1E5.   When parallel titles are involved, other title information follows the title proper or the parallel title that it accompanies. Example:

La nuit : Etüde für Klavier = Night : piano study : op. 31, Nr. 3

1.1E6.   In cases where a title proper needs explanation, an explanatory term or phrase is added in brackets as other title information in the same language as the title proper. Such additions are preceded by a colon so as to distinguish them from GMDs. Example:

Beginnings : [poems]

X.1F.   Statements of responsibility (subfield c, MARC 21 field 245)

1.1F1.   Statements of responsibility that appear prominently in an item are recorded as they appear. They are separated from the title or GMD information preceding them by a space-slash-space. Just as for title information, statements of responsibility that do not come from the chief source of information must be enclosed in square brackets. An LC rule interpretation suggests that only statements "that are of bibliographic significance" should be recorded, and guidelines are provided for making such a determination. (*CSB* 13: 4-6). Examples:

And then there's always the possibility of disappearing altogether [motion picture] / Pegarty Long.

Bath Alum quadrangle, Virginia–Bath Co. / mapped, edited, and published by the Geological Survey

Ben Oliel and Seeley / [Dorothy Wood Ewers].

6.1F1 Sound recordings: This rule is somewhat different from that for other materials. The cataloger must make a decision as to whether the participation of the person(s) or body(ies) involved in the recording goes beyond that of performance, execution, or interpretation of a work. If so, the statement is given as statement of responsibility. If not, the statement is given in a note. Thus, the statement on the chief source of information shown in figure 4.17 (p. 77), "Nils-Erik Sparf, The Drottningholm Baroque Ensemble," would be relegated to note position because participation seems to be "confined to performance, execution, or interpretation." Writers of spoken words, composers of music, and collectors of field material for sound recordings are included in statements of responsibility. Examples:

Is there enough to go around? [sound recording] / Buckminster Fuller

(This recording consists of an interview in which Fuller is the primary speaker. In the case of a group of poems by e. e. cummings read by Spencer Tracy, for example, only e. e. cummings would be given in the statement of responsibility.)

Sounds of inner peace [sound recording] / composed and performed by Nawang Khechog

7.1F1 / 8.1F1 Films and Graphics: These rules state that names should be given in the statement of responsibility when a person or body has had a major role in the creation of works in these media. Producers, directors, and writers (and, for graphics, artists, designers, and sponsors) are among the roles assumed to have some degree of overall responsibility. Person(s) or body(ies) with responsibility for only segments or one aspect of a work are named in the note area.

1.1F2.   Unlike titles proper, a statement of responsibility is not essential to a description, and if one is not prominent in the item, one is not constructed.

It should be noted that serials and other items often have identical titles proper (e.g., Bulletin). When no statement of responsibility is given, non-distinctive titles become a problem when the title is the main entry and when it is necessary to make an added entry for that title on the record for another work. This problem has been solved with uniform titles. (*See* discussion in chapter 7.)

1.1F5.   Often an information package names more than three persons or corporate bodies that have all performed the same function or have had the same degree of responsibility for the work. If there are three such persons or bodies, all are given in the statement of responsibility. If there are more than three, only the first person or corporate body of each group is listed. The omission of the others is indicated by ". . . [et al.]" (or the equivalent of "et al." in nonroman scripts). Example:

> Studies in modality / Nicholas Rescher ; with the collaboration
> of Ruth Manor . . . [et al.].

1.1F6.   Multiple statements of responsibility (i.e., for different kinds of responsibility for a work) are transcribed in the order in which they appear in the information source. They are separated from each other by a space-semicolon-space. If the layout is such that the statements are not in an obvious order, the cataloger is instructed to use "the order that makes the most sense." Example:

> Looking backwards / Colette ; translated from the French by
> David Le Vay ; with an introduction by Maurice Goudeket.

1.1F7.   Most titles of address, honor, and distinction; qualifications; dates of founding; etc., are omitted from statements of responsibility. There are four exceptions:

1. when the title is necessary grammatically
2. when only a given name or only a surname is accompanied by a title
3. when a title is necessary for identification
4. when a title of nobility or British title of honor is involved.

In the following example the title "Mrs." is necessary for identification:

> Suppression of Mutiny, 1857-1858 / Mrs. Henry
> Duberly.

1.1F8.   In instances where the relationship of the person or body in the statement of responsibility to the work is not clear, a word or phrase of explanation may be added in brackets. This does not allow, however, for the former practice of adding "by" and/or "and" in statements of authorship. Examples:

Addition with an explanatory phrase:

> About interpretation : from Plato to Dilthey : a
> hermeneutic anthology / [compiled by] Barrie A. Wilson.

Statement of responsibility without addition:

> Potters of Southern Africa / G. Clark, L. Wagner.

1.1F12.   Noun phrases sometimes appear between titles and statements of responsibility that are not clearly part of either. One has to decide whether such a noun or noun phrase seems to indicate the nature of the work or the role of the person or body responsible. If it seems to indicate the nature of the work, it is transcribed as other title information. Example:

> Walt Whitman's poetry : a study & a selection / by
> Edmond Holmes.

Otherwise it is transcribed as part of the statement of responsibility. Example:

> Innovative funding : the ABC's of supplementing LMI
> budgets / a collaborative effort initiated by the ICESA
> LMI Committee.

Preference is given the latter treatment when in doubt.

1.1F13.   The rules for transcription of title information include instructions to give statements of responsibility as part of the title when they are inseparable grammatically. When this has been done, no separate statement of responsibility is given unless there is a separate statement in the chief source of information. Examples:

No statement of responsibility:

> Horowitz in concert [sound recording] : recorded at his
> 1966 Carnegie Hall recitals.

Separate statement of responsibility:

> McGuffey's new third eclectic reader for young
> learners / by Wm. H. McGuffey.

X.1F for AACR2R Chapters 11 and 12:

11.F Microforms: As with other areas of the description, transcription of title and statement of responsibility may varying according to whether one is following *AACR2R* or LC policy. Examples:

Transcription of title and statement of responsibility area for the microfiche from figures 4.32–4.34 according to *AACR2R*:

> The impact of feminist thought on American librarianship,
> 1965-1985 [microform] / Christina Diane Baum

The impact of feminist thought on American librarianship,
1965-1985 [microform] / by Christina D. Baum

12.1F2 Serials: When a title includes a full or abbreviated statement of responsibility as part of the title proper no separate statement is given. Example:

ALCTS Newsletter. —

12.1F3. Personal editors are not recorded in statements of responsibility for serials.
If considered important, they may be given in a note.

X.1G.   Items without a collective title

Items that lack a collective title may or may not have a predominant part. If
such a predominant part is present, the title of that part is given as the title proper for
the work, and other titles are given in a note. If there is no predominant part, the rule
calls for describing the item as a unit, with the option of describing each part separately and linking the separate descriptions with notes. When the item is described as
a unit, the titles are transcribed in the order given in the chief source of information
(or in the order in which they appear, if there is no chief source). The GMD is given
following the first title, as stated in rule 1.1C2. If the parts are all by the same person(s) or body(ies), their titles are separated by semicolons, and the statement of responsibility follows the last one. Examples:

Transcription of titles of two sides of a recording by the same person with each title taken
from a separate label, and there being no linking word:

African politics [sound recording] ; More songs from Kenya /
David Nzomo.

Transcription of titles of two works that are published in the same book with the title page
giving the linking word *and*:

Fantazias ; and, In nomines / by Henry Purcell ; edited with a
foreword by Anthony Ford.

If different persons or bodies were responsible for the various parts, or if it is
not known whether all parts were by the same person(s) or body(ies), each title is
followed by its other title information, statement of responsibility, and a period.
Example:

The suicide meet / Mary Humphrey Baldridge. Pickle /
by Sheila Junor-Moore. The saga of the elk / by Jim
Taylor. What it means to me to be a Canadian / compiled
from Calgary school children, grades 6 and 7.

Added entries made for this work:

I. Junor-Moore, Sheila. Pickle. II. Taylor, Jim,
1937-   . The saga of the elk. III. What it means to me
to be a Canadian. IV. Title.

3.1G1 Cartographic materials: This rule allows the cataloger to supply a collective title for an item that consists of a large number of physically separate parts. Example:

> [Maps of the United States]

[4.1G] Manuscripts: A collective title may also be supplied for manuscript collections, but this is authorized in rule 4.1B2 rather than here. Example:

> [Papers] / William Alexander Smith

6.1G1 Sound recordings: LC has made a decision to describe a sound recording as a unit in all cases. (*CSB* 11: 15) Example:

> Rhapsody in blue [sound recording] ; An American in Paris / Gershwin

11.1G Microforms: It is common to find several different serial titles on the same roll of microfilm. These are given separate descriptions in most libraries.

AREA 2.   EDITION AREA (MARC 21 field 250)

X.2B.   Edition statement (subfield a, MARC 21 field 250)

1.2B1.   If there is an edition statement, it is transcribed as found, with the exception that standard abbreviations found in Appendix B of *AACR2R* and numerals as found in Appendix C of *AACR2R* are used in place of the actual words from the source of information. Example:

> Export/import traffic management and forwarding / by Alfred Murr. — 3rd ed., rev. and enl.

2.2B Books: AACR2R does not give instructions for transcribing edition statements for multi-part sets when the various parts show different edition statements. An LC rule interpretation for rule 2.2 addresses this issue. (*CSB* 41: 14)

X.2C.   Statements of responsibility relating to the edition (subfield b, MARC 21 field 250)

1.2C.   Statements of responsibility relating to the edition

1.2C1.   A statement of responsibility that applies to the edition in hand, but not to all editions of a work, is given following the edition statement, if there is one. Example:

> The Oxford school dictionary / compiled by Dorothy C. Mackenzie. — 3rd ed. / revised by Joan Pusey.

1.2C2.   When there is no edition statement, when there is doubt about whether a statement of responsibility applies to all editions, or when one is describing a first edition, all statements of responsibility are transcribed into the title and statement of responsibility area.

General notes on Area 2 in AACR2R Chapters 5, 9 and 11:

5.2 Music: An LC rule interpretation discusses the care that must be taken with music publications to distinguish between edition statements and musical presentation statements. The latter often include the word *edition*, but should not be taken as edition statements. Musical presentation statements indicate the version, arrangement, music format, etc., in which a work is presented. These go in the statement of responsibility when the music itself is meant (i.e., a version, arrangement, or transposition of the music) because an "author" is responsible for changing the original work, even if such a person is not named. When the music format is meant (e.g., edition as a set of parts), the statement is transcribed in Area 3 (see below). (*CSB* 33: 32) Only when edition statements of the book type appear are they transcribed into the edition area. Example:

> Drei Sonaten für Klavier zu vier Händen / Johann Christian
> Bach ; herausgegeben von Wilhelm Weismann. — Ed. Peters

9.2 Computer files: It may sometimes be difficult to interpret "edition" when cataloging computer files. Changes can be made to a computer file very quickly and easily (e.g., data can be added, changed, or deleted). While published software has fairly standard edition statements (e.g., Version 5.6 or Release 3.0), data files do not. Published data files that are reissued on a regular basis contain a cumulation of all older data plus new data acquired since the previous issue. These are sometimes advertised as being, for example, "a complete new edition each quarter." Most libraries treat these as serials. Rule 9.2B4 instructs the cataloger not to treat as a new edition an issue including such minor changes as corrections of misspelled data, rearrangement of contents, changes in output format or display medium, and changes in physical characteristics (e.g., recording density). If deemed important, such changes may be given in a note. Examples:

> Microsoft word [computer file]. — Version 6.0

> Science citation index [computer file]. — Compact disc ed.

On the Internet a work changes every time a change is overlaid. With Web pages, one catalogs from one "edition." Two weeks later changes may be made to those Web pages. The catalog can then no longer give access to the "edition" first cataloged; the catalog can only give access to the "new edition," which is not now represented in the catalog. *AACR2R* states that an edition statement is for a file that contains differences from other editions of that file, implying existence of both files, not an overlay. Minor changes are not counted as a new edition. How can one tell if the changes are minor if one cannot compare a version with the previous version? This matter has yet to be resolved, and the reader should watch for a rule interpretation or rule change on this issue.

11.2 Microforms: A statement relating to an edition of a microform, rather than the edition of an original that is being reproduced, is called for in this rule. Example:

> Die Kataloge der Frankfurter und Leipziger Buchmessen
> 1759-1800 [microform] / hrsg. von Bernhard Fabian. —
> Microfiche-Ed.

However, for reproduction of previously existing materials under current policy, LC would reverse this rule.

AREA 3. MATERIAL (OR TYPE OF PUBLICATION) SPECIFIC DETAILS AREA

This area, so far, is used only for cartographic materials, music, computer files, and serials. It is also used in describing microforms of cartographic materials, music, and serials. Therefore, the content of this area is discussed in the *AACR2R* chapters specifically devoted to description of these materials.

Cartographic materials:

3.3. MATHEMATICAL DATA AREA (MARC 21 field 255)

3.3B. Statement of scale (subfield a, MARC 21 field 255)

3.3B1. The first part of this area is "Statement of scale." Scale is given as a representative fraction expressed as 1:_____ and preceded by the word *scale*. If the statement of scale on the item is not expressed as a representative fraction (e.g., "1 inch to 76 miles"), it is given as a representative fraction in square brackets (e.g., [1:4,815,360]). If any statement of scale is found outside the item, it also is given as a representative fraction in square brackets. If no statement is found, the scale is computed and given preceded by "ca." If it cannot be computed, the statement "scale indeterminable" is used.

3.3B2. An option allows giving additional scale information found on the item. LC is applying this option. (*CSB* 8: 10) Example:

> West Indies and Central America / compiled and drawn
> in the Cartographic Division of the National Geographic
> Society, for The national geographic magazine. — Scale
> 1:4,815,360. 1 in. to 76 miles.

3.3B3-3.3B8. Detailed instructions for recording more than one scale value, and for handling other problems, are given in these rules, which should be consulted when one is doing in-depth map cataloging.

3.3C. Statement of projection (subfield b, MARC 21 field 255)
If a statement of projection is found on the item or any of the accompanying materials, it is given following the scale, using abbreviations and numerals where appropriate. Example:

> Bath Alum quadrangle, Virginia–Bath Co. / mapped,
> edited, and published by the Geological Survey. — Scale
> 1:24,000 ; Polyconic proj.

Music:

5.3. *Optional area.* MUSICAL PRESENTATION STATEMENT AREA (MARC 21 field 254)

This area for music was added to *AACR2* in 1984. It calls for recording a statement found in the chief source that indicates the physical presentation of the music.

As discussed above under the edition area, it is necessary to distinguish among statements that are true edition statements, those that are statements of responsibility, and those that indicate the physical presentation. LC is applying this optional area. (*CSB* 34: 25) Example:

> Aubade : trio for flute, oboe & clarinet in B^b / DeWailley ;
> [edited by] Jerry Kirkbride. — Score and parts

Computer files:

9.3.   FILE CHARACTERISTICS AREA (MARC 21 field 256)
This area calls for recording the type of file (computer data, computer program[s], or both) followed by the number or approximate number of files when the latter information is readily available. Other details that may be given include number of records and/or bytes of data, number of statements and/or bytes, or statements/bytes for each part of multipart files. Examples:

> The magic flute [interactive multimedia] / Mozart ; conducted by Nikolaus Harnoncourt ; annotated by Warner New Media. — Computer data and program

> OCLC names project [computer file] / principal investigator, Arlene G. Taylor. — Computer data (3 files : 450, 457, 128 records)

The revised ISBD for computer files [ISBD(ER)] provides a greatly expanded list of terms which may be used in Area 3. Olson, in *Cataloging Internet Resources*,[22] encourages the cataloger "to follow the provisions of ISBD(ER)" in using these terms. One such term, "computer online service," is used in the full description of the American Memory Web site. Example:

> American memory [computer file] : historical collections for the National Digital Library / The Library of Congress. — Computer online service

General note on Area 3 in AACR2R Chapters 3–10:

Aside from Chapters 3, 5 and 9, these state that area 3 is not used for the types of material described in them. The implication is that use of this area is not permitted for the types of material in question. However, although the need is rare, nonbook materials may be produced serially, and occasionally their content is cartographic (e.g., slides of maps). The scope note for Chapter 12, description of serials, says that the rules in that chapter are to be used for serial publications of all kinds in all media. Clearly, then, it is permissable, and certainly desirable, to use area 3 when describing other nonbook materials. For example, sound recordings that are available on a subscription basis require serial cataloging. Example:

> Musicworks [sound recording]. — No. 52 (1992)-

Microforms:

11.3. SPECIAL DATA FOR CARTOGRAPHIC MATERIALS, MUSIC, AND SERIALS (MARC 21 field 255, 254, OR 362)

Material specific details for cartographic materials, music, or serials are recorded as instructed in the chapters for those materials. When reproductions of previously existing works are cataloged, this area contains data relating to the original regardless of the policy being followed. Examples:

> Bulletin of the American Economic Association [microform]. — 4th ser., no. 1 (Mar. 1911)-no. 6 (Dec. 1911)

> Viewpoint [microform]. — Vol. 1 (1976)-

Serials:

12.3. NUMERIC AND/OR ALPHABETIC, CHRONOLOGICAL, OR OTHER DESIGNATION AREA (MARC 21 field 362)

12.3B Numeric and/or alphabetic designation (subfield a, MARC 21 field 362)

The numeric and/or alphabetic designation of a serial is given as it appears in the first issue of the serial, using standard abbreviations and numerals. The numeric and/or alphabetic designation of the original is used when a facsimile or reprint is in hand. When a serial title changes but continues its previous numbering, the numbering of the first issue with the new title is used. LC comments that numbering used alone in this area should be unique to the issue. (*CSB* 71: 21)

Rules 12.3B1–12.3B3 provide for transcription of a numeric and/or alphabetic designation. Rules 12.3C1–12.3C3 treat the transcription of a chronological designation when there is no numeric or alphabetic designation. Rule 12.3C4 covers transcription of both numeric and/or alphabetic designation *and* chronological designation. It would have been clearer if this rule had been accorded a boldface rule heading. There are relatively few instances in which there is a numeric and/or alphabetic designation without also having a chronological designation; however, it is relatively common for serials of the "advances in" and "progress in" type to be dated only with an imprint date. The following title page transcription illustrates such a situation:

ADVANCES IN CHEMICAL PHYSICS

Edited by I. PRIGOGINE
University of Brussels, Brussels, Belgium

With a Preface by P. DEBYE
Cornell University, Ithaca, New York

VOLUME 1

INTERSCIENCE PUBLISHERS, INC., NEW YORK
INTERSCIENCE PUBLISHERS LTD., LONDON   1958

Such a date is recorded as part of the publication area rather than part of the numeric, alphabetic, chronological area:

> Advances in chemical physics. — Vol. 1 -   — New
> York : Interscience Publishers, 1958-

For other examples of numeric designations see the examples under rule 12.3C4.

12.3C.   Chronological designation (subfield a, MARC 21 field 362)

12.3C1.   A chronological designation that identifies the first issue of a serial is recorded as it appears, using standard abbreviations and numerals. Examples:

> Index to Title 40 of the Code of federal regulations : protection of environment. — 1978-

> HRA, HSA, CDC, OASH, & ADAMHA public advisory commitees : authority, structure, functions, members. — Mar. 1978-

12.3C4.   When the first issue of a serial has both numbering and a chronological designation, both are given, with the numbering given first, and the chronological designation given in parentheses. Examples:

> Developmental medicine and child neurology. — Vol. 4 (1962)-

> Gas turbine electric plant construction cost and annual production expenses. Annual supplement / Office of Energy Data and Interpretation, Energy Information Administration, U.S. Dept. of Energy. — 2nd (1974)-

> ALCTS newsletter. — Vol. 1, no. 1 (1990)-

A difficulty with this rule is that it does not refer to the potential confusion caused by a situation in which the numbering sequence is repeated every year so that there is no overall numbering, but only the dates to distinguish issues (e.g., issues published in 1998 are numbered 1 through 4, issues for 1999 are also numbered 1 through 4, etc.). If the numbering is given first, as is called for in the rules, the implication is that the numbering is continuous and a completed serial could appear to have published only a few numbers over a span of many years [e.g., No. 1 (Winter 1960)-no. 4 (Fall 1999)].

An LC rule interpretation says that in such a case the date should be followed by the number as if both were a single numeric designation. Example:

> — 1960, no. 1-1999, no. 4

In such a case a chronological designation would be recorded only when a separate one also appears on the issue. (*CSB* 23: 20)

12.3D.   No designation on first issue

When a serial lacks any designation, the cataloger is instructed to record "[No. 1] -" or its equivalent in the language of the title proper, and then if later issues appear with numbering, one is to change to the later form. If an item lacks a numerical designation, but has a date, rule 12.3C1 should be applied.

12.3F. Completed serials
When the serial is completed (e.g., ceases publication, or its title changes) the designation of the last issue is given following the designation of the first. Example:

> RTSD newsletter. — Vol. 1, no. 1 (Jan. 1976)-v. 14,
> no. 6 (1989)

AREA 4. PUBLICATION, DISTRIBUTION, ETC., AREA (MARC 21 field 260)

X.4B General rule
All details about place(s), name(s), and date(s) of the activities involved in the publishing, distributing, issuing, releasing, and manufacture of information packages are recorded in this area. When there is more than one place, name, and/or date, they are recorded in an order appropriate to the item in hand. Names of places, persons, or bodies are given as they appear, except that prepositions that are not integral parts of the name are usually omitted, and abbreviations from Appendix B of *AACR2R* are used.

X.4C Place of publication, distribution, etc. (subfield a, MARC 21 field 260)

1.4C1. The place of publication (or production, etc.) is recorded as it appears in a prescribed source of information.

1.4C3. The name of the country, state, province, etc., is added to the name when necessary to distinguish between places or if necessary for identification. It is added in brackets if it does not appear in the source of information. Examples:

Name of country added when city alone appeared
in prescribed source of information:

> Vanished fleets : sea stories from old Van Dieman's
> land / by Alan Villiers. — Cambridge [England]

Name of state added when name of state appeared
in prescribed source of information:

> Hans in luck [motion picture]. — Santa Monica,
> Calif.

Name of state not considered necessary to identify the city:

> Troll tales of Tumble Town [filmstrip] / Don Arthur
> Torgersen. — Chicago

1.4C5. When more than one place is given for a publisher, distributor, etc., the first named place is transcribed. If another place is typographically prominent, it is also transcribed. In addition, if neither the first named place nor a typographically prominent place are in the home country of the cataloging agency, the first place given that *is* in the home country is also transcribed. Places are separated from each other by a space-semicolon-space. Example:

> Educational theory : an introduction / T.W.
> Moore. — London ; Boston

Rule 1.4D5 treats two or more places that relate to two or more publishers, etc.

1.4C6.   A probable place is given in brackets with a question mark when the place of publication, etc., is uncertain. Example:

> A century in Singapore : 1877-1977 / Hongkong
> and Shanghai Banking Corporation. — [Singapore?]

If the place is unknown but the country, state, province, etc., is known or probable, the country, state or province, etc., is given in brackets (with a question mark if uncertain). If no country, etc., or probable country can be given, the abbreviation "s.l." (*sine loco*), or its equivalent in nonroman scripts, is given. Example:

> Precious cargo / by Ralph Byrne. — [S.l. : R. Byrne]
>
> [Note: Uppercase "S.l." results from its beginning an area of the description.]

1.4C8.   Neither place of publication, distribution, etc., nor "s.l." is recorded for unpublished items (e.g., art originals) or for unpublished collections. *See* examples under 1.4F9-1.4F10 below.

X.4D   Name of publisher, distributor, etc. (subfield b, MARC 21 field 260)

7.4D   Sound recordings: The functions of "releasing agency," "production agency," and "producer" are included in this rule.

1.4D1.   The name of the publisher, distributor, etc., follows the name of the place to which it relates, separated from the place by a space-colon-space.

1.4D2.   The name of the publisher, distributor, etc., is given in the shortest form it can take to be understood internationally. Example:

> Living with loss : a dramatic new breakthrough in
> grief therapy / Ronald W. Ramsay, Rene Noorbergen. —
> New York : W. Morrow
>
> [Note: Publisher statement on title page reads: William Morrow and
> Company, Inc.]

It is important to note the term *internationally*. Because there is now more emphasis on creating bibliographic records for an international audience, the publisher, distributor, etc., area sometimes needs fuller information than was adequate in the past.

LC generally does not omit parts of a hierarchy for any corporate bodies except in the case of some commercial publishers. Also, such words as *Inc.* that appear after a serial title being recorded as a publisher are retained. (*CSB* 84: 12)

6.4D2 Sound recordings: This rule in *AACR2R*, chapter 6, deals with the issue of trade names, brand names, of subdivision names used by recording companies. In cases where these are used, they are recorded as the name of the publisher. Example:

Label on disc reads:
   SUNSET, a product of Liberty Records
   A division of Liberty Records, Inc., Los Angeles,
      California

Description should read:
— Los Angeles, Calif. : Sunset

6.4D3. By contrast, if a trade name seems to be the name of a series, it is recorded as a series rather than as the name of a publisher.

1.4D3. Two particular parts of names of publishers, distributors, etc., that are to be retained are:

a) Words that indicate function other than only a publishing function. Examples:

> At the edge of megalopolis : a history of Salem, N.H., 1900-1974 / [Noyes, Turner]. — Canaan, N.H. : Published for the Town of Salem, N. H., by Phoenix Pub.

> The National labor relations act : a guidebook for health care facility administrators / Dennis D. Pointer and Norman Metzger. — New York : Spectrum Publications : distributed by Halsted Press

b) Parts of a name that distinguish between publishers, etc. For example:

> Encyclopaedia Britannica Educational Corp.
> Encyclopaedia Britannica, Inc.
>
> **[These are separate bodies and cannot be identified simply as Encyclopaedia Britannica.]**

5.4D3 Music: This rule has an instruction to record plate numbers and publishers' numbers in the note area.

1.4D4. A person or corporate body that appears in both the statement of responsibility and the publication area is given in the publication area in a shortened form if the name is in a recognizable form in the title and statement of responsibility area. Example:

> The Dexter Avenue Baptist Church, 1877-1977 / edited by Zelia S. Evans, with J.T. Alexander. — 1st ed. — [Montgomery, Ala.] : The Church

When a person is both author and publisher, the form used in the publisher, etc., area is the initial(s) and surname of the person. *See* example under rule 1.4C6 above.

1.4D5. There are four situations in which the transcription of a subsequently named publisher, distributor, etc. (and its place, if different from the first), is to be added after the first named body:

a) when the two bodies are linked in a single statement, e.g.,

> — London: Published for the Institute of Mediaeval Studies by Sheed & Ward.

b)   when a distributor, etc., is named first, while a publisher is named later,

c)   when a publisher, distributor, etc., is clearly the principal one (as shown by layout or typography) but is not named first,

d)   when the first body is not in the country of the cataloging agency, while a later one is. Example:

> **Cataloging done by a U.S. cataloging agency:**
>
> Genetics of forest ecosystems / Klaus Stern, Laurence Roche. — London : Chapman and Hall ; New York : Springer-Verlag

LC, in applying rule 1.4D5, records both entities when two are named. The situations prescribed in the rule, then, are used as guidelines when three or more names are given. (*CSB* 67: 14-17)

1.4D6.   An option allows addition of the name (and place if different) of a distributor when the first name is for a publisher. LC is applying this option. (*CSB* 66:11) Example:

> The plow that broke the Plains [videorecording] / United States Resettlement Administration. — Washington, D.C. : National Archives and Records Service : distributed by National Audiovisual Center

1.4D7.   When the name of the publisher, etc., is not known, the abbreviation s.n. (*sine nomine*) is given in brackets. Example:

> The story of Lanark / prepared and written by Elizabeth L. Jamieson. — [S.l. : s.n.]

1.4D9.   Neither name of publisher, distributor, etc., nor "s.n." is recorded for unpublished items or for unpublished collections. *See* examples under 1.4F9–1.4F10 below.

X.4F.   Date of Publication, distribution, etc. (subfield c, MARC 21 field 260)

1.4F1.   The date of publication of the edition in hand is the next element of this area and follows a comma-space.

1.4F2.   The date given in the item is used even if it is known to be incorrect, in which case the correct date is added in brackets and an explanation is given in a note if necessary.

7.4F2 Films and videorecordings / 8.4F2 Graphics: In these rules there is a provision for giving in a note a date of original production that differs from the date in Area 4. LC is applying this option when the difference is greater than two years. (*CSB* 33: 33 & 37) Example:

> — Washington, [D.C.] : Division of Audiovisual Arts : distributed by National Audiovisual Center, 1989.

> **Note on this record:**
>
> Made in 1985.

10.4F2 Three-dimensional artifacts and realia: This rule calls for giving only the date for artifacts not intended primarily for communication (e.g., clothing, money, furniture). Example:

> [White treadle sewing machine] [realia]. — 1890.

1.4F5.   An option allows adding the latest copyright date to the publication, distribution, etc., date if it is different. LC has applied this option since the inception of *AACR2*, but does not presently do so for books and printed serials. (*CSB* 47: 15) Example:

> Attracting birds to your backyard [videorecording] / with Roger Tory Peterson. — Carrboro, N.C. : Nature Science Network, 1990, c1986.

Note that a copyright date is always preceded by a "c," and a phonogram copyright date (the date of "pressings" of sound recordings) is preceded by a "p".

1.4F6.   If the date of publication or distribution is not given in the item, the copyright date is used. Example:

> Multimedia Beethoven [interactive multimedia] : the ninth symphony, an illustrated interactive musical exploration / [by Robert Winter with the Voyager Company]. — [Santa Monica, Calif.] : Microsoft Corporation, c1992.

If there is no copyright date, a manufacturing date, if present, is given. In the latter case, a word such as *printing* or *pressing* is added, e.g., 1996 pressing.

LC has issued a rule interpretation for when to use copyright date, probable date of publication, and/or date of manufacture. (*CSB* 47: 15-16)

1.4F7.   If no date of publication, etc., copyright, or manufacture can be found, the cataloger is instructed to give an approximate date. Example:

> Carrier Air Wing [videorecording]. — Seattle : Pool & Crew Communications, [1987?]

1.4F8.   When a multipart information package has been published during more than one year and thus two or more dates are found on different parts, the earliest and latest dates are given. Only the earliest date and a hyphen followed by four spaces is given when a multipart package is incomplete. LC often places the date of a second or later volume that is not the last volume within angle brackets. Example:

> Christ in Christian tradition / Aloys Grillmeier ; translated by John Bowden. — 2nd rev. ed. — London : Mowbrays, 1975- <1987>

An option allows adding the latest or later date when the package is complete. LC follows this option. (*CSB* 45: 12). Example:

> The narrative unity of Luke-Acts : a literary interpretation / by Robert C. Tannehill. — Philadelphia : Fortress Press, c1986-1990.
>   2 v. ; 25 cm.

1.4F9–1.4F10.   No date is given for naturally occurring objects unless they have been packaged for commercial distribution. For the latter and other unpublished items the date of production is given. A date or inclusive dates are given for unpublished collections. Examples:

> [Polar bears] [art original] / Dorothy S. Taylor. — 1985.

> [Photographs of blue ribbon pigs, Iowa State Fair] [picture]. — 1927-1947.

1.4G.   Place of manufacture, name of manufacturer, date of manufacture
(subfields e, f, and g, MARC 21 field 260)

1.4G1.   If the name of the publisher, distributor, etc., is not known and the place and name of the manufacturer are given, the latter are transcribed into the record after the date. (The date given in the publication date position is often the date of manufacture in this situation; if so, it is not repeated here.) Example:

> The offensive side of Lou Holtz / by Lou Holtz. — [S.1. : s.n.], c1978 (Little Rock, Ark. : Parkin Print. Co.)

10.4G2 Three-dimensional artifacts and realia: If the person or body that has manufactured an object is named in the statement of responsibility (as is the case with handmade items such as hand-woven tapestries or handmade pottery), that information is not repeated in this area.

General notes on Area 4 in AACR2R Chapters 4, 11, and 12:

4.4C-F Manuscripts: This area in the manuscripts chapter is called the "Date Area." It omits details of place and name of publisher (this being unpublished material) and includes only date, and then only if it is not already in the title. The date of a single manuscript is given as a year, optionally followed by the month and day.
    For a manuscript collection, inclusive years are given. Example:

> [Papers] / William Alexander Smith. — 1765-1849.

11.4 Microforms: The details of this area are recorded as instructed in the general chapter of *AACR2R*. Again, if one is following *AACR2R* policy, it should be remembered that the details recorded here are those of the publication of the *microform*, not those of an original being reproduced. Examples:

> Women and/in health [microform] / filmed by the Women's History Research Center. — Berkeley, Calif. : The Center, 1974.

> The impact of feminist thought on American librarianship, 1965-1985 [microform] / Christina Diane Baum. — Ann Arbor, Mich. : University Microfilms International, 1987.

If one is following LC policy, the details of the original are given here for a microform of a previously existing work. Example:

> The impact of feminist thought on American librarianship,
> 1965-1985 [microform] / by Christina D. Baum. — 1987.

12.4F1-2 Serials: The date of publication is given even if it coincides with the date given as the chronological designation in the preceding area. The date of first issue is followed by a hyphen and, if the serial is completed, the date of publication of the last issue. Example:

> RTSD newsletter. — Vol. 1, no. 1 (Jan. 1976)-v. 14,
> no. 6 (1989). — Chicago, IL : Resources and Technical
> Services Division, American Library Association,
> 1976-1989.

AREA 5.   PHYSICAL DESCRIPTION AREA (MARC 21 field 300)

1.5A3.   This preliminary rule calls for giving the physical description for the information package if the work is available in different formats. Optionally, notes are made to describe the other physical formats in which a work is available.

The part of this rule that calls for describing text on microfilm as microfilm has caused much controversy in the library community. It is believed by many librarians that the importance of text on microfilm is as a version of the text. The fact that the version is in microform rather than regular print is, to these persons, less important than the description of the original in terms of number of pages of text. On the other side, there are those who say that the purpose of bibliographic description is to describe the item in hand. If it is two sheets of microfiche, it is not the same as a 350-page bound volume.

This debate has been resolved for now by LC's decision to catalog microreproductions of certain printed items by transcribing the physical details of the original work in the body of the description while giving the details of the microreproduction in a note. (*CSB* 77: 22–23) This practice has not been adopted as a rule revision because the other countries involved in responsibility for *AACR2R* have not had as much problem about the issue.

The option of making a note describing other formats is being applied by LC. (*CSB* 84: 12) Example:

> Macumba, trance, and spirit healing [videorecording] /
> producer, Madeleine Richeport. — New York, NY :
> Filmakers Library, 1984.
> 1 videocassette (43 min.) : sd., col.
> Issued as U-matic ¾ in. or Beta ½ in. or
> VHS ½ in.
> Issued also as motion picture.

X.5B   Extent of item (including specific material designation)
(subfield a, MARC 21 field 300)

1.5B1.   The extent of item consists of the number of physical units in Arabic numerals followed by the specific material designation. It answers the question: How many of what? The word *identical* is added before the specific material designation when appropriate (e.g., 10 identical study prints). How to record the extent of item for different types of materials is covered in detail in each *AACR2R* chapter on a type of material. Additions or qualifications to the extent are placed within parentheses.

1.5B5.   A multipart information package that is not yet complete is described with the specific material designation preceded by three spaces. An option allows adding the number of physical units after completion. Example:

> Spy. — Oct. 1986–   . — New
> York, N.Y. : Spy Pub. Partners, c1986-
> v. : ill. ; 28 cm.

LC is applying the option; so if the work in the example becomes complete in, say, 30 volumes, the physical description area will read (according to *CSB* 8:9):

> 30 v. : ill. ; 28 cm.

2.5B Books: This rule is called "Number of volumes and/or pagination."

Single volumes

2.5B1.   The following terms are used in recording the number of pages or leaves in a publication.

TERM USED	SITUATION
pages (abbreviated "p.")	[volume with leaves printed on both sides]
leaves	[volume with leaves printed on only one side]
columns	[volume with more than one column to a page and numbered in columns]
leaves, pages, and/or columns (in sequence)	[volume that contains sequences of leaves, pages, and/or columns]
broadside	[broadside]
sheet	[folded and other single sheets]
case	[case]
portfolio	[portfolio]

2.5B2.   Numbers of pages, leaves, or columns are recorded in accord with the numbered or lettered sequences represented. The number on the last page, leaf, or column of each sequence is recorded, followed in each case by the appropriate term or abbreviation. Examples:

92 p.	[46 leaves printed on both sides]
62 leaves	[62 leaves printed only on one side]
ix, 289 p.	[last numbered page in Roman numerals sequence and in Arabic numerals sequence]
iv leaves, 224 p.	[last numbered leaf and last numbered page]

2.5B3. Unnumbered sequences are disregarded unless the whole item or a substantial part of a publication is unnumbered (*see* rule 2.5B7 and rule 2.5B8). An exception is made when pages in an unnumbered sequence must be referred to in a note, in which case either the estimated number is given preceded by "ca." or the exact number is given enclosed in square brackets. Example:

79, [1], 64 p.	[unnumbered page referred to in the note]
Bibliography: p. [80]	[note requiring use of the unnumbered page]

2.5B5. When a single sequence is numbered in more than one way (e.g., when numbering changes from Roman to Arabic numerals), the first numbering scheme is ignored, and only the last number of the sequence is recorded. Example:

252 leaves	[item numbered i-vii followed by leaves 8-252, for a total of 252 leaves—not 7 leaves followed by 252 leaves as would be indicated by: vii, 252 leaves]

2.5B7. When an entire volume is unnumbered, if it is not too large, the pages are counted and given in square brackets. The number of pages of larger items are estimated and recorded following "ca." Examples:

[12] p.	[unnumbered pages counted]
ca. 200 p.	[unnumbered pages approximated]

LC does not follow the rule except in the case of rare books. Instead, the extent statement is recorded as "1 v. (unpaged)." (*CSB* 52: 15)

The reader should consult *AACR2R*, rule 2.5B8, if dealing with complicated or irregular paging.

2.5B10. Leaves or pages of plates
The number of leaves or pages of plates is recorded at the end of the numbers given for paging sequences regardless of whether the plates are placed together or are scattered through the publication. If there is only one plate, it is described as "1 leaf of plates." If plates are unnumbered, rule 2.5B7 is followed. If there are both leaves and plates, the term that is predominant is used. Examples:

vi, 224, [9] p., 26 leaves of plates	[numbered leaves of plates]
176 p., [16] p. of plates	[unnumbered pages of plates]
74 leaves, [33] leaves of plates	[unnumbered leaves of plates]

Publications in more than one volume

2.5B17.-2.5B18. A printed monograph in more than one physical part is described with the number of whichever of the following terms is appropriate:

volumes—each bibliographic unit in its own binding

parts—bibliographic units bound several to a volume

pamphlets—collections of pamphlets bound together or assembled in a portfolio pieces—items of varying character published, or assembled for cataloging, as a collection

case(s)—box(es) containing bound or unbound material

portfolio(s)—container(s), usually consisting of two covers joined at the back and tied at the front, top, and/or bottom, holding loose papers, illustrative materials, etc.

Examples:

5 v.	[each of five bibliographic units bound separately]
25 pts.	[each part issued separately but specified by the publisher that they should be bound several to a volume when complete]
2 cases	[unbound material held together as a bibliographic unit in two boxes]

2.5B19.   When the number of bibliographic volumes is different from the number of physical volumes, the number of bibliographic volumes is given first followed by "in" and the number of physical volumes. Example:

> 3 v. in 1

2.5B20.   When the volumes of a multi-volume set are paged so that the first page numbers of a succeeding volume follow the last page number of the preceding volume (ignoring any preliminary pages in the succeeding volume that may be separately paged), the total number of pages or leaves is given in parentheses after the number of volumes. Example:

> 2 v. (ix, 1438 p., 32 leaves of plates)

2.5B23.   Braille or other tactile systems
    If appropriate, an appropriate term, such as one of the following phrases, is added to the number of volumes or leaves:

of braille	of press braille
of Moon type	of print and braille [eye-readable
of jumbo braille	print and braille]
of microbraille	of print and press braille

Examples:

> 3 v. of jumbo braille
>
> 484 leaves of braille

2.5B24.   Large print
    Items in large print meant for use by the visually impaired should be described by adding "(large print)" to the statement of extent. Example:

> 58 leaves (large print)

3.5B1 Cartographic materials: The following specific material designations are provided:

atlas	profile
diagram	relief model
globe	remote-sensing image
map	view
map section	

Examples:

1 globe (tactile)

1 atlas (20 leaves)

4.5B Manuscripts: The manuscripts chapter directs the cataloger to record the extent of single manuscripts as one would for books. The term *bound* is added if the manuscript has been bound. Example:

128 leaves, bound

A collection that occupies one linear foot or less of shelf space is described in terms of the number of items or the number of containers or volumes. LC is applying the option to add the number of items if the collection is described in number of volumes or containers. (*CSB* 47: 35) Examples:

1 v. (208 items)

2 boxes (110 items), 2 v. (68 items)

ca. 600 items

A collection that occupies more than one linear foot of shelf space is described in terms of the number of linear feet occupied. LC is applying the option to add the number of items or containers or volumes. (*CSB* 47: 35)

5.5B1 Music: The following specific material designations are provided:

score	vocal score
condensed score	piano score
close score	chorus score
miniature score	part
piano [violin, etc.] conductor part	

Normally, specific material designations are given to different classes of materials that represent different kinds of physical objects. In the case of published music, specific material designations vary under different circumstances, one of them being whether the music is written for a solo instrument or for several instruments. The physical extent of a piece of music written for a solo instrument is described, as for any monograph, in terms of leaves, pages, or volumes. If the option of using the GMD [music], is not applied, then the term *music* is incorporated in the extent of item statement. Example:

36 p. of music.

A specific material designation using the terms *score(s)* and/or *part(s)* is to be given to a piece of music written for several instrumental or vocal parts. The type of score it is—miniature, piano, vocal, etc.—as well as its pagination and the number of copies of it issued by the publisher are to be recorded. (Definitions of different types of scores are given in the Glossary of *AACR2R*.) If the score is accompanied by parts, the number of these issued by the publisher is to be recorded.

6.5B1 Sound recordings: The following specific material designations are provided:

sound cartridge	sound tape reel
sound cassette	sound track film
sound disc	

6.5B2. As specified in general rule 1.5B4, playing times are given as stated, if stated explicitly on the item. If the playing time is not explicitly stated, it should be given if easily determined. As an option, an approximate time may be given if neither of these conditions apply. LC is applying this option on a case-by-base basis. (*CSB* 33: 27) In addition, the playing times of a multipart item may be given followed by the word "each" if the parts have a stated or approximate uniform playing time. Examples:

1 sound disc (73 min.)

3 sound cassettes (ca. 40 min. each)

An LC rule interpretation provides guidance for giving playing times under circumstances where there are either multiple parts, or not all durations are stated on the item. (*CSB* 33: 36)

7.5B1 Films and videorecordings: The following specific material designations are provided:

film cartridge	videocartridge
film cassette	videocassette
film loop	videodisc
film reel	videoreel

7.5B2.   Playing times are given, as in the rule for sound recordings. Examples:

1 videocassette (88 min.)

3 film cassettes (20 min. each)

For videodiscs, the rule specifies information to be provided for discs consisting of moving images, still frames or a combination.

8.5B1 Graphics: The following specific material designations are provided (as distributed by LC among the GMDs appropriate to this chapter. *CSB* 64: 12-13):

activity card	flash card	radiograph
activity card	flash card	study print
chart	picture	slide
chart	art print	slide
flip chart	art reproduction	stereograph
wall chart	photograph	technical drawing
filmstrip	picture	technical drawing
filmstrip	postcard	transparency
filmslip	poster	transparency

9.5B1 Computer files: The following specific material designations are provided:

computer cartridge	computer optical disc
computer cassette	computer reel
computer disk	

The spelling "disc" is used for optical media, reflecting the standardized spelling used by the computer industry. The spelling "disk" is to be used for magnetic media only.

No physical description is given for a computer file or digital resource that is available only by remote access. This applies, for example, to World Wide Web pages.

10.5B1 Three-dimensional artifacts and realia: The following specific material designations are provided:

art original	game
art reproduction	microscope slide
braille cassette	mock-up
diorama	model
exhibit	toy

10.5B2. The number and name(s) of component pieces are added to the specific material designation. The term *(various pieces)* may be added where they cannot be concisely named, or where their number is not ascertainable. In the latter case, an option allows detailing the pieces in a note. Examples:

1 game (1 board, 7 markers, 60 cards, 3 dice)

1 diorama (various pieces)

General notes on Area 5B in AACR2R Chapters 3–10:

The rules for all materials covered in these chapters, except for manuscripts, allow the cataloger to use terms other than those listed if needed. Examples:

Music	Realia
choir book	jigsaw puzzle
table book	hand puppet
Sound recordings	quilt
piano roll	tapestry
organ roll	statue
Computer files	sculpture
computer card	bowl (cup, jar, handle holder, etc.)
computer chip cartridge	dress (coat, belt, suit, etc.)

As shown in the previous examples various pieces of information may be added in parentheses after the statement of extent of most nonbook materials if easily ascertainable from the item in hand. Numbers of pages are added after statements of extent of atlases and music. Examples:

1 atlas (20 leaves)

1 score (35 p.) + 4 parts

Information about systems intended for the visually impaired may be given for cartographic items, music, and graphic materials. Examples:

1 globe (tactile)

1 score (20 leaves, braille)

228 p. of music (large print)

Numbers of items may be given for collections of manuscripts, some kinds of graphics, and realia. Examples:

2 ft. (ca. 300 items)

1 transparency (3 overlays)

3 flip charts (10 sheets each)

1 game (1 board, 1 timer, 500 word cards, 1 die, 4 markers, 4 category cards, 4 pads of paper, 4 pencils)

2 dioramas (various pieces)

1 jigsaw puzzle (ca. 500 pieces)

Running/playing time may be given for sound recordings, films, and videorecordings. Examples:

2 sound cassettes (ca. 150 min.)

1 videocassette (15 min.)

The number of frames may be given for filmstrips, filmslips, stereographs, or video-discs consisting of still images. Example:

4 filmstrips (ca. 40 fr. each)

In a few cases the number of intellectual units may differ from the number of physical pieces, and this may be specified. Examples:

8 maps on 2 sheets

1 aerial chart in 6 segments

Specific rules in *AACR2R* for any of the above situations should be consulted when cataloging nonbook materials.

11.5B Microforms: The following specific material designations are provided:

aperture card

microfiche

microfilm

microopaque

LC has chosen not to follow the *AACR2R* option to drop the prefix micro when the GMD "microform" is used. The reason for LC's decision is that the resulting bibliographic description will be complete regardless of whether another library chooses to use the GMD.[23]

If the item is described in terms of "microfilm," one of the following terms is added: *cartridge, cassette,* or *reel.* Example:

13 microfilm reels

If the item is described in terms of "microfiche," the term *cassette* may be added if appropriate, and the number of frames is added in parentheses if the number can be determined easily. Example:

3 microfiches (276 fr.)

12.5B Serials:

12.5B1.   A printed serial still in progress is described as *v., no.,* or *pt.* preceded by three spaces. (An LC rule interpretation mandates the use of "v." as the only specific material designation for printed serials. *CSB* 71: 24) For a serial still in progress that is of a type of material other than print, the specific material designation relevant to that type of material, preceded by three spaces, should be used.

12.5B2.   When the serial is completed, the specific material designation is preceded by the number of parts in arabic numerals. An LC rule interpretation says that "parts" is to be interpreted as bibliographic units rather than physical units. (*CSB* 71: 24–25) Example:

> The Christian's magazine [microform]. — Vol. 1
> (1806)-v. 4 (1811). — Ann Arbor, Mich. : University
> Microfilms, 1946-1949.
>   4 v. on 2 microfilm reels ; 35 mm.

X.5C.   Other physical details (subfield b, MARC 21 field 300)

Physical details other than extent of item or dimensions are given following the extent and separated from it by a space-colon-space. These vary by type of material.

2.5C Books: This rule is called "Illustrative matter."

2.5C1.   If a monograph has illustrations, the abbreviation "ill." is given in the physical description. Tables are not treated as illustrations. Illustrated title pages and minor illustrations (e.g., decorations) are ignored.

2.5C2.   *Optionally*, if all of the illustrations are of one or more of the types mentioned below, the appropriate term(s) or abbreviation(s) may be given, in alphabetical order.

TERM	ABBREVIATION (IF ALLOWED)
coats of arms	
facsimiles	facsim., facsims.
forms	
genealogical tables	geneal. table(s)
maps	
music	
plans	
portraits (use for both single and group portraits)	port, ports.
samples	

If there are illustrations in addition to these types (including graphs and diagrams), they are described as "ill.," and "ill." precedes the other types in the list. Examples:

47 p. : ill., ports.	[contains illustrations, some of which are portraits]
280 p. : facsims.	[the only illustrations are facsimiles]
176 p., [24] p. of plates : ill., coats of arms, maps, plans	[illustrations include three of the specific types in rule 2.5C2, in addition to other illustrations]

LC uses only "ill." to describe an illustrated printed monograph unless there are maps present, or the publication consists wholly or predominantly of one type of illustration. (*CSB* 76: 20)

2.5C3.   If illustrations are in two or more colors, they are described as "col." or "some col." Examples:

48 p. : ill. (some col.)	[some illustrations in color]
216 p. : ill., maps (some col.), col. ports.	[some maps in color, all portraits in color]
xiv, 182 p. : col. ill.	[all illustrations in color]

2.5C4–2.5C6. Treatment of special cases (e.g., number of illustrations known, special locations of illustrations, works consisting of all or nearly all illustrations) is delineated in these rules in *AACR2R*, which should be consulted when such special cases arise.

General note on Area 5C in AACR2R Chapters 3–12:

Different kinds of "other physical details" are given for each of the materials covered in these chapters. The following outlines indicate the kinds of details specified for each type of material. These details are called for only where appropriate. Where there are several kinds of details for one type of material, they are to be given in the order specified in the list.

3.5C Cartographic materials:

number of maps in an atlas
color
material
mounting
Examples:

1 atlas (5 v.) : 250 col. maps

1 relief model : col., plastic

1 globe : col., plastic, mounted on wooden stand

1 map: col., mounted on linen

4.5C Manuscripts:

material other than paper for a single manuscript
illustrations (as noted in rule 2.5C or rule 8.5C)
Example:

42 leaves : parchment, col. ill.

5.5C Music:

illustrations (as noted in rule 2.5C)
Example:

1 score (x, 77 p., [1] leaf of plates) : facsim.

6.5C Sound recordings:

type of recording
playing speed
groove characteristic (analog discs)
track configuration (sound track films)
number of tracks (tapes)
number of sound channels
recording and reproduction characteristics [*optional addition*]
Examples:

1 sound disc (42 min.) : digital, stereo.

2 sound cassettes (ca. 150 min.) : 1-1/2 ips, mono.

1 sound disc : analog, 78 rpm, microgroove, mono.

7.5C Films and videorecordings:

> aspect ratio and special projection characteristics (motion pictures)
> sound characteristics
> color
> projection speed (motion pictures)

> Examples:

>> 1 videocassette (15 min.) : sd., col.

>> 1 videodisc (ca. 35 min.) : sd., b&w

>> 2 film reels (25 min.) : multiprojector, multiscreen, si., col.

8.5C Graphics: The other physical details required in the description depend upon the kind of graphic material being cataloged. Some require only an indication of color (e.g., col., b&w, sepia). These are:

pictures	study prints
postcards	transparencies
posters	wall charts
stereographs	

Others require some description of a characteristic in addition to color. These are:

> art prints—process in general terms (e.g., engraving, lithograph) or specific terms (e.g., copper engraving) and color

> art reproductions—method of reproduction (e.g., photogravure, collotype) and color

> charts and flip charts—indication of double-sided sheets (if applicable) and color

> filmstrips, filmslips, flash cards, and slides—indication of sound if it is integral (if sound not integral, it is described as accompanying material) and color

> photographs—indication if photograph is a transparency not designed for projection or if it is a negative print and color. Optionally, the process used may be given. LC applies this option on a case-by-case basis.

Two kinds of items require description of a characteristic, but no indication of color. These are:

> art originals—medium (chalk, oil, pastel, etc.) and base (board, canvas, fabric, etc.) are given

> technical drawings—method of reproduction if any (blueprint, photocopy, etc.) is given

One kind of graphic item—radiograph—requires no description for other physical details.

> Examples of other physical details for graphics:

>> 8 study prints : col.

>> 5 filmstrips : sd., col.

>> 1 art original : oil on board

9.5C Computer files:

> encoded sound
> encoded to display in two or more colors

Optional additions, if readily available and considered to be important:

> number of sides used
> recording density
> sectoring

Examples:

> 2 computer disks : sd., col., double sided, high density
>
> 1 computer optical disc : sd., col.

10.5C Three-dimensional artifacts and realia:

> material
> color

Examples:

> 1 jar : clay, brown and red
>
> 1 jigsaw puzzle (500 pieces) : wood, col.
>
> 1 pair of socks : white

11.5C Microforms:
A negative microform is indicated here, followed by a statement of illustration using instructions in rule 2.5C. If illustrations are in color, the term *col. ill.* is used. If the microform itself is colored, terms used are *col. & ill.* Example:

> 15 microfiches : negative, ill.

12.5C Serials:
Since serials may be issued in many forms, other physical details are recorded according to the rule numbered "5C" in the appropriate chapter for the type of material being treated.

The term most often used here for printed serials is *ill.* The first issue (or issue used for cataloging) may not be totally representative of details found in later issues, but it is unlikely that one will keep returning to the record to add more details. It is better to be more general with this area of a serial.

X.5D. Dimensions (subfield c, MARC 21 field 300)
The dimensions of an information package serve as an aid in finding it on the library shelves. Dimensions are especially valuable for libraries with separate storage areas for oversized pieces. They also serve the user who wishes to borrow an item through interlibrary loan. Dimensions are separated from either the extent or physical details by a space-semicolon-space.

2.5D Books:

2.5D1. Size of printed monographs is given in terms of the height of volumes in centimeters. The height of the binding (or the height of the item, if unbound) is measured and recorded as the *next* whole centimeter *up* (*not* the *nearest* centimeter). Size of volumes that measure less than 10 centimeters is given in millimeters. Example:

Critical guide to Catholic reference books / James Patrick
McCabe ; with an introduction by Russell E. Bidlack. — 3rd
ed. — Englewood, Colo. : Libraries Unlimited, Inc., 1989.
xiv, 323 p. ; 25 cm.

[Note: Book actually measures 24.2 centimeters but is recorded as 25.]

2.5D2.   Width of a volume is recorded only when it is less than half the height or
greater than the height. Examples:

ca. 150 p. : ill. ; 34 x 16 cm.   [width less than half the height]

ii, 97 p. : ill., ports. ; 18 x 21 cm.   [width greater than the height]

2.5D3-2.5D5.   These rules in *AACR2R* cover unusual cases and should be consulted when one is cataloging sets with items of varying sizes, or single sheets.

General notes on Area 5D in AACR2R Chapters 3–12:

For book-like materials, dimensions are given as instructed in rule 2.5D. This
applies to atlases, single manuscripts, and music.

For large, flat items the height x width is given in centimeters; and if the item is
stored folded, the dimensions of the folded item follow the dimensions of the extended item. This applies to maps, plans, large manuscripts, technical drawings, and
wall charts. Example:

1 map : col. ; 67 x 97 cm. folded to 15 x 22 cm.

Round items are described in terms of the diameter, specified as such. Sound
discs and videodiscs are measured in inches, while other items are measured in centimeters. Exception: No measurements are given for stereographs, including stereograph reels, or for computer reels. Examples:

1 globe : col., cardboard, mounted on metal stand ; 32 cm.

1 computer optical disc ; 4¾ in.

The gauge (width) is given for motion pictures, videotapes, filmstrips, and
filmslips. All are given in millimeters except for videotapes, which are given in
inches. Examples:

1 film cartridge (4 min.) : si., col. ; super 8 mm.

1 film reel (12 min.) : sd., col. with b&w sequences ; 16 mm.

1 videocassette (15 min.) : sd., col. ; ¾ in.

5 filmstrips : col. ; 35 mm.

For a computer cartridge the length of the side that is to be inserted into the machine is given in inches to the next ¼ inch up. Example:

1 computer cartridge : sd., col. ; 3¼ in.

Most other items are measured in terms of height x width or height x depth or
height x width x depth, and most are recorded in centimeters to the next whole centimeter up. This is true for relief models; manuscript collections when the containers
are uniform; sound cartridges and cassettes when the dimensions are other than the
standard ones (measured in fractions of inches); all graphic materials (except filmstrips, filmslips, stereographs, and slides whose dimensions are 5 x 5 cm.); computer

cassettes (measured in inches to the next $\frac{1}{8}$ inch up), computer cards, and other appropriate physical carriers of computer files; three-dimensional artifacts and realia. Examples:

>1 relief model : col., wood ; 50 x 35 x 4 cm.

>2 ft. (2 boxes, ca. 300 items) ; 44 x 30 x 15 cm.

>1 sound cassette (60 min.) : analog, stereo. ; 7¼ x 3½ in.

>1 art original : oil on canvas ; 31 x 41 cm.

For three-dimensional artifacts and realia it may be necessary to give only one dimension. In such a case the dimension being given is specified. Examples:

>1 jar : clay, brown and red ; 32 cm. high

>1 paperweight : glass, col. ; 8 cm. in diam.

Three-dimensional artifacts and realia in containers should have the name of the container and its dimensions given after the dimensions of the object or as the only dimensions. Dimensions of a container are an optional addition for cartographic materials. LC is applying the option on a case-by-case basis. (*CSB* 84: 13) Examples:

>1 relief model : col., wood ; 50 x 35 x 4 cm. in box
>26 x 19 x 9 cm.

>1 jigsaw puzzle (ca. 60 pieces) : cardboard, col. ; 18 cm. in
>diam. in box 11 cm. in diam. x 4 cm.

No dimensions are given for sound recordings on rolls, or for sound cartridges, sound cassettes, or slides that are of standard dimensions.

The dimensions of a microfiche, a microopaque, and an aperture card mount are given as height x width in centimeters to the next whole centimeter up. Example:

>12 microfiches ; 11 x 15 cm.

The width of a microfilm is given in millimeters. Example:

>8 microfilm reels ; 35 mm.

Dimensions for serials are recorded according to the rule numbered "5D" in the appropriate chapter for the type of material being treated.

X.5E. Accompanying material (subfield e, MARC 21 field 300)

Accompanying material includes answer books, teacher's manuals, atlases, portfolios of plates, slides, phonodiscs, booklets explaining audiovisual materials, and other such items. These materials often are placed in pockets inside the cover of the work being cataloged, or they may be loose inside the container. Their description may make up the fourth element of the physical description area and is separated from the dimensions by a space-plus sign-space.

1.5E1. Four methods are suggested for handling accompanying material:

>a) It may be described in a separate entry.

>b) It may be described in a multilevel description as outlined in Chapter 13 of *AACR2R*.

>c) Details may be given in a note.

>d) Details may be given as the last element of the physical description area.

If the last method is used, an option allows addition in parentheses of further physical description of the accompanying material. LC is applying this option on a case-by-case basis, usually to items that are substantial in extent or are significant for some reason. (*CSB* 50: 23–24) Example:

> Evolution of the Arctic-North Atlantic and the Western Tethys : Peter A. Ziegler. — Tulsa, Okla., U.S.A. : American Association of Petroleum Geologists, c1988.
> viii, 198 p. : ill. (some col.), maps ; 29 cm. + 1 portfolio (30 plates : col. maps ; 28 cm.).

9.5E Computer files: Because no physical description is given for a computer file that is available only by remote access, the details of any accompanying material for such files are given in a note.

12.5E Serials: Accompanying material is described only if it is intended to be issued regularly and used with the serial. Its frequency is given in a note. If issued only once or irregularly, such material could be described in a note, ignored, or cataloged separately if judged to be important.

AREA 6.   SERIES AREA (MARC 21 fields 4XX)

The first definition of *series* as it appears in the *AACR2R98* Glossary is: "A group of separate items related to one another by the fact that each item bears, in addition to its own title proper, a collective title applying to the group as a whole."[24] LC has issued a lengthy rule interpretation regarding situations in which a series statement is to be given. It in turn refers to other rule interpretations that discuss LC practice in areas such as sources of information for the series statement, data elements in a series statement, multiple series statements and access points for series. (*CSB* 81: 11–17)

This area is not used for manuscripts (Chapter 4). When cataloging microform reproductions (Chapter 11), a series statement for an original is recorded with other details of the original. If one is following *AACR2R*, this means placing the original series in a note. If one is following LC practice, the original series is transcribed in the series area.

X.6B.   Title proper of series (subfield a, MARC 21 fields 4XX)

1.6B1.   The title proper of a series is transcribed according to the rules for transcribing the title proper of the information package and is enclosed within parentheses. Example:

> Vegetable suite : for flute and piano / Graham Powning. — London : Chester Music ; New York : W. Hansen/Chester Music, c1986.
> 1 score (6 p.) + 1 part (3 p.) ; 31 cm. — (The Chester woodwind series)

Other examples:

Sound recording: (CBS masterworks)

Game: (Instructo activity kit)

Microform: (British publishers' archives on microfilm)

Other title information is seldom recorded for series. It is recorded only if valuable for identifying the series. When other title information or parallel titles for series are recorded, they are transcribed according to the same rules used for the title and statement of responsibility area.

1.6B2. This rule gives a hierarchy for choice among variant series titles that may appear in an information package. A title in the first of the prescribed sources of information for the series is preferred. If the series title does not appear in the first prescribed source, but there are different forms in other parts of the item, the order of preference for sources dictates which form should be used.

X.6E. **Statements of responsibility relating to series** (subfield a, MARC 21 fields 4XX)

1.6E1. Statements of responsibility that appear "in conjunction with the series title" are to be recorded if "they are considered to be necessary for identification." LC's rule interpretation states "in conjunction with" means on the same source as the series title. (*CSB* 76:16) Example:

> Post-war food and cash crop production in former
> colonial territories / compiled by B.J. Silk. — [Oxford :
> Oxford Development Records Project, 1985]
> 64 p. ; 30 cm. — (Report / Oxford Development
> Records Project ; 8)

X.6F. **ISSN of series** (subfield x, MARC 21 fields 4XX)
The ISSN is the International Standard Series Number, assigned to a serial as an internationally agreed-upon unique identifier. It is useful for identification and ordering purposes. It is recorded in the series area if it appears in the item and follows a comma-space. Example:

> Religion, intergroup relations, and social change in South
> Africa / G.E. Oosthuizen . . . [et al.] ; Human Sciences
> Research Council, Work Committee: Religion. — New
> York ; London : Greenwood, 1988.
> xii, 237 p. ; 23 cm. — (Contributions in ethnic studies,
> ISSN 0196-7088 ; no. 24)

An LC rule interpretation states that, when using MARC format, one may not input letters "ISSN" in this subfield. (*CSB* 74: 20)

X.6G. **Numbering within series** (subfield v, MARC 21 fields 4XX)

1.6G1. Numbering given with the series in the item is recorded as part of the series area. Abbreviations as found in Appendix B of *AACR2R* are used and Arabic numerals are substituted for non-Arabic numerals. Numbering is separated from preceding information by a space-semicolon-space. Examples:

Music: (Hortus Musicus ; 240)

Videorecording: (OCLC ; no. 6)

Computer file: (SRC/CPS American national election series ; no. 13)

Microform: (Columbia University oral history collection ; pt. 2, no. 24)

LC has issued a lengthy rule interpretation concerning transcription of series numbering. (*CSB* 79: 12–14)

12.6G Serials: Series numberings are not given when each issue has a separate series number. Example:

> Wage chronology : Ford Motor Company / U.S. Bureau of
> Labor Statistics....
>   v. ; 28 cm. — (Bulletin / Bureau of Labor Statistics)

X.6H.   Subseries (subfields n and p, MARC 21 field 440)
    AACR2R98 defines subseries: "A series within a series (i.e., a series that always appears in conjunction with another, usually more comprehensive, series of which it forms a section). Its title may or may not be dependent on the title of the main series."[25]
    Such a subseries, if present, is transcribed after the details of the main series. Parallel titles, other title information, statements of responsibility, ISSN, and numbering are transcribed for subseries in the same way as for series. An LC rule interpretation gives guidelines for judging whether an item is part of a subseries and for transcribing subseries into a bibliographic record. (*CSB* 83: 23) Example:

> About interpretation : from Plato to Dilthey : a
> hermeneutic anthology / [compiled by] Barrie A. Wilson.
> —New York : P. Lang, c1989.
>   xii, 208 p. ; 23 cm. — (American university studies.
> Series V, Philosophy, ISSN 0739-6392 ; v. 30)

X.6J.   More than one series statement

1.6J1.   If there is more than one series, each series is recorded in a separate series statement in its own set of parentheses. An LC rule interpretation gives guidelines for application of this rule. (*CSB* 74: 26–27) Example:

> Conducting a successful capital campaign : a comprehensive
> fundraising guide for nonprofit organizations / Kent E. Dove.
> — 1st ed. — San Francisco : Jossey-Bass Publishers, 1988.
>   xxii, 292 p. : ill. ; 24 cm. — (The Jossey-Bass management
> series)   (The Jossey-Bass higher education series)

AREA 7.   NOTE AREA (MARC 21 fields 5XX)
    Many works require description beyond that presented formally in the title and statement of responsibility area through the series area. Notes qualify or amplify the formal description. Some notes contribute to identification of a work (e.g., a note giving the original title of a translated work). Some contribute to the intelligibility of the record (e.g., a note explaining the relationship of the work of a person who has been given an added entry). Other notes aid the reader who does not have in hand an exact citation (e.g., a summary or contents note). Still other notes characterize an information package (e.g., a thesis note) or give its bibliographic history (e.g., notes giving previous titles). Each *AACR2R* chapter gives rules for notes for the kind of materials covered by that chapter.

1.7A.   Preliminary rule

1.7A3.   Form of notes

This rule gives general guidelines for the formulation of notes.

Order of information. In any one note, data that correspond to data found in descriptive areas preceding the notes area are transcribed in the same order in the note. The prescribed punctuation is used with the exception that a period (full stop), space, dash, space is replaced simply by a period (full stop). Example:

> Trees and shrubs of the Southeast / Blanche Evans Dean ; illustrated by Forrest Bonner. — 3rd ed., rev. and expanded. — Birmingham, Ala. : Birmingham Audubon Society Press, c1988.
> xx, 264 p. : ill. ; 23 cm.
> Rev. and expanded ed. of: Trees and shrubs in the heart of Dixie. Rev. ed. Birmingham, Ala. : Southern University Press, 1968.

> [Note contains information in the same order it would be in a description, but the period, space, dash, space area separators are omitted between areas.]

Quotations. Quotations in notes are given in quotes followed by an indication of the source, unless the chief source of information is the source of the quotation.

Formal notes. Standard format is used for certain notes because uniformity can assist in recognition of some types of information.

Informal notes. Informal notes should be as brief as they can be without sacrificing clarity, understandability, or good grammar.

1.7A4.   Notes citing other editions and works

When notes are made citing other works or other manifestations of the same work, the notes should give enough information to identify the work cited. When giving a note for an original work from which the work in hand is reproduced, all notes relating to the original are combined into one note. An LC rule interpretation gives guidance and examples for applying this rule. (*CSB* 60: 14–15)

X.7B.   Notes (MARC 21 field 500 is used unless otherwise noted.)

Notes are to be given in the order listed here, except that a note that has been decided to be of primary importance for a particular type of material should be given first (e.g., publishers' stock numbers for sound recordings). Upon examination, one can determine the logic of the order. First come notes concerning the nature and language of the information package. Then come notes that relate to the areas of description from title through series in the order in which they appear in the body of the entry. These are followed by notes that characterize and summarize the information package.

For serials, many notes (called "linking notes" by LC) refer to another serial. *AACR2R* (rule 12.7A2) gives instructions for citing another serial in a note. It suggests using the title or heading-title that is the catalog entry for the serial. If the serial is not in the catalog, or if main entry is not used, the title proper and statement of responsibility are to be cited. An LC rule interpretation changes these instructions to include uniform title when this is appropriate, if needed by identification. Statements of responsibility are not used in LC's linking notes. (*CSB* 81:22) Another rule interpretation for serials notes clarifies the information to be provided when it is known that data in a note do not apply to all issues of a serial. (*CSB* 71:26)

X.7B1.   Nature, scope, or artistic form (MARC 21 field 500 [520 for manuscripts; 500 and 538 for computer files; 310 for serials])

When the nature, scope, or artistic form of a work is not apparent from the rest of the description, notes may be made. Examples:

Book:	Catalog of an exhibition held Aug. 16-Nov. 2, 1986, at the Fine Arts Museum of San Francisco.
Map:	Shows locations of important historical events.
Sound recording:	Organ music to demonstrate the instrument: various organists and organs.
Computer file:	Data base manager.
Microform:	Extensive collection of feminist serial literature published 1956 through June, 1974.

2.7B1 Books: LC generally restricts this type of note for books to those that contain one or more literary works by one personal author *and* fall into one of several categories of languages (e.g. Turkish, Hebrew alphabet, or language indigenous to Africa and in the roman script). LC also makes notes recording the literary forms of belles lettres when their titles are misleading. Fanciful titles are not necessarily considered to be misleading. (*CSB* 54: 29–30)

4.7B1 Manuscripts: This note prescribes terms to be used for originals and copies. The word *signed* is added if appropriate. Examples:

Printout, signed.

Mss. (photocopies)

Ms., signed (carbon copy)

Holograph (photocopy)

For collections of manuscripts, the cataloger is instructed to name the types of information packages that compose the collection and to mention any other characterizing features. Example:

[Papers] / William Alexander Smith. — 1765-1849.
51 boxes (11,573 items), 101 v. ; 44 x 30 x 9 cm.

Mss.
Capitalist and businessman operating mainly in North Carolina from ca. 1866 to 1934. Includes correspondence, reports, financial statements, writings, legal papers, volumes, clippings, genealogy, pictures, bills, receipts, and promissory notes.

5.7B1 Music: This note is called "Form of composition and medium of performance." Musical form not apparent from the rest of the description is given briefly. Examples of forms of composition are carol, opera, concerto, and symphony. The medium of performance is given unless it has been given earlier in English or in an easily understood term in a foreign language. Example:

>For harpsichord, 2 violins, viola, and violoncello.

9.7B1 Computer files: This note is called "Nature and scope and system requirements." Information on system requirements is given, when readily available, in a note beginning "System requirements:" and followed by information about the make and model of the computer(s) for which the file is designed, the amount of memory required, the name of the operating system, the software requirements, and the kind of characteristics of required or recommended peripherals. Example:

>System requirements for Macintosh: 68030 processor or higher ; System 7 or higher ; 4 MB RAM (8 MB preferred) ; 256-color monitor ; CD-ROM drive ; mouse.

12.7B1 Serials: This note is called "Frequency." *AACR2R* prescribes making a frequency note unless frequency is apparent from the title and statement of responsibility area or is unknown. However, an LC rule interpretation calls for a note on the known frequency even if it is apparent from the rest of the item. (*CSB* 71: 27) Examples:

>Eight issues yearly.

>Bimonthly.

>Semiannual.

X.7B2.   Language of the item and/or translation or adaptation
>(MARC 21 field 546) (*See also CSB* 78:38–40)

If the language is not evident from the description or if the fact of translation or adaptation is not apparent, notes may be made. Examples:

Book:	Translation of: Das adoptierte Kind.
Map:	Place names in Arabic and English.
Music:	German and English words.
Sound recording:	Sung in Latin.
Film:	In English; also issued in Portuguese and Spanish.
Videorecording:	Closed-captioned.
Serial:	Summaries in English, 1987-Mar./Apr. 1988; summaries in English and Spanish, May/June 1988-

An LC rule interpretation provides guidance for making language and script notes in common and less common situations. (*CSB* 81: 18–20)

X.7B3.   Source of title proper
The source of the title proper is noted if it is taken from a title page substitute. In addition is it given for sound recordings and graphic materials if it is the container and also is given for sound recordings if it is accompanying textual material. The source of the title proper is *always* given for computer files. Examples:

Book:	Cover title.
Sound recording:	Title from publisher's catalog.

Graphic:	Title from later reproductions.
Computer file:	Title from disc label.
Realia:	Title supplied by cataloger.

12.7B3 Serials: LC has issued a rule interpretation stating that, for remote-access electronic serials, the date the title was viewed should be given in parentheses. (*CSB* 79:15) Example:

Title from title screen (viewed on August 12, 1998).

X.7B4.   Variations in title (first indicator 0 or 1, MARC 21 field 246; 2nd indicator 0, MARC 21 field 247) (*See also CSB* 39: 11–12)

Titles on an item that differ from the title proper should be noted. Examples:

Book:	Spine title: 1988 International Display Research Conference.
Map:	Title in lower right hand corner: Bath Alum, Va.
Sound recording:	Title on container: The last sixteen piano trios.

[Label reads: The last sixteen trios.]

Computer file:	Title on container: Pro-Cite for the Macintosh.

[Title proper: Pro-Cite.]

Serial:	Each issue has a distinctive title.
Serial:	Running title: Chemical engineering catalog census.

[Title proper is: CEC census of buyers in the chemical process industries.]

X.7B5.   Parallel titles and other information. Example:

Serial: "An international journal of palaeobotany, palynology and allied sciences."

X.7B6.   Statements of responsibility (MARC 21 fields 500, 508, and 511)

Here is a place for statements of responsibility (e.g., significant persons or bodies connected with previous editions, or persons or bodies not named in the chief source) that were not given in the title and statement of responsibility area. Examples:

Book:	Prepared by the Oceanography Course Team.

[Note: The statement of responsibility did not appear in the chief source of information but was composed by the cataloger from information that appeared elsewhere. Had it appeared in the chief source of information it would have been transcribed in the statement of responsibility area.]

Map:	Grid and marginal information added by the Army Map Service.
Manuscript:	Holography signed note by William Pitt appended to letter.
Music:	Text based on the drama of the same name of Pushkin.
Sound recording:	Violoncello: Raphael Wallfisch ; piano: Richard Markham.
Serial:	Official journal of: American Academy for Cerebral Palsy and Developmental Medicine.
Serial:	Issued by graduate students in the Dept. of French at the Pennsylvania State University.

7.7B6 Motion pictures and videorecordings: An LC rule interpretation lists (in prescribed order) the functions for which persons or bodies will be given in a "credits" statement. It also lists the functions that will not be given. (*CSB* 22: 21) Examples:

> Cast: John Howard Davis, Alec Guinness, Robert Newton.

> Credits: Editor, Lars Floden ; voices, Hans Conreid, June Forray ; music, Larry Wolff.

X.7B7.   Edition and history (MARC 21 fields 500, 518, and 580)

Bibliographic history notes and notes relating to the edition in hand are recorded here. Examples:

Book:	Reprint. Originally published: New York : Pantheon Books, 1986.
Book:	Companion vol. to: The IMF and stabilization. 1984.
Map:	First published under title: Geographic map of the . . . Kingdom of Saudi Arabia.
Music:	Edited from ms. sources in the National Library of Turin.
Sound recording:	Recorded in San Francisco in 1999.
Sound recording:	Reissue of: Capitol SW-1804.
Videorecording:	Videorecording of play produced at Kathryn Bache Miller Theatre, Columbia University, New York, N.Y., March 10, 1998.

Computer file (Interactive multimedia):
> Full digital recording of the performance recorded in Nov. 1987 in Kirche Altstetten, Zürich, Switzerland and released on Teldec 35766.

Microform:	Filmed from the H.G. Wells collection in the Bromley Public Libraries.

2.7B7 Books: An LC rule interpretation is helpful for constructing notes about reprint editions. (*CSB* 58: 14–15)

4.7B7 Manuscripts: This note is called "Donor, source, etc., and previous owner(s)." Example:

> Gift of the estate of Mrs. Theodora Cabot, 1955.

12.7B7 Serials: This note is called "Relationships with other serials."

Continuation. When a serial changes title and a new record is created, a note is made for the preceding title whether or not the numbering continues or is different (MARC 21 field 780). Example:

> Continues: Cerebral palsy bulletin.

Continued by. The record for the serial before the title change should have a note added that names the succeeding title (MARC 21 field 785). Optionally, the date of change may also be added. LC does not apply the option. (*CSB* 71: 28) Example:

> Continued by: Industrial vegetation, turf and pest management.

Merger. When two or more serials are merged, the names of the previously separate serials are given on the record for the new serial (MARC 21 fields 580 and 787). Example:

> Merger of: Mariah, and: Outside.

Each of the serials that were merged should have a note added to give the title of the new serial and the title(s) with which it has merged (MARC 21 fields 580 and 787). Example:

> Merged with: Outside, to become: Mariah/Outside.

Split. A note is made on the record for a serial that is the result of a split of a serial into two or more parts. The note should name the serial that was split (MARC 21 fields 580 and 787). Example:

> Continues in part: Transportation research.

An option allows also naming the other serial(s) resulting from the split. LC is not applying the option. (*CSB* 71: 28) The serial that was split should have a note added that gives the names of the resulting serials (MARC 21 field 580). Example:

> Split into: Transportation research. Part A, General, and: Transportation research. Part B, Methodological.

Absorption. The record for a serial that has absorbed another serial should have added to it a note giving the title of the serial that has been absorbed (MARC 21 fields 580 and 787). An option allows giving also the date of the absorption. LC applies the option when the information is readily available. (*CSB* 71: 28) Example:

> Absorbed: American Association of Stratigraphic Palynologists. Proceedings of the annual meeting.

The record for the serial that has been absorbed should have a note added that gives the title of the serial that absorbed it (MARC 21 field 580). Example:

> Absorbed by: Palynology.

Supplements (MARC 21 fields 580 and 770). Examples:

> Supplement to: Dictionary of literary biography.
> Supplements, including laws, ordinances, bills, etc., accompanying some numbers.

X.7B8.   Material (or type of publication) specific details

3.7B8 Cartographic materials: This note is called "Mathematical and other cartographic data." Examples:

> "Contour interval 50 feet."
> Relief shown by hachures, shading, spot heights, etc.

4.7B8 Manuscripts: This note is called "Place of writing." Example:

> At top of letter: Brooklyn.

5.7B8 Music: This note is called "Notation." Example:

> Shape-note notation.

9.7B8 Computer files: This note is called "File characteristics." Examples:

> File size unknown.
>
> Weighted sample size is 2523.

12.7B8 Serials: This note is called "Numbering and chronological designation." (MARC field 515) Examples:

> Report year ends Mar. 31.
>
> Numbering begins each year with no. 1.

A rule interpretation from LC discusses the case of a remote-access electronic serial, which reproduces some but not all volumes of an existing serial in another format. In this situation, make a note giving the date of cataloging and the beginning of electronic coverage as of that date. If coverage changes, the note may be changed. (*CSB* 81: 23)

X.7B9. Publication, distribution, etc. (MARC 21 field 500 or 550)
Important publication, distribution, etc., details that cannot be given in the publication, distribution, etc., area are recorded in a note. Examples:

> *Book:*   Printed at the Tabard Private Press, Oxshott, by Philip Kerrigan.
>
> *Map:*   Based on 1972 data.
>
> *Film:*   First released in France.
>
> *Graphic:* Issued in 3 parts.

2.7B9 Books: LC interprets a date that consists of month and year or month, day, and year, and that appears in a prominent position, to be a date of release or transmittal and records it in a note in quotation marks. It is not considered to be a publication date, although the publication date may be inferred from it and given in brackets (*CSB* 44: 21–22) Example:

> "March 1990."

4.7B9 Manuscripts: This note is called "Published versions." Example:

> Published in: Some letters of George III / W.B. Hamilton. p. 416.
> *In* The South Atlantic quarterly. Vol. 68, no. 3 (Summer 1969).

X.7B10. Physical description
Important physical details not given in the physical description area may be recorded here. Examples:

> *Book:*   Maps on lining papers.
>
> *Map:*   Maps issued in envelopes bearing copies of inset maps of cities.
>
> *Music:*   Duration: 13:20.
>
> > [given only if stated in the item; a cataloging decision made in the Music Section, Special Materials Cataloging Division, Library of Congress, indicates that for music and sound recordings, hours, minutes, and seconds are to be expressed in the note area as numerals separated by colons.[26]]

Sound recording:	Impressed on pliable surface with rectangular edge attached to hard paper cover for support.
Graphic:	For flannel board.
Puzzle:	Vertical sides in straight lines; horizontal sides form wavy lines.

11.7B10 Microforms: Reduction ratio is given if it is outside the 16X-30X range, using one of the following terms:

Low reduction	*For less than 16X*
High reduction	*For 31X-60X*
Very high reduction	*For 61X-90X*
Ultra high reduction	*For over 90X; for ultra high reduction give also the specific ratio, e.g.,* Ultra high reduction, 150X

Reduction ratio varies

X.7B11.   Accompanying material and supplements

Rule 1.5E1 gives four options for treating accompanying material. When giving details in a note is chosen, the details are recorded here. Examples:

Book:	Overlay grid in pocket inside back cover.
Map:	Accompanied by: Index to maps of Arabia / issued by Army Map Service. 1 sheet ; 25 x 36 cm.
Sound recording:	Program notes by Anthony Hodgson on container.
Film:	With teacher's guide and supplementary material.
Computer file:	Accompanied by printed Index to documents relating to the committee's hearing on the proposed tobacco settlement, November 13, 1997.
Microform:	With companion print index: American public opinion index.

X.7B12.   Series

Series data that cannot appropriately be given in the series area may be recorded in a note. Examples:

Originally issued in series: Research studies in library science.

Part 1 in a series.

Series statement supplied by producer.

11.7B12 Microforms: A note is made here only for a microform series of which the item has been part. The rule for a note for any series relating to the original of which the microform is a reproduction is included in Rule 11.7B22.

Example:

Originally issued in series: Archives on microfilm.

X.7B13.   Dissertations (MARC 21 field 502)

Dissertations or theses are described with a formal note. The English word *thesis* is followed by the degree for which the author was a candidate (e.g., Ph.D., M.A., Master's), the name of the institution or faculty, and the year the degree was granted. Example:

> Thesis (Ph. D.) — Texas A & M University, 1988.

Revisions, abridgments, edited editions, and publications lacking formal thesis notes are noted in MARC field 500. Example:

> Revision of thesis (Ph. D.) — Yale University, 1989.

X.7B14.   Audience (MARC 21 field 521)

If the intended audience is stated in the publication, it may be noted here. Examples:

> For adults learning to read.
>
> Grades 3-6.
>
> For nurses' training.

4.7B14 Manuscripts: This note is called "Access and literary rights." Example:

> Information on literary rights available in the repository.

X.7B15.   Reference to published descriptions (MARC 21 field 510)

4.7B15 Manuscripts: This rule number appears only in the general chapter and in Chapter 4. Example:

> Described in: Manuscripts for research / report of the director, 1961–1974, North Country Historical Research Center, Feinberg Library, State University College, Plattsburgh, New York. 1975. p. 31–32.

X.7B16.   Other formats (MARC 21 field 530)

If the content of the information package has been issued in other formats, they may be noted here. Examples:

Book:	Issued also as computer optical disc.
Videorecording:	Available as cartridge or disc.
Slide:	Issued also as filmstrip.
Microform:	Library also has volumes in printed form and on microfilm.

X.7B17.   Summary (MARC 21 field 520)

Summary notes may be given when the contents of an information package are not specified in the rest of the description. Such notes are often given for nonbook materials because of the difficulty of browsing them (as can be done with books) to determine what they contain. Examples:

| *Sound recording:* | Summary: The author presents an overview and introduction to the area of human potentialities and its implications for humankind. |
| *Film:* | Summary: A sports documentary covering three snowmobile races. |

Computer file (electronic journal):

> Summary: Provides image and full-text online access to back issues. Consult the online table of contents for specific holdings.

Puzzle:

> Summary: The picture shows a battle scene on the deck of a British war ship during the Revolutionary War. The officers are in full dress uniforms for the 1787-1795 period.

2.7B17 Books: LC practice has generally limited summary notes on printed monographs to children's books. Example:

> Summary: By falling down a rabbit hole, Alice experiences unusual adventures with a variety of nonsensical characters.

Since 1984, however, some summary notes created by LC's overseas offices have been included in LC bibliographic records. (*CSB* 60: 15)

12.7B17 Serials: This note is called "Indexes" (MARC 21 field 555). Example:

> Indexes: Vols. 4 (1982)-8 (1986) published separately.

X.7B18.   Contents (MARC 21 fields 504 and 505)

When parts of an information package are titled and would be useful to the user of a bibliographic record, they are brought out in notes. Examples:

Map:

> Each sheet includes: "Index to adjoining sheets," glossary, and "Sources of base compilation."

Music:

> Contents: Sonate C dur, op. 15, Nr. 15 — Sonate A dur, op. 18, Nr. 5 — Sonate F dur, op. 18, Nr. 6.

Film:

> Contents: The black league (20 min.) — Doing your own thing (22 min.) — Teamwork against the odds (18 min.) — A new era (15 min.)

2.7B18 Books: The LC rule interpretation for contents notes is lengthy and should be consulted when such notes seem appropriate. (*CSB* 47: 31–34) Examples:

Contents note for collection of works of one author:

> Contents: Third girl — Poirot loses a client — Funerals are fatal.

Contents note for collection of works by different authors:

> Contents: Introduction / William Zinsser — We are not excused / Robert Stone — Writing as an act of hope / Isabel Allende — A strip of exposed film / Charles McCarry — Active in time and history / Marge Piercy — The agreed-upon facts / Gore Vidal.

Contents note for multi-volume work:

> Contents: v. 1. The gathering storm — v. 2. Their finest hour — v. 3. The Grand Alliance — v. 4. The hinge of fate — v. 5. Closing the ring — v. 6. Triumph and tragedy.

Two parts of an item that are often titled are "Bibliography" and "Index." By example, they fall under rule 2.7B18 in *AACR2R*. In LC practice formal bibliographies were traditionally given as "Bibliography:" with the page numbers on which they fall, and other bibliographical references were given as either "Includes bibliographies" or "Includes bibliographical references." The most recent policy at LC, however, is to use one form of note for bibliographical citations in any form: "Includes bibliographical references." In the case of one formal bibliography, its inclusive page numbers are given in parentheses following the note. "Discography" and "Filmography" are still given as a formal note with page numbers. (*CSB* 47: 32–33) Examples:

> Includes bibliographical references (p. 298–301).
>
> Discography: p. [109] – 111.

While the simplification is welcome, bibliography notes on past LC catalog records are now difficult to interpret. For many years "Includes bibliographical references" meant the book had citations with footnote-type numbering in the order referred to in the text, whether at the bottoms of pages or at the ends of chapters or at the end of the book. Starting in 1984 the note was used only for true footnotes at the bottoms of pages. Then in 1989 it was broadened to be the only form of note used for citations in any form. Bibliography notes in various forms continue to be shown in this text, because they are allowed by *AACR2R*.

8.7B18 Graphic materials: An LC rule interpretation for projected graphics allows the addition, after the number of frames, slides, etc., of the duration of any accompanying sound. (*CSB* 13: 17) Example:

> Contents: Return to the sea (130 fr., 25 min., 15 sec.) —
> To save a living sea (153 fr., 30 min., 25 sec.)

X.7B19.   Numbers borne by the item (other than those covered in area 8)
            (MARC 21 fields 024-032, 036, 037 and 500)
Numbers found in the item other than ISBNs or ISSNs are recorded as notes — often quoted. Examples:

Book:	"IEEE catalog number 88CH2542-9."
Map:	Publisher's no.: AMS 5060 II SW-Series V834.
Music:	Pl. no.: B.S.I. no. 31.
Graphic:	Packet no. A 792.
Realia:	"No. 1014."

6.7B19 Sound recordings: An LC rule interpretation for the transcription of a label name and number of a sound recording calls for making this note the first one. (*CSB* 14: 17) Example:

> Angel: S 37309.

X.7B20.   Copy being described, library's holdings, and restrictions on use
            (MARC 21 field 506 for restrictions on access pertaining to *all* copies;
            local MARC field 590 for local copy information [in OCLC])
Notes are made about the particular copy in hand, including notes about imperfections or notes giving incomplete holdings of a multipart information package. These notes are "copy specific." That is, such a note is applicable only to the copy

held by the cataloger who is creating the description. This works well in an individual library. However, if the library belongs to a network and creates online original cataloging that other libraries eventually use as a basis for their cataloging, this type of note can be a source of difficulty, as is known by libraries that have had to change LC's copy-specific notes to reflect local cataloging. Such notes are tagged 590 in an OCLC MARC record and thus are readily identifiable. Examples:

Book:	Library's copy autographed by the author.
Book:	Library lacks. v. 3.
Music:	Library has 2 copies of the score and 1 copy of each part.

This rule also calls for notes about any restrictions there may be on use of the item. Such a note may or may not be copy-specific. Example:

Book:	Restricted use until 2001.
Computer file:	Available by lease arrangement. Also available through commercial online vendors.

X.7B21.   "With" notes (MARC 21 field 501) (*See also CSB* 38: 31–32)
For information packages lacking a collective title and described separately, a note is given beginning "With:" and then listing the other separately titled parts. Examples:

Music:	With: La plus que lente / Claude Debussy.
Sound recording:	With: Suite italienne / Igor Stravinskii — Vocalise, op. 34, no. 14 / Sergei Rachmaninoff.
Serial microform:	Filmed with: BYU studies. Vol. 11, no. 1-v. 13.

Note: a problem in the "With" note has been commented on by music librarians. Because the rules for notes call for referring to another bibliographic item by its title proper and statement of responsibility, musical works that are entered under a uniform title may be "lost" to the user of the "With" note. Such musical works seldom have added entries for the title proper, and the filing arrangement under the main entry is usually by uniform title, not title proper. This problem, however, may be mitigated in online systems that index all MARC 245 fields in the title index.

X.7B22.   Combined notes relating to the original (MARC 21 fields 500 and 534)
Two chapters besides the general chapter have this rule.

8.7B22 Graphic materials: This note is called "Note relating to the original" and calls for description of the original of a reproduced art work.

11.7B22 Microforms: This note also is called "Note relating to the original." Example:

> Reproduction of: New York : Teachers College, Columbia University, 1927. xix, 166 p. : ill. ; 24 cm.

X.7B23.   Two chapters have a rule "7B23."

4.7B23 Manuscripts: This note is called "Ancient, medieval, and Renaissance manuscripts" and gives instructions for more detailed notes for these manuscripts.

12.7B23 Serials: This note is called "Item described." It is used when the description is not based on the first issue. Example:

Description based on: Vol. 36, no. 1 (Winter 1989).

Figures 4.39–4.43 show examples of complete cataloging for several kinds of information packages, illustrating the use of notes.

Fig. 4.39. Rule 2.7B. Transcriptions of notes for a literary work.

The poetry of Singapore / editors, Edwin Thumboo . . . [et al.] — [Singapore?] : ASEAN Committee on Culture and Information, c1985.
560 p. : col. maps ; 25 cm. — (Anthology of ASEAN literatures ; v. 1
1 →   Poems.
2 →   In Chinese, English, Malay, and Tamil.
3 →   Maps on lining papers.
4 →   Includes index.

[1]Nature, scope, or artistic form (1.7B1)
[2]Language (1.7B2)
[3]Physical description (1.7B10)
[4]Index note (1.7B18)

Fig. 4.40. Rule 2.7B. Transcriptions of notes for a treatise.

Properties of impurity states in superlattice semiconductors / edited by C.Y. Fong, Inder P. Batra, and S. Ciraci. — New York : Plenum Press, c1988.
xi, 351 p. : ill. ; 26 cm. — (NATO ASI series. Series B, Physics ; v. 183)

1 →   "Proceedings of a NATO Advanced Research Workshop on the Properties of Impurity States in Superlattice Semiconductors, held September 7-11, 1987, at the University of Essex, Colchester, United Kingdom"—Verso t.p.
2 →   "Published in cooperation with NATO Scientific Affairs Division."
3 →   Includes bibliographies and index.

[1]Quoted note on nature of item (1.7B1)
[2]Publication information note (1.7B9)
[3]Bibliography and index note (1.7B18)

Fig. 4.41. Rule 7.7B. Transcriptions of notes for a motion picture.

Berlin [motion picture] / Polonius Film Productions ; directors, writers, John Dooley, Tessa Dooley. — Chicago, Ill. : International Film Bureau, 1985.
   1 film reel (25 min.) : sd., col. ; 16 mm. + 1 guide.

1 → In German.
2 → Title from data sheet.
3 → Credits: Photographer, Nicholas Struthers ; narrator, Jurgen Schweckendiek.
4 → A foreign film (England)
5 → Junior high school through adults.
6 → Issued also as videorecording.
7 → Summary: A foreign language teaching program that introduces beginning German students to the history of Berlin and to aspects of contemporary life in the city.

[1]Language (1.7B2)
[2]Source of title proper (1.7B3)
[3]Statements of responsibility (1.7B6)
[4]Edition and history (1.7B7)
[5]Audience (1.7B14)
[6]Other formats (1.7B16)
[7]Summary (1.7B17)

Fig. 4.42. Rule 7.7B. Transcriptions of notes for a videorecording.

The Alphabet theatre proudly presents The Z was zapped [videorecording] : a play in twenty-six acts / written and directed by Chris Van Allsburg ; produced by King Productions. — New Rochelle, N.Y. : Spoken Arts, 1988.
   1 videocassette (9 min.) : sd., col. ; ½ in. +1 guide.

1 → Title on container and guide: Spoken Arts presents The Z was zapped.
1 → Spine title on cassette and container: The Z was zapped.
2 → Credits: Music by Wayne Abravanel ; performed by the Caslon Players.
3 → Based on the book of the same title by Chris Van Allsburg.
4 → VHS format.
5 → Summary: As a player in a play, each letter of the alphabet meets a fate described by a word that begins with that letter.
6 → "SAV 9010."

[1]Variations in title (1.7B4)
[2]Statements of responsibility (1.7B6)
[3]Edition and history (1.7B7)
[4]Physical description (1.7B10)
[5]Summary (1.7B17)
[6]Numbers borne by the item (1.7B19)

Fig. 4.43. Rule 9.7B. Transcriptions of notes for a computer file.

Multimedia Beethoven [interactive multimedia] : the ninth
symphony, an illustrated interactive musical exploration / [by
Robert Winter with the Voyager Company. — Version 1.10,
academic ed. — Computer data and program. — [Santa
Monica, Calif.] : Microsoft Corporation, c1992.

1 computer optical disc : sd., col. ; 4 ¾ in. + 1 users' guide.

1 → System requirements: multimedia PC or equivalent (includes
386SX or higher processor, 2 MB of RAM, 30 MB hard disk,
CD-ROM drive, audio board, mouse, and VGA or VGA+ display);
Microsoft Windows operating system 3.1 or higher; MS-DOS
CD-ROM extension (MSCDEX) version 2.2 or higher; headphones
or speakers.

2 → Title from disk label.

3 → Credits: Viennese State Opera, with Wilhelm Pitz, chorus
master ; Viennese Philharmonic, conducted by Hans Schmidt-
Isserstedt.

4 → Summary: The program is an illustrated, interactive
exploration of Beethoven's Ninth Symphony, which examines the
music and historical setting in which it was created, and the
concepts behind the music.

5 → Contents: Pocket guide — Beethoven's world — Art
of listening — A close reading — Ninth game.

6 → "CDAC 021200."

[1]Nature and scope and system requirements (9.7B1)
[2]Source of title proper (1.7B3)
[3]Statement of responsibility (1.7B6)
[4]Summary (1.7B17)
[5]Contents (1.7B18)
[6]Numbers (other than Standard Numbers) (1.7B19)

AREA 8.   STANDARD NUMBER AND TERMS OF AVAILABILITY
AREA (MARC 21 fields 020 and 022)

An LC rule interpretation should be consulted when applying this rule using
standards set by LC. (*CSB* 47:28–29). When cataloging microforms, it should be remembered that only a standard number assigned to the microform itself is placed
here. A standard number for the original should be included in the note on details of
the original. This area is not used for manuscripts.

X.8B.   Standard number (subfield a, MARC 21 field 020 or 022)

X.8B1.   An internationally agreed-upon standard number for the information
package is given in the standard number area following the notes. The numbers usually given here are the International Standard Book Number (ISBN) or the International Standard Serial Number (ISSN). Example:

> The Battle of Britain : the greatest air battle of World War II /
> Richard Hough and Denis Richards. — 1st American ed.
> — London : Hodder & Stoughton ; New York : Norton, c1989.
> xvii, 413 p., [40] p. of plates : ill. (some col.), maps ; 25 cm.
> Includes index.
> ISBN 0-393-02766-X

X.8B2.   If there are two or more standard numbers, the one that applies to the item being described should be given. An option allows recording more than one number and adding a qualification (as prescribed in rule 1.8E). LC is applying this option. (*CSB* 8: 9) Example:

> ISBN 0-8032-3093-1 (alk. paper) —
> ISBN 0-8032-8167-6 (pbk. : alk. paper)

When ISBNs are inserted into a MARC record, each is input into its own 020 field, each number is recorded as a block without hyphens, and the acronym *ISBN* is omitted. An ISSN is placed in a 022 field with its hyphen, but omitting the acronym *ISSN*.

X.8C. Key-title (MARC 21 field 222)

1.8C1.   The key-title of a serial, if found on the item, is added after the ISSN, even if it is the same as the title proper. It is separated from the ISSN by a space-equal sign-space. Example:

> ALCTS newsletter. — Vol. 1, no. 1 (1990)-v. 9, no. 4-6 (1998).
> — Chicago, IL : Association for Library Collections &
> Technical Services, American Library Association, 1990-
> 9 v. : ill. ; 28 cm.
>
> Eight no. a year.
> Title from caption.
> Continues: RTSD newsletter.
> Continued by: ALCTS newsletter online.
> ISSN 1047-949X = ALCTS newsletter

X.8D.   *Optional addition.* **Terms of availability** (subfield c, MARC 21 field 020)
    It is optional to add the price or other terms of availability, separated from the ISBN or ISSN by a space-colon-space. LC does not exercise this option for current items. (*CSB* 67: 19) Example:

> ISBN 0-87287-621-7 : $45.00

[*Books:* In the books chapter, the terms of availability rule is placed at 2.8C. In all other chapters which have this rule, it is placed at X.8D.]

X.8E.   Qualification (subfield a, MARC 21 field 020)

1.8E1.   A brief qualification is added after the standard number or terms of availability when there are two or more (*see* example under X.8B2, above).

RULE X.9.   SUPPLEMENTARY ITEMS (MARC 21 field 525 [for serials]
                or separate record)
    All *AACR2R* chapters except that for manuscripts have this rule. Many supplementary items are described as separate entities and are given complete independent

bibliographic records. The rule that identifies which supplementary works should be cataloged separately is 21.28.

In the cases where a supplementary work is described dependently, one of three methods may be chosen: 1) the supplementary item may be recorded as accompanying material (rule 1.5E1d) (*see* example under 1.10B below); 2) the item may be described in the note area (rule 1.7B11); multilevel description may be used (rule 13.6)

RULE X.10.   ITEMS MADE UP OF SEVERAL TYPES OF MATERIALS

All *AACR2R* chapters except that for manuscripts have this rule, which deals with the description of information packages with components that belong to more than one group or type of material (e.g., printed text and slides).

1.10B.   If one of the components is so predominant that the item is of no use without that component (e.g., a slide set with an accompanying script that has little value without seeing the slides), the item should be described in terms of the predominant component with details of the other component(s) given as accompanying material or in a note. Example:

> Bushy the squirrel [filmstrip] / Cathedral Films, Inc. ;
> producers, Jim Friedrich ... [et al.] ; writer, John Calvin
> Reid. — Niles, IL : United Learning, 1987.
>   1 filmstrip (33 fr.) : col. ; 35 mm. + 1 sound cassette
> (9 min., 10 sec. : analog) + 1 study guide. — (Parables
> from nature)

> [Note: Predominant component is the filmstrip; the sound cassette and
> study guide are subsidiary components.]

1.10C.   If there is no predominant component, the item is cataloged as a kit as described below.

1.10C1.   General material designation

The instructions in rule 1.1C4 are followed except when an item has no collective title. Then the appropriate GMD is given after each individual title.

1.10C2.   Physical description

The cataloger is instructed to choose the most appropriate of three methods of providing the physical description:

a)   listing the extent of each of the individual parts. An option allows adding the name of the container and its dimensions. LC is applying the option on a case-by-case basis. (*CSB* 84: 13) Example:

> Who were the Pilgrims? [kit] / National Geographic
> Society. — Washington, D.C. : The Society, c1989.
>   30 identical booklets, 1 sound cassette, 6 activity sheets
> (2 copies each), 8 duplicating masters, 1 teacher's guide ; in
> box 29 x 24 x 5 cm. — (Wonders of learning)

b)   giving separate physical descriptions on separate lines for each type of component. Again, naming the container and giving its dimensions is given as an option. Example:

Element probe [kit] : an A/V game for teaching the
chemical elements / United Learning, Inc. ; writer,
Richard S. Treptow. — Niles, IL : United Learning, 1988.
100 slides : col.
1 sound cassette (44 min.) : analog, stereo.
10 duplicating masters ; 28 x 22 cm.
1 teacher's guide (28 p.) ; 24 cm.
All in container 30 x 23 x 7 cm.

c)   giving a general term with the number of pieces as the extent of item for
items with a large number of different types of materials. The same option
for naming the container and giving its dimensions is allowed, and LC applies it on a case-by-case basis. Example:

Safety begins with you [kit]. — New York : Children's
Media Productions, c1979.
24 various pieces. — (School craft kits)

12.10 Serials: This rule is called "Sections of Serials." It states that sections of a
serial should be described as separate serials rather than using the "multilevel" structure described in chapter 5 of this text, "Description of Analytical Materials." Rules
12.1B4–12.1B6 give instructions for recording separate titles proper for sections of
a serial.

RULE X.11.   FACSIMILES, PHOTOCOPIES, AND OTHER REPRODUCTIONS

The *AACR2R* chapters for printed texts, cartographic materials, music and
graphics have this rule. Facsimiles, photocopies, or other reproductions of these
items are described in such a way that the details of the facsimile, etc., are given in all
areas except the note area. If the title of the facsimile, etc., is different from the original, the title of the facsimile, etc., is given as title proper. The same is true for edition,
publication details, or series. In these cases, the details of the original are given in a
single note in the notes area in the same order as they would appear in the main part
of the description. Example:

Frederic Remington / by Ernest Raboff. — 1st Harper
trophy ed. — New York : Harper & Row, 1989.
[31] p. : ill. (some col.) ; 29 cm.

"A Harper trophy book."
Summary: A brief biography of the artist and sculptor
accompanies fifteen color reproductions and critical
interpretations of his works.
Reprint of: Frederic Remington / by Adeline Peter
and Ernest Raboff. Garden City, N.Y. : Doubleday, 1973.
(Art for children)

If the facsimile, etc., is in a form of material different from the original, the
chapter relating to the form of the facsimile, etc., is used. For a manuscript reproduced as a book, the chapter on description of books would be used. For maps reproduced on microfilm, the chapter on description of microforms would be used.

COMPLETE DESCRIPTIONS AND MACHINE-READABLE CATALOGING (MARC RECORDS) FOR ILLUSTRATIVE EXAMPLES

Fig. 4.44. *AACR2R* **description of the book whose title page and other preliminaries are shown in figures 4.6–4.8.**

A guide to the Library of Congress classification / Lois Mai Chan. — 5th ed. — Englewood, Colo. : Libraries Unlimited, 1999.
xviii, 551 p. ; 25 cm. — (Library and information science text series)

"Based on the fourth edition of Immroth's Guide to the Library of Congress classification."
Includes bibliographical references (p. 531-537) and index.
ISBN 1-56308-499-6 (cloth) — ISBN 1-56308-500-3 (pbk.)

Fig. 4.45. Complete bibliographic record for the printed monograph in Fig. 4.44 coded according to the MARC format and spaced and formatted for the OCLC system.

```
   OCLC: 41211262         Rec stat:   c
   Entered: 19990406      Replaced:   19990914     Used: 19990924
 > Type: a    ELvl:        Srce:      Audn:     Ctrl:       Lang: eng
   BLvl: m    Form:        Conf:  0   Biog:     MRec:       Ctry: cou
              Cont: b      GPub:      Fict:  0  Indx:  1
   Desc: a    Ills:        Fest:  0   DtSt: s   Dates: 1999,        <
 >    1 010       99-15279 <
 >    2 040       DLC $c DLC $d UKM $d C#P <
 >    3 015       GB99-Y0841 <
 >    4 020       1563084996 (cloth) <
 >    5 020       1563085003 (pbk.) <
 >    6 050 00    Z696.U4 $b C47 1999 <
 >    7 082 00    025.4/33 $2 21 <
 >    8 090 $b    <
 >    9 049       DD0A <
 >   10 100 1     Chan, Lois Mai. <
 >   11 245 12    A guide to the Library of Congress classification / $c
 Lois Mai Chan. <
 >   12 250       5th ed. <
 >   13 260       Englewood, Colo. : $b Libraries Unlimited, $c 1999. <
 >   14 300       xviii, 551 p. ; $c 25 cm. <
 >   15 440  0    Library and information science text series <
 >   16 500       "Based on the fourth edition of Immroth's Guide to the Library
 of Congress classification." <
 >   17 504       Includes bibliographical references (p. 531-537) and index. <
 >   18 650  0    Classification, Library of Congress. <
 >   19 650  4    Classification, Library of Congress. <
 >   20 700 1     Chan, Lois Mai. $t Immroth's Guide to the Library of
 Congress classification. $s 4th ed. <
```

Fig. 4.46. *AACR2R* description of the map shown in figures 4.9–4.12.

Bath Alum quadrangle, Virginia–Bath Co. / mapped, edited, and published by the Geological Survey. — Scale 1:24,000 ; Polyconic proj. — Washington, D.C. : For sale by U.S. Geological Survey, 1968.
1 map section : col. ; 58 x 43 cm. — (7.5 minute series : topographic)

Title in lower right corner: Bath Alum, Va.
"Topography by photogrammetric methods from aerial photographs."
Includes quadrangle location map.
Publisher's no.: AMS 5060 II SW-Series V834.
"N3800—W7937.5/7.5."

Fig. 4.47. MARC record for the map.

```
    Entered:    19980505     Replaced:   19990518    Used:     19980505
>   Type: e     ELvl: I    Srce:  d    Relf: a    Ctrl:        Lang: eng
    BLvl: m     SpFm:      GPub:  f    Prme:      MRec:        Ctry: dcu
    CrTp: a     Indx: 0    Proj:  cp   DtSt: s    Dates: 1968,
    Desc: a <
>    1 040      MFS $c MFS $d OCL <
>    2 007      a $b j $d c $e a
>    3 034 1    a $b 24000 <
>    4 043      n-us-va <
>    5 052      3883 $b B3 <
>    6 090      G3883.B3 1968 $b .U5 <
>    7 049      DD0A <
>    8 110 2    Geological Survey (U.S.) <
>    9 245 10   Bath Alum quadrangle, Virginia—Bath Co. / $c mapped,
edited, and published by the Geological Survey. <
>   10 246 1    $i Filing title: $a Bath Alum, Va. <
>   11 255      Scale 1:24,000 ; $b Polyconic proj. <
>   12 260      Washington, D.C. : $b For sale by the U.S. Geological
Survey, $c 1968. <
>   13 300      1 map section : $b col. ; $c 58 x 43 cm. <
>   14 490 0    7.5 minute series : topographic <
>   15 500      Title in lower right corner: Bath Alum, Va. <
>   16 500      "Topography by programmetric methods from aerial
photographs." <
>   17 500      Includes quadrangle location map. <
>   18 500      Publisher's no.: AMS 5060 II SW-Series V834. <
>   19 500      "N3800--W7937.5/7.5." <
>   20 651  0   Bath Alum (Va.) $v Maps, Topographic. <
```

Fig. 4.48. *AACR2R* description of the single manuscript shown in figures 4.13–4.15.

[Letter] 1793 Feb. 3, Windsor [to Henry] Dundas / G.R. [George III].
1 leaf ; 38 x 46 cm. folded to 23 x 19 cm.

Holograph signed.
Purchase, 1961.
Published in: Some letters of George III / W.B. Hamilton. p. 416. *In* The South Atlantic quarterly. Vol. 68, no. 3 (Summer 1969)

Fig. 4.49. MARC record for the manuscript.

```
    Entered:     19850324      Replaced:     19970605      Used: 19970605
>   Type: t       ELvl: I    Srce:  d    Audn:       Ctrl:  a   Lang: eng
    BLvl: m       Form:      Conf:  0    Biog:       MRec:      Ctry: xx
                  Cont:      GPub:       Fict:  0    Indx:  0
    Desc: a       Ills:      Fest:  0    DtSt:  s    Dates: 1793,   <
>    1 040        DD0 $c DD0 <
>    2 045        v9v9 $b d17930203
>    3 090        DA506.A2 $b 1793 <
>    4 049        DD0A <
>    5 100 1      George $b III, $c King of Great Britain, $d 1738-1820. <
>    6 245 10     [Letter] 1793 Feb. 3, Windsor [to Henry] Dundas / $c G.R.
[George III]. <
>    7 300        1 leaf ; $c 38 x 46 cm. folded to 23 x 19 cm. <
>    8 500        Holograph, signed. <
>    9 590        Purchase, 1961. <
>   10 500        Published in: Some letters of George III / W.B. Hamilton. p. 416.
In The South Atlantic quarterly. Vol. 68, no. 3 (Summer 1969) <
>   11 651 0      Great Britain $x History $y George III, 1760-1820. <
```

Fig. 4.50. *AACR2R* description of the score shown in figure 4.16.

> Triosonate H-moll für zwei Violinen und Basso Continuo = Trio
> sonata in B minor for two violins and basso continuo : op. I/8 / Tommaso
> Albinoni ; herausgegeben von Stefan Altner. — Kassel ; New York :
> Bärenreiter, 1987.
> 1 score (12 p.) + 3 parts ; 30 cm. — (Hortus Musicus ; 240)

> Pref. in German and English.
> Continuo realized in score for keyboard.
> Pl. no.: HM 240.

Fig. 4.51. MARC record for the score.

```
    OCLC:   17336099          Rec stat:     c
    Entered:     19880112      Replaced:     19990506    Used:    19990515
>   Type: c       ELvl: I    Srce:  d    Audn:       Ctrl:      Lang: N/A
    BLvl: m       Form:      Comp:  ts   AccM:       MRec:      Ctry: gw
    Desc: a       FMus: a    LTxt:  n    DtSt:  s    Dates: 1987,   <
>    1 040        FUG $c FUG $d OCL $d RES $d OCL <
>    2 028 22     HM 240 $b B"arenreiter <
>    3 041 0      $g gereng <
>    4 045        u9u9 <
>    5 048        sa02 $a ke <
>    6 090        M312.4 $b .A421 op. 1, no. 8, 1987 <
>    7 049        DD0A <
>    8 100 1      Albinoni, Tomaso, $d 1671-1750. <
>    9 240 10     Trio sonatas, $m violins, continuo, $n op. 1. $n No. 8 <
>   10 245 10     Triosonate H-moll f"ur zwei Violinen und Basso Continuo =
$b Trio sonata in B minor for two violins and basso continuo : $b op. I/8 /
$c Tommaso Albinoni ; herausgegeben von Stefan Altner. <
>   11 260        Kassel ; $a New York : $b B"arenreiter, $c 1987. <
>   12 300        1 score (12 p.) + 3 parts ; $c 30 cm. <
>   13 440  0     Hortus Musicus ; $v 240 <
```

(Figure 4.51 continues on page 150.)

Fig. 4.51—*Continued*

```
>   14 500        Pref. in German and English. <
>   15 500        Continuo realized in score for keyboard. <
>   16 650   0    Trio sonatas (Violins (2), continuo) $v Scores and parts. <
>   17 700   1    Altner, Stefan. <
```

Fig. 4.52. *AACR2R* **description of the sound recording shown in figures 4.17–4.18.**

The four seasons [sound recording] / Antonio Vivaldi. —
Djursholm, Sweden : BIS, p1985.
    1 sound disc (ca. 40 min.) : digital, stereo. ; 4¾ in. + 1 booklet
([10] p. ; 12 cm.)

    BIS: CD-275.
    Compact disc.
    Nils Erik Sparf, baroque violin ; Drottningholm Baroque Ensemble.
    Program notes in Swedish by Stig Jacobsson with English, French,
and German translations inserted in container.
    Recorded June 7 and Sept. 11, 1984, in the Petrus Church, Stocksund,
Sweden.

Fig. 4.53. MARC record for the sound recording.

```
    OCLC:  21788480         Rec stat:      n
    Entered:   19880510     Replaced:      19950506    Used:   19990920
>   Type: j        ELvl: I    Srce:  d    Audn:       Ctrl:        Lang: N/A
    BLvl: m        Form:      Comp:  co   AccM:       MRec:        Ctry: sw
    Desc: a        FMus: n    LTxt:       DtSt:  s    Dates: 1985,    <
>    1 040         CUY $c CUY <
>    2 007         s $b d $c u $d f $e s $f n $g g $h n $i n $j m $k l $l n $m e <
>    3 028  01     $b Bis $a CD-275 <
>    4 033  1      19840607 $a 19840911 $b 6954 <
>    5 048         oa <
>    6 090         $b <
>    7 049         DD0A <
>    8 100  1      Vivaldi, Antonio, $d 1678-1741. <
>    9 240  10     Cimento dell'armonia e dell'inventione. $n N. 1-4. <
>   10 245  14     The four seasons $h [sound recording] / $c Antonio Vivaldi. <
>   11 260         Djursholm, Sweden : $b BIS, $c p1985. <
>   12 300         1 sound disc (ca. 40 min.) : $b digital, stereo. ; $c 4 3/4
in. + $e 1 booklet ([10] p. ; 12 cm.) <
>   13 500         Compact disc. <
>   14 511  0      Nils Erik Sparf, baroque violin ; Drottningholm Baroque
Ensemble. <
>   15 500         Program notes in Swedish by Stig Jacobsson with English,
French, and German translations inserted in container. <
>   16 518         Recorded June 7 and Sept. 11, 1984, in the Petrus Church,
Stocksund, Sweden. <
>   17 650  0      Concertos (Violin with string orchestra) <
>   18 650  0      Seasons $x Songs and music. <
>   19 700  1      Sparf, Nils Erik. $4 prf <
>   20 710  2      Drottningholms barockensemble. $4 prf <
```

Fig. 4.54. *AACR2R* description of the videorecording shown in figures 4.19–4.21.

The Martian space party [videorecording]. — Bloomington, IN :
More Sugar from the Firesign Theatre [distributor], 1996, c1972.
1 videocassette (27 min.) : sd., col. ; 1/2 in.

Cast: Phil Austin, Peter Bergman, David Ossman and Phil Proctor.
Credits: Directed by Stephen Gillmor ; produced and edited by The
Firesign Theater and Stephen Gillmor.
Videocassette release of the 1972 film.
"Not insane! in '96" — container.
VHS format.
Summary: Filmed excerpts from a 1972 live performance by the
comedy group, The Firesign Theatre, "on location at the Natural
Surrealist Light Peoples' Party convention." A satirical look at political
conventions and news coverage is combined with parodies of Shake-
speare and low-budget television shows. The performance concludes
with the liftoff of the incumbent President in a rocket to Mars,
accompanied by a Japanese movie monster.

Fig. 4.55. MARC record for the videorecording.

```
  OCLC:  34346718        Rec stat:     c
  Entered: 19960312       Replaced:     19960312    Used:  19980911
> Type: g    ELvl: I    Srce:  d    Audn:      Ctrl:      Lang: eng
  BLvl: m    TMat: v    GPub:       AccM:      MRec:      Ctry: inu
  Desc: a    Time: 027  Tech:  1    DtSt:  r   Dates: 1996,1972    <
>   1 040      CGL $c CGL <
>   2 007      v $b f $d c $e b $f a $g h $h o <
>   3 043      n-us--- <
>   4 045 0    PN1995.9.C55 $b F57 1996 <
>   5 049      CUMM <
>   6 110 0    Firesign Theatre (Performing group) <
>   7 245 14   The Martian space party $h [videorecording]. <
>   8 260      Bloomington, IN : $b More Sugar from the Firesign Theatre
[distributor], $c 1996, c1972. <
>   9 300      1 videocassette (27 min.) : $b sd., col. ; $c 1/2 in. <
>  10 511      Phil Austin, Peter Bergman, David Ossman and Phil Proctor. <
>  11 508      Directed by Stephen Gillmor ; produced and edited by The
Firesign Theatre and Stephen Gillmor. <
>  12 500      Videocassette release of the 1972 film. <
>  13 500      "Not insane! in '96" --container. <
>  14 538      VHS format. <
>  15 520      Filmed excerpts from a 1972 live performance by the comedy
group, The Firesign Theatre, "on location at the Natural Surrealist Light
Peoples' Party convention." A satirical look at political conventions and
news coverage is combined with parodies of Shakespeare and low-budget
television shows. The performance concludes with the liftoff of the
incumbent President in a rocket to Mars, accompanied by a Japanese movie
monster. <
>  16 650 0    Political conventions $v Humor. <
>  17 650 0    Presidents $z United States $x Election $y 1972 $v Humor. <
>  18 655 7    Comedy variety. $2 mim <
>  19 700 1    Gillmor, Steve. <
```

Fig. 4.56. *AACR2R* **description of the stereograph reel shown in figures 4.22–4.24.**

Smithsonian Institution, Washington, D.C. [slide]. — Portland, Or. : Sawyer's Inc., [196-?]
3 stereograph reels (7 pairs of fr. each) : col. + 1 booklet (16 p. : col. ill. ; 11 cm.). — (View-master guided picture tour)

Booklet edited by Lowell Thomas.
For use with View-master.
Summary: Shows and describes some of the major exhibits housed in three of the buildings of the Smithsonian.
Contents: Reel 1. Air and space exhibits — Reel 2. Natural history exhibits — Reel 3. History & technology exhibits.
"Packet no. A 792."

Fig. 4.57. MARC record for the stereograph reel.

```
    Entered: 19810922        Replaced: 19990616        Used: 19870601
>   Type: g      ELvl: I    Srce:  d    Audn: g    Ctrl:       Lang: eng
    BLvl: m      TMat: s    GPub:       AccM: m    MRec:       Ctry: oru
    Desc: a      Time: 021  Tech:  n    DtSt: q    Dates: 1960,1969    <
>    1 040       DD0 $c DD0 <
>    2 007       g $b s $c r $d c $e n $h z <
>    3 090       Q11.S8 $b S64 <
>    4 049       DD0A <
>    5 245 00    Smithsonian Institution, Washington, D.C. $h [slide] <
>    6 260       Portland, Or. : $b Sawyer's Inc., $c [196-?] <
>    7 300       3 stereograph reels (7 pairs of fr. each) : $b col. + $e 1
booklet (16 p. : col. ill. ; 11 cm.) <
>    8 490 0     View-master guided picture tour <
>    9 500       Booklet edited by Lowell Thomas. <
>   10 500       For use with View-master.
>   11 520       Shows and describes some of the major exhibits housed in
three of the buildings of the Smithsonian.
>   12 505 0     Reel 1. Air and space exhibits -- Reel 2. Natural history
exhibits -- Reel 3. History & technology exhibits. <
>   13 500       "Packet no. A 792." <
>   14 610  0    Smithsonian Institution. <
>   15 700 1     Thomas, Lowell, $d 1892-1981. <
```

Fig. 4.58. *AACR2R* **description of the computer disc shown in figures 4.25–4.26.**

The Annenberg Washington Program electronic library [computer file]. — Computer data. — Washington, D.C. : Annenberg Washington Program in Communications Policy Studies, Northwestern University, c1996.

1 computer optical disc : sd., col. ; 4¾ in. + 1 user guide (15 p. ; 12 cm.).

System requirements: IBM-compatible PCs, 80386 processor or better, Windows 3.1 or higher, 4 MB of RAM, 3 MB of hard disk space; Macintosh computers, 68020 processor or higher, system 6 or higher, 8 MB of RAM, 4 MB of hard disk space.

Title from title screen.

Summary: Contains more than ninety Program publications, previously published in print, addressing issues in communications, information technology, political science, medicine, and many other critical areas. Most publications include full text of the original reports.

Fig. 4.59. MARC record for the computer disc.

```
  OCLC:   34777512        Rec stat:    c
  Entered:   19960523     Replaced:    19990117    Used:   19990914
> Type: a      ELvl: I    Srce:  d    Audn:     Ctrl:       Lang: eng
  BLvl: m      Form:      Conf:  0    Biog:     MRec:       Ctry: dcu
               Cont:      GPub:       Fict: 0   Indx:  0
  Desc: a      Ills:      Fest:  0    DtSt: s   Dates: 1996,        <
>    1 040     ZHM $c ZHM $d OCL <
>    2 006     [m   u   ] <
>    3 007     c $b o $d u $e g $f u <
>    4 090     P92.U5 $b A5 1996 <
>    5 049     CUMM <
>    6 245 04  The Annenberg Washington Program electronic library $h
[computer file]. <
>    7 256     Computer data. <
>    8 260     Washington D.C. : $b Annenberg Washington Program in
Communications Policy Studies, Northwestern University, $c c1996. <
>    9 300     1 computer optical disc : $b sd., col. ; $c 4 3/4 in. +
$e 1 user guide (15 p. ; 12 cm.). <
>   10 538     System requirements: IBM-compatible PCs, 80386 processor
or better, Windows 3.1 or higher, 4 MB of RAM, 3MB of hard disk space;
Macintosh computers, 68020 processor or higher, system 6 or higher, 8 MB
of RAM, 4 MB of hard disk space. <
>   11 500     Title from title screen. <
>   12 520     Contains more than ninety Program publications, previously
published in print, addressing issues in communications, information
technology, political science, medicine, and many other critical areas.
Most publications include full text of the original reports. <
>   10 650  0  Communication policy $z United States. <
>   11 650  0  Communication $z United States. <
>   12 710 2   Northwestern University (Evanston, Ill.). $b Annenberg
Washington Program in Communication Policy Studies. <
```

Fig. 4.60. *AACR2R* description of the Web site shown in figure 4.27.

American memory [computer file] : historical collections for
the National Digital Library / The Library of Congress. —
Computer online service. — [Washington, D.C.] : National
Digital Library Program, Library of Congress, [1994-].

Mode of access: World Wide Web.
Access: http://lcweb2.loc.gov/ammem/
Title from home page.
Title on title bar: Home page: American Memory from the
Library of Congress.
Summary: Provides information on, and access to, digitized
versions of the Library's primary-source collections on American
history and culture, including photographs, documents, sound
recordings, and motion pictures.
Description based on home page, as viewed on April 13,
2000.

Fig. 4.61. MARC record for the Web site.

```
  OCLC:   34374164        Rec stat:   c
  Entered:   19960315      Replaced:   19990322     Used:   19990921
> Type: m    ELvl: I    Srce:  d   Audn:       Ctrl:       Lang: eng
  BLvl: m    File: j    GPub:  f             MRec:       Ctry: dcu
  Desc: a                        DtSt:  m    Dates: 1994,9999      <
>   1 040      VFL $c VFL $d ZBL <
>   2 007      c $b r $d m $e n $f a <
>   3 043      n-us--- <
>   4 090      E151 $b .L5 <
>   5 049      CUMM <
>   6 110 2    Library of Congress. $b National Digital Library Program. <
>   7 245 10   American Memory $h [computer file] : $b historical collections
for the National Digital Library / $c The Library of Congress. <
>   8 246 1    $i Title on title bar: $a Home page : American Memory
from the Library of Congress <
>   9 246 13   American Memory from the Library of Congress <
>  10 256      Computer online service. <
>  11 260      [Washington, DC] : $b National Digital Library Program,
Library of Congress, $c [1994- ] <
>  12 538      Mode of access: World Wide Web. <
>  13 500      Title from home page. <
>  14 520      Provides information on, and access to, digitized versions
of the Library's primary-source collections on American history and culture,
including photographs, documents, sound recordings, and motion pictures. <
>  15 500      Description based on home page, as viewed on April 13, 2000. <
>  16 651  0   United States $x Civilization $v Sources. <
>  17 651  0   United States $x Social life and customs $v Sources. <
>  18 651  0   United States $x History $v Sources. <
>  19 856 40   $u http://lcweb2.loc.gov/ammem/ <
```

Fig. 4.62. *AACR2R* **description of the game shown
in figures 4.28–4.29.**

Double nine dominoes [game]. — Premier ed. —
L[ong] I[sland] C[ity], NY : Cardinal Industries, c1993.
    1 game (55 pieces) : plastic ; in case 12 x 20 x 5 cm. + 1
instruction sheet.

Instructions in English and Spanish.
Title on carrying case: Domino by Cardinal.
Ages 4 to adult.
"No. 511."

Fig. 4.63. MARC record for the game.

```
  OCLC:  29713225        Rec stat:     c
  Entered: 19940131        Replaced:     19980909    Used:   19940131
> Type: r      ELvl: I    Srce:  d    Audn: g    Ctrl:      Lang: eng
  BLvl: m      TMat: g    GPub:       AccM:      MRec:      Ctry: nyu
  Desc: a      Time: nnn  Tech:  n    DtSt: s    Dates: 1993,     <
>   1 040      CUM $c CUM <
>   2 041      engspa <
>   3 090      GV1467 <
>   4 092      510.7 $b DOUBLE <
>   5 049      CUMM <
>   6 245 00   Double nine dominoes $h [game]. <
>   7 246 1    Domino by Cardinal <
>   8 250      Premier ed. <
>   9 260      L[ong] I[sland] C[ity], NY : $b Cardinal Industries, $c c1993. <
>  10 300      1 game (55 pieces) : $b plastic ; $c in case 12 x 20 x 5
cm. + $e 1 instruction sheet. <
>  11 500      Instructions in English and Spanish. <
>  12 500      Title on carrying case: Domino by Cardinal. <
>  13 521      Ages 4 to adult. <
>  14 500      "No. 511." <
>  15 655  7   Dominoes. $2 lcsh <
>  16 710 2    Cardinal Industries. <
```

Fig. 4.64. Description of the microfilm shown in figures 4.30–4.31.

Women and/in health [microform] / filmed by the Women's
History Research Center. — Berkeley, Calif. : The Center, 1974.
14 microfilm reels : ill. ; 35 mm. + 1 guide (88 p. in various
pagings ; 28 cm.)

Collection of microfilmed clippings from newspapers, professional
journals, alternative newspapers, academic research papers, theses, and
conference speeches. Includes leaflets, poetry and graphic material.
Title on containers: Women and health/mental health.
Low reduction (15:1).
Guide issued under title: Guide to the microfilm edition of the
Women and health collection.
Contents: Section 1. Physical and mental health of women (3 reels)
— Section 2. Physical and mental illnesses of women (2 reels) —
Section 3. Biology, women, and the life cycle (1 reel) — Section 4.
Birth control/population control (3 reels) — Section 5. Sex and
sexuality (2 reels) — Section 6. Black and third world
women—health (1 reel) — Section 7. Special issues of mass
periodicals relating to sections I, II, III, IV, V, VI of Women and
health (2 reels).

Fig. 4.65. MARC record for the microfilm.

```
  OCLC:  28588259          Rec stat:    c
  Entered:    19930729     Replaced:    19980129     Used:   19990927
> Type: a     ELvl:        Srce:  d     Audn:        Ctrl:       Lang: eng
  BLvl: m     Form:  a     Conf:  0     Biog:        MRec:       Ctry: cau
              Cont:        GPub:        Fict:  0     Indx:  0
  Desc: a     Ills:        Fest:  0     DtSt:  s     Dates: 1974,     <
>    1 040     NLM $c NLM <
>    2 007     h $b d $d a $e f $f a015 $g b $h b $i c $j a <
>    3 060 00  WA 300 $b W8715 1974 <
>    4 090     HQ1426 $b .W68 1974 <
>    5 049     DD0A <
>    6 245 00  Women and/in health $h [microform] / $c filmed by the
Women's History Research Center. <
>    7 246 3   Women and, in health <
>    8 246 3   Women and health/mental health <
>    9 246 3   Women and health, mental health <
>   10 260     Berkeley, Calif. : $b The Center, $c 1974. <
>   11 300     14 microfilm reels : $b ill. ; $c 35 mm. + $e 1 guide (88 p.
in various pagings ; 28 cm.) <
>   12 500     Collection of microfilmed clippings from newspapers, profes-
sional journals, alternative newspapers, academic research papers, theses,
and conference speeches. Includes leaflets, poetry, and graphic material. <
>   13 500     Title on containers: Women and health/mental health. <
>   14 500     Low reduction (15:1). <
>   15 500     Guide issued under title: Guide to the microfilm edition
of the Women and health collection. <
```

```
>   16 505 0    Section 1. Physical and mental health of women (3 reels)
-- Section 2. Physical and mental illnesses of women (2 reels) -- Section
3. Biology, women, and the life cycle (1 reel) -- Section 4. Birth control/
population control (3 reels) -- Section 5. Sex and sexuality (2 reels)
-- Section 6. Black and third world women -- health (1 reel) -- Section
7. Special issues of mass periodicals relating to sections I, II, III,
IV, V, VI of Women and health (2 reels). <
>   17 650  0    Women $x Health and hygiene. <
>   18 650  0    Women's health services. <
>   19 650  0    Women $x Psychology. <
>   20 650  2    Health $v collected works. <
>   21 650  2    Women's Health Services $v collected works. <
>   22 650  2    Women's Health $v collected works. <
>   23 710 2     Women's History Research Center. <
```

Fig. 4.66. Description of the microfiche shown in figures 4.32–4.34, according to *AACR2R*.

The impact of feminist thought on American librarianship, 1965-1985 [microform] / Christina Diane Baum. — Ann Arbor, Mich. : University Microfilms International, 1987.
 3 microfiches (276 fr.) ; 11 x 15 cm.

Thesis (Ed.D.)—University of Kentucky, 1987.
Includes bibliographical references.
"87-15914."
Reproduction of: x, 255 leaves ; 28 cm.
Typescript. Includes bibliographical references (leaves 245-254).

(If one is following LC policy, the description shown in figure 4.66 would appear as in figure 4.68.)

Fig. 4.67. MARC record for the microfiche, according to *AACR2R*.

```
    OCLC:  22772600        Rec stat:    n
    Entered:   19901204     Replaced:    19930330    Used:    19950131
>   Type: a    ELvl: I    Srce:  d    Audn:       Ctrl:       Lang: eng
    BLvl: m    Form: b    Conf:  0    Biog:       MRec:       Ctry: miu
               Cont: b    GPub:       Fict: 0     Indx: 0
    Desc: a    Ills:      Fest:  0    DtSt: r     Dates: 1987,1987    <
>    1 040     DD0 $c DD0 <
>    2 007     h $b e $d a $e m $f b--- $g b $h u $i c $j u <
>    3 090     Z665 $b .B38 1987 <
>    4 049     DD0A <
>    5 100 1   Baum, Christina D. <
>    6 245 14  The impact of feminist thought on American librarianship
1965-1985 $h [microform] / $c Christina Diane Baum. <
>    7 260     Ann Arbor, Mich. : $c University Microfilms International,
$c 1987. <
>    8 300     3 microfiches (276 fr.) ; $c 11 x 15 cm. <
>    9 502     Thesis (Ed.D.) -- University of Kentucky, 1987. <
>   10 504     Includes bibliographical references. <
>   11 500     "87-15914." <
>   12 534     Reproduction of: $e x, 255 leaves ; 28 cm. $n Typescript.
$n Includes bibliographical references (leaves 245-254). <
>   13 650  0  Library science $z United States $x History. <
>   14 650  0  Women in library science $z United States $x History. <
>   15 650  0  Feminism $z United States $x History. <
```

Fig. 4.68. Description of the microfiche shown in figures 4.32–4.34, according to LC policy.

The impact of feminist thought on American librarianship, 1965-1985 [microform] / by Christina D. Baum. — 1987.
   x, 255 leaves ; 28 cm.
   Typescript.
   Thesis (Ed.D.)—University of Kentucky, 1987.
   Includes bibliographical references (leaves 245-254).
   Microfiche. Ann Arbor, Mich. : University Microfilms International, 1987. 3 microfiches (276 fr.) ; 11 x 15 cm.
   "87-159145."

Fig. 4.69. MARC record for the microfiche, according to LC policy.

```
   OCLC:  22772600         Rec stat:     n
   Entered: 19901204        Replaced:     19930330    Used:   19950131
>  Type: a      ELvl: I    Srce:  d    Audn:       Ctrl:       Lang: eng
   BLvl: m      Form: b    Conf:  0    Biog:       MRec:       Ctry: xx
                Cont: b    GPub:       Fict: 0     Indx:  0
   Desc: a      Ills:      Fest:  0    DtSt: s     Dates: 1987,    <
>    1 040      SUC $c SUC <
>    2 007      h $b e $d a $e m $f b--- $g b $h u $i c $j u <
>    3 090      Z655 $b .B38 1987 <
>    4 049      DD0A <
>    5 100 1    Baum, Christina D. <
>    6 245 14   The impact of feminist thought on American librarianship
1965-1985 $h [microform] / $c by Christina D. Baum. <
>    7 260      $c 1987. <
>    8 300      x, 255 leaves ; 28 cm. <
>    9 500      Typescript. <
>   10 502      Thesis (Ed.D.) -- University of Kentucky, 1987. <
>   11 504      Includes bibliographical references (leaves 245-254). <
>   12 533      Microfiche. $b Ann Arbor, Mich. : $c University Microfilms
International, $d 1987. $e 3 microfiches (276 fr.) ; 11 x 15 cm.
"87-15914." <
>   13 539      s $b 1987 $d mi $e n <
>   14 650  0   Library science $z United States $x History. <
>   15 650  0   Women in library science $z United States $x History. <
>   16 650  0   Feminism $z United States $x History. <fs20
```

Fig. 4.70. *AACR2R* description of the print serial shown in figures 4.35–4.36.

Journal of Internet cataloging. — Vol. 1, no. 1 (1997)– . —
Binghamton, NY : Haworth Press, 1997-
   v. ; 25 cm.
   Quarterly.
   Title from cover.
   ISSN 1091-1367 = Journal of Internet cataloging

Fig. 4.71. MARC record for the print serial.

```
OCLC:  34108984          Rec stat:     c
    Entered:   19960131        Replaced:    19971224    Used:   19990930
>   Type: a      ELvl:      Srce:  d    GPub:       Ctrl:        Lang: eng
    BLvl: s      Form:      Conf:  0    Freq:  q    MRec:        Ctry: nyu
    S/L:  0      Orig:      EntW:       Regl:  r    ISSN: 1 .  Alph: a
    Desc: a      SrTp: p    Cont:       DtSt:  c    Dates: 1997,9999 <
>    1 010        97-655064 $z sn96-4762 <
>    2 040        UOK $c UOK $d NSD $d DLC $d NYG $d AGL $d HLS $d EYM $d DLC <
>    3 012        $i 9711 $k 1 $l 1 <
>    4 022  0     1091-1367 <
>    5 037        $c |$|65.00 (institutions) <
>    6 042        nsdp $a lc <
>    7 043        n-u--- <
>    8 050 00     Z695.24 $b .J68 <
>    9 072  0     X200 <
>   10 082 00     025.3/44 $2 21 <
>   11 082 10     025 $2 12 <
>   12 049        CUMM <
>   13 210 0      J. Internet cat. <
>   14 222  0     Journal of Internet cataloging <
>   15 245 00     Journal of Internet cataloging. <
>   16 260        Binghamton, NY : $b Haworth Press, $c 1997- <
>   17 270        Haworth Press $a 10 Alice St. $b Binghamton $c NY $e
13904-1580 <
>   18 300        v. ; $c 25 cm. <
>   19 310        Quarterly <
>   20 362 0      Vol. 1, no. 1 (1997)- <
>   21 500        Title from cover. <
>   22 650  0     Cataloging of computer network resources $v Periodicals. <
>   23 650  0     Cataloging of computer network resources $z United States
$v Periodicals. <
>   24 850        DLC $a DNAL $a MiU $a N <
>   25 890        Journal of internet cataloging. <
>   26 856 7      $3 Table of contents and abstracts $u
http://jic.libraries.psu.edu $2 http <
>   27 901        $c SER <
```

**Fig. 4.72. *AACR2R* description of the electronic serial shown
in figures 4.37–4.38.**

Journal of Buddhist ethics [computer file]. — Vol. 1 (1994)–   . —
University Park, PA : [s.n.], 1994-
Text (electronic journal).
Mode of access: Electronic mail, FTP, gopher, and World Wide Web.
For email subscription, send to: listserv@lists.psu.edu, the message: sub
JBE-L [first name last name].
Title from title screen.
ISSN: 1076-9005 = Journal of Buddhist ethics

Fig. 4.73. MARC record for the electronic serial.

```
OCLC:   30635286          Rec stat:      c
Entered:    19940621      Replaced:      19971223    Used:    19990904
> Type: m      ELvl:       Srce:  d    Audn:      Ctrl:        Lang: eng
  BLvl: s      File: d     GPub:                   MRec:        Ctry: pau
  Desc: a                              DtSt:  c    Dates: 1994,9999    <
>    1 010       sn94-2649 <
>    2 040       NSD $c NSD $d EYM $d OCL $d UMC <
>    3 006       [suu1    0  a0] <
>    4 007       c $b r $d c $e n $f u <
>    5 012       $k 1 $l 1 <
>    6 022 0     1076-9005 <
>    7 037       $b Journal of Buddhist ethics, c/o Charles S. Prebish,
Pennsylvania State University, Religious Studies Program, University
Park, PA 16802-5500 $c Free <
>    8 042       nsdp $a lcd <
>    9 082 10    181 $2 12 <
>   10 090       BQ2 <
>   11 049       CUMM <
>   12 210 0     J. Buddh. ethics <
>   13 222  0    Journal of Buddhist ethics <
>   14 245 00    Journal of Buddhist ethics $h [computer file]. <
>   15 246 13    JBE <
>   16 246 3     JBE-L <
>   17 260       University Park, PA : $b [s.n.], $c 1994- <
>   18 362 0     Vol. 1 (1994)- <
>   19 516 8     Text (electronic journal) <
>   20 538       Mode of access: Electronic mail, FTP, gopher, and World Wide
Web. For email subscription, send to: listserv@lists.psu.edu, the message:
sub JBE-L [first name last name]. <
>   21 500       T    itle from title screen. <
>   22 650  0    Buddhist ethics $v Periodicals. <
>   23 856 0     lists.psu.edu $f JBE-L $h listserv $i sub $z Internet
email subscription <
>   24 856 1     ftp.cac.psu.edu $d /pub/jbe $1 anonymous $n Pennsylvania
State University <
>   25 856 1     scorpio.gold.ac.uk $d /pub/jbe $1 anonymous $n University
of London (Goldsmiths College) <
>   26 856 7     ftp.cac.psu.edu $p 70 $2 gopher <
>   27 856 7     scorpio.gold.ac.uk $p 70 $2 gopher <
>   28 856 7     $u http://jbe.la.psu.edu/ $2 http <
>   29 856 7     $u http://scorpio.gold.ac.uk/jbe/jbe.html $2 http <
>   30 936       Vol. 2 (1995) LIC <
```

NOTES

1. *Anglo-American Cataloging Rules, Second Edition, 1998 Revisions*, prepared under the direction of the Joint Steering Committee for Revision of AACR (Chicago: American Library Association, 1998), p. 620.

2. *MARC 21 Format for Bibliographic Data: Including Guidelines for Content Designation* (Washington, D.C.: Cataloging Distribution Service, Library of Congress, 1999). 2v.; *MARC 21 Concise Format for Bibliographic Data* (available: http://lcweb.loc.gov/marc/bibliographic/ecbdhome.html [accessed 3/5/00]).

3.   *Library of Congress Rule Interpretations*, 2nd ed. (Washington, D.C.: Cataloging Distribution Service, Library of Congress, 1990–), looseleaf, with updates.

4.   *Cataloging Service Bulletin* no. 1– (Washington, D.C.: Processing Services, Library of Congress, 1978–).

5.   *Library of Congress Rule Interpretations for AACR 2, 1988 Revision: A Cumulation Through Cataloging Service Bulletin* . . , compiled with quarterly looseleaf supplements by Alan Boyd and Elaine Druesdow (Oberlin, Ohio: Oberlin College Library, 1989–).

6.   A discussion of these problems in relation to *AACR2* may be found in Michael Gorman, "Cataloging and Classification of Film Study Material," in Nancy Allen, *Film Study Collections* (New York: F. Ungar Publishing, 1979), pp. 113–123.

7.   American Library Association, Committee on Cataloging: Description and Access, *Guidelines for Using AACR2 Chapter 9 for Cataloging Microcomputer Software* (Chicago: American Library Association, 1984).

8.   *Anglo-American Cataloguing Rules, Second Edition, Chapter 9, Computer Files*, edited for the Joint Steering Committee for Revision of AACR2 by Michael Gorman, draft revision (Chicago: American Library Association, 1987).

9.   American Library Association, Interactive Multimedia Guidelines Review Task Force, *Guidelines for Bibliographic Description of Interactive Multimedia* (Chicago: American Library Association, 1994).

10.   Nancy B. Olson, ed., *Cataloging Internet Resources: A Manual and Practical Guide*, 2nd ed. (Dublin, Ohio: OCLC Online Computer Library Center, Inc., 1997).

11.   Janet Swan Hill, "Descriptions of Reproductions of Previously Existing Works: Another View," *Microform Review* 11 (Winter 1982): 14–21; and Nancy R. John, "Microforms," *Journal of Library Administration* 3 (Spring 1982): 3–8.

12.   *Cataloging Service Bulletin*, no. 14 (Fall 1981): 56–58; a revised version is in *Cataloging Service Bulletin*, no. 81 (Summer 1998): 20–21.

13.   *The Principles and Future of AACR: Proceedings of the International Conference on the Principles and Future Development of AACR*, edited by Jean Weihs (Chicago: American Library Association, 1998).

14.   Jean Hirons, *Revising AACR2 to Accommodate Seriality: Report to the Joint Steering Committee for Revision of AACR*, 1999 (available: http://www.nlc-bnc.ca/jsc/ser-rep0.html [accessed 9/16/99]).

15.   *Union List of Serials in Libraries of the United States and Canada*, 3rd ed. (New York: H. W. Wilson, 1965); coverage through 1949. *New Serial Titles: A Union List of Serials Commencing Publication After December 31, 1949* (Washington, D.C.: Library of Congress, 1953–). *Standard Periodical Directory* (New York: Oxbridge Communications, 1964/65–). *Ulrich's International Periodicals Directory* (New York: Bowker, 1965–). *Ulrich's Update* (New York: Bowker, 1988–). *British Union Catalogue of Periodicals* (London: Butterworths, 1955–58). *British Union Catalogue of Periodicals. New Periodical Titles* (London: Butterworths, 1964–80). *Serials in the British Library* (London: British Library, Bibliographic Services Division, 1981–).

16.   Eleanora A. Baer, *Titles in Series: A Handbook for Librarians and Students*, 3rd ed. (Metuchen, N.J.: Scarecrow Press, 1978). *Books in Series in the United States* (New York: Bowker, 1977–79). *Books in Series* (New York: Bowker, 1980–1989).

17.   *Library of Congress Catalogs: Monographic Series* (Washington, D.C.: Library of Congress, 1974–1982). *National Union Catalog. Books* (Washington, D.C.: Library of Congress, 1983–).

18.   Bohdan S. Wynar and Arlene G. Taylor, *Introduction to Cataloging and Classification*, 8th ed. (Englewood, Colo.: Libraries Unlimited, 1992), pp. 558–571.

19.   *AACR2R98*, p. 621.

20.   *AACR2R98*, p. 616.

21.   As an occasional exception to the policy of using only GMDs on List 2 in this text, some examples will use the GMD [interactive multimedia], following the *Guidelines* cited in note 9 above.

22.   Olson, p. 14.

23.   "AACR 2 Options Proposed by the Library of Congress: Chapters 2–11," *Library of Congress Information Bulletin* 38 (August 10, 1979): 316.

24.   *AACR2R98*, p. 622.

25.   *AACR2R98*, p. 623.

26.   Richard P. Smiraglia, *Cataloging Music: A Manual for Use with AACR2*, 2nd ed. (Lake Crystal, Minn.: Soldier Creek Press, 1986), p. 29.

SUGGESTED READING

American Library Association, Interactive Multimedia Guidelines Review Task Force. *Guidelines for Bibliographic Description of Interactive Multimedia*. Chicago: American Library Association, 1994.

Cartographic Materials: A Manual of Interpretation for AACR2. Chicago: American Library Association, 1982.

Chan, Lois Mai. *Cataloging and Classification: An Introduction*. 2nd ed. New York: McGraw-Hill, 1994. Chapters 1–3.

Ferguson, Bobby. *Cataloging Nonprint Materials: Blitz Cataloging Workbook*. Englewood, Colo.: Libraries Unlimited, 1999.

———. *MARC/AACR2/Authority Control Tagging: Blitz Cataloging Workbook*. Englewood, Colo.: Libraries Unlimited, 1998.

Fritz, Deborah A. *Cataloging with AACR2R and USMARC for Books, Computer Files, Serials, Sound Recordings, Videorecordings*. Chicago: American Library Association, 1998.

Frost, Carolyn O. *Media Access and Organization: A Cataloging and Reference Sources Guide for Nonbook Materials*. Englewood, Colo.: Libraries Unlimited, 1989.

Gamble, Betsy, ed. *Music Cataloging Decisions: As Issued by the Music Section, Special Materials Cataloging Division, Library of Congress in the Music Cataloging Bulletin, Through December 1991*. Canton, Mass.: Music Library Association, 1992.

Geer, Beverley, and Beatrice L. Caraway. *Notes for Serials Cataloging*. 2nd ed. Englewood, Colo.: Libraries Unlimited, 1998.

Graham, Crystal. "What's Wrong with AACR2: A Serials Perspective." In *The Future of the Cataloging Rules*, edited by Brian E. C. Schottlaender. Chicago: American Library Association, 1998.

Hagler, Ronald. *The Bibliographic Record and Information Technology*. 3rd ed. Chicago: American Library Association, 1997. Chapter 2.

Hensen, Steven L. *Archives, Personal Papers, and Manuscripts: A Cataloging Manual for Archival Repositories, Historical Societies, and Manuscript Libraries*. 2nd ed. Chicago: Society of American Archivists, 1990.

Hill, Janet Swan. "Descriptions of Reproductions of Previously Existing Works: Another View," *Microform Review* 11 (Winter 1982): 14–21.

Hirons, Jean L., ed. *CONSER Cataloging Manual*. Washington, D.C.: Serial Record Division, Library of Congress, 1993– .

Intner, Sheila S., and Richard P. Smiraglia, eds. *Policy and Practice in Bibliographic Control of Nonbook Media*. Chicago: American Library Association, 1987, pp. 103–181.

John, Nancy R. "Microforms," *Journal of Library Administration* 3 (Spring 1982): 3–8.

Liheng, Carol, and Winnie S. Chan. *Serials Cataloging Handbook: An Illustrative Guide to the Use of AACR2R and LC Rule Interpretations*. 2nd ed. Chicago: American Library Association, 1998.

Maxwell, Robert L., with Margaret F. Maxwell. *Maxwell's Handbook for AACR2R*. Chicago: American Library Association, 1997. Chapters 1–12.

Olson, Nancy B. *Cataloging Computer Files*, edited by Edward Swanson. Lake Crystal, Minn.: Soldier Creek Press, 1992.

———. *Cataloging Computer Files: 1996 Update*, edited by Edward Swanson. Lake Crystal, Minn.: Soldier Creek Press, 1996.

———. *Cataloging Motion Pictures and Videorecordings*, edited by Edward Swanson. Lake Crystal, Minn.: Soldier Creek Press, 1992.

———. *Cataloging Motion Pictures and Videorecordings: 1996 Update*, edited by Edward Swanson. Lake Crystal, Minn.: Soldier Creek Press, 1996.

———. *Cataloging of Audiovisual Materials and Other Special Materials: A Manual Based on AACR 2*. 4th ed., edited by Sheila S. Intner and Edward Swanson. DeKalb, Ill.: Minnesota Scholarly Press, 1998.

———, ed. *Cataloging Internet Resources: A Manual and Practical Guide*. 2nd ed. Dublin, Ohio: OCLC Online Computer Library Center, Inc., 1997.

Rogers, JoAnn V., with Jerry D. Saye. *Nonprint Cataloging for Multimedia Collections: A Guide Based on AACR2*. 2nd ed. Littleton, Colo.: Libraries Unlimited, 1987.

Sandberg-Fox, Ann, and John D. Byrum. "From ISBD(CF) to ISBD(ER): Process, Policy, and Provisions." *Library Resources and Technical Services* 42 (April 1998): 89–101.

Saye, Jerry D., and Sherry L. Vellucci. *Notes in the Catalog Record Based on AACR2 and LC Rule Interpretations*. Chicago: American Library Association, 1989.

Smiraglia, Richard P. *Cataloging Music: A Manual for Use with AACR2*. 2nd ed. Lake Crystal, Minn.: Soldier Creek Press, 1986.

———. *Music Cataloging: The Bibliographic Control of Printed and Recorded Music in Libraries*. Englewood, Colo.: Libraries Unlimited, 1989. Chapters 2 and 3.

Soper, Mary Ellen. "Description and Entry of Serials in *AACR2*." *Serials Librarian* 4 (Winter 1979): 167–176.

Tseng, Sally C. "Serials Cataloging and AACR2: An Introduction." *Journal of Educational Media Science* 19 (Winter 1982): 177–216.

Weihs, Jean, ed. *The Principles and Future of AACR: Proceedings of the International Conference on the Principles and Future Development of AACR*. Chicago: American Library Association, 1998.

Weihs, Jean, with Shirley Lewis. *Nonbook Materials: The Organization of Integrated Collections*. 3rd ed. Ottawa: Canadian Library Association, 1989.

5 〉 Description
of Analytical Materials

INTRODUCTION

Whether or not to describe parts of a work is an ever-present problem in cataloging. When does a part of a larger work deserve description of its own? When such description is warranted, how is it accomplished in relation to the larger work? These are questions addressed by *Anglo-American Cataloguing Rules, Second Edition,* Chapter 13, "Analysis." As in the preceding chapter specific cites to the 1998 print version are referred to as *AACR2R98*, but the work with its additions and changes is referred to as *AACR2R*.

In the Glossary of *AACR2R98*, "analytical entry" is defined as "an entry for a part of an item for which a comprehensive entry is also made."[1] "Analytical note" is defined as "the statement in an analytical entry relating the part being analyzed to the item of which it is a part."[2] Analytical entries vary from complete bibliographic descriptions to simple added entries for parts mentioned in the description of the larger work. Obviously, preparing additional entries requires time. Usually, the decision in this matter depends on the administrative policy of an individual library and the local needs. In deciding whether analytical entries are needed, certain general situations may be taken into consideration:

- The availability of printed indexes, bibliographies, and abstracting services that will locate the material to be analyzed.

- The availability of analytics from the Library of Congress (LC) or other sources.

- The quantity and quality of material on the given subject already in the catalog.

- The quantity of material by the same creators already in the catalog. The best example in this category is provided by the library's policy regarding books in sets that usually represent various types of collections or compilations of one or more authors—e.g., *Harvard Classics* or *Harvard Shelf of Fiction*. If the library has little material by an author, the need for analytics may be greater.

- The significance of the parts to be analyzed for a given library (e.g., parts written by local noted authors, performed by local musicians, produced by locally-born actors, etc.).

- The significance of the parts in a given work.

In addition, the rules in *AACR2R* give some guidance in deciding when and how analysis should be accomplished.

A basic descriptive question that must be answered before making the decision to analyze a multi-part information package, and one for which there is no guidance in *AACR2R*, is: What is to be considered a multi-part information package rather than two or more separate packages for cataloging purposes?

A publication issued in two or more volumes may be defined as a set. Usually, monographs in collected sets represent various types of collections or compilations by one or more authors. Many reference books are examples of monographs in collected sets. The number of physical volumes making up such a set may cause problems in cataloging and classification. If the works of a single author are collected in several volumes, the cataloger may be tempted to class each volume separately. On the other hand, the cataloger may only have one volume of a multi-volume set to catalog and may consider classing it as if the library had the entire set. Although both of these approaches are arguable, the fact remains that neither is really right or wrong. There are no established codes for cataloging and classifying individual titles of information packages that come in sets. The approaches presented below are provided merely for the consideration of the cataloger; they are not meant to be followed slavishly.

One usually catalogs and classes a set of information packages together if:

- They are issued in a uniform format

- The individual packages are numbered in consecutive order

- There is a general index to the entire set

Two additional criteria are:

- If patrons are likely to expect to find the information packages together as a set

- If there is a possibility that supplements and/or additional numbers will appear at a later date

However, one usually catalogs and classes a set of information packages separately if:

- Not all the packages of the set are in the library, nor are likely to be added to the library's collection

- Each package has a separate title, especially in the case of literary works.

Obviously, these two sets of approaches are somewhat contradictory and demand individual application in actual practice. The following examples are designed to clarify these problems. First, it should be quite obvious that a set of books comprising an encyclopedia should be cataloged and classed together. An encyclopedia is uniform in format; the individual volumes are consecutively numbered; there is usually a general index to the entire encyclopedia; patrons do expect to find these books together as a set; and supplements and/or yearbooks often appear at a later date. Second, it similarly follows that a set of monographs that is a collection of great works (such as the *Harvard Classics* or the *Great Books of the Western World*) should be both cataloged and classed together. In these examples, however, individual items have one or more separate titles. Should individual items in such a set (both of which, for example, include the plays of William Shakespeare) be classed with other collections of Shakespeare's plays or not? Either choice will create some problems. It is unwise in either case to try to avoid a record in the catalog for each separate bibliographical unit. The catalog may be the only key the patron uses for discovering the library's holdings. Analysis is one method of solving this particular problem. The use of analytical entries under rules 13.5A and 13.6, as described below, allows these sets of monographs to be cataloged and classed together while also providing separate entries for individual bibliographical units.

The collected or complete works of one author present another problem of titles in sets. For example, Winston Churchill's *A History of the English-speaking Peoples* may be cataloged together or separately. If this work is cataloged together as a set, the individual parts or volumes are listed in a contents note, and the set receives general subject added entries and a general subject classification number (*see* figure 5.1). On the other hand, if each of the parts of this work is cataloged separately, the relationship of each part to the main work is shown by a series note. This latter approach allows for a complete publication area, including the date, for each part, and for separate specific subject added entries (*see* figure 5.2). Cataloging each part separately allows the cataloger to choose whether to classify each part separately or in the more general number. The classification problems of collected sets versus cataloging as monographs are dealt with in chapter 9 of this textbook.

Fig. 5.1. Churchill's *History of the English-speaking Peoples* cataloged as a set using a contents note for the individual bibliographical units and having a general subject heading.

Churchill, Winston, Sir, 1874-1965.
    A history of the English-speaking peoples / Winston S. Churchill.
— Toronto : McClelland and Stewart, 1988, c1956.
    4 v. : ill., maps, geneal. tables ; 22 cm.

    Includes bibliographical references and index.
    Contents: v. 1. The birth of Britain — v. 2. The new world —
v. 3. The age of revolution — v. 4. The great democracies.
    ISBN: 0-8103-4573-0.

    1. Great Britain—History. I. Title.

Fig. 5.2. One part of Churchill's work cataloged as a separate bibliographical unit using a series note to relate to the collected set and having specific subject headings.

Churchill, Winston, Sir, 1874-1965.
 The age of revolution / Winston S. Churchill. — Toronto : McClelland and Stewart, 1988, c1956.
 xi, 395 p. : ill., maps ; 22 cm. — (A history of the English-speaking peoples / Winston S. Churchill ; v. 3)

 Includes bibliographical references and index.

 1. Great Britain—History—1689-1714. 2. Great Britain—History—18th century. I. Title. II. Series: Churchill, Winston, Sir, 1874-1965. A history of the English-speaking peoples.

The nature of many World Wide Web sites, where an agency's home page serves as a gateway to a number of documents or other resources maintained by the same agency, presents another situation calling for decision making. Should one catalog the home page alone, representing the resource at the highest level of abstraction? If so, should a contents note be provided (keeping in mind that many Web sites continually expand or alter their content)? If analytic records are provided for individual documents, will this be in addition to, or in place of, a general record for the site? As with the other cases examined here, the answers to these questions will depend on the nature of the resource, the collection for which it is being cataloged, and the needs of the library's constituency.

Figure 5.3 shows an *AACR2R* description for one of the resources found at LC's American Memory Web site. The description for the entire site is shown at figure 4.60 (page 154).

Fig. 5.3. Resource linked to the Library of Congress's American Memory site, cataloged as a separate bibliographical unit, using an added title entry to relate to the larger site.

America from the Great Depression to World War II [computer file] : photographs from the FSA-OWI, 1935-1945 / Prints and Photographs Division, Library of Congress. — Computer data and programs. — [Washington, D.C.] : Library of Congress, [1998-   ]

 Mode of access: World Wide Web.
Access: http://memory.loc.gov/ammem/fsowhome.html
 Title from title screen (viewed on August 6, 1998).
 HTML source title: Documenting America.
 Part of the American Memory World Wide Web site, compiled by the National Digital Library Program of the Library of Congress.
 Summary: Photographs from the Farm Security Administration-Office of War Information Collection, created by a group of U.S. government photographers. Subjects include rural life and the negative impact of the Great Depression, farm mechanization, the Dust Bowl, and the later mobilization effort for World War II. The collection consists of about 164,000 black-and-white photographs. The initial online release includes approximately 45,000 of these images, with more to be added.

Description based on: 1st release.

1. United States—History—1933-1945—Pictorial works. 2. United States—Social conditions—1933-1945—Pictorial works. 3. United States—Rural conditions—Pictorial works. 4. Rural population—United States—History—20th century—Pictorial works. 5. Farm life—United States—History—20th century—Pictorial works. 6. World War, 1939-1945—United States—Pictorial works. I. Library of Congress. Prints and Photographs Division. II. Library of Congress. National Digital Library Program. III. United States. Farm Security Administration. IV. United States. Office of War Information. I. Title. II. Title: Documenting America. III. Title: American memory.

SELECTED RULES AND EXAMPLES

RULE 13.1. SCOPE

The scope of the analysis chapter in *AACR2R* is to give instructions for describing a part or parts of a larger information package. Various methods are suggested for doing this. Some of the suggestions here are also referred to in other chapters, but the point of this chapter is to gather together all the methods and to give suggestions for choosing one over another.

RULE 13.2. ANALYTICAL ADDED ENTRIES

When the title of a part appears either in the title and statement of responsibility area or in the note area of the bibliographic record for a more comprehensive work, an added entry may be made to provide direct access to the part without having to make a separate bibliographic record for the part. Such an added entry is composed of the main entry heading and title, if title is not main entry. The title used is the uniform title if there is one, otherwise it is the title proper. *See* figure 5.4.

Fig. 5.4. Rule 13.2. Record for a comprehensive work with analytical added entry made for the second part.

Mozart, Wolfgang Amadeus, 1756-1791.
[Symphonies, K. 543, Eb major]
Symphony no. 39 in E flat, K. 543 / Wolfgang Amadeus Mozart. Symphony no. 2 in D, op. 36 / Ludwig van Beethoven [sound recording]. — [Netherlands] : Philips, p1989.
1 sound disc (64 min.) : digital, stereo. ; 4¾ in. — (Digital classics)

Philips: 422 389-2.
Orchestra of the 18th century (on period instruments) ; Frans Bruggen, conductor.
Recorded June 1988, Concertgebouw, Amsterdam.
Compact disc.
Durations: 32:00 ; 32:00.   analytical
                                                           added entry

1. Symphonies. I. Bruggen, Frans, 1932-   . II. Beethoven, Ludwig van, 1770-1827. Symphonies, no. 2, op. 36, D major. 1989. III. Orchestra of the 18th century.

RULE 13.3.   ANALYSIS OF MONOGRAPHIC SERIES AND MULTI-PART MONOGRAPHS

The suggested criterion for deciding to describe a part of a monographic series or a multi-part monograph independently concerns title. If the title of the part is not dependent on the title of the whole, a complete description of the part should be created, giving the title (and statement of responsibility, if applicable) of the whole set in the series area. The volume number of the part is also given in the series area. *See* figure 5.5.

Fig. 5.5. Rule 13.3. Complete independent description of a monographic title with the title of the comprehensive series given in the series area.

Austrian fiction writers after 1914 / edited by James Hardin and Donald G. Daviau. — Detroit, Mich. : Gale Research, c1989.

xi, 394 p. : ill., 29 cm. — (Dictionary of literary ◄——— comprehensive title
biography ; v. 85)

Includes bibliographical references.
ISBN: 0-8103-4563-3.

Rule 13.3 does not go on to say what one should do if the title of an individual part is dependent on the comprehensive title or if there is no individual title. The implication is that such works would not be described separately. However, when such items appear as parts of series that are analyzed in full or that are classified separately, a separate record is necessary. An LC rule interpretation gives rules and examples for handling such situations; it should be consulted when needed. (*CSB* 44: 34–36) Its basic idea is that the comprehensive title becomes part of the title proper, no series statement is given, and an explicitly traced series added entry is made.

RULE 13.4.   NOTE AREA

If it is decided to describe the comprehensive work as a set, individual parts may be named in a contents note. This method was shown in figure 5.1 (page 167).

RULE 13.5.   "IN" ANALYTICS

Another possible way to describe a part is to provide an "In" analytic record. This is useful when one wishes to provide more information than can be given in the note area of the record for the set.

LC makes "In" analytics only in very special cases. (*CSB* 44: 36)

13.5A.   An "In" analytic shows first a description of the part. This is followed by a short description of the comprehensive work.

The description of the part contains all the elements of the eight areas of description that apply to the part, with the exception that in the publication, distribution, etc., area, only those elements that differ from the whole item are given.

The description of the whole information package begins with the word *In*, emphasized in a manner appropriate to the medium of the catalog. For printed catalogs, this may be accomplished through underlining or italicizing; Web-based catalogs may have other options available for display. *In* is followed by the name and/or uniform title heading (if appropriate); title proper; statement(s) of responsibility necessary for identification; edition statement; and numeric or other designation (if a serial) or publication details (if a monographic item). *See* figures 5.6 and 5.7.

Fig. 5.6. Rule 13.5A. "In" analytic where the part is contained in a monographic item.

The crisis in cataloging / Andrew D. Osborn. — p. 90-103 ; 25 cm.
In Foundations of cataloging / edited by Michael Carpenter and Elaine Svenonius. — Littleton, Colo. : Libraries Unlimited, 1985.

Fig. 5.7. Rule 13.5A. "In" analytic where the part is contained in a serial item.

Uniform titles for music : an exercise in collocation / Richard P. Smiraglia. — p. 97-114 ; 22 cm.
In Cataloging & classification quarterly. — Vol. 9, no. 3 (Spring 1989)

RULE 13.6.   MULTILEVEL DESCRIPTION
An alternative to "In" analytic records is a technique called multilevel description. It is useful when one wishes to provide complete identification of both part and whole in a single record.

The first level of descriptive information shows the description of the whole item. The second level contains description (not repeating information given at the first level) of an individual part or groups of parts. If the second level describes a group of parts, then a third level may describe an individual part. *See* figure 5.8.

Fig. 5.8. Rule 13.6. Multilevel description showing three levels from most to least comprehensive.

The Library of America. — New York, N.Y. : Literary Classics of the U.S. : Distributed to the trade in the U.S. and Canada by Viking Press, 1982-   . —   v. : 21 cm.

Vols. 26-27 : [Selections. 1985]. The leatherstocking tales / James Fenimore Cooper ; [edited by] Blake Nevius. — c1985.

The last of the Mohicans : a narrative of 1757. — vol. 26, p. 467-878.

LC does not use the technique of multilevel description. (*CSB* 11: 17)

NOTES

1. *Anglo-American Cataloging Rules, Second Edition, 1998 Revisions*, prepared under the direction of the Joint Steering Committee for Revision of AACR (Chicago: American Library Association, 1998), p. 615.

2. Ibid.

SUGGESTED READING

Hagler, Ronald. *The Bibliographic Record and Information Technology*. 3rd ed. Chicago: American Library Association, 1997, pp. 332–347.

Maxwell, Robert L., with Margaret F. Maxwell. *Maxwell's Handbook for AACR2R*. Chicago: American Library Association, 1997. Chapter 13.

O'Neil, Rosanna M. "Analysis and 'In' Analytics," *Serials Review* 13, no. 2 (Summer 1987): 57–63.

Choice of
Access Points

INTRODUCTION

The rules in *Anglo-American Cataloguing Rules, Second Edition*, Chapter 21, deal with the choice of access points and not the form of entry. As in Chapters 4 and 5, specific cites to the 1998 print version are referred to as *AACR2R98*, but the work with its additions and changes is referred to as *AACR2R*. Choice *of access points* means choosing all names and titles under which the description of an information package may be sought by a user. (Subject headings are also chosen as access points, but the only subjects affected by *AACR2R* are names and titles used as subjects. *See* Chapters 8–17 for discussions of subject access.)

For any one item, one of the access points is chosen as a main entry, and the others become added entries. Originally this choice was necessary, in part, so that there could be one place in a printed catalog where all information about a work or item could be found, while other entries for the item in that catalog could be much shorter. Eventually, when *unit cards* (i.e., every card in a card set contains identical information) became standard, this need for a main entry became obsolete. And with MAchine-Readable Cataloging (MARC) records, where there is only one master record stored in a catalog, there is no need for the concept of main entry as a place to put all information. However, the main entry *heading* is also frequently used as a secondary filing element (e.g., all items under the subject heading "Psychology" are subarranged by main entry). In the introduction to *AACR2R98* there is a recognition that designation of one entry as "main" may not be considered important in some libraries.[1] There is lack of agreement on this point in the cataloging community.[2]

Proponents of the main entry concept assert that one of the major outcomes of cataloging is to identify the works embodied in the information packages cataloged. This can only be done, they believe, by using one consistent means for citing any given work. This, in turn, can only be done by adhering to a set of rules for choosing the main access point and then using this access point, or main entry heading, in conjunction with other necessary elements to form a unit that identifies the work (e.g., if the main entry is the first of two authors, that name is combined with the title to form a unit that identifies the work). The unit thus formed is often referred to as the *uniform title*, although this can be misleading, since the term "uniform title" is also used to refer to a standardized title for a work that may have variant titles or that may have only a generic title. In any case, the unit formed to identify the work is used to collocate all editions, translations, criticisms, etc., of that work that may appear.

The introduction to *AACR2R98* points out that it is necessary to distinguish the main entry from the others when one is creating a listing in which each record will be given only once, or in any other situation when one must make a single citation for a work.[3] The latter situation occurs, for example, when a related work needs to be cited on the bibliographic record for the work to which it is related, or when one work is the subject of another. *AACR2R* also points out that the concept of main entry is useful in creating uniform titles to draw those related works together. At one time it was thought that related works were probably a small proportion of all works, and therefore a great deal of time was being spent choosing main entries for many works that would never have editions, translations, etc. However, recent research indicates that nearly half of information packages cataloged embody works which are related to other works. The percentage may be as high as 75% for items held by general academic libraries, and even higher for collections of musical scores.[4]

Proponents of the idea that all access points for an information package are basically equal question the need to designate one access point as primary. They say that in most catalogs all access points are equally accessible; in online systems, the main entry is not necessarily used to subarrange records retrieved under other access points (e.g., subarrangement may be by date).

Much has been written about this controversy,[5] and its resolution may not come about without changes in the relationship between the recording of cataloging data and the means by which systems index and display such data. For example, most library systems that use MARC 21 format, either for online access or for printed products, create the rough equivalent of uniform titles by linking the main entry headings entered in 100–111 fields with title data entered in the 240 or 245 fields. (For information packages given title main entry, a 130, 240, or 245 field will be used on its own.) If catalogers no longer designate any entry as "main," the data now entered in the 100–130 fields would be moved to 700–730. This might create little difficulty where an item contains an expression of one and only one work, though for many systems some reprogramming would be necessary. For the many items which contain expressions of more than one work, and with multiple persons or bodies associated with each work, new coding would be needed to link the appropriate 7XX fields to the data entered in the 240 or 245 field. This is particularly, though not exclusively, true for music recordings. The purpose of this discussion is not to provide a detailed analysis of this technical problem, nor to suggest that this is the only aspect of the question, but rather to indicate that the "main entry debate" is not simply of theoretical interest.

This chapter covers basic choice of main entry under personal author, corporate body, and title (rule 21.2). More specific guidance is then given for choice of entry for:

1. Works where there have been changes in title proper (rule 21.2) or in persons or bodies responsible for the work (rule 21.3)

2. Works of single responsibility (rules 21.4–21.5)

3. Works of shared responsibility (rule 21.6)

4. Collections and works produced under editorial responsibility (rule 21.7)

5. Works of mixed responsibility (rules 21.8–21.27)

6. Works that are related to other works (rule 21.28)

7.   General rules for added entries are given (rules 21.29–21.30), followed by special rules for certain legal and religious publications (rules 21.31–21.39).

The rules covered in this text deal only with basic or general instances; for more complex problems and special cases, the student should consult *AACR2R*, chapter 21. Examples in this text allow the student to see not only the choice of main entry, but also the form of entry and the added entries. The following chapters deal with the rules for these specific forms.

GENERAL RULES:
SELECTED RULES AND EXAMPLES

RULE 21.0.   INTRODUCTORY RULES

21.0B.   Sources for determining access points
Access points for the information package being cataloged are determined from the chief source of information or its substitute (*see* rule 1.0A). Other statements appearing formally in one of the prescribed sources of information should be taken into account, but the emphasis is to be on the chief source of information, making it unnecessary for the cataloger to search in the contents or outside the item for potential access points. A rule interpretation from the Library of Congress (LC) indicates that when information in the prescribed sources is ambiguous, information may be taken from the contents or from outside the item. (*CSB* 45: 19–20)

21.0D.   *Optional addition*. Designations of function
This option allows for abbreviated designations of function, such as *ed.* for *editor* and *tr.* for *translator*, to be added to a heading for a person. LC has decided not to apply this option, with one exception: the abbreviation *ill.* is added to the headings for illustrators that appear as added entries on bibliographic records in the annotated cards (AC) series (i.e., for children's books). (*CSB* 18: 29–30)

RULE 21.1.   GENERAL RULE

21.1A.   Works of personal authorship
Personal author is defined as "the person chiefly responsible for the creation of the intellectual or artistic content of a work."[6] This can include composers, cartographers, photographers, and performers, as well as writers and other creators. The general rule is to enter works by one or more persons under the heading for the personal author according to the specific instructions given in rules 21.4A, 21.5B, 21.6, and 21.8–21.17 and to make added entries as instructed in rules 21.29–21.30. For example, the sound recording entitled "Where the Blue of the Night Meets the Gold of the Day," which includes songs from the original sound tracks of Bing Crosby's early films, would be entered under the heading:

Crosby, Bing, 1904–1977.

There would be an added entry for the title.

21.1B.   Entry under corporate body
A corporate body is defined as "an organization or a group of persons that is identified by a particular name and that acts, or may act, as an entity."[7] Guidelines dictate that a corporate body should be considered to have a name: if the words referring to

it are a specific appellation, not just a description; if the initial letters of important words are capitalized; and/or if the words are associated with a definite article. Corporate bodies include, for example, associations, institutions, business firms, governments, conferences, ad hoc events (e.g., exhibitions, festivals), and vessels (e.g., spacecraft).

LC has issued a rule interpretation that gives assistance in determining whether a conference is named. This interpretation should be consulted when needed. (*CSB* 71: 31–33)

21.1B2.   The general rule states that a corporate body may be chosen as main entry if it falls into one or more of six categories:

- a.   A work that deals with the body itself, such as a report on finances or operations, or a listing of staff, or a catalog of the body's resources

- b.   Certain legal, governmental, or religious types of works listed in this rule with rule numbers to consult for more guidance

- c.   Works that deal with official pronouncements that represent the body's position on matters other than those covered in a) above

- d.   Works of a *collective* nature that report on activities of conferences, expeditions, or events that can be defined as corporate bodies and whose names appear prominently in the publication

- e.   Sound recordings, films, videorecordings, or written records of performances in which the responsibility of the group for the existence of the performance is more than a performance or execution of a previously existing script, score, etc. (e.g., improvised jazz or drama)

- f.   Cartographic materials for which a body does more than merely publish or distribute the materials.

A lengthy LC rule interpretation gives guidance in applying this rule, and should be consulted for more information. The rule interpretation adds a seventh category, "named individual works of art by two or more artists acting as a corporate body" (e.g., General Idea). (*CSB* 81: 23–26) *See* examples below under rule 21.4B.

21.1B3.   If a work falls outside the above categories, the main entry is chosen as if no corporate body were involved, but added entries may be made. Thus, the World Wide Web home page for the Columbus Museum of Art would be entered under the heading "Columbus Museum of Art," and an added entry would be made under the title. However, a monograph entitled "Benue through Pictures" that has been put together in the Information Division of Benue, Nigeria, does not fall under one of the five categories of rule 21.1B2; therefore, the main entry would be under the title, with an added entry under the heading: Benue (Nigeria). Information Division.

21.1C.   Entry under title
Entry under title is prescribed when there is no known personal author, or personal authorship is diffuse (*see* rule 21.6C2), *and* the work is not eligible for entry under corporate body; when the work is a collection of multiple authorship; or when the work is a text that a religious group accepts as sacred scripture.

An LC rule interpretation adds a case for title entry that is not listed in *AACR2R*. It is the situation where a work seems to give technical credit of more than one kind to several persons, and the position and typography of the statement indicates lesser importance in relation to the title. (*CSB* 18: 34–35)

RULE 21.2.   CHANGES IN TITLES PROPER

This rule and the next one fill a need for guidance about when separate main entries should be chosen for different parts of a multipart monograph or of a serial. The cataloger is instructed to choose separate main entries (and thus make separate records) for each edition when the title proper of a monograph changes between editions. However, if the title proper of a multipart monograph changes between *parts*, one title proper (the one that predominates) is to be used for the whole monograph. If the title proper of a serial changes, a separate main entry is chosen for each title, and separate records are made.

The cases in which a title proper is considered to have changed occur when:

1. Any important words are added, deleted, or changed (e.g., *Cataloging Service* changed to *Cataloging Service Bulletin*)

2. The order of the first five words (not counting an initial article) changes (e.g., *Sell's Directory of Products & Services* changed to *Sell's Products and Services Directory*).

A title proper is not to be considered changed, however, if:

1. The change is one of word representation (e.g., *Teaching, Learning and Technology* versus *Teaching, Learning + Technology*)

2. The change is after the first five words (not counting an initial article) *and* does not change meaning or indicate different subject coverage

3. The only change involves addition or deletion of issuing body at the end of the title

4. The only change involves punctuation (e.g., *Out of Line!* versus *Out of Line*)

An LC rule interpretation adds cases to these categories and should be consulted as needed. (*CSB* 81: 26) A note should report changes not considered to constitute a change in title proper. Title added entries may also be made.

A rule interpretation from LC gives guidance for treatment of fluctuating serial titles. (*CSB* 78: 40–41)

RULE 21.3   CHANGES OF PERSONS OR BODIES RESPONSIBLE FOR A WORK

21.3A.   Monographs

Monographs that have been modified by a person or body different from the one responsible for the original edition are to be treated according to rules 21.9–21.23. This means that in some cases, when the nature and/or content has been changed, the main entry will be different from that of the original. Example:

Title main entry for a work whose nature has changed:

> Bambi's fragrant forest : based on the original story by Felix Salten / Walt Disney Productions

Added entries for the person responsible for the original and the corporate body responsible for modification:

> I. Salten, Felix, 1869-1945. Bambi. II. Walt Disney Productions.

(If a person had modified the work, main entry would be under the person. This is explained below under corporate entry rules.)

In other cases, when the modification abridges or rearranges, for example, the main entry of the original will be used. Example:

Main entry for original author for an abridged work:

> Salten, Felix, 1869-1945.
>   Bambi [sound recording] / abridged by Marianne Mantell. Read by Glynis Johns

Added entries for person responsible for the modification, for the reader, and for title:

> I. Mantell, Marianne. II. Johns, Glynis. III. Title.

21.3B.   Serials

AACR2R gives two conditions under which changes in persons or bodies could require a new entry for a serial:

a.   When the serial has a corporate body main entry and the name of that body changes (e.g., *Financial Report* of the Board of Trustees of the Firemen's Pension Fund, formerly the Firemen's Pension and Relief Fund)

b.   When the serial has a corporate body or personal author as main entry, and the person or body is no longer responsible for the serial

An LC rule interpretation adds two other conditions:

c.   When the serial's main entry is under a uniform title heading that must be changed either because a corporate body used as a qualifier changes or because the title used in the heading for a translation changes

d.   When there is a change in the serial's physical format (as compared with a reproduction in another format). (*CSB* 50:34–35)

RULE 21.4.   WORKS FOR WHICH A SINGLE PERSON OR CORPORATE BODY IS RESPONSIBLE

21.4A.   Works of single personal authorship (MARC 21 field 100)

An information package that contains a work or works by one personal author should have the heading for that person as its main entry. Example:

Personal author main entry:

Bennetts, Pamela.
My dear lover England / Pamela Bennetts

Added entry for title:

I. Title.

21.4B. Works emanating from a single corporate body (MARC 21 field 110 or 111)

An information package that contains a work or works that emanate from one corporate body should have the heading for that body as its main entry if one or more of the categories given under rule 21.1B2 applies. Examples:

Corporate body main entry for a work of single corporate responsibility (21.1B2, type a):

Al-Anon Family Group Headquarters.
World directory of Al-Anon Family Groups and
Ala-teens

Added entry for title:

I. Title.

A work of single corporate responsibility (21.1B2, type c):

United States. Congress. House. Select Committee to
Investigate Covert Arms Transactions with Iran.
Report of the congressional committees investigating the
Iran-Contra Affair : with the minority views

Added entry for title:

I. Title.

A work of single corporate responsibility (21.1B2, type d):

AIAA International Communication Satellite Systems Conference
and Exhibit (13th : 1990 : Los Angeles, Calif.)
A collection of technical papers : 13th AIAA International
Communication Satellite Systems Conference and Exhibit, Los
Angeles, CA, March 11-15, 1990

Added entry for title:

I. Title.

21.4D. Works by heads of state, other high government officials, popes, and other high ecclesiastical officials

21.4D1. Official communications

Two categories of official works are entered under the corporate heading (*see* rules 24.20 and 24.27B) for the official:

"a)   an official communication from a head of state, head of government, or head of an international body (e.g., a message to a legislature, a proclamation, an executive order other than one covered by 21.31)

b) an official communication from a pope, patriarch, bishop, etc. (e.g., an order, decree, pastoral letter, bull, encyclical, constitution, or an official message to a council, synod, etc.)."[8]

An added entry is made under the personal heading for the person. Example:

Official communication entered under corporate heading:

> Maine. Governor (1975-1979 : Longley)
> Budget message address of James B. Longley, Governor of Maine, to the One hundred and seventh Legislature, State of Maine, February 6, 1975

Added entries including personal heading for the man who was governor:

> I. Maine. Legislature. II. Longley, James B. III. Title:
> Budget message address of James B. Longley, Governor of Maine . . .

21.4D2.   Other works

Other works by a government or religious official are given the personal heading for the person as main entry. One explanatory reference is made under the corporate heading rather than making an added entry under the corporate heading for each such work. Example:

Work by a government official entered under personal heading:

> Jefferson, Thomas, 1743-1826.
> The portable Thomas Jefferson / edited and with an introduction by Merrill D. Peterson

Added entries for person responsible for this edition of the work and for title:

> I. Peterson, Merrill D. II. Title.

For examples of explanatory references *see* rule 26.2D in chapter 7 of this text.

RULE 21.5.   WORKS OF UNKNOWN OR UNCERTAIN AUTHORSHIP OR BY UNNAMED GROUPS

21.5A.   A work of unknown or uncertain responsibility or one that emanates from a body that lacks a name is entered under its title. Example:

Work of unknown authorship entered under title:

> The old non-conformist, touching the book of common-prayer and ceremonies. . . . — London : [s.n.], 1660.

21.5C.   A work is entered under a characterizing word or phrase or under a phrase naming another work by the person, if that is the only clue to authorship and it appears in the chief source of information. For example, the title page of the following work shows only a "characterizing phrase" for the name of the author. The phrase would be used as the main entry:

Work of unknown authorship entered under characterizing phrase:

> One who has tested the receipts.
>> The manual of French cookery : dedicated to the housekeepers and cooks of England who wish to study the art : simplified for the benefit of the most unlearned / by one who has tested the receipts

Added entry for title:

> I. Title.

RULE 21.6.   WORKS OF SHARED RESPONSIBILITY

21.6A.   Scope

This rule is used for situations in which two or more persons or corporate bodies have made the same kind of contribution to a work. It also applies when the same kinds of contributions come from one or more persons *and* one or more corporate bodies.

Special types of collaborations are covered by rules on mixed responsibility (rules 21.8–21.27), but when those rules prescribe main entry under the heading for an adapter, for example, and when there is shared responsibility among two or more adapters, then this rule of shared responsibility is applied. This rule does not apply to works that are collections of previously existing works; these are covered by rule 21.7.

21.6B.   Principal responsibility indicated

21.6B1.   A work of shared responsibility is entered under the heading for the principal person or body if one is indicated by wording or typography. Added entries are made under the headings for other persons or bodies involved, if there are not more than two. An added entry is always made under the heading for the person or body, other than the principal one, whose name appears first on the title page. Example:

Main entry under principal author:

> Haynes, Connie
>> Speed, strength, and stamina : conditioning for tennis / by Connie Haynes, with Eve Kraft and John Conroy ; illustrated by George Janes

Added entries for subsidiary authors and for title:

> I. Kraft, Eve F. II. Conroy, John, 1908-   . III. Title.

[Since the principal author, Connie Haynes, is indicated on the title page of this work by the wording of the subsidiary authorship statement, the choice of main entry is the principal author.]

21.6B2.   When the chief source of information indicates that two or three persons or bodies have principal responsibility, main entry is made for the first named of these. Added entries are made under headings for the other principal author(s) and for a collaborator if there are two principal authors and one collaborator (i.e., there may be no more than two added entries).

21.6C.   Principal responsibility not indicated

21.6C1.   If principal responsibility is not indicated and if there are not more than three names, entry is made under the one that is named first, and added entries are made for the others. Example:

> **Main entry under first named author when principal author is not indicated, and there are not more than three authors:**
>
> Cheney, Gay.
>   Modern dance / Gay Cheney, Janet Strader
>
> **Added entries for second named author and for title:**
>
> I. Strader, Janet. II. Title.

If different editions of a work have the responsible persons or bodies appearing in a different order in the chief sources of information, each edition is entered under the heading for the person or body named first in that edition.

21.6C2. If principal responsibility is not indicated and there are more than three persons or bodies, the work is entered under the title and an added entry is made for the heading for the person or body named first in the chief source of information. If editors are named prominently and there are not more than three, an added entry is made for each. If there are more than three editors named prominently, an added entry is made for the first named. Example:

> **Title main entry when principal author is not indicated and there are more than three:**
>
> Europe reborn : the story of Renaissance civilization / contributors, Julian Mates . . . [et al.]
>
> **Added entry for first named author:**
>
> I. Mates, Julian, 1927-

RULE 21.7.   COLLECTIONS OF WORKS BY DIFFERENT PERSONS OR BODIES

21.7A.   Scope

This rule is used for situations in which contributions by different persons or corporate bodies are brought together:

1.   As collections of previously existing, independent works

2.   As collections of extracts from such works

3.   As combinations of existing independent works and new contributions by different persons or bodies.

One should not apply this rule to works that emanate from a corporate body and fall in the scope of rule 21.1B2 or to papers or proceedings of conferences. For the latter, one should use rule 21.1B2d if the conference, etc., is named prominently; rule 21.1B3 if it is not named prominently; or rule 21.5A if it is unnamed.

21.7B. With collective title

Main entry for a work covered by this rule is title if there is a collective title. Added entries are made under the headings for prominently named editors or compilers, if there are not more than three, or for the principal one or the one named first if there are more than three. Example:

Title main entry for a collection with a collective title:

> Modern music librarianship : essays in honor of Ruth Watanabe / edited by Alfred Mann.

Added entry for the prominently named editor:

> I. Mann, Alfred, 1917-

Name-title added entries are made if there are only two or three contributions or independent works included in a work covered by this rule. A name-title added entry is composed of the name of a person or corporate body followed by the title of a work for which the person or body is responsible. *See* example under 21.7C for an example of name-title added entries.

An added entry is made for each contributor when only two or three have contributed four or more works. In this case if one or two contributors have contributed only one work each, a name-title added entry is made for each.

An added entry is made for the first contributor named when more than three are named in the chief source of information.

21.7C. Without collective title

The main entry for a work that falls under this rule but does *not* have a collective title is the heading appropriate for the first work named in the chief source of information. If a chief source is lacking, the first work in the item is noted. Added entries are made as instructed in rule 21.7B. Example:

Main entry under first named author for a collection without a collective title:

> Ellsworth, Ralph E., 1907-
>   Buildings / by Ralph E. Ellsworth. Shelving / by Louis Kaplan. Storage warehouses / by Jerrold Orne

Name-title added entries for second and third works plus title added entries for all three works:

> I.   Kaplan, Louis, 1909-   . Shelving. II. Orne, Jerrold, 1921-   . Storage warehouses. III. Title. IV. Title: Shelving. V. Title: Storage warehouses.

Note: The rule does not mention separate title added entries for the separate titles in a collection without a collective title, nor does rule 21.30J suggest such title added entries. However, an LC rule interpretation for rule 21.30J gives instructions to make separate title added entries for each of the titles listed in the title and statement of responsibility area if there are not more than three. (*CSB* 78: 52–55)

WORKS OF MIXED RESPONSIBILITY: SELECTED RULES AND EXAMPLES

RULE 21.8.   WORKS OF MIXED RESPONSIBILITY

21.8A.   Scope

In many works the responsibility is divided. This occurs when different persons or bodies have contributed to the intellectual or artistic content performing different kinds of functions, e.g., writing, adapting, illustrating, translating, etc. Determination of main entry depends to a large extent on the relative importance of such contributions.

The rules in this section are divided into two basic categories of mixed responsibility:

1.   Modifications of previously existing works, such as revised editions, adaptations, or translations (rules 21.9–21.23)

2.   New works that consist of different kinds of contributions, such as illustrated texts or musical works with words by persons other than the composers (rules 21.24–21.27).

Works That Are Modifications of Other Works

RULE 21.9.   GENERAL RULE

Works that are modifications of other works may be entered under the heading appropriate to the new work or that appropriate to the original, depending upon the nature of the modification. If the modification has changed the nature or content of the original in a substantial way, or if the medium of expression is different, the new heading is chosen. However, if the modification is a rearrangement, abridgment, etc., where the original person or body is still seen as being responsible, the original heading is chosen. Rules 21.10–21.23 give specific guidance in applying this general rule.

Modifications of Texts (Rules 21.10–21.15)

RULE 21.10.   ADAPTATIONS OF TEXT

Adaptations of texts are entered under the heading for the adapter or under title if the adapter is unknown. A name-title added entry is made for the original work. Examples of adaptations are paraphrases, changes of literary form (e.g., dramatization), and adaptations for children. Example:

Adapter as main entry:

> Taylor, Helen L. (Helen Louisa)
> Little Pilgrim's progress / by Helen L. Taylor

Note expanding upon statement of responsibility:

> Adaptation for children of: The Pilgrim's progress / John Bunyan.

Name-title added entries for original author and title and for title page title:

> I. Bunyan, John, 1628-1688. Pilgrim's progress. II. Title.

RULE 21.11.   ILLUSTRATED TEXTS

21.11A.   General rule

When an illustrator has added illustrations to a text, the main entry is under the heading appropriate to the text. Example:

Main entry under author:

> Day, Jenifer W.
>> What is a bird? / by Jenifer W. Day ; illustrated by
> Tony Chen

Added entries for artist and for title:

> I. Chen, Tony. II. Title.

An added entry for the illustrator is made if appropriate (*see* rule 21.30K2). Works of collaboration between an artist and a writer are treated in rule 21.24.

RULE 21.12.   REVISIONS OF TEXTS

21.12A.   Original author considered responsible

The main entry for the original work is used for a revision if *either* the name of the original author appears in a statement of responsibility in the revision *or* the name of the original author appears in the revision's title proper and no other person is named in a statement of responsibility or other title information. The reviser, condenser, etc., is given an added entry. Such revisions include condensations, enlargements, revisions, and updates. Abridgments, however, are always entered under the original author, with an added entry made for the abridger, as explained above under rule 21.3A. Condensations that involve rewriting are considered to be adaptations and are entered according to rule 21.10. Example:

Revised work entered under original author:

> Gray, Henry, 1827-1861.
>> Anatomy of the human body / by Henry Gray. — 30th
> American ed. / edited by Carmine C. Clemente.

Added entries for reviser and for title:

> I. Clemente, Carmine D. II. Title.

21.12B.   Original author no longer considered responsible

If the wording of the chief source indicates that the original person or body is no longer responsible (i.e., it does not meet the conditions given in rule 21.12A), then entry is under the reviser, etc., or under title as appropriate. A name-title added entry is made under the original author and, if possible, the title of the latest edition to be entered under that name. Example:

Revised work entered under reviser.

> Bedingfeld, A.L.
>> Oxburgh Hall, Norfolk : a property of the National Trust / by
> A.L. Bedingfeld. — 2nd ed.

Note expanding upon statement of responsibility:

"First edition, 1953, by Professor F. de Zulueta."

Name-title added entry for original author and added entry for title:

I. Zulueta, Francis de. Oxburgh Hall, Norfolk. II. Title.

RULE 21.13.   TEXTS PUBLISHED WITH COMMENTARY

This rule applies to information packages comprising a text or texts by one person or body and a commentary or interpretation by another person or body. In essence, the rule calls for entry under the heading appropriate to the commentary if the chief source of information presents the work as a commentary, and entry under the heading for the original work if the chief source of information presents the work as an edition of the original. If the chief source is ambiguous, entry is determined by (in order of preference) emphasis in the preface, the typographic presentation of the text and commentary, or the relative extent of text and commentary. If there is still doubt, the work is treated as an edition with an added entry appropriate to the commentary. Example:

Text with commentary entered under commentator:

Fischer, John L.
Annotations to the Book of Luelen / translated and edited by John L. Fischer, Saul H. Riesenberg and Marjorie G. Whiting

Note explaining the statement of responsibility:

Annotations by J.L. Fischer, S.H. Riesenberg, and M.G. Whiting.

Added entries appropriate to the text:

I. Riesenberg, Saul H. II. Whiting, Marjorie G. III. Bernart, Luelen. Book of Luelen. IV. Title.

RULE 21.14.   TRANSLATIONS

A single translation is entered under the heading appropriate to the original. An added entry for the translator may be made in accordance with rule 21.30K1. Example:

Translation entered under original author.

Flohr, Salo, 1908-
Twelfth chess tournament of nations / Salo Flohr ; [translated from the Russian by W. Perelman]

[Note: added entries are not usually made for translators.]

A collection of translations of works by different authors is treated as a collection (*see* rule 21.7).

RULE 21.15.   TEXTS PUBLISHED WITH BIBLIOGRAPHICAL/CRITICAL MATERIAL

Works that consist of a writer's work or works accompanied by bibliographical or critical material written by someone else are treated according to the way they are represented in the chief source of information. If the chief source presents the work as biography and/or criticism, the main entry is the biographer/critic. If the chief source presents the work as an edition with an editor, compiler, etc., then the original writer is used as main entry. In either case an added entry is made for the one not chosen as main entry. Examples:

Biographical work entered under biographer.

> Morse, John T. (John Torrey), 1840-1937.
> Life and letters of Oliver Wendell Holmes / by John T. Morse

Added entries for Holmes both as subject of the biography and as personal author and title added entry:

> 1. Holmes, Oliver Wendell, 1809-1894. I. Holmes, Oliver Wendell, 1809-1894. II. Title.

Edited biographical work entered under author:

> Dover, Thomas, 1660-1742.
> Thomas Dover's life and Legacy / edited and introduced by Kenneth Dewhurst

Added entries for editor and for title:

> I. Dewhurst, Kenneth, ed. II. Title.

Art Works (Rules 21.16–21.17)

RULE 21.16.   ADAPTATIONS OF ART WORKS

AACR2R98 defines art works as including "paintings, engravings, photographs, drawings, sculptures, etc., and any other creative work that can be represented pictorially (e.g., ceramic designs, tapestries, fabrics)."[9]

21.16A.   When an art work is adapted from one medium to another, the main entry is the adapter, or the title if the adapter is unknown. A name-title added entry is made for the original. Example:

Adaptation entered under heading for title because adapter is unknown.

> [Mona Lisa] [picture] / [computer representation of the original by Leonardo da Vinci, produced via program written at IBM]

Note explaining existence of work:

> Copies distributed at demonstration of IBM equipment.

Name-title added entry for original work:

> I. Leonardo, da Vinci, 1452-1519. Mona Lisa.

Added entry for responsible corporate body:

> II. International Business Machines Corporation.

21.16B.   When an art work is reproduced, however, the main entry is the heading for the original, with an added entry for the person or body responsible for the reproduction, unless that person or body is only the manufacturer or publisher. Example:

Reproduction of art work entered under heading for the artist.

> Hobbema, Meindert, 1638-1709.
> View on a high road [picture] / Hobbema ; National Gallery of Art

Added entries for body responsible for reproduction and for title:

> I. National Gallery of Art (U.S.). II. Title.

RULE 21.17.   REPRODUCTIONS OF TWO OR MORE ART WORKS

21.17A.   Without text

If a work consists of reproductions of an artist's works and there is no text, the main entry is the artist.

21.17B.   With text

When text accompanies reproductions of an artist's works, entry is under the personal heading for the author of the text if that person is represented as author in the chief source of information; an added entry is made under the heading for the artist. Otherwise, or in case of doubt, entry is made under the heading for the artist with an added entry for the person mentioned in the chief source of information as having written the text. Catalogs of the holdings of a corporate body are governed by rule 21.1B2a. Art catalogs often present difficult choices. An LC rule interpretation gives guidance in this area. (*CSB* 45: 27–28) Examples:

Art reproductions with text entered under author of text.

> Cassou, Jean, 1897-
> Rembrandt / par Jean Cassou

Added entry for artist:

> I. Rembrandt Harmenszoon van Rijn, 1606-1669.

Art reproductions with text entered under artist.

> Rembrandt Harmenszoon van Rijn, 1606-1669.
> More drawings of Rembrandt / introduction by Stephen Longstreet

Added entries for author of text and for title:

> I. Longstreet, Stephen, 1907-   . II. Title.

Musical Works (Rules 21.18–21.22)

RULE 21.18.   GENERAL RULE

21.18A.   Scope

This rule applies to all kinds of arrangements of musical works where medium of performance has been changed; the original has been simplified; the new work is described as "based on," etc.; new material has been incorporated; or the harmony or style of the original has been changed.

21.18B.   Arrangements, transcriptions, etc.

A musical arrangement is a musical work or part of a musical work that has been rewritten either for a different medium of performance or to provide a simplified version. The general rule for a musical arrangement is to enter it under the heading for the original composer whenever possible. An added entry is made for the name of the arranger. Example:

Arrangement of musical work entered under original composer.

> Mozart, Wolfgang Amadeus, 1756-1791.
>> Eighth quintet, k. 614, fourth movement / W.A. Mozart ; arranged for 2 B^b trumpets, horn, trombone & tuba by Ralph Lockwood

Added entry for arranger:

> I. Lockwood, Ralph.

[A uniform title would be constructed instead of a title added entry. *See* rule 25.25]

21.18C.   Adaptations

A musical work that is an adaptation represents a more serious departure from the original work than does an arrangement. Thus, generally, the main entry is made under the heading for the adapter, with an added entry given to the author of the original work. Three types of adaptations of music are specified for entry under adapter:

"a)   a distinct alteration of another work (e.g., a free transcription)

b)   a paraphrase of various works or of the general style of another composer

c)   a work merely based on other music (e.g., variations on a theme.)"[10]

In case of doubt about whether a work is an adaptation, it is to be treated as an arrangement, transcription, etc. Example:

Adaptation of musical work entered under adapter.

> Brahms, Johannes, 1833-1897.
>> Variations and fugue on a theme by Handel, op. 24 / Johannes Brahms

Note explaining the scope of the item:

>> The theme is that of the Aria con variazioni from Handel's Suite for harpsichord, 2nd collection, no. 1.

Name-title added entry for original work:

>> I. Handel, George Frideric, 1685–1759. Suites, harpsichord, HWV 434, B^b major. Aria con variazioni.

RULE 21.19.   MUSICAL WORKS THAT INCLUDE WORDS

21.19A.   General rule

If a musical work includes words, the main entry is for the composer with an added entry for the writer of the words, if the writer's work is represented, as in a full score or a vocal score, for example. A name-title added entry is made for an original text upon which the words have been based. Librettos are treated under another rule: 21.28. Example:

> **Musical comedy entered under composer.**

> Adler, Richard.
>   The pajama game : a musical comedy / music and lyrics by
> Richard Adler and Jerry Ross ; book by George Abbott

> **Note expanding statement of responsibility:**

> "Based on the novel '7½ cents' by Richard Bissell."

> **Added entries for co-composer, writer, and title, and an added name-title entry for original text:**

> I. Ross, Jerry, 1926-1955. II. Abbott, George,
> 1889-   III. Bissell, Richard. 7½ cents.
> IV. Title.

21.19C.   Writer's works set by several composers

If the work or works of one writer are set in a collection of songs, etc., by two or more composers, entry is made according to the rule for collections, rule 21.7. Example:

> **Collection of songs with words by one writer and music by several composers; entered as a collection under title.**

> A Shakespeare song book / edited by H.A. Chambers.

> **Added entries for writer of words and for editor:**

> I. Shakespeare, William, 1564-1616. II. Chambers,
> H.A. (Herbert Arthur), 1880-

RULES 21.20–21.22.

These rules discuss main entry problems for musical settings for ballets, etc. (21.20), the addition of accompaniments or parts to a musical work (21.21), and liturgical music (21.22).

Sound Recordings (Rule 21.23)

RULE 21.23.   ENTRY OF SOUND RECORDINGS

It should be noted that this rule applies only to sound recordings that are modifications of other works. This includes readings of texts and performances of musical works. There is no rule specifically for sound recordings considered to constitute new works, such as recordings of improvisations and lectures. These items would be entered according to the principles of responsibility found in the basic rules. Such works as interviews made as oral history could be entered according to the principles in rule 21.25.

It should be noted also that this rule must be used in conjunction with rule 6.1G. If under rule 6.1G it is decided that a sound recording lacking a collective title should be described as a unit, then one of rules 21.23B–21.23D will be applied. If, however, it is decided to make a separate description for each separately titled work, rule 21.23A will be applied.

21.23A. One work

Main entry for a sound recording of one work is the heading appropriate to that work. The rule specifically calls for added entries for the principal performers unless there are more than three, in which case an added entry is made for the first named principal performer. A rule interpretation from LC points out that added entries should also be made for those prescribed by the rules under which the choice of main entry for the work is made. (*CSB* 44: 37) Example:

Sound recording entered under author of original work:

> Rey, Margret.
> Curious George learns the alphabet [sound recording] /
> Margret & H.A. Rey

Note expanding statement of responsibility:

> Read by Julie Harris.

Added entries for shared author, for reader, and for title:

> I. Rey, H.A. (Hans Agusto), 1898-   . II.
> Harris, Julie. III. Title.

21.23B.   Two or more works by the same person(s) or body(ies)

Main entry for a sound recording of works that are all the responsibility of the same person(s) or body(ies) is the heading appropriate to those works. Added entries are made for performers and for additional responsible persons or bodies as explained above under rule 21.23A. Example:

Sound recording entered under composer of the several works performed.

> Chopin, Frédéric, 1810-1849.
> The 24 preludes [sound recording] / Chopin

Note expanding statement of responsibility:

> Alexander Brailowsky, pianist.

Added entries for performer and for title:

> I. Brailowsky, Alexander, 1896-1976. II. Title.

21.23C.   Works by different persons or bodies. Collective title

Main entry for a sound recording of works by different persons or bodies that has a collective title is the person or body represented as principal performer. If there are two or three principal performers, main entry is the first named, with added entries for the others. A rule interpretation from LC gives guidance in deciding whom to consider "principal performers." This rule interpretation should be consulted for further detail. (*CSB* 45: 28–31) Example:

Sound recording entered under first-named principal performer.

> Boston Pops Orchestra.
> Greatest hits of the '50s [sound recording]

Note expanding statement of responsibility:

> Boston Pops Orchestra ; Arthur Fiedler, conductor.

Added entries for second named principal performer and for title:

> I. Fiedler, Arthur, 1894-1979. II. Title.

A sound recording with four or more principal performers or no principal performers is given main entry under title. Example:

Sound recording with more than three principal performers entered under title:

> Stay awake [sound recording]

Other title information from jacket:

> "Various interpretations of music from vintage Disney films."

Note expanding statement of responsibility:

> Performances by Betty Carter, Garth Hudson, Los Lobos,
> Natalie Merchant, NRBQ, Harry Nilsson, Bonnie Raitt, Sun Ra,
> Ringo Starr, James Taylor, Tom Waits and others.

21.23D.   Works by different persons or bodies. No collective title

This rule applies to a sound recording that contains works by different persons or bodies, that has no collective title, and that is to be cataloged as a unit. Treatment depends upon the decision about whether participation of the performer(s) goes beyond mere performance, execution, or interpretation.

Popular, rock, and jazz music are usually considered to have participation of performers beyond execution or interpretation. In these cases main entry is under principal performer, if there is one; under the first of two or three principal performers; or under the heading appropriate to the first work if there are four or more principal performers. Added entries are made for the performers not named as main entry if there are not more than three. Examples:

Sound recording entered under principal performer:

> Alan, Buddy.
> When I turn twenty-one [sound recording] / Merle Haggard.
> Adios, farewell, goodbye, good luck, so long / Buck Owens.

Note expanding statement of responsibility:

> Buddy Alan, vocals ; James Burton's orchestra.

Sound recording entered under main entry [title] for first work:

> Little white duck [sound recording]. Mary had a little lamb

Note expanding statement of responsibility:

> Recording sung by Betty Wells, Bill Marine and The
> Playmates with orchestra directed by Maury Laws (side A),
> The 4 Cricketones with orchestra and chorus (side B).

Classical and other "serious" music is usually considered to have participation of performers that does not go beyond execution or interpretation. For these works, main entry is under the heading appropriate to the first work with added entries for the other works if appropriate as explained under rule 21.7C.

Mixed Responsibility in New Works

RULE 21.24. COLLABORATION BETWEEN ARTIST AND WRITER

If a work appears to be a collaborative effort between an artist and a writer, rather than an artist's illustrations of a writer's text (covered by rule 21.11A), main entry is under the one named first in the chief source of information, unless the other one is given greater prominence by typography, etc. Example:

Collaborative work entered under artist named first on title page:

> Mair, A.J. (Alice Joy)
> More homes of the pioneers and other buildings : pen and wash drawings / by A.J. Mair ; with text by J.A. Hendry

Added entries for author of text and for title:

> I. Hendry, J.A. (John A.). II. Title.

RULE 21.25. REPORTS OF INTERVIEWS OR EXCHANGES

Whether to give main entry to the reporter or to one of the other participants in an interview or exchange depends upon how much the words are those of the reporter and how much those of the other participant(s). If the report gives essentially the words of the interviewee or other participant, main entry is the principal participant, first named participant, or title if there are more than three equal participants. An added entry is made for an openly named reporter. If the report, for the most part, consists of the words of the reporter, main entry is for the reporter, with added entry(ies) for the persons interviewed if they are named in the chief source of information (or for only the first if there are more than three). Examples:

Interview entered under the first named participant:

> Scott, David Randolph.
> Interview from deep space [sound recording] / by David Randolph Scott, Alfred Merrill Worden, and James Benson Irwin

Added entries for other participants and for title:

> I. Worden, Alfred Merrill. II. Irwin, James B. (James Benson). III. Title.

Interview entered under reporter:

> Schneider, Duane.
> An interview with Anaïs Nin / Duane Schneider

Added entry for person interviewed and for title:

> I. Nin, Anaïs, 1903-1977. II. Title.

RELATED WORKS:
SELECTED RULES AND EXAMPLES

RULE 21.28.   RELATED WORKS

21.28A.   Scope

According to rule 1.9, supplementary items may be described separately or dependently (i.e., described as accompanying material; or in a note; or in a multi-level description, further described in rule 13.6). This rule (21.28) applies only to separately cataloged works that are related to another work. It includes continuations, sequels, supplements, indexes, concordances, incidental music to dramatic works, cadenzas, scenarios, screenplays, choreographies, subseries, special numbers of serials, and collections of extracts from serials. It does not apply to works that have only subject relationship to other works or to the particular types of relationships covered in rules 21.8–21.27.

In *AACR2R* proper, this rule includes librettos, but an alternative rule for librettos is given in a footnote. LC has decided to apply the alternative rule for librettos because "librettos are normally sought as an adjunct to the music."[11] Therefore, librettos are entered by LC under the heading for the musical work, with an added entry under the personal heading for the librettist. A name-title added entry is also made under the heading for the original text on which the libretto is based, if this applies. Example:

Libretto entered under heading appropriate to the musical work [composer] according to rule 21.28A, footnote 7:

> Laderman, Ezra.
> [Galileo Galilei. Libretto. English]
> Galileo Galilei : an opera-oratorio in three acts / libretto by Joe Darion ; music by Ezra Laderman

Note providing other title information:

> Original title: The trials of Galileo.

Added entries for librettist and for titles:

> I. Darion, Joe, 1917-   . II. Title. III. Title:
> The trials of Galileo.

21.28B.   General rule

Main entry for a related work is the heading appropriate to it as if it were an independent work. An added entry is made for the name-title or title (whichever is main entry) of the related work. An added entry is not made, however, for the related work in the case of a sequel by the same author. LC has made some other exceptions to making added entries for the related works that apply to excerpts from serials, indexes, census data, and Bible texts. (*CSB* 47: 46–47) Examples:

Supplement cataloged separately and entered under author:

> Gore, Marvin.
> Elements of systems analysis for business data processing.
> Instructional supplement / Marvin Gore, John Stubbe

Added entries for co-author of supplement and for title:

I. Stubbe, John. II. Title.

[Note that a name-title added entry for the related work is not made because it would, in essence, be a duplication of the main entry and title given before the words *Instructional supplement*.]

Concordance entered under its own author:

Williams, Mary.
    The Dickens concordance, being a compendium of names and characters and principal places mentioned in all the works of Charles Dickens . . . / by Mary Williams

Added entries for author of works to which this work is related and for title:

I. Dickens, Charles, 1812-1870. II. Title.

Collection of extracts from a serial entered as a collection under title as appropriate to the related work in hand. [Joyce is the subject of these essays.]:

James Joyce essays / by Brian Nolan . . . [et al.]

Note providing bibliographic history:

"These essays were first published in Envoy, 1951."

Added entries for first named author and for serial from which essays were extracted:

I. O'Brien, Flann, 1911-1966. II. Envoy (Dublin).

[Note: Flann O'Brien has written under many names, including Brian Nolan. All works are brought together by LC under: O'Brien, Flann, 1911-1966.]

ADDED ENTRIES:
SELECTED RULES AND EXAMPLES

RULE 21.29.   GENERAL RULE

The preceding rules have indicated the added entries required in typical circumstances to supplement the main entry by providing additional bibliographical access to materials represented in the catalog. In general, added entries are suggested to provide access to other names of persons or titles under which a work may be known and under which catalog users might reasonably search. Persons, corporate bodies, and works related to the work at hand are considered, providing these are openly stated in the work. It is a matter of local library policy to establish whether or not to make all required added entries, a decision that must be related to the extent of the collection, the needs it serves, and some economic considerations.

It is prescribed here that if the cataloger believes an added entry is needed, and if the reason for an added entry is not clear from the body of the description, a note should be provided to justify the added entry.

An option provides for explanatory references in place of certain added entries (as in rule 26.5); LC is not applying this option. (*CSB* 8: 12)

LC has given guidelines in addition to those in *AACR2R* for making added entries for audiovisual materials and for sound recordings. These should be consulted when appropriate. (*CSB* 45: 32–34)

RULE 21.30.   SPECIFIC RULES

21.30A–21.30H, 21.30K, 21.30M.   These specific rules for added entries for collaborators, writers, editors and compilers, corporate bodies, other related persons or bodies, related works, other relationships, translators, illustrators, and analytical entries have been touched on in the rules for choice of main entry. When particular guidance is needed for one of these cases, these rules in *AACR2R* should be consulted. One should also consult LC rule interpretations for rule 21.30E, Corporate bodies (*CSB* 79: 17–18); rule 21.30F, Other related persons or bodies (*CSB* 59: 11); rule 21.30G, Related works (*CSB* 77: 23–24); rule 21.30H, Other relationships (*CSB* 52: 19–20); rule 21.30K, Translators (*CSB* 77: 44); and rule 21.30M, Analytical entries (*CSB* 63: 11–12). Examples:

Bibliographic entry with an added entry for editor:

> Shakespeare, William, 1564-1616.
>   As you like it / [by William Shakespeare] ; edited by Peter Hollindale

Added entries made:

> I. Hollindale, Peter. II. Title.

Bibliographic entry with an added entry for translator:

> Busch, Wilhelm, 1832-1908.
>   The bees : a fairy tale / by Wilhelm Busch ; translated by Rudolph Wiemann

Notes providing information on translation:

> Translation of: Schnurrdiburr.

Added entries made:

> I. Wiemann, Rudolph. II. Title.

Two added entry rules are used with such frequency that they warrant special mention:

21.30J.   Titles

According to *AACR2R98* there are only four instances in which an added entry for a title proper (that is not a main entry) should not be made:

"a)   the title proper is essentially the same as the main entry heading or a reference to that heading   *or*

b)   the title proper has been composed by the cataloguer   *or*

c)   in a catalogue in which name-title and subject entries are interfiled, the title proper is identical with a subject heading assigned to the work, or a direct reference to that subject heading   *or*

d) a conventionalized uniform title has been used as the uniform title for a musical work (*see* 25.25–25.35)."[12]

Added entries should be made for any other version of the title (e.g., cover title) that differs significantly (according to rule 21.2A) from the title proper.

LC applies only restriction b) without exceptions. An extensive rule interpretation gives guidelines for making title added entries and for tracing them. Guidance is also given for added entries for spelled-out forms of abbreviations, numerals, etc., as well as the non-spelled-out forms. (*CSB* 78: 41–61)

See examples throughout this chapter.

21.30L. Series

An added entry is made for a series on each record for each work in the series if it is judged to be a useful access point. Adding the numeric or other designation to each added entry is optional. This option is applied at LC. (*CSB* 74: 29) Example:

Bibliographic entry with an added entry for series:

Dundes, Alan.
Analytic essays in folklore / by Alan Dundes

Use of series area:

— (Studies in folklore ; 2)

Added entries made:

I. Title. II. Series.

According to *AACR2R*, series added entries are not made if the series shares only common physical characteristics or if the series numbering appears to be only publisher's stock control numbers. For a number of years LC placed certain additional restrictions on tracing series, but at the end of 1989 a decision was made to begin tracing every series. The cataloger should consult LC's rule interpretation for assistance with the form of series added entry tracings. (*CSB* 74: 29–32)

SPECIAL RULES: SELECTED RULES AND EXAMPLES

Certain Legal Publications

Rules 21.31 through 21.36 cover the following legal publications:

21.31 — legislative enactments and decrees that have the force of law except for ones that are covered by later rules

21.32 — administrative regulations

21.33 — constitutions and charters

21.34 — court rules

21.35 — treaties and intergovernmental agreements

21.36 — court decisions and cases

The reader is referred to these rules for choice of entry for these publications. Examples:

Laws governing a single jurisdiction entered under name of jurisdiction:

> United States.
> [Tax reduction act of 1975]
> Tax reduction act of 1975, P.L. 94-12, as signed by the President on March 29, 1975 : law and explanation. — Chicago : Commerce Clearing House, [1975]

Added entries for corporate body issuing or compiling the law and for title:

> I. Commerce Clearing House. II. Title.

[For Uniform titles for laws, *see* rule 25.15A] `

U.S. administrative regulation entered under promulgating agency:

> United States. Internal Revenue Service.
> Estate tax regulations under the Internal Revenue Code of 1954 / [United States Treasury Department, Internal Revenue Service]

Added entries for heading for uniform title for authorizing law and for title:

> I. United States. [Internal Revenue Code of 1954] II. Title.

Treaty involving two countries entered under country alphabetically first:

> France.
> [Treaties, etc. United States, 1984 Jan. 3]
> Atomic energy, radioactive waste management : arrangement between the United States of America and France, signed at Washington and Paris January 3 and 10, 1984.

Added entries for the second named country and for title:

> I. United States. Treaties, etc. France, 1984 Jan. 3. II. Title.

Certain Religious Publications

Rules 21.37 through 21.39 cover the following religious publications:

21.37 — sacred scriptures

21.38 — theological creeds, confessions of faith, etc.

21.39 — liturgical works

The reader is referred to these rules for choice of entry for these publications. Examples:

Sacred scripture entered under uniform title main entry:

> Tipiṭaka. Suttapiṭaka. English. Selections.
> Some sayings of the Buddha, according to the Pali canon / translated [from the Pali] by F. L. Woodward ; with an introduction by Christmas Humphreys

Added entries for persons associated with the work and for title page title:

I. Woodward, F. L. (Frank Lee), 1870 or 71-1952.
II. Humphreys, Christmas, 1901–   . III. Tipitaka.
Vinayapitaka. English. Selections. IV. Title.

Liturgical work entered under heading for the church:

Catholic Church.
[Rite of ordination. English]
The ordination of deacons, priests, and bishops : provisional
text prepared by the International Committee on English in the
Liturgy, approved for interim use by the Bishops' Committee on
the Liturgy, National Conference of Catholic Bishops, and
confirmed by the Apostolic See.

Added entry for title:

I. Title.

NOTES

1. *Anglo-American Cataloging Rules, Second Edition, 1998 Revisions*, prepared under the
direction of the Joint Steering Committee for Revision of AACR (Chicago: American Library
Association, 1998), p. 2 (paragraph 0.5).

2. For further discussion of "main entry" as a theoretical concept *see* Arlene G. Taylor, *The
Organization of Information*, Englewood, Colo.: Libraries Unlimited, 1999, chapter 6.

3. *AACR2R98*, p. 2 (paragraph 0.5).

4. Richard P. Smiraglia, Barbara B. Tillett, and Sherry L. Vellucci have done recent notable
research in this area:

Smiraglia: "Authority Control and the Extent of Derivative Bibliographic Relation-
ships," Ph.D. dissertation, University of Chicago, 1992; and "Derivative Bibliographic
Relationships: Linkages in the Bibliographic Universe," in *Navigating the Networks:
Proceedings of the ASIS Mid-Year Meeting, Portland, Oregon, May 21–25, 1994*
(Medford, N.J.: Learned Information, 1994), pp. 167–183.

Tillett: "Bibliographic Relationships: Toward a Conceptual Structure of Bibliographic
Information Used in Cataloging." Ph.D. dissertation, University of California, Los An-
geles, 1987; "A Taxonomy of Bibliographic Relationships," *Library Resources and
Technical Services*, 35 (April 1991), pp. 150–158; "A Summary of the Treatment of
Bibliographic Relationships in Cataloging Rules," *Library Resources and Technical
Services*, 35 (October 1991), pp. 393–405; "The History of Linking Devices," *Library
Resources and Technical Services*, 36 (January 1992), pp. 23–36; and "Bibliographic
Relationships: An Empirical Study of the LC Machine-Readable Records," *Library Re-
sources and Technical Services*, 36 (April 1992), pp. 162–188.

Vellucci: "Bibliographic Relationships Among Musical Bibliographic Entities: A Conceptual Analysis of Music Represented in the Library Catalog with a Taxonomy of the
Relationships Discovered." D.L.S. dissertation, Columbia University, 1995; and "Bibliographic Relationships," in *The Principles and Future of AACR2*, ed. Jean Weihs
(Chicago: American Library Association, 1998), pp. 105–146.

5.   For example, see Seymour Lubetzky, "The Fundamentals of Bibliographic Cataloging and AACR2," in International Conference on AACR2, Florida State University, 1979, *The Making of a Code* (Chicago: American Library Association, 1980), pp. 18–23; Michael Gorman, "AACR2: Main Themes," in ibid., pp. 45–46; and Elizabeth L. Tate, "Examining the 'Main' in Main Entry Headings," in ibid., pp. 109–140. More recent discussions include Michael Carpenter, "Does Cataloging Theory Rest on a Mistake?" in Smiraglia, Richard P., editor, *Origins, Content, and Future of AACR2 Revisited* (Chicago: American Library Association, 1992), pp. 95–102; and Ronald Hagler, "Access Points for Works," in *The Principles and Future of AACR2*, ed. Jean Weihs (Chicago: American Library Association, 1998), pp. 214–228.

6.   *AACR2R98*, p. 312.

7.   *AACR2R98*, p. 312.

8.   *AACR2R98*, p. 320.

9.   *AACR2R98*, p. 338.

10.   *AACR2R98*, p. 340.

11.   "AACR 2 Options to Be Followed by the Library of Congress, Chapters 1–2, 12, 21–26," *Library of Congress Information Bulletin*, 37 (July 21, 1978): 425.

12.   *AACR2R98*, pp. 356–357.

SUGGESTED READING

Chan, Lois Mai. *Cataloging and Classification: An Introduction.* 2nd ed. New York: McGraw-Hill, 1994. Chapter 4.

Fritz, Deborah A. *Cataloging with AACR2R and USMARC for Books, Computer Files, Serials, Sound Recordings, Videorecordings.* Chicago: American Library Association, 1998. Chapter 9.

Hagler, Ronald. *The Bibliographic Record and Information Technology.* 3rd ed. Chicago: American Library Association, 1997, pp. 247–252.

Maxwell, Robert L., with Margaret F. Maxwell. *Maxwell's Handbook for AACR2R.* Chicago: American Library Association, 1997. Chapter 14.

Tate, Elizabeth L. "Examining the 'Main' in Main Entry Headings." In International Conference on AACR2, Florida State University, 1979, *The Making of a Code.* Chicago: American Library Association, 1980, pp. 109–140.

7 Form of Headings for Names and Titles

INTRODUCTION

The previous chapter dealt with choice of access points; this chapter presents rules for the form of heading regardless of whether the access point is to be a main entry or an added entry. Once it has been decided what is to be the main entry or heading and what are to be added entries, it must be determined how those entries are to be displayed in the record. Choice of entry rules deal with who or what is to be the entry; form of entry rules deal with how an entry is to be recorded as a heading.

NAMES OF PERSONS

Most headings in American library catalogs consist of a personal name entered under the surname followed by forenames (like the white pages of a telephone directory). However, as the following rules for headings for persons show, there are certain complexities that must be considered in a library catalog. Rules—i.e., principles and practices—must be followed consistently for those persons known by more than one name. There are many possible instances when a person may be known and/or even write under more than one name. Some authors deliberately disguise their real names and write under a pseudonym or pen name—such as Charles Lutwidge Dodgson, who wrote his children's fantasies under the pseudonym of Lewis Carroll. Others consistently write under initialized forenames (e.g., H. G. Wells), while still others, such as Bernard Shaw (also known as George Bernard Shaw), consistently omit one of their forenames. If someone's original name is written in a nonroman alphabet, different romanization systems may create different spellings of the name (such as Chekhov, Chekov, or Tchekhov). A married woman traditionally may have two possible surnames—her birth surname and her husband's surname. Further, compound surnames—i.e., surnames consisting of two or more parts—create problems. Granville-Barker is an example of a compound, hyphenated English surname. Prefixes to surnames create another type of compound surname. De Gaulle and von Goethe are examples of surnames with prefixes; O'Brien and MacPherson are other examples. Individuals who are members of nobility may have two names—a titled name and a common surname (such as Lord Byron, George Gordon Byron). Certain individuals are known under their bynames or forenames rather than their surnames;

these include royalty (Elizabeth II), saints (Joan of Arc), popes (Paul VI), and individuals in ancient and medieval periods prior to the development of surnames (Horace). Bynames or forenames often exist in different forms in different languages (such as Horace in English, but Horatius in Latin). The purpose of this section is to demonstrate the general rules used to resolve all of these problems. For more complicated problems of personal names, the student should carefully examine Chapter 22 in the *Anglo-American Cataloguing Rules, Second Edition* in one of its formats. (As in chapters 4–6, specific cites to the 1998 print version are referred to as *AACR2R98*, but the work with its additions and changes is referred to as *AACR2R*.)

AACR2R Chapter 22 is divided into four sections, the first three of which suggest the order of the steps taken by the cataloger to establish the form in which the name will appear as a heading in the catalog. The first section, rules 22.1–22.3, is entitled "Choice of name." This "choice" is a separate action from "choice of access points," discussed in the preceding chapter. Once it has been decided through choice of access points that a person will be given an access point, rules 22.1–22.3 prescribe the choice of name when that person has used more than one name or different manifestations of the same name. After making a choice of name, the cataloger uses the next section, rules 22.4–22.11, "Entry element," to decide which element of the chosen name will be the first and in what order the other elements will follow. The third step is to make any additions to the name that may be necessitated because of the kind of name involved (rules 22.12–22.16) or because two or more names are identical (rules 22.17–22.20). The fourth section of *AACR2R*, Chapter 22, is "Special Rules for Names in Certain Languages." These are for selected languages in which heading form does not follow the typical "western" style.

It should be noted that the rules in this section apply to the choice and form of personal names whether they are access points because of some kind of responsibility for the creation of a work or because they are the subject of a work. That is, a personal name subject heading is constructed in the same manner and according to the same rules as is a personal name main or added entry heading for an author, painter, performer, etc.

The Library of Congress (LC) adopted *Anglo-American Cataloguing Rules, Second Edition (AACR2)* for new names beginning January 2, 1981. It also abandoned the policy of *superimposition* at that time so that a number of already established name forms were changed to agree with the prescribed *AACR2* form. Superimposition was a policy established with the adoption of *Anglo-American Cataloging Rules (AACR)* in 1967. Under that policy any name that had been established prior to *AACR* continued to be used on new cataloging as already established, even if its form according to *AACR* would have been different. Even though this policy was officially abandoned with the adoption of *AACR2*, in certain defined categories, established names were considered to be "*AACR2* compatible," and the established form continued to be used even on new records. After the initial impact of adopting *AACR2* was over, it became counterproductive to continue the "compatible" policy, because it took more time to decide on such headings than to change the old forms. Therefore, the "compatible" policy was abandoned on September 1, 1982.[1] All pre-*AACR2* headings coded as compatible between January 2, 1981, and September 1, 1982, remain in that form at LC. Thus, it is useful to be aware of some of the major cases. These are summarized with examples in an issue of *Cataloging Service Bulletin*, which should be consulted by anyone who works with cataloging copy from LC.[2]

A heading created using *AACR2R*, Chapter 22, is coded 100, 600, 700, or 800 in the MARC 21 (MAchine-Readable Cataloging) format in use by the United States and Canada, depending upon whether it functions as a main entry, a subject heading, or an added entry or begins a series added entry.

Choice of Name: Selected Rules and Examples

RULE 22.1.   GENERAL RULE

22.1A.   The name by which a person is commonly known is the one that should be chosen, whether that name be the person's real name, nickname, pseudonym, shortened form of name, or other form of name customarily used by a person. Thus the following choices might be made:

Pseudonym

> Mathew James
>
> *not* birth name: James D. Lucey

Nickname

> Billy Graham
>
> *not* William Franklin Graham

Name in religion

> Maria Teresa dell'Eucaristia
>
> *not* birth name: Maria Teresa Tosi

Short form of name

> Virginia Knight Nelson
>
> *not* Alyce Virginia Knight Nelson

Real name

> Sally Benson
>
> *not* pseudonym: Esther Evarts

22.1B.   The name by which a person is commonly known is to be determined from chief sources of information of works in that person's language. This, of course, may not be possible if the person is only a subject of works or creates only nonverbal works (e.g., unsigned paintings). In these cases the name is to be determined from reference sources in the person's language or from the person's country of residence or activity. A footnote to this rule in *AACR2R* indicates that "reference sources" include books and articles written about a person.

A rule interpretation from LC indicates that chief sources used for this rule may be from works published both during and after a person's lifetime. There are special instructions, also, about treatment of music composers, names without forenames, names containing abbreviations rather than initials, and other more unusual situations. (*CSB* 44: 38–41)

Throughout this chapter of *AACR2R* there are references to "commonly known" and "predominant" when referring to choosing one name or one form of name. *AACR2R98* defines predominant name as, "The name or form of name of a person or corporate body that appears most frequently (1) in the person's works or works issued by the corporate body, or (2) in reference sources, in that order of preference."[3] At the time of implementation of *AACR2* in 1981 there was indication from those involved in its creation that "most frequently" should not be taken to mean 51 percent of the instances; yet there were no guidelines otherwise. For a number of years, LC had used 75 percent in interpreting the "fullness of name" rule. That is, until a name appeared in a different form in an author's works 75 percent of the time (counting works by the person issued after the person's death as well as during the person's lifetime), the form of heading was not changed. They continued to apply this concept with *AACR2*, except the percentage was changed to 66⅔ percent during the early years of *AACR2* and later was changed to 80 percent. They are continuing this policy with *AACR2R*. A note with the interpretation that gives the figure of 80 percent to be used with the rule for fullness (22.3A) cautions that this figure is to be applied only to rule 22.3A—that no formula has been assigned to the other rules. (*CSB* 64: 23–24) However, other libraries might still use this as a guideline for changes. When a name is first established, "predominant" could be 51 percent or more; but a change would not be called for until the name had appeared differently 80 percent of the time.

22.1C–22.1D.   Terms and punctuation associated with a name

Rules 22.1C–22.1D refer to inclusion of titles of nobility or honor, diacritical marks, and hyphens. At first glance it may not be clear how these relate to choice of name. However, the intention here is to give rules for choosing those elements that should be included in the heading. The order in which these elements appear is the subject of rules 22.4–22.17.

The principle again is to follow the form customarily used by the person. Titles, words, or phrases that commonly appear with the name are included, as are accents, other diacritical marks, and hyphens used by the person, except that a hyphen that is used between a forename and a surname is not included.

RULE 22.2.   CHOICE AMONG DIFFERENT NAMES

Rules 22.2 and 22.3 give more specific guidelines for adhering to the principle stated in rule 22.1. Rules in 22.2 help choose among different names for the same person, and those in rule 22.3 help in the choice among different forms of the same name. Both may have to be used in a particular instance, because a name chosen from among different names may itself appear in varying degrees of fullness or with variant spellings. For example, once it has been decided that the name used should be George Novack, not William Warde, one then has to decide whether to use George Novack, George E. Novack, or George Edward Novack.

22.2A.   Predominant name

This rule applies only when a pseudonym is *not* involved. If a person is *known* by more than one name, and if there is a name that is clearly most common, it is used. If not, the following order of preference is used in making a choice:

"a)   the name that appears most frequently in the person's works

b)   the name that appears most frequently in reference sources

c)   the latest name."[4]

LC has issued a rule interpretation to be used for an author who simultaneously uses different forms of a real name. (*CSB* 44: 41) Another rule interpretation notes that if a person's name is shown with a nickname in quotation marks or parentheses, the nickname should be omitted in the heading. (*CSB* 43: 32)

22.2B.   Pseudonyms

22.2B1.   One pseudonym

When a person has used one pseudonym on all works, it is used for the heading, with a reference from the real name, if known. Example:

> Ford, Ford Madox, 1873-1939.
> It was the nightingale / Ford Madox Ford

[Note: Refer from[5] real name: Hueffer, Ford Madox.]

22.2B2.   Separate bibliographic identities

The concept in this rule was new with *AACR2R*. When works of one type always appear under one pseudonym and works of another type always appear under the person's real name or under another pseudonym, the person is considered to have established different bibliographic identities, and each separate group of works is entered under the name used for that identity. The cataloger is instructed to consult also rule 22.2B3 if the person involved is contemporary. Example:

Entry under real name:

> Clemens, Samuel Langhorne, 1835-1910.
> Republican letters / by Samuel L. Clemens

Note on bibliographic record:

> Articles published in the Chicago Republican in 1868.

Entry under pseudonym:

> Twain, Mark, 1835-1910.
> A Connecticut Yankee in King Arthur's court / Mark Twain

[Note: References are made from each name to the other and to Snodgrass, Quintus Curtius, 1835-1910—another pseudonym used by this author.]

The impetus for a rule establishing bibliographic identities came from those who were dissatisfied with the previous provision for entering all works of a person using two or more names under the name that had been used predominantly in the person's works or had become predominant in reference sources. The result was that the scholarly works written under a person's real name (e.g., Charles L. Dodgson) sometimes were entered under the name that person used on works of fiction (e.g., Lewis Carroll). In addition manuscript writings from a person's personal life (e.g., letters to family members) could be entered under a pseudonym used in published works. Establishing bibliographic identities solves these problems, and with advances in authority control in online systems, the need for pulling a person's works together in the same catalog drawer is no longer urgent.

22.2B3.   Contemporary authors

When a contemporary author uses more than one pseudonym or a real name and one or more pseudonyms, each work is given a heading based upon the name used in it. References are made to connect the names. Example:

Entry under pseudonym:

Cross, Amanda, 1926-
    Death in a tenured position / Amanda Cross

Entry under real name:

Heilbrun, Carolyn G., 1926-
    Hamlet's mother and other women / Carolyn G. Heilbrun

[Note: References are made from each name to the other. It should be noted that if this author were not a contemporary, both names would still be used because of separate bibliographic identities. She writes mysteries under the pseudonym of Cross and literary criticism under her real name of Heilbrun.]

When different editions of a work of a contemporary author have appeared with different names of the author, the name most often used should be the heading for all editions. If no one name is predominant, one should use the name that appears in the latest available edition. In all cases name-title references are made from the other name(s) used for editions of that work.

22.2B4. When a person who falls under rule 22.2B is not a contemporary and does not have separate bibliographic identities under different names, one name is chosen based on the following order of preference:

1.   The name used in later editions of his or her works

2.   The name most used in critical works

3.   The name by which the person has come to be identified in reference sources

References are made from other names not chosen.
    In a rule interpretation for all of rule 22.2B, LC points out that the intent of this rule is that for contemporaries who use at least one pseudonym, there will be as many headings as there are names. For non-contemporaries, the same may be true, but only if the cataloger can establish that there are separate bibliographic identities. If such identities cannot be identified, then there will be only one heading for non-contemporaries, regardless of number of names. The rule interpretation then gives guidelines for identifying "contemporary" and "separate bibliographic identities." (*CSB* 71: 53–55)

22.2C.   Change of name
    When a person who has not used a pseudonym has changed his or her name or has acquired and become known by a title of nobility, the latest name should be used for the heading. Example:

Latest name used:

Cochrane, Pauline A. (Pauline Atherton), 1929-
    Improving LCSH for use in online catalogs ; exercises
for self-help with a selection of background readings /
Pauline A. Cochrane

[Note: Refer from Atherton, Pauline, 1929- , name used in writings before author's marriage.]

RULE 22.3. CHOICE AMONG DIFFERENT FORMS OF THE SAME NAME

22.3A. Fullness

When a name is found in forms that vary in fullness, the form most commonly found should be used as the heading, with references from the other forms when they would be useful. Example:

> **Predominant form:** John P. Hamilton
> **Occasional form:** J.P. Hamilton
> **Rare form:** "Bud" Hamilton
> **Heading:** Hamilton, John P.
>
> [Note: Because Hamilton is a common surname, the second forename, Peter, may be required in parentheses to distinguish between two identical names (*see* rule 22.18). Also, references are needed from the two forms of name not chosen.]

When a form cannot be decided upon as most common, *AACR2R* prescribes using the latest form; but if the latest form is in doubt, then one should use the fullest form. LC skips the possibility of "latest form" and goes directly to fullest form if one form cannot be determined to be most common. (*CSB* 64: 23)

LC's rule interpretation also suggests that if the name appears in two or more forms in the same work, one should choose the form in the chief source. If the name does not appear in the chief source, then a form in another prominent source should be used, if the name appears only once in a prominent source. Otherwise, the fullest form should be chosen. (*CSB* 64: 24)

LC applies the "80% rule" when a heading is already coded as "AACR" but subsequent items are received showing the name in a different form. If an established heading is coded "AACR2 compatible," LC generally will not reconsider the heading, although exceptions are made in a few instances (e.g., when an author has notified LC that another form of name is preferred). (*CSB* 64: 23–24) Examples:

> **Established heading:** Rouse, John Edward, 1942-
> **Has written later as:** John E. Rouse
> **Heading coded "AACR2 compatible."**
> **Established heading retained.**

> **Established heading:** Sánchez E., Rodrigo.
> **Has now written over 80% as:** Rodrigo Sánchez Enríquez
> **New heading:** Sánchez Enríquez, Rodrigo.

22.3B. Language

22.3B1. Persons using more than one language

The heading for a person who writes in more than one language should be the form that corresponds to the language of most of the works. Example:

> **Names found on works:** William More
>   Guillermo Mora
> **Lived and worked in both U.S. and Venezuela.**
> **Most works in Spanish.**
> **Heading:** Mora, Guillermo.

If there is doubt about which language is used in most of the works, the form found most in reference sources of the person's country of residence or activity should be used. LC practice when reference sources cannot be found, or the person is not listed, is to use the form of the name in the person's native language but to change to another language if 80% of the works eventually use the name in that language. (*CSB* 47: 52) The choice made according to this rule may be altered by application of rules 22.3B2, 22.3B3, or 22.3C.

22.3B2.   Names in vernacular and Greek or Latin forms
The heading for a name that appears in both Latin or Greek and the vernacular in reference sources and/or in the person's works should be given in the form found most often in reference sources. For cases of doubt, the Latin or Greek is chosen for persons active before 1400 A.D. and the vernacular for persons active after 1400. Example:

> **Name in vernacular:** Dante Alighieri (with various spellings)
> **Name in Latin:** Dantes Aligerius
> **Form most commonly found in reference sources:** Dante
>   Alighieri
> **Heading:** Dante Alighieri, 1265-1321.

22.3B3.   Names written in the roman alphabet and established in an English form
The heading for a person entered under given name according to rule 22.8 or for a Roman of classical times is the English form if an English form is well established in English-language reference sources. The vernacular or Latin is used in cases of doubt. Example:

> **Name of saint in Latin:** Justinus
> **Name in English-language reference sources:** Justin
> **Heading:** Justin, Martyr, Saint.

22.3B4.   Other names
The heading for all other names found in two or more languages is the form found most often in reference sources of the person's country of residence or activity. Example:

> **Name on original work:** John Boyer Noss
> **Name on translation of original work:** Jān B. Nūs
> **Place of author's residence:** U.S.
> **Heading:** Noss, John Boyer.

22.3C.   Names written in a nonroman script
Names that must be romanized or transliterated present many problems. Some languages have a number of systems for romanization, and use of the different systems results in different spellings. In addition, there may be one or more English-language forms of some better known names. The rules in 22.3C give some guidance.

22.3C1.   Persons entered under given name, etc.
This rule, like 22.3B3, calls for entry under an English-language form, if one has become well established in English-language reference sources. (If more than one exists, choose the one that appears most frequently.) Example:

Romanizations of name: Movses Khorenãtsi
                        Moses Xorenc'i
English-language form of name: Moses of Khoren
Heading: Moses, of Khoren, 5th cent.

If there is no English form, or if one romanization cannot be determined to be predominant, the name should be romanized according to the cataloging agency's adopted romanization table.

A single LC rule interpretation addresses both rule 22.3C1 and rule 22.3C2. LC's policy for nonroman alphabet names entered under a given name or a surname is to search the name in *Academic American Encyclopedia*, *The Encyclopedia Americana*, and *Encyclopaedia Britannica* (15th ed.). If the name is in all three sources in a single form, that form is used. If it varies, the form in *Encyclopaedia Britannica* is used. If it is not found in all three sources, the systematic romanization is used. An exception is made for persons entered under *given* name who are not found in all three sources because of "specialized fame." In such cases major specialized encyclopedias, such as *New Catholic Encyclopedia*, are used. Another exception is for persons of very recent fame. For these, yearbooks to the encyclopedias and indexes to major newspapers are consulted. (*CSB* 40: 29–31)

22.3C2.   Persons entered under surname
Unlike the preceding rule, this one directs the cataloger to romanize a name entered under surname according to the table adopted by the cataloging agency. References are made from other romanized forms. If a name is found only in romanized form in the works involved, that form is used.

An alternative rule is given for 22.3C2: An English form, well established in English-language reference sources, may be used for the heading. This corresponds to the treatment of persons entered under given name, but is counter to the principle of entry under the name elements most commonly found in writers' works or in reference works in the language or country of residence or activity for persons other than writers. The Library of Congress is following the alternative rule. (*CSB* 40: 29–31) Their policy for application of the alternative rule is discussed above under discussion of rule 22.3C1. Example:

> **Heading in romanized form found in English-language reference sources:**
> Dostoyevsky, Fyodor, 1821-1881.
> **Romanized form appearing in the item:** Fyodor Dostoevsky
> **Systematic romanization according to LC's adopted tables:**
> Dostoevskiĭ, Fedor
> **Form most often found in English-language reference sources:**
> Dostoyevsky, Fyodor
> **Refer from:**
> Dostoevsky, Fyodor.
> Dostoevskiĭ, Fedor.

It should be noted that the alternative rule makes no provision for names for which there are no entries in English-language reference sources, unless the person uses Hebrew or Yiddish, in which case the romanized form found in the person's works is called for. Otherwise, when there are no entries in English-language sources, presumably, one should use the provision given in rule 22.3C1 for persons entered under given name: "If no English romanization is found ... romanize the name according to the table for the language adopted by the cataloguing agency."[6] Example:

> **Romanizations found in chief sources of information,**
> **but not in reference sources:**
>   Maîsiûte, Regina
>   Maciūte, Regina [romanization according to adopted table]
> **Heading:** Maciūte, Regina
>   **Refer from:** Maîsiûte, Regina.

22.3D.   Spelling

If variant spellings occur that are not the result of different romanizations, the form that represents an official orthographic change should be used, if this is applicable. Otherwise, one should choose the predominant spelling, or, in case of doubt, the spelling found in the first item cataloged. Example:

> **Variant spellings found:**   Thomas Decker
>   Thomas Dekker
>   Thomas Deckar
> **Predominant spelling:** Thomas Dekker
> **Heading:** Dekker, Thomas, ca. 1572-1632.

Entry Element: Selected Rules and Examples

RULE 22.4.   GENERAL RULE

22.4A.   When a person's name consists of more than one part, a choice must be made about which part will be the entry element. In general the entry element is the one that would usually be used in authoritative alphabetic lists in the person's own country or language. "Authoritative" is defined as meaning "who's who" type publications, not telephone directory type publications. However, if it is known that the person prefers some other entry element than would be the usual usage for that language or country, the person's preference is followed.

22.4B. Order of elements

The entry element is chosen according to rules 22.5–22.9, but the order of other elements is given here, covering the entry element as the first element in a name (22.4B1–22.4B2), the entry element not the first element of a name (22.4B3), or the entry element as the proper name in a title of nobility (22.4B4).

RULE 22.5.   ENTRY UNDER SURNAME

22.5A.   General rule

If a name contains a surname, the entry element should be the surname unless one of the following rules provides for a different entry element. (*See also* rules 22.6, 22.10, and 22.28.) Example:

> **Name on chief source of information:** Jill S. Slattery
> **Surname entry element:** Slattery
> **Heading:** Slattery, Jill S., 1943-

22.5B.   Element other than the first treated as a surname

A name that functions as a surname, even though it is not really a surname, is treated as if it were. Example:

> **Name on chief source of information:** Muḥammad Sa'īd Bāyirlī
> **Heading:** Bāyirlī, Muḥammad Sa'īd.
> **Refer from:** Muḥammad Sa'īd Bāyirlī.

22.5C.   Compound surnames

22.5C1.   Preliminary rule

Compound surnames consist of two or more proper names. The rules under rule 22.5C treat these and also some names that appear to be compound surnames. The rules are applied in the order given. References should be made from elements of a compound surname not chosen for entry.

22.5C2.   Preferred or established form known

The entry element for a compound surname of a person with a known preference should be the person's preferred entry element. Otherwise, the entry element should be the element under which it is given in reference sources from the person's country or in the person's language. Example:

> Lloyd George, David, 1863-1945.
> War memoirs of David Lloyd George

> [Note: Refer from: George, David Lloyd. George is his paternal surname.]

22.5C3.   Hyphenated surnames

Compound surnames that are hyphenated (even if only sometimes) should be entered under the first element. Example:

> **Heading under first part of hyphenated surname:**
> Boswell-Taylor, Harold.
> **Refer from:** Taylor, Harold Boswell- .

22.5C4-22.5C5.

Rules 22.5C4–22.5C5 cover all other compound surnames, including those of married women whose surnames consist of a surname before marriage and a husband's surname.

22.5D.   Surnames with separately written prefixes

LC's rule interpretation should be consulted for guidance on placement of constituent parts of a name in headings and references once the appropriate entry element has been determined according to the following rules. (*CSB* 23: 31–33)

22.5D1.   Articles and prepositions

Names that contain an article or a preposition or a combination of the two as part of the surname should be entered under the element that would normally be used in alphabetical lists from the person's country or in the person's language.

In *AACR2R* this rule contains many specific examples of names in different languages. Only the most basic of those rules are cited here.

DUTCH. Dutch names are entered under the part following the prefix with one exception: a name with the prefix *ver* is entered under the prefix. Example:

> **Heading:** Beek, Jan M. van der.
> **Refer from:** Van der Beek, Jan M.

ENGLISH. English names are entered under the prefix. Example:

> **Heading:** Van Buren, Ariane.
> **Refer from:** Buren, Ariane van

FRENCH and GERMAN. French and German names in which the prefix is an article or a contraction of an article and a preposition are entered under the prefix. Examples:

> **Heading:** Le Bihan, Alain.
> **Refer from:** Bihan, Alain Le
> **Heading:** Vom Scheidt, Jürgen, 1940-
> **Refer from:** Scheidt, Jürgen vom

All other French and German names with prefixes are entered under the element following the prefix. Examples:

> **Heading:** La Fontaine, Jean de, 1621-1695.
> **Refer from:** Fontaine, Jean de la
> **[Note: Entry is under the article following the preposition.]**

> **Heading:** Weizsäcker, Carl Christian von

ITALIAN. Modern Italian names are entered under the prefix. Example:

> **Heading:** De Filippo, Peppino.
> **Refer from:** Filippo, Peppino de

In order to determine the correct entry element for medieval and early modern Italian names, reference sources should be consulted. Example:

> **Heading:** Medici, Lorenzo de'

SPANISH. Spanish names that have a prefix that consists only of an article are entered under the prefix. Otherwise, a name is entered under the element following the prefix. Example:

> **Heading:** Lorenzo, Pedro de.

22.5D2-22.5E.   Other prefixes

In all languages, when the prefix is not an article or a preposition or a combination of the two, or when the prefix is hyphenated or combined with the name, the entry element should be the prefix. Example:

> **Heading:** MacIntyre, Elisabeth.

RULE 22.6. ENTRY UNDER TITLE OF NOBILITY

If a person is commonly known by a title of nobility, the proper name in that title should be the entry element. This rule applies to persons who use titles rather than surnames in their works or, if there are no textual works to consult, to those persons who are listed by title in reference sources that do not list all members of the nobility under title. The proper name in the title is followed by the personal name in direct order, and the personal name is followed by the term of rank. Unused forenames are not included. A reference is made from the personal surname unless it is the same as the proper name in the title. The rule in *AACR2R* should be consulted for further details.

This rule is closely related to rules 22.4B4 and 22.12. The three result in the same form of name, but they approach this type of name from the three viewpoints of order of elements, entry element, and additions to names.

RULE 22.8. ENTRY UNDER GIVEN NAME, ETC.

If a person is not identified by a title of nobility and the name does not include a surname, the entry element should be the part of the name that is the entry element in reference sources. Any words or phrases that are commonly associated with the name in that person's works or in reference sources should be included, preceded by a comma. Example:

Heading: Paul, of Aleppo, Archdeacon, fl. 1654-1666.

Specific parts of this rule address names that include a patronymic and names of royal persons. LC rule interpretations give guidelines for more complicated given name entries and should be consulted for more guidance. (*CSB* 44: 46; *CSB* 71: 55–56)

22.10–22.11.

Rules 22.10–22.11 give instructions for entry elements when all one has for a name are initials, letters, numerals, or phrases. These are to be entered in direct order if they do not contain a real name. More specialized rules cover entry of phrases that contain names, and these should be consulted when needed.

Additions to Names: Selected Rules and Examples

General

RULE 22.12. TITLES OF NOBILITY AND TERMS OF HONOUR

22.12A. If a nobleman or noblewoman is not entered under title according to rule 22.6, but the title or a part of the title usually appears with the name, the title of nobility should be added in the vernacular to the personal name. Example:

Heading: John, of Gaunt, Duke of Lancaster, 1340-1399.

22.12B. British terms of honour

There are four British terms of honour that are to be added to a name if they usually appear with the name in the person's works or in reference sources. They are: Sir, Dame, Lord, Lady. Note that the terms "Hon." and "bart." formerly used in headings are not now authorized.

In *AACR2R* this rule goes on to distinguish the times when such terms should be added after the forenames and when they should be inserted before forenames. However, LC, due to the historical incapability of its computer systems to handle these as nonfiling characters, places all terms of honour and address after the forenames. (*CSB* 18: 55) This situation may change with the implementation of LC's new integrated library system. Example:

Heading: Stephen, James Fitzjames, Sir, 1829-1894.

[Note: Position of term is LC practice. According to *AACR2R*, heading should be: Stephen, Sir James Fitzjames, 1829-1894.]

Heading: Hepworth, Barbara, Dame, 1903-1975.

[Note: Position of term is LC practice. *AACR2R* form: Hepworth, Dame Barbara, 1903-1975.]

RULE 22.13.   SAINTS

The word *Saint* is added after a saint's given name unless the person was a pope, emperor, empress, king, or queen. In those cases the latter epithet takes precedence over *Saint*, and one follows rules 22.16A–22.16B. Example:

Heading: Joan, of Arc, Saint, 1412-1431.

RULE 22.15.   ADDITIONS TO NAMES ENTERED UNDER SURNAME

22.15A.   When a name consists only of a surname with an accompanying word or phrase in the person's works or in reference sources, the associated word or phrase should be added after the surname. A reference is made from the name in direct order if it would be useful. LC generally makes the direct order reference only when such a heading is a pseudonym or assumed name. (*CSB* 39: 13) Example:

Heading: Jefferson, Mr., of Gray's Inn.
Refer from: Mr. Jefferson of Gray's Inn.

22.15B.   **Terms of address of married women**

When a woman is identified only by "Mrs." with her husband's name, the term "Mrs." is added. Example:

Heading: Bruce, William, Mrs.

[Note: Form above is LC practice. *AACR2R* form: Bruce, Mrs. William.]

22.15C.   Titles or terms other than those in the preceding rules are not added to names entered under surname except when necessary to distinguish between otherwise identical names for which dates are not available. Example:

Name on chief source of information: Dr. Mary Lyon
Heading: Lyon, Mary.

RULE 22.16.   ADDITIONS TO NAMES ENTERED UNDER GIVEN NAME, ETC.

22.16A.   **Royalty**

This rule in *AACR2R* has four specific subsections with accompanying examples. The essence of the rule is that royal persons are entered under the names by which they are known. A royal name may include a house, dynasty, or surname (*see* rule 22.8C in *AACR2R*) or a Roman numeral. A phrase (in English, if possible) consisting of title and state governed follows the name of a person with the highest royal status in a state. Other epithets are not added, but are "referred from." Consorts, children, and grandchildren of rulers have a title added to their names (again in English, if possible) plus the name of the ruler to whom related. Examples:

> **Heading:** Nikolaĭ Mikhaĭlovich, Grand Duke of Russia, 1859-1919.
> **Heading:** William, Prince, grandson of Elizabeth II, Queen of Great Britain, 1982-

22.16B. Popes

22.16C. Bishops, etc.

22.16D. Other persons of religious vocation
Rules 22.16B–22.16D call for addition of the words *Pope*, *Bishop*, *Archbishop*, *Cardinal*, and other titles in English (if there is an English equivalent) to the names of persons who are high ecclesiastical officials. The name of the latest see is also added to some titles. For other persons of religious vocation who are entered under given name, titles or terms of address are added in the vernacular. Initials of a Christian religious order regularly used by the person are also added. Examples:

> **Heading:** John Paul II, Pope, 1920-
> **Heading:** Maria Crocifissa di Gesu, madre, 1713-1787.

Additions to Distinguish Identical Names

RULE 22.17. DATES
Birth and death dates are added as the last element of a heading in order to distinguish between two otherwise identical headings. An option to this rule allows adding the date(s) even when there is no conflict. LC is applying this option when the date is known at the time the heading is first established or later if the heading must be revised anyway. For persons living in the twentieth century or later, LC only adds precise dates. Less precise dates may be added to the headings for pre-twentieth century persons. (*CSB* 83: 23–24) Examples:

Addition of dates for a living person:

> Vieweg-Marks, Karin, 1957-

Addition of dates when references differ as to year of birth; 1496 is probable:

> Fox, Edward, Bishop of Hereford, 1496?-1538.

Addition of dates when year of birth unknown:

> Timberlake, Henry, d. 1626.

Addition of dates when years of birth and death unknown, but date of activity is known. (Not used for twentieth century):

> Gardiner, Richard, fl. 1599-1603.

[Note: "fl." is the *AACR2R* abbreviation for "flourished."]

Day, month, and year of birth added to distinguish from others of same name and same year of birth:

Fischer, John, 1910 Apr. 27-

Addition of probable dates:

Ford, John, 1586-ca. 1640.

RULE 22.18.   FULLER FORMS

When two names as prescribed by the preceding rules are identical and a fuller form of one or both names is known, the fuller form is added in parentheses in order to distinguish between the two names. The rule calls for a reference from the full form when appropriate. In many catalogs such references are superfluous, especially when the initial in the name is for a second or later forename. Example:

Heading: Roberts, J.O. (Jack O.)
Refer from: Roberts, Jack O.

This rule allows the option of making the above additions even when not necessary to distinguish identical names except that, when following the option, one is not to add:

"unused forenames to headings that contain forenames

initials of names that are not part of the heading

unused parts of surnames to headings that contain surnames."[7]

LC is following the option when the information is known with certainty. A rule interpretation gives guidelines for how much of the name to include in the parenthetical statement and where to place it. Once a heading has been established without the names in parentheses, they are not added if they become known later unless the heading must be changed for some other reason (e.g., it comes in conflict with another heading). (*CSB* 57: 20–21)

RULE 22.19.   DISTINGUISHING TERMS and
RULE 22.20.   UNDIFFERENTIATED NAMES

When dates or fuller forms are not available to distinguish between identical names, certain other additions may be made following rule 22.19. For given names, a brief term may be devised (e.g., "poet") and added in parentheses. For surname entries, a term of address, title of position, initials of academic degree, etc., that appears with the name in works or reference sources may be added. Example:

Heading: Chapman, William H., M.A.

Otherwise, according to rule 22.20 the same heading is used for all persons with the same name.

22.21–22.28.

Rules 22.21–22.28 are special rules for names in certain languages and should be consulted as needed.

GEOGRAPHIC NAMES

This section covers chapter 23 in *AACR2R*, which treats the form of heading for any geographic name that may be used as a main or added entry heading. This includes names for places that now are or once were jurisdictional entities. It does not include names that cannot be jurisdictions, such as continents, mountains, and rivers. Yet there is an attempt in *AACR2R* to separate rules for place names that are "only" geographic names from those that are names of jurisdictions. Therefore, one rule in chapter 24, "Headings for Corporate Bodies" (rule 24.6), deals with what seem to be geographic names; but the rule actually deals with jurisdictions. Another rule, 24.3E, covers "conventional" names of governments and gives instructions to use the geographic name as constructed in chapter 23. Other rules throughout chapter 24 cover additions of geographic names to corporate names for the purpose of identification or distinction. It can be seen, then, that the cataloger cannot rely solely on chapter 23 for the construction of names that appear to be geographic.

In chapter 23 of *AACR2R* there are rules for choice of name (rules 23.2–23.3), additions to place names (rule 23.4), and modification of place names (rule 23.5). Problems involved in choice of name often involve choice between an English form and a form in some other language. Choice may also involve which name to use when the name of a place has changed. For additions to place names, problems may involve decisions about which larger place names are most useful for identification. (For example, should the name of the county, state, and/or country be added to the name of a town?) A problem that may require modification of a name involves the use of a term indicating type of jurisdiction. The problem is whether that term comes first, while the name is commonly known or listed under another element of the name (e.g., Kreis Lippe, a county in Germany, is commonly listed under Lippe). The purpose of this chapter is to demonstrate the rules used to resolve these problems.

A heading created using *AACR2R*, Chapter 23, is coded 110, 651, 710, or 810 in the MARC 21 format, depending upon whether it functions as a main entry, subject heading, or added entry or begins a series. Codes 110, 710, and 810 are for corporate names, and in these cases the name of a jurisdiction alone is coded as a corporate name. However, in the subject fields there are separate numbers for corporate names (610) and geographic names (651). Jurisdictions that stand alone are coded as geographic names.

Selected Rules and Examples

RULE 23.2.   GENERAL RULES
These general rules involve choice of a name from among variant forms of a name that may be found.

23.2A.   English form
AACR2R calls for use of the English form of a place name and specifies that this form should be determined from gazetteers and other reference sources from English-speaking countries. When there is doubt as to whether the English form is generally used, the vernacular form is to be used. Examples:

Forms of name found:	Brasil
	Brazil
Heading: Brazil	
Forms of name found:	Bucharest
	Bucuresti
	Bucurescĭ
	Bukharest
	Bucarest
Heading:	Bucharest (Romania)

LC bases headings for United States names on the Geographic Names Information System (GNIS), the United States Board on Geographical Names' (BGN) domestic names system. The *Rand McNally Commercial Atlas and Marketing Guide* is used as backup when Web access is unavailable. Names from Australia and New Zealand, are based on the GEOnet Names Server (GNS) of the Defense Mapping Agency, again with a recent gazetteer used as backup. Names from Great Britain are based on a recent edition of the *Bartholomew Gazetteer of Place in Great Britain*; headings for place names in Canada are those provided by the National Library of Canada. For other names, the heading is based on the form found in the work being cataloged, in consultation with the form found on the GNS Web site. An English form in general use is always used, even when the BGN-approved form is in the vernacular. LC's rule interpretation provides the current Web address for the resources mentioned in this paragraph. (*CSB* 83: 25–26)

LC has issued special decisions in a number of complicated cases, even where they contradict the prescriptions of *AACR2R*. These include China, Germany (pre- and post-unification), Great Britain, Korea, the several entities referred to as "London", the former Soviet Union, and Washington, D.C. (*CSB* 83: 28–29)

23.2B.   Vernacular form

23.2B1.   If there is no English form in general use, the form in the official language of the country is used. Examples:

> **Headings:**   [no English form in use]
> Pistoia (Italy)
> Tétaigne (France)
> Tromsø (Norway)
> **Heading:**   [English form, Brunswick, not in general use]
> Braunschweig (Germany)

In cases where there is more than one official language in a country, the most common form found in English-language reference sources is used. Example:

> **Forms of name found:**   Bruxelles
> Brüssel
> Brussels
> **Form most often found in English-language sources:**   Brussels
> **Heading:**   Brussels (Belgium)

Note: There is no rule for variations of spelling of the name in the same language. Because of the close association in the rules of geographic names and corporate names, it is assumed that needed rules, such as the one for spelling, may be taken from *AACR2R* chapter 24 and applied to geographic names. Rule 24.2C states that for a name with variant spellings, the one that represents an official change in orthography should be used if this applies or else the predominant spelling should be used. Example:

Original spelling:	Tandjungpinang, Indonesia
New official spelling:	Tanjungpinang, Indonesia
Variants also found:	Tandjoengpinang
	Tandjung Pinang
	Tanjung Pinang
Heading:	Tanjungpinang (Indonesia)

RULE 23.3. CHANGES OF NAME

The essence of this rule is that if the name of a place changes, one should use on catalog records as many of the names as are required by rules in *AACR2R*, chapter 24. The rule mentions specifically rules 24.3E, 24.4C6, and 24.7B4 but allows for other relevant rules as well. Examples:

> **In 1971, the Town of Whitchurch-Stouffville was created, incorporating the Village of Stouffville in Ontario.**
> **A work requiring Stouffville as a heading prior to 1971 would use the heading:**
> Stouffville (Ont.)

> **A work requiring Stouffville as a heading in 1971 or later would use the heading:**
> Stouffville (Whitchurch-Stouffville, Ont.)

> **In 1971 East Pakistan became Bangladesh. A corporate body whose lifetime spanned the change would have the latest name of the country added, even for items relevant only to the body during the time the country was known as East Pakistan, e.g.,**
> Institution of Engineers (Bangladesh)
> *not* Institution of Engineers (East Pakistan)

RULE 23.4. ADDITIONS

23.4A. Punctuation

Additions to place names that are used as entry elements are made in parentheses. Example:

> Staunton (Va.)

When the whole place name is used as an addition, it is enclosed in parentheses with a comma preceding the larger place. Example:

> Second Presbyterian Church (Staunton, Va.)

23.4B. General rule

Any place name (other than that of a country or that of a state, etc., listed in rule 23.4C1 or rule 23.4D1) should have added to it the name of a larger place, following rules 23.4C–23.4F. Additional instructions for place names used as headings for governments are given in rule 24.6. Instructions for abbreviations for additions are given in Appendix B of *AACR2R*.

In a rule interpretation for this rule, LC addresses three situations not covered by rules 23.4C–23.4F: (*CSB* 41: 44–45)

1) If an island or island group is a jurisdiction, the name of the larger jurisdiction should be added only when the island or island group is located near the larger jurisdiction. Example:

> Guardia Island (Spain)
> Madeira Islands

2) When a larger place that is being added has changed its name and if the smaller place existed through the name change, the current larger place name should be added, with a reference from the place with the earlier larger place name. Example:

> Georgetown (Guyana)

with a reference from:

> Georgetown (British Guiana)

3) The additions prescribed in rule 24.6 should not be added as part of the qualifier being added under rule 23.4B. Example:

> St. Romuald (Québec)
> *not* St. Romuald (Québec, Province)

23.4C. Places in Australia, Canada, Malaysia, United States, U.S.S.R., or Yugoslavia

23.4C1. States, etc.

No addition should be made to the name of a state, province, etc., of one of the countries covered by this rule. Examples:

> California
> *not* California (U.S.)

> Hrvatska Croatia
> *not* Hrvatska Croatia (Yugoslavia)

LC makes references from the names of states of Malaysia qualified with "(Malaysia)." (*CSB* 41: 46) Example:

> Kedah

with reference from:

> Kedah (Malaysia)

For the constituent republics of the former Soviet Union (before 1992), and their successor states (after 1991), LC uses the following headings: (*CSB* 81: 33)

Armenian S.S.R.	Armenia (Republic)
Azerbaijan S.S.R.	Azerbaijan
Byerlorussian S.S.R.	Belarus
Estonia	Estonia
Georgian S.S.R.	Georgia (Republic)
Kazakh S.S.R.	Kazakhstan
Kirghiz S.S.R.	Kyrgyzstan
Latvia	Latvia
Lithuania	Lithuania
Moldavian S.S.R. [before 1990]	Moldova [after 1989]
Russian S.F.S.R.	Russia (Federation)
Tajik S.S.R.	Tajikistan
Turkmen S.S.R.	Turkmenistan
Ukraine	Ukraine
Uzbek S.S.R.	Uzbekistan

23.4C2.   Other places

Add the name of the state, province, or territory to a place located in one of the countries covered by this rule. Places located in cities are treated according to rule 23.4F2. Examples:

> Delmont (Pa.)
> Montreal (Québec)
> Melbourne (Vic.)

23.4D.   Places in the British Isles

23.4D1.   No addition should be made to the names of the parts of the British Isles: England, the Republic of Ireland, Northern Ireland, Scotland, Wales, the Isle of Man, and the Channel Islands.

23.4D2.   For a place located in one of the above-named parts of the British Isles, one of the following names is added to the heading, as appropriate: England, Ireland (for the Republic of Ireland), Northern Ireland, Scotland, Wales, Isle of Man, or Channel Islands. Examples:

> Antrim (Northern Ireland)
> Warwickshire (England)
> Ayrshire (Scotland)
> Cambridge (England)
> Mold (Wales)
> Tralee (Ireland)

23.4E.   Other places

If a place is not covered by 23.4C–23.4D, the name of the country in which it lies is added. Examples:

> Lund (Sweden)
> Siena (Italy)
> Rio de Janeiro (Brazil)

23.4F.   Further additions

If two places with the same name are not sufficiently distinguished with additions as instructed in rules 23.4C–23.4E, a word or phrase commonly used with them may be used or an appropriate smaller place may be added before the larger place. Examples:

> Mount Vernon (Westchester County, N.Y.)
> Mount Vernon (Erie County, N.Y.)

A place otherwise difficult to identify, such as a community within a city, may also have an appropriate smaller place added before the larger place. Examples:

> Bregninge (Svendborg, Denmark)
> Chinatown (San Francisco, Calif.)

RULE 23.5.   PLACE NAMES INCLUDING OR REQUIRING A TERM INDICATING A TYPE OF JURISDICTION

23.5A.   When the first element of a place name indicates a type of jurisdiction but the place is usually listed under another name element in reference sources of the country, the term indicating type of jurisdiction should be omitted. Example:

> **Kreis Lippe in Germany is commonly listed under Lippe in German lists.**
> **Heading:** Lippe (Germany : Kreis)
>
> [Note: In this example, *Kreis* is omitted from the first element according to this rule, but it is added in the qualifier to distinguish it from the principality that had the name *Lippe*, as called for in the *AACR2R* chapter on corporate names.]

The type of jurisdiction is included in all cases that do not fit the above criteria. Example:

> Dutchess County (N.Y.)

Note: The term *county* should be included for U.S. counties, even though many U.S. atlases list counties by name only under the caption *counties* and therefore omit the word *county* with the name. Note that *county* is spelled out. Most U.S. counties have been established by LC and other libraries in the past using *Co.* and are being changed by LC as new occasions for use of each county name arise.

23.5B.   Occasionally a place name does not include a term indicating type of jurisdiction, but such a term is required for differentiating between two identical names. If this is the case, rule 24.6 should be applied. Example:

> Chimaltenango (Guatemala : Dept.)
>
> [Note: There is also a municipality named Chimaltenango.]

Note: LC continues to abbreviate *Department* as *Dept.*, even though it is not allowed to be abbreviated in headings according to *AACR2R*, Appendix B, "Abbreviations." (*CSB* 32: 58)

CORPORATE NAMES

This section covers the rules for construction of names of corporate bodies. *Corporate body* is defined in rule 21.1B1 of *AACR2R98* as "an organization or a group of persons that is identified by a particular name and that acts, or may act, as an entity."[8] In general, entry of a corporate body is under the name the body itself uses except when the rules specify entry under a higher or related body or under the name of a government. Like the principle in use for personal names, the principle for corporate names is to choose the name the corporate body itself generally uses (including conventional names), even if that name is not the official one. Unlike personal names, however, when the name of a corporate body changes, a new heading is made under that name with cross references to and from various other former and related names.

Following the general rule (rule 24.1), there are rules for choice of names (rules 24.2–24.3) and for additions, omissions, and modifications (rules 24.4–24.11). These are followed by rules for subordinate and related bodies in general (rules 24.12–24.16), for government bodies and officials (rules 24.17–24.26), and for religious bodies and officials (rule 24.27). Problems involved in choice of name include choice among variant forms found in items issued by a body, such as official name or acronym or short form, choice among variant spellings (including differences in romanization), and choice among different languages. Problems requiring additions, omissions, or other modifications include the need to distinguish between two or more bodies with the same name, the need to provide adequate identification for a name that does not convey the idea of a corporate body, and the desire to omit unnecessary or excess terms such as *incorporated* or *biennial*. In dealing with a subordinate body, the cataloger must decide whether the body can be entered directly under its own name or must be entered under its higher body, and because government and religious bodies present special problems in this area, the cataloger must know whether a subordinate body belongs in one of these two groups before applying the rules. The purpose of this section is to demonstrate only the most important problems of corporate entry. For more detail, the cataloger should consult *AACR2R*, chapter 24.

As with personal names, there are certain previously established headings for corporate bodies that LC considered "*AACR2* compatible" from January 2, 1981, to September 1, 1982 (*see* discussion on page 202 in the personal names section of this chapter). These are summarized with examples in *Cataloging Service Bulletin.* (*CSB* 76: 29–30)

A heading created using *AACR2R*, Chapter 24, is coded 110, 111, 610, 611, 710, 711, 810, or 811 in the MARC 21 format, depending upon whether it functions as a main entry, subject heading, or added entry or begins a series. The codes ending in "11" are for conference names. The codes ending in "10" are for all other corporate names.

General Rules: Selected Rules and Examples

RULE 24.1.   GENERAL RULE

24.1A.   A corporate body is to be entered directly under its own name unless later rules instruct that it be entered subordinately to a higher body or to a government. Although the rule does not say so, there are also religious bodies that must be entered subordinately. Therefore, the cataloger must first determine whether a body is a government or religious body and start with those rules if it is: rules 24.17–24.26 for government bodies; rule 24.27 for religious bodies. If a body is neither government nor religious but is subordinate to another body, rules 24.12–24.16 must be consulted. In many cases one will be referred back to this rule (rule 24.1), because the body can be entered under its own name even though it is a subordinate body.

The form of the name of a corporate body is determined from items issued by the body in its language, if possible, or from reference sources. The punctuation usage of the body should be followed (e.g., whether or not periods are included after initials depends upon the predominant usage by the body).

References from different forms of a corporate body name are prescribed in the *AACR2R* reference chapter, rule 26.3. Examples:

> **Heading:** Lawyer's Committee for Civil Rights Under Law.

> **Heading:** W.K. Kellogg Arabian Horse Center.
> **Refer from:** Kellogg Arabian Horse Center.

> **Heading:** Nelliston Community Group.

> **Heading:** Pro Musica Antiqua, Prague.
> **Refer from:** Symposium "Pro Musica Antiqua" Prag.

A rule interpretation from LC gives guidance for punctuating and spacing corporate names. (*CSB* 76: 28–29)

It should also be noted here that for a corporate name that itself includes the name of a place at the end, the punctuation used by the body is retained. This means that some names may be established ending with a place preceded by a comma and a space, and others may be established with a place enclosed in parentheses. These have nothing to do with the additions prescribed in rule 24.4 and should not be interpreted as "errors." Example:

> California State University, San Diego
> *not* California State University (San Diego)

24.1B.   Romanization

The name of a body that is written in a nonroman script is romanized using the table adopted by the cataloging agency. This means that even if a romanized form of the name appears in items issued by a body, that form may be used only if it corresponds to the table adopted by the cataloging agency. References are made from other romanizations. Example:

> **Romanization of name originally in nonroman script**
> **with reference from the English form of the name:**
> **Heading:** Akademiia nauk SSSR.
> **Refer from:** Academy of Sciences of the U.S.S.R.

A footnote in *AACR2R* allows an alternative to this rule: a romanized form appearing in items issued by the body is used with references from other romanizations. LC is not applying the alternative rule. (*CSB* 44: 53)

24.1C.   Changes of name

When a corporate body changes its name, a new heading is established for the new name. A bibliographic record for an item relating to the old name has the old name as a heading, while a bibliographic record for an item relating to the new name has the new name as a heading. References are made referring to each name from the other. Example:

Explanatory reference showing each name a corporate body has used:

> The Long Range Planning Service of the Stanford Research Institute became the Business Intelligence Program in April 1976. On May 16, 1977, the Institute changed its name to S.R.I. International.
> Works by these bodies are found under the following headings according to the name used at the time of publication:
> Stanford Research Institute. Long Range Planning Service.
> Business Intelligence Program (SRI International)

RULE 24.2.   VARIANT NAMES. GENERAL RULES

Variant names here do not include those resulting from official changes of names. Such changes are covered by 24.1. LC has a rule interpretation that explains what are to be treated as variant names. (*CSB* 47: 54–55)

24.2B.   When different name forms are found in various places in items issued by a corporate body, the form found in chief sources of information should be used. Example:

> **Name on title page:** Michael Bradner Associates
> **Forms of name found elsewhere in work:**
> Mike Bradner & Associates
> Mike Bradner and Associates
> **Heading:** Michael Bradner Associates.
> **Refer from:**   Mike Bradner and Associates.
> Bradner Associates.

24.2C.   When there are variant spellings of a name in items issued by the body, the one that represents an official change in orthography should be used, if this applies, or if not, the predominant spelling should be chosen. Example:

> **Name on some title pages:** Allgemeines deutsches Commersbuch
> **Name on most title pages:** Allgemeines deutsches Kommersbuch
> **Heading:** Allgemeines deutsches Kommersbuch.
> **Refer from:** Allgemeines deutsches Commersbuch.

24.2D.   When different name forms appear in the chief source of information, the one presented formally should be used if that is applicable, or the predominant form should be used if no form is presented formally or all are equally presented. *AACR2R* prescribes that if no form is predominant, a short form that distinguishes this body from others with a similar name should be used in preference to a longer form. However, a rule interpretation from LC indicates that if a body's initials or acronym appear formally with the full form, the full form should be chosen for the heading. (*CSB* 44: 53–54) Example:

> **Names on title page:** GAAG, the Guerrilla Art Action Group
> **Neither form formally presented. No predominant form.**
> *AACR2R* **heading:** GAAG.
> **Refer from:** Guerrilla Art Action Group
> **LC choice of heading:** Guerrilla Art Action Group.
> **LC reference from:** GAAG

If a brief form does not differentiate a body from another with the same name, a form found in reference sources or the official form, in that order of preference, should be used. For example, the short form *NEA* for the National Education Association of the United States does not distinguish it from other bodies known as NEA: Nouvelles Editions africaines, National Endowment for the Arts, or the OECD Nuclear Energy Agency.

RULE 24.3   VARIANT NAMES. SPECIAL RULES

24.3A.   Language

This rule sets up an order of precedence to follow when the name of a body appears in different languages:

1. The form in the official language of the body

2. An English-language form if there is more than one official language and one is English

3. The predominant language

4. English, French, German, Spanish, or Russian, in that order

5. The language that comes first in English alphabetic order

An LC rule interpretation inserts another criterion between 3 and 4: if one does not know the official language of the body, the official language of the country in which the body is located is used (if the country has a single official language). (*CSB* 45: 54) Example:

> **Names on publications:**
> Schweizerische Hochschulrektoren-Konferenz, Kommission für Hochschulplanung
> Commission de planification de la Conférence des recteurs des universités suisses
> **Official language:** German
> **Heading:** Schweizerische Hochschulrektoren-Konferenz.
> Kommission für Hochschulplanung.
> **Refer from French form.**

An alternative to this rule allows use of a form of language appropriate to the catalog's users if the application of the rule results in a language not familiar to the users. LC is not following this alternative. (*CSB* 45: 54)

24.3B.   Language. International bodies

The English form of an international body is used if the name appears in English in its publications. Otherwise, the preceding rule, rule 24.3A, is used. Example:

> **Names on title page:**
> al-Maṣrif al-'Arabi lil-Tanmiyah al-Iqtiṣādiyah fī Afrīqyā
> Arab Bank for Economic Development in Africa
> Banque Arabe de développement économique en Afrique
> **Heading:** Arab Bank for Economic Development in Africa.
> **Refer from the names in Arabic and French.**

24.3C.   Conventional name

24.3C1.   General rule

A conventional name that is often used to identify a corporate body in reference sources in its own language should be used in place of an official name. Example:

> **Conventional name:** Abbey of Bury St. Edmunds.
> **Official name:** Benedictine Abbey of Bury St. Edmunds
>   in Suffolk

[Heading consists of conventional name, with reference from official name.]

24.3C2.   Ancient and international bodies

When an English form of name of an ancient body or of a body of international character has become very well known in English-language usage, this form should be used. A footnote comments that this rule applies to such bodies as religious bodies, fraternal and knightly orders, church councils, and diplomatic conferences. Examples:

> **Heading:** Orthodox Eastern Church.
> **Refer from:** [Hēmerologion tēs Ekklēsias tēs Hellados]
>   Ἡμερολόγιον τῆς Ἐκκλησίας τῆς Ἑλλάδος

> **Heading:** Catholic Church. Canadian Catholic Conference.
> **Refer from French forms of name.**

24.3D.   Religious orders and societies

The best known form of name for a religious order or society should be used. An English form is preferred, if one exists. Otherwise, the language of the country of origin is used. Example:

> **Heading:** White Fathers.
> **Refer from:** Pères blancs

24.3E.   Governments

The conventional name of a government is preferred unless there is an official name in common use. The name of the geographic area over which the government has jurisdiction serves as the conventional name. Examples:

> Jersey City (N.J.)
> *not* City of Jersey City

> Korea (North)
> *not* Democratic People's Republic of Korea

> San Marino
> *not* Most Serene Republic of San Marino

24.3F.   Conferences, congresses, meetings, etc.

When variant forms of a conference name appear in the chief source of information, one that includes the name (or initials) of a body associated with the conference should be chosen, if possible. If, however, the meeting is *subordinate* to the body, rule 24.13A, Type 6 should be applied. Example:

> **Name of meeting:** ALI-ABA Course of Study: Partnerships:
> UPA, ULPA, Securities, Taxation, and Bankruptcy
> **Name appears both with and without the initials of the**
> **American Law Institute and the American Bar Association.**
> **Heading:** ALI-ABA Course of Study: Partnerships: UPA, ULPA,
> Securities, Taxation, and Bankruptcy (1990 : Seattle)
> **Refer from:** Course of Study: Partnerships: UPA, ULPA,
> Securities, Taxation, and Bankruptcy.

Additions, Omissions, and Modifications:
Selected Rules and Examples

RULE 24.4.   ADDITIONS

24.4A.   General rule

The subrules under rule 24.4 give general directions for making additions to corporate names. Special types of corporate names may need more specialized types of additions, which are covered in rules 24.6–24.11. All additions to corporate names are enclosed in parentheses.

24.4B.   Names not conveying the idea of a corporate body

When a corporate body name does not sound like that of a corporate body, a designation is added in English. A rule interpretation from LC that gives guidance in determining when such designations are needed (e.g., for ships, performing groups, etc.) should be consulted when needed. (*CSB* 49: 30–32) Examples:

ABBA (Musical group)

International Road Safety (Association)

But (Yacht)

24.4C.   Two or more bodies with the same or similar names

24.4C1.   General rule

When two or more corporate name headings are identical or so similar that they could be easily confused, a word or phrase must be added to each according to the subrules under rule 24.4C. Such additions may also be made when they would merely assist understanding. A rule interpretation explains how LC is applying this rule. In general additions are made to every government body name that is entered under its own name unless the government's name (or an understandable substitute for it) is already part of the name. An exception is made for government institutions (e.g., schools, libraries, hospitals). If one of these or if a nongovernment body is entered under its own name, a qualifier is added if it is needed for understanding the nature or purpose of the body. The rule interpretation goes on to elaborate upon choice of qualifiers and the forms qualifiers should take. (*CSB* 65: 20-21)

24.4C2–24.4C7.   Rules 24.4C2–24.4C4 authorize addition of place names— country, state, province, etc.—for a body that is national, provincial, etc., in character or of local place names for a body whose character is essentially local. If a place is not appropriate, rules 24.4C5–24.4C7 provide for addition of the name of an institution, the inclusive years of existence, or some other appropriate general designation in English. Example:

Addition of country to corporate name:

> National Committee on the Status of Women (India)
>
> [Note: This name could be held by similar groups in several countries. Therefore, the name of the country is added.]

It should be noted that when a place is used as a qualifier, if it is a place that is itself qualified by a larger place according to *AACR2R* chapter 23, the smaller and the larger place are both used in the qualifier of the corporate body. Thus, for a corporate body in Oklahoma City, the name of the city alone cannot be used as qualifier. It must be: (Oklahoma City, Okla.).

RULE 24.5.   OMISSIONS

24.5A–24.5C.   These rules require omission of certain elements from corporate names: initial articles are omitted unless the heading is to be filed under the article; terms indicating incorporation, etc., are omitted unless they are an integral part of the name or are needed to clarify the fact that the name is that of a corporate body. Other required omissions occur in rare instances, and the cataloger should consult *AACR2R* for them. Examples:

Entry of name omitting initial article:

> **Note giving title as shown on item in hand:**
> At head of title: The Daily Telegraph.

> **Heading made with initial article omitted:**
> Daily Telegraph (London, England).

Entry of name omitting term indicating incorporation:

> **Name appearing on publications:**
> Firestone Tire and Rubber Company, Inc.

> **Cataloger's judgment:** *Inc.* not necessary for clarification
> as a corporate body

> **Heading:** Firestone Tire and Rubber Company.

Entry of name retaining term indicating incorporation.

> **Information in source about corporate body:**
> [Produced and distributed by Alternate Choice, Inc.]

> **Heading made for body with term of incorporation retained:**
> Alternate Choice, Inc.

RULE 24.6.   GOVERNMENTS. ADDITIONS

As mentioned in the geographic names section of this chapter, this rule is an attempt to give directions for entry of names of jurisdictions—distinct from the rules given for strictly geographic names. However, they are not totally separate, because this rule says that if names have not been differentiated by use of rule 23.4, then further addition according to rule 24.6 should be made.

LC has elaborated upon how it interprets this rule (*CSB* 78: 62–63), because it is not clear from the rule whether additions should be made to *both* conflicting names in all cases.

A succession of jurisdictions that have had the same name are all entered under one heading. Examples:

North Carolina   Hawaii
not   North Carolina (Colony)   *not*   Hawaii (Kingdom)
         North Carolina (State)   Hawaii (Republic)
                                                 Hawaii (State)

The name of a sovereign nation that is the same as the name of another place is not qualified. Example:

Italy
Italy (Tex.)

A third elaboration on this rule distinguishes between situations where the name of a place within a jurisdiction conflicts with the name of the jurisdiction and situations where the name of a jurisdiction conflicts with the name of a place in another jurisdiction. In the first situation, the name of the larger jurisdiction is qualified with the name of the type of government. Example:

Québec (Québec)   **[name of city]**
Québec (Province)   **[name of larger jurisdiction]**

In the second situation, only the name of the place in another jurisdiction is qualified. Example:

Alberta (Va.)
Alberta
not Alberta (Province)

An exception is made for the state of Washington. It is entered:

Washington (State)

24.6B.   If a jurisdiction is not a city or town and must have an addition because of conflict with another name, the type of jurisdiction is given in English, if there is an English equivalent; otherwise, it is given in the vernacular. Examples:

São Paulo (Brazil)
São Paulo (Brazil : State)
Alessandria (Italy : Province)
Esberg (Denmark : Kommune)

RULE 24.7.   CONFERENCES, CONGRESSES, MEETINGS, ETC.

24.7A.   Omissions
Words that express number, frequency, or year of meeting are omitted from the name of a conference. Example:

Name on title page: II Jornadas de Derecho Natural
Heading: Jornadas de Derecho Natural

An LC rule interpretation states that, with some exceptions, an abbreviated form of the year will be retained as part of a conference name when that abbreviation is combined with an acronym or initialism. (*CSB* 77: 50)

24.7B.   Additions

The number of a conference, etc., the year, and the place in which it was held are added in parentheses to the name. If any of these elements are not known, they are omitted. Examples:

Heading: International Ocular Trauma Conference
(1st : 1988 : Zhengzhou, Henan, China)
Heading: International Symposium on Viral Hepatitis
and Liver Disease (1987 : Barbican Centre for Arts
and Conferences)

For further guidance in selecting qualifiers for conferences, etc., the LC rule interpretation on this rule should be consulted. (*CSB* 77: 50–51)

Subordinate and Related Bodies

The problem of entry of corporate bodies that are subordinate to or closely related to other bodies is a difficult one. No completely unambiguous set of rules (including *AACR2R*) has yet been devised to handle it. The last sixteen rules in chapter 24 of *AACR2R* (rules 24.12–24.27) deal with this issue; yet even with this exhaustive treatment the end result may still depend upon the judgment of the individual cataloger.

There are three parts to this section: general rules, government body rules, and religious organization rules. The cataloger must first know if a body is a government or religious body. This is important because, in some cases, the results of applying the nongovernment rules to a government body may yield a heading not intended by the makers of the code. However, once into the sequence for government or religious bodies, the cataloger may be referred back to the general sequence for further instructions.

If it is determined that a body is a government body, rules 24.17–24.26 must be consulted before any others in chapter 24, because a government body is always a subordinate body—that is, it is always subordinate to a jurisdiction. Once into the rules, the cataloger may find that the result is the same as if subordination were not involved—that is, the body may be entered under its own name. (For example, the University of California, Los Angeles, a state institution, and the University of Southern California, a private institution, both end up entered under "University of....") But if the body is one of the types listed in rule 24.18, it will be entered subordinately, and then rule 24.19 for direct or indirect subheading must be consulted; and if it is one of Types 6 through 11, one of rules 24.20–24.26 must also be consulted. The cataloger must also be concerned with the level of subordinate body involved. If it is subordinate to another government body that is entered under its *own name* because it is not one of the types listed in rule 24.18, then general rules 24.12–24.14 must be consulted for formulation of the heading for the subordinate body. If it is subordinate to another body that is entered under *jurisdiction*, then the cataloger continues to use government body rules 24.17–24.19 for formulation of the heading for the subordinate body.

If it is determined that a body is a religious body, rule 24.27 and its subparts are consulted first. Certain kinds of religious subordinate bodies are specified for subordinate entry in these rules. All others are to be treated according to general rules 24.12–24.14.

For all subordinate bodies other than government or religious, the cataloger uses general rules 24.12–24.16, which refer back to rules 24.1–24.3 for construction of headings for subordinate bodies that should be entered under their own names.

Subordinate and Related Bodies: Selected Rules and Examples

RULE 24.12.   GENERAL RULE

If a subordinate body is not a government body entered under jurisdiction, it is to be entered under its own name according to rules 24.1–24.3 unless it is one of the types listed under rule 24.13. A reference is made from the name formulated as a subheading of its higher body to the name as an independent heading. (Note the similarity of this rule to rule 24.17 for government bodies.) Examples:

Headings for subordinate bodies under their own names:

Information on title page of exhibition catalog: Baxter Art
Gallery, California Institute of Technology, Pasadena
Heading: Baxter Art Gallery.
Refer from: California Institute of Technology. Baxter Art
Gallery.
Information on chief source of information: National
Affiliation for Literacy Advance, Laubach Literacy
International's programming arm in the U.S. and Canada
Heading: National Affiliation for Literacy Advance.
Refer from: Laubach Literacy International. National
Affiliation for Literacy Advance.

RULE 24.13.   SUBORDINATE AND RELATED BODIES ENTERED SUBORDINATELY

When a subordinate or related body's name belongs to one of Types 1–6 below, the heading for that body is constructed so that the higher body is named first, followed by the name of the subordinate or related body. If the name or abbreviation of the higher body is included in the name of the subordinate body in noun form, it is omitted from the subheading, unless it does not make sense to omit it. There may or may not be names of intervening bodies that are part of the hierarchy, depending on the application of rule 24.14. (Note the similarity of this rule to rule 24.18 for government bodies. Note also that Types 1–4 in the two rules are nearly identical, but that the other types are quite different.)

Type 1.   If a name contains a term that implies the body is part of another body, it is entered subordinately. Examples of such terms: *department*, *division*, *section*, *branch*, and their equivalents in other languages. Example:

Name on chief source: Section of International Law and Practice,
American Bar Association
Heading: American Bar Association. Section of International Law
and Practice.

A major LC departure from *AACR2R* affects headings constructed by many rules, but it can be illustrated here. LC continues to abbreviate *Department* as *Dept.* even though this is not authorized for use in headings by *AACR2R*, Appendix B, "Abbreviations," (*CSB* 32: 58) Example:

Previously established heading: Notre Dame, Ind.
University. Dept. of Economics.
LC's heading under *AACR2R*: University of Notre
Dame. Dept. of Economics.

**[Note: Even though the heading had to be reconstructed for other reasons,
the abbreviation *Dept.* was retained.]**

Type 2.   If a name contains a term that implies that the body is subordinate to another in an administrative sense, it is entered subordinately *if* the name of the higher body is required to identify the subordinate body. *AACR2R* gives two words as examples: *committee* and *commission*. LC has created lists of words in English, French, and Spanish that imply administrative subordination. (*CSB* 71: 64–65) For the second part of the rule, judgment is to be used by LC's catalogers to determine whether the name of the higher body is required for identification. Example:

Information on chief source: NAIS Teacher Services Committee
Heading: National Association of Independent Schools. Teacher
Services Committee.
Refer from: NAIS Teacher Services Committee.

Type 3.   If a name is "general in nature" or indicates only that it is a geographic, chronological, numbered, or lettered subdivision of a higher body, it is entered subordinately. For LC "general in nature" means that the name has no distinctive elements, such as proper names, nor does it have subject words. (*CSB* 25: 67–68) Example:

Name in credits of motion picture: Brigham Young University,
Media Productions
Cataloger's judgment: *Media Productions* is general in nature
Heading: Brigham Young University. Media Productions.

Type 4.   If a name does not give the impression of being that of a corporate body, it is entered subordinately. Example:

Name on title page: National Student Ministries
Cataloger's judgment: Name does not clearly give the impression
of being that of a corporate body
Heading: Southern Baptist Convention. National Student Ministries.

Type 5.   If a name of a unit of a university simply indicates that it encompasses a particular field of study, it is entered subordinately. A rule interpretation adds *college* as well as *university* and also adds *interest* and *activity* to *field of study* as criteria for the type of field encompassed by the unit. (*CSB* 44: 58) Example:

Name on title page: School of Graduate and Professional Studies,
Emporia State University
Heading: Emporia State University. School of Graduate and
Professional Studies.

Type 6.   If the name of a subordinate or related body includes the entire name of the higher or related body, it is entered subordinately. LC has issued a lengthy rule interpretation for rule 24.13, Type 6, including exceptions and exclusions and discussing its application to named meetings. (*CSB* 44: 58–62) Example:

> **Name on title page:** Chaucer Group of the Modern Language Association of America
> **Heading:** Modern Language Association of America. Chaucer Group.

RULE 24.14.   DIRECT OR INDIRECT SUBHEADING

A body that belongs to one of the types listed in rule 24.13 and that, therefore, is to be entered subordinately is entered as a subdivision of the element closest above it in its hierarchy that is entered under its own name. If there are elements in the hierarchy that fall between the subdivision and the name that is to be the entry element, they are omitted unless they are needed to distinguish this body from another that does or might have the same entry form (e.g., several sections of the same institution might have an office called the "Personnel Office"). A reference is made from the form that includes the name of an intervening body that has been omitted from the heading. (Note the similarity of this rule to rule 24.19 for government bodies.) Examples:

> **Name on title page:** University of Washington Libraries, Manuscripts Section
> **Heading:** University of Washington. Libraries. Manuscripts Section.
>
> [Note: Even though the University of Washington is a government body, its subordinate bodies are entered according to rules 24.12–24.14 because the university is entered under its own name, not under jurisdiction.]
>
> **Name on title page:** Radiological Research Laboratory, Department of Radiology, Columbia University, New York, N.Y.
> **Heading:** Columbia University. Radiological Research Laboratory.
>   **Refer from:** Columbia University. Dept. of Radiology. Radiological Research Laboratory.

Omission of elements of a hierarchy is another area where the results of different catalogers' judgments may vary. The words *or is likely to be* often mean differences in judgment. LC has identified for its catalogers two categories where judgment should not vary. In the first category, names of bodies performing functions common to many higher bodies (e.g., Personnel Office; Planning Dept.), the hierarchy should be included. In the second category, names of bodies performing major functions unique to the higher body (e.g., Division of Fisheries; Division of Transport [under the Ministry of Transport, Industry, and Engineering]), intervening elements of the hierarchy should be omitted. Common sense must dictate the inclusion of hierarchy for the great middle ground. The cataloger should consider whether the name would be appropriate for another subordinate body within the same higher body structure and whether some word or phrase in a name in the hierarchy expresses an idea necessary to the identification of the subordinate body. (*CSB* 18: 76–78)

Government Bodies and Officials:
Selected Rules and Examples

RULE 24.17.   GENERAL RULE

A government body that is not one of Types 1–11 below is entered under its own name according to rules 24.1–24.3 or is entered subordinately to a higher body that is entered under its own name according to rules 24.12–24.14. A reference is made from the form the name would have if it were a subheading under the name of the government. Example:

> **Heading:** National Institutes of Health (U.S.)
> **Refer from:** United States. National Institutes of Health.
> N.I.H.
> United States. Public Health Service. National Institutes of Health.
> United States. Federal Security Agency. National Institutes of Health.

LC treats the United Nations as a government body when applying these rules. (*CSB* 45: 58)

RULE 24.18.   GOVERNMENT AGENCIES ENTERED
SUBORDINATELY

When a government body's name belongs to one of Types 1–11 below, it is entered subordinately. If the name or abbreviation of the government is included in the name of the subordinate body in noun form, it is omitted from the subheading, unless it does not make sense to omit it. There may or may not be names of intervening bodies between the name of the government and the name of the subordinate body being established, depending on the application of rule 24.19.

A rule interpretation from LC should be consulted for guidance when a government agency name contains the entire name of its parent body (there is no equivalent to rule 24.13, Type 6, under rule 24.18). (CSB 44: 62–64)

Type 1.   If a name contains a word that implies the body is part of another body, it is entered subordinately. The same terms given as examples under rule 24.13, Type 1, apply here. Example:

> **Name on title page:** Division of Planning, City of Jersey City
> **Heading:** Jersey City (N.J.). Division of Planning.

Type 2.   If a name contains a word that implies that the body is subordinate to the government in an administrative sense, it is entered subordinately *if* the name of the government is required to identify the agency. Example:

> **Information on title page:** Legislative Commission on Correctional Programs [seal]: The Great Seal of the State of North Carolina
> **Heading:** North Carolina. Legislative Commission on Correctional Programs.

In LC's rule interpretation for catalogers at LC, there are two tests to be applied here. One is a judgment as to whether the name contains a word that implies "administrative subordination." The cataloger should ask whether the word is commonly used in a particular jurisdiction for names of government subdivisions. If in doubt, the word is considered not to have such an implication. The same list of terms in English, French, and Spanish given for rule 24.13, Type 2, is given under the rule interpretation for this rule and should be consulted when needed. (*CSB* 71: 65–67)

If the name passes the first test, it is then evaluated as to whether the name of the government is required for identification. "If the name of the government is stated explicitly or implied in the wording of the name, enter it independently; in all other cases, enter the name subordinately."[9] Thus, the United States Travel Service, which includes the government in its name, is entered independently: United States Travel Service. The Soil Conservation Service, however, is entered subordinately: United States. Soil Conservation Service.

If the body is entered independently according to this interpretation, the name of the government is added as a qualifier unless the name or an understandable surrogate for the name of the government (e.g., *American* for U.S.) appears in the name. (*CSB* 71: 67) *See* example under rule 24.17 above.

Type 3.   If a name is "general in nature" or indicates only that it is a geographic, chronological, numbered, or lettered subdivision of a government or a government agency, it is entered subordinately. Example:

> **Name on title page:** U.S. Public Health Service. Region V
> **Cataloger's judgment:** Region V is a name that is general in nature
> **Heading:** United States. Public Health Service. Region V.

LC policy for interpreting this rule states that if the body is at the national level, it is to be considered general and entered subordinately if the name contains neither distinctive words nor subject words and does not contain either the term *national* or *state* or one of their foreign language equivalents. (*CSB* 44: 63) For example, enter subordinately:

> Research Center
> Library
> Technical Laboratory

but enter independently:

> Population Research Center (U.S.)
> Nuclear Energy Library (U.S.)
> Technical Laboratory of Oceanographic Research (U.S.)
> National Gallery (U.S.)

If the body is below the national level and it is not any of the other types under rule 24.18, LC enters it under the name of the government unless that name is explicitly or implicitly included in the subordinate body's name or the name contains some other word that tends to make it absolutely unique (e.g., a proper noun). (*CSB* 44: 63)

As under rule 24.18, Type 2, a body entered independently under Type 3 will have the name of the government added as a qualifier unless it is already part of the body's name. (*CSB* 44: 63)

Type 4.   If the name does not give the impression of being that of a corporate body *and* it does not contain the name of the governing jurisdiction, it is entered subordinately. Example:

Name on title page: Naval Oceanography and Meteorology
Heading: United States. Naval Oceanography and Meteorology.

Type 5. If the name represents a major executive agency (as defined by official publications of the government) it is entered subordinately. Example:

Name on title page: Oyo State Executive Council
Heading: Oyo State (Nigeria). Executive Council.

LC restricts application of this rule to major executive agencies of *national* governments. (*CSB* 44: 63)

Type 6. Government legislative bodies are entered subordinately according to the provisions in rule 24.21. *See* example under rule 24.21.

Type 7. Government courts are entered subordinately according to the provisions in rule 24.23. *See* example under rule 24.23.

Type 8. Principal armed services are entered subordinately according to the provisions in rule 24.24. *See* example under rule 24.24

Type 9. Chiefs of state and other heads of government are entered subordinately according to the provisions in rule 24.20. *See* example under rule 24.20.

Type 10. Embassies, consulates, etc., and **Type 11**, Delegations to international and intergovernmental bodies, are also entered subordinately.

RULE 24.19. DIRECT OR INDIRECT SUBHEADING

This rule is the same as rule 24.14 except that the body is entered under the heading for the government instead of under the lowest element in the hierarchy that is entered under its own name. Other elements in the hierarchy are interposed or omitted in the same way and with the same difficulties in judgment. (*See* discussion under rule 24.14.) Examples:

Indirect subordinate entry of an office:

Name on title page: Office of the Executive Director,
Colorado Department of Natural Resources
Heading: Colorado. Dept. of Natural Resources. Office
of the Executive Director.

Direct subordinate entry of an office:

Name on title page: U.S. Department of Commerce Maritime
Administration, Office of Commercial Development, Office
of Port and Intermodal Development
Heading: United States. Office of Port and Intermodal
Development.
Refer from: United States. Maritime Administration. Office
of Port and Intermodal Development.

United States. Maritime Administration. Office
of Commercial Development. Office of Port and
Intermodal Development.

Special Rules

RULE 24.20.   GOVERNMENT OFFICIALS

24.20B.   Heads of state, etc.

The heading for a head of state who is acting in an official capacity is made up of the name of the government followed by the title of the office in English, if possible, the inclusive years the person held that office, and a brief form of name of the person in the language used for the person's personal heading. Non-gendered terminology is used, e.g., *Sovereign*, not *Queen* or *King*. Example:

> **Heading for governor as an official:** New York (State).
> Governor (1983-1994 : Cuomo)

An explanatory reference should be made to the incumbent as a person (*see* rule 26.3C1 in *AACR2R*).

RULE 24.21.   LEGISLATIVE BODIES

A legislature is entered under the name of the jurisdiction for which it makes laws. Chambers of legislative bodies are entered subordinately to the legislative body, and committees are entered subordinately to the legislature or to a chamber, whichever is appropriate. A subcommittee of the U.S. Congress is entered as a subheading of the committee to which it is subordinate. If legislatures are numbered, the number and year(s) are added. Session numbers may also be added [e.g., United States. Congress (106th, 1st session : 1999)]. Example:

> **Entry of a state legislative committee:**
>
> **Name on title page:** Committee on Motor Vehicles, Illinois
> House of Representatives
> **Heading:** Illinois. General Assembly. House of Representatives.
> Committee on Motor Vehicles.

It should be noted that, although *AACR2R* shows in its examples "United States. Congress. House of Representatives," which is the official name of that body, LC continues to use the conventional name "House" in its headings for the body. (*CSB* 44: 64)

RULE 24.23.   COURTS

Civil and criminal courts are entered as subheadings of the jurisdiction. A place name for the place a court sits or the area it serves is omitted but added as a conventional addition if needed to distinguish it from others of the same name. Example:

> **Name on title page:** Court of Common Pleas of Crawford County, Pa.
> **Heading:** Pennsylvania. Court of Common Pleas (Crawford County).

RULE 24.24.   ARMED FORCES

A principal service of the armed forces of a government is entered as a subheading of the government. A branch, district, or unit is entered as a subheading for the principal service, and if it is numbered, the numbering in the style used in the name follows the name. Example:

> **Name on chief source of information:** Air Defense Command,
> U.S. Air Force
> **Heading:** United States. Air Force. Air Defense Command.

RULE 24.27.   RELIGIOUS BODIES AND OFFICIALS

24.27A.   Councils, etc., of a single religious body

Councils, etc., of a single religious body are entered as subheadings of that body. Appropriate additions may be made as for conferences, etc. (rule 24.7B). General councils are entered according to the general rules for subordinate bodies (rules 24.12–24.13). Example:

> **Name on title page:** Il Concilio romano del 1725
> **Heading:** Catholic Church. Concilio romano (1725)

24.27B.   Religious officials

The heading for a religious official acting in an official capacity looks very much like the heading for a head of state (rule 24.20B). It consists of the heading for the diocese, order, patriarchate, etc., followed by the title in English (unless there is no English equivalent), the inclusive years of incumbency, and the name of the person. Example:

> **Name on title page:** His Holiness John Paul II
> **Heading:** Catholic Church. Pope (1978-   : John Paul II)

> [Note: An explanatory reference should refer to the personal heading for John Paul II.]

24.27C.   Subordinate bodies

Provinces, dioceses, synods, and other subordinate units having jurisdiction over geographic areas are entered as subheadings of the religious body. For the Catholic Church, the English form of name should be used. Example:

> **Name on title page:** Arzobispado del Cuzco
> **Heading:** Catholic Church. Archdiocese of Cuzco (Peru)
> **Refer from:** Catholic Church. Arzobispado del Cuzco.

UNIFORM TITLES

When a work has appeared under more than one title, a uniform title may be used for cataloging purposes in order to bring all editions of the work together. Uniform titles may also be used to *distinguish* different works which have the same titles proper. Uniform titles of the first type have traditionally been used for sacred scriptures, creeds, liturgical works, and anonymous classics. In more recent practice, uniform titles of the second type have been found useful for distinguishing works such as serials with generic titles (such as *Report*). *Bible* is a very common example in library catalogs of the first type of uniform title; similarly, editions of the Mother Goose verses are assembled under the uniform title *Mother Goose*. In these cases the uniform titles represent main entry headings. In other instances the uniform title follows the main entry, as in the cases of music, laws, liturgical works, and translations. *AACR2R*, chapter 25, contains many further suggestions for extending these rules to other instances.

One of the problems faced in constructing uniform titles of the first type is the choice of a title when titles of a work appear in more than one form. Titles may be in different languages, in one or more long forms and one or more short forms, or in two simultaneous versions (as when a work is published simultaneously in England and the United States under different titles). Some works may be published in parts and need identification of the part *without* identification of the whole (as in the case of one title from a trilogy) or *with* identification of the whole (as in the case of a book from Homer's *Iliad*, called only "Book 1"). Additions may be needed to distinguish uniform titles from each other or from other headings, to identify the language in which the work appears, to identify the version, or to date the particular edition. The purpose of this chapter is to demonstrate the general rules used to resolve these problems. Much more detail can be found in *AACR2R*, chapter 25.

In addition to the first rule, which sets down the conditions for use of uniform titles, the *AACR2R* chapter comprises three groups of rules: basic rules for choice and form of the title itself (rules 25.2–25.4 and 25.12), rules for additions to uniform titles (rules 25.5–25.11), and special rules for certain materials (rules 25.13–25.35). The materials given special treatment are manuscripts (rule 25.13), incunabula (rule 25.14), legal materials (rules 25.15–25.16), sacred scriptures (rules 25.17–25.18), liturgical and other religious works (rules 25.19–25.24), and music (rules 25.25–25.35).

A heading created using *AACR2R*, Chapter 25, is coded 130, 240, 630, 730, or 830 in the MARC 21 format, depending upon whether it functions as a main entry, a supplementary title between main entry and the title proper, a subject heading, an added entry, or a series added entry.

RULE 25.1.   USE OF UNIFORM TITLES

Whether or not uniform titles are used may depend on the type and size of catalog one has. *AACR2R98* gives six criteria to use in deciding whether to use uniform titles:

"1)   how well the work is known

2)   how many manifestations of the work are involved

3)   whether another work with the same title proper has been identified (*see* 25.5B)

4)   whether the main entry is under title (*see* 21.1C)

5)   whether the work was originally in another language

6)   the extent to which the catalogue is used for research purposes."[10]

In essence this rule states that the entire set of rules on uniform titles is optional, and a policy decision should be made in each cataloging agency as to whether some or all of the rules should be applied.

General Rules: Selected Rules and Examples

RULE 25.2.   GENERAL RULE

25.2A.   In a printed record the uniform title is given before the title proper and enclosed in square brackets. If the main entry is title, *AACR2R* calls for it also to be enclosed in brackets, but an option allows omitting the brackets if the uniform title is used as main entry. The Library of Congress is following the option, which is a continuation of LC's past practice. In addition it is LC practice not to enclose uniform titles in brackets when used in added entries. (*CSB* 64: 28–29) It is also LC practice in the case of anonymous classics that have been published in many editions, translations, and differing titles to use the uniform title for all editions, even when it does not differ from the title proper. (*CSB* 64: 28–29) Example:

Uniform title as main entry without square brackets—LC practice:

> Beowulf.
> Beowulf : an edition with manuscript spacing notation
> and graphotactic analyses : Robert D. Stevick

[Note: In MARC records the square brackets are not recorded, and display is dependent upon the programming of the system.]

25.2B. Uniform titles are not used for revisions or updated versions of a work in the same language as the original. Instead, these are related by giving a note about the earlier edition in the bibliographic record for the later edition. Example:

New title, not uniform title, used for new edition in the same language:

> Hawker, Pat.
> Amateur radio techniques / Pat Hawker. — 6th ed. — London :
> Radio Society of Great Britain, 1978.
> 336 p. : ill. ; 25 cm.
> First ed. published with title: Technical topics for the radio
> amateur.

25.2C. Initial articles

Initial articles are omitted unless the uniform title is to be filed under that article. Example:

Initial article not included in uniform title:

> Dickens, Charles, 1812-1870.
> [Pickwick papers]
> The Pickwick papers / Charles Dickens ; edited with
> an introduction and notes by James Kinsley

Individual Titles

RULE 25.3. WORKS CREATED AFTER 1500

25.3A. For a work created after 1500 the title in the original language by which the work has become known is used as its uniform title. The "known" title is judged from its use in manifestations of the work or in reference sources. Example:

Uniform title in original language:

> Suder, Joseph, 1892-
> [Dona nobis pacem]
> Festmesse in D [sound recording] / Joseph Suder

Other titles given to this work:

> Messe Dona nobis pacem
> Grosse Messe Dona nobis pacem

25.3B.   If none of the titles in the original language can be established as being the "best known," the title proper of the original edition is used. In using such original titles, one should omit introductory phrases and statements of responsibility that can be grammatically separated. LC also omits alternative titles. (*CSB* 44: 65) Example:

Use of title proper of the original edition when there are variant titles in the original language:

> Cross, Amanda, 1926-
>   [Death in a tenured position]
>   A death in the faculty / Amanda Cross. — London :
> Virago, 1988, c1981.

Note explaining uniform title:

> Originally published as: Death in a tenured position. New York : Dutton, 1981.

25.3C.   Simultaneous publication under different titles

25.3C1.   When a work is published in two or more editions simultaneously in the same language with different titles, the cataloger should use as uniform title the one for the edition published in the cataloging agency's country, if this applies. If it does not apply, the title of the edition received first should be used. Example:

American title used as uniform title for work whose British title is different:

> Mansfield, Peter, 1928-
>   [Arab world]
>   The Arabs / Peter Mansfield. — Harmondsworth :
> Penguin, 1928.

Note explaining uniform title:

> American ed. published under title: The Arab world.

RULE 25.4.   WORKS CREATED BEFORE 1501

25.4A.   If a work was created before 1501, the title in the original language by which the work is identified in modern reference sources is used. If none of the titles can be established in reference sources, the title found most frequently in modern editions, early editions, or manuscript copies (in that order of preference) is used. This rule, however, is superseded by rules 25.4B–25.4C and 25.14, if they apply. Example:

Uniform title for pre-1501 work as identified in reference sources:

> Gawain and the Grene Knight.
>   Sir Gawain and the Green Knight / translated with an introduction by Brian Stone

25.4B–25.4C.   In general, a well-established English title, if there is one, is used for a pre-1501 Greek work or anonymous work in nonroman script. Example:

**Anonymous pre-1501 work originally in nonroman script entered under
established English title with the language of the translation in hand added
(rules 25.4 and 25.5C1):**

> Arabian nights. English.
> More fairy tales from the Arabian nights / edited and
> arranged by E. Dixon ; illustrated by J.D. Batten

RULE 25.5. ADDITIONS TO UNIFORM TITLES

25.5B. Conflict resolution

25.5B1. If uniform titles used as main entries are identical to each other or to the
form used as the heading for a person, corporate body, or reference, additions are
made in parentheses to the uniform title. Example:

**Additions in parentheses to distinguish between two otherwise
identical uniform titles:**

> Jungle book (1942)
> Jungle book [motion picture]
> Jungle book (1967)
> The jungle book [motion picture]

Identical uniform titles that are entered under the same personal or corporate
heading also need additions in parentheses to distinguish them. Example:

> United States.
> [Census (1960)]
> United States.
> [Census (1970)]

For this rule LC has made a lengthy rule interpretation that prescribes the kinds
of additions that are to be made to distinguish between otherwise identical titles of
different serials, including monographic series. (*CSB* 84: 15–26) In general such
conflicts are handled by adding a uniform title to the bibliographic record for the
serial in hand, not to the one cataloged earlier.

Place of publication is LC's preferred qualifying term for conflicting serial
titles. Example:

> Times (Charleston, S.C.)
> Times (Kansas City, Mo.)

However, if the title consists only of an indication of type and/or periodicity of publication, or if the place is inadequate to resolve the conflict, or if the conflicting titles
include initials of their issuing bodies' names, then the heading for the body that
originated or issued the serial is used as the qualifying term. Examples:

> Occasional paper (Canberra College of Advanced Education. Library)
> Occasional paper (London Public Library and Art Museum (Ont.))
> European physics series (McGraw-Hill)
> European physics series (Wiley)

[Note: both works published in New York, N.Y.]

Other qualifiers may be added when the above provisions do not suffice. Other qualifiers may be place and date, corporate body and date, date, edition statement, other title information, etc. The LC rule interpretation should be consulted for elaboration on these qualifiers and on other special situations such as may occur with radio and television programs, comics, motion pictures, computer programs, choreographic works, named individual works of art, and other situations in which conflict may arise.

25.5C.   Language

25.5C1.   When the item in hand is in a different language from the original, the name of the language of the item is added to the uniform title. LC catalogers use the language name as established in the latest edition of *MARC 21 Code List for Languages*. (*CSB* 78: 75) Example:

> **Modern translation with original title as uniform title, followed by language of translation:**
>
> > Leys, Simon, 1935-
> > [Habits neufs du président Mao. English]
> > The Chairman's new clothes : Mao and the cultural
> > revolution / Simon Leys ; translated by Carol Appleyard
> > and Patrick Goode

AACR2R rule 25.5C and LC's rule interpretation on multilingual works should be consulted when more than one language is involved. (*CSB* 78: 75–76)

25.5D.   An option allows addition of General Material Designations (GMDs) at the end of uniform titles. LC is not applying this option. (*CSB* 44: 67)

RULE 25.6.   PARTS OF A WORK

This rule is not applied to parts of the Bible and certain other sacred scriptures (*see* rules 25.17–25.18) or to parts of musical works (*see* rule 25.32).

25.6A.   One part

25.6A1.   When a separately cataloged part of a work has a title that is not dependent for its meaning upon the title of the collected work, the title of the part alone is used as the uniform title. A reference is made from the form the heading would have if the title of the part were a subheading of the title of the whole work. Example:

> **Separately cataloged part with its own title as uniform title:**
>
> > Hesse, Hermann, 1877-1962.
> > [Tractat vom Steppenwolf. English]
> > Treatise on the Steppenwolf / Hermann Hesse ; [translated from the German] ; paintings by Jaroslav Bradac
>
> **[Note: The title of the whole work is *Der Steppenwolf*.]**
>
> > **Refer from:** Hesse, Hermann, 1877-1962.
> > Steppenwolf. Tractat vom Steppenwolf. English

25.6A2.   When a separately cataloged part of a work has a title that *is* dependent for its meaning upon the title of the whole work, the uniform title is the title of the whole work followed by the title of the part as a subheading. Arabic numerals are used to record part numbers. Example:

Separately cataloged part given as subheading of the title of the whole work:

> Milton, John, 1608-1674.
> [Paradise lost. Book 4]
> Paradise lost, book IV / John Milton ; edited by S.E. Goggin

25.6B. More than one part

When an item consists of consecutively numbered parts, the designation of the parts in the singular is used as a subheading of the title of the whole work and is followed by the inclusive numbering of parts. Example:

Separately cataloged consecutive parts of a work given as subheading of the title of the whole work:

> Milton, John, 1608-1674.
> [Paradise lost. Book 9-10]
> Paradise lost, books IX and X / John Milton ; edited by Cyril Aldred

When an item has two parts not consecutively numbered, the uniform title is made for the first part, and a name-title added entry is made for the second. When an item has three or more parts not consecutively numbered, the uniform title of the whole work is used, followed by "Selections."

RULE 25.7.   TWO WORKS ISSUED TOGETHER

25.7A.   When an item contains two works entered under a personal or corporate main entry, uniform titles are assigned to the two works. The uniform title of the first work is given following the main entry, and a name-title added entry using the second uniform title is made for the second work. Example:

Separate uniform titles made for two works appearing in the same item:

> Poe, Edgar Allan, 1809-1849.
> [Tell-tale heart]
> The telltale heart ; and, The cask of Amontillado [sound recording]

Added entry for second work:

> I. Poe, Edgar Allan, 1809-1849. Cask of Amontillado.

Collective Titles

Collective titles can be general (e.g., "Works," "Selections") or more specific (e.g., "Novels," "Poems," "Laws, etc."). When these are used alone, the effect is to separate originals from translations, different editions from each other, etc., if the titles proper are different. They also are inadequate when being used in added entries. Therefore, LC emphasizes using the principle found in rule 25.5B in conjunction with collective titles when needed to bring together items with different titles proper or to refer to a work in an added entry. The designation to be enclosed in parentheses may be title proper, editor, translator, publisher, etc.—whichever best fits each case. Example:

> Maugham, W. Somerset (William Somerset), 1874-1965.
>   [Short stories (Heinemann)]
>   Complete short stories

This technique is applied only after the need arises; thus, earlier entries must be revised. (*CSB* 46: 52–53)

RULE 25.8.   COMPLETE WORKS
If an information package contains, or claims to contain, the complete works of a person, the collective title "Works" is used as uniform title. Example:

> Posada, José Guadalupe, 1852-1913.
>   [Works. English & German. 1976]
>   Das Werk von Jose Guadalupe Posada = The works of José Guadalupe Posada / edited and with an introduction by Hannes Jähn

A rule interpretation from LC indicates that "Works" occurs so frequently that there should always be additions made to such uniform titles to make them distinctive. The interpretation outlines the additions to be made. (*CSB* 63: 17–19)

RULE 25.9.   SELECTIONS
When an item contains three or more works in various forms, all by the same person, the collective title "Selections" is used as uniform title. Example:

> Twain, Mark, 1835-1910.
>   [Selections. 1987]
>   The outrageous Mark Twain : some lesser-known but extraordinary works : with "Reflections on religion" now in book form for the first time / selected and edited, with an introduction, by Charles Neider

LC calls for the same additions here that are made to the collective title "Works." (*CSB* 60: 22)

RULE 25.10.   WORKS IN A SINGLE FORM
The following collective titles are used for collections of the works of a person all in one form:

Correspondence	Poems
Essays	Prose works
Novels	Short stories
Plays	Speeches

LC applies this rule only when the title proper of the collection is not distinctive or when there is no collective title proper. (*CSB* 60: 22–23)

Special Rules for Certain Types of Work:
Selected Rules and Examples

Laws, Treaties, Etc.

RULE 25.15.   LAWS, ETC.

25.15A.   Modern laws, etc.

25.15A1.   Collections
A collection of legislative enactments is given the uniform title "Laws, etc.," unless the compilation is on a particular subject. LC, when using "Laws, etc.," makes further additions, in parentheses, and revises existing records that lack the additions. The additions may consist of a brief title and, if needed, edition or date. The LC rule interpretation should be consulted. (*CSB* 36: 33–38) Example:

> India.
> [Laws, etc. (Statutes of India)]
> The statutes of India : a manual of central arts & rules :
> exhaustive commentary on all central acts with important central
> rules

When a compilation of laws is on a particular subject, a citation title, if there is one, should be used as uniform title. If there is no citation title, a uniform title should be constructed according to rule 25.3. LC adds that if a subject compilation lacks both a citation title and a collective title, the uniform title of the first law in the collection should be used. (*CSB* 36: 38)

25.15A2.   Single laws, etc.
Single laws are assigned, as uniform title, one of the following (in order of preference): an official citation title (or official short title), an unofficial short or citation title used in legal literature, the official title, or any other official designation. Example:

> **Official short title used as uniform title:**

> Québec (Province)
> [Labour code. English & French]
> Code du travail : Titre 1, des relations du travail =
> Labour code : Title, labour relations

RULE 25.16.   TREATIES, ETC.
The uniform title for treaties is "Treaties, etc." Various additions are made depending upon the circumstances: the second party for a collection of treaties between two parties or for single treaties between two parties; the date or earliest date of signing (in the form: year, abbreviated name of the month, number of the day) for a single treaty. A single treaty between four or more parties is entered under the name by which the treaty is known (in English, if possible) followed by the year of signing in parentheses. Added entries for individual signers, if made, are formulated with the uniform title "Treaties, etc.," followed by date of signing. *See* treaty example following rule 21.36 on p. 198 in chapter 6.

Sacred Scriptures

RULE 25.17.   GENERAL RULE

The uniform title for a sacred scripture should be the title that is usually used in English-language reference sources that discuss the particular religious group that uses the scripture.

RULE 25.18.   PARTS OF SACRED SCRIPTURES AND ADDITIONS

25.18A.   Bible

When appropriate, the testaments (designated O.T. and N.T.) are added after the word "Bible." Then books are designated. If the books are numbered, the number is given as an ordinal Arabic numeral after the name. The name of a group of books may also be a subdivision of the testament (e.g., Minor Prophets, Apocrypha, Gospels). Next are added, as appropriate: 1) language; 2) version, translator, name of manuscripts or repository, or reviser; and 3) year. A single selection with a distinctive title is entered directly under that title with a reference from the appropriate "Bible" uniform title. If a work consists of more than two selections, they are entered under the most specific Bible heading appropriate to all, with the term *Selections* added after language and version but before the year. Examples:

Bible.   **[parts] [language] [versions] [selections] [date]**
Bible.   N.T. Corinthians, 1st . . .
Bible.   N.T. English. Stern. 1989.
Bible.   N.T. Gospels . . .
Bible.   O.T. Esther. Hebrew. 1990.
Bible.   O.T. Genesis XII, 1 - XXV, 11 . . .
Bible.   O.T. Historical books . . .
Bible.   O.T. Leviticus. Hebrew. Samaritan. 1959.
Bible.   English. New Century. Selections. 1990.
Bible.   English. New Jerusalem Bible. 1990.
Bible.   English. New Life. 1990.

25.18B–25.18M.   Rules 25.18B–25.18M are special rules for the Talmud, Mishnah and Tosefta, Midrashim, Buddhist scriptures, Vedas, Aranyakas, Brahmanas, Upanishads, Jaina Agama, Avesta, and Koran. Rules are given for parts and additions as for the Bible.

Liturgical Works, Theological Creeds, Confessions of Faith, Etc.

RULE 25.19.   GENERAL RULE

When a liturgical work is entered under an English-language corporate body name, the uniform title should also be in English if there is an established English title; if not, the uniform title is given in the language of the liturgy. Example:

Uniform title for a liturgical work:
Catholic Church.
[Mass, Epiphany. German]
Messe an Epiphanias

RULES 25.20–25.23.
Rules 25.20–25.23 are special rules for Catholic and Jewish liturgical works, for variant and special texts, and for parts of liturgical works.

Musical Works

RULE 25.25.   GENERAL RULE
The general rule outlines the rules in the remainder of the chapter.

Uniform titles for:	Rule(s):
one musical work	25.26–25.31
one or more parts of a musical work	25.32
two works of a composer issued together	25.33
collections of music	25.34

The last rule, rule 25.35, is for additions to a uniform title to designate a particular manifestation. The cataloger is instructed to use rules 25.1–25.7 whenever they are applicable and are not contradicted by rules 25.26–25.35.

Individual Titles

RULE 25.26.   GENERAL RULE
The initial title element of the uniform title for a musical work is created as instructed in rules 25.27–25.29. Rules 25.30–25.32 and 25.35 give instructions for additions to the initial title element, although additions are not always required.

RULES 25.27–25.31.
Uniform titles are frequently used in cataloging music because the same musical composition is often issued in numerous editions with variations in the language and the wording of the title pages. Composer-title references are made from forms of the title not used as uniform title, as needed. Examples:

Beethoven, Ludwig van, 1770-1827.
   Battle of Vitoria
      see
   Beethoven, Ludwig van, 1770-1827.
     Wellingtons Sieg

Beethoven, Ludwig van, 1770-1827.
   Cantata on the death of Emperor Joseph II
      see
   Beethoven, Ludwig van, 1770-1827.
     Kantate auf den Tod Kaiser Josephs II

In the selection and construction of uniform titles the most reliable bibliographical sources are consulted, such as thematic indexes, bibliographies, music encyclopedias, etc. Information given in the work cataloged is not used without an attempt at verification. LC catalogs are useful in constructing a uniform title, but only after the cataloger has identified the work in thematic or other musical sources.

Rules 25.27–25.31 give the principles for construction of a uniform title for a single work. The basic rule for choice of uniform title instructs the cataloger to use the composer's original title unless a later title in the same language has become better known. If the title is distinctive, it is left unmodified unless there is a conflict. Example:

Bach, Johann Sebastian, 1685-1750.
[Kunst der Fuge]

If the title is distinctive and there *is* a conflict, the title is followed by some modification as instructed under rule 25.31B1. Example:

Bach, Johann Sebastian, 1685-1750.
[Wachet auf, ruft uns die Stimme (Cantata)]

Bach, Johann Sebastian, 1685-1750.
[Wachet auf, ruft uns die Stimme (Chorale prelude)]

However, if the title consists solely of the name of one type of composition, the title is constructed as instructed under rule 25.29A. Additions are then made according to rule 25.30: the medium of performance (the instruments for which it was written), followed by further identifying elements to distinguish the work from other compositions by the same composer, generally the serial number, opus (or thematic index) number, and the key. Examples:

Mozart, Wolfgang Amadeus, 1756-1791.
[Quartets, strings, K. 387, G major]
Quartett für 2 Violinen, Viola und Violoncello

Dvořák, Antonín, 1841-1904.
[Symphonies, no. 8, op. 88, G major]
From the new world : symphony no. 8 by Dvořák

Titles of works in the larger vocal forms (operas, oratorios, etc.) generally require additional modification because of the various versions in which they are likely to be issued. Example:

Puccini, Giacomo, 1858-1924.
[Manon Lescaut]
[Manon Lescaut.   Vocal score]
[Manon Lescaut.   Libretto.   English]

RULE 25.32.   PARTS OF A WORK
A separately published part of a musical work uses the title of the whole work, followed by the title of the part. This is counter to rule 25.6A1 for other types of works. Examples:

Arne, Thomas Augustine, 1710-1778.
[Artaxerxes.   Soldier tir'd]
Schumann, Robert, 1810-1856.
[Fantasiestücke, piano, op. 12. Nr. 7. Traumes Warren]

Collective Titles

RULES 25.33–25.34

These rules give principles for construction of a uniform title for items containing more than one work. Two works published together (rule 25.33) are treated as in rule 25.7. Complete works (rule 25.34A) are treated as in rule 25.8. A collection of selections of various types of compositions originally composed for various instrumental and/or vocal media is assigned the uniform title "Selections" (rule 25.34B). However, if a collection contains works of various types all in a broad or specific medium, the designation of that medium is used (rule 25.34C1). For example:

[Instrumental music]
[Vocal music]
[Brass music]
[Piano music]
[Violin, piano music]

If the collection contains works of one type, the name of that type is used, with the addition of medium in appropriate cases (rule 25.34C2). For example:

[Operas]
[Quartets, strings]
[Sonatas, piano]

Additions

RULE 25.35.   ADDITIONS FOR MUSICAL WORKS

Further additions are made to distinguish sketches for a musical composition, arrangements of a musical work, translations of texts of vocal works, etc. Example:

Cowell, Henry, 1897-1965.
[Concerto brevis; arr.]
Concerto brevis : for accordion and orchestra

REFERENCES

All the rules in the preceding sections of this chapter have referred to "references" needed when one name or form of heading is chosen from among more than one possible name or form of heading. This section is a summary of all those situations where references are called for explicitly or implicitly in the earlier rules. This section also gives examples of the different types of references. Chapter 26 of *AACR2R*, "References," begins with introductory notes that define different kinds of references, explain the form to use, and set up the conditions under which references should be made. Following this introduction are specific rules for and examples of references for persons, corporate bodies and geographic names, and uniform titles. Finally, there is a rule allowing references instead of certain added entries that are common to many editions.

References are not included in the bibliographic records for the information packages being cataloged when the references are made. Instead they are recorded in a record called an authority record. An authority record is a separate record for each name or title established as a heading to be used in the library's public catalog. It contains the established form for the heading, the forms from which references should be made to the established form, and, often, notes about the sources of information used in establishing the heading. In manual authority files the forms from which references are to be made are preceded by x's—one x precedes a *see from* reference, and two x's precede a *see also from* reference. In a machine-readable authority file headings and references are preceded by codes similar to those used in bibliographic records. There is a separate MARC 21 format for authority records. In this format 1XX codes precede headings, 4XX codes precede *see from* references, and 5XX codes precede *see also from* references. Sample authority records and further information about authority files are given in chapter 18 of this text.

Selected Rules and Examples

RULE 26.1.   GENERAL RULE

26.1A.   References are to be made as instructed in the previous sections of this chapter and also according to the more general instructions in *AACR2R*, chapter 26. References should be made only to a heading for which there is an entry in the catalog. (References made to headings that are not there are called *blind references* because they direct a user to something that cannot be seen.) A record of every reference made should be kept under the heading to which the reference refers. (This record is usually kept on an authority record for the heading that is being referred to. The record, among other things, enables one to correct or delete a reference when the heading is changed or deleted.)

26.1B.   *See* references
     See references are used to direct users from a form of name or title of a work that they have looked under to the form that has been chosen as the heading for that name or title. A *see* reference says to the user, "No, you won't find what you're looking for here; but if you'll look under _____, you will find something."

26.1C.   *See also* references
     See also references are used to direct users from a name or uniform title heading to a related name or uniform title heading. A *see also* reference says to the user, "Yes, there is some information here, and you may also be interested in related information that you can find under _____."

26.1D.   Name-title references
     Name-title references are used when a title has been entered under a personal or corporate name and either *see* or *see also* references are needed from another form of the title. When such references are needed, the name is given before the title in both the form referred from and the form referred to.

26.1E.   Explanatory references
     Explanatory references are used when more guidance or explanation than can be given in simple references is necessary.
     Terminology used in references is undergoing change with the expansion of online catalogs. In an online environment the codes 4XX and 5XX can be translated into other words or phrases than *see* and *see also*, if the creator of the system believes that other terminology would be more understandable to users. Popular substitutes are "search under" or "the heading used in this catalog is" for *see*, and "search also under" or "related information may be found under" for *see also*. Because *AACR2R*

uses *see* and *see also*, these terms are used in the remainder of this chapter for ease of explanation.

There is a lengthy LC rule interpretation that explains the forms that references should take on LC authority records, explaining, for example, how references for "compatible headings" might differ from those for "pure" *AACR2* headings. (*CSB* 47: 57–60)

26.1F.   Form of references

AACR2R suggests that the form of name from which a reference is made should have the same structure it would have if it were the heading rather than a reference to the heading. *AACR2R* also calls for making only one reference rather than two or more when one form is used to refer to more than one catalog heading. Examples:

Taylor, J. R.
   see also
Taylor, James Robert.
Taylor, John Roberts.

ACU
   see
Arbeitskreis Computer im Unterricht (Germany)
Association of Commonwealth Universities.
Association of Computer Users (U.S.)

LC makes individual references rather than combined references in these instances. (*CSB* 47: 60) Presumably this is because of the difficulty of maintaining records of such combined references in an automated system. However, in most online systems that have access to authority records a search for initials brings up a response screen that lists all the headings with authority records that have a reference from those initials. The wording of the examples of references in *AACR2R* and in this text is not intended to be prescriptive, but only to provide examples.

RULE 26.2.   NAMES OF PERSONS

26.2A.   *See* references

26.2A1.   Different names

When a person has used a name different from that chosen for the heading for that person, or when a different name is found in reference sources, a reference is made from the different name to the heading. (*See also* rule 26.2C1 and rule 26.2D1.) Examples:

Tosi, Maria Teresa, 1918-
   see
Maria Teresa dell'Eucaristia, suor, 1918-

Beyle, Marie Henri, 1783-1842
   see
Stendhal, 1783-1842.

Skłodowska-Curie, Maria, 1867-1934
   see
Curie, Marie, 1867-1934.

26.2A2.   Different forms of the name

If a form of name used by a person is significantly different from the form used for the heading for the person, a reference is made. For LC catalogers the policy for normal inverted headings is to make references from forms that have any variations to the left of the comma or in the first element to the right of the comma. (*CSB* 64: 44) Examples:

Burt, Stanley G.
> see
> Burt, S.G. (Stanley G.)

Abe, Suehisa, 1622-1709
> see
> Abe, Suenao, 1622-1709.

Ruth, George Herman, 1895-1948
> see
> Ruth, Babe, 1895-1948.

Homerus
> see
> Homer

26.2A3.   Different entry elements

A reference should be made from any element of a name heading under which a user might reasonably look for a name. Examples:

Van Zuidam, R. A.
> see
> Zuidam, R. A. van.

Buren, Ariane van
> see
> Van Buren, Ariane.

Damas, Bernardo Valverde
> see
> Valverde Damas, Bernardo.

Ram Acharya
> see
> Acharya, Ram.

Wellesley, Arthur, Duke of Wellington, 1769-1852
> see
> Wellington, Arthur Wellesley, Duke of, 1769-1852.

26.2C.   *See also* references

When a person is entered under two headings (e.g., two pseudonyms), *see also* references are made at each heading to direct the user also to search under the other heading. Example:

Baker, Ray Stannard, 1870-1946
   see also
Grayson, David, 1870-1946.

Grayson, David, 1870-1946
   see also
Baker, Ray Stannard, 1870-1946.

26.2D. Explanatory references

26.2D1.   Explanatory references are provided when more information is needed for guidance than can be given with a *see* or *see also* reference. Examples:

Stone, Rosetta
   The joint pseudonym of Michael K. Frith and Dr. Seuss.
For separate works entered under each name search also under:
   Frith, Michael K.
   Seuss, Dr.

Hunter, Evan, 1926-
      For works of this author written under pseudonyms, see
Collins, Hunt, 1926-
McBain, Ed, 1926-
Marsten, Richard, 1926-

26.2D2.   An option allows making an explanatory reference under each separately written prefix that can be used in a number of surnames. The purpose of such a reference is to explain how names with this prefix are entered in the catalog. Example:

Van
   Some names beginning with this prefix are also entered under the
   name following the prefix (e.g., Zuidam, R. A. van)

LC is not applying this option. Instead, individual references are traced for each heading. (*CSB* 30: 22)

RULE 26.3.   GEOGRAPHIC NAMES AND NAMES OF CORPORATE BODIES

26.3A.   *See* references

26.3A1.   Different names

When a corporate body or place has appeared in works or reference sources with a different name or names than that used for the catalog heading, a reference is made from the different name. If, however, the name represents a name *change*, use rule 26.3C1. Example:

Detroit (Mich.). Police Dept. God Squad
   see
Detroit (Mich.). Police Dept. Chaplain Corps.

26.3A3.   Different forms of the name

If a different form of name for a body or place is found in works or reference sources or if different romanizations result in different forms, references are made from the differing form(s). Examples:

A.B.E.D.I.A.
> see
> Arab Bank for Economic Development in Africa.

Wien (Austria)
> see
> Vienna (Austria)

Pharmaceutical Society of Korea
> see
> Taehan Yakhakhoe.

Kellogg Arabian Horse Center
> see
> W.K. Kellogg Arabian Horse Center.

General Aniline and Film Corp. Ansco
> see
> Ansco.

Society of Jesus
> see
> Jesuits.

Bradner Associates
> see
> Michael Bradner Associates.

26.3A5.   Numbers

If headings are arranged so that numbers expressed as words are displayed in a different place than numbers expressed as numerals, make references from the opposite form to the one used in the heading, if the number is in a position to affect the arrangement. Example:

3 Bridges Reformed Church (Three Bridges, N.J.)
> see
> Three Bridges Reformed Church (Three Bridges, N.J.)

26.3A6.   Abbreviations

If headings are arranged so that abbreviations are displayed in a different place than the equivalent words, refer from the full form to an abbreviation, if the abbreviation is in a position to affect the arrangement. Example:

Mount Auburn Associates (Somerville, Mass.)
> see
> Mt. Auburn Associates (Somerville, Mass.)

LC includes ampersands or other symbols that represent *and* here. If such a symbol occurs in the first five words, a reference from the name using *and* or its equivalent in the language of the heading is made. For other abbreviations to have a reference made, LC requires that they be in the first five words, not be listed in Appendix B.9 of *AACR2R, and* not represent a proper name. (*CSB* 21: 45)

26.3A7. Different forms of heading

References are made from different forms of a corporate name that seem to be reasonable forms under which a user might search. Examples:

Cambridge University
> see
> University of Cambridge.

California Institute of Technology. Baxter Art Gallery
> see
> Baxter Art Gallery.

Project Introspection
> see
> Virgin Islands of the United States. Project Introspection.

United States. Maritime Administration. Office of Commercial Development. Office of Port and Intermodal Development
> see
> United States. Office of Port and Intermodal Development.

Treviso (Italy). Cathedral
> see
> Treviso Cathedral.

26.3B. *See also* references

26.3B1. *See also* references are made between corporate headings that are related. This includes names that represent corporate name changes. LC calls these "earlier/later heading references," and instead of reading *see also*, the message of the reference reads "search also under the earlier heading" or "search also under the later heading." (*CSB* 59: 19) Examples:

Gemeentelijke Archiefdienst Amsterdam
> see also
> Amsterdam (Netherlands). Gemeentearchief.

Automotive Transport Association of Ontario
> search also under the later heading
> Ontario Trucking Association.

Ontario Trucking Association
> search also under the earlier heading
> Automotive Transport Association of Ontario

26.3C.   Explanatory references

26.3C1.   General rule

Explanatory references are made when more guidance is required. Examples:

United Nations. Missions.
   Delegations, missions, etc. from member nations to the United Nations and to its subordinate units are entered under the name of the nation followed by the name of the delegation, mission, etc., e.g.
      United States. Mission to the United Nations.
      Uruguay. Delegación en las Naciones Unidas.

A. Harris & Co.
   Sanger Brothers was established in 1857. A. Harris & Co. was established in 1886. In 1961 they merged to form Sanger-Harris.
   Works by these bodies are found under the following headings according to the name used at the time of publication:
      Sanger Brothers.
      A. Harris & Co.
      Sanger-Harris.

LC no longer makes references of this type. Instead each related body is connected with the earlier or later name by a *see also* reference. References like the "United Nations. Missions" example above are handled by placing specific *see* references on each applicable authority record. (*CSB* 59: 29)

26.3C2.   Acronyms

When a system arranges initials separated by periods in a different place from initials not separated by periods, *AACR2R* allows for making an explanatory reference. Examples:

N.A.C.
      see
   National Automobile Club
   Naval Avionics Center (U.S.)
      When these initials occur in a title or other heading without spaces or periods, they are arranged as a single word.

NAC
      see
   National Automobile Club
   Naval Avionics Center (U.S.)
      When these initials occur in a title or other heading with spaces or periods, they are arranged as if each initial is a single word.

LC no longer makes explanatory references for acronyms. They are converted to simple *see* references on the authority record for each name involved. (*CSB* 59: 29–30)

RULE 26.4.   UNIFORM TITLES

26.4A.   A rule calling for a reference to or from a uniform title, in some cases, means that the reference may require a name heading preceding the uniform title.

26.4B.   *See* **references**

26.4B1.   Different titles or variants of the title
When different titles have been used in other editions of a work than the one(s) held by the library, or when variant titles have been used to cite a work in reference sources, references may be made from these variants. Examples:

Laderman, Ezra.
   Trials of Galileo
     see
Laderman, Ezra.
   Galileo Galilei

Córdoba (Argentina : Province)
   Ley no. 4051
     see
Córdoba (Argentina : Province)
   Ley orgánica del poder judicial (1942)

Suder, Joseph, 1892-
   Festmesse, in D
     see
Suder, Joseph, 1892-
   Dona nobis pacem

Revueltas, Silvestre, 1899-1940.
   Chit-chat music
     see
Revueltas, Silvestre, 1899-1940.
   Música para charlar

> **[Title page title: Música para charlar = Chit-chat music. Title added entries would be made for both titles. In the other cases, a title added entry would be made for the title proper of the edition being cataloged.]**

When translated titles are involved, the reference is made from the translated version of the title to the uniform title followed by the appropriate language subheading. Examples:

Song of Roland
     see
Chanson de Roland. English

Naft, Stephen, 1878-1956.
   Kyōsanshugi ni taisura nijū no shitsumon
     see
Naft, Stephen, 1878-1956.
   Answer please! Questions for communists. Japanese

26.4B2.   Titles of parts of a work cataloged independently
When a part of a work is cataloged so that the part is entered independently, a reference is made from the uniform title of the whole work with the part as a subheading to the title of the part as an independent entry. Example:

Hesse, Hermann, 1877-1962.
    Steppenwolf. Tractat vom Steppenwolf
    see
Hesse, Hermann, 1877-1962.
    Tractat vom Steppenwolf

26.4B3. Titles of parts cataloged under the title of the whole work

When a part of a work is cataloged so that the part is a subheading of the whole work, and if the title of the part is distinctive, a reference is made from the title of the part to the uniform title of the whole work with the part as a subheading. Examples:

Strauss, Richard, 1864-1949.
    Breit über mein Haupt dein schwarzes Haar
    see
Strauss, Richard, 1864-1949.
    Lieder, op. 19. Breit über mein Haupt dein schwarzes Haar

Mu`awwidhatan
    see
    Koran. Mu`awwidhatān.

26.4B4. Collective titles

If a collection or selection of works of one person has been given a collective uniform title, and if the title proper is distinctive, a name-title reference is made from the title proper to the uniform title. Example:

Shepp, Archie.
    Further fire music
    see
Shepp, Archie.
    Instrumental music. Selections

RULE 26.5.   REFERENCES TO ADDED ENTRIES FOR SERIES AND SERIALS

This rule states that, when making an added entry for either a series to which individually cataloged parts belong, or under the heading for a serial, references should be made from different forms of the series or serial heading that users might reasonably search under. A lengthy LC rule interpretation for rule 26.5A provides guidance for making such references in the case of series added entries. (*CSB* 78: 76–85)

NOTES

1. *Cataloging Service Bulletin*, no. 17 (Summer 1982): 31.

2. *Cataloging Service Bulletin*, no. 81 (Summer 1998): 27–28.

3. *Anglo-American Cataloging Rules, Second Edition, 1998 Revisions*, prepared under the direction of the Joint Steering Committee for Revision of AACR (Chicago: American Library Association, 1998), p. 621.

4.   *AACR2R98*, p. 384.

5.   For examples of references, *see* the section on references in this chapter: "References" (p. 251).

6.   *AACR2R98*, p. 389.

7.   *AACR2R98*, p. 417.

8.   *AACR2R98*, p. 312.

9.   *Cataloging Service Bulletin*, no. 41 (Summer 1988): 54.

10.   *AACR2R98*, p. 484.

SUGGESTED READING

Chan, Lois Mai. *Cataloging and Classification: An Introduction.* 2nd ed. New York: McGraw-Hill, 1994. Chapters 5–6.

Hagler, Ronald. *The Bibliographic Record and Information Technology.* 3rd ed. Chicago: American Library Association, 1997. Chapter 6.

Maxwell, Robert L., with Margaret F. Maxwell. *Maxwell's Handbook for AACR2R.* Chicago: American Library Association, 1997. Chapters 15–18.

Smiraglia, Richard P. *Cataloging Music: A Manual for Use with AACR2.* 2nd ed. Lake Crystal, Minn.: Soldier Creek Press, 1986. Chapter 3: Uniform Titles.

———. *Music Cataloging: The Bibliographic Control of Printed and Recorded Music in Libraries.* Englewood, Colo.: Libraries Unlimited, 1989, pp. 54–61.

Part IV
SUBJECT ANALYSIS

8 Subject Access to Library Materials

INTRODUCTION

Subject analysis is the part of cataloging that deals with determining what the intellectual content of an item is "about," translating that "aboutness" into the conceptual framework of the classification or subject heading system being used, and then translating the conceptual framework into the specific classificatory symbols or specific terminology used in the classification or subject heading system.

First, one must have a clear idea about the level of exhaustivity that is to be applied. Exhaustivity has to do with the number of concepts that will be considered in the conceptual framework of the system. A. G. Brown identifies two basic degrees of exhaustivity: depth indexing and summarization.[1] Depth indexing aims to extract all the main concepts dealt with in an item, recognizing many subtopics and subthemes. Summarization recognizes only a dominant, overall subject of the item, recognizing only concepts embodied in the main theme. In library cataloging subject analysis has traditionally been carried out at the summarization level, reserving depth indexing for other enterprises such as periodical indexes.

Determining what an item is about at the summarization level can be a difficult matter. In chapter 1 Charles A. Cutter's statement of the basic functions of a catalog was quoted, including "To show what the library has . . . on a given subject." (*See* p. 7.) The implication of this is that it is obvious what being "on a given subject" means. Patrick Wilson has discussed this matter at some length and has suggested that part of the problem is that catalogers and others are taught to look for *the* subject of an item.[2] He observes that if a person is writing a book or paper, and you ask what the person is writing about, he or she can tell you. If you go further and ask what is the subject about which the person is writing, this seems to be an equivalent question; but using the definite article *the* in front of *subject* implies that there will be just one thing to mention in answer to the question. Wilson's further explication demonstrates the fallacy of this assumption.[3]

Although some items *seem* to have an easily determined subject, it may not be so. A work entitled *History of Mathematics* is about the discipline of mathematics; but it is more specifically about mathematics from a historical perspective while not being about the discipline of history. This distinction has a certain subtlety that is learned through education in our present-day Western tradition. It is possible that in another place and time history would be considered to be the major subject of anything historical, regardless of the specific topic. Let us take another example: *Nature in Italian Art: A Study of Landscape Backgrounds from Giotto to Tintoretto*. This work is about landscape painting—specifically in Italian art during a set period of time. Is it *about* Italian art? Who is to say that it would not be useful to someone searching for information on Italian art? Is it about Giotto and Tintoretto and all the landscape artists in between? Of course it is, and if one were doing depth indexing, all would be indexed; but if one is looking for *the* subject, a listing of names of numerous artists will not do.

Determining what something is about depends to some extent upon one's knowledge or opinions about the world and upon understanding a work in different ways depending upon one's experiences. Many people could read a list of names that included Giotto and Tintoretto and not know that the list was a list of Italian artists, not to mention that they were landscape painters. A person could understand each individual sentence in a writing and still not know what the writing as a whole was about.

In addition determination of "aboutness" may depend on judgment. This problem has been elaborated upon by W. C. Berwick Sayers:

> If [a] book on Scotland is not mainly geographic and historical, but consists of descriptive and narrative chapters together with a melange of literary and scientific observations and reflections on the national traits and institutions, also considerable social philosophy in the last chapters, the judgment is indeed complex and the decisions may be uncertain.[4]

Because it is difficult to define what "on a given subject" means, and because determining "aboutness" depends upon the indexer's or cataloger's knowledge, opinions, experiences, and judgment, Marcia Bates has observed that "it is practically impossible to instruct indexers or catalogers [on] how to find subjects when they examine documents. Indeed, we cataloging instructors usually deal with this essential feature of the skill being taught by saying such vague and inadequate things as 'Look for the main topic of the document.' "[5]

Although there is no one correct way to determine "aboutness," one suggested method is presented in A. G. Taylor's *The Organization of Information*.[6] The book also includes an appendix that gives a workform listing concepts to consider.[7] Two other works that are useful for someone faced with the need to determine "aboutness" are *Documentation: Methods for Examining Documents, Determining Their Subjects and Selecting Indexing Terms*, published by the International Organization for Standardization, and *Subject Analysis: Principles and Procedures*, by D. W. Langridge.[8] These give suggested guidelines on what to look for when doing subject analysis.

Prior to the 1980s there was considerable antipathy toward subject access in the United States based in part on studies that showed that academic library card catalog users used a subject approach only about 30 percent of the time. However, Karen Markey constructed a grid of card catalog use studies in several types of libraries completed between 1967 and 1981 that shows that subject approaches in card catalogs varied from 10 percent to 62 percent and the median was about 40 percent.[9] More recent studies of online catalog users have showed that subject access in online catalogs is quite popular—one study of many types of libraries with different online systems showed that subject approaches were about 59 percent of all catalog uses.[10] It must be assumed, therefore, that subject analysis has been done well enough that people find it useful, if not perfect.

Once the cataloger has decided what he or she thinks an item is about, that "aboutness" must be translated into the conceptual framework of the system. If one is classifying, this usually means one must determine disciplines, subdisciplines, subtopics, space (i.e., place in which the subject is set), time, and form (e.g., historical treatment, dictionary). A. G. Brown gives an excellent introduction to the process of learning to place one's subject into a conceptual framework necessary for classification.[11] If one is using a verbal subject system, completion of a sentence beginning, "This information package is about . . ." serves well as a translation device into the conceptual framework of thinking about words that can be used to identify the intellectual content of the information package.

Finally, the cataloger assigns classification symbols from the particular classification scheme being used and subject headings either according to a set of rules, as is the case with PRECIS headings (*see* discussion of PRECIS in chapter 17), or from a controlled list of headings, which may also have rules for using the list, as is the case with *Library of Congress Subject Headings (LCSH)* or with the *Sears List of Subject Headings (Sears)*. (*See* discussion of *LCSH* and *Sears* in chapters 15 and 16.) The classification notation is usually used as the basis for a call number for a physical information package, that will determine the position of the item on the library's shelves. The subject term(s) most often appear as access points for the item in the library's catalog.

CLASSIFIED VERSUS ALPHABETIC APPROACH TO INFORMATION

During cataloging, the cataloger must take into account the dual manifestations of the physical items to be added to the collection. Such items are both intellectual and physical entities. In descriptive cataloging the physical description addresses the physical entity while access points are constructed to allow for approach to the intellectual work. In subject analysis, classifiers traditionally choose only one classification, which will place in one location on the shelves all copies of a given physical item. On the other hand, catalogers may choose more than one subject term or classification under which to represent an item in a catalog or index. Classifiers strive for the optimum location in view of the content of the item, the accepted classification schedule, and the needs of the clientele. Such decisions are not always easy to make. For instance, the same historical treatise might go equally well into political or economic history, or perhaps under social history or biography. In the choice of subjects to be represented in the catalog or index for this hypothetical treatise, all the aspects can be brought out through choice of multiple access points. And, of course, virtual information packages (e.g., Web pages) are not limited to only one place on any shelf.

Inquirers who want information on a certain subject will approach the catalog with questions formulated in their own words. These terms must be translated into the predetermined access categories of the catalog. Such communication between inquirer and catalog, with the possible intervention of a librarian, must take place regardless of the type of catalog consulted or the arrangement of its entries.

Two systems of arranging entries in a library catalog were discussed in chapter 1. Classified catalogs were said to be the older of the two, although in present-day libraries they are less numerous than alphabetical approaches. If classified catalogs are to make a comeback, it probably will be because the alphabetical "index" will be combined with the classified display arrangement. Getting to a subject area using words, the user will be able to browse up and down a hierarchy and will be able to explore related concepts through hyperlinks. The connection between inquirers and subject headings (the "alphabetical" approach) has been greatly facilitated by the use of keyword searching. Instead of the user's terminology having to coincide with that of a controlled list, the user enters the system with his or her own terminology. Seldom is there no match unless the terminology used is misspelled. Once a record has been identified that seems to match the user's subject need, subject headings on the record can be searched specifically to find other records on the subject and to find the subject's reference structure of broader terms, narrower terms, and related terms.

Each approach in a catalog requires a different pattern of communication. The classified catalog offers a "vertical" (hierarchical) approach to the collection through its closely related classes and categories, under which materials can be identified by means of logical, orderly sequences from general to specific. The alphabetical catalog gives a "horizontal" approach through its random scattering of access points throughout the entire linguistic finding apparatus.

With online catalogs it is possible to have both approaches in the same catalog, and some experimentation with this is being done. For the most part, so far, access by classification notation in online catalogs is a shelflist approach—that is, there is only one classification notation for any one item. Karen Markey and Anh Demeyer experimented with making the verbal terms associated with *Dewey Decimal Classification (DDC)* numbers in the scheme itself searchable alongside the subject headings assigned. They found that searchers locate approximately equal numbers of relevant items using either the traditional subject headings or the terminology associated with the classification, but the groups of relevant items retrieved by the two methods are different from each other.[12]

It may be that keyword searching will soon be enhanced by the power of ontologies. The field of Natural Language Processing (NLP) uses lexical ontologies to provide analysis of language. Ontologies include terms with an analysis of each term into its usage as different parts of speech, and within each part of speech, it gives the various senses in which a term may be used. For example, a fence may be a structure built to set off a particular area, or a fence may be a receiver of stolen goods. Then within each sense, synonyms, antonyms, related terms, broader terms, narrower terms, etc., are given. The potential for ontologies in catalogs is that when a user searches the catalog for a particular keyword, the system could present the user with the various senses of that word, from which the user could choose the one wanted. A further step could be to ask the user if he or she wishes to search for all synonyms to the sense chosen.[13]

CONCLUSION

This chapter has discussed the topic of subject analysis and arrangement of library materials both by classification and by verbal/alphabetical approaches. In the chapters that follow, these two approaches are considered separately along with systems and schemes for implementing each approach. The student should remember, however, that these are two sides of the same coin and that both are attempts to provide users with access to the intellectual contents of the items being analyzed. For more discussion of controlled vocabularies, ontologies, and classification theory and concepts, the reader is referred to Taylor's *The Organization of Information*.[14]

NOTES

1.   A. G. Brown, in collaboration with D. W. Langridge and J. Mills, *An Introduction to Subject Indexing*, 2nd ed. (London: Bingley, 1982), frames 48 and 51.

2.   Patrick Wilson, "Subjects and the Sense of Position," in *Theory of Subject Analysis: A Sourcebook*, edited by Lois Mai Chan, Phyllis A. Richmond, and Elaine Svenonius (Littleton, Colo.: Libraries Unlimited, 1985), p. 309.

3.   Wilson, "Subjects and the Sense of Position," pp. 309–320.

4.   W. C. Berwick Sayers, *Sayers' Manual of Classification for Librarians*, 3rd ed. rev. by Arthur Maltby (London: Andre Deutsch, 1955), pp. 235–236.

5.   Marcia Bates, "Subject Access in Online Catalogs: A Design Model," *Journal of the American Society for Information Science* 37, no. 6 (November 1986): 360.

6.   Arlene G. Taylor, *The Organization of Information* (Englewood, Colo.: Libraries Unlimited, 1999), pp. 131–143.

7.   Ibid., pp. 229–232.

8.   *Documentation: Methods for Examining Documents, Determining Their Subjects and Selecting Indexing Terms* (Geneva, Switzerland: International Organization for Standardization, 1985); D. W. Langridge, *Subject Analysis: Principles and Procedures* (London: Bowker-Saur, 1989).

9.   Karen Markey, *Subject Searching in Library Catalogs: Before and After the Introduction of Online Catalogs* (Dublin, Ohio: OCLC, 1984), pp. 75–77.

10.   *Using Online Catalogs: A Nationwide Survey*, edited by Joseph R. Matthews, Gary S. Lawrence, and Douglas K. Ferguson; sponsored by the Council on Library Resources (New York: Neal-Schuman, 1983), p. 144.

11.   Brown, *Introduction to Subject Indexing*, frames 91–130.

12.   Karen Markey and Anh Demeyer, *Dewey Decimal Classification Online Project: Evaluation of a Library Schedule and Index Integrated into the Subject Searching Capabilities of an Online Catalog: Final Report to the Council on Library Resources* (Dublin, Ohio: OCLC, 1986).

13.   For more about ontologies *see*: Vickery, B. C. "Ontologies," *Journal of Information Science* 23, no. 4 (1997): 277–286.

14.   Arlene G. Taylor, "Verbal Subject Analysis," Chapter 8, and "Classification," Chapter 9 in *The Organization of Information* (Englewood, Colo.: Libraries Unlimited, 1999).

SUGGESTED READING

Brown, A. G., in collaboration with D. W. Langridge and J. Mills. *An Introduction to Subject Indexing*. 2nd ed. London: Bingley, 1982 [programmed text].

Chan, Lois Mai. *Cataloging and Classification: An Introduction*. 2nd ed. New York: McGraw-Hill, 1994. Chapter 7.

Documentation: Methods for Examining Documents, Determining Their Subjects and Selecting Indexing Terms. Geneva, Switzerland: International Organization for Standardization, 1985.

Foskett, A. C. *The Subject Approach to Information*. 5th ed. London: Library Association Publishing, 1996.

Fugmann, Robert. *Subject Analysis and Indexing: Theoretical Foundation and Practical Advice*. Frankfurt am Main: Indeks Verlag, 1993.

Hagler, Ronald. *The Bibliographic Record and Information Technology*. 3rd ed. Chicago: American Library Association, 1997. Chapter 7.

Langridge, D. W. *Subject Analysis: Principles and Procedures*. London: Bowker-Saur, 1989.

Subject Indexing: Principles and Practices in the 90's: Proceedings of the IFLA Satellite Meeting Held in Lisbon, Portugal, 17–18 August 1993. Munich: Saur, 1995.

Taylor, Arlene G. *The Organization of Information*. Englewood, Colo.: Libraries Unlimited, 1999. Chapters 8 and 9.

Wilson, Patrick. "Subjects and the Sense of Position." In *Theory of Subject Analysis: A Sourcebook*, edited by Lois Mai Chan, Phyllis A. Richmond, and Elaine Svenonius. Littleton, Colo.: Libraries Unlimited, 1985.

9 Classification of Library Materials

INTRODUCTION

Collections in libraries of any appreciable size are arranged according to some system, and the arrangement is generally referred to as classification. Classification provides formal, orderly access to the shelves.

No matter what scheme is chosen, or how large the library, the purpose of classification is to bring related items together in a helpful sequence from the general to the specific. Ease of access is especially important if the collection is heterogeneous. It is convenient and desirable—particularly in the open-shelf collections to which many libraries in the United States are committed—to have, for example, all histories of the United States together, or all items on symbolic logic, or all symphony scores, so that the patron, who may or may not have one title in mind, can find related works in one location.

The ultimate aim of any classification system is to lead the patron to the information packages required. Traditionally in the United States this has been accomplished either through direct search of the shelves (open stacks) or through the help of a library attendant whose duty is to retrieve the materials on demand (closed stacks). Each system has its virtues. Open stacks encourage browsing, and thus stimulate intellectual awareness and foster serendipity. They work best with a logical, fairly comprehensible system of classification that encourages the patron's self-reliance in seeking items on a particular subject or its specific aspects. Closed stacks lessen the chances that materials will be mishandled, misplaced, or stolen, but they force the patron to limit his or her own searching to the catalog (and perhaps the shelflist) and to wait for a library employee to bring items specifically requested. Closed stacks are valuable in a storage library situation where items may not be shelved in subject groups at all, but ranged in more or less fixed location by size, with consecutive numbers assigned as addresses. ["Fixed location" means that each item has one specific, fixed position on the shelf in the library as was the case in many libraries prior to the mid-nineteenth century. "Relative location" is a fluid, constantly changing arrangement of items according to their relationship to one another and resulting from the addition of new materials or the removal of old, weeded, or lost materials. In this system items may be moved from shelf to shelf without altering or disturbing their classified sequence.] Now, in addition to the traditional approaches, libraries offer classified access to Internet resources through the catalog. And many Web sites, themselves, offer a classified arrangement to the hyperlinks accumulated at the site.

271

LIBRARY CLASSIFICATION

Organized documentary collections have existed since early civilizations learned to convert their spoken languages to written forms. Even before the codex book appeared, early record depositories received some form of utilitarian arrangement. Groupings were made by title, by broad subject, by chronology, by author, by order of acquisition, by size, etc. One of the earliest catalogs was the one known as *Pinakes* (Greek for "tablets with wax in the middle") compiled for the great Alexandrian library by the poet Callimachus in the third century B.C. Although this catalog did not survive, it is known that it arranged the entries in at least 10 (and possibly more) main classes, subdivided alphabetically by author. In the Middle East and in the Byzantine Empire it served as a model for other catalogs and bibliographies until the early Middle Ages. The monastery libraries of that time in Western Europe were mostly small and had almost no need for classification, but the university libraries of the late Middle Ages arranged books corresponding to the Trivium and Quadrivium, the traditional seven subject fields taught. Within the classes, books had fixed locations on the shelves.

Beginning in the sixteenth century, librarians devised many different classification schemes for the arrangement of books, but fixed locations predominated in most European and early American libraries until the mid-nineteenth century. The most substantive developments in the arrangement of library collections were concurrent with the rapid growth of libraries and their use during the nineteenth century. At that time librarians felt a definite need for better methods of arrangement, so that the content of their holdings would be available, and more apparent, to the user.

The history of modern library classification corresponds to the various attempts to adapt and modify existing philosophical systems of knowledge to the arrangement of materials and to users' needs. One of the best known early American classifiers was Thomas Jefferson, third president of the United States. He adapted certain elements of Francis Bacon's outline of knowledge, not only to his own library, but also to his plans for the organization of the University of Virginia and the reorganization of the College of William and Mary.

Bacon's system classified materials as functions of the three basic faculties: history (natural, civil, literary, ecclesiastical) as the function of memory; philosophy (including theology) as that of reason; and poetry, fables, and the like as that of imagination.[1] Its influence was widespread. Jean Le Rond d'Alembert used the Baconian system for the arrangement of the famous *Encyclopédie ou dictionnaire raisonné des sciences des arts et des métiers* of the French Enlightenment (1751–1765). Jefferson's classification was based on that modification as was the *Catalogue* of Benjamin Franklin's Library Company of Philadelphia (1789). Three years before Jefferson's *Catalogue of the Library of the United States* was installed at the Library of Congress (LC), a variant of the Philadelphia scheme was used to produce the 1812 *Catalogue of the Library of Congress*.[2]

Among other early followers of the Baconian system were Thaddeus Mason Harris, librarian at Harvard (1791–1793); Edward William Johnson, librarian of the College of South Carolina and later of the St. Louis Mercantile Library; and, finally, Johnson's successor, William Torrey Harris, a Hegelian who inverted the Baconian system, creating an independent American classification. At the same time, various adaptations of the Brunet utilitarian classification scheme existed in several American libraries as a direct result of its use to arrange parts of the British Museum and the Bibliothèque Nationale.

In 1876 Melvil Dewey devised his famous *Dewey Decimal Classification* (*DDC*), based in large part on W. T. Harris's system, with a decimal notation. Soon *DDC* was spreading its influence throughout the world. At about the same time, Charles A. Cutter began his work at the Boston Athenaeum. Cutter sought to achieve, not a classification of knowledge, but a practical, useful method for arranging library materials. Nevertheless, his *Expansive Classification* shows the definite influence of Spencer and Comte, especially in the development of its subordinate classes.

Toward the end of the 19th century, when LC had grown from several thousand books to nearly one million, it was apparent that the library would need a new classification system. After much deliberation, J. C. M. Hanson and Charles Martel decided to design an independent system governed by the actual content of the collection (literary warrant). This form of classification differed from a purely philosophical approach in that it was based on the books as entities. For this reason *Library of Congress Classification* (*LCC*) is enumerative. An *enumerative* classification attempts to assign designations for (to enumerate) all the single and composite subject concepts required in the system. Hierarchical classification is based on the assumption that the process of subdivision and collocation must exhibit as much as possible the "natural" organization of the subject, proceeding from classes to divisions to subdivisions and following, at least in part, the rules of division as set down by "logic." *Faceted* classifications confine their explicit lists of designations to single, unsubdivided concepts, giving the local classifier generalized rules with which to construct headings for composite subjects (*see* the section of this chapter below, "Faceted Classification").

In summary, established philosophical systems of knowledge, with various modifications, underlie most traditional library classifications. The frequent distinction between classification of knowledge and classification of materials seems to have confused the thinking of many librarians. The two processes have important interactions. Even cursory examination of any library classification, including those purporting to organize "the items themselves," reveals an intellectual concept of the item as an expression of certain ideas in one of many available media. Philosophical classification organizes knowledge itself—registering, evaluating, and classifying thoughts, ideas, and concepts for the universal purpose of adequately representing the field of human learning. Library classification arranges the records that express and preserve knowledge, making adjustments as needed because of the physical format of such records.

For more discussion of classification theory and concepts, the reader is referred to Taylor's *The Organization of Information*.[3]

TRADITIONAL CLASSIFICATION SCHEMES

Most traditional classification systems are basically both hierarchical and enumerative. By contrast, the more recent schemes tend to be faceted. In this introductory text the discussion will apply generally all three types. It is well to remember that materials on shelves or in files are arranged in a single order. Most items can be requested by author, title, subject, or form, but they can be organized by only one of these at a time. Linear arrangement imposes certain limitations on the classifier. Over the years efforts to meet such limitations have resulted in techniques or features that are characteristic of nearly every library classification.

One such feature is a generalia or general works class, which accommodates items that are too broad in scope for inclusion in any single class. Such works usually overlap several traditional disciplines or "classes," e.g., encyclopedias, dictionaries, general periodicals, etc. In addition, genre classes organize materials according to their form of presentation rather than to their subject content. Literary works, e.g., poetry, drama, fiction, etc., are the most obvious, but books of etchings, photographs, musical scores, etc., also fall into this group. Form divisions group items in a class according to their form or mode of treatment. For example, notations for outlines, dictionaries, or periodicals are used to pull together those presentations; and notations for philosophical treatments, research in a subject, histories, and biographies show the "inner form" of items.

A notation is a shorthand code for the class, division, and subdivisions chosen for an item. It may be composed of letters, numerals, arbitrary signs, or a mixture of these. Notation can be of two types, pure or mixed. Pure notation uses only one kind of symbol. *DDC*, for example, uses numbers only (e.g., 974.1, meaning history of Maine). Mixed notation uses two or more kinds of symbols. *LCC*, for example, uses letters and numbers (e.g., BF575.G7, meaning psychology of the emotion of grief).

A final feature of traditional classification schemes is the index. The index provides an alphabetical approach to the classified part of the scheme.

FACETED CLASSIFICATION

A faceted classification differs from a traditional one in that it does not assign fixed slots to subjects in sequence, but uses clearly defined, mutually exclusive, and collectively exhaustive aspects, properties, or characteristics of a class or specific subject. Such aspects, properties, or characteristics are called *facets* of a class or subject, a term introduced into classification theory and given this new meaning by the Indian librarian and classificationist, S. R. Ranganathan, and first used in his *Colon Classification* in the early 1930s. Although the term was then new to classification, the idea was not (as Ranganathan freely admitted). It had its roots in Dewey's device of place (location) using a standard number (e.g., the United States always being 73) appended to any subject number by means of digits 09, a device now known as a *facet indicator*. Dewey recognized three things:

1. That certain characteristics such as "belonging to a place," "being in the form of a periodical," and some others are general and should be applicable to all subjects

2. That such a number must be clearly distinguished from the class notation for the main subject to avoid confusion

3. That two or more facets could be combined to express a complex subject—his "number building" device (e.g., the subject "frost damage to oranges" can be expressed by adding to the class notation 634.31 for oranges the facet indicator 9 and the last two digits taken from the subject "plant injuries: low temperatures" 632.11, to result in 634.31911)

Most other classification schemes designed after Dewey also provided generally applicable facets for places and time periods, and often also for forms. Even *LCC*, which is an entirely enumerative scheme, included such facets, although they were specially developed for each class as a part of the enumerative structure and are not uniformly applicable in all classes. The *Universal Decimal Classification* (*UDC*) expanded Dewey's "standard subdivisions" to about a dozen generally applicable "auxiliaries" (*see* the section on *UDC* in chapter 10). Finally, the *Colon Classification* introduced the fully faceted approach by means of class notations constructed entirely from individual facets in a prescribed sequence from the most specific to the most general.

Originally, Ranganathan postulated five basic facets: personality (i.e., the focal or most specific subject), material, energy (i.e., any activity, operation, or process), space, and time, known as the "PMEST formula." These basic facets were used to analyze a class or subject and to construct a composite class notation for it. For example, the subject "the design of metal ploughshares in the 19th century U.S." shows all five facets: from the most general to the most specific, 19th century is the time facet; U.S. is the space (or place) facet; design (an activity) is the energy facet; metal is the material facet; and ploughshares, the focal subject, is personality. It was soon found that these five basic facets were too broad and that most classes or disciplines needed tailor-made facets; e.g., the field of education can be broken down into facets for students, educators, teaching methods, subjects taught, level of instruction, etc.; agriculture has the facets crops, operations (sowing, harvesting, etc.), implements and tools, etc.

Each facet must have a distinctive notation and a facet indicator to show the sequence of facets unambiguously. For example, a classification notation from Ranganathan's *Colon Classification* is: J , 381 ; 4 : 5 . 42 ' N70.[4] It is for a book on the eradication of virus in rice plants in Japan, 1971. Each punctuation mark shows what facet is coming next:

, (comma)	personality
; (semicolon)	matter
: (colon)	energy
. (period)	space
' (apostrophe)	time

In the notation given, the first category is for a main subject, not part of the PMEST formula. Main subjects correspond roughly to academic areas. The breakdown of the notation is:

J	agriculture	(main subject)
381	rice plant	(personality)
4	virus disease	(matter)
5	eradication	(energy)
42	Japan	(space)
N70	1970s	(time)

A faceted structure relieves a classification from a rigid hierarchical arrangement and from having to create thousands of fixed "pigeonholes" for subjects that happened to be known or were foreseen when a system was designed. Such systems often left no room for future developments and made no provision for the expression of complex relationships. Enumeration is, however, not entirely absent from faceted schemes: the *Colon Classification* has some 50 main classes, largely corresponding to traditional disciplines.

All traditional schemes are essentially based on the strictly hierarchical genus-species relationship for most of their subdivisions. Faceted schemes recognize this relationship where warranted, but also display others, such as whole-part, operations and processes, agents and tools, substances, physical forms, organizational aspects, and many more as needed, for each specific field or subject. The design of faceted classification schemes is treated in detail by B. C. Vickery.[5]

A faceted class notation, such as those in the examples above, is not necessarily meant to serve as a shelving device or "call number" (although all or part of it may be so used) but rather for the arrangement of items in bibliographies and access service databases, where the faceted notation provides a helpful sequence, and the individual facets can be accessed and retrieved either alone or in any desired combination. This feature is especially important for online retrieval, which has been successfully applied to faceted classification,[6] as a complement to verbal retrieval methods by subject headings or keywords.

The faceted approach is, indeed, not limited to the construction and assignment of class notations. It is clearly discernible also in verbal subject indication, e.g., a subject heading such as "**Newspapers—United States—Bibliography**" shows "United States" as the place facet and "bibliography" as the form facet. The "List of subdivisions" in the *Sears List of Subject Headings* (*Sears*) is actually a list of generally applicable facets (although it is not arranged systematically as it would be in a faceted classification).

Since the 1960s all major classification schemes (with the exception of *LCC*) either have been partially restructured on a faceted basis or display a fully faceted structure. The influence of faceted classification theory has been most conspicuous in *DDC*, which now offers facets not only for its traditional "standard subdivisions" and areas, but also for individual literatures and languages, for racial, ethnic, and national groups, for persons, and in completely revised schedules for such areas as music and biology that rely heavily on faceting in their internal structures. Special faceted classifications have been designed for broad fields such as education or business management, as well as for more specialized ones such as occupational safety, the diamond industry, library and information science, and many others (*see* the section titled "Special Classification Schemes" in chapter 13).

CRITERIA FOR A SUCCESSFUL CLASSIFICATION SCHEME

Classification schemes, as indicated earlier, vary widely. Besides providing for the subject organization of the collection, a successful classification scheme may also contain devices for indicating method of treatment or form of materials treated, time periods, places, peoples, various types of persons, and other special categories.

Any or all of these devices may be justifiably and successfully used for a special situation such as a rare book collection or a collection concerned with a particular subject area or period. Following is a list of a few criteria that may be generally applied to judge a successful general knowledge classification system:

- **It must be inclusive as well as comprehensive.** That is, it must encompass the whole field of knowledge as represented in collectible media of communication and information. It must therefore include all subjects that are, have been, or may be recognized, allowing for possible future additions to the body of knowledge. It must make provision, not only for the records themselves, but also for every actual and potential use of the records.

- **It must be systematic.** Not only must the division of subjects be exhaustive, but it must also bring together related topics in logical, comprehensible fashion, allowing its users to locate easily whatever they want that is available. It must be so arranged that each aspect of a subject can be considered a separate, yet related, part of the scheme, and it must be so arranged that new topics and aspects can be added in a systematic manner.

- **It must be flexible and expansible.** It must be constructed so that any new subject may be inserted without dislocating the general sequence of classification. It must allow for recognized knowledge in all its ramifications, and it must be capable of admitting new subjects or new aspects of well-established subjects. The flexibility of the notation is of first importance if the classification scheme is to be expansive and hospitable in the highest degree. It should also be current. *DDC*, for example, is kept up-to-date with the publication of *Decimal Classification Additions, Notes, and Decisions (DC&)* on the Dewey Web site.[7] These notices and revisions are especially important in subject areas in which a great deal of new work is being done.

- **It must employ terminology that is clear and descriptive, with consistent meaning for both the user and the classifier.** The arrangement of terms in the schedule and the index should help reveal the significance of the arrangement. The terms themselves should be unambiguous and reasonably current, correctly identifying the concepts and characteristics present in the materials being classified.

BROAD AND CLOSE
CLASSIFICATION

Close classification means classing each work as specifically as possible, using all available subdivisions in the classification scheme. Broad classification groups works under the main divisions and main subdivisions of the scheme, without using its minute breakdowns into narrower concepts. When a library has relatively few items in a given subject area, broad classification might actually be more useful than isolating each item under its own specific class. A library using the *DDC* with a large collection of Bibles, for example, may need to classify the King James Version in 220.5203, whereas a smaller collection might cut back to the broad number 220. Generally speaking, *DDC* provides small libraries with more opportunities than does *LCC* to cut back to broader notations, because its enumeration stresses hierarchies of subject matter, while *LCC* has relatively few notations that signify broad categories.

GENERAL PRINCIPLES OF CLASSIFYING

Most of this chapter has been directed to the broad principles, methods, and problems of constructing classification systems. Some attention should now be given to choosing the optimum location for each item.

When classifying an item with respect to a particular library's holdings, it is often tempting to arrange items with local needs in mind, but classification schemes vary in their hospitality to local manipulation. It is assumed that such possibilities and difficulties were considered when the choice was made of one scheme over all others for use in a local library.

Once the particular system of arrangement is chosen, certain general precepts enable the classifier to apply it meaningfully to the information packages being organized by the library. The following summary is designed to aid that process. These principles apply primarily to both the *DDC* and the *LCC* schemes.

- **In general class the item first according to subject, then by the form in which the subject is represented.** There are exceptions, of course. For example in *DDC*, in literature, classification is first by country/language, then by form, then by time period, then by author; in *LCC*, classification is first by country/language, then by time period, then by author, then by form. Subject does not figure into the classification in either case.

- **Class an item where it will be most useful.** The classifier has to consider the nature of the collection and the needs of the user. For example, should a sports biography be classified with sports or with biography? The answer to this question might be quite different in a school library than in a library that specializes in sports materials.

- **Place the item in the most specific subject division that will contain it, rather than with the general topic.** This principle, of course, may be affected by a decision to use broad rather than close classification. Most libraries, for example, classify general French histories together and then subdivide the rest of the items dealing with the history of France by the specific time periods or local places they cover. To assign the same notation to all would result in a discouragingly large assortment of volumes under one notation. On the other hand, small libraries might prefer to classify all of their few volumes dealing with this subject in the general classification.

- **When the book deals with two or three subjects, place it with the predominant subject or with the one treated first. When the book deals with more than three subjects, place it in the general class that combines all of them.** This principle requires little explanation. The subject that is treated most fully should take predominance over secondary subjects. If two subjects are coordinate (e.g., electricity and magnetism treated equally in the same volume) the information package should be classified with whichever topic comes first.

    There are some refinements to this general principle. For example, if the work covers two subjects, one of which is represented as acting upon or influencing the other, such a work should be classed under the subject influenced or acted upon. Thus, a work discussing French influence on English literature should be classed with English literature. On similar grounds a work such as *Religious Aspects of Philosophy* should be classed under philosophy, not religion, since a treatment of some particular aspect of a subject should be classed with the subject, not with the aspect.

Another, perhaps more involved difficulty arises with the monographic series or collected set. (*See* chapter 5.) Winston Churchill's *History of the English-Speaking Peoples* can be classed as an author's collection of four related volumes under a broad "history" number. Or the classifier can place volume 1 with other works on very early Britain, volume 2 with those on discovery and growth of the New World, and so on. LC, as mentioned earlier, often classifies series and collected sets together, but has in recent years provided, for optional use by other libraries, an alternative, volume-specific class notation on most of its separate records for monographs belonging to serial sets.

CONCLUSION

Critics have noted limitations in existing classification systems used by most libraries today.[8] A few are summarized here only as a basis for further study. There is a long-standing argument over the logical arrangement of various systems. Although a scheme may be logical within itself, it can also have inconsistencies. For example, in *DDC*, language is separated from literature, and history from social sciences. In *LCC* language is classified with literature, and history is shelved close to the social sciences. Arguments can be advanced for both approaches. Language is closely related to literature, but it is also an essential to all disciplines. History throws much light on the social sciences, but every discipline and every literature has its own history that influences, and is influenced by, general social history. There is some evidence that the current trend away from hierarchical enumeration toward faceting has lessened concern over achieving the one incontestably correct logical arrangement.

As mentioned above, *DDC* and *LCC*, the two most popular library classifications, are both linear and therefore uni-dimensional. However, concepts found in works are multi-dimensional, but because classification is most often used to arrange items on shelves, only one number is assigned to each title whether it covers one subject or many. Classified catalogs address this problem to a certain extent because they allow the classifier to assign as many numbers to the catalog record as are appropriate. But classified catalogs have not gained acceptance in the United States. Instead, the many subject relationships among items and works are shown through a verbal, alphabetical approach—i.e., subject headings with references (*see* chapters 14–17).

Other limitations include problems of reorganization and relocation arising from the need to keep any classification scheme up-to-date. *DDC* and *LCC* both are regularly revised with new numbers being added for new concepts and with some concepts being moved to more logical locations in the scheme (e.g., computer science in *DDC* was moved from 001.6 to 004–006, and in *LCC* a new class, ZA, was created, to give this rapidly growing area room to expand). Occasionally, a section of a scheme is completely reorganized so that the old numbers are reused with new meanings (e.g., 560–590 for life sciences was completely reorganized for the twenty-first edition of *DDC*). While such reorganizations and relocations are very logical from a theoretical point of view, they may wreak havoc for orderly browsing in libraries. Most libraries cannot afford to reclassify older items, so they either push all items belonging to a reorganized section together on the shelves and start a new section for the new items, or they simply give up and say that the number is only a location address in any case. A more in-depth discussion of this problem may be found in *Subject Analysis in Online Catalogs*, by Rao Aluri, Alasdair Kemp, and John J. Boll.[9]

Another problem arising from the process of keeping a classification scheme up-to-date is that the notation tends to become more complex and awkward as the schedules are expanded to include new subjects and to define old topics more specifically. In *LCC*, for example, digits are added after decimal points to place a new concept with older equivalent concepts. For example, in Z665–Z674.2, Library and information science, Z666 is for "Bibliography," and Z667 is for "Information retrieval systems." When "Information organization," an equivalent concept to "Information retrieval," was added, it was placed at Z666.5.

Related to the problem of keeping up with revisions in classification schemes is the fact that in most libraries, most of the classification numbers are taken from cataloging provided by an outside agency (e.g., a centralized processing facility or LC). These numbers are only as current as the time period in which they were assigned. A more in-depth discussion of this problem may be found in Taylor's *Cataloging with Copy*.[10]

In an international context classification is taken much more seriously than it has been in the United States. In a setting where many languages are involved it is believed that numerical and other symbols can transcend the language barriers imposed upon verbal subject approaches. As computer technology becomes more sophisticated many of the limitations mentioned above have the potential to be overcome, and classification may become an international means for subject communication.[11]

In chapters 10–13 some of the better-known modern classifications devised by librarians and used in various contexts are discussed. Their resemblances and differences are briefly examined, to show their actual and possible uses, strengths, and limitations.

NOTES

1.   Cf. Bacon's *Advancement of Learning* (1605) and his Latin translation of it: *De augmentis* (1621).

2.   Leo E. LaMontagne, "Historical Background of Classification," in *The Subject Analysis of Library Materials* (New York: Columbia University School of Library Service, 1953), p. 20.

3.   Arlene G. Taylor, *The Organization of Information* (Englewood, Colo.: Libraries Unlimited, 1999), pp. 173–198.

4.   S. R. Ranganathan, *Colon Classification: Basic Classification*. 6th ed., completely revised (Bombay; New York: Asia Publishing House, 1960).

5.   B. C. Vickery, *Faceted Classification: A Guide to the Construction and Use of Special Schemes* (London: Aslib, 1960).

6.   R. R. Freeman, "The Management of a Classification Scheme: Modern Approaches Exemplified by the UDC Project of the American Institute of Physics," *Journal of Documentation* 23 (1967): 304–320.

7.   OCLC Forest Press, *DC&: Changes and Corrections for DDC21 and Abridged Edition 13* (available: http://www.oclc.org/fp/dcand/dc_toc.htm [accessed 2/24/99]).

8.   A helpful list of articles and books on classification theory can be found in the brief bibliography: Phyllis A. Richmond, "Reading List in Classification Theory," *Library Resources & Technical Services* 16 (Summer 1972): 364–382.

9.   Rao Aluri, D. Alasdair Kemp, and John J. Boll, *Subject Analysis in Online Catalogs* (Englewood, Colo.: Libraries Unlimited, 1991), pp. 184–187.

10.   Arlene G. Taylor, *Cataloging with Copy*, 2nd ed. (Englewood, Colo.: Libraries Unlimited, 1988), pp. 170–246.

11.   Russell Sweeney, "The Atlantic Divide: Classification Outside the United States," in *Classification of Library Materials*, edited by Betty G. Bengtson and Janet Swan Hill (New York: Neal-Schuman, 1990), pp. 40–51.

SUGGESTED READING

Dunkin, Paul S. *Cataloging U.S.A.* Chicago: American Library Association, 1969. Chapter 6.

Foskett, A. C. *The Subject Approach to Information.* 5th ed. London: Library Association Publishing, 1996. Chapter 10: General Classification Schemes and Chapter 21: The Colon Classification.

Herdman, M. M. *Classification: An Introductory Manual.* 3rd ed., revised by Jeanne Osborn. Chicago: American Library Association, 1978.

Mann, Thomas. *Library Research Models: A Guide to Classification, Cataloging, and Computers.* New York: Oxford University Press, 1993. Chapter 3: The Traditional Library Science Model. Part One: The Classification Scheme.

Marcella, Rita, and Robert Newton. *A New Manual of Classification.* Aldershot, England; Brookfield, Vt.: Gower, 1994.

Taylor, Arlene G. *The Organization of Information.* Englewood, Colo.: Libraries Unlimited, 1999. Chapter 8: Classification.

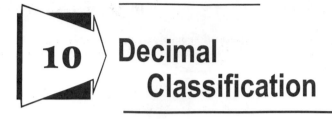

10 Decimal Classification

INTRODUCTION

Of modern library classification schemes, the *Dewey Decimal Classification* (*DDC*) is both the oldest and the most widely used in the United States. It also has a substantial following abroad. Such widespread use is a tribute to Melvil[le Louis Kossuth] Dewey, whose original plan was adaptable enough to incorporate new subjects as they emerged and flexible enough to withstand the changes imposed by the passage of time. Born on December 10, 1851, and graduated from Amherst in 1874, Dewey became assistant college librarian. He developed the first draft of his system for arranging books at that time. He soon became a leader in American librarianship, helping to found both the American Library Association (ALA) and the first American library school at Columbia University. Being a man of many interests, he was also an advocate of spelling reform. He shortened his forename to "Melvil," dropped his two middle names, and even attempted to change the spelling of his surname to "Dui." Throughout his career he promoted librarianship by his teaching, writing, and speaking. In recognizing and acting upon the need to systematize library collections for effective use, he knew of various previous attempts, but found them inadequate.

Dewey never claimed to have originated decimals for classification notation, but earlier systems used them merely as shelf location devices with no significant relation to the subject matter. What Dewey did claim as original, and with some justification, was his "relativ [relative] index," compiled as a key to the "diverse material" included in his tables. His most significant contribution was perhaps the use of decimals for hierarchical divisions. Combined with the digits 0 to 9, decimals provide a pure notation that can be subdivided indefinitely.

The first edition of Dewey's scheme, prepared for the Amherst College Library, was issued anonymously in 1876 under the title *A Classification and Subject Index for Cataloguing and Arranging the Books and Pamphlets of a Library*. It included schedules to 1,000 divisions numbered 000–999, together with a relative index and prefatory matter—a total of 44 pages. The second, "revised and greatly enlarged" edition was published under Dewey's name in 1885. Since that time 19 more full editions and 13 abridgments have appeared. The fourteenth edition, published in 1942, remained the standard edition for many years because an experimental index to the fifteenth edition, published in 1951, was unsuccessful. In 1958 the sixteenth edition appeared with many changes and additions, including a complete revision of sections 546–47, "Inorganic and Organic Chemistry." Since that time each successive edition has carried, besides other, less sweeping changes, totally new developments of one or more targeted portions of the system. The present twenty-first edition (*DDC21*) was published in 1996.[1] The associated thirteenth abridged edition was published in 1997.[2]

DDC notations are assigned the tag 082 in *MARC 21* (the current U.S./Canadian MAchine-Readable Cataloging format) when they have been created for a particular item by the Library of Congress (LC). A *DDC* notation created by a local library participating in a network is placed in MARC field 092. *DDC* complete call numbers are also placed in field 092, regardless of who assigned the *DDC* notation to the item involved.

Closely related to *DDC* is the *Universal Decimal Classification* (*UDC*), which was based originally on *DDC*. It is discussed briefly at the end of this chapter.

BASIC CONCEPTS

The system is called "decimal" because it arranges all knowledge as represented by library materials into ten broad subject classes numbered from 000 to 900. Using Arabic numerals for symbols, it is flexible only to the degree that numbers can be expanded in linear fashion to cover special aspects of general subjects. Theoretically, expansions may continue indefinitely. The more specific the work being classified, the longer the number combination will tend to grow. LC records have been known to carry suggested Dewey numbers containing 21 digits, i.e., 18 decimal places. Such long numbers, however accurate, are unwieldy; it is hard to crowd them onto book spines and audio-visual containers, and dangers of miscopying and mis-shelving are multiplied. For these and related reasons many larger libraries have turned from *DDC* to some other system, such as *Library of Congress Classification* (*LCC*), which has a more economical notation.

Nevertheless, the *DDC* system has many advantages. Its content is compact, consisting in *DDC21* of a volume for introductory matter, auxiliary tables, and a list of relocations and schedule reductions; two volumes for schedule summaries and schedule development; and a fourth volume for the index and the manual. It incorporates many mnemonic devices that can be transferred from one class to another (e.g., "–03" at the end of a class number of any length often indicates a dictionary of the subject at hand). The classifier, once familiar with the system, can apply it to incoming materials quite rapidly. It provides a limited number of optional alternative locations and allows for great detail of specification. The patron is likely to be familiar with it, because it is the system most frequently used in school and public libraries. Furthermore, it arranges subjects from the general to the specific in a logical order, which often can be traced by analogy through more than one class. It is philosophical in conception, being based on a systematic outline of knowledge that allows for subjects not yet known. Even so, the overall arrangement is not preemptively theoretical or logical. Dewey's intent was to provide a practical system for classifying books. This primary application to the books generally found in American libraries remains one of its notable limitations, although efforts have been made in later editions to rectify that bias.

A basic premise of the Dewey approach is that there is no one class for any given subject. The primary arrangement is by discipline. Any specific topic may appear in any number of disciplines. Various aspects of such a topic are usually brought together in the relative index. For example, a work on "families" may be classed in one of several places depending on its emphasis, as can be seen in the table below. Besides the aspects shown there, other material on families may be found in still different *DDC* numbers. Use of the relative index would lead the classifier to some of them.

Some *DDC* Class Numbers Pertaining to the Family

173	Ethics of family relationships
241.63	Christian family ethics
296.4	Religious family rites, celebrations, services
304.666	Family planning
306.8	Marriage and family
362.82	Families with specific problems
392.3	Dwelling places [including those for families]
616.89156	Family psychotherapy
796	Sports for families
929.2	Family histories

The basic concepts of the system are covered in two places in *DDC21*: the introduction in volume 1 and the manual in volume 4. The introduction gives detailed explanations of the schedules and tables and detailed instructions in classifying and building numbers with *DDC*. The manual is devoted to a discussion of the tables and schedules by number, pointing out areas of difficulty and explaining what should or should not be included in certain numbers.

In addition to the manual in *DDC21*, two outside sources provide guidance: *Dewey Decimal Classification: A Practical Guide*, by Lois Mai Chan, John P. Comaromi, Joan S. Mitchell, and Mohinder P. Satija[3]; and *Dewey Decimal Classification, 21st Edition: A Study Manual and Number Building Guide*, by Mona L. Scott.[4]

SCHEDULE FORMAT

Summaries

At the beginning of volume 2, *DDC21* provides three summaries, showing successively the 10 main classes, the 100 divisions, and the 1,000 sections of the basic scheme. Each class from 100 to 900 consists of a group of related disciplines. The 000 class is reserved for materials too general to fit anywhere else.

Summary of the 10 Main *DDC* Classes

000	Generalities
100	Philosophy & psychology
200	Religion
300	Social sciences
400	Language
500	Natural sciences & mathematics
600	Technology (Applied sciences)
700	The arts Fine and decorative arts
800	Literature & rhetoric
900	Geography & history

Each main class is separated into 10 divisions, although a few of these, as well as some further subdivisions, may seem to be rather artificially located within the class. The hundred divisions are shown in the "Second Summary," e.g.,

Summary of the Divisions of a Typical *DDC* Class

600	Technology (Applied sciences)
610	Medical sciences Medicine
620	Engineering & allied operations
630	Agriculture & related technologies
640	Home economics & family living
650	Management & auxiliary services
660	Chemical engineering
670	Manufacturing
680	Manufacture for specific uses
690	Buildings

Each division is subdivided into 10 sections. Again some of these may seem artificially located. The one thousand sections are shown in the "Third Summary," e.g.,

Summary of the Sections of a Typical *DDC* Division

610	Medical sciences Medicine
611	Human anatomy, cytology, histology
612	Human physiology
613	Promotion of health
614	Incidence & prevention of disease
615	Pharmacology & therapeutics
616	Diseases
617	Surgery & related medical specialties
618	Synecology & other medical specialties
619	Experimental medicine

Volume 2 presents in detail the subjects placed in 000 through 599. Fully detailed schedules for subjects placed in 600 through 999 are in volume 3. In the full schedules, each of the 1,000 numbers that has subdivisions extending over more than two pages gives a summary of the "tens" place past the decimal point, e.g.,

612   Human physiology

SUMMARY

612.001–.009	Standard subdivisions
.01–.04	[Biophysics, biochemistry, control processes, tissue and organ culture, physiology of specific activities]
.1	Blood and circulation
.2	Respiration
.3	Digestion
.4	Secretion, excretion, related functions
.6	Reproduction, development, maturation
.7	Musculoskeletal system, integument
.8	Nervous functions Sensory functions
.9	Regional physiology

At a few places within the schedules, multilevel summaries are provided. An example of this can be found at "610   Medical sciences   Medicine."

Entries in Schedules

In the full schedules the 1,000 sections are listed separately, followed in detail by any subdivisions they may have. There are often asymmetrics attesting to the fact that the phenomena of the world cannot always be subdivided and re-subdivided into groups of 10:

Extended Decimal Subdivision of a *DDC* Topic

612	Human physiology
612.1	Blood and circulation
612.11	Blood
612.12	Blood chemistry
612.13	Blood vessels and vascular circulation
612.14	Blood pressure
612.17	Heart
612.18	Vasomoters

Successive lengthening of the base number by one (occasionally two or three) digit(s) achieves step-wise division. This pyramidal structure means that, in subject relationships, what is true of the whole is true of the parts. For instance, the medical sciences are a branch of technology; physiology is a medical science, etc.

A Typical *DDC* Hierarchical Sequence

600	Technology (Applied sciences)
610	Medical sciences Medicine
612	Human physiology
612.1	Blood and circulation
612.11	Blood
612.112	White corpuscles (Leukocytes)

As the notation expands beyond the decimal point, *DDC* editors introduce a space after every third number. The spaces are inserted merely to facilitate reading the closely listed digits. On library materials and bibliographic records they should be omitted, so that the number will occupy no more space than is absolutely necessary. Thus, the schedules show "331.873 2 Membership [in labor unions]" or "572.864 59 DNA repair [Biosynthesis — DNA — Biochemical genetics — Biochemistry]." The schedules rarely display numbers with more than four decimal places, although the relative index sometimes expands numbers to eight or even nine decimals. Thus, in the index we find "Radiation injury (Biology) — veterinary medicine 636.089 698 97." Yet the schedules proper expand "636 — Animal husbandry" only as far as "636.089 — Veterinary sciences Veterinary medicine." Instructions at 636.089 in the schedules allow the building of the longer number found in the index. The concept of building numbers is explained later in this chapter.

Certain places in the schedules where fully symmetrical expansion cannot be maintained are given *centered entries*, which represent concepts for which there is no specific number in the notational hierarchy and which, therefore, cover an abbreviated span of numbers. These appear with centered inch-long lines immediately above them and with the symbol ">" at their left margins. Centered entries are always followed by a note that tells where to class comprehensive works that cover the subject represented by the centered entry, e.g.:

A Typical *DDC* Centered Entry

> 439.7–439.8   East Scandinavian languages

Class comprehensive works in 439.5

Other useful formatting devices are the section numbers and running titles at the top of each page of volumes 2 and 3 (the schedules), the use of boldface and light-face type in various sizes, lefthand marginal indentions to indicate hierarchical structure, and the use of square brackets for numbers from which a topic has recently been shifted (or "relocated").

Notes

Perhaps the most helpful sources of information for the *DDC* classifier are the notes. There are seven major kinds of notes in the twenty-first edition: 1) notes that tell what is found at a classification, 2) notes that tell what is found at other classifications, 3) notes that identify topics in "standing room," 4) notes that explain changes in schedules and tables, 5) notes that instruct the classifier in number building, 6) notes that prescribe citation and preference order, and 7) notes that explain options.

1. Notes that tell what is found at a classification include scope notes, definition notes, former heading notes, variant name notes, and class-here notes. An example of a scope or definition note is found at "025.6 Circulation services." The first note there reads, "Lending and renting materials, keeping records of loans and rentals." The second note at this classification is an example of a class-here note: "Class here document delivery." Such notes are used to list major topics that are included at a class and also to indicate where interdisciplinary and comprehensive works are to be classified. Former heading and variant name notes begin with those words and seem self-explanatory.

2. Notes that tell what is found at other classifications begin with the words *class*, *for*, or *see also*. For example, at "070.9 Historical and persons treatment of journalism and newspapers" is found the note, "Class geographical treatment in 071–079." At "338.5 General production economics" is the note, "For organization of production, see 338.6."

    Notes found in categories 1 and 2 have what is called "hierarchical force." This means that they are applicable to all the subdivisions under the number that has the note, as well as to the number with the note. For example, the two previously quoted notes found at "025.6 Circulation services" would apply also to the subdivision "025.62 Interlibrary loans." That is, a work about keeping records of loans carried out via interlibrary loans would be appropriate at 025.62, even though there is no specific note to this effect at 025.62.

3.   Notes that identify topics in "standing room" provide a location for topics that do not yet have enough works about them to justify a separate number. It is assumed that there may be more works in the future, in which case the topics could be assigned their own number. Therefore, the rules for applying *DDC* do not allow number building of any kind (including additions of standard subdivisions) for topics in "standing room." The assumption is that the number in which the topic stands will be subdivided to create a number for the topic, and so, if no number building has been done, all items on that topic can be classed in the new number for the topic simply by adding new digits to the general number. Standing-room notes begin with the word *including*. For example, in the library and information sciences section at "025.313 Form [of the catalog]" is the note, "Including book, card, microform catalogs." The topic "Online catalogs" has its own number: "025.3132."

4.   Notes explaining changes in schedules and tables tell a user of the schedules that there have been changes at a particular number since the last edition of *DDC*. There may have been revisions of contents covered, a discontinuation of coverage either for a whole number or for a part of its contents, or a relocation of all or part of the contents.

5.   Notes that instruct the classifier in number building provide ways to gain greater depth of analysis at a particular classification. Number building is discussed in detail below.

6.   Notes that prescribe citation and preference order help a classifier decide which of more than one aspect or characteristic to use for classification. Citation order allows the use of two or more characteristics (i.e., facets) in a specified order. Preference order establishes the order in which one chooses a facet when only one can be chosen. For example:

> 006   Special computer methods
>   . . .
>   Unless other instructions are given, class complex subjects with aspects in two or more subdivisions of 006 in the one coming last, e.g., natural language processing in expert systems 006.35 (*not* 006.33)

7.   Notes that explain options are given in parentheses and may be of benefit in providing alternative methods for handling certain situations. International users find that options for religions, languages, and literatures allow them to give preferred treatment for local needs. One option often followed even in the United States is:

016   Bibliographies and catalogs of works on specific subjects or in specific disciplines

. . .

(Option: Class with the specific discipline or subject, using notation 016 from Table 1, e.g., bibliographies of medicine 610.16)

COMPLETELY REVISED SCHEDULES

In *DDC21* there are three significant areas that have undergone complete remodeling: 350–354 — Public administration, 370 — Education, and 560–590 — Life sciences. For two of these areas, public administration and life sciences, facets and facet indicators are a basic part of the design. Faceting in this form was introduced in the music schedule that was completely revised for the twentieth edition. It allows building of numbers through use of the indicators 0 and 1. Faceting makes possible the identification of meaningful components in a number both in the classification process and in the retrieval process.

In addition to those complete revisions, the twenty-first edition relocates the standard subdivisions of Christianity from 201–209 to 230–270. In future editions more will be done to reduce bias toward Christianity. Judaism in 296 and Islam in 297 have been revised and expanded. Also dealt with in the twenty-first edition are political and social changes such as revision of the geographic area numbers for the countries of the former Soviet Union. New topics such as rap music and snowboarding have been added, terminology has been updated, and attention has been given to international needs.

NUMBER BUILDING

A premise in working with *DDC* is that all possible numbers are not specifically printed in the schedules, but more precise numbers than those printed can be built or synthesized using tables or other parts of the schedules.

Adding from Auxiliary Tables

Auxiliary tables 1 through 7, found in volume 1 of *DDC21*, give the classifier one way to expand existing numbers in the schedules. Each number in these tables is preceded by a dash to show that it cannot stand alone as a class number. The dash should be omitted when the number is attached to a class notation.

Table 1. Standard Subdivisions

As was noted under the "General Principles of Classifying" section of chapter 9, all shelf classifications provide a dual approach. Some items are grouped on the basis of their subject content, while others are placed according to their form or genre. The standard subdivisions supplied in auxiliary Table 1 derive from what was called in earlier editions a table of "form divisions." The present-day "standard subdivisions" include examples other than form. Some actually do treat form (e.g., dictionaries, encyclopedias, periodicals, etc.). Others represent "modes of treatment," covering theoretical or historical aspects of the subject, such as philosophy and theory, history, etc. The following illustrates some of the categories to be found in Table 1.

– 01   **Philosophy and theory.** An exposition of any subject treated from the theoretical point of view.
  Example: 701   Philosophy of the Arts

– 03   **Dictionaries, encyclopedias, concordances.**
  Example: 720.3   Dictionary of Architecture

– 05   **Serial publications.** Used for publications in which the subject is treated in articles, papers, etc.
  Example: 720.5   Architectural Record

– 08   **History and description with respect to kinds of persons.**
  Example: 720.8   Architectural Adaptations for People with Specific Needs

– 09   **Historical, geographic, persons treatment.**
  Example: 720.9   Fletcher's History of Architecture

Most of the standard subdivisions are further subdivided in Table 1. For example, under "–01   Philosophy and theory" the following subtopics are listed:

– 011   Systems
– 012   Classification
– 013   Value
– 014   Language and communication
– 015   Scientific principles
– 019   Psychological principles

The –09 standard subdivision can be geographically divided, through the addition of area digits from Table 2, e.g., "720.973   History of Architecture in the United States." This is explained in detail below in the section titled "Table 2. Geographic Areas, Historical Periods, Persons."

Unless specific instructions indicate otherwise, standard subdivisions may be used with any number if such application is meaningful. One specific instruction not to add standard subdivisions is found only in the introduction in volume 1 and is often overlooked. When a work does not "approximate the whole of the subject of the number," the standard subdivision usually should not be added. This was mentioned above in the discussion of notes that identify topics in "standing room." If, for example, a book is about research on card catalogs, it should be given the number "025.313" for "Form" of catalogs. Because the book is not about research on all forms of catalogs, and because there is no specific number for card catalogs, the standard subdivision "–072" for research should not be attached to the number.

Although in the table each number is preceded by a single zero, e.g., "–03   Dictionaries, etc.," it is sometimes necessary in the schedules to apply a double or triple zero to introduce the subdivision. This happens when single zero subdivisions are already appropriated in the schedules for special purposes. The instructions that cover such situations are explicit and should be followed carefully. A few examples will illustrate certain basic principles:

a) **Standard subdivisions printed in the schedules**

In some parts of the schedules a concept that is ordinarily expressed as a standard subdivision is printed with its own number. For example, "805   Serial publications" is printed in the schedule following "800   Literature . . ." Therefore, this is the number used for a serial about literature, not 800.5 or 800.05. Likewise, "501   Philosophy and theory" is printed after "500   Natural sciences and mathematics." None of the standard subdivision breakdown for –01 found in Table 1 is printed after "501," but one can use this breakdown at this number if appropriate. Thus, a work on the concept of theoretical value in the natural sciences would be classed "501.3."

b) **Standard subdivisions not printed and no instructions given**

The most common situation is that in which standard subdivisions are not printed and no instructions are given. In such cases a single-0 introduces the standard subdivision. For example, the schedules give the number "371.4" for student guidance and counseling. A work on the philosophy and theory of student guidance and counseling would be given the class number "371.401."

c) **0-divisions utilized for a specific purpose; standard subdivision to be introduced by a double-0**

An example of the double-0 appears at "271   Religious congregations and orders in church history." Single-0 subdivisions are used for specific kinds of religious congregations, e.g., "271.01   Contemplative," "271.03   Teaching," "271.04   Preaching," etc. Here the instruction is to use 271.001–271.008 for standard subdivisions. Therefore, an encyclopedia of religious congregations and orders in general is classed in 271.003.

d) **00-divisions utilized for special purposes; standard subdivisions to be introduced by a triple-0**

An example of the triple-0 appears at "230   Christianity   Christian theology." 230.1–230.9 (single-0) are reserved for "Doctrines of specific denominations and sects. 230.01–230.09 (double-0) are reserved for "Standard   subdivisions   of   Christian   theology."   Therefore 230.001-230.009 (triple-0) are used for "Standard subdivisions of Christianity." An encyclopedia of Christianity would be classed as 230.003.

Table 2. Geographic Areas, Historical Periods, Persons

When a given heading can be subdivided geographically and the library has many books dealing with that subject, it is recommended that the classifier use Table 2 (the area table), which allows one to expand the number systematically by region or site. It is by far the bulkiest of the seven auxiliary tables accompanying the DDC schedules. Its general arrangement is as follows:

– 01–05	Historical periods
– 1	Areas, regions, places in general
– 2	Persons regardless of area, region, place
– 3	The ancient world
– 4	Europe Western Europe
– 5	Asia Orient Far East
– 6	Africa
– 7	North America
– 8	South America
– 9	Other parts of world and extraterrestrial worlds
Pacific Ocean islands

Area –1 is used for the treatment of any subject geographically but not limited by continent, country, or locality. It allows diverse elements that have natural ties to regions or groups (e.g., frigid zones, temperate zones, land forms, or types of vegetation) to be brought together under certain subjects. Area –2 permits subdivision by biography, diaries, reminiscences, correspondence, and the like of persons associated with any subject for which the schedule instructions say to add the "areas" notation directly instead of adding "standard subdivision" notation –092 from Table 1. Area –3 offers specific subdivisions for ancient countries and areas up to the fall of the Roman Empire. Area notations –4 through –9 are for specific continents and modern countries. For example, area number "–4   Europe" has the following summary subtopics:

– 41	British Isles
– 42	England and Wales
– 43	Central Europe Germany
– 44	France and Monaco
– 45	Italian Peninsula and adjacent islands Italy
– 46	Iberian Peninsula and adjacent islands Spain
– 47	Eastern Europe Russia
– 48	Scandinavia
– 49	Other parts of Europe

The area notations –41 and –42 were extensively revised in the nineteenth edition to reflect a thorough reorganization of British local administration. The area concepts of "British Isles," "United Kingdom," and "Great Britain" were at the same time relocated from area –42 to area –41. Area notation –47 was extensively revised in the twenty-first edition in order to make a more logical organization for the countries of the former Soviet Union.

Area notations may be added directly to schedule numbers where so instructed. For example, a general treatise on higher education in Dundee, Scotland, will be classed in 378 in the Dewey Decimal Classification. The schedule at 378.4–.9 instructs "Add to base number 378 notation 4–9 from Table 2." In Table 2 one finds "–412 7" as the number for "Dundee (Scotland)." This number is therefore applied to 378, giving 378.4127, as the following analysis shows:

378	Higher education
378.4	Europe
378.41	British Isles
378.412	Northeastern Scotland
378.4127	City of Dundee

Where specific instructions (as in 378.4 .9) are not given for geographical treatment in the schedules, the classifier can apply the standard subdivision "–09   Historical and geographical treatment" to any number that lends itself to that approach, unless localized instructions mandate a double- or triple-0 in place of the single-0. For example, the specific DDC number for savings banks is 332.21. To class a work on savings banks in London, the schedule gives no specific direction to use Table 2, nor does it give any direction for specific subdivisions. So the standard subdivision –09 may be used directly. In Table 1 a note under "–093–099   Treatment by specific continents, countries, localities; extra-terrestrial worlds" says to "Add to base number –09 notation 3–9 from Table 2." So works on savings banks in London will be classed in 332.2109421. The number may be analyzed to show:

332.21	Savings banks
332.2109	Standard subdivision for historical and geographical treatment
332.21094	In Europe
332.210942	In England and Wales
332.2109421	In Greater London

Although these examples result in long numbers, they are quite simple to construct.

Table 3. Individual Literatures and the Arts

Table 3, "Subdivisions for the Arts, Individual Literatures, for Specific Literary Forms," is actually three tables: Table 3–A, "Subdivisions for Works by or about Individual Authors," Table 3–B, "Subdivisions for Works by or about More than One Author," and Table 3–C, "Notation to be Added Where Instructed in Table 3–B, 700.4, 791.4, and in 808–809." The titles of these tables are descriptive of their uses. They are never used alone, but are used following specific instructions. Numbers "–1–8   Specific forms" in Tables 3–A and 3–B develop and expand the summary form numbers that appear in the full schedules under "810   American literature in English." These mnemonic form divisions for kinds of literature are:

– 1	Poetry	(e.g., 831	German poetry)
– 2	Drama	(e.g., 842	French drama)
– 3	Fiction	(e.g., 839.313	Dutch fiction)
– 4	Essays	(e.g., 869.4	Portuguese essays)
– 5	Speeches	(e.g., 845	French speeches)
– 6	Letters	(e.g., 836	German letters)
– 7	Humor and satire	(e.g., 869.7	Portuguese humor & satire)

[–7 does not appear in Table 3-A and is not used for individual authors.]

| – 8 | Miscellaneous writings | (e.g., 839.318 | Dutch miscellaneous writings) |

Flow charts for building literature numbers can be found at the Table 3 instructions in the Manual in volume 4 of *DDC21*. These are of great assistance in following the massive amount of instructions found in the literature schedules and with Table 3.

Table 4. Individual Languages

Table 4, "Subdivisions of Individual Languages and Language Families," is used with base numbers for individual languages, as explained under 420–490. In a fashion similar to that of Table 3 it provides mnemonic form divisions for languages, e.g.:

– 1   Writing systems and phonology of the standard form of the language
       (e.g., 431   Writing systems and phonology of standard German)

– 2   Etymology of the standard form of the language
       (e.g., 442   Etymology of the standard form of French)

– 3   Dictionaries of the standard form of the language.
       (e.g., 439.313   Dictionaries of the standard form of Dutch)

etc.

Table 5. Racial, Ethnic, National Groups

Table 5, "Racial, Ethnic, National Groups," is used according to specific instructions at certain places in the schedules or in other tables, or through the interposition of "–089   [Treatment among specific] racial, ethnic, national groups" from Table 1. These applications are exactly parallel to the use of Table 2, which is used either on direct instructions in the schedule or on interposition of "–09   Historical and geographical treatment" from Table 1. The Table 5 summary includes:

– 03–04   [Basic races, mixtures of basic races]
– 1   North Americans
– 2   British   English   Anglo-Saxons
– 3   Nordic (Germanic) people
– 4   Modern Latin peoples
etc.

Table 6. Languages

Table 6, "Languages," is a basic mnemonic table used to indicate the particular language of a work or the language that is the subject matter of a work. It is used as instructed in the schedules or other tables. The summary includes:

– 1   Indo-European (Indo-Germanic) languages

– 2   English and Old English (Anglo-Saxon)

– 3   Germanic (Teutonic) languages

– 4   Romance languages

etc.

To illustrate the application of this table let us class a Bible in French, starting from the entry given in both index and schedules, "220.5   Modern versions and translations [of the Bible]." For "220.53–59   Versions in other languages [than English]" the schedule direction says, "Add to base number 220.5 notation 3–9 from Table 6." The notation for French in Table 6 is –41. The resulting whole number for a modern French Bible may be analyzed as follows:

220	The Bible
220.5	Modern versions and translations
220.54	In the Romance languages
220.541	In modern French

Table 7. Groups of Persons

Table 7, "Groups of Persons," is used as instructed in the schedules or other tables. It deals with various characteristics of persons, as the following partial summary shows:

– 01	Individual persons	
– 02	Groups of persons	
– 03– 08	Persons by various nonoccupational characteristics	
	– 03	Persons by racial, ethnic, national background
	– 04	Persons by sex and kinship characteristics
	– 05	Persons by age
	etc.	

– 1–9	Specialists	
	– 1	Persons occupied with philosophy, parapsychology and occultism, psychology
	– 2	Persons occupied with or adherent to religion
	– 3	Persons occupied with the social sciences and socioeconomic activities
	etc.	

From –09 to –9 this table is based on the 10 main classes of *DDC*. A work on Shakers as a social group furnishes the following example. The number for adherents of religious groups in social contexts is 305.6. The directions in the schedule at the number say, "Add to base number 305.6 the numbers following –2 in notation 21–29 from Table 7." The Table 7 number for Shakers is –288. Thus the work would be classed 305.688. The analysis of the number is as follows:

305	Social groups
305.6	Religious groups
305.688	Shakers

Adding from Other Parts of the Schedules

There are a number of places in the schedules where the classifier is instructed to find a number elsewhere in the schedules and to add it whole to the number at hand, as demonstrated by the following example:

750   Painting and paintings

. . .

758   Other subjects

. . .

758.9   Other
                     Add to base number 758.9 notation
                     001–999, e.g., paintings of historical
                     events 758.99 . . .

If one wanted to classify paintings of library buildings, the number for the architecture of library buildings, 727.8, would be attached to 758.9, resulting in 758.97278.

In many other places the classifier is instructed to take a part of another number and add to a base number given in the instruction. The following example will illustrate:

296.47   Sermons and preaching (Homiletics)
                     Add to base number 296.47 the numbers following
                     296.4 in 296.41–296.44, e.g., High Holy Day
                     sermons 296.4731

At 296.41 we find:

296
        .41   Sabbath
        .412   Prohibited activity

. . .

        .43   Festivals, holy days, fasts
        .431   High Holy Days
        .432   Yom Kippur (Day of Atonement)

. . .

        .44   Rites and customs for occasions that occur generally once
                 in a lifetime
        .442   Special rites for male Jews
        etc.

So, for a work on Sabbath sermons, the notation would be 296.471.

More complicated instructions may give more than one directive for building a number. For example:

616.99411–.99415   Cancers of cardiovascular organs
                          Add to base number 616.9941 the numbers
                          following 611.1 in 611.11–611.15, e.g.,
                          cancer of heart 616.99412; then add further
                          as instructed under 618.1–618.8

At 611.1 is found:

.1	Cardiovascular organs
.11	Pericardium
.12	Heart
.13	Arteries
.14	Veins
.15	Capillaries

At 618.1–618.8 is a table of digits to be added where instructed. This table may be summarized as follows:

001–009	Standard subdivisions
01–04	Microbiology, special topics, rehabilitation, special classes of diseases
05	Preventive measures and surgery
06	Therapy
07	Pathology

So a work on therapy for cancer of the heart could be given the classification number 616.9941206, that is, 616.9941 (base number) followed by 2 (for heart) followed by 06 (for therapy). "Add tables" of this type are found in many places in the schedules and must be used only as instructed.

When a single work treats multiple aspects of a subject, such as age, gender, and physical characteristics, the classifier must be careful, as mentioned above, to observe citation and preference order. As mentioned earlier, citation order allows a number to be built that takes into account two or more of the aspects. Instructions are given in such cases as to the order in which the aspects may be represented in the number. If a citation order is not given, then one must choose among the aspects according to instructions for preference. Sometimes one is instructed to prefer the aspect that comes first (or last) in the schedule, while at other times there may be a table of preference given. The important point to remember is to follow instructions. More detail about number building can be found in the Introduction to *DDC21*.

THE RELATIVE INDEX

The "relative" index is so called because it is claimed to show relationships of each specific topic to one or more disciplines and to other topics. It contains terms found in the schedules and tables, and synonyms for those terms; names of countries, states, provinces, major cities, and important geographic features; and some names of persons. It does not have phrases that contain concepts represented by standard subdivisions (e.g., "Medical education"). Many *see also* references are given (e.g., "Organizations . . . *see also* Religious organizations"). Geographic name entries usually refer the user to the appropriate area table [e.g., "Macerata (Italy : Province) T2–456 73"]. A few referrals occur to the standard subdivisions and to other auxiliary tables (e.g., "Repairs ...T1–028 8").

The *DDC* relative index enumerates alphabetically all the main headings in the classification schedules, plus certain other specific entries not actually listed in the schedules. One such instance was discussed on page 286.

In other places index terminology varies from that found in the schedules for the same class number, although the general meanings coincide. Thus, the schedule entry "612.792 1   Glands and glandular secretions, Including perspiration" is a generalized representation of the index entry "Sebaceous glands–human physiology 612.792 1."

The classifier should, of course, consult the index, especially in cases in which the location of the desired topic, or the precise nature of its relation to other topics, is in doubt. Yet the relative index should never become a substitute for the schedules. It is coordinated with them, but is limited for reasons of space and cannot show hierarchical progressions or topical groupings. It will guide the classifier to some, but not necessarily all, aspects of a given subject. The next important step in the classification process is to consult the schedules for verification, perspective, and possible further instructions. Only by using the two types of display together can the full potential of the scheme be realized.

BROAD AND CLOSE CLASSIFICATION

Because it offers a wide variety of techniques and nearly limitless expansions in number building, *DDC* is hospitable to all the titles that a large library might add in any subject. It also offers various ways to meet the limited needs of smaller libraries. The classifier must remember that, in general, when there are relatively few works in a given subject area, *DDC* encourages broad classification. Digits in class notations after decimal points may be cut off at any appropriate place. The present policy of the Library of Congress is to provide bibliographic records with *DDC* numbers of from one to three segments. The segments are indicated by slash marks, e.g., "940.53/1743/092," which stands for "World War II—Concentration camps in Germany—Biographies." A small library with a limited collection of materials on World War II might prefer to keep them all together under 940.53. If the library has several dozen items on the war, it might keep the ones on concentration camps in Germany together by using 940.531743. If it maintains a separate resource collection for use by researchers, it could add the standard subdivision "–092" to distinguish the biographies. When a library decides to retain one or more of the *DDC* segments to achieve close classification at a particular point in the collection, it omits the slash marks, which were used in the LC record merely to suggest break-points.

In catalog records created by other members of a network, the *DDC* classification numbers do not have slash marks. If a shorter number is desired, one must consult the schedules to find an appropriate break-point. For example, in the World War II concentration camp number above, breaking the number at 940.531 would place the item with other works on social, political, and economic history of the war—not a very logical option. Breaking it at 940.5317 would place it with items on concentration camps, not subdivided by place—quite logical. The number 940.53174 would be for concentration camps in all of Europe, not subdivided by country. The classifier needs to check the schedules and not just cut the number at an arbitrary number of digits past the decimal point, which could result in an illogical placement.

UPDATING

New editions of *DDC* have been published every few years. Between editions, updating is accomplished via the publication of *Dewey Decimal Classification Additions, Notes and Decisions* (affectionately known as *DC&*, "&" being the symbol for

"AND," the acronym for "Additions, Notes and Decisions").[5] *DC&* is published annually. It contains corrections of errors, clarifications, updating, and expansions. Starting with volume 6, number 1, December 1997, it is available on the OCLC Forest Press Dewey home page.[6] Also available on the Dewey home page are other kinds of updating tools such as "Application Notes," "New and Changed Entries," and "New LCSH/DDC Headings." A policy for "continuous revision" has been adopted by OCLC Forest Press, which means that major revisions are released as separates between editions, and new editions appear as cumulations.

ABRIDGED EDITIONS

The first *Abridged Decimal Classification and Relativ Index for Libraries, Clippings, Notes, etc.*, appeared in 1894, the year in which the fifth edition of the full schedules was published. Abridged edition 13 is based on *DDC21* and was published in 1997. Like its predecessors, it is designed primarily for general collections of 20,000 titles or fewer, such as are found in small public and school libraries. It contains many fewer entries than the full edition, and tables, schedules, index, and manual all appear in one volume. The numbers used are compatible with *DDC21* so that growing libraries can expand from the abridged to the full edition as their collections increase.

DIFFICULTIES:
LONG NUMBERS AND TOPIC RELOCATIONS

Among the difficulties built into the *DDC* system are its long numbers, which increase rather than diminish as the system grows, nullifying much of the mnemonic character of the basic system. Thus the number 636.08969897, which was cited on page 286 as coming from the relative index entry for radiation injury in veterinary medicine, is so long that any mnemonic associations between it and the number 616.9897 (from which it was built) are obscured. Librarians who wish to retain these long numbers because of extensive holdings in one or more fields should write them on cards and items to be shelved in several lines. The above number could be written in short segments as follows:

636
.089
698
97

Related to the long number difficulties are the rapid, often sweeping, topical relocations from one edition to another. Such drastic surgery is forced upon the system by its limited notational base and the swift growth and change in the world of knowledge and of publication. An article by Pat Thomas in the first *DC&* to appear after *DDC20* gives pointers on adjusting to *DDC*'s expansions, reductions, relocations, and revised schedules.[7] While the big rush, particularly in academic libraries, to change from *DDC* to *LCC* seems to have run its course, no library can afford to ignore all efforts to keep shelf arrangement contemporary with the shifts in knowledge as reflected in the literature.

UNIVERSAL DECIMAL CLASSIFICATION (UDC)

UDC was begun in 1885 by two Belgian lawyers, Paul Otlet and Henri LaFontaine, for the classification of a huge catalog of the world's literature in all fields of knowledge. It was based on the *DDC* (then in its fifth edition) but was, with Dewey's permission, expanded by the addition of many more detailed subdivisions and the use of typographical signs to indicate complex subjects and what we know today as facets. *DDC*'s decimal notation was retained (except for final zeros), and the 10 main classes as well as some subdivisions are still the same in *UDC* as they are in *DDC*, but class 4 (i.e., *DDC* 400) has been amalgamated with class 8 and is currently vacant. Many major and almost all minor subdivisions are now quite different from those in *DDC*. The main difference lies, however, in the synthetic structure of *UDC*. Thus, a work dealing with two or more subjects can be classed by two or more *UDC* class notations, linked by a colon sign (the most commonly used of the typographical symbols), as in the following example:

362.1 : 658.3 : 681.31 Hospital : Personnel management : Computers

for a work on the use of computers in the management of hospital personnel. Such a class notation is, however, not a "call number" but is intended for a classified catalog in which each of the three class notations may serve as an access point, while the other two are shown in rotation, e.g.:

658.3 : 681.31 : 362.1 and *681.31* 362.1 : 658.3

If *UDC* is to be used for shelf classification, one of the three class notations may be chosen as a call number for a work on this complex subject.

UDC's faceted structure has its roots in *DDC*'s device for indication of place, namely, the intercalation of –09 followed by the class notation for a country or region, e.g., –0973 for the United States. *UDC* uses largely the same place notations as *DDC* but encloses them in parentheses. Thus, "plant cultivation in the U.S." is 631.50973 in *DDC* but 631.5(73) in *UDC* (note that the main class notation is the same in both). In addition to the place facet *UDC* has also specific symbols and notations for the language of a work, its physical form, races and peoples, time periods, materials, persons, specific points of view, and recurring subdivisions in certain classes, all of which can be appended to basic notations either alone or in combination, as in the following example:

631.5	Plant cultivation—written in Russian
631.5(038)	—Glossary
631.5"17"	—18th century
631.5(= 97)(85)	—By American Indians in Peru

Due to this highly faceted structure and largely expressive notation the *UDC* has been used successfully in computerized information retrieval.[8]

UDC schedules were first published from 1904 to 1907 in French, followed later by full editions in English. *UDC* has since been published in whole or in part in 23 languages. It is widely used in many countries where English is the main or a co-official language (e.g., Great Britain, Canada, Australia, New Zealand, India) and in countries using other languages (e.g., Germany, Japan, Russia, Spanish-speaking countries).

Until 1992 *UDC* was managed by the International Federation of Documentation (FID) in the Hague (Netherlands). When it became apparent in the 1980s that a more broadly based organization was needed to administer *UDC*, FID and the publishers of the Dutch, English, French, Japanese, and Spanish editions combined to found a new body, the UDC Consortium (UDCC). An early action of the UDCC was to create an international database that would be a master file. The database, called the Master Reference File (MRF) and containing about 61,000 entries, is held at the Royal Library in the Hague and is updated once a year. An Editor-in-Chief and an Editorial Board of international membership oversee the continuous revision and expansion.

Since 1992, UDCC has maintained the scheme by reviewing its content and initiating revisions and extensions. The results are published in *Extensions and Corrections to the UDC*.[9] A two-volume, easy-to-use edition of *UDC* was published in its second edition by the British Standards Institution in 1993.[10] It is referred to as BS 1000M. It was derived from the MRF. Supplements are issued each year, each one cumulating all previous ones so that one has only to look in two places for the latest notations. The newest edition is a compact one-volume "pocket edition" published in 1999.[11] It contains about 4,000 entries and is referred to as PD 1000.

In the United States *UDC* is used mainly in some scientific and technical libraries and by one abstracting database.[12] A U.S. Information Center for the *UDC* exists at the College of Library and Information Services of the University of Maryland in College Park, Maryland, where a complete collection of current English *UDC* editions and their updating as well as pending proposals for revision are available. More detailed descriptions of the *UDC*, its development, and its application may be found in a number of publications.[13]

NOTES

1.   *Dewey Decimal Classification and Relative Index*, 21st ed., edited by John P. Comaromi, et al. (Albany, N.Y.: Forest Press, 1996), 4v.

2.   *Abridged Dewey Decimal Classification and Relative Index*, 13th ed. (Albany, N.Y.: Forest Press, 1997).

3.   Lois Mai Chan, John P. Comaromi, Joan S. Mitchell, and Mohinder P. Satija, *Dewey Decimal Classification: A Practical Guide*, 2nd ed., revised for *DDC21* (Dublin, Ohio: OCLC Forest Press, 1996).

4.   Mona L. Scott, *Dewey Decimal Classification, 21st Edition: A Study Manual and Number Building Guide* (Englewood, Colo.: Libraries Unlimited, 1998).

5.   *Dewey Decimal Classification Additions, Notes and Decisions*, vol. 5, no. 1– (Albany, N.Y.: Forest Press, 1990–   )

6.   OCLC Forest Press, *DC&: Changes and Corrections for DDC21 and Abridged Edition 13* (available: http://www.oclc.org/oclc/fp/dcand/dc_toc.htm [accessed 3/12/00]).

7.   Pat Thomas, "Implementing *DDC20*," *DC&,* vol. 5, no. 1 (March 1990): 7–8.

8.   Malcolm Rigby, *Automation and the UDC, 1948–1980*, 2nd ed. (The Hague: FID, 1981). FID 565.

9.   *Extensions and Corrections to the UDC* (The Hague: FID, 1951–   ). Annual.

10.   British Standards Institution, *Universal Decimal Classification, International Medium ed., English text, ed.* 2 (Milton Keynes, England: BSI Standards, 1993). BS 1000M.

11.   British Standards Institution, *Universal Decimal Classification, Pocket Edition* (London: BSI, 1999).

12.   *Meteorological and Geoastrophysical Abstracts* (Boston: American Meteorological Society, 1950–   ).

13.   I. C. McIlwaine, *Guide to the Use of the Universal Decimal Classification*, FID Occasional Paper No. 5, FID Publication No. 703 (The Hague: FID on behalf of the UCC Consortium, 1995); W. Boyd Rayward, "The UDC and FID: A Historical Perspective," *Library Quarterly* 37 (July 1967): 259–278; A. C. Foskett, "The Universal Decimal Classification," in *The Subject Approach to Information*, 5th ed. (London: Library Association Publishing, 1996), pp. 281–294.

SUGGESTED READING

Chan, Lois Mai, John P. Comaromi, Joan S. Mitchell, and Mohinder P. Satija. *Dewey Decimal Classification: A Practical Guide.* 2nd ed., revised for *DDC21*. Dublin, Ohio: OCLC Forest Press, 1996.

Ferguson, Bobby. *Subject Analysis: Blitz Cataloging Workbook.* Englewood, Colo.: Libraries Unlimited, 1998. Chapter 3: Dewey Decimal Classification.

Foskett, A. C. *The Subject Approach to Information.* 5th ed. London: Library Association Publishing, 1996. Chapter 17: The Dewey Decimal Classification and Chapter 18: The Universal Decimal Classification.

McIlwaine, I. C. *Guide to the Use of the Universal Decimal Classification.* FID Occasional Paper No. 5, FID Publication No. 703. The Hague: FID on behalf of the UCC Consortium, 1995.

Miksa, Francis L. *The DDC, the Universe of Knowledge, and the Post-Modern Library.* Albany, N.Y.: Forest Press, 1998.

Scott, Mona L. *Dewey Decimal Classification, 21st Edition: A Study Manual and Number Building Guide.* Englewood, Colo.: Libraries Unlimited, 1998.

Library of Congress Classification (LCC)

INTRODUCTION

The Library of Congress (LC) was founded in 1800. Its earliest classification system was by size (folios, quartos, octavos, etc.), subdivided by accession numbers. By 1812 the collection had grown to about 3,000 volumes, and a better method of classification was needed. The solution was to arrange the works under 18 broad subject categories similar to the Bacon-d'Alembert system used in the 1789 *Catalogue* of Benjamin Franklin's Library Company of Philadelphia. Soon after, in 1814, British soldiers burned the Capitol, where the collection was housed. To reestablish it, Thomas Jefferson offered to sell Congress his library of around 7,000 volumes. Jefferson had cataloged and classified the works himself, using 44 main classes and divisions based on a different interpretation of the Bacon-d'Alembert system. After some debate, Congress agreed to purchase the Jefferson books. Although many were destroyed in a later fire, the classification that came with them was used until the end of the nineteenth century. By that time it had undergone so much ad hoc modification, largely based on shelving and other physical limitations, that it was barely recognizable and completely inadequate.

Many significant changes occurred at LC near the turn of the century. In 1899 Dr. Herbert Putnam, the new Librarian, with many new staff appointments and a brand new building, decided to reorganize and reclassify his rapidly growing collection. Since it was to be moved into more adequate shelving areas, the time was right to develop a better, more detailed classification system. There were already in existence the first five editions of the *Dewey Decimal Classification* (*DDC*) and the first six expansions of Charles A. Cutter's *Expansive Classification*. LC classifiers studied both, as well as the German *Halle Schema* devised by Otto Hartwig. They did not adopt any in full, but the experience they gained was invaluable, and their debt, especially to Cutter, is implicit in the basic structure of their system. While the outline and notation of their main classes are very similar to those of the *Expansive Classification*, there are no main classes I, O, W, X, or Y, as there are in the Cutter system.[1] All five letters do appear, however, as second or third symbols in the notation for various LC subclasses. The other major similarity to the *Expansive Classification* is in the structure of class "Z—Bibliography and Library Science," which was the first class devised and was adopted from Cutter with only minor variations.

After Putnam and his Chief Cataloger, Charles Martel, determined the broad outlines of the new classification, different subject specialists were asked to develop each individual schedule, or portion of the system. Within a broad general framework set up to ensure coordination, each topic or form of presentation identified as a class or subclass was further organized to display the library's holdings and to serve anticipated research needs. Schedules comprising single classes or parts of classes were separately published as they were completed. Most of them first appeared between 1899 and 1940. Many have since gone through several editions. In one sense, the scheme represents a series of special classifications. Yet special libraries, with narrowly defined collecting and service goals, often find the *Library of Congress Classification (LCC)*, which serves broader, more interdisciplinary uses, unsatisfactory for their purposes.

To keep the system functionally up-to-date, individual schedule volumes are frequently reviewed in committee. Revisions, reallocations, and additions keep it flexible and hospitable to new subjects or points of view. For example, in the 1960s interest in Eastern religions and the increase in materials from Asia occasioned a reallocation in 1972 of the topic "Buddhism" from the span BL1400–1495 into a whole new subclass, BQ. Revisions were likewise made in subclass PL, particularly in the sections for Chinese, Japanese, and Korean literatures. Number spans now reflect political changes in Albania, Bangladesh, Korea, Namibia, Somalia, and the like. A triple-letter subclass "DJK—Eastern Europe" was developed in 1976. Intensified foreign acquisitions programs under PL480, the National Program for Acquisitions and Cataloging (NPAC), the revised copyright law, and other developments, stimulated increased expansion and revision of the system.

Hundreds of different number-letter combinations compatible with the notation have not yet been employed or have been retired in favor of new locations. The scheme will continue to accommodate for a long time the many new subjects and aspects of subjects not yet anticipated. It is particularly useful for large university and research collections because of its hospitality and inherent flexibility. It has been used effectively in smaller academic and public libraries, although its adaptability for broad classification is limited. Even special libraries frequently base their own more technical constructs on it, extending its schedules or parts of schedules to cover their unique materials. Some foreign libraries also use the system, although, in spite of LC's large foreign holdings, it is primarily designed from an American perspective.

In MARC 21 (MAchine-Readable Cataloging format for the U.S. and Canada) call numbers based on LCC that are assigned by LC or the British Library are placed in field 050. Those assigned by the National Library of Canada, the National Library of Medicine, or the National Agricultural Library are entered in field 055, 060, or 070, respectively. In the OCLC system, members are asked to enter locally assigned call numbers based on *LCC* in field 090.

CLASSIFICATION TOOLS AND AIDS

The working schedules are contained in over 40 separate volumes. Besides the basic schedules, there are a separately published partial index, for P-PM subcategories in the Language and Literature class, and a short general *Outline*, now in its sixth edition, which gives the secondary and tertiary subclass spans for most classes. Several volumes are devoted to subclass coverage of broad areas, such as related language and literature groups. They comprise:

A	General Works, 1998 Edition
B-BJ	Philosophy; Psychology, 1996 Edition
BL, BM, BP, BQ	Religion: Religions, Hinduism, Judaism, Islam, Buddhism (3rd ed., 1984)
BR-BV	Religion: Christianity, Bible (1987)
BX	Religion: Christian Denominations (1985)
[BR-BX	Christianity (to be published 2000)]
C	Auxiliary Sciences of History, 1996 Edition
D-DJ	History (General): History of Europe, Part 1 (3rd ed., 1990)
DJK-DK	History of Eastern Europe: General, Soviet Union, Poland (1987)
DL-DR	History of Europe, Part 2 (3rd ed., 1990)
DS-DX	History of Asia, Africa, Australia, New Zealand, etc., 1998 Edition
E-F	History: America, 2000 Edition
G	Geography; Maps; Anthropology; Recreation (4th ed., 1976)
[GA-GV	Geography, Anthropology, Recreation (to be published 2000)]
Subclass GE	Environmental Science (1976)
H	Social sciences, 1997 Edition
J	Political Science, 1997 Edition
K	Law (General), 1998 Edition
K Tables	Form Division Tables for Law, 1999 Edition
KD	Law of the United Kingdom and Ireland, 1998 Edition
KDZ, KG-KH	Law of the Americas, Latin America, and the West Indies (1984) [new edition to be published 2000]
KE	Law of Canada, 1998 Edition
KF	Law of the United States, 1999 Edition
KJ-KKZ	Law of Europe, 2000 Edition
KJV-KJW	Law of France, 1999 Edition

KK-KKC	Law of Germany (1982)
KL-KWX	Law of Asia and Eurasia, Africa, Pacific Area and Antarctica (1st ed., 1993)
KZ	Law of Nations, 1998 Edition
L	Education, 1998 Edition
M	Music and Books on Music, 1998 Edition
N	Fine Arts, 1996 Edition
P-PZ Tables	Language and Literature Tables, 1998 Edition (supersedes the tables in the P Schedules)
P-PA	Philology and Linguistics (General). Greek Language and Literature. Latin Language and Literature (1997)
PB-PH	Modern European Languages, 1999 Edition
PJ-PK	Oriental Philology and Literature, Indo-Iranian Philology and Literature, 2000 Edition
PL-PM	Languages of Eastern Asia, Africa, Oceania; Hyperborean, Indian, and Artificial Languages (2nd ed., 1988)
P-PM supplement	Index to Languages and Dialects (4th ed., 1991)
PN	Literature (General) (1997)
PR, PS, PZ	English and American Literatures. Juvenile Belles Lettres, 1998 Edition
PQ	French, Italian, Spanish, and Portuguese Literatures, 1998 Edition
PT, pt. 1	German Literature (2nd ed., 1989)
PT, pt. 2	Dutch and Scandinavian Literatures (2nd ed., 1992)
Q	Science, 1996 Edition
R	Medicine, 1999 Edition
S	Agriculture, 1996 Edition
T	Technology, 1999 Edition
U-V	Military Science. Naval Science, 1996 Edition
Z	Bibliography and Library Science, 1995 Edition
A-Z	Outline (6th ed., 1990)

Updating is accomplished by a variety of publications, most of which are available directly from LC.[2]

- **Revised editions of individual schedules.** As the above list shows, the various schedules differ widely in the number and kinds of revisions made. All schedules and the *Outline* are sold individually by LC's Cataloging Distribution Service (CDS) at nominal prices.

- *Library of Congress Classification—Additions and Changes.* This publication reports quarterly on the latest adjustments in all schedules and schedule indexes of *LCC*. Subscriptions may be placed with CDS. The additions and changes are also available on the Web. Substantial changes, such as the revisions of subclass HM1–299, are posted on the Web in addition to appearing in *Library of Congress Classification: Additions and Changes.*[3]

- *SUPERLCCS™ . . . : Library of Congress Classification Schedules Combined with Additions and Changes.* These cumulations of the schedules combined with the quarterly *Additions and Changes* have been published since 1988, first by Gale Research Company, and since 1998 by The Gale Group (a company formed from the merger of Gale Research with other companies).[4]

- *Cataloging Service Bulletin.* This channel for recent decisions and experiments in technical processing at LC has been offered since 1945.[5] It has a regular quarterly publication schedule, carrying valuable data on *LCC* and shelflisting practice, as well as other aspects of subject and descriptive cataloging. Subscriptions may be placed with CDS.

- *Library of Congress Subject Headings (LCSH).* There is no official comprehensive index to the *LCC* scheme. Most of the schedules carry their own indexes, which are largely self-contained, although they occasionally refer to other schedules where related materials can be found on an indexed topic. For example, the index to class "T—Technology" provides the following entries under "Baths, Public":

> Baths, Public
> Building construction: TH4761
> Plumbing: TH6518.B3

At best, this type of cross-schedule indexing is spotty. The class "N—Fine Arts" index entry reads:

> Bath houses:
> Architecture: NA7010

and the class "R—Medicine" entry reads:

> Public baths:
> Public health: RA605 +

The most obvious substitute for an official comprehensive index is *LCSH*.[6] While it was never designed to function as a true index, many entries and subdivisions refer in brackets to one or more class numbers, often including terminology used in the schedules. In it, under the heading "Public Baths" one finds the following:

Public baths   *(May Subd Geog)*
[*RA605-RA606 (Public health)*]

LC makes no effort to maintain class notations in *LCSH*, and it can be seen that under the heading, "Public baths" one would miss the entries from the N and T schedules. Sometimes though, *LCC* notations relating to a given concept can be grouped more quickly through *LCSH* than through the many schedule indexes, as shown in the following example:

Schedule B-BJ—Philosophy; Psychology:
    Hypnotism (Parapsychology): BF1111 +
Schedule BL, BM, BP, BQ—Religion: Religions, Hinduism,
Judaism, Islam, Buddhism:
    Hypnotism: BL65.H9
Schedule H—Social Sciences:
    Hypnotism and crime: HV6110
Schedule Q—Science:
    Hypnotic conditions
            Physiology: QP425+
Schedule R—Medicine:
    Hypnotics: RM325
    Hypnotism and hypnosis
        Anesthesiology: RD85.A9
            Dentistry: RK512.H95
        Forensic medicine: RA1171
        Psychiatry: RC490 +

LCSH:
    Hypnotics   *(May Subd Geog)*
        [*RM325*]
        . . .
    Hypnotism
        [*BF1111-BF1156 (Parapsychology)*]
        [*HV6110 (Hypnotism and crime)*]
        [*RC490-RC499 (Psychiatry)*]
        . . .
    Hypnotism in dentistry   *(May Subd Geog)*
        [*RK512.H95*]
        . . .
    Hypnotism in surgery   *(May Subd Geog)*
        [*RD85.H9*]

It can be seen that one would miss the entries at BL, QP, and RA when using *LCSH*, but more entries are grouped there than are not.

- **Library of Congress Shelflist in Microform.** In 1978 the six and one-half million cards of the LC shelflist, arranged by call number, were offered for purchase in various microformats (35mm roll film, 16mm cartridge, and microfiche) as well as in Copyflo hard copy. The United States Historical Documents Institute, Inc., and University Microfilms International jointly sponsored the filming and respectively sell different formats of the full shelflist, or selected portions of it. This tool can be used most effectively for fine-tuning class number and shelflist assignments through comparison of proposed numbers for new materials with those already grouped in a given area.

- **Commercially prepared indexes.** Just as the Gale cumulations and the LC shelflist reproductions are commercial aids based on official, publicly accessible LC data, so a number of indexing ventures have reflected similar trade manipulation of publications or automated processing available from LC. Their problem has been in keeping up-to-date. A recent publication that can serve as a kind of index is Scott's *Conversion Tables: LC–Dewey, Dewey–LC, and LC Subject Headings–LC and Dewey.*[7]

- **Texts and general discussions.** Through the years many perceptive discussions of *LCC* have appeared. The list of suggested readings at the end of this chapter gives those titles that are most likely to help introduce the scheme to the beginning student.

BASIC FEATURES

Because *LCC* was developed as a utilitarian scheme for books at LC, it is an enumerative, rather than a deductive, system. Among the basic features borrowed from Cutter are its order of main classes, its use of capital letters for main and subclass notation, its use of Arabic numerals for further subdivision, and its modification of the Cutter author-mark idea to achieve alphabetic subarrangements of various kinds.

All the LC schedules have similar, but not identical, sequencing arrangements and physical appearance. Within each sequence of class numbers the order proceeds, as a rule, from general aspects of the topic or discipline to its particular divisions and subtopics. Chronological sequences may trace historical events, publication dates, or other useful time frames. Geographical arrangements are frequently alphabetical, but just as frequently are given in a "preferred order," starting with the Western Hemisphere and the United States. Class "G—Geography, etc." is distinct from the history classes, although located next to them. This distribution is similar to the *DDC* location of "910—Geography and Travel" within class "900—History." Neither scheme quite succeeds in solving the problem of ambiguous relationships between popular works of description and travel and other, perhaps more scholarly, books on national or regional social life and customs. The user must search both the history and the geography shelves to find all available materials on these topics.

There are some significant differences between *LCC* and *DDC* in organizing some materials. For example, *LCC* provides broad subclasses in class P for the various national literatures, subdividing next by chronology and then by individual author. Seldom, except for anthologies, does it group literary works by form. *DDC* also starts in its 800 class with a basic separation into national literatures, but it subdivides next by form, e.g., poetry, drama, fiction, etc. Only subordinately does it provide for time divisions or individual authors.

The LC preference for grouping national literatures by time period and author extends to class "B—Philosophy" but not to music or the graphic arts. In subclass "M—Music and Scores" works are classed first by form (e.g., opera, oratorio, symphony, chamber music), then by composer. There is no attempt to keep time periods, national schools, or genres of expression (e.g., classical, romantic, modern) distinct. Subclass "ML—Literature, History and Criticism of Music" does use national, chronological, and similar groupings. In class "N—Fine Arts" materials are grouped first by form (e.g., sculpture, drawing, painting), then by nationality or chronology, and finally by artist.

The major LC use of literary grouping by form formerly was its subclass "PZ—Fiction in English; Juvenile Belles Lettres." Here a concession was made to a "reader interest" orientation that proved to be most controversial and a stumbling block to the full use of *LCC* by other research libraries with large holdings in literature. Therefore, beginning July 1, 1980, LC discontinued use of PZ1, PZ3, and PZ4. American fiction is now classed in PS, English fiction in PR, and translations of fiction into English with the original national literature. Otherwise, LC's handling of literature has met with general approval. A recurring pattern of organization within each literature affords the shelf or shelflist browser a useful guide:

1. History and criticism, subdivided
    a. Chronologically
    b. Then by form
2. Collections or anthologies, subdivided by form
3. Individual authors, subdivided
    a. Chronologically
    b. Then alphabetically by author
        1) Collective works
        2) Individual works
        3) Biography and criticism

LCC breaks the "Generalia" class familiar to *DDC* users into two classes at opposite ends of the alphabet. The "A—General Works" schedule employs for its subclasses rare instances of mnemonic notation. General encyclopedias are located in subclass AE, general indexes in AI, general museum publications in AM, and so forth. By contrast, the Z class, containing bibliographies and works on the book industries and on libraries, has, until very recently, had no two-letter subclasses at all. While its subject bibliographies are arranged alphabetically by topic in the Z5001–Z8000 span, there is nothing mnemonic about their notation. A need for a new classification area for "Information Resources" precipitated the creation of subclass ZA in 1996.[8] The only other notable instances of mnemonic class letter associations are for class "G—Geography, etc.," class "M—Music," subclass "ML—Music Literature," and class "T—Technology."

SCHEDULE FORMAT

Most of the *LCC* schedules exhibit certain common features of external and internal format. Many of these format features are missing from certain schedules, a reminder that the scheme was intentionally decentralized in its development. Subject specialists were encouraged to adopt standard modes of organization, but were never forced to maintain a rigid formal pattern.

External Format

The gross physical format, or external appearance, of the schedules has already been described. Both old and new editions, regardless of typography or binding, tend to follow a familiar pattern of organization:

1. **A preface or prefatory note** nearly always follows the title page. These introductory remarks in recent editions have become briefer and less helpful for classification purposes than they formerly were.

2. **Brief synopses** next appear in many of the schedules, to show the primary subdivisions contained in those volumes. In most cases these broad subclasses are readily identifiable by their brief double-letter notation, but class "K—Law" is issued in double-letter subclass volumes with synopses that frequently show mnemonic triple-letter divisions. We can learn at a glance that the law of Ontario is found in subclass KEO, while that of Quebec is in KEQ. A similar mnemonic arrangement applies to the American states in subclass KF, but their notation is more complicated since several states share certain initial letters. A typical synopsis is shown in figure 11.1.

   Fig. 11.1. An example of the LCC feature known as a "Synopsis."

   SYNOPSIS

H	SOCIAL SCIENCES (GENERAL)
HA	STATISTICS
HB	ECONOMIC THEORY. DEMOGRAPHY
HC	ECONOMIC HISTORY AND CONDITIONS
HD	ECONOMIC HISTORY AND CONDITIONS
HE	TRANSPORTATION AND COMMUNICATIONS
HF	COMMERCE
HG	FINANCE
HJ	PUBLIC FINANCE
HM	SOCIOLOGY
HN	SOCIAL HISTORY AND CONDITIONS. SOCIAL PROBLEMS. SOCIAL REFORM
HQ	THE FAMILY. MARRIAGE. WOMAN
HS	SOCIETIES: SECRET, BENEVOLENT, ETC.
HT	COMMUNITIES. CLASSES. RACES
HV	SOCIAL PATHOLOGY. SOCIAL AND PUBLIC WELFARE. CRIMINOLOGY
HX	SOCIALISM. COMMUNISM. ANARCHISM

3. **An outline,** consisting not only of alphabetic subclasses, but also of significant alphanumeric subspans, is present in nearly every schedule. In schedules without synopses the outlines tend to be briefer and to show broader subdivisions; in schedules with synopses, they are longer and more detailed. Occasionally, as in the schedule for class "J—Political Science," the "synopsis" is really an outline. These two kinds of preliminary overview offer the user supplementary techniques for arriving quickly at any given portion of the schedules. The outline for the first two subclasses of class H appears in the schedule as shown in figure 11.2.

Fig. 11.2. An example of the LCC feature known as an "Outline."

OUTLINE

H		Social Sciences (General)
HA		Statistics
	29-32	Theory and method of social science statistics
	36-37	Organizations. Bureaus. Service
	38-39	Registration of vital events. Registration (General)
	154-4737	Statistical data
	154-155	Universal statistics
	175-4737	By region or country
HB		Economic theory. Demography
	71-74	Economics as a science. Relation to other subjects
	75-130	History of economics. History of economic theory *Including special economic schools*
	131-145	Methodology
	135-145	Mathematical economics. Quantitative methods *Including econometrics, input-output analysis, game theory*
	201-206	Value. Utility
	221-236	Price.
	238-251	Competition. Production. Wealth
	501	Capital. Capitalism
	522-715	Income. Factor shares
	531-551	Interest. Usury
	601	Profit
	615-715	Entrepreneurship. Risk and uncertainty. Property
	801-843	Consumption. Demand
	846.846.8	Welfare theory
	848-3697	Demography. Vital events
	3711-3840	Business cycles. Economic fluctuations

4. **The schedule proper** enumerates specific class number assignments and sequences in their most explicit form. Page formatting devices, although slightly different in each of the schedule formats (i.e., published schedules available from CDS, schedules available in *Cataloger's Desktop/Classification Plus*, and schedules available from the Gale Group), demonstrate hierarchical subordinations and progressions. *LCC* schedules show left-margin indentions, with nested running titles on nearly every page or screen display to demonstrate hierarchy. These devices are not so carefully worked out, nor so consistently displayed, as they are in *DDC*. Many broad headings not listed in the schedule outline, but which offer a useful survey of subtopics, are interpolated just ahead of the specific numbers that they embrace. They often carry no single class number of their own. For this and related reasons *LCC* does not work well for classifying small general collections or parts of collections. Nor are these spans very often accompanied by internal summary tables such as *DDC* uses.

   Most schedules do carry internal tables at key junctures, to provide schematic patterns for further localized development of class numbers or sequences. While *LCC* is basically enumerative (that is, its topical number assignments are usually not made until there is at least one work to go into the category), these generalized tables open up patterned arrangements that are usually not fully realized on the shelves.

   Users of older schedules will find the "Divide like" or "Subarranged like" note, which appears infrequently, but very specifically, in simple one-to-one equivalencies, without the complications encountered in the more abstractly contrived *DDC* notation. Scope notes and footnotes occasionally refer to auxiliary tables, etc., or they sometimes give useful instructions for number building. An excerpt from the "T—Technology" schedule (*see* figure 11.3, page 314) shows most of these features.

5. **Auxiliary tables** designed for use with more than one specific class notation or span are located externally to the schedules proper in many volumes. They appear after the full schedule, immediately preceding the index. (Class P-PZ tables are published in a completely separate volume.) Sometimes a table number is given in parentheses beside an entry in the schedule, to warn the user that the entry should be further subdivided. Sometimes a footnote cites the table with its page number and occasionally indicates how the interpolation should be made. Sometimes the instructions for interpolation are right in the schedule. Such is the case in figure 11.3 from the TD subclass shown on page 314.

   The excerpt in figure 11.4, page 315, from the "N—Fine Arts" external Table I and Table II shows how spans of 100 and 200 numbers can be distributed among the same list of terms. Table I distributes America and the United States among numbers 1 to 10, while Table II distributes the same span among numbers 1 to 25. The span "N5801–5896.3—Classical art in other [i.e., non-Greek or Italian] countries" is to be distributed according to Table N1, adding the appropriate table number to N5800. On the other hand, "NB1501–1685—[Sculptured monuments in] Special countries" uses Table N2 as a guide for adding country numbers to NB1500.

Fig. 11.3. Sample excerpt from the *LCC* "T" schedule showing many typical schedule features.

TD	**Environmental technology. Sanitary engineering**
	Including the promotion and conservation of the public health, comfort, and convenience by the control of the environment
	Cf. GE170+, Environmental policy
	Cf. GF51, Human beings and the environment
	Cf. RA565+, Environmental health
	Cf. TH6014+, Environmental engineering in buildings
	Periodicals and societies. By language of publication
1	English
2	French
3	German
4	Other languages (not A-Z)
5	Congresses
6.A1-Z	Exhibitions. Museums
6.A1	General works
6.A2-Z	By region or country, A-Z
	Under each country:
	.x General works
	.x2A-Z Special. By city, A-Z
7	Collected works (nonserial)
9	Dictionaries and encyclopedias
12	Directories
	History
15	General works
16	Ancient
17	Medieval
18	Modern to 1800
19	Nineteenth century
20	Twentieth century
21-127	Country and city subdivisions (Table T1 modified)
	Including municipal reports of public sanitary works
	Add country number in table to TD0
	Under each two number country, unless otherwise specified:
	1.A1 General works
	1.A6-Z States, provinces, etc., A-Z
	2.A-Z Local (Cities, etc.), A-Z
	Biography
139	Collective
140.A-Z	Individual, A-Z
	General works
144	Early to 1850
145	1850-
146	Elementary textbooks
148	Popular works
151	Pocketbooks, tables, etc.
153	General special
155	Addresses, essays, lectures
156	Environmental and sanitary engineering as a profession

Fig. 11.4. Distribution of the same terms among different spans of numbers.

TABLES TO Class N

TABLE N1: TABLES OF REGIONS OR COUNTRIES (100 NUMBERS)

01	America
01.5	Latin America
02	North America
	United States
03	General works
03.5	Colonial period; 18th (and early 19th) century
03.7	19th century
04	20th century
04.5	Northeastern States
04.7	Atlantic States
05	New England
05.5	Middle Atlantic States
06	South
07	Central
08	West
08.5	Northwestern States
08.6	Southwestern States
09	Pacific States
10.A-W	States, A-W

Under each:

.x	General works	
.x2	Local (other than cities), A-Z	

. . .

TABLE N2: TABLES OF REGIONS OR COUNTRIES (200 NUMBERS)

01	America
02	Latin America
03	North America
	United States
05	General works
06	Colonial period; 18th (and early 19th) century
07	19th century
08	20th century
08.5	Northeastern States
08.7	Atlantic States
10	New England
10.5	Middle Atlantic States
11	South
14	Central
17	West
18	Northwestern States
18.6	Southwestern States
19	Pacific States
25.A-W	States, A-W

Under each:

.x	General works	
.x2	Local (other than cities), A-Z	

. . .

Auxiliary Table I from the N schedule is "simple" because it carries only one sequence of numbers that can be interpolated directly into the corresponding number spans in the schedule. In the past many tables were "compound." That is, they supplied more than one number sequence for the same list of subtopics. Someone using older copies of schedules will still find these compound tables. All tables in new schedules and in the version available in *Cataloger's Desktop/Classification Plus* are now "simple" tables. Number spans from the schedule and the table are matched according to the quantity of materials that the LC classifiers anticipate at any given location.

Geographical and chronological subdivisions are often relegated to auxiliary tables. The two concepts may be combined as shown in figure 11.4 on page 315. Other principles of division may also be found in tabular form. Tables in class "J—Political Science" contain such categories as "Periodicals," "Public administration," "Political participation," and the like. The heavily used PR, PS, PZ schedule has a separately published extensive set of tables designed for use with literary author numbers, running the gamut from long spans for prolific, often translated and discussed authors to brief expansions of cutter designations for recent or little-published authors.

6. **A detailed index** accompanies each schedule except Parts 1 and 2 of the PT subclass. These indexes vary in coverage and depth, but most of them list specific topics from their schedule. References from synonyms or related terms, alphabetized and indented subordinate topical lists, and suggestions for placing related materials in other schedules are occasionally included.

7. **Supplementary pages of additions and changes** appear at the back of the few remaining schedules published before 1970.

Internal Format

While Herbert Putnam and Charles Martel left the local arrangement of topical and form divisions very much to the discretion of their subject specialists, they nevertheless identified certain basic orientation features for use throughout the system. These organizational concepts were generally known as "Martel's Seven Points" of internal format. They could be incorporated into the schedules at any level of hierarchical subdivision appropriate within the given context. They encompassed:

1. **General form divisions.** The approach here was similar to Dewey's Form Division Table, which has evolved in recent *DDC* editions into the Table of Standard Subdivisions. It assumes that library materials can often be effectively grouped according to their mode of presentation. Examples are periodicals; society publications; collections; dictionaries or encyclopedias; conference, exhibition, or museum publications; annuals or yearbooks; directories; and documents. Because of their general application they belong near the beginning of any disciplinary or topical

section, but *LCC* imposes no rigid order upon their location. Their importance in subclass "L—Education (General)" is observed in the following schedule outline:

L	**EDUCATION (GENERAL)**
7-97	Periodicals. Societies
101	Yearbooks
106-107	Congresses
111-791	Official documents, reports, etc.
797-899	Educational exhibitions and museums
999-991	Directories of educational institutions

By contrast, subclasses "LD-LG—Individual Educational Institutions" show no obvious use of the form division concept. Only in their auxiliary tables do a few of the forms emerge as useful ordering concepts.

2. **Theory.   Philosophy.**

3. **History.   Biography.**

4. **Treatises.   General works.**   Works falling under points 2–4 of Martel's Seven Points are often intermixed with those arranged according to physical form and with other locally useful groupings, as shown in the excerpt from QE—Geology in figure 11.5.

Fig. 11. 5. Excerpt showing intermixture of different kinds of form subgroupings for the Geology subclass.

QE	**GEOLOGY**
1	Periodicals, societies, congresses, serial collections, yearbooks
3	Collected works (nonserial)
4	Voyages and expeditions
5	Dictionaries and encyclopedias
6	Philosophy
7	Nomenclature, terminology, notation, abbreviations
	History
11	General works
13	By region or country, A-Z
	Biography
21	Collective
22	Individual, A-Z
	e.g. .D25 Dana, J.D.
	.L8 Lyell
	.S77 Steno, Nicolaus, Bishop
23	Directories
25	Early works through 1800
	General works, treatises, and advanced textbooks
26	1801-1969
.2	1970-
	Elementary textbooks
28	General
.2	Physical geology
.3	Historical geology

5. **Law.   Regulation.   State relations.**   Until the publication in 1969 of the first "K—Law" subclass, this ordering principle was handy for grouping legal materials with their related topics, especially in the social sciences. The development of class K inverts the relationship. Whenever possible we now classify such works first as legal materials and only subordinately as being discipline-oriented. For example, books dealing with government regulations for control of drugs as economic commodities were originally classed in HD9665.7–9. Those dealing with regulations for the manufacture, sale, and use of drugs were classed in RA402. Subclass "KF—Law of the United States" now places drug laws in KF3885–3895. Now, most works dealing with U.S. drug legislation and regulation are placed there.

6. **Study and teaching.   Research.   Textbooks.**   Unlike *DDC*, *LCC* sometimes allows a unique place for textbooks, as well as for more theoretical works on how to study, teach, or research a topic. Thus, under "QL—Zoology" (*see* figure 11.6) QL47–QL48.2 are numbers for textbooks. In other disciplines, *LCC* explicitly groups textbooks with general works and treatises, as shown under QH581 in figure 11.7.

Fig. 11. 6. Excerpt showing a unique place for textbooks.

QL	ZOOLOGY
	General works and treaties
41	Early through 1759
45	1760-1969
.2	1970-
46	Pictorial works and atlases
.5	Zoological illustrating
	Textbooks
	Advanced
47	Through 1969
.2	1970-
	Elementary
48	Through 1969
.2	1970-
49	Juvenile works
	Cf. SF75.5, Domestic animals
50	Popular works
	For stories and anecdotes, *see* QL791+
.5	Zoology as a profession. Vocational guidance
	Study and teaching. Research
51	General works
.2	By region or country, A-Z
	Each region or country subarranged by author
.5	Problems, exercises, examinations
52	Outlines, syllabi
.55	Activity programs
.6	Experiments
53	Laboratory manuals

Fig. 11.7. Excerpt showing textbooks grouped with general works and treatises.

QH	CYTOLOGY
573	Periodicals, societies, congresses, serial collections, yearbooks
574	Collected works (nonserial)
575	Dictionaries and encyclopedias
	History
577	General works
578	By region or country, A-Z
	General works, treatises, and textbooks
581	Through 1969
.2	1970-
.5	Addresses, essays, lectures
582	Pictorial works and atlases
.4	Popular works
	Study and teaching. Research
583	General works
.2	Laboratory manuals

7. **Subjects and subdivisions of subjects.** Most modern classification systems are disciplinary rather than topical. That is, they normally proceed from broad general divisions of knowledge to narrower subdivisions, with more or less comprehensive coverage provided for each special topic in relation to the hierarchy. Any linear arrangement of books or other materials on shelves must resort to a series of cyclic progressions if it displays subject-related groupings based on logical considerations or practical associations. Just as Martel's fourth point reminds classifiers that "general works" should be shelved together, usually near the beginning of each new topical group, so this seventh point provides for further subject breakdown based on "literary warrant" or the amount of material requiring classification in such a group. One intermediate type that *LCC* frequently places just after "general works" is a potpourri called "general special" or "special aspects." These works treat the topic from particular points of view. Sometimes, as in TD153 (*see* figure 11.3 on page 314), such works have a single class number. At other places they must be spread out over several pages of the schedules.

NOTATION

The typical *LCC* notation contains a mixed notation of one to three letters, followed by one to four integers, and possibly a short decimal. Decimal numbers were not used much until it became necessary to expand certain sections where no further integers were available. Decimals do not usually indicate subordination, but allow a new topic or aspect to be inserted into an established context. In the excerpt from the "QH573–583.2—Cytology" schedule (*see* figure 11.7) the decimals belie the left-margin indentions of their associated topics. Clearly, "QH581.5—Addresses, essays, lectures" is hierarchically equivalent to "QH575—Dictionaries and encyclopedias," and is not subordinate to "QH581—General works . . . Through 1969."

Another method of expanding *LCC* notations is by means of mnemonic letter-number combinations, which look like Cutter's "Author numbers" but are derived from a different matrix (*see* chapter 12, "Creation of Complete Call Numbers"). These "cutter numbers" may represent geographic, personal, corporate, or topical names. They are subordinated to schedule notations where an instruction to subdivide "A-Z" appears. Since they are part of the class notation, many of the actual LC assignments, or at least a significant number of examples, are included within the schedule (*see* "QE22—Individual [biography of geologists], A-Z" in figure 11.5 on page 317). Geographic cutter numbers are generally omitted, however (*see* "QH578—[History of cytology] By region or country, A-Z" in figure 11.7 on page 319).

Alphabetic geographic sequences normally appear at subordinate places in the schedules, where they subdivide a single integer or decimal number. For broader disciplines or subjects, where the geographic arrangement covers an extensive number span, the organization follows a preferred pattern as was noted in the section on external format (*see* page 313). Class N, Tables I and II (*see* figure 11.4 on page 315), show how such sequences begin with "home base" (i.e., the Western Hemisphere and the United States), and then follow a pattern that covers the earth pretty much according to our American perceptions of the nearness and importance of our neighbors.

LC interpretation of "cutter numbers" is always decimal. In a typical letter(s)-number(s)/letter-number(s) combination, the primary letter(s)-number(s) group should be arranged first alphabetically, then by integer(s) until a digit is introduced following a decimal point. All schedules make the basic ordering by integer quite evident, as when PR509 follows PR51, but precedes PR5018. The secondary letter-number(s) combination, by contrast, should be filed decimally. LC carefully inserts a decimal point in front of it, even if, as at "QH541.15.M3—Mathematical Models in Ecology," a decimal is already part of the primary notation. Some libraries using *LCC* drop the cutter decimal from their notation, on the premise that users will remember to follow the convention. The practice may possibly cause confusion in long cutter number runs where it is not clearly understood that a class notation like PR4972.M33 should follow PR4972.M3 but precede PR4972.M5.

Occasionally a class notation, or series of notations, appears in the schedules in parentheses. These were formerly termed "shelflist numbers," but today more often are called "alternative class numbers." Some of them represent locations once actively used, but now retired by LC. Other class notations appear to have been reserved in parentheses for possible future use and have since been activated. "PA2025—Collections [dealing with Latin philology and language]" was so reserved in the original 1928 edition of the P-PA schedule, but now the parentheses have been removed. Alternative class notations are nearly always accompanied by "prefer notes." Subclass SF (Animal culture), for example, has an entry "SF(112) Weight tables, *see* HG5716.C62, etc." Libraries using *LCC* are welcome to adopt these alternative class notations if their own classification needs are better realized by so doing.

Following are a few examples of classification using *LCC*.

Example 1

DC203.4	Ashton, John, b. 1834.
	English caricature and satire on Napoleon I . . .

D	History and Topography (except America)
DC	France
139–249	Revolutionary and Napoleonic period, 1789–1815
203–212.5	Biography of Napoleon
203	[General works]
203.4	Caricature and satire

Example 2

QL696	Turner, Angela K.
.P247	Swallows & martins . . .

Q	Science
QL	Zoology
605–739.3	Chordates. Vertebrates
671–699	Birds
696	Systematic divisions. By order and family, A-Z
.P2	Passeriformes
.P247	Hirundinidae (Swallows)

Example 3

RA407.3	American Hospital Association
	Comparative statistics on health facilities and population : metropolitan and nonmetropolitan areas . . .

R	Medicine (General)
RA	Public aspects of medicine
1–418.5	Medicine and the state
407–409.5	Health status indicators. Medical statistics and surveys
407.3–407.5	By region or country
407.3–4	United States.
407.3	General works

Example 4

HB1237	Marriage statistics for Sweden . . .

H	Social sciences
HB	Economic theory. Demography
848–3697	Demography. Population. Vital events
1111–1317	Marriages. Nuptiality
1121–1317	By region or country. Table H2
	[Add country number in table to HB1120]
	[Table H2: 117-118 Sweden]
1237	Sweden [General works]

CONCLUSION

Most libraries using *LCC* will continue to use officially assigned call numbers for any of their own materials that LC has already classified. However, it is a rare library that holds only information packages also available in the LC collection. Classifiers should be able to create reasonably consistent notations with which to fit their unique holdings into the system. They may stumble over special practices at local points, but the general principles of arrangement are nearly always decipherable, especially if a shelflist of LC call numbers is available to compare with the schedules. Highly specific shelflisting (i.e., the rationale underlying many cutter numbers, as explained in chapter 12) is, on the other hand, not always so easy to explain. *LCC* is loosely coordinated and essentially pragmatic. It aims first to class closely, then to identify uniquely, particular works, or issues of works, using the most economical notation available within its broad parameters of theory and practice.

NOTES

1.   A table comparing the main classes of the Cutter and the LC schemes is given on page 334.

2.   Library of Congess, Cataloging Distribution Service. "Bibliographic Products & Services" (available: http://lcweb.loc.gov/cds/ [accessed 3/5/00]).

3.   For connections to these changes *see*: *The Library of Congress Cataloging Policy & Support Office* (available: http://lcweb.loc.gov/catdir/cpso/ [accessed 3/5/00]).

4.   For information regarding The Gale Group and its publication of the cumulated editions of the *Library of Congress Classification, see*: *The Gale Group* (available: http://www.galegroup.com/ [accessed 3/12/00]).

5.   Library of Congress, *Cataloging Service*, bulletin 1 (June 1945)–125 (Spring 1978); *Cataloging Service Bulletin*, no. 1 (Summer 1978)– .

6.   *Library of Congress Subject Headings*, 13th– eds. (Washington, D.C.: Library of Congress, Office for Subject Cataloging Policy, 1990–). Also available in *Classification Plus* (Washington, D.C.: Cataloging Distribution Service, Library of Congress, current issue supersedes all previous issues). For a detailed discussion of this work, *see* chapter 15 of this text.

7.   Mona L. Scott, *Conversion Tables: LC–Dewey, Dewey–LC, and LC Subject Headings–LC and Dewey*, 2nd ed. (Englewood, Colo.: Libraries Unlimited, 1999).

8.   In addition to its being published in *Library of Congress Classification: Additions and Changes*, subclass ZA is available on the Web: http://lcweb.loc.gov/catdir/cpso/ (accessed 8/28/99).

SUGGESTED READING

Chan, Lois M. *A Guide to the Library of Congress Classification*. 5th ed. Englewood, Colo.: Libraries Unlimited, 1999.

Dittmann, Helena. *Learn Library of Congress Classification*. Lanham, Md.: Scarecrow Press, 2000.

Ferguson, Bobby. *Subject Analysis: Blitz Cataloging Workbook*. Englewood, Colo.: Libraries Unlimited, 1998. Chapter 4: Library of Congress Classification.

Foskett, A. C. *The Subject Approach to Information*. 5th ed. London: Library Association Publishing, 1996. Chapter 22: The Library of Congress Classification.

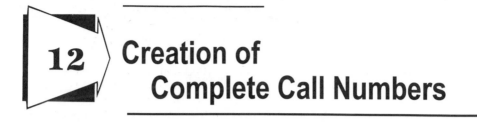

Creation of
Complete Call Numbers

INTRODUCTION

Library call numbers serve a double function. The class notation portion groups related materials together. The second portion of the complete call number uniquely identifies different works in the same class. Traditionally, this second part of the call number is based on the main entry, which has been chosen for the work through descriptive cataloging. Various terms such as *author number*, *book number*, and *cutter number* have been applied, but *author number* does not allow for those works with title main entries, while *book number* implies that it cannot be applied to nonbook materials. *Cutter number* is also misleading because the Library of Congress (LC) method of deriving it differs from the original tables devised by Charles A. Cutter.

However, the name *cutter number* has come into general use in practice regardless of the classification scheme used. Its general usage is a tribute to Cutter, who conceived the idea of using alphanumeric symbols to keep items in alphabetical order within a particular classification notation. In this text *cutter number* is used for any notation serving this function.

CUTTER NUMBERS DEVISED BY
CHARLES A. CUTTER

Providing a classification notation with a supplementary cutter number enables the cataloger to design a fully unique call number for each title in a collection. The cutter numbers most often used with *Dewey Decimal Classification* (*DDC*) class notations are taken from a set of tables devised by Cutter. These tables equate surnames and other words with alphanumeric sequences. Cutter initially produced a table in a single alphabet of all consonants except *S*, followed by an alphabet of vowels and the letter *S*.[1] This "two-figure" table (most of its combinations consist of a capital letter plus two digits) was later expanded by Kate E. Sanborn to provide more differentiation among names for use with larger collections.[2] Since she did not adhere to Cutter's schema, Cutter then developed his own expansion to permit growing libraries to assign more specific book numbers without disrupting the sequences they had already established from his two-figure table.[3] There are thus three different "Cutter" tables. The Cutter-Sanborn version is perhaps the most widely used today, being preferred by many larger libraries because of its simpler design and notation.

While cutter numbers are most commonly used to arrange material by main entries (usually authors' surnames, but occasionally forenames, corporate names, or titles), they are also used in some instances to alphabetize material by subject, as in the case of biography. To illustrate the use of each table, let us suppose that we wish to assign a cutter number for the English poet, John Donne. The three tables carry the following sequences:

Cutter Two-figure Table

Doll	69	Foh
Dom	71	Folg
Doo	72	Foll

Cutter Three-figure Table

Donk	718	Folk
Donnet	719	Folke
Doo	72	Foll

Cutter-Sanborn Table

Donk	684	Fonti
Donn	685	Fontr
Donner	686	Foo

According to the Cutter two-figure table, the number for Donne is D71. By the Cutter three-figure table it is D718 (an expansion of the D71 assignment). But by the Cutter-Sanborn table it is D685. The above examples also demonstrate the typical three-column display used in the original form of the tables. In 1969 Paul K. Swanson of the Forbes Library, Northampton, Massachusetts, and Esther M. Swift, editor of the H. R. Huntting Company, revised this arrangement into single continuous alphabets of two columns, with letters on the left corresponding to numbers on the right. The new arrangement appears to be easier to use.

The work letter (or workmark) is the first letter of the title of the work, exclusive of articles. It follows the cutter number on the second line of the call number. For example, the complete Dewey Decimal call number of Henry James's novel *Wings of the Dove* is 813.4 J27w. Work letters do not inevitably ensure that a book will be placed in alphabetical sequence within the author grouping; this depends upon the sequence of acquisition of the books. One additional letter from the title may be added if necessary. Thus, a copy of James's *Washington Square* might be classified 813.4 J27wa. If the third acquisition is a volume entitled *The Works of Henry James*, it would most probably be given the call number 813.4 J27, with no workmark, as most libraries prefer to place collected works of an author ahead of the individual works.

With an author such as Erle Stanley Gardner, who began the title of all of his Perry Mason mysteries with *The Case of the* ..., such a scheme is not feasible. Depending on the library's policy, the cataloger can choose one of several alternatives. For example, the cataloger can ignore completely the common phrase *the case of the* and proceed directly to the distinctive part of the title, or use two work letters: *c* for *case*, plus an additional letter for the distinctive title (e.g., *The Case of the Mischievous Doll* might be assigned the work letters *cm*).

Biographies and criticism of a specific author pose a particular problem of library policy. Two procedures are common. In the Dewey schedule, 928 is the biography number for literary figures (920 for Biography; 8 for Literature). Thus, biographies of authors might be classified in 928, with subdivision for nationality. Another way of classifying biography is to use the standard biography subdivision, 092. A third possibility is to classify biographies of authors with their work, in order to keep everything by and about a literary figure in one place. In such cases, a common method of distinguishing works "by" from works "about" an author is to insert an arbitrary letter—usually one toward the end of the alphabet—after the cutter number and to follow it with the initial of the author of the biography. This device puts all books about an author directly behind all books by that author. Thus, if the letter *z* is chosen as the biographical letter, a biography or criticism of Henry James by Leon Edel could be cuttered J27zE, and it would follow, in shelflist order, J27w. If James had written a novel beginning with the letter *z* only the work letter *z* would be used for the novel; thus, the novel would still come before all criticism and biography.

The problem of a variety of editions occurs most frequently in literature, but classic works in all other fields are also reprinted by the same or another publisher, especially since paperbacks and audio books have revived many worthwhile books that have been long out of print. One cataloging practice is to assign the date of publication as part of the call number to all editions of a single work issued by the same publisher and to assign a number following the work letter to all editions of the same work published by different publishers. Thus, the first acquired copy of *Wings of the Dove* would be classified 813.4 J27w. If the library acquired a second copy of the novel, issued by a different publisher, the number would be 813.4 J27w2. Assume that the second publisher was Modern Library and that the library received another edition of the novel, also published by Modern Library, in 1985. The call number might then be 813.4 J27w2 1985. A completely different edition published by a third publisher would be classified 813.4 J27w3. Many variations of these practices exist.

CUTTER NUMBERS DEVISED BY THE
LIBRARY OF CONGRESS (LC)

LC call numbers also consist, in general, of two principal elements: class notation and cutter number, to which are added, as required, symbols designating a particular work. While it is possible to use Cutter-Sanborn numbers with LC classification, most libraries prefer to use LC cutter numbers constructed from a table composed by LC for this purpose.

Policies and procedures used at LC in completing call numbers have been published in the form of a shelflisting manual.[4] This manual should be consulted for more detailed information than is discussed below.

LC cutter numbers are composed of the initial letter of the main entry heading, followed by Arabic numerals representing the succeeding letters on the following basis:

LC Cutter Table

(1) After initial *vowels*
for the second letter:

	b	d	l-m	n	p	r	s-t	u-y
use number:	2	3	4	5	6	7	8	9

(2) After initial letter *S*
for the second letter:

	a	ch	e	h-i	m-p	t	u	w-z
use number:	2	3	4	5	6	7	8	9

(3) After initial letters *Qu*
for the second [i.e. next] letter:

	a	e	i	o	r	t	y
use number:	3	4	5	6	7	8	9

For initial letters *Qa-Qt*, use: **2-29**

(4) After other initial *consonants*
for the second letter:

	a	e	i	o	r	u	y
use number:	3	4	5	6	7	8	9

(5) For *expansion*
for the letter:

	a-d	e-h	i-l	m-o	p-s	t-v	w-z
use number:	3	4	5	6	7	8	9

The following examples show cutters that would be used in entries already shelflisted conform to the table [above]. In most cases, cutters must be adjusted to file an entry correctly and to allow room for later entries.

Vowels		S		Q		Consonants	
IBM	.I26	Sadron	.S23	*Qadduri	.Q23	Campbell	.C36
Idaho	.I33	*Scanlon	.S29	*Qiao	.Q27	Ceccaldi	.C43
*Ilardo	.I4	Schreiber	.S37	Quade	.Q33	*Chertok	.C48
*Import	.I48	*Shillingburg	.S53	Queiroz	.Q45	*Clark	.C58
Inman	.I56	*Singer	.S57	Quinn	.Q56	Cobblestone	.C63
Ipswich	.I67	Stinson	.S75	Quorum	.Q67	Cryer	.C79
*Ito	.I87	Suranyi	.S87	Qutub	.Q88	Cuellar	.C84
*Ivy	.I94	*Symposium	.S96	*Qvortrup	.Q97	Cymbal	.C96

*These cutters reflect the adjustments made to allow for a range of letters on the table, e.g., **l-m**, or for letters not explicitly stated, e.g., **h** after an initial consonant.[5]

Some points need further comment. Note first of all that the numeral *1* appears nowhere in the table. LC avoids its use, and the use of zeros, as decimals to preserve alphabetic order. If, for instance, the name *Abbott* were given the cutter *.A1*, a subsequent cutter at the same location for *Aamondt* would have to be, say, *.A09*, while *Aagard* would go to *.A085* or something like it. While most type-fonts distinguish between the digit zero and the capital letter *O*, it is still sometimes difficult for the human eye to distinguish them. In actual practice, LC shelflisters would more likely give *Abbott* a cutter such as *.A2* so later assignments for names such as *Aagard* and *Aamodt* could have *.A12* and *.A15*, or similar decimals to ensure space for unlimited further alphabetical expansion if needed.

All this brings out another trait of LC shelflisting. There is nothing sacrosanct about the above table. It has been officially changed as shelflisting problems were encountered and new needs were perceived. The present LC shelflist contains a jumble of old and new assignments. Recently devised numbers may reflect accommodation to outmoded practices, to avoid extensive re-shelflisting, rather than following current practice as outlined in the table. Cutter numbers assigned for the same person may also vary significantly from one class notation to another. The examples below illustrate such a variation:

TL561	Splaver, Sarah, 1921–
.S65	Some day I'll be an aerospace engineer . . .

. . . .

Z682	Splaver, Sarah, 1921–
.S735	Some day I'll be a librarian . . .

Since cutter numbers are used by LC to extend some class notations, as well as for shelflisting alphabetically by main entry, many works have at least two cutter segments in their call numbers. One example is Niles M. Hansen's *French Regional Planning*, for which the LC call number HT395.F7H35 can be analyzed as follows:

H	Social sciences
HT	Communities. Classes. Races
395	Regional planning: countries or regions other than the United States, A-Z
.F7	France
H35	The cutter number for Hansen

While double cutters are commonplace, triple cutters are exceedingly rare. They have been used in class G for certain kinds of subject maps, but with a special disclaimer added. An example is the *New York City Community Health Atlas 1988* prepared by Melvin I. Krasner, et al. Its call number, G1254.N4 E55 K7 1988, is analyzed as follows:

G	Geography. Anthropology. Recreation
1-9980	Geography (General). Atlases. Maps
1000.3-3122	Atlases
1254	New York State sub-area atlas
.N4	New York City
E55	Public Health [from Table IV—Subject subdivisions: "These numbers are not Cutter numbers and have no alphabetical significance."]
K7	Cutter number for Krasner
1988	Date of atlas publication

In the few instances where double cutters are prescribed in the schedules to stand for two separate subdivisions of the subject, the second cutter is made to accommodate both the subject for which it stands and the alphabetical arrangement for which it stands. For example:

HD3561	Hanel, Alfred.
.A6N55	Genossenschaften in Nigeria

In the classification schedules under HD3441–3570.9, the notation run assigned to industrial cooperation by country, the notation for the country is first cuttered by *.A6* for general cooperative societies and then is subdivided further "by state, province, etc." Thus, *N55* stands both for Nigeria and for the alphabetical arrangement of *Hanel* among other works on the subject.

Reserved cutter numbers. The LC schedules and tables frequently set aside the first few *.A* or the last several *.Z* possibilities in a cutter sequence for special purposes. Observe the example at "TD21–127—Country and City Subdivisions [of Environmental technology and Sanitary engineering]" in figure 11.3 on page 314. Assume that class T, Table I, and the internal table in the schedule have been applied to derive the class number TD28.A1 for a general work on sanitary engineering in Mexico. Let us suppose that the first book classified here was written by a Ricardo Gomez. Using the LC cutter number table, we could complete the call number as TD28.A1G6 or TD28.A1G65. A second work on the same topic by a Rachael Goode might then receive the call number TD28.A1G66, while still a third treatise by a Ralph Goddard could be given something like TD28.A1G58.

Assume now that we have a book on sanitary engineering in the Mexican state of Aguascalientes. It cannot receive the usual cutter *.A3* or *.A33* because the internal table at TD21–126 has "reserved" .A1 through .A5 for general works and other possible future needs. One knows this because the direction for cuttering for "States, provinces, etc." is to use ".A6–Z," meaning that the first cutter that can be used for a state beginning with the letter "A" is "A6." Therefore we must accommodate the reservation by assigning the class number TD28.A68 or TD28.A7, followed by an appropriate cutter number for main entry. Now suppose that still another book covers sanitary engineering in the city of Aguascalientes. Our class number will probably be TD29.A38, plus a second cutter for the main entry.

.Z cutter reservations are most common in class P, where researchers like to have biography and criticism of an author shelved immediately following that author's works. In this class, separate integers frequently designate all authors of a given period whose surnames start with the same initial. The first cutter number is then based on the second letter of the surname (i.e., the letter beginning the cutter is the second letter of the author's name, followed by a number representing the third, or third and fourth, letter[s]). A second cutter, based usually on an auxiliary table of reserved numbers, identifies collected works, selections, titles of separate works, adaptations, translations, or biography and criticism. *The Selected Letters of Rebecca West* carries the LC call number PR6045.E8Z48 1999, exemplifying application of auxiliary Table 40 in the *P-PZ Language and Literature Tables* of the LC classification schedules.

Additions to LC call numbers. Workmarks, in the traditional sense of lowercase letters added to book numbers to alphabetize titles or writers of biographies, are not used by LC. Lowercase letters do serve a few special purposes in LC call numbers. They are sometimes used following dates, as discussed below. In addition, in subclass "PZ   Fiction in English.   Juvenile Literature" a unique combination of upper- and lowercase letters (instead of second cutter numbers) alphabetizes the titles of a given author, while dates designate reissues or new editions. For example, the original 1938 Vanguard Press edition of Dr. Seuss's *The 500 Hats of Bartholomew Cubbins* was given the call number PZ8.G326 Fi, while the 1990 Random House edition has the call number PZ8.G326 Fi 1990. (*Fi* was used in the time when this title was to be filed as if spelled out: "Five Hundred Hats. . . .") Formerly, numerals were used with juvenile literature call numbers to designate new editions, so the 1966 Collins edition of this work was given the call number PZ8.G326 Fi2.

The adding of dates to LC call numbers has increased with multiple publication in more than one country, in different imprints, in paperback as well as hardcover, in later editions, and in reprints. LC began in 1982 to add dates to all monographic call numbers.[6] One use of lowercase letters is to identify bibliographically distinct issues of the same title published in the same year. For example, Andrew M. Greeley's *Love Song* was published by G. K. Hall in a large print version the same year it was published by Warner Books. The second one to be cataloged was assigned the call number PS3557.R358 L68 1989b, the use of the letter "b" being the only difference between the two call numbers. Another use of lowercase letters following dates is to distinguish among works on the same subject and published in the same year that have the same corporate body as main entry.[7]

A few other exceptional notations show up in some schedules. For example, dates are used not only as final elements, to distinguish issues of the same title. In addition they occasionally become secondary elements of class numbers, taking precedence over cutter numbers. Class numbers "BX830–831—General and Ecumenical Councils [within Roman Catholicism]" use this device to arrange church councils by date of opening. An example is John W. O'Malley's *Tradition and Transition: Historical Perspectives on Vatican II*, which carries the LC call number BX830 1962 .O45 1989. Also, in schedule "BL-BX—Religion" some Bible texts are so specifically classed that LC shelflisters merely add dates (no cutter numbers) to keep them in order. For example, the *NRSV-NIV Parallel New Testament in Greek and English*, with interlinear translation by Alfred Marshall, has been assigned the LC call number BS1965.5 1990.

CONCLUSION

Call numbers are of particular concern in libraries with open stacks where browsing allows patrons to find materials on similar subjects in proximity, to find works of one author on a subject together, and to find editions of a work together. Where there are closed stacks, an accession number can serve as well as a call number for retrieval, although a greater burden is then placed on the verbal subject headings to guide users to information packages in particular subject areas.

While use of cutter numbers is the most common method of creating complete call numbers, other means may sometimes be found more useful. In a science and technology collection, for example, where recency of material may be of utmost importance, subarrangement under each class notation may be by year of imprint. In very small general collections, on the other hand, one or more letters of the first word of the main entry may be added after the class notation, with no additional numbers given. This method, however, will usually not result in unique call numbers, which may be needed for shelving management.

NOTES

1,   Charles Ammi Cutter, *Two-Figure Author Table*, Swanson-Swift revision, 1969. Distributed by Libraries Unlimited, Inc., Littleton, Colo. (formerly distributed by H. R. Huntting Co.).

2.   *Cutter-Sanborn Three-Figure Author Table*, Swanson-Swift revision, 1969. Distributed by Libraries Unlimited, Inc., Littleton, Colo. (formerly distributed by H. R. Huntting Co.).

3.   Charles Ammi Cutter, *Three-Figure Author Table*, Swanson-Swift revision, 1969. Distributed by Libraries Unlimited, Inc., Littleton, Colo. (formerly distributed by H. R. Huntting Co.).

4.   *Subject Cataloging Manual: Subject Headings*, 5th ed. (Washington, D.C.: Cataloging Distribution Service, Library of Congress, 1996). Updates, 1997–

5.   *Subject Cataloging Manual: Shelflisting*, G 60, pp. 14–15.

6.   *Cataloging Service Bulletin*, no. 19 (Winter 1982): 25–26.

7.   *Subject Cataloging Manual: Shelflisting*, G220.

SUGGESTED READING

Comaromi, John P. *Book Numbers: A Historical Study and Practical Guide to Their Use*. Littleton, Colo.: Libraries Unlimited, 1981.

Lehnus, Donald J. *Book Numbers: History, Principles, and Application*. Chicago: American Library Association, 1980.

Taylor, Arlene G. *The Organization of Information*. Englewood, Colo.: Libraries Unlimited, 1999. Chapter 9: Arrangement and Display.

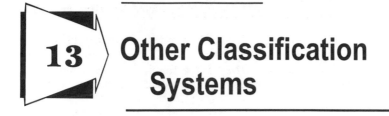

13 ⟩ Other Classification Systems

INTRODUCTION

This chapter provides a brief overview of some of the more significant modern classifications besides *Dewey Decimal Classification* (*DDC*) and *Library of Congress Classification* (*LCC*). Those discussed are Cutter's *Expansive Classification*, Brown's *Subject Classification*, Bliss's *Bibliographic Classification*, and some special classifications. *Universal Decimal Classification* (*UDC*) was discussed at the end of chapter 10, "Decimal Classification," and Ranganathan's *Colon Classification* was used as an example in the discussion of faceted classification in chapter 9. While the classifications discussed here by no means exhaust modern classification research and practice, they do illustrate many of the problems and solutions, or failures, of both the seminal and the well-entrenched systems discussed in the contemporary literature.[1]

CUTTER'S *EXPANSIVE CLASSIFICATION*

The *Expansive Classification*, like the *DDC*, is the brainchild of an eminent library pioneer. Charles A. Cutter (1837–1903) was 15 years older than Melvil Dewey (1851–1931), but took 15 years longer to publish his scheme. Both men devised their systems as practical efforts to organize collections that they knew and served. Just as *DDC* came out of Dewey's student employment in the Amherst College Library, so Cutter's cataloging efforts in the Harvard College Library, and for much longer at the Boston Athenaeum, flowered into his *Expansive Classification*.

While the lives and achievements of the two men show many parallels, there are also significant differences. In classification, Dewey chose his pure decimal notation early on, making it such a key feature of his approach that it more or less governed all subsequent growth patterns. He saw that a simple basic design, easy-to-master mnemonic devices, and a certain sturdy inflexibility could provide a general system that would be applicable to the many libraries that were being established. With characteristic energy, he started a schedule of periodic revision to keep his system responsive to the rapidly changing cultural and publishing milieu. And he marketed his invention with zest and conviction. Cutter was of a more delicate physique and temperament, less exuberant, more institution-oriented. He, too, imbued with the gregarious optimism of his era, worked diligently to establish librarianship as a helping profession, with "scientific" organization as one of its basic assumptions.

Cutter's scheme stressed a sequence of "classifications," or expansions, from a very simple set of categories for a small library to an intricate network of interrelated, highly specific subdivisions for the library of over a million volumes.[2] He did not live to finish his ultimate seventh expansion or to embark on a successive-edition program, but he did have the satisfaction of seeing the Library of Congress (LC) prefer many features of his scheme to that of his friendly rival. His willingness to take suggestions, and to compromise, worked to his credit and to the continuing influence of his system in spite of its limited adoption.

Cutter found the 10 broad classes of *DDC* too narrow a base for large collections. He therefore turned to the alphabet, with its easily ordered sequence of up to 26 primary groupings. For collections that "could be put into a single room" his first "classification" used only seven letters, with an eighth double-letter subclass, as follows:

A   Works of reference and general works that include several of the following sections, and so could not go to any one

B   Philosophy and Religion

E   Biography

F   History and Geography and Travels

H   Social sciences

L   Natural sciences and Arts

Y   Language and Literature

YF   Fiction

If a small library should grow to require closer, more specific classes, Cutter's second classification, or expansion, introduced a mixed alphanumeric notation. It also subdivided the "F—History" and the new "G—Geography" classes by adding two Arabic numerals to the letter to signify identical geographic areas for each class. For example, F30 means History of Europe, while G30 means Geography of Europe. The second expansion holds 14 main classes, some redefinition of the original seven, and further differentiation of two classes along geographic lines.

The third expansion completes all but "P—Vertebrates" of the base 26 divisions and separates Religion from Philosophy, moving it to a second double-letter subclass. Part of the debt that *LCC* owes to Cutter can easily be traced through the outline comparison shown on page 334.

The fourth expansion subdivides 12 main classes for the first time, increasing the double-letter subclasses to 50. It also carries an extensive supplementary table expanding the double-digit geographic numbers from the F and G classes into a "place" or "local" list.

The fifth expansion introduces the twenty-sixth single-letter class "P—Vertebrates" and subdivides all remaining undivided classes, using many triple- and a few quadruple-letter sections. The sixth "classification" introduces no new techniques—only new expansions of existing classes and subclasses.

The seventh classification was published in 18 parts, edited and to some extent developed by William Parker Cutter after the originator's death.[3] All expansions were prepared on the theory that as a library outgrew its simpler modes of organization, partial dislocation and reclassification of the existing collection was preferable to complete reorganization. Although some books would have to be reclassed and relocated, not all would be, and certainly not all at once.

Cutter's *Expansive Classification*		Library of Congress Classification *(LCC)*	
A	General works	A	General works
B	Philosophy	B	Philosophy. Religion
BR	Non-Judaeo-Christian religions		
C	Judaism and Christianity	C	History. Auxiliary sciences
D	Ecclesiastical history	D	History (except America)
E	Biography	E-F	History of the Americas
F	History		
G	Geography	G	Geography. Anthropology
H	Social sciences	H	Social sciences
I	Sociology		
J	Political science	J	Political science
K	Law	K	Law
L	Natural sciences	L	Education
M	Natural history	M	Music
N	Botany	N	Fine arts
O	Zoology		
		P	Language and literature
Q	Medicine	Q	Science
R	Technology	R	Medicine
S	Engineering	S	Agriculture
T	Manufactures and Handicrafts	T	Technology
U	Defensive and preservative arts	U	Military science
V	Athletic and recreative arts	V	Naval science
W	Fine arts		
X	Languages		
Y	Literature		
YF	Fiction		
Z	Book arts	Z	Bibliography and Library science

While it was never widely adopted, some 67 American, Canadian, and British libraries have been identified as past or present Cutter System users.[4] Perhaps even more important is the influence it exerted on later, more popular classifications, such as that developed soon after at LC.

BROWN'S *SUBJECT CLASSIFICATION*

Next in chronological development is a British scheme. James Duff Brown (1864–1914) was a Scottish counterpart of Dewey and Cutter, if somewhat younger. Coming to the profession from an early apprenticeship to publishers and booksellers, he became deeply involved in the public library movement in Great Britain. It is debatable whether his advocacy of open stacks was directly influenced by his travels in the United States, in 1893. Without benefit of a university education, his breadth of knowledge was legendary, and his interest in music resulted in several music reference tools that he either compiled or sponsored.

Brown recognized the lack of good organization of materials in most British libraries. To make open stack access feasible he and John Henry Quinn published in 1894 a "Classification of Books for Libraries in Which Readers Are Allowed Access to Shelves." Brown's own "Adjustable Classification" followed in 1898. As the name implies, it allowed for insertion of new divisions or topics as needed, but it was not worked out or indexed in much detail. Growing out of it, in 1906, was the first edition of the *Subject Classification*. In 1914, shortly after Brown's death, came a second edition, and in 1939 James Douglas Stewart issued a revised and enlarged third edition.[5]

The basic scaffold of Brown's *Subject Classification* consists of 11 main classes, expressing four broad divisional concepts in orderly sequence. Primary notation is alphabetical, with some classes assigned more than one capital letter, to cover all subtopics without making the notation unduly long:

A	Generalia	} Matter and force
B C D	Physical Science	
E F	Biological Science	
G H	Ethnological and Medical Science	} Life
I	Economic Biology and Domestic Arts	
J K	Philosophy and Religion	
L	Social and Political Science	} Mind
M	Language and Literature	
N	Literary forms	
O - W	History, Geography	} Record
X	Biography	

Each initial letter is followed by three Arabic numerals. Sequence, rather than length of number, reveals hierarchy, e.g.,

D600	METALLURGY
601	Smelting
602	Blast Furnaces
603	Open Hearth Furnaces
604	Ores

These schedule numbers may be expanded like decimals (without the decimal point) when new topics require insertion. The scheme allows several methods of building numbers: geographic numbers from the O-W classes may be attached to topical numbers when needed. There is a "Categorical Table" of "forms, etc. for the subdivision of subjects." Numbers from this table are attached after a period, which is not to be regarded as a decimal point. A plus sign is used to connect two facets from the same class. The underscore is used to "stack" parts of a number. Its purpose is to keep an extended notation compact.

While Brown's *Subject Classification*, like Cutter's *Expansive Classification*, never received the widespread adoption received by its American rivals, timing and the lack of a consistent, continuing update program may be the explanation, rather than the comparative merits of the four schemes. Brown's system stimulated research and development in British classification theory, much as Cutter's did in the United States. Both are now milestones of classification history, rather than popular modern schemes for arranging library materials.

BLISS'S
BIBLIOGRAPHIC CLASSIFICATION

Henry Evelyn Bliss (1870–1955) was Librarian of the College of the City of New York, where he spent some 30 years developing and testing his ideas on library classification. After several periodical articles and books, he finished publication of his magnum opus only two years before his death.[6]

A "bibliographic" classification is, in Bliss's terminology, one designed to organize documentary materials (i.e., library collections, chiefly in print format). The sequence of main classes nonetheless preserves the discipline (rather than topical) orientation that Bliss interpreted as the basic structure of knowledge. Paul Dunkin called it "a sort of reader interest classification for scholars."[7]

According to Bliss, it is important in classifying a book to decide in what main classes it falls. The literature on concrete topics like "bees" is not kept in one place (as Brown would try to do) but is distributed, as in *DDC*, according to the "aspect" from which it is viewed. For example, a book on bees from a scientific aspect goes to class "G—Zoology," whereas a book on beekeeping is classed in "U—Useful Arts."

The Bliss system soon grew more popular in Great Britain than in the United States.[8] A British Committee for the Bliss Classification, which changed its name in 1967 to the Bliss Classification Association (BCA), draws its membership largely from libraries using the scheme. It publishes an annual *Bliss Classification Bulletin* and has an annual meeting in November each year. The Association arranges lectures and visits to libraries using the scheme. The BCA official Web site[9] links to several *Bibliographic Classification (BC)* sites, some of which are particular colleges of Cambridge University and of Oxford University.

The second edition (*BC2*) is so radically revised that it is more accurately described as a new system, although it uses the broad outline developed by Bliss. It derives techniques of facet analysis, as well as of explicit citation and filing orders, from Ranganathan's monumental contributions to classification theory. The outline of *BC2* is as follows:

Introduction & Auxiliary schedules. 1977

2/9	Generalia, Phenomena, Knowledge, Information science & technology
A/AL	Philosophy & Logic. 1991
AM/AX	Mathematics, Probability, Statistics. 1993
AY	General science. 1999
B	Physics. 1999
C	Chemistry, Chemical Engineering. 2000
D	Space & Earth sciences
	Astronomy
	Geology
	Geography
E/GQ	Biological sciences
E	Biology
	Biochemistry
	Genetics
	Virology
F	Botany
G	Zoology
GR	Agriculture
GU	Veterinary Science
GY	Ecology
H	Physical Anthropology, Human biology
	Health sciences. 1980
I	Psychology & Psychiatry. 1978
J	Education. 1990
K	Society (includes Social sciences, sociology & social anthropology). 1984
L/O	History, (includes Archaeology, biography and travel)
P	Religion, Occult, Morals and ethics. 1977
Q	Social welfare & Criminology. Rev. ed. 1994
R	Politics & Public administration. 1996
S	Law. 1996
T	Economics & Management of economic enterprises. 1987
U/V	Technology, Engineering. 2000
W	Recreation, Arts, Music.
X/Y	Language, Literature

The dates following the titles indicate the 16 volumes that have appeared to date. Detailed draft schedules have been completed for all remaining classes, and publication is expected to be complete in 2003.[10]

Second edition notation consists of capital letters and numerals, omitting zero because of its similarity to the letter O. The numbers are as brief as possible, consistent with full expression of the various aspects of a topic. Each main class and each subclass is fully faceted. A comprehensive and consistent citation order is observed throughout; although it is suggested that if that order is not appropriate in a particular local situation, another order may be adopted. The notation is fully faceted and does not attempt the task of always reflecting hierarchy. The notation uses only letters and numbers divided into blocks of three. The first letter indicates the discipline of the information package, as shown in the outline above. The next letter categorizes the subject into the broad areas of the discipline. It can be subdivided again for more specificity. An example of a notation for the nursing of children with cancer is HXO QEM Y:

HXO   Pediatrics

HQE   Cancer

HMY   Nursing

The initial letter for the class is dropped when combining subclasses.

The future of the *Bibliographic Classification* is dependent in large part on the timing and public acceptance of the new edition. That Bliss's theory and practice had many advantages is a fact recognized by anyone who knows it well enough to compare it with more widely accepted schemes. That it badly needed updating and further development is also clear. The gargantuan job of complete overhaul by a few aficionados on a shoestring budget, if finished, should permit future sequential revision of different class schedules as needed (somewhat resembling the present revision program at LC). Meanwhile, some libraries using the original schedules have fallen away.[11] Establishment of the Bliss scheme as a major contender for library adoption will require not only efficient, dedicated work, but also a great deal of luck.

SPECIAL CLASSIFICATION SCHEMES

Classification schemes comprising the entire universe of knowledge must of necessity be general and cannot deal with specialties or fine detail. They are also largely inflexible, presenting the particular viewpoint of their designers (which in the case of *DDC* and *LCC* represents the late nineteenth century), and they often disperse subjects that, for the purposes of specialists, ought to be dealt with in close proximity (e.g., *DDC* has chemistry in 540 but chemical technology in 660, which is very unhelpful for a chemistry library). Even *UDC*, although providing for very fine detail, suffers from many of the faults inherited from *DDC* (e.g., the chemistry dispersal) and often has long notations.

Librarians of collections devoted mainly or exclusively to one specific field of knowledge, a discipline, or one of its subfields have therefore often found it necessary to design special classification schemes. The British Classification Research Group (CRG) was particularly active in designing special faceted classifications during the 1960s and 1970s, whereas in the United States special classifications were more often the work of individuals and organizations.

Special classification schemes are mainly of two types: "general-special" schemes, which classify a special field or subject exhaustively while providing only very general class marks to peripheral or extraneous subjects, and "special" schemes, dealing only with a particular specialty in sometimes very fine detail but leaving the classing of other subjects to one of the general schemes. Hybrids of the two types are those schemes that expand an existing class of a general scheme or make use of an unused notation under which a special subject field is developed in detail.

Two examples of the latter type are widely used in U.S. libraries. *The National Library of Medicine Classification*[12] uses class W (which is vacant in *LCC*) and the medical parts of *LCC*'s class Q for the entire biomedical field. Subdivision of W is by all letters of the alphabet, including even I and O (which are avoided by *LCC* because of possible confusion with the digits 1 and 0), followed by up to three digits used enumeratively and an occasional fourth digit used decimally, followed by more detailed subdivision using cuttering, e.g.,

WD 200   Metabolic diseases

WD 205.5.A5   Amino acid metabolism

Since NLM's W class notations appear on many MAchine-Readable Cataloging (MARC) records for medical books, most medical libraries use the W special classification.

A *Classification Scheme for Law Books*,[13] which expands class K of *LCC*, found wide acceptance in law libraries after its publication in 1968, but completion of many parts of class K by LC in recent years has reduced the need for the separate scheme. Another expansion of *LCC* is for a highly specialized subject. *An Alternative Classification for Catholic Books*[14] takes a section of the LC classification that was not in use by LC when the schedule was developed in 1937 and develops it as Christian literature with three major subclasses: BQT, theology; BQV, canon law; and BQX, church history, all further subdivided by enumerative digits and cuttering. The introduction gives detailed instructions on how to integrate these schedules into either *LCC* or *DDC* when these are used to class other subjects in a library.

The following examples are representatives of the special type that combine a faceted structure and high flexibility with brief notations. The *London Education Classification*[15] fulfills a double role as a classification and thesaurus and uses a letter notation, with uppercase letters serving as facet indicators, e.g.,

Mab   Curriculum

Mabb   Curriculum development

Mabf   Curriculum classification

The *Physics and Astronomy Classification Scheme*[16] of the American Institute of Physics (AIP) uses a mixed notation of two decimal groups followed by a letter, e.g.,

84   Electromagnetic technology
84.30   Electronic circuits
84.30 L   Amplifiers

Except for two sections, the AIP scheme closely resembles the *International Classification for Physics*,[17] and parts of it have been adopted by the Institution of Electrical Engineers in London for its *Classification for the INSPEC Database*.[18] Thus, a physics library could choose among three major special schemes, all of which have the backing of professional societies.

The *London Classification of Business Studies*[19] has five major classes: management responsibility in the enterprise (A-G), environmental studies (J-R), analytical techniques (S-X), library and information science (Y), and auxiliary schedules (1-7). The notation consists of up to four uppercase letters, e.g.,

K	Industries
KCL	Alcoholic drinks industry
KCLB	Wine industry

and notations can be combined by a forward slash, e.g.,

EE/KCLB Financial management in the wine industry

The scheme is used in about 40 British libraries and more than 20 libraries elsewhere. The London Business School is responsible for updating and development of the scheme.

An example of a special scheme relying on another classification for extraneous subjects is the *Classification of Library & Information Science*,[20] designed by the Classification Research Group. This scheme, too, makes use of a letter notation with capitals as facet indicators, resulting in notations such as TogsNjrFv, which expresses the topic "Online systems:centralized:Public libraries," or ZmRnM(57), "Databases:Information Services:By subject:Biology," with 57 taken from *UDC* for a subject not germane to the central topic of library and information science.

Special classifications are sometimes developed for extremely narrow subjects, such as the *Classification for London Literature*,[21] concerned with works only on that city, with decimal subdivisions for every place and event in its long history, e.g.,

10	Religion
12	St. Paul's Cathedral
12.4	Dome and roof

A bibliography of classification schemes and subject heading lists for hundreds of different subjects lists 2,250 items in several languages.[22]

A special classification scheme may initially have the advantage of being more detailed and more up-to-date than any of the general schemes, but it is unfortunately often the case that such schemes, once designed, are not further developed and therefore become obsolete and lacking in detail much quicker than general schemes. When adopting a special scheme, one must take care to choose a scheme that has a reasonably good chance of being further developed and updated—that is, one that is backed by an organization rather than being the one-time effort of a librarian in a special collection. Such homemade classification schemes are generally motivated by the fact that sooner or later almost any librarian will find that the scheme he or she uses, whether general or specific, is insufficiently detailed or does not contain a class notation for a new subject. It is then easy to succumb to the temptation to create a new subdivision or an entirely new scheme for the missing topics or for sections of a scheme that seem to be misplaced. The proper design of a special classification is, however, a task best left to someone thoroughly familiar with the theory and principles of classification design, and the novice should refrain from attempting this enterprise until some considerable experience has been gained. Many a hastily conceived and improperly designed special classification scheme has had to be abandoned sooner or later, to be replaced with an existing and proven scheme at great cost and inconvenience to the library and its users.

CONCLUSION

The classification systems briefly reviewed here differ from each other, and from the better known *DDC* and *LCC* systems, in many ways. In basic theory of the organization of knowledge, some emphasize the specific subject approach, clustering these unitary topics in related sequences, whereas most start from a broad disciplinary orientation, subdividing hierarchically, so that the various aspects or unitary topics become scattered to different parts of the system. In providing a schedule framework to arrange items on shelves, some systems (the more traditional) are primarily enumerative, whereas most newer ones are synthetic or faceted. Some maintain a comparatively pure notation, whereas others use combinations of letters and Arabic numerals, while upper- and lowercase letters, Roman numerals, Greek letters, and a variety of arbitrary relational signs and symbols appear in still others. Timeliness is a constant problem. Some systems maintain a serials program to announce additions and changes or issue new editions at intervals of 5 to 25 years. Many have outlived their originators, but some suffer more than others from age and lack of funds or organized promotion. Each has unique attractive features; each has practical and theoretical problems. Some are more useful for shelf arrangement of books and related formats. Others are better suited to in-depth indexing of periodical articles, technical reports, books, and the like. Centripetal forces such as networking seem at the moment to favor general acceptance of one or two well-known, widely used schemes, overlooking functional disadvantages to achieve standardization and administrative coherence. Yet classification research, like that in all other areas of bibliographic organization, is very brisk and busy in the modern world of information science. Time may show that all the schemes we study and use today, regardless of their present achievements or popularity, are chiefly important for the historic part they play as heralds of still better solutions to the problems of subject access.

NOTES

1.   Four examples of specific applications using the systems discussed in this chapter, as well as *DDC* and *LCC*, are given in Bohdan S. Wynar, *Introduction to Cataloging and Classification*, 5th ed., prepared with the assistance of John Phillip Immroth (Littleton, Colo.: Libraries Unlimited, 1976), pp. 314–328.

2.   Charles A. Cutter, *Expansive Classification, Part I: The First Six Classifications* (Boston: Cutter, 1891–1893).

3.   Charles A. Cutter, *Expansive Classification, Part II: Seventh Classification*, largely edited by William Parker Cutter (Boston and Northampton, Mass.: Cutter, 1896–1911), 2v. with supplementary pages.

4.   Robert L. Mowery, "The Cutter Classification: Still at Work," *Library Resources & Technical Services* 20 (Spring 1976): 154.

5.   James Duff Brown, *Subject Classification: With Tables, Indexes, etc. for the Subdivision of Subjects*, 3rd ed., rev. and enl. by James Douglas Stewart (London: Grafton, 1939).

6.   Bliss's major works are the following: *The Organization of Knowledge and the System of the Sciences* (New York: Holt, 1929); *The Organization of Knowledge in Libraries*, 2nd ed., rev. and partly rewritten (New York: H. W. Wilson, 1939); *A Bibliographic Classification: Extended by Systematic Auxiliary Schedules for Composite Specification and Notation* (New York: H. W. Wilson, 1940–1953), 4v.

7.   Paul S. Dunkin, *Cataloging U.S.A.* (Chicago: American Library Association, 1969), p. 126.

8.   *See*, for instance: School Library Association (England), *The Abridged Bliss Classification: The Bibliographical Classification of Henry Evelyn Bliss Revised for School Libraries*, with corrections and minor amendments (London: The Association, 1970).

9.   Bliss Classification Association, "Bliss Classification Association: homepage" (available: http://www.sid.cam.ac.uk/bca/bcahome.htm [accessed 5/11/00]).

10.   Bliss Classification Association, "The Bliss Bibliographic Classification: Outline of Bliss Classification (2nd ed.)" (available: http://www.sid.cam.ac.uk/bca/bcoutline.htm [accessed 5/11/00]).

11.   *See*, for instance: "Ibadan Abandons Bliss," *Library Association Record* 79 (May 1977): 241, which tells how the University of Ibadan (Nigeria), after using Bliss for 25 years, was converting to *LCC* because of the inadequacy of outdated, unrevised Bliss schedules.

12.   *National Library of Medicine Classification: A Scheme for the Shelf Arrangement of Books in the Field of Medicine and Its Related Sciences*, 5th ed., rev. (Bethesda, Md.: NLM, 1994).

13.   *Moys Classification Scheme for Law Books*, 2nd ed. (London: Butterworths, 1982).

14.   Jeannette Murphy Lynn, *An Alternative Classification for Catholic Books*, 2nd ed., rev. by G. C. Peterson; supplement (1965) by Thomas G. Pater (Washington, D.C.: Catholic University of America Press, 1965).

15.   D. J. Foskett and J. Foskett, *The London Education Classification: A Thesaurus/ Classification of British Education Terms*, 2nd ed. (London: University of London Institute of Education Library, 1974).

16.   American Institute of Physics, *Physics and Astronomy Classification Scheme, 1999* (Woodbury, N.Y.: AIP, 1999).

17.   International Council of Scientific Unions, Abstracting Board, *International Classification for Physics* (Paris: ICSU/AB, 1975).

18.   Institution of Electrical Engineers, *Classification: A Classification Scheme for the INSPEC Database* (London: IEE, 1991–   ).

19.   K. D. C. Vernon and V. Lang, *The London Classification of Business Studies*, 2nd ed., rev. by K. G. B. Bakewell and D. A. Cotton (London: Aslib, 1979).

20.   Classification Research Group, *A Classification of Library & Information Science*, 2nd ed. (London: CRG, 1975).

21.   Guildhall Library, *Classification for London Literature*, 3rd ed. (London: The Library, 1966).

22.   *Classification Systems and Thesauri, 1950–1982* (Frankfurt, West Germany: Indeks Verlag, 1982). International Classification and Indexing Bibliography 1.

SUGGESTED READING

Chan, Lois Mai. *Cataloging and Classification: An Introduction*. 2nd ed. New York: McGraw-Hill, 1994. Chapter 14.

Foskett, A. C. *The Subject Approach to Information*. 5th ed. London: Library Association Publishing, 1996. Chapter 10: General Classification Schemes, Chapter 19: The Bibliographic Classification, and Chapter 20: The Broad System of Ordering.

Koch, Traugott, and Michael Day. *The Role of Classification Schemes in Internet Resource Description and Discovery*. Available: http://www.ukoln.ac.uk/metadata/desire/classification/ (accessed 5/11/00).

McKiernan, Gerry. *Beyond Bookmarks: Schemes for Organizing the Web*. Online, Ames, Iowa, G. McKiernan. Available: http://www.public.iastate.edu/~CYBERSTACKS/CTW.htm (accessed 5/11/00).

Miksa, Francis. *The Subject in the Dictionary Catalog from Cutter to the Present*. Chicago: American Library Association, 1983. Chapter 6: Cutter's Subject Rules.

14 > Verbal Subject Access

INTRODUCTION

We have seen in the preceding chapters that classification provides a library with a systematic arrangement of materials according to their subject content, mode of treatment, or even their physical format. In addition to classification, there is another commonly used means of access to the intellectual contents of a library—namely indexing through the use of a subject heading list of controlled vocabulary terms and references. Whereas classification provides a logical, or at least a methodical, approach to the arrangement of documentary materials, subject headings give a more random alphabetic approach to the concepts inherent in those materials, thus adding another dimension to the linear arrangement characteristic of classification. The two techniques offer alternative, and to some extent complementary, modes of access to the collection, comprising that aspect of bibliographic control and access known as subject cataloging.

BASIC CONCEPTS AND STRUCTURE
OF SUBJECT HEADINGS

Subject heading has been defined as a "subject concept term or phrase found in a subject heading list and used in catalog records."[1] Their use in catalog records is as access points by which works can be searched. Most such subject headings in library catalogs are precoordinated, while their counterparts in indexes, which are called "descriptors," are meant to be used in postcoordinated systems. Information analysts distinguish precoordinate indexing, by which appropriate terms are chosen and coordinated at the time of indexing or cataloging, from postcoordinate indexing, with which coordination takes place after the encoded documents have been stored. All standard published lists of "subject headings" were developed with precoordinate indexing techniques. Lists called "thesauri" are used in postcoordinate systems.

Subject headings have dual objectives: 1) to identify pertinent material on a given subject or topic; 2) to enable the inquirer to find material on related subjects. Both objectives pose problems of communication; both demand a set of terms that match, as far as possible, the terms likely to be in the minds of inquirers wishing to locate material on a given topic or in a given discipline. E. J. Coates warns:

This would be fairly simple to achieve if there were an uncomplicated, one-to-one relationship between concepts and words: that is to say, if there were a single word corresponding to each separate concept and a single concept corresponding to each separate word. In fact, we have on the one hand concepts that can be rendered by any one of a number of words, and on the other hand, concepts for which no single word equivalent exists in the natural language.[2]

Modern subject heading practice has its roots in Charles A. Cutter's *Rules for a Dictionary Catalog*.[3] Immroth reminds us that Cutter's "rules for subject entries are the basis for two major American lists of subject headings—the *Library of Congress Subject Headings (LCSH)* and the *Sears List of Subject Headings*."[4] Later theorists refined and expanded Cutter's work in various ways. David Judson Haykin, former Chief of the Library of Congress (LC) Subject Cataloging Division, enumerates the principles on which the choice of terms for a subject list must rest.[5] They may be summarized as follows:

1. *The reader as focus.* "[T]he heading, in wording and structure, should be that which the reader will seek in the catalog, if we know or can presume what the reader will look under.... [In] the face of a lack of sufficient objective, experimental data, we must rely for guidance in the choice of terms upon the experience of librarians and such objective findings as are available."

2. *Unity.* "A subject catalog must bring together under one heading all the books which deal principally or exclusively with the subject, whatever the terms applied to it by the authors of the books and whatever the varying terms applied to it at different times. [It] must [use] a term which is unambiguous and does not overlap in meaning other headings in the catalog, even where that involves defining the sense in which it is used."

3. *Usage.* "The heading chosen must represent common usage or, at any rate, the usage of the class of reader for whom the material on the subject within which the heading falls is intended. . . . Whether a popular term or a scientific one is to be chosen depends on several considerations. If the library serves a miscellaneous public, it must prefer the popular to the scientific term."

4. *Specificity.* "The heading should be as specific as the topic it is intended to cover. As a corollary, the heading should not be broader than the topic; rather than use a broader heading, the cataloger should use two specific headings which will approximately cover it."

The following discussion touches on some of the most important problems encountered in construction and use of subject headings.

The Choice of Subject Headings

Linguistic usage determines correctness of form in natural language, as all grammarians and dictionary compilers well know. Language changes constantly, not only in response to new discoveries and formulations of knowledge, but also in response to dynamic forces of its own, some but not all of which have been codified by linguists. In choosing subject terms, librarians try to consider both the author's usage and the patron's needs and preferences; but authors and patrons are likely to use different terms for the same subject. Without a record of choices, the cataloger may enter the same subject under two or more different headings. Two types of decision are especially likely to miscarry: those for which more than one adequate term is available and those for which no adequate term is available.

Selecting a term from among verbal equivalents. The cataloger or compiler of a subject heading list must sometimes choose one subject term from among several synonyms or very similar terms. Cutter suggests the following sequence of preferences when selecting from synonymous headings:[6]

1. *The term most familiar to the general public.* Cutter no doubt was thinking of the local library's public. We shall see that one of the major differences between *LCSH* and *Sears* is that *LCSH*, being designed for use in a comprehensive research library, favors scientific terminology (e.g., "**Arachnida** NT Spiders"), whereas *Sears* tends to use more popular terms (e.g., "Arachnida *USE* **Spiders**").

2. *The term most used in other catalogs.* Since patrons frequently change libraries or consult more than one library catalog, it is comforting to find that terminology remains stable, even standardized, so long as it does not violate the usage of the local library's public. Broad automated networks, using consolidated computer files, make reliably standardized terminology even more desirable. A different, but related, argument is that new concepts and terms are often introduced into the periodical literature before they form the topics of full-scale books. If a library's subject heading list does not yet include such a term, the cataloger might well consult the *New York Times Index*, or commonly used periodical indexes and abstracting tools, to discover what usage, if any, has been established.

3. *The term that has fewest meanings.* The clear intent here is to avoid ambiguity wherever possible.

4. *The term that comes first in the alphabet.* This is the type of arbitrary, procedural decision that can be invoked when semantic considerations have been exhausted.

5. *The term that brings the subject into the neighborhood of other, related subjects.* It was previously noted that a serious drawback of alphabetic arrangement is its fragmentation of subject matter and that most alphabetic subject lists indulge in some "classing." Here is Cutter's recognition that the technique is valid, but only after all other modes for choosing among synonymous terms have been exhausted.

Supplying a term that is not contained in a single word. Some concepts must be expressed by phrases (combinations of words). Phrase headings present certain disadvantages. As Coates indicates, most catalog users try to formulate search topics in single words, even when a phrase would be used in natural language.[7] Various uncertainties shadow the introduction of phrases into a controlled vocabulary. In determining the order of words, should a heading always retain the order of natural language, or should modifications and transpositions be allowed in the interests of brevity and clarity? Should a variety of syntactic forms be used, or should the syntax of phrase headings be confined to a few simple forms that occasionally make them seem awkward and artificial? Some theorists feel that, lacking cleanly enunciated rules, phrase-makers have produced a number of troublesome headings. Modern usage condones several varieties, which different subject lists usually adapt to their own uses. The specific rules printed in *Sears List of Subject Headings* (*Sears*) and in *LCSH* simplify but do not solve this problem, since they are purely arbitrary.[8] The problem of communication still exists. Many information packages are listed under subject headings that patrons would not immediately think of as the appropriate ones under which to search. For the most part they can be roughly categorized as follows. All examples are taken from the LC list:

1. *Modified nouns.* Modifiers can take different syntactic forms:

    a. Nouns preceded by adjectives or other modifiers, e.g., **"Regional planning," "Fur-bearing animals,"** or **"Country life"**
    b. Nouns followed by adjectives or other modifiers, e.g., **"Insurance, Malpractice,"** or **"Molds (Fungi)"**

2. *Conjunctive phrases.* The conjunction is nearly always *and*, e.g., **"Mills and mill-work," "Instrumentation and orchestration,"** or **"Mind and body"**

3. *Prepositional phrases. In* and *of* are most common, but other prepositions may be used to form phrases, e.g., **"Segregation in education,"** or **"Freedom of speech"**

4. *Serial phrases*, e.g., **"Plots (Drama, novel, etc.)"**

5. *Complex phrase forms*, e.g., **"Artificial satellites in telecommunication," "Glass painting and staining," "Justice, Administration of," "Right and left (Political science),"** or **"Fortune-telling by tea leaves"**

6. *Subdivided topical phrases*, e.g., **"Book industries and trade—Exhibitions," "Mines and mineral resources—United States,"** or **"Military service, Voluntary—Law and legislation"**

The Number of Subject Headings

The number of subject headings entered into a catalog for a single item depends on many factors. As long as library catalogs were in card form, rapidly increasing bulk was both an economic and a use hazard. Maintenance costs (housing, filing, revising) were high, while users grew confused, or wasted considerable time, moving from one point to another in a roomful of several thousand trays.

The larger the number of subject entries provided, the greater the cost of cataloging a title. On the other hand, the assignment of more headings per item makes the total resources of the library more available and may bring out special aspects and bits of unusual or significant information. Current online catalogs make increasing the number of subject entries proportionately less expensive in time, effort, or cost of retrieval. Catalogs in either book form or microform also occupy little space and can be consulted in one spot. Moreover, the simultaneous display of either complete or truncated entries in an ordered column often makes filing practices self-evident.

In the early 1980s LC was adding about two subject entries per cataloged item. This was up from fewer than two entries per record prior to the implementation of *Anglo-American Cataloguing Rules, Second Edition (AACR2)*. The tendency over the decades prior to 1980 was to reduce the average number of subject entries. However, this trend has reversed, and more entries per record are being made. Indexes and abstracting tools in science and technology, by contrast, tend to use specific subject entries to a point of minute analysis. Twenty to forty subject terms for one brief article are not rare. Subject analysis of library titles has expanded with the increased use of automated bibliographic control.

The computer is facilitating more, and better, studies of library use, to discern optimum types and quantities of subject headings for full subject retrieval. A Council on Library Resources (CLR) study of online catalog use of 15 online catalogs showed that in catalogs with subject access, about 59 percent of all searches were for subject information rather than for "known items."[9] This is quite different from studies of card catalog use, many of which showed that over two-thirds of searches in academic libraries were known-item searches (although subject searching in public libraries was often higher).[10] The CLR study recommended that system designers implement keyword searching for subjects and browsing of the subject index or thesaurus. It also recognized that such systems can only find subject terms that exist in bibliographic records and recommended increased subject information in bibliographic records along with strict authority control to restrict the number of synonymous and related terms.[11]

Location of Material on Related Subjects

Consistency is one of the most important criteria for assigning subject headings. The cataloger should choose one subject term, and one alone, to index all materials on the same topic. References should then be made to the chosen heading from all other likely terms. They help the inquirer to locate available material on the topic, plus collateral topics, at the level of specificity and from the point of view most useful for the particular need. References consist primarily of three types: references from unused terms, hierarchical references, and coordinate references.

An unused term is one under which no items are entered. Instead, a reference is made from that term to the one that is used, e.g., "Lunar expeditions *See* **Space flight to the moon**." The instruction given may be something other than the word *See*, e.g., "For material on this subject search under" or "use." It is also possible for an online catalog to give no reference at all in a situation where a *see* reference would be given in a manual catalog. A user searching under "lunar expeditions" might be given automatically a list of the library's material that had been given the heading "space flight to the moon." This practice is called "invisible referencing."

Hierarchical references and coordinate references are most often related term references that suggest to the user that if the material already located is more or less relevant, there are other related headings that might also yield some relevant material. The instruction given is often "*See also*" or "Related material on this topic may be found under"; e.g., "**Hearing disorders.** *See also* **Deafness**" or "**Deafness.** Related material on this topic may be found under **Hearing**."

Hierarchical references move vertically, rather than horizontally, leading the user to topics at a different level of specificity. In current library practice references of this type nearly always move "down" from a general term to one or more specific topics subsumed under it, e.g., "**Cruelty** NT Atrocities," although in indexing practice, many systems provide for moving either up or down the hierarchy. (*See* discussion of this issue in chapter 15.)

The connections and relationships shown by coordinate references (often called "related terms") are horizontal rather than vertical. They usually overlap in such ways that reciprocal or multilateral entries are deemed to be necessary, e.g., "**Reforestation** *See also* **Tree planting**," "**Tree planting** *See also* **Reforestation**." Others suggest associative rather than overlapping relationships, e.g., "**Political corruption** *See also* **Misconduct in office**," "**Misconduct in office** *See also* **Political corruption**."

While unused term references are most often synonymous terms, they are occasionally hierarchical or coordinate in their relationship to the used term. A few of them move "up" from a specific term that is not used to the broader term that contains it, e.g., "Heirs *Use* **Inheritance and succession**." A few others show an "illustrative" relationship, e.g., "Economic entomology *Use* **Beneficial insects**."

Besides simple references, subject heading lists sometimes include scope notes to define and delimit a subject term. These may or may not suggest further terms for the user to consult. Some catalog systems allow these notes or guides to be displayed preceding all subject entries under those given terms in their catalogs. Other systems do not allow such display and the libraries involved may keep one or more copies of the printed list near the catalog for public consultation. The following two examples come from *LCSH*:

Community and school
> Here are entered works on ways in which the community at large, as distinct from government, may aid the school program.

Migrant labor
> Here are entered works on laborers who migrate from one section to another section of the same country. Works on nationals of one country working in another country are entered under "**Alien labor**." Works on employment opportunities in foreign countries are entered under "**Employment in foreign countries**."

Some lists include key headings or pattern headings, with instructions to the cataloger on how to construct other headings of similar form that have been omitted from the list for reasons of brevity. The following example is from *Sears*:

Hijacking of airplanes
> Use same form for the hijacking of other modes of transportation.

To assure maximum consistency, a careful, up-to-date record of all subject term selections and references should be kept, either by checking the terms used and the additions made in a standard printed list or by maintaining a separate subject authority file.

The Concept of Specific Entry

One of Haykin's principles on which the choice of terms for a subject list must rest was "specificity." The idea had been enunciated a half century earlier by Cutter:

> Enter a work under its subject heading, not under the heading of the class which includes that subject. . . . Put Lady Cust's book on "the cat" under "Cat," not under Zoology or Mammals, or Domestic animals. . . . Some subjects have no name. They are spoken of by a phrase or phrases not definite enough to be used as headings. It is not always easy to decide what is a *distinct* subject. . . . Possible matters of investigation . . . must attain a certain individuality as objects of inquiry and be given some sort of *name*, otherwise we must assign them class-entry.[12]

It should be noted that the concept of specific entry is not the same as the concept of coextensive entry. At least one system for subject analysis, *PRECIS* (discussed in greater detail in chapter 17), attempts to make subject headings coextensive with the concept/topics covered in the item analyzed. That is, the subject heading will cover all, but no more than, the concepts or topics covered in the item. A very simple example can be drawn by elaborating upon the idea from Cutter above. If one had a book about cats and dogs, the concept of *specific* entry would require two headings: "Cats" and "Dogs." There is no one specific term to cover these two kinds of animal. In order to have a heading that is *coextensive* with the subject of the items the heading would have to be "Cats and dogs."

A great weakness of the concept of specific entry is that subjects must be described in terms that are constantly changing. Material very often has to be cataloged before a suitable term has been added to any standard list. Many subjects now represent a cross-fertilization among once traditional disciplines. As Coates indicates,

> New subjects are being generated around us all the time, and while subjects may still be more or less distinct, there can be no hard and fast separation of the "distinct" subjects from the others.[13]

Not only do particular terms fluctuate in meaning, but a constant, obtrusive tendency of any alphabetic subject list based on the ideal of specific entry is to develop sequences of topical subdivisions or modifications that, as was previously noted, convert true random access into an inadvertent classing device. All such lists show marks of a split personality in this respect. The two most popular American lists, *LCSH* and *Sears*, are reviewed in the next two chapters; chapter 17 presents some indexing systems that have been proposed as supplements to, or replacements for, these two lists as a primary mode of subject access to organized library collections.

NOTES

1.   Arlene G. Taylor, *The Organization of Information* (Englewood, Colo.: Libraries Unlimited, 1999), p. 251.

2.   E. J. Coates, *Subject Catalogues: Headings and Structure* (London: Library Association, 1960), p. 19.

3.   Charles Ammi Cutter, *Rules for a Dictionary Catalog*, 4th ed. (Washington, D.C.: GPO, 1904), republished, London: Library Association, 1972). The original version of this work was Charles A. Cutter, "Rules for a Printed Dictionary Catalogue," in *Public Libraries in the United States of America: Their History, Condition, and Management*, U.S. Bureau of Education (Washington, D.C.: GPO, 1876), Part II.

4.   John Phillip Immroth, "Cutter, Charles Ammi," in *Encyclopedia of Library and Information Science*, vol. 6 (New York: Marcel Dekker, 1971), p. 382.

5.   David Judson Haykin, *Subject Headings: A Practical Guide* (Washington, D.C.: GPO, 1951), pp. 7–9.

6.   Cutter, *Dictionary Catalog*, p. 19.

7.   Coates, *Subject Catalogues*, p. 19.

8.   For the development of phrase heading forms in *Sears List of Subject Headings* and in *Library of Congress Subject Headings*, *see* chapters 15 and 16 of this text.

9.   *Using Online Catalogs: A Nationwide Survey*, edited by Joseph R. Matthews, Gary S. Lawrence, and Douglas K. Ferguson (New York: Neal-Schuman, 1983), pp. 144–146.

10.   Karen Markey, *Subject Searching in Library Catalogs: Before and After the Introduction of Online Catalogs* (Dublin, Ohio: OCLC Online Computer Library Center, 1984), pp. 75–87.

11.   *Using Online Catalogs*, pp. 177–179.

12.   Cutter, *Dictionary Catalog*, pp. 66–67.

13.   Coates, *Subject Catalogues*, p. 32.

SUGGESTED READING

Chan, Lois Mai, Phyllis A. Richmond, and Elaine Svenonius. *Theory of Subject Analysis: A Sourcebook*. Littleton, Colo.: Libraries Unlimited, 1985.

Coates, E. J. *Subject Catalogues: Heading and Structure*. London: Library Association, 1960.

Foskett, A. C. *The Subject Approach to Information*. 5th ed. London: Library Association Publishing, 1996. Chapter 8: Alphabetical Subject Headings: Cutter to Austin.

Mann, Thomas. *Library Research Models: A Guide to Classification, Cataloging, and Computers*. New York: Oxford University Press, 1993. Chapter 4: The Traditional Library Science Model. Part Two: The Vocabulary-Controlled Catalog.

Pettee, Julia. *Subject Headings: The History and Theory of the Alphabetical Approach to Books*. New York: H. W. Wilson, 1946.

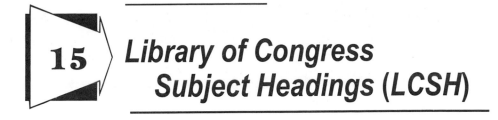

15 Library of Congress Subject Headings (LCSH)

INTRODUCTION

The official list, *Library of Congress Subject Headings* (*LCSH*), consists of terms, with references, that have been established over the years since 1898 for use in the Library of Congress's (LC's) subject catalogs. Although developed to give subject access to the vast collections of one particular library, this list can be, and has been, adopted by libraries of all sizes, including many with non-LC classification schemes. The National Library of Canada, for example, has for many years used it as basic, supplementing it with a special set of terms for Canadian material.[1] It is used by most large public libraries, college and university libraries, and special libraries that do not have technical subject lists of their own. Since bibliographic records created by LC often carry *Dewey Decimal Classification* (*DDC*) numbers as well as LC call numbers, but have only LC subject headings, some smaller libraries also use the LC subject list. Others retain the shorter, less frequently revised *Sears List of Subject Headings* (*Sears*) list as their primary source, but consult the LC list for suggestions when *Sears* cannot provide the specificity or the diversity they want.[2] (*Sears* is discussed in chapter 16.)

BACKGROUND

Library of Congress subject headings come from a long tradition of theory and practice that is generally held to begin with Charles A. Cutter's *Rules for a Dictionary Catalog*.[3] A brief review of Cutter's approach and of the major developments stemming from his work can be found in chapter 14, "Verbal Subject Access." The purpose in the present chapter is to highlight trends leading directly to the current manifestations of LC subject headings.[4]

On July 1, 1909, J. C. M. Hanson, Chief of the Catalog Division of LC, addressed the Catalog Section of the American Library Association (ALA) at its Bretton Woods Conference "The Subject Catalogs of the Library of Congress."[5] He alluded to a two-volume subject catalog published by LC in 1869, but called the subject heading developments of the intervening 40 years too radical to permit a meaningful comparison. The many changes attendant upon the new classification scheme and the move into a new building required a new approach to subject indexing. LC catalogers agreed to start from the ALA *List of Subject Headings for Use in Dictionary Catalogs* (1895)[6], which embodied much of Cutter's theory and which originally formed an appendix to his *Rules*. It was designed for smaller libraries of "generally popular character," but with LC's printed card distribution plans, such an orientation was not altogether disadvantageous.

When the first cards carrying the new headings were published, subject terms were given only if an LC call number was available to print. Since many class schedules were still undeveloped, the list of subject headings grew slowly in the first decade. Proposed new headings were compared to those in the ALA *List* before final selection. Separate publication of the new list did not start until 1909, when the annotated and interleaved copies of the ALA *List* grew unwieldy. It was assumed from the first that cumulations of additions and changes would be issued periodically to supplement the main list, which itself appeared in parts until March 1914.

The practice of subordinating place to subject in scientific and technical headings, as well as under many economic and educational topics, was established at this time. But other subjects—historical, political, administrative, social, and descriptive—were to be subordinated to place, although Hanson admitted to "a number of subjects so nearly on the border line, that it has been difficult in all cases to preserve absolute consistency in decisions."[7] Besides the place/subject versus subject/place precedents, other syntactic forms evolved:

> There is undeniably a strong tendency in the Library of Congress catalog to bring related subjects together by means of inversion of headings, by combinations of two or more subject-words, and even by subordination of one subject to another.[8]

Hanson recognized that subordination within the dictionary arrangement of his new subject list was a concession to the alphabetico-classed or systematic organization of the 1869 catalog. He argued:

> the student and the investigator . . . are best served by having related topics brought together so far as that can be accomplished without a too serious violation of the dictionary principle.[9]

The practice of inversion of certain types of modified headings was firmly established by 1951 when David Judson Haykin wrote:

> It is unlikely that the reader will look under an adjective denoting language, ethnic group, or place for material on a subject limited by language, ethnic group, or place, although, in the case of ethnic groups particularly, the interest in the group may outweigh that in the subject. On this basis it has been assumed, although it has not been demonstrated, that a reader interested in French art . . . would be much more likely to look under *Art, French* (or *Art—France*) . . . than under the respective uninverted forms.[10]

These and other practices have been questioned and modified in recent years but were basic premises in the establishment of subject headings at LC for many years and are still reflected in the list.

FORMATS AND SUPPLEMENTARY TOOLS

LC subject headings are made available in several forms. The longest running format is the printed and bound version. For many years these lists were published in new editions every five years or so, but starting in 1988 with the eleventh edition, they have been published annually.[11] Beginning with the ninth edition, it was necessary to publish the list in two volumes, which quickly expanded, and the last few editions have been published in five volumes. The volumes have for many years been published in red bindings and are affectionately known as "The Big Red Books." The print format can be supplemented with *LC Subject Headings Weekly Lists*, available on the World Wide Web.[12] These give information about new and changed subject headings, class numbers, references, and scope notes. A fully updated list can be purchased each quarter on microfiche,[13] and the fully updated version is also available on *Classification Plus*, a CD-ROM cataloging tool often used in conjunction with *Cataloger's Desktop*.[14]

MAchine-Readable Cataloging (MARC) format authority records for LC subject headings became available online through OCLC in 1987 and through RLIN in 1988. The online version is updated at least weekly and so provides the most current data.

The concept of the official headings authorized by LC is referred to in this chapter as LCSH (standing for Library of Congress subject headings). The online version available at the time of writing yields the examples found in this chapter.

When catalogers make use of LCSH there are several supplementary tools that must be used. The rules and guidelines used by LC catalogers when applying LCSH have been published as *Subject Cataloging Manual: Subject Headings (SCM: SH)*, issued in looseleaf form with periodic updates.[15] It is an essential tool for anyone who wishes to apply the subject headings correctly. It is also available and kept up-to-date through *Classification Plus*.

Catalogers can also keep up-to-date on LCSH through the *Cataloging Service Bulletin (CSB)*.[16] *CSB* gives information about changes to *SCM: SH*, lists some new subject headings that have been established, lists headings that have been changed, and gives information about new publications that may be useful to the subject cataloger.

TYPES OF TOPICAL SUBJECT HEADINGS
(MARC 21 bibliographic field 650, 2nd indicator 0;
MARC 21 authority field 150)

Library of Congress topical subject headings are constructed in a variety of ways, ranging from a single noun to complex descriptive phrases. As was discussed in chapter 14, Cutter enumerated six varieties according to their grammar or syntax.[17] They covered only primary headings, i.e., headings without further subdivision. The categories below are his, but the examples come from the current LCSH:

- A single word (e.g., "**Skating**")

- A noun preceded by an adjective (e.g., "**Administrative law**")

- A noun preceded by another noun used like an adjective (e.g., "**Energy industries**")

- A noun connected with another by a preposition (e.g., **"Radioisotopes in cardiology"**)

- A noun connected with another by *and* (e.g., **"Libraries and society"**)

- A phrase or sentence (e.g., **"Show driving of horse-drawn vehicles"**)

While Cutter did tolerate modifier inversions (e.g., **"Etching, Anonymous"**) "only when some other word is decidedly more significant or is often used alone with the same meaning as the whole name," he made no explicit provision for parenthetical qualifiers (e.g., **"Kairós (The Greek word)"**) or other such complicated forms as **"Internal combustion engines, Spark ignition,"** which, like subdivisions, are usually reminiscent of the alphabetico-classed approach. There are various alternative groupings. This discussion follows those used by Lois Mai Chan in her treatise on subject headings.[18]

Single Noun Headings

Cutter's Rule No. 172 reads: "Enter books under the word which best expresses their subject, whether it occurs in the title or not." He worked primarily in terms of the simple concept-name relationship on which the noun forms of all languages are based. LC over the years has experimented with slight variations of this single-word heading, for example, inclusion of an initial article (e.g., **"The West"**), sometimes inverted (e.g., **"State, The"**) in the interests of clarity. Subject headings are no longer established with an English article in the initial position. **"The West"** has been changed to **"West (U.S.)."**[19]

Another variation was the distinction drawn, particularly in literature and art, between singular nouns (denoting the activity or the form, e.g., **"Essay"** and **"Painting"**) and plural nouns (denoting the objects, e.g., **"Essays"** and **"Paintings"**). In general no new plural noun headings are being established, and some old plurals (e.g., **"Paintings"**) have been cancelled in favor of the singular form.

Adjectival Headings

These headings start with a modifier followed by a noun or noun phrase (e.g., **"Municipal officials and employees"**). The modifier may be an adjective or it may be a noun used as an adjective. Examples of some of these are:

Common adjective (e.g., **"Dental records"**)

Ethnic, national, or geographic adjective (e.g., **"Afro-American Librarians"**)

Participial modifiers (e.g., **"Applied anthropology"** or **"Hearing aids"**)

Common noun used as a modifier (e.g., **"Household pests"**)

Proper noun used as a modifier (e.g., **"Bernstein polynomials"**)

Conjunctive Phrase Headings

Headings composed of two or more nouns, with or without modifiers, connected by *and* or ending with *etc.* belong in this group. Those that are additive may comprise similar elements (e.g., **"Wit and humor"** or **"Charitable uses, trusts, and foundations"** or **"Chapters, Cathedral, collegiate, etc."**) or the elements may be contradictory (e.g., **"Right and wrong"**). Headings of this type are now established only when a work being cataloged discusses a relationship between two topics from both perspectives and in such broad terms that the relationship could not be described by use of a main heading with a subdivision.[20] Many older additive headings have been separated, (e.g., **"Buddha and Buddhism"** has been replaced by **"Buddhism"** and **"Gautama Buddha"**).

Prepositional Phrase Headings

Prepositions sometimes enable the subject cataloger to express single but complex ideas for which there is no one word. Some express relationships for which an "and" phrase would be artificial (e.g., **"Photography in psychiatry"** or **"Police services for juveniles"**). Some are inverted (e.g., **"Plants, effect of heat on"**). Examples of other prepositions used are:

against (e.g., **"Offenses against the person"**)

as (e.g., **"Alfalfa as feed"**)

from (e.g., **"Theft from motor vehicles"**)

to (e.g., **"Ceramic to metal bonding"**)

with (e.g., **"Double bass with band"**)

Many of these circumlocutions are replaced when a simpler expression gains currency (e.g., **"Psychoanalysis in historiography"** was replaced by **"Psychohistory"**). "As" headings for classes of persons have been restricted to certain situations where the resulting connotation will not be seen as disparaging (e.g., **"Physicians as authors"**). Old headings in which men or women are identified as professionals (e.g., **"Men as nurses"** or **"Women as teachers"**) have been replaced by adjectival phrases (e.g., **"Male nurses"** and **"Women teachers"**).[21]

Parenthetical Qualifiers

Nouns or phrases in parentheses following primary terms have in the past occasioned a variety of linguistic ineptitudes. LC no longer adds them to designate special applications of a general concept, although it has no plans to change established headings such as:

Vibration (Marine engineering)
Cookery (Frozen foods)
Excavations (Archaeology)

For newly established situations, three different techniques are available:

- "In" and "of" headings:

  Information theory in biology (*not* **Information theory (Biology)**)
  Abandonment of automobiles (*not* **Abandonment (Automobiles)**)

- Phrase headings:

  Combinatorial enumeration problems (*not* **Enumeration problems (Combinatorial analysis)**)

- Subdivisions under a primary heading (preferred when practicable):

  Public health—Citizen participation (*not* **Citizen participation (Public health)**)

A few situations are recognized in which it may be necessary to use parenthetical qualifiers:

- To specify a definition if several can be found in the dictionary:

  "Analysis (Philosophy)"

- To remove ambiguity or to make an obscure word or phrase more explicit:

  "Cluttering (Speech pathology)"

- To identify the category if a heading designates a kind of "object"

  "Trunks (Luggage)"

- To identify the category for a named entity:

  "Arulo (Artificial language)" [22]

Parenthetical expressions are also used for some headings for musical works.

Inverted Headings

Inversions, while awkward syntactically (e.g., "**Aged, Writings of the, American**"), serve the alphabetico-classed function of subordinating specific descriptors under their broad generic categories (e.g., "**Education, Bilingual**" or "**Asylum, Right of** "). Here too, much inconsistency is apparent.

In the course of its efforts to modernize and systematize LCSH, LC has attempted to set policy for creation of new inverted headings. For example, topical headings modified by adjectival qualifiers referring to ethnic groups are to be established in the inverted form (e.g., "**Proverbs, Korean**") with certain exceptions, one of which is for ethnic groups of the United States (e.g., "**Mexican American proverbs**").[23] LC occasionally changes an existing heading, especially in cases where every instance of the concept but one is in direct order.

SEMANTICS

Not only have syntactic forms of subject headings come under close scrutiny and revision in recent years, but also LCSH terminology has been reconsidered. Word meanings, particularly their connotative aspects, mutate rapidly; social and political upheavals cause many changes, and scientific and technological developments account for many more. The problem of shifting terminology is particularly troublesome for a subject access list based on specific entry, avoidance of synonyms, and controlled references, designed for use with card or printed book catalogs.

A ringing complaint that LCSH terminology was obsolete and prejudicial came from Sanford Berman in 1971.[24] As Head of the Hennepin County, Minnesota, Library Catalog Department for many years, Berman edited the *HCL Cataloging Bulletin*, a bimonthly carrying lists of subject headings and references added to the HCL catalogs.[25] Many new concepts have been added as headings at HCL before being added by LC, and LC subject catalogers frequently consult the *HCL Cataloging Bulletin* when establishing new headings.

Other writers criticized the stance at LC on conceptual and linguistic shifts. Doris Clack's 1975 analysis of black literature resources started from a critique of LC subject analysis. She observed:

> Inadequate subject analysis is not just a problem with black literature—though admittedly there the level of adequacy is critically low—nor has it only in recent years been brought to the attention of the library world.[26]

Clack devoted the bulk of her treatise to various lists of LC class numbers and subject terms from the black perspective. Since her book was published, LC has made many changes. The one cited below involved changing approximately 12,000 cards:

> A basic function in the maintenance of a subject heading system is that of updating headings to conform to changing terminology or altered concepts. In general, the Library of Congress is and has been conservative in making changes since it involves altering reference structures surrounding a given heading as well as accommodating the change in both the card catalogs and the machine-readable data base. However, after a long period of great reluctance in effecting major changes, the Library has recently been involved in a number of changes represented in the following list . . .
>
> **Negroes.** This heading discontinued February 1976.
> See **Afro-Americans** for later materials on the permanent residents of the United States. See **Blacks** for later materials on persons outside the United States. . . .[27]

It can be seen in this statement that a major deterrent to LC's making changes was the card catalog. Since they closed the card catalog at the beginning of 1981 and have had only machine-readable records to update, terminology changes have been made more readily; but because LC's home-grown computer system did not have global search and replace capabilities, changes still had to be made record by record. This made it difficult to consider massive changes such as changing "Afro-Americans" to the more popular "African Americans" of the 1990s. At the end of 1999, the implementation of a new integrated library system (ILS) means that such changes can be implemented with one command instead of thousands. The impact of this capability has yet to be felt.

Reflecting another socio-linguistic revolution was Joan K. Marshall's 1977 critique of gender bias in LCSH.[28] She used six principles developed by ALA's Social Responsibilities Round Table Task Force Committee on Sexist Subject

Headings to replace logically and consistently the guesswork that evolved over the years from Cutter's concern for the "convenience of the public." Basing her work on the six principles, she submitted an alphabetical, annotated "Thesaurus for Nonsexist Indexing and Cataloging." As in the case of the subject concepts for Blacks, LC has overhauled most of its more obsolete or offensive sexist headings.

PROPER NAME HEADINGS

Any proper name can be used as a subject heading in the LC system. Names are not, however, all included in the subject list or given subject authority records. The only ones appearing in the list are those that are used as pattern headings (*see* discussion below), or as examples, or that need special subject subdivisions or instructions printed under them.

Personal and Corporate Names and Uniform Titles
(MARC 21 bibliographic fields 600, 610, 611, 630;
MARC 21 authority fields 100, 110, 111, 130)

The correct forms of personal names, names of corporate bodies, names of jurisdictions, names of conferences and meetings, and uniform titles are found in LC's Name Authority File (LCNAF). (If one thinks of a uniform title as the "name" of a *work*, then this file is correctly named.) When any of these is the subject of a work, the correct form is taken from LCNAF and placed in a subject field in the bibliographic record. These names are established in accordance with LC's interpretation of *Anglo-American Cataloguing Rules, Second Edition* (*AACR2R*).

Geographic Names
(MARC 21 bibliographic field 651;
MARC 21 authority field 151)

Geographic, jurisdictional, and physiographic names form a large part of any library's subject network. Prior to the mid-1970s, only key examples to illustrate modes of entry and types of subdivision were listed in LCSH. Libraries had to locate bibliographic records using the names to verify them. With the acceptance of *AACR2* in 1981 it was decided to create subject geographic names in a form consistent with the jurisdictional forms controlled by *AACR2*. Subject authority records are now created for all non-jurisdictional geographic and physiographic names, except for those that are created as free-floating phrase headings (*see* discussion below), and they are listed in the printed versions of LCSH. Although the form of jurisdictional names is taken from LCNAF, subject authority records are sometimes made and printed when needed in order to add a topical or chronological subdivision (e.g., "**Chicago (Ill.)—History—To 1875**").

Place names reflecting political or jurisdictional changes are treated somewhat differently as subject headings than as descriptive cataloging access points. In descriptive cataloging, the name used for the place at the time of the creation of the work is used as the access point. In subject cataloging, however, when the name of a country, state, city, etc., has been changed without substantially affecting the jurisdictional area covered, it is LC's policy to make all subject entries under the new name regardless of the time period covered. Subject entries under an old name are changed to the new name. These changes are referred to as "linear name changes."[29] This policy is followed regardless of whether the government changed the jurisdiction name or the change was made to accommodate cataloging rules. Examples:

Old Form	Latest Form
Argentine Republic	Argentina
British Honduras	Belize
Ceylon	Sri Lanka
Zaire	Congo (Democratic Republic)
Formosa	Taiwan

GENRE/FORM TERMS
(MARC 21 bibliographic field 655; MARC 21 authority field 155)

"Form" is a concept that has been associated with subject analysis from the inception of the idea that books could be entered in catalogs and placed on shelves according to the category they belonged to. Early categories included such things as encyclopedias, biographies, and histories, as well as chemistry and religion. Later, as subject headings evolved to mean what an item is "about" instead of a category to which the book belonged, the idea of "form" remained as part of the subject heading process. Because it was often difficult to separate the ideas of "aboutness" and form, as in the case of "history," which seems to incorporate elements of both, the concept of form has only recently begun to be treated differently in bibliographic records.

A definition, created by a Subcommittee of ALA's Subject Analysis Committee, was approved by appropriate ALA bodies in January, 1993:

Form data are those terms and phrases that designate specific kinds or genres of materials. Materials designated with these terms or phrases may be determined by an examination of:

their physical character (e.g., videocassettes, photographs, maps, broadsides)

the particular type of data that they contain (e.g., bibliographies, questionnaires, statistics)

the arrangement of information within them (e.g., diaries, outlines, indexes)

the style, technique, purpose, or intended audience (e.g., drama, romances, cartoons, commercials, popular works)

or a combination of the above (e.g., scores)

A single term may be modified by other terms, in which case the whole phrase is considered to be form data (e.g., aerial photographs, French dictionaries, conversation and phrase books, wind ensemble suites, telephone directories, vellum bound books, science fiction).[30]

LC does not yet create form/genre headings that they treat differently from topical headings (i.e., that are coded 655 in the MARC format instead of 650). There are a number of specialized lists of form terms in the rare books, art, and audio-visual communities, among others. One commonly used list in public and school libraries is the *Guidelines on Subject Access to Individual Works of Fiction, Drama, Etc.*[31] Terms from this list are added in 655 fields to catalog records by many public libraries.

HEADINGS OMITTED FROM
LIBRARY OF CONGRESS SUBJECT HEADINGS (LCSH)

A troublesome corollary of the principle of specific entry is the inevitable, and seemingly endless, proliferation of subject terms for individual members of certain subject categories. Until the early 1980s LC omitted from its printed list a wide variety of such terms. These terms were included in the library's official records but were not spelled out in the printed editions of *LCSH*. They included such categories as names of sacred books, fictitious and legendary characters, works of art, chemicals, geographic regions, archaeological sites, and buildings. Authority records are now being made for the individual names in such groups, but only those established after 1976 (1981 if affected by *AACR2*) are in the file. There are still many general *See also* references to cover such situations (e.g., "**Lumber**, SA *kinds of lumber*, e.g. Cypress; Walnut"). These are gradually being replaced as the narrower headings are established.

Categories of headings currently intentionally omitted from *LCSH* include headings residing in the LCNAF and free-floating phrase headings. Headings in the LCNAF are discussed above. Free-floating phrase headings are composed as needed without creation of authority records. In free-floating phrase headings the initial word changes. This type is still limited to a very few pattern phrases. The following are listed in the *Subject Cataloging Manual*:

[topic or name heading (except personal names)] in art
> e.g., **Manhattan (New York, N.Y.) in art**

[name of city] Metropolitan Area ([geographical qualifier])
> e.g., **Atlanta Metropolitan Area (Ga.)**

[name of city] Region ([geographical qualifier])
> e.g., **Dallas Region (Tex.)**

[name of city] Suburban Area ([geographic qualifier])
> e.g., **Atlanta Suburban Area (Ga.)**

[name of geographic feature] Region ([geographic qualifier, if part of the name as established])
> e.g., **Himalaya Mountains Region**

[name of river] Region ([geographic qualifier, if part of name as established])
> e.g., **Tweed River Region (Scotland and England)**[32]

The local cataloger should not take any other "... in ..." phrase found in *LCSH* as a pattern phrase. For example, the heading "**Color in clothing**" does not of itself give license to coin other phrases ending with "... **in clothing**." LC formerly used pattern phrases of the form "... **as a profession**" (e.g., "**Medicine as a profession**"). It now uses the subdivision "**—Vocational guidance**" instead (e.g., "**Medicine— Vocational guidance**").

It should be pointed out that this list of categories of headings omitted from *LCSH* refers only to main headings. In the discussion under "Subdivisions" below it can be seen that there are *many* headings with subdivisions that are not individually listed in the subject authority file.

GENERAL CHARACTERISTICS OF *LIBRARY OF CONGRESS SUBJECT HEADINGS (LCSH)*

Physical characteristics of LCSH differ depending upon whether one is dealing with a printed version or with an online version. In the printed book version all primary subject terms appear in boldface type, while subdivisions and reference tracings, as well as references interfiled with the main headings, are in lightface type. References interfiled with primary terms are followed by the instruction USE, which is in turn followed by the preferred term. The instruction SA (*See also*) is given in some entries and precedes terms, phrases, etc., that show related headings or subdivisions. The directions UF (used for), BT (broader term), RT (related term), and NT (narrower term) precede reference tracings in printed entries.

In the MARC 21 authorities format, functions of terms are identified by coding. Primary terms are given a three-digit code beginning with *1* (e.g., 150, 151). "Used for" terms are assigned codes beginning with *4* (e.g., 450, 451); "see also" references are coded 360; and broader and related terms are assigned codes beginning with *5* (e.g., 550, 551). Narrower terms are not shown in MARC 21 authority records except in the relatively few cases where general "reference records" are made showing the unused term coded 150 and the preferred term in a field coded 260. In such a record there is a fixed field code to show that the record is a reference record and that the term in the 150 field should not be used as a heading.

Syndetic (Reference) Structure

Figures 15.1 (page 364) and 15.2 (page 366) illustrate the usages of the abbreviations in the print formats and of the codes in the MARC format.

Fig. 15.1. Printed entry for subject heading "Maintenance."

Maintenance
UF   Preventive maintenance
        Upkeep
BT   Maintainability (Engineering)
RT   Repairing
        Service life (Engineering)
SA   *subdivision* Maintenance and repair *under kinds*
        of objects, including machinery, vehicles, structures,
        etc., e.g. Automobiles—Maintenance and repair;
        Dwellings—Maintenance and repair; Nuclear
        reactors—Maintenance and repair
NT   Buildings—Repair and reconstruction
        Grounds maintenance
        Military bases—Maintenance
        Plant maintenance

In figure 15.1 the two terms following UF serve as tracings to indicate that there are references that read:

Preventive maintenance
    USE   Maintenance

Upkeep
    USE   Maintenance

This also serves as an instruction that when the heading "Maintenance" is first entered into the catalog, these two references should be added to the catalog also. In online systems with linked authority files, this is done automatically.

The BT line not only indicates that the term following BT is a broader term in the hierarchy of the concept, but also serves as a tracing to indicate that there should be a reference in the catalog that reads:

Maintainability (Engineering)
    See also   Maintenance

In traditional library practice it has been considered improper to provide a reference from a narrower term to its broader term, on the assumption that there would be no place to stop until one arrived at "General Knowledge," and the catalog would be overflowing with reference cards. Now that catalogs are mostly online, however, there is no reason to limit references, and there is evidence that users like to be able to browse "up" a hierarchy to the broader terms in addition to being able to browse narrower and related terms.

The terms following RT are related terms. Neither is hierarchically above the other. The instruction here is to make references both from and to these terms:

Maintenance
 See also Repairing
     Service life (Engineering)

Repairing
 See also Maintenance

Service life (Engineering)
 See also Maintenance

SA means "see also" and is currently used for special instructions concerning how the concept embodied in this heading may be used as a subdivision or to refer to groups of headings that are all related to the heading concept. In the example shown above, the concept as a subdivision may be expressed as "Maintenance and repair" under kinds of objects.

The terms following NT are narrower in the concept hierarchy, and there is an implicit instruction to make a reference that reads:

Maintenance
 See also Buildings—Repair and reconstruction
     Grounds maintenance
     Military bases—Maintenance
     Plant maintenance

This last reference, in some cases, would be combined with the "related terms" reference from "Maintenance" shown above unless the wording of the reference is of the type that refers specifically to related terms and/or narrower terms.

The MARC 21 format version of the same record (see figure 15.2, page 366) shows the heading coded 150. The "used for" terms are coded 450. In some records a term coded 450 may be followed by "$w nne" ("e" meaning "earlier"), which indicates that the now unused term was once used as the heading for the concept, but the correct heading now is the one in the 150 field. The broader term and the related terms are all coded 550. The broader term is distinguished from the two related terms by the "$w g" following the term. The special instructions about the concept used as a subdivision are coded 360. Narrower terms are not included in MARC 21 authority records on the assumption that if all references are made from broader terms listed in all authority records in an online system, references to the narrower terms will automatically be taken care of. This does, in fact, work, as can be seen in the sample screen display from OCLC (see figure 15.3, page 366) in which references beginning with "MAINTENANCE" are displayed.

Fig. 15.2. MARC 21 Subject Authority Record as formatted in OCLC.

```
    ARN: 2080919
    Rec stat: c        Entered:    19860211
>   Type:     z        Upd status: a       Enc lvl:   n        Source:
    Roman:    _        Ref status: b       Mod rec:              Name use: b
    Govt agn: _        Auth status: a      Subj:      a        Subj use: a
    Series:   n        Auth/ref:   a       Geo subd:  _        Ser use:  b
    Ser num:  n        Name:       n       Subdiv tp: _        Rules:    n <
>    1 010             sh 85079931 <
>    2 040             DLC $c DLC $d DLC <
>    3 005             19891011120233.6 <
>    4 150   0         Maintenance <
>    5 360             $i subdivision $a Maintenance and repair $i under kinds
of objects, including machinery, vehicles, structures, etc., e.g. $a
Automobiles--Maintenance and repair; Dwellings--Maintenance and repair;
Nuclear reactors--Maintenance and repair <
>    6 450   0         Preventive maintenance <
>    7 450   0         Upkeep <
>    8 550   0         Maintainability (Engineering) $w g <
>    9 550   0         Repairing <
>   10 550   0         Service life (Engineering) <
```

Fig. 15.3. Display of narrower terms and related terms in OCLC.

AUTH   su "MAINTENANCE - "   Records: 6
Rec#   Field accessed >>> Established heading
>   1<   Maintenance >> Buildings Repair and reconstruction
>   2<   Maintenance >> Grounds maintenance
>   3<   Maintenance >> Military bases Maintenance
>   4<   Maintenance >> Plant maintenance
>   5<   Maintenance >> Repairing
>   6<   Maintenance >> Service life (Engineering)

The instructions for references imbedded in the abbreviations and codes are not to be followed blindly, but should be applied where useful and needed. If, for example, a catalog lacks entries under the narrower terms "Grounds maintenance," "Military bases—Maintenance," and the related term "Service life (Engineering)," then the *See also* reference from "Maintenance" would omit these and read only:

Maintenance
 See also Buildings—Repair and reconstruction
     Plant maintenance
     Repairing

If all six headings are lacking, then the reference should not be made at all.
  The related and broader term references to "Maintenance" present a complicated problem. If there were no entries in the catalog under "Repairing," strictly speaking it would be inaccurate to make a reference reading:

Repairing
 See also Maintenance

Some theorists argue that it is nonetheless justifiable to make such *See also* references on the assumption that the term referred from will eventually be activated. Even if it is not, they say, the reference serves to move users from a term not included in the catalog to one where there may be pertinent materials. Some libraries convert such ambiguous *See also* references into *See* references:

Repairing
  See Maintenance

If the term referred from is later activated, they add the word *also* to *See* on the reference. This system is difficult to handle, and as more catalogs are automated it is necessary to write unambiguous programs that create references only as authorized in the authority file. The problem can be solved by using *Broader terms*, *Narrower terms*, etc., in catalogs instead of *See also*, or *Search also under* (a phrase currently used in numerous systems). There should be no semantic problem with telling a user that a related term for "Repairing" is "Maintenance," even if there are no entries under "Repairing." In fact, the traditional ban on referring users from narrower terms to broader terms should also be lifted. The problem is also being solved in some systems by giving the number of postings beside each term. Listing a referred-to term with zero postings alerts the user to the term's presence in the subject heading list, but indicates that the particular database in use does not have any records with the term.

A number of writers have criticized LCSH's syndetic structure and its lack of ability to show hierarchical relationships. Coates wrote in 1960 that LCSH merely linked an "indeterminate selection" of related terms—that at times there was more than one level of hierarchy in a list under one primary term, while at other times intermediate hierarchical terms were omitted from the chain of references.[33] Sinkankis demonstrated in his 1972 study, in which he followed the *See alsos* under the heading "Hunting," that a user was quickly led away from the subject. By following the references he was led to "Migrant labor," "Pimps," "Liturgy and drama," and "Panic," among other terms.[34] Petersen wrote in 1983 that during a project to create the *Art and Architecture Thesaurus* (*AAT*), the designers chose to keep LCSH terms as a base and to modify and expand them. But the *See alsos* and *See also froms* in LCSH had to be ignored because they could not be converted to broader, narrower, and related terms. There were too many types of reference present.[35] Mary Dykstra was critical in 1989 of the format LC began using in *LCSH11* (*LCSH, eleventh edition*), the first edition to use the abbreviations BT, RT, NT, etc., instead of the previous system that used *x* and *xx* to trace *See* and *See also* references. Dykstra believed that LC was trying to make *LCSH* look like a true thesaurus, which it is not because of its use of "headings" instead of "terms."[36]

LC has recognized the problems but has not been able to eliminate all inappropriate references created in the past; staff time has not always been available for "clean-up" projects. However, beginning in the mid-1980s, subject catalogers at LC put into effect a fairly strict policy for creating new references for all *new* headings created. The general rule is to make a broader term reference from the class of which the heading is a class member (e.g., "**Cinematography**, BT Photography"), to make a reference for a whole/part relationship (e.g., "**Toes**, BT Foot"), and to make a reference for cases in which a specific heading is an instance or example of a broader category (e.g., "**Erie, Lake**, BT Lakes—United States"). Broader term references are made only from the next broader level in a hierarchy. Related terms are used to link two headings not in the same hierarchy (e.g., a concept and an object). One of the headings should be strongly implied whenever the other is considered (e.g., **"Boats and boating**, RT Ships").[37] While this reference policy moves LCSH toward answering its critics, the problem will not be solved completely until all "clean-up" projects have been completed.

Scope Notes

Scope notes are sometimes inserted into the subject authority records. In printed versions they are between the heading and its references; in MARC 21 records they are tagged 680. Such notes specify the range of application for a term or draw distinctions between related terms. Some libraries with card catalogs copy these notes on cards and file them in the catalog just ahead of the subject entries under the same heading. Other libraries provide one or more copies of *LCSH* near the catalog for reference use by patrons doing subject searches. Although most online catalogs do not yet display scope notes, some do, and there is encouragement to provide more such information to users. A typical example of an entry with a scope note is figure 15.4 from *LCSH21 (LCSH, twenty-first edition)*.

Fig. 15.4. Printed entry for a subject heading with a scope note.

Sexism   *(May Subd Geog)*
    Here are entered works on sexism as an attitude as
well as works on attitude and overt discriminatory behavior.
Works dealing solely with discriminatory behavior directed
toward both of the sexes are entered under Sex discrimination.
UF   Sex bias
BT   Attitude (Psychology)
       Prejudices
       Sex (Psychology)
       Social perception
RT   Sex role
NT   Heterosexism
       Sex discrimination

In the MARC 21 authorities format the scope note is in a field coded 680 as can be seen in figure 15.5, the record for "Sexism" as it is formatted in the OCLC database.

Fig. 15.5. MARC 21 authority record showing a scope note in the 680 field.

```
   ARN: 2102436
   Rec stat: c        Entered:    19860211
>  Type:      z        Upd status: a      Enc lvl:   n      Source:
   Roman:     _        Ref status: b      Mod rec:          Name use: b
Govt agn:     _        Auth status: a     Subj:      a      Subj use: a
Series:       n        Auth/ref:   a      Geo subd:  i      Ser use:  b
   Ser num:   n        Name:       n      Subdiv tp: _      Rules:    n <
>   1 010            sh 85120678 <
>   2 040            DLC $c DLC $d DLC <
>   3 005            19870326163626.7 <
>   4 150   0        Sexism <
>   5 450   0        Sex bias <
>   6 550   0        Attitude (Psychology) $w g <
>   7 550   0        Prejudices $w g <
>   8 550   0        Sex (Psychology) $w g <
>   9 550   0        Social perception $w g <
>  10 550   0        Sex role <
>  11 680            $i Here are entered works on sexism as an attitude as well
as works on attitude and overt discriminatory behavior. Works dealing
solely with, discriminatory behavior directed toward both of the sexes
are entered under $a Sex discrimination. <
>  12 681            $i Note under $a Sex discrimination <
```

Subdivisions
(MARC 21 subfields $x, $y, $z, and $v)

It was mentioned earlier that the practice of establishing subdivisions for headings was firmly set in Hanson's time as a concession to alphabetico-classed organization of catalogs. The introduction to *LCSH* states:

> The application of Library of Congress subject headings requires extensive use of subject subdivisions as a means of combining a number of different concepts into a single subject heading. Complex topics may be represented by subject headings followed by subdivisions. Some subdivisions are printed in *LCSH* but a greater number of subdivisions may be assigned according to rules specified in the *Manual*. Only a fraction of all possible heading-and-subdivision combinations are listed in *LCSH*.[38]

Subdivisions fall into several broadly defined categories: topical and chronological subdivisions specific to particular headings; geographic subdivisions; form subdivisions; free-floating subdivisions; and subdivisions under pattern headings.

Topical Subdivisions Specific to Particular Headings
(MARC 21 bibliographic and authority subfield $x;
MARC 21 subdivision authority record field 180)

Some headings need topical subdivisions that are specific to the concepts in the headings and that, therefore, must be authorized specifically for the headings. Such subdivisions in printed versions of *LCSH* are introduced by a long dash; if two subdivisions are used, there are two long dashes; etc. Figure 15.6, page 370, shows printed subdivisions for the heading "**Lumber**."

Fig. 15.6. Printed entry for subject heading "Lumber" and its subdivisions.

Lumber
>*[TS800-TS837]*
>BT   Forests and forestry
>   Wood products
>RT   Timber
>SA   *kinds of lumber, e.g.* Cypress; Walnut
>NT   Hardwoods
>   Pit-wood
>   Planing-mills
>   Sawmills
>—Advertising
>   USE Advertising—Lumber
>**—Drying**
>>*[TS837]*
>>UF   Lumber—Seasoning
>>   Lumber drying
>>   Wood—Drying
>>BT   Wood—Preservation
>
>**—Law and legislation**   *(May Subd Geog)*
>**—Mensuration**
>**—Rate-books**
>>*[HE2116.L8]*
>—Seasoning
>   USE   Lumber—Drying
>**—Storage**
>**—Transportation**
>>*[HE199.5.L]*
>— —**Law and legislation**
>>*(May Subd Geog)*

The interpretation of the subdivisions in figure 15.6 should be:

>Lumber—Advertising
>   USE **Advertising—Lumber**
>**Lumber—Drying**
>**Lumber—Law and legislation**
>**Lumber—Mensuration**
>**Lumber—Rate-books**
>Lumber—Seasoning
>   USE **Lumber—Drying**
>**Lumber—Storage**
>**Lumber—Transportation**
>**Lumber—Transportation—Law and legislation**

In the MARC version of LCSH, each of these headings is given a separate authority record. The MARC records for the main heading and four of its subdivision records are shown as figures 15.7 to 15.11. In these records the dashes that appeared in the printed list are represented by the code $x.

Fig. 15.7. MARC record for the main heading "Lumber."

```
ARN: 2070743
  Rec stat: c        Entered:    19860211
> Type:     z         Upd status: a    Enc lvl:   n     Source:
  Roman:    _         Ref status: b    Mod rec:         Name use: b
  Govt agn: _         Auth status: a   Subj:      a     Subj use: a
  Series:   n         Auth/ref:   a    Geo subd:  _     Ser use:  b
  Ser num:  n         Name:       n    Subdiv tp: _     Rules:    n <
>   1 010            sh 85078804 <
>   2 040            DLC $c DLC $d DLC <
>   3 005            19871021111358.5 <
>   4 053            TS800 $b TS837 <
>   5 150   0        Lumber <
>   6 360            $i kinds of lumber, e.g. $a Cypress; Walnut <
>   7 550   0        Forests and forestry $w g <
>   8 550   0        Wood products $w g <
>   9 550   0        Timber <
```

Fig. 15.8. MARC record that generates a "USE" reference from "Lumber—Advertising" (*see* line 7).

```
ARN: 3645412
  Rec stat: c        Entered:    19940607
> Type:     z         Upd status: a    Enc lvl:   n     Source:
  Roman:    _         Ref status: a    Mod rec:         Name use: b
  Govt agn: _         Auth status: a   Subj:      a     Subj use: a
  Series:   n         Auth/ref:   a    Geo subd:  i     Ser use:  b
  Ser num:  n         Name:       n    Subdiv tp: _     Rules:    n <
>   1 010            sh 94004017 <
>   2 040            DLC $c DLC $d DLC <
>   3 005            19961004125910.7 <
>   4 053            HF6161.L9 <
>   5 150   0        Advertising $x Lumber <
>   6 450   0        Advertising $x Lumber trade $w nne <
>   7 450   0        Lumber $x Advertising <
>   8 670            Work cat.: NUCMC data from Forest History Soc. for
Laughead, W.B. Papers, 1897-1958 $b (William B. Laughead, advertising
manager for Red River Lumber Company, popularizer of folk hero Paul
Bunyan through advertising pamphlets of the company) <
```

Fig. 15.9. MARC record for "Lumber—Drying."

```
ARN: 2070757
Rec stat: c        Entered:    19860211
> Type:      z      Upd status: a      Enc lvl:    n      Source:
  Roman:     _      Ref status: b      Mod rec:           Name use: b
  Govt agn:  _      Auth status: a     Subj:       a      Subj use: a
  Series:    n      Auth/ref:   a      Geo subd:   i      Ser use:  b
  Ser num:   n      Name:       n      Subdiv tp:  _      Rules:    n <
>   1 010           sh 85078805 <
>   2 040           DLC $c DLC $d DLC <
>   3 005           19950918171534.2 <
>   4 053           TS837 <
>   5 150   0       Lumber $x Drying <
>   6 450   0       Lumber $x Seasoning <
>   7 450   0       Lumber drying <
>   8 450   0       Seasoning of lumber <
>   9 450   0       Wood $x Drying <
>  10 550   0       Wood $x Preservation $w g <
```

Fig. 15.10. MARC record for "Lumber—Transportation."

```
ARN: 2070790
Rec stat: c        Entered:    19860211
> Type:      z      Upd status: a      Enc lvl:    n      Source:
  Roman:     _      Ref status: n      Mod rec:           Name use: b
  Govt agn:  _      Auth status: a     Subj:       a      Subj use: a
  Series:    n      Auth/ref:   a      Geo subd:   i      Ser use:  b
  Ser num:   n      Name:       n      Subdiv tp:  _      Rules:    n <
>   1 010           sh 85078810 <
>   2 040           DLC $c DLC $d DLC <
>   3 005           19960305120606.5 <
>   4 053           HE199.5.L84 $c Freight <
>   5 053           HE595.L8 $c Ships <
>   6 053           HE2321.L8 $c Railroads <
>   7 150   0       Lumber $x Transportation <
```

Fig. 15.11. MARC record for "Lumber—Transportation—Law and Legislation."

```
ARN: 2070794
Rec stat: n        Entered:    19860211
> Type:      z      Upd status: a      Enc lvl:    n      Source:
  Roman:     _      Ref status: n      Mod rec:           Name use: b
  Govt agn:  _      Auth status: a     Subj:       a      Subj use: a
  Series:    n      Auth/ref:   a      Geo subd:   i      Ser use:  b
  Ser num:   n      Name:       n      Subdiv tp:  _      Rules:    n <
>   1 010           sh 85078811 <
>   2 040           DLC $c DLC <
>   3 005           19860211000000.0 <
>   4 150   0       Lumber $x Transportation $x Law and legislation <
```

Chronological Subdivisions Specific to Particular Headings
(MARC 21 bibliographic and authority subfield $y;
MARC 21 authority record field 182)

Chronological subdivisions are sometimes assigned in LCSH. The most common assigned time periods are for historical or political time periods under particular jurisdictions. It is also possible to have time periods assigned under topical headings. The assignment of century time periods is "free-floating" and is discussed below. Chronological subdivisions appear in the printed list as in figure 15.12.

Fig. 15.12. Printed entry for a place with established chronological subdivisions.

Irian Jaya (Indonesia) *(Not Subd Geog)*
   • • •
—Politics and government
— —To 1963
— —1963-

In MARC 21 authority records chronological subdivisions are preceded by the code $y. Again, every heading/subdivision combination has its own separate authority record. MARC records for Irian Jaya and its chronological subdivisions are shown in figures 15.13 to 15.16.

Fig. 15.13. MARC name authority record for "Irian Jaya, Indonesia."

```
     ARN: 448370
     Rec stat: c        Entered:    19800703
>    Type:     z         Upd status: a      Enc lvl:  n      Source:
     Roman:    _         Ref status: a      Mod rec:         Name use: a
     Govt agn: _         Auth status:a      Subj:     a      Subj use: a
     Series:   n         Auth/ref:   a      Geo subd: n      Ser use:  b
     Ser num:  n         Name:       n      Subdiv tp: _     Rules:    c <
>     1 010         n 80066811 $z sh 85068057 <
>     2 040         DLC $c DLC $d DLC $d OrU $d DLC $d NIC <
>     3 005         19970122051941.3 <
>     4 151  0      Irian Jaya (Indonesia) <
>     5 451  0      West Papua (Indonesia) <
>     6 551  0      Irian Barat (Indonesia) $w a <
>     7 667         Old catalog heading: Irian Jaya, Indonesia <
>     8 667         In 1963 Dutch New Guinea became Irian Barat, which in
1973 changed its name to Irian Jaya. <
>     9 670         Indonesia. Direktorat Jenderal Perindustrian Kimia. $b
Laporan survey industri ... 1973. <
>    10 670         Fox, C. Environmental politics, indigenous nations and
the changing state, 1994: $b p. 3 (West Papua, called Irian Jaya by the
Indonesian government) <
```

Fig. 15.14. MARC subject authority record for the "Politics and government" subdivision.

```
ARN: 2121129
Rec stat: n      Entered:    19860211
> Type:      z    Upd status: a      Enc lvl:   n     Source:
  Roman:     _    Ref status: n      Mod rec:         Name use: b
  Govt agn: _     Auth status: a     Subj:      a     Subj use: a
  Series:    n    Auth/ref:   a      Geo subd:  _     Ser use:  b
  Ser num:   n    Name:       n      Subdiv tp: _     Rules:    n <
>   1 010        sh 85068061 <
>   2 040        DLC $c DLC <
>   3 005        19860211000000.0 <
>   4 151   0    Irian Jaya (Indonesia) $x Politics and government <
```

Fig. 15.15. MARC record for the first chronological subdivision.

```
ARN: 2121131
Rec stat: n      Entered:    19860211
> Type:      z    Upd status: a      Enc lvl:   n     Source:
  Roman:     _    Ref status: n      Mod rec:         Name use: b
  Govt agn: _     Auth status: a     Subj:      a     Subj use: a
  Series:    n    Auth/ref:   a      Geo subd:  _     Ser use:  b
  Ser num:   n    Name:       n      Subdiv tp: _     Rules:    n <
>   1 010        sh 85068062 <
>   2 040        DLC $c DLC <
>   3 005        19860211000000.0 <
>   4 151   0    Irian Jaya (Indonesia) $x Politics and government $y To 1963 <
```

Fig. 15.16. MARC record for the second chronological subdivision.

```
ARN: 2121132
Rec stat: n      Entered:    19860211
> Type:      z    Upd status: a      Enc lvl:   n     Source:
  Roman:     _    Ref status: n      Mod rec:         Name use: b
  Govt agn: _     Auth status: a     Subj:      a     Subj use: a
  Series:    n    Auth/ref:   a      Geo subd:  _     Ser use:  b
  Ser num:   n    Name:       n      Subdiv tp: _     Rules:    n <
>   1 010        sh 85068063 <
>   2 040        DLC $c DLC <
>   3 005        19860211000000.0 <
>   4 151   0    Irian Jaya (Indonesia) $x Politics and government $y 1963- <
```

Geographic Subdivisions

(MARC 21 bibliographic and authority subfield $z;
MARC 21 subdivision authority record field 181)

The code words "*(May Subd Geog)*" in parentheses after any entry in the printed list tell us that place names may be added without having been spelled out in the list and without separate MARC authority records having been created. In a MARC authority record the code for geographic subdivision is given in a byte of the fixed field. The letter *i* indicates that geographic subdivision is allowed. In the OCLC system the fixed field byte is labeled "Geo subd:". The printed and MARC codes are illustrated in figures 15.17 and 15.18.

Fig. 15.17. Printed entry showing a heading that may be subdivided geographically.

Lumbering   *(May Subd Geog)*
  [TS800-TS837 (Manufactures)]
  Here are entered works on the manufacturing of
logs into lumber. Works on the felling of trees through
the transporting of logs to sawmills or to a place of sale
are entered under Logging.
  BT   Forest products industry
  RT   Lumber trade
  NT   Communication in lumbering
       Explosives in lumbering
       Logging
       Lumbermen

Fig. 15.18. MARC record showing "i" in subfield "Geo subd:" meaning that the heading can be subdivided geographically.

```
  ARN: 2070847
  Rec stat: c
> Type:       z        Upd status: a     Enc lvl:   n      Source:
  Roman:      _        Ref status: b     Mod rec:          Name use: b
  Govt agn: _          Auth status: a    Subj:      a      Subj use: a
  Series:     n        Auth/ref:   a     Geo subd:  i      Ser use:  b
  Ser num:    n        Name:       n     Subdiv tp: _      Rules:    n <
>   1 010            sh 85078820 <
>   2 040            DLC $c DLC $d DLC <
>   3 005            19970902143428.1 <
>   4 053            TS800 $b TS837 $c Manufactures <
>   5 150   0        Lumbering <
>   6 550   0        Forest products industry $w g <
>   7 550   0        Lumber trade <
>   8 680            $i Here are entered works on the manufacturing of logs
into lumber. Works on the felling of trees through the transporting of
logs to sawmills or to a place of sale are entered under $a Logging. <
>   9 681            $i Note under $a Logging <
```

It will be noted that in the earlier example shown for the heading "Lumber" (*see* figure 15.7 on page 371), geographic subdivision is not called for. The code shown following "Geo subd:" in that record is a "fill character" (shown in the example as "_").

The code "i" stands for the word "indirect" which was a former term used to indicate that geographic subdivision was allowed. It still describes the manner in which LCSH goes about providing geographic subdivision. Indirect subdivision means that the elements of the geographic name are to be arranged hierarchically, with a broader place name preceding the local name, e.g., "**Chestnut—Oregon—Portland.**" Each sequential part of the subdivision follows the broader place name regardless of its political, administrative, or regional scope.

Formerly, "direct" subdivision was allowed (and is still used in *Sears*, as explained in chapter 16). This meant that the place name was written as it would be written to address a letter (e.g., "**Opera—Santa Fe, N.M.**"). Late in 1976, "direct" subdivision was abandoned by LC, although there are a few exceptions, which are well defined. The advantage of indirect subdivision is the collocation of material on one topic for one country or state, while direct subdivision separated such material by the first letters of the names of cities. On the other hand, indirect subdivision can sometimes be difficult to apply (e.g., when a geographic entity falls within two countries), whereas direct subdivision allowed use of the established name without alteration.

The following are subdivided "direct" in exception to the "indirect" policy:[39]

- Names of countries (not divided through continent)

- Names of first-order subdivisions (e.g., states) of the United States, Canada, and Great Britain (while there are five countries that are qualified by first-order subdivision rather than country under *AACR2R*, only three of these are subdivided indirectly this way in LCSH)

- Inverted headings for regions (e.g., "**Italy, Northern**")

- Names of geographical entities not wholly within one country

- Two cities: Washington, and Jerusalem. (Hong Kong and Vatican City are treated as countries and are thus also assigned directly)

- Islands "at a distance" from "owning" land masses

- Antartica (entities on the continent are divided through "**Antartica**")

The following list shows some results of the above policy:

> **Catholic Church—France—Paris**
> **Lumbering—Pyrenees (France and Spain)**
> **Children—Ontario—Toronto**
> **Children—Australia—New South Wales** [only two
>   levels are allowed; so a city in New South Wales
>   would follow "**Australia—**":
>   **Children—Australia—Newcastle (N.S.W.)**]
> **Education—Washington (D.C.)**
> **Geology—Islands of the Aegean**
> **Geology—Indonesia—Ambon Island**

For geographic subdivisions, as for geographic headings, local name changes are observed. For instance, works that formerly would have received the heading "**Banks and banking—Leopoldville, Belgian Congo**" are now found under "**Banks and banking—Congo (Democratic Republic)—Kinshasa**." In card catalogs it was very difficult to keep up with such subdivision changes because of the difficulty of finding all occurrences of, for example, "Belgian Congo" used as a subdivision. In online catalogs, keyword searching is making such changes easier, although some critics still object to making such changes "regardless of the form of the name used in the work cataloged."[40]

If both geographical and topical subdivisions are established in the same heading, the last provision for geographical subdivision prevails. For example, the subject heading "Children" may be subdivided geographically. The subdivision "Quotations" is not divided. Therefore, a correct heading would be:

Children—Illinois—Quotations

The subdivision "Dental care" under "Children" *is* divided. Therefore, a correct heading would be:

Children—Dental care—Illinois

Other explanations and illustrations of geographic headings and subdivision practice are issued from time to time. Their best sources are the *Cataloging Service Bulletin*, and the *Subject Cataloging Manual: Subject Headings*.

Form/Genre Subdivisions
(MARC 21 bibliographic and authority subfield $v;
MARC 21 authority record field 185)

While form/genre subdivisions have been assigned in subject heading strings from the beginning of LCSH, they have only been coded separately in the MARC format since February 1999. The need to code form subdivisions differently has occasioned the reevaluation of the use of these subdivisions and their location in subject strings. At the current time, wording of form subdivisions is such that quite often the same word form is used to indicate that the work is about a particular form as the word form used to indicate that the work is an example of a particular form. Coding is according to the function of the word in the subject string, resulting in the possibility of identical subject string constructions being coded differently. For example, "**Science $x Periodicals**" represents a work about science periodicals, while "**Science $v Periodicals**" represents a work that is a periodical that deals with scientific subjects. LC's publication, *Free-Floating Subdivisions: An Alphabetical Index*[41] includes a column for subfield codes, in which a letter "v" appears beside each subdivision that may be coded as a form subdivision.

Free-Floating Subdivisions
(MARC 21 bibliographic and authority subfield $x and/or $v)

For many kinds of primary headings there are a number of identical, or nearly identical, subdivisions that can be applied in specifically defined situations, according to LC's rules, policies, and practices, and that, therefore, do not have separate authority records made for each heading with subdivision combination in which they appear. These are collectively designated "free-floating," but they may not be assigned indiscriminately, for they fall into different groups, each with its own rules and examples. There are five broad groups: general free-floating subdivisions; subdivisions used under classes of persons and ethnic groups; subdivisions used under names of corporate bodies, persons, and families; subdivisions used under place names; and subdivisions controlled by pattern headings. Each group is explained briefly below. All free-floating subdivisions are listed in *Free-Floating Subdivisions: An Alphabetical Index*.[42] In this list they are in alphabetical order, each with a reference to the category in which it appears in *SCM: SH* and with citations to special instructions in the manual when applicable.

- General Free-Floating Subdivisions

General free-floating subdivisions are listed in *SCM: SH*, H1095. Along with each subdivision is a scope note, followed by *See also* references to other subdivisions, when applicable. With some there are also references to other memo numbers in the manual, because the concept represented by the subdivision has an entire instruction sheet about it. Some also include the instruction *"(May Subd Geog)."* Example:

> **—Political aspects** *(May Subd Geog)*   *(H1942)*   *sh85-104440*
> Use under individual religions and topical headings for works on the political dimensions or implications of nonpolitical topics.
> See also **—Politics and government** under names of countries, cities, etc., and under ethnic groups.

An example of a heading using this subdivision is:

Environmental education—Political aspects

- Subdivisions Used under Classes of Persons and Ethnic Groups

These subdivisions are listed in *SCM: SH*, H1100 and H1103. The primary headings under which the list in H1100 may be used include all kinds of classes of persons except ethnic groups and nationalities, which is covered by H1103. Examples of classes of persons are: **Mothers; Youth; Political prisoners; Lungs—Cancer—Patients; Baseball coaches**; and **Afro-American dentists**. Examples of ethnic groups are: **French-Canadians; Dinka (African people); Jews**. Headings for nationalities (e.g., **Ukrainians**) are included when they designate those nationalities *outside* their native countries. Many of the subdivisions in these two lists carry the instruction *"(May Subd Geog)."* Only a few have scope notes. Examples: **Women—Information services; Cuban Americans—Job stress**.

- Subdivisions Used under Names of Corporate Bodies, Persons, and Families

Subdivisions to be used under names of corporate bodies are given in H1105. H1110 lists subdivisions used under names of persons, and H1631 lists those for family names. The subdivisions in H1105 may be used under all types of corporate bodies except conferences, congresses, meetings, or names of jurisdictions. The list has no scope notes as such, but does have footnotes that limit the use of some subdivisions. Example: **Princeton University. Art Museum—Catalogs**.

Subdivisions listed in H1110 may be used under persons of all categories except literary authors. The latter are covered by a pattern heading and are discussed below. This list is like the one for general subdivisions in that there are scope notes and references to other subdivisions. Example: **Lincoln, Abraham, 1809-1865—Correspondence**.

The list of subdivisions to be used under family names is relatively short with no notes. Example: **Lull family—Coin collections**.

- Subdivisions Used under Place Names

Subdivisions to be used under place names are given in two lists: H1140 lists subdivisions used under names of regions, countries, cities, etc., and H1145.5 lists those to be used with names of bodies of water. As for subdivisions under corporate bodies, the list of subdivisions in H1140 is simply a list with no scope notes but with footnotes that limit the use of some subdivisions. Example: **Chicago (Ill.)—Ethnic relations**. The list of subdivisions used with names of bodies of water is very short. Example: **Okmulgee Lake (Okla.)—Recreational use**.

- Subdivisions Controlled by Pattern Headings

Pattern headings are examples of a particular primary heading type that have been entered into the *LCSH* authority file to show all the possible subdivisions that might be used with other specific headings of the same type. A very few may not even apply to the heading under which they are found. For instance, under "**Shakespeare, William, 1564-1616**" a scope note warns us:

> The subdivisions provided under this heading represent for the greater part standard subdivisions usable under any literary author heading, and do not necessarily pertain to Shakespeare.

Besides literary authors, several other categories of specific subjects have distinctive sets of subdivisions applicable to all examples of their genre. These include such categories as educational institutions, monastic and religious orders, languages, musical instruments, industries, military services, animals, diseases, and sports. Pattern headings are represented by examples in the printed LCSH and in the online authority file, but one must have a table to find them. A table in alphabetical order by category is found in the introduction to the printed list. A table grouped by subject field is found in *SCM: SH*, H1146. There is also a separate memo in *SCM: SH* for each pattern heading that explains what is included in the category and lists all allowable subdivisions for that category.

The following table shows some of the pattern headings available:

Subject Field	Category	Pattern Heading(s)
Religion	Religions	**Buddhism**
History and geography	Legislative bodies	**United States. Congress**
Social sciences	Individual educational institutions	**Harvard University**
The arts	Music compositions	**Operas**
Science and technology	Organs and regions of the body	**Heart; Foot**

Following the pattern, if one were cataloging a work about "football" it would be appropriate to find "**Soccer** " in LCSH and choose appropriate subdivisions found there to be used with the heading "**Football**." General free-floating subdivisions are not usually printed under pattern headings, but they may also be used as appropriate.

Subdivision Authority Records

In February 1999 LC began distributing subdivision records for the more than 3,000 topical, form, and chronological free-floating subdivisions in LCSH. These records contain subdivision data in 18x fields. Codes in 073 fields identify location of instructions concerning the subdivisions in *SCM: SH*. All records contain a basic usage statement, and some have references. A typical subdivision record is shown in figure 15.19.

Fig. 15.19. MARC authority record for the subdivision "Indexes."

```
  ARN: 4933911
  Rec stat: n      Entered:     19990225
> Type:      z     Upd status: a     Enc lvl:   n     Source:
  Roman:     _     Ref status: a     Mod rec:         Name use: b
  Govt agn: _      Auth status: a    Subj:      a     Subj use: a
  Series:    n     Auth/ref:   d     Geo subd:  _     Ser use:  b
  Ser num:   n     Name:       n     Subdiv tp: n     Rules:    n <
>    1 010     sh 99001477 <
>    2 040     IEN $b eng $c DLC <
>    3 005     19990226144823.2 <
>    4 073     H 1095 $a H 1100 $a H 1103 $a H 1105 $a H 1110 $z lcsh <
>    5 185     $v Indexes <
>    6 485     $v Bibliography $v Indexes <
>    7 485     $v Dictionaries, indexes, etc. $w nne <
>    8 680     $i Use as a form subdivision under subjects. <
>    9 681     $i Reference under the heading $a Indexes <
```

Classification Aids
(MARC 21 bibliographic field 053)

Many primary subject terms, and some subject subdivisions under those terms, are accompanied by *LC Classification* (*LCC*) notations. Sometimes more than one *LCC* notation is given, with a term from the schedule to show the various aspects of classification represented by the subject heading. Frequently a range of notations is supplied as shown in figure 15.20.

Fig. 15.20. Printed entry showing *LCC* notations in three different areas for the subject heading "Chestnut."

> **Chestnut**   *(May Subd Geog)*
> *[QK495.F14 (Botany)]*
> *[SB401.C4 (Nut trees)]*
> *[SD397.C5 (Forestry)]*
> UF   Castanea sativa
>   Castenea vesca
>   Castanea vulgaris
>   Chestnut tree
>   Common European chestnut
>   English chestnut
>   European chestnut
>   Italian chestnut
>   Spanish chestnut
>   Sweet chestnut
> BT   Castanea
> RT   Cookery (Chestnuts)

In the MARC 21 authorities format the class numbers are given in a field with the tag 053 as shown in figure 15.21. When a term is used to identify the particular aspect the classification represents, that term is coded $c in the 053 field.

Fig. 15.21. MARC authority record showing LCC notations in 053 field.

```
  ARN: 2140296
  Rec stat: c       Entered:     19860211
> Type:     z       Upd status: a      Enc lvl:   n      Source:
  Roman:    _       Ref status: b      Mod rec:          Name use: b
  Govt agn: _       Auth status: a     Subj:      a      Subj use: a
  Series:   n       Auth/ref:   a      Geo subd:  i      Ser use:  b
  Ser num:  n       Name:       n      Subdiv tp: n      Rules:    n <
>    1 010      sh 85023154 <
>    2 040      DLC $c DLC $d DLC <
>    3 005      19910620144255.2 <
>    4 053      QK495.F14 $c Botany <
>    5 053      SB401.C4 $c Nut trees <
>    6 053      SD397.C5 $c Forestry <
>    7 150      Chestnut <
>    8 450      Castanea sativa <
>    9 450      Castanea vesca <
>   10 450      Castanea vulgaris <
>   11 450      Chestnut tree <
>   12 450      Common European chestnut <
>   13 450      English chestnut <
>   14 450      European chestnut <
>   15 450      Italian chestnut <
>   16 450      Spanish chestnut <
>   17 450      Sweet chestnut <
>   18 550      Castanea $w g <
>   19 550      Cookery (Chestnuts) <
>   20 681      $i Example under $a Nuts <
```

These notations are usually supplied when a term is first established. Occasionally they are added at a later time. But there is no systematic checking or revision of these notations unless changes are being made in an existing record for some other reason. Thus, a classification notation could be changed or its meaning revised in the *LCC* schedules, but it might not be changed in LCSH Therefore, these notations are only a guide and should not be assigned without verification.

Filing Arrangement

The list proper in printed versions is given in alphabetical order. Filing rules were revised in 1980 to facilitate computer manipulation, and the revised rules continue to be used. Basic arrangement is word by word. Numbers given in digits precede alphabetic characters in the order of increasing value. Initials separated by punctuation file as separate words. Abbreviations without interior punctuation file as single whole words:

4-H clubs
A3D bomber   USE Skywarrior bomber
A4D (Jet attack plane)   USE Skyhawk (Jet attack plane)
A-36 (Fighter-bomber planes)   USE Mustang (Fighter planes)
A.L.F. Fentress (Va.)   USE Naval Auxiliary Landing Field Fentress (Va.)
A priori
Aage family   USE Agee family
ACI test   USE Adult-child interaction test
ACTH
AK 8 motion picture camera
Alaska
ALGOL (Computer program language)

Punctuation of subject terms affects filing order more immediately than it does in lists such as *Sears*, which sacrifice categorical to straight alphabetical arrangement. Subject headings from LCSH that contain subordinate elements preceded by one or more dashes fall into three groups:

a)   period subdivisions (MARC subfield $y), arranged chronologically according to explicit dates, regardless of whether a descriptive term is used,

b)   topical and form subdivisions (MARC subfield $x and subfield $v), arranged alphabetically, and

c)   geographical subdivisions (MARC subfield $z), arranged alphabetically.

The secondary subdivisions under "**United States—Foreign relations**" illustrate all three groups in order:

a)   **United States—Foreign relations—1775-1783**
United States—Foreign relations—1783-1865
United States—Foreign relations—1789-1809
United States—Foreign relations—War of 1812

b)   **United States—Foreign relations—Executive agreements**
United States—Foreign relations—Historiography
United States—Foreign relations—Juvenile literature
United States—Foreign relations—Law and legislation
United States—Foreign relations—Speeches in Congress
United States—Foreign relations—Treaties

c)   **United States—Foreign relations—Iran**
United States—Foreign relations—Latin America
United States—Foreign relations—Middle East

In actual practice these three groups generally collapse into two, for nearly all period subdivisions follow such topical subdivisions as "**—Civilization,**" "**—Economic conditions,**" "**—Politics and government,**" or "**—History.**" All period subdivisions have explicit dates to allow for computer filing:

United States—History—1849-1877
United States—History—Civil War, 1861-1865
United States—History—1865-
United States—History—1865-1898
United States—History—1865-1921

Prior to 1974 period subdivisions were sometimes indicated only by descriptive terminology (e.g., "**United States—History—Civil War**"), and one may still find these forms in old card catalogs.

In *LCSH* printed versions all subject subdivisions (identified by dashes) file ahead of inverted modifiers, which are punctuated by commas. Inverted modifiers, in turn, file ahead of parenthetical qualifiers. Last of all come phrases that start with the primary term:

Children
Children—Attitudes
Children—Growth
Children—Quotations
Children, Ashanti
Children, Blind
Children, Yoruba
Children (Christian theology)
Children (International law)
Children (Roman law)
Children and animals
Children and strangers
Children as inventors
Children in literature
Children of working parents

In OCLC's display of the online authority file, the inverted modifiers come last in the list after the phrases, rather than right after the heading and its subdivisions.

SUBJECT HEADINGS FOR
CHILDREN'S LITERATURE
(2nd MARC 21 indicator "1" in bibliographic record 650 field;
authority record fixed field 008/17 code "b")

Since 1965 LC has issued a special service for children's catalogers. Known as the Annotated Card Program, it was originated in order to provide "more appropriate and in-depth subject treatment of juvenile titles."[43] A list of specially tailored subject headings is accompanied by a review of commonly used subdivisions, another of subdivisions and qualifiers not used, and general instructions for applying and modifying standard LC subject terms. In the MARC 21 format they are tagged specifically as subject terms for children with a second indicator of *1* in 6XX fields. Some comparative examples are:

LCSH	**Annotated Card List**
Cliff-dwellers	**Cliff dwellers**
Enuresis	**Bedwetting**
Navel	**Belly button**
Phytogeography	**Plant distribution**
Zoogeography	**Animal distribution**

CONCLUSION

In spite of perennial criticisms on grounds of its outdated terminology, illogical syntax, and general inefficiency for precise subject retrieval, LCSH is the most widely accepted controlled vocabulary list in use in English-language libraries today. LC, with considerable prompting from interested bystanders, now and again assesses its virtues and disadvantages, in comparison with other, more scientifically constructed systems. *PRECIS* (*PREserved Context Index System*), inaugurated for the *British National Bibliography* in 1971, received perhaps the strongest consideration as an alternative to, if not a replacement for, LCSH. After cost studies, however, the decision went against any such replacement or supplement. Instead, more intensive efforts are under way to modernize and systematize the existing tool. Many of the features discussed in this chapter represent steps in that direction. For the foreseeable future, this venerable subject list gives every sign of retaining its vitality and preeminence for subject access to library collections.

In the spring of 1991 a special conference was sponsored by LC to bring together experts to discuss possible ways of restructuring *LCSH*. A number of improvements have resulted and are still being accomplished. These and other changes are outlined each quarter in the *Cataloging Service Bulletin* along with lists of changed headings and new headings created that quarter.[44]

NOTES

1.   *Canadian Subject Headings*, 3rd ed. (Ottawa: National Library of Canada, 1992).

2.   *Sears List of Subject Headings*, 17th ed., edited by Joseph Miller (New York: H. W. Wilson, 2000).

3.   Charles Ammi Cutter, *Rules for a Dictionary Catalog*, 4th ed., rewritten (Washington, D.C.: GPO, 1904; republished, London: The Library Association, 1972). The original version of this work was: Charles A. Cutter, "Rules for a Printed Dictionary Catalogue," in *Public Libraries in the United States of America: Their History, Condition, and Management*, United States Bureau of Education (Washington, D.C.: GPO, 1876), Part II.

4.   For fuller information on the origin and development of the LC subject list, *see* Lois Mai Chan, *Library of Congress Subject Headings: Principles and Application*, 3rd ed. (Englewood, Colo.: Libraries Unlimited, 1995); and Richard S. Angell, "Library of Congress Subject Headings—Review and Forecast," in *Subject Retrieval in the Seventies: New Directions*, edited by Hans (Hanan) Wellisch and Thomas D. Wilson (Westport, Conn.: Greenwood Publishing Co., 1972), pp. 143–163.

5.   J. C. M. Hanson, "The Subject Catalogs of the Library of Congress," *Bulletin of the American Library Association* 3 (September 1909): 385–397.

6.   American Library Association, *List of Subject Headings for Use in Dictionary Catalogs* (Boston: Library Bureau, 1895).

7.   Hanson, "Subject Catalogs," p. 387.

8.   Hanson, "Subject Catalogs," p. 389.

9.   Hanson, "Subject Catalogs," p. 390.

10.   David Judson Haykin, *Subject Headings: A Practical Guide* (Washington, D.C.: GPO, 1951), p. 11.

11.   *Subject Headings Used in the Dictionary Catalogues of the Library of Congress*, [1st]–3rd eds. (Washington, D.C.: Library of Congress, Catalog Division, 1910–1928); *Subject Headings Used in the Dictionary Catalogs of the Library of Congress*, 4th–7th eds. (Washington, D.C.: Library of Congress, Subject Cataloging Division, 1943–1966); *Library of Congress Subject Headings*, 8th–12th eds. (Washington, D.C.: Library of Congress, Subject Cataloging Division, 1975–1989); *Library of Congress Subject Headings*, 13th– eds. (Washington, D.C.: Library of Congress, Office for Subject Cataloging Policy, 1990–).

12.   *Library of Congress Subject Headings Weekly Lists* (Washington, D.C.: Library of Congress, Cataloging Policy and Support Office, January 1984–). 1997, no. 1–date (available: http://lcweb.loc.gov/catdir/cpso/cpso.html [accessed 3/5/00]).

13.   *Library of Congress Subject Headings in Microform* (Washington, D.C.: Library of Congress, Cataloging Distribution Service, current issue supersedes all previous issues).

14.   *Classification Plus* (Washington, D.C.: Library of Congress, Cataloging Distribution Service, current issue supersedes all previous issues).

15.   *Subject Cataloging Manual: Subject Headings*, 5th ed. (Washington, D.C.: Cataloging Distribution Service, Library of Congress, 1996). Updates, 1997–   .

16.   *Cataloging Service Bulletin*, no. 1–   (Washington, D.C.: Library of Congress, Processing Services, 1978–   ).

17.   Cutter, *Rules*, 4th ed., pp. 71–72.

18.   Chan, *Library of Congress*, pp. 48–59.

19.   *Subject Cataloging Manual: Subject Headings*, H290; H690, p. 7.

20.   *Subject Cataloging Manual*, H310.

21.   *Subject Cataloging Manual*, H360.

22.   *Subject Cataloging Manual*, H357.

23.   *Subject Cataloging Manual*, H320, H350, H351.

24.   Sanford Berman, *Prejudices and Antipathies: A Tract on the LC Subject Heads Concerning People* (Metuchen, N.J.: Scarecrow, 1971).

25.   Hennepin County Library, Cataloging Section, *Cataloging Bulletin*, May 1973–   .

26.   Doris H. Clack, *Black Literature Resources: Analysis and Organization* (New York: Marcel Dekker, 1975), p. 10.

27.   *Cataloging Service*, bulletin 119 (Fall 1976): 22, 24.

28.   Joan K. Marshall, comp., *On Equal Terms: A Thesaurus for Nonsexist Indexing and Cataloging* (Santa Barbara, Calif.: American Bibliographical Center–Clio Press, 1977).

29.   *Subject Cataloging Manual*, H708.

30.   American Library Association, Subject Analysis Committee, 1993, "Definition of Form Data" (available: http://www.pitt.edu/~agtaylor/ala/form-def.htm [accessed 3/5/00]).

31.   Subject Analysis Committee, Subcommittee on Subject Access to Individual Works of Fiction, Drama, etc., *Guidelines on Subject Access to Individual Works of Fiction, Drama, Etc.* (Chicago: American Library Association, 1990). New edition to be published in 2000.

32.   *Subject Cataloging Manual*, H362.

33.   E. J. Coates, *Subject Catalogues: Headings and Structure* (London: Library Association, 1960).

34.   George M. Sinkankis, "A Study in the Syndetic Structure of the Library of Congress List of Subject Headings" (Pittsburgh, Pa.: University of Pittsburgh, 1972).

35.   Toni Petersen, "The AAT: A Model for the Restructuring of LCSH," *Journal of Academic Librarianship* 9 (September 1983): 207–210.

36.   Mary Dykstra, "LC Subject Headings Disguised as a Thesaurus," *Library Journal* 113 (March 1, 1988): 42–46.

37.   *Subject Cataloging Manual*, H370.

38.   *Library of Congress Subject Headings*, "Introduction" in *Cataloger's Desktop/Classification Plus,* issue 2 (May 1999).

39.   *Subject Cataloging Manual*, H830, H807.

40.   *Cataloging Service*, bulletin 120 (Winter 1977): 10.

41.   *Free-Floating Subdivisions: An Alphabetical Index*, 1st ed.–   (Washington, D.C.: Library of Congress, 1989–   ).

42.   Ibid.

43.   *LCSH*, "Introduction."

44.   *Cataloging Service Bulletin.*

SUGGESTED READING

Berman, Sanford. *Prejudices and Antipathies: A Tract on the LC Subject Heads Concerning People*. Jefferson, N.C.: McFarland & Co., 1993.

Chan, Lois Mai. *Library of Congress Subject Headings: Principles and Application*. 3rd ed. Englewood, Colo.: Libraries Unlimited, 1995.

Ferguson, Bobby. *Subject Analysis: Blitz Cataloging Workbook.* Englewood, Colo.: Libraries Unlimited, 1998. Chapter 1: Library of Congress Subject Headings.

Foskett, A. C. *The Subject Approach to Information*. 5th ed. London: Library Association Publishing, 1996. Chapter 23: Library of Congress Subject Headings.

Library of Congress Subject Headings: "Introduction." Washington, D.C.: Library of Congress, Cataloging Distribution Service, [current issue].

Mann, Thomas. *Doing Research at the Library of Congress: A Guide to Subject Searching in a Closed Stacks Library*. Washington, D.C.: Library of Congress, Humanities and Social Sciences Division, 1994.

———. *Library Research Models: A Guide to Classification, Cataloging, and Computers*. New York: Oxford University Press, 1993.

Studwell, William E. *Library of Congress Subject Headings: Philosophy, Practice and Prospects*. New York: Haworth Press, 1990.

16 > Sears List of Subject Headings (Sears)

INTRODUCTION

The *Sears List of Subject Headings* (*Sears*), now in its seventeenth edition, is widely used by small public libraries and by school libraries. It is very much smaller in scope and more general in treatment than *Library of Congress Subject Headings* (*LCSH*), which is commonly used in academic and research libraries. Its history of continuous publication is not so long-standing as that of the Library of Congress (LC) list. The preface states:

> Minnie Earl Sears prepared the first edition of this work in response to demands for a list of subject headings that was better suited to the needs of the small library than the existing American Library Association and Library of Congress lists. Published in 1923, the *List of Subject Headings for Small Libraries* was based on the headings used by nine small libraries that were known to be well cataloged.[1]

For many years *Sears* followed *LCSH* fairly closely, differing mainly in level of specificity (although its principles encourage specific entry and creation of headings of greater specificity when needed). In its earlier editions *Sears* used the broader headings from *LCSH*. However, in the most recent editions, *Sears* has shown more independence.

TERMINOLOGY

New headings for recent editions of *Sears* were suggested by librarians representing various sizes and types of libraries and by H. W. Wilson catalogers responsible for the Standard Catalog series, *Book Review Digest*, and various periodical indexes. (Wilson also has published a special interest companion volume for Canadian libraries and a Spanish language translation.[2]) *LCSH* was consulted, but modifications of *LCSH* were made to meet the needs of smaller collections. Included among the terms in *Sears* are some terms from LC's "Subject Headings for Children's Literature." Examples of *Sears*'s comparative brevity and simplicity are: *Sears* uses "**Crisis centers**" and "**Litigation**"; LCSH uses "**Crisis intervention (Mental health services)**" and "**Actions and defenses**" as primary headings. *Sears* uses "**Hallucinogens**" and "**Silk screen printing**"; LCSH uses only narrower terms:

"Hallucinogenic drugs," "Hallucinogenic plants," "Screen process printing," and "Serigraphy."

Modernization of Terminology

Sears has undergone the same attempts to eliminate racist, sexist, and pejorative headings that have been made with LCSH. For example, the heading "**Negro actors**," was replaced by "**Black actors**," while "**Air lines—Hostesses**" became "**Flight attendants**," and **Man (Theology)** was changed to **Human beings (Theology)**. Other headings with prejudicial connotations disappeared or underwent purification rites. The tenth edition's "**Jewish question**" disappeared along with "**Women in aeronautics**" and most other "**Women in ...** " and all "**Women as ...** " headings. "**Underdeveloped areas**" was downgraded into a USE reference to "**Developing areas**" in the eleventh edition, changed to a USE reference to "**Third World**" in the twelfth edition, and then became a USE reference to "**Developing countries**" in the thirteenth edition. "**Insanity**" was converted into a USE reference to "**Mental illness—Jurisprudence**" in the fourteenth edition, which, in turn, became "**Insanity defense**" in the sixteenth edition. "**Man, Primitive**" became "**Non-literate man**" in the fourteenth edition, followed by becoming "**Primitive societies**" in the sixteenth edition.

Modernization has also occurred with time periods. "**Renaissance**" has been replaced by the subdivision "**15th and 16th centuries**" (e.g., "**Renaissance decoration and ornament**" became "**Decoration and ornament—15th and 16th centuries**"). The adjective "Modern" has been eliminated (e.g., "**Modern architecture—1800–1899 (19th century)**" has been replaced by "**Architecture—19th century**," and the former "**Modern art**" is now either "**Modernism in art**" or "**Art—20th century**," or both).

Other updating of terminology includes subdividing headings for policy geographically rather than having the term as a subdivision under geographic heading (e.g., "**Social policy—United States**" rather than "**United States—Social policy**") and making compound headings that include the word "state" into the term subdivided by "Government policy" ("**Science—Government policy**" instead of "**Science and state**").

Problems of Updating Terminology

Some linguistic change would have occurred, no doubt, regardless of the social climate. However, formal subject lists have tended to be conservative in their response to new terminology. In attempting to retain the goodwill of their constituents, they are understandably sensitive to the disruptions caused to a library's cataloging routines when an unduly large number of new subject forms are mandated at one time. Still, the argument that an obsolete form reflects usage in the bulk of the literature indexed is specious. Furthermore, it becomes misleading as new materials with new terminology are added. On the other hand, librarians with card catalogs fear not only the time and effort required to change large numbers of entries, but also the stresses placed on the filing apparatus when revised cards must be moved from one section of the catalog to another. As online catalogs have become the norm, this problem has eased.

SEARS LIST OF SUBJECT HEADINGS' (SEARS)
USE OF SUBJECT HEADING THEORY

The general philosophy of *Sears* is contained in two phrases, both of which the cataloger should remember as he or she makes specific application of the list to the individual materials in the library's collection.[3]

"The principle of specific entry" means that a specific heading is preferred to a general one. For a book about cats alone, "**Cats**" is preferred to "**Domestic animals.**" On the other hand, the headings "**Siamese cats**" or "**Seal-point Siamese cats**" might be too specific for some libraries, although the principle of specific entry would place a work on Siamese cats under that heading, and *Sears* has a general reference under "**Cats**" that reads: "See Also names of specific breeds of cats, to be added as needed." The cataloger must know the collection, know its emphases, and know something of the way people use it to be prepared to assign subject headings to it. Are users likely to look for very specific headings, or do they expect to find information under a more general collocating category?

"The principle of unique heading" means that one subject heading, and one alone, is chosen for all items on that subject. The choice of subject headings must be logical and consistent. References should be inserted in the catalog wherever it is anticipated that patrons are likely to approach the topic through different terminology. A few general principles or guidelines are useful for constructing subject headings:

- Prefer the English word or phrase unless a foreign one best expresses the idea. *Sears*, for example, carries the reference "Laissez faire. USE **Free enterprise**; **Industrial policy**."

- Try to use terms that are used in other libraries as well, unless the library in question is highly specialized or otherwise unique.

- Try to use terms that will cover the field, i.e., terms that will apply to more than one item.

References

Sears breaks down references into three main categories, and the introduction discusses each in some detail: specific *See* references; specific *See also* references; and general references.[4] (References in *Sears* carry the same designations as in *LCSH*, that is, USE, UF, SA, BT, NT, and RT; however, the introduction still identifies these as "see," "see also," and "general" references, possibly because of the number of smaller catalogs that still contain references designated in this way rather than "search also under" or other newer reference forms.)

See references are considered essential to the success of the catalog. Yet the cataloger in a local library may not find necessary every *See* reference suggested in the list. For example, *Sears* proposes "Plants, Edible USE **Edible plants**." There is also a narrower term reference under "**Plants**" to "**Edible plants**," and in a small catalog, the inverted reference could be superfluous. The most frequent and helpful varieties of *See* references direct the user from:

- Synonyms or terms so nearly synonymous that they would cover the same kind of material, e.g., "Chemical geology USE **Geochemistry**" and "Pay equity USE **Equal pay for equal work**."

- The second part of a compound heading, e.g., "Illusions USE **Hallucinations and illusions**" and "Motels USE **Hotels and motels**."

- Variant spellings or initialisms to the accepted spelling or full form, e.g., "Gipsies USE **Gypsies**" and "ESP USE **Extrasensory perception**."

- Opposites when they are included without being specifically mentioned, e.g., "Disobedience USE **Obedience**" and "Truth in advertising USE **Deceptive advertising**."

- The singular to the plural when the two forms would not file together, e.g., "Goose USE **Geese**."

See also references pose theoretical and practical problems that jeopardize their efficacy. Yet both *Sears* and *LCSH* make heavy use of them. The above warning against making references simply because they are suggested in a standard list holds as true for *See also* references as it does for *See* references.

It was stated in chapters 14 and 15 that *See also* references normally move downward from a general term to a more specific term or terms, e.g., "**Conservation of natural resources** *See also* **Energy conservation; Nature conservation**." In this example the general term refers to two more specific terms. The user who pursues the reference by looking under "**Nature conservation**" will find a still more specific downward reference to more headings: "**Nature conservation** *See also* **Endangered species; Landscape protection; Natural monuments; Plant conservation; Wildlife conservation**." While the reference in the catalog may appear as just shown, the designation in the list for these terms is "NT," for "narrower term(s)." The list also includes terms designated "BT," for "broader term(s)." As mentioned in chapter 15, some catalogs also make *See also* references to broader terms.

Sears also indulges in a high number of bilateral or reciprocal references, where the movement is horizontal, between related subjects of more or less equal specificity. These terms are designated "RT," for "related term(s)," in the list. The following examples have been pruned of extraneous terms, to make their reciprocity more visible:

Gods and goddesses *See also* **Mythology; Religions**

Mythology *See also* **Gods and goddesses**

Religions *See also* **Gods and goddesses**

Mollusks *See also* **Shells**

Shells *See also* **Mollusks**

In the case of general *See* and *See also* references, the more specific terms being referred to are so diverse or numerous that it is suggested that specific references be made from a broader term to all narrower terms on the next level of specificity.

General references to terms with subdivisions present another problem. That is, when the list gives "Illustrations *See* subjects with the subdivision *Pictorial Works*; e.g. **Animals—Pictorial works; United States—History—1861–1865,**

Civil War—Pictorial works; etc." and the library that has subject entries for both referrals adds a book consisting largely of pictures of children, should the cataloger revise the reference entry by inserting "**Children—Pictorial works**" as a third illustration? Or can he or she depend on the "etc." to cover all subsequent examples? Most libraries follow the second option, thus throwing the burden of search on the user, who probably either will not understand the instructions or, after a bit of desultory searching, will give up, unless the catalog is online and the system allows the possibility of doing a search on just the "Pictorial works" segment of headings. However well the user copes, valuable materials may be overlooked.[5]

Sears enumerates seven major types of general references:[6]

1. Common names of various members of a class, e.g., "**Dogs** *See also* types of dogs, e.g. **Guide dogs**; and names of specific breeds of dogs, to be added as needed"

2. Names of individual persons, etc., e.g., "**Presidents—United States** *See also* names of presidents, to be added as needed"

3. Names of particular institutions, buildings, societies, etc., e.g., "**Bridges** *See also* names of individual bridges, to be added as needed"

4. Names of particular geographic features, e.g., "**Natural monuments** *See also* names of individual natural monuments, to be added as needed"

5. Names of places subdivided by subject, e.g., "Defenses USE types of defenses, e.g. **Air** defenses; and names of continents, regions, countries, and individual colonies with the subdivision *Defenses*, e.g. **United States—Defenses**; to be added as needed"

6. Subjects followed by form subdivisions, e.g., "Case studies USE subjects with the subdivision *Case studies*, e.g. **Juvenile delinquency—Case studies**; to be added as needed"

7. Subjects with national adjectives, e.g., "**Essays** . . . Collections of literary essays by American authors are entered under **American essays**; by English authors, under **English essays**; etc."

STRUCTURE OF SUBJECT HEADINGS

Like LCSH, *Sears* terms consist of a variety of forms, ranging from a single noun to different kinds of complex descriptive phrases:[7]

- The single noun is the most desirable form of subject heading if it is specific enough to fit the item at hand and the needs of the library. In general, if there is a significant difference between the singular and plural forms, the plural is preferred (e.g., "Mouse USE **Mice**"). However, there are situations where the singular form is used to cover abstract ideas or general usage (e.g., "**Essay**" as a literary form), while the plural designates individual examples of the form.

- The modified noun takes at least two forms: a) normal word order (e.g., "**Health maintenance organizations**"), and b) explanatory modifier added in parentheses (e.g., "**Hotlines (Telephone counseling)**"). Formerly, inverted word order was used, but now it is only used as a "used for" term from which a reference is made to the normal word order (e.g., "Technical assistance, American USE **American technical assistance**").

- The compound heading is usually two nouns joined by *and*, but the nouns are sometimes also modified (e.g., "**Coal mines and mining**"). The terms are conjoined for various reasons:

    —To link related topics. Usually both ideas are covered in a single treatise, e.g., "**Anarchism and anarchists**," "**Clocks and watches**," and "**Puppets and puppet plays**."

    —To link opposites. Again, the pairs are often discussed together, e.g., "**Corrosion and anticorrosives**," "**Good and evil**," and "**Joy and sorrow**."

- In most cases, usage dictates the order of terms, but when that fails, alphabetical order is preferred. If a library should acquire enough materials under one of two such terms to make searching difficult or tiresome, the cataloger might consider splitting the subject heading into its two components, with linking references. For example, *LCSH* has broken its former heading "**Antigens and antibodies**" into "**Antigens**" and "**Immunoglobulins**."

- The phrase heading may be prepositional (e.g., "**Cost and standard of living**"), serial (e.g., "**Plots (Drama, fiction, etc.)**"), or an intriguing combination of forms (e.g., "**Superhero comic books, strips, etc.**" or "**Life support systems (Medical environment)**").

TYPES OF SUBDIVISIONS

Subject subdivisions indicate a specialized aspect of a broad subject or point of view (e.g., "**Artificial satellites—Orbits**"). They are set off from the primary heading by a dash. Unlike the *LCSH* printed versions, *Sears* does not separate the category from references that are inverted with commas (e.g., "Artificial satellites, American USE **American artificial satellites**") or from phrases beginning with the same words (e.g., "**Artificial satellites in telecommunication**"), but interfiles all entries in straight alphabetical order, letter by letter to the end of each word, disregarding punctuation, following the American Library Association (ALA) filing rules that are discussed in chapter 20 and in the Appendix. [8]

A primary purpose of the subject subdivision is to subdivide topics that are broad in scope or that have much written about them (e.g., "**Education**"). Without subdivision, there would be many entries under such headings subarranged only by main entry or by date. Such headings with large numbers of entries can be tedious for a catalog user to search. Subdivision allows grouping of the entries in meaningful ways, e.g.,

Education—Aims and objectives

Education—Curricula

Education—Experimental methods

Subdivisions may be compounded under a given topic. As many as three are used for such a subtopic as "**United States—History—1861-1865, Civil War—Medical care**." In it are displayed several of the different types of subdivisions:

1. Form subdivisions are used, like the Dewey Decimal Classification form divisions, to indicate the physical (e.g., ". . . **—Bibliography**") or philosophical (e.g., ". . . **—Research**") form of the work and may be used by the cataloger to divide practically any subject heading in the list, if local policy allows the cataloger to add such subdivisions even if they are not "established" in the list. In addition there are many general and topical subdivisions that may be used under subjects as appropriate. These are given in the list with instructions for their use as subdivisions with appropriate subject headings.

2. *Sears*, like *LCSH*, has a group of headings that serve as patterns for the subdivisions that may be used under all headings of the same type. Some of these "Key Headings" are:[9]

    Persons:
    Presidents—United States (to illustrate subdivisions that may be used under presidents, prime ministers, and other rulers)

    Shakespeare, William, 1564–1616 (to illustrate subdivisions that may be used under any voluminous author)

    Places:
    United States; Ohio; Chicago (Ill.) (to illustrate subdivisions—except for historical periods—under geographic names)

    Languages and Literatures:
    English language (to illustrate subdivisions that may be used with any language)

    English literature (to illustrate subdivisions that may be used with any literature)

    In order to use the subdivisions under the key headings, one finds the appropriate example (e.g., "**English language—Idioms**") and then applies the subdivision to the heading for the item in hand (e.g., "**French language—Idioms**").

3. Some special topic divisions cannot readily be transferred from one heading to another because they are specially tailored to bring out important aspects of individual topics, e.g., "**Deaf—Means of communication**" or "**Airplanes—Piloting**." One could not reasonably use "**Deaf—Piloting**" or "**Airplanes—Means of communication**." Such divisions are listed in full in the body of the list, being for the most part nontransferable.

4. Time divisions, which apply most frequently to history, define a specific chronology for the primary topic. Some consist merely of dates (e.g., "**Europe—History—1789–1900**"). Often the date or dates are followed by a descriptive phrase (e.g., "**Church history—30–600, Early church**"). Prior to the twelfth edition the descriptive phrase preceded the dates in such headings. The change in position facilitates filing in chronological order both manually and by machine. Occasionally the chronological designation is an inverted qualifier rather than a subdivision (e.g., "**Gettysburg (Pa.), Battle of, 1863**").

5. Geographic divisions are of two forms: a) area—subject, e.g., "**Chicago (Ill.)—Census**," and b) subject—area, e.g., "**Geology—Bolivia**." *Sears* adds parenthetical instructions to those headings in its list that may be divided by place, e.g., "**Geology** (May subdiv. geog.)." Under some headings the instructions are more detailed, e.g., "**American Hostages** (May subdiv. geog. except U.S.)."

   Unlike LCSH, *Sears* does not dictate the form of geographic subdivisions. The introduction to the sixteenth edition specifies that *Sears* prefers direct place subdivision (in which the name of the place discussed in the work is used directly as the subdivision) over indirect place subdivision (in which the name of a larger geographic area is interposed between the subject and a smaller area discussed in the work). *Sears* uses the *AACR2* form of a place name in using direct subdivision (i.e., "**—Chicago (Ill.)**," not just "**—Chicago**"), but it does not mandate this usage for the libraries using its list. Some libraries may wish to follow LCSH practice and use indirect place subdivision. If direct place subdivision is chosen, it is wise to use *AACR2* form for the sake of consistency.

   Geographic area subdivided by subject situations are less conspicuous in the list, but play an important role in most library catalogs. Instructions may take the form: "**Italy** . . . May be subdivided like U.S. except for *History*."

   Subject headings in various fields, especially in the fields of science, technology, and economics, usually are subdivided by place. Those in history, geography, and politics usually are made subdivisions under place.[10] It is assumed that the real subject of a book about Colorado history, and the one the patron will most likely consult, is "**Colorado**," not "**History**." In *Sears*, the subject entry "**History**" is used only for general works on history as an intellectual discipline.

HEADINGS FOR BELLES-LETTRES

Individual works of belles-lettres (e.g., novels, plays, and poetry) are not always assigned subject headings. It is assumed that patrons are more likely to seek access to these materials through author or title. However, there are many themes of literature that may be used as subject headings. In the list of form subdivisions supplied by *Sears* ". . . —**Fiction**" appears as a suggested option for libraries that prefer to make subject headings for fictionalized history or biography. Thus, a novel about the Six Day War in the Middle East might be given the subject heading, "**Israel-Arab War, 1967—Fiction**." In addition other genre headings, such as "**Mystery fiction**" or "**Science fiction**," can be assigned to these works.

For literary anthologies it is common to give a genre heading with the subdivision "**—Collections**" (e.g., "**Poetry—Collections**"; "**American drama—Collections**"), but *Sears* sometimes uses the plural noun (e.g., "**Essays**") rather than using the subdivision.[11] Topical headings reflecting themes of the work as a whole are also common (e.g., "**Love poetry**"; "**Dogs—Fiction**").

PHYSICAL CHARACTERISTICS AND FORMAT OF *SEARS LIST OF SUBJECT HEADINGS (SEARS)*

The sixteenth edition of *Sears* opens with a preface that gives its historical setting and identifies the authoritative sources and the new features incorporated in it. It is followed by an explanatory essay that has become a Sears tradition, undergoing considerable expansion in scope and detail over the years. This essay is called "Principles of the Sears List of Subject Headings."[12] It treats both the theoretical and practical aspects of subject heading work. It merits careful reading, not only by those planning to use the *Sears* list, but also by anyone wishing to gain knowledge of traditional subject list usage.

In the list proper, subject entries are printed in boldface type. USE references appear in lightface type in the same alphabet. Filing in *Sears* has already been discussed under "Types of Subdivisions." The following excerpt shows the various elements that may be included under a subject entry, although not every entry requires all of these elements:

Children's poetry   **808.81; 809.1; 811, etc.; 811.008, etc.; 811.009, etc.**
> Use for individual poems, collections, or materials about poetry written for children. Individual works and collections of poetry written by children are entered under the form heading **Children's writings**. Materials about poetry written by children are entered under **Child authors**.
> UF   Poetry for children
> BT   **Children's literature**
>   **Poetry**
> NT   **Children's songs**
>   **Lullabies**
>   **Nonsense verses**
>   **Nursery rhymes**
>   **Tongue twisters**

DDC numbers from the thirteenth edition of the *Abridged Dewey Decimal Classification* are given with the permission of the publisher, Forest Press, a division of OCLC. The above example shows the associated *DDC* numbers in their customary place, on the same line with the subject entry. Note that three numbers are specifically included, together with an "etc.," to remind the user that he or she might profitably seek further in the *DDC* to find the best number for the particular need.

Scope notes have been used more extensively in each new edition of *Sears*. The one in the example above is typical. The reader receives first a positive instruction on appropriate use of the entry. Then comes a negative instruction (albeit stated positively) on the kinds of material that should be placed under a different entry.

The initials UF (standing for "used for") normally follow the scope note or, if there is no scope note, the entry proper. The letters UF before one or more terms mean that a *See* reference is recommended from each such term to the heading under which the UF appears. Terms preceded by UF are never used as subject headings. Next come the letters BT followed by terms in boldface type that represent concepts broader than the concept represented in the heading. Next come the letters NT. They precede a list in boldface type of more specific headings that the user might like to explore. Each boldface entry in this list is a legitimate subject heading. Reference to these *See also* headings might very well lead to further *See also* headings that could help expand or modify the search to reveal the full range of materials available in the particular collection. But a *See also* reference is not usually made unless the catalog actually has material under the heading referred to (*see* discussion of this issue in chapter 15).

Thus, *Sears* suggests the following references for the subject entry "**Children's poetry**," but the local cataloger is expected to consider each on its merits, in view of the terminology used by the library's clientele and the presence of other subject entries in the catalog:

Poetry for children
    See **Children's poetry**

Children's literature
    See also **Children's poetry**

Poetry
    See also **Children's poetry**

Children's poetry
    See also **Children's songs**
            Lullabies
            Nonsense verses
            Nursery rhymes
            Tongue twisters

Sears includes a list of "Headings to Be Added by the Cataloger."[13] Nine varieties of proper names and five of common names, are identified, for which there is no attempt to include all possibilities in the printed list. One or two obvious names of each variety can be found in the list proper, to serve as examples or because important or typical subdivisions have been given. The cataloger is also reminded that general *See also* references imply other specific names that the cataloger is to add as needed, using available reference sources to establish correct entry forms.

UPDATING

Sears updates its usage by successive editions. New print editions are published every three years or so. A machine-readable version, available on tape, is updated annually. The relatively limited scope of *Sears*, for use in small and medium-size libraries, makes comprehensive revision manageable for both editors and users. The results are more coherently integrated than the ad hoc revisions issued for *LCSH*. However, some may believe that one to three years is too long to wait for updated terminology in today's rapidly changing environment. LC's publication of the "Weekly Lists" and weekly updating of the online LCSH permit (if they do not always ensure) easy professional response on the part of one enormous library to inevitable, but generally unpredictable, shifts in publishing interests and emphases. Actually neither approach monopolizes all the advantages. What matters is that every viable subject access mode remain under constant surveillance and revision, offering a dynamic compromise between rigid custom and assimilative change.

CONCLUSION

The assigning of subject headings is a discipline that inevitably seems complicated and bewildering to the neophyte cataloger. Unlike other cataloging disciplines, it has no logical progression other than the linguistic development of knowledge itself. Even the assigning of a classification number to a book is less forbidding, for the novice usually has some sort of previous orientation to the Dewey system and can see, if dimly, the divisions of knowledge and why they should exist. Subject headings are, however, not difficult once the cataloger learns to handle them. Both *Sears* and *LCSH* are quite explicit in their directions; both contain lists of general subdivisions with specific instructions for their use. If followed consistently, they will provide useful reference guides for the user, including the reference librarian.

A beginning cataloger should study the subject list used in the local library. It would be helpful to choose a subject in which he or she is personally interested, tracing it throughout the list and observing the interrelation of references. There are other aids, such as the reference tools in the library. They amplify subjects and clarify aspects not immediately understood, especially in an age when no one can expect to know everything. The library's shelflist and public catalog are also helpful. The former can suggest subject headings if the cataloger has a classification number in mind, since most shelflists consist of full unit records, with tracings for the subject entries of each cataloged item. The public catalog can suggest classification numbers if the would-be cataloger has a subject heading in mind. Neither is a completely reliable crutch. Books are very often written about new subjects and about more than one subject. The vagaries of past and present individual catalogers, however experienced, may mislead. Yet both resources are generally helpful; both serve to characterize the practices of the local library. To become a successful cataloger, one must know what is current local practice and work within that frame of reference. Major changes should not be put into effect until the reasons for what is done are fully understood and the reactions of other users and fellow librarians can be anticipated.

NOTES

1. *Sears List of Subject Headings*, 16th ed., edited by Joseph Miller (New York: H. W. Wilson, 1997), p. vii. (The 16th ed. is cited because of unavailability of the 17th ed. at the time of writing.)

2. Lynne Isberg Lighthall, *Sears List of Subject Headings; Canadian Companion*, 4th ed. (New York: H. W. Wilson, 1992); *Sears—Lista de Encabezamientos de Materia: Traducción y Adaptación de la 12a. Edición en Inglés*, ed. por Barbara M. Westby; trans. por Carmen Rovira (New York: H. W. Wilson, 1984) [Spanish translation now out-of-print].

3. For more detailed discussion of the theory of subject headings, refer to chapter 14, "Verbal Subject Access."

4. The list of reference types is adapted from *Sears*, p. xxx–xxxiv, but the examples are changed, to give alternative insights.

5. *Sears*, pp. xxxiii–xxxiv, also discusses this problem.

6. *Sears*, p. xxxiii.

7. For a review of the structure of *LCSH* and further comment on some of the points mentioned here, *see* "Types of Topical Subject Headings" in chapter 15 and "The Choice of Subject Headings" in chapter 14.

8. *See* pp. 382–383 of this text to compare the filing used in the printed versions of *LCSH* with that found in *Sears*.

9. *Sears*, p. xl.

10. *Sears*, p. xxiii–xxiv.

11. *Sears*, p. xxvii–xxix.

12. Much of the foregoing discussion is based on this essay.

13. *Sears*, p. xxxix.

SUGGESTED READING

Ferguson, Bobby. *Subject Analysis: Blitz Cataloging Workbook*. Englewood, Colo.: Libraries Unlimited, 1998. Chapter 2: Sears List of Subject Headings.

Foskett, A. C. *The Subject Approach to Information*. 5th ed. London: Library Association Publishing, 1996, pp. 348–353.

"Principles of the Sears List of Subject Headings." In *Sears List of Subject Headings*. 17th ed., edited by Joseph Miller. New York: H. W. Wilson, 2000, pp. xv–xxxvi.

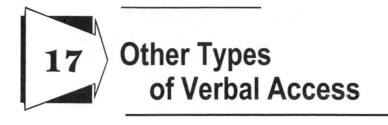

Other Types
of Verbal Access

INTRODUCTION

For well over a century libraries have provided subject retrieval from their holdings through the use of pre-coordinate lists of integrated and cross-referenced topical headings. The preceding chapters have discussed *Sears Lists of Subject Headings* (*Sears*) and *Library of Congress Subject Headings* (*LCSH*), which remain the most universally recognized linguistic tools for analyzing library collections. Recent developments in information science offer new modes of indexing that throw both practical and theoretical light on traditional subject lists. Some of the techniques are offered as supplements, or even substitutes, for traditional subject catalogs. This chapter reviews those enterprises most pertinent to library subject retrieval and explains briefly the applications of the more successful ones.

DEVELOPMENTS IN DOCUMENT
INDEXING

The word *index* still connotes book and periodical indexes more often than it does subject catalogs for library collections. However, library indexes and catalogs are nearly as old as alphabets, being present in some form with almost every organized collection of written records as far back as the early Mesopotamian and Egyptian archives. In the final years of the nineteenth and the early years of the twentieth centuries, catalogers frequently made numerous "analytics" to significant informational works in their libraries. Books were expensive. The high cost of acquisitions and the relative scarcity of printed materials were countered with efforts to exploit collections intensively. Librarians were a captive labor force, often with "disposable time" on the job. And what more profitable "pick- up work" could there be than making analytic indexes to anthologies and treatises? If the cards followed standard cataloging practices they were filed into the official catalog. If they were less carefully constructed, they might be kept in a desk drawer or a shoe box in the reference department. John Rothman points to a continuing reciprocity between library classification and indexing:

Although indexing is often clearly differentiated from cataloging and classification, there is considerable overlapping in practice, and the development of new cataloging techniques or new classification systems is bound to affect indexing practices. Thus the development of the Dewey and other decimal classification systems for library catalogs was paralleled by the development of decimal, coded, and faceted topical indexing systems.[1]

Coordinate Indexing

The post-World War II information explosion dramatized the values of good indexing. Older methods that had gone into eclipse were revived and improved. New theories sprang up to support other techniques. A major departure from the relatively simple hierarchical use of subordinate divisions and inverted modifiers in traditional subject heading lists was the idea of postcoordinate searching, in which the searcher could play a more active role. A coordinate index consists of a list of subject terms in a standard format. Each term is independent of all others, except for cross references, and is designed to retrieve all documents for which it is specifically relevant. A user can stop at the single-term level of search if he or she is satisfied with the results. True postcoordinate searching moves on to a second level. Taking two or more terms that together delimit a still more specific search topic, and comparing the records indexed under each, the searcher retrieves only those items that have been indexed under all the chosen terms.

Suppose the searcher is looking for material on the use of solar energy for drying grain. The index might offer the terms "Solar energy," "Heat engines," and "Grain." Perhaps five document citations emerge because they are all entered under all three terms. The searcher makes the matches and consults those documents. In a traditional printed subject catalog this type of postcoordinate searching is awkward and difficult. The underlying assumption is that the list itself is precoordinate. That is, the assimilation and matching of concepts has already been done by the cataloger and is implicit in the terminology of the list. Thus, *LCSH* offers the subject headings **"Solar energy in agriculture"** and **"Grain—Drying"** as subject identifiers for the above items. In a printed catalog there would be no way of matching the two concepts to specify the available items except by comparing subject entries under each heading or examining full bibliographic records to find those on which both headings were traced.

In postcoordinate indexing, the coordination of terms is the responsibility of the searcher, rather than of the subject cataloger. The terms are usually single nouns, and the specific document citations frequently take the form of accession numbers (rarely hierarchical class or call numbers). In 1953 Mortimer Taube introduced what he called the Uniterm index, to emphasize its postcoordinate use of single terms as opposed to composite headings.[2] It was primarily a manual system, using cards with headings displayed at the top and 10 columns in which document accession numbers could be entered according to the number's final digit. For example, documents 56A, 306, 96, 1176, and 1006 might all be listed in column 6 of each of the three cards bearing the Uniterms "Solar energy," "Heat engines," and "Grain." The technique, known as terminal digit posting, has been most successful in its computerized applications, where some of the tediousness and error-proneness of manual listing is forestalled.

To overcome the disadvantages of a visual search, other modes of post-coordinate indexing soon developed. Mechanical scanning devices were based on the fact that cards could be precisely gridded for punched holes to replace the columns of written or printed numbers. Two or more of these punched cards (e.g., the three carrying the headings "Solar energy," "Heat engines," and "Grain") could be laid together and held up to the light, or otherwise probed, to extract the reference numbers that they indexed in common. Various brands of these cards have been marketed, variously called optical coincidence cards, peek-a-boo cards, or feature cards.

A newer form of coordinate indexing is that created by keyword access in online catalogs and other databases. This has been described by Bates (italics original):

> [I]n fact, *online search capabilities themselves constitute a form of indexing*. Subject access to online catalogs is thus a combination of original indexing and what we might call "search capabilities indexing." ...
>
> Typical online search capabilities are keyword searching, Boolean searching, truncation, and multi-index searching (that is, combining query terms from more than one index, e.g., "FIND TITLE Grapes AND FIND AUTHOR Steinbeck").
>
> ... When an online catalog simply possesses the capability of being searched by title keyword, in effect a whole new index is added to the catalog, with every title word an index term, even though the whole index is not seen printed out.[3]

Typically, online catalogs with keyword access allow the user to input several search terms to be searched at once with an implicit Boolean "and" in operation. That is, a keyword search may be "solar energy grain," which the system interprets to mean "Find bibliographic records that have the words 'solar' AND 'energy' AND 'grain'." While this method can yield false drops (e.g., "Electrical energy characterization of grain boundaries in gallium arsenide and their relationship to solar cell performance"), it can also yield a number of useful retrievals in much less time than that needed for manual indexing. It cannot be a complete substitute for manual indexing, however, because keyword vocabulary is not controlled (i.e., no connections are made between synonyms, variant word forms, related terms, etc.), not all titles contain subject-content words, and authors writing on the same concepts use different words to express those concepts.

Hierarchic or Subordination Indexing

The subsuming of narrower terms or subdivisions under broader terms is familiar to librarians in many contexts. We spoke in previous chapters of its use for library subject catalogs. Printed indexes frequently indent secondary words under primary ones and make use of *see* and *see also* references. The rapid growth of online databases that analyze periodical articles, books, report literature, patents, and the like for rapid retrieval in nearly all disciplines led to the publication of search-oriented thesauri to aid users with their search strategies.

The terms *thesaurus* and *subject heading list* are often used interchangeably in the literature, but they are not really the same. Since 1974 there have been international standard guidelines for thesauri.[4] There are no such standards for subject heading lists. Another difference is that thesauri are composed of "terms," while subject heading lists are composed of "subject headings." This difference has been described by Dykstra.[5] She says that in general a term denotes a single concept, while a subject heading may consist of composites of terms, although a subject heading may also consist of a single concept. Yet another difference lies in the way terms and subjects are related to each other (i.e., the syndetic structure). The guidelines for thesauri give rules for establishing hierarchical relationships and for assigning related (or associative) terms. While LCSH also has rules that are used when establishing new headings, composite headings are more difficult to relate than terms, and there remain many headings and relationships that were established before the rules were made. Dykstra argues that by adopting the abbreviations used by thesauri to show these relationships, LCSH has exacerbated the confusion that already exists.[6] A final difference is that a thesaurus is likely to cover a limited discipline or cross-disciplinary area, whereas subject heading lists tend to be designed for unrestricted subject application.

Thesaurus of Psychological Index Terms

Thesauri usually have introductory material that explains how to use them. One very simple example of a search strategy manual is the *Thesaurus of Psychological Index Terms*.[7] Its users' guide explains:

Each *Thesaurus* term is listed alphabetically and, as appropriate, is cross-referenced and displayed with its broader, narrower, and related terms (i.e., subterms). In many cases, a scope note (**SN**) provides a definition and/or information on proper use of the term. The date of the term's inclusion in the *Thesaurus* appears as a superscript. . . .

Term Relationships
The terms in the Relationship Section are displayed to reflect the following relationships:

Use. Directs the user from a term that cannot be used (nonpostable) to a postable term that can be used in indexing or searching. The use reference indicates preferred forms of synonyms, abbreviations, spelling, and word sequence:

> **Facilitated Communication** [94]
>   **Use**   Augmentative Communication

UF (used for). Reciprocal of the **Use** reference. Terms listed as **UF** (used for) references represent some but not all of the most frequently encountered synonyms, abbreviations, alternate spellings, or word sequences:

> **Augmentative Communication** [94]
>   **UF**   Facilitated Communication

B (broader term) and **N (narrower term)**. Reciprocal designators used to indicate hierarchical relationships:

Academic Achievement [67]
>   **B**   Achievement [67]

Achievement [67]
>   **N**   Academic Achievement [67]

R (related term). Reciprocal designators used to indicate relationships that are semantic or conceptual but not hierarchical. Related-term references indicate to searchers (or indexers) terms that they may not have considered but that may have a bearing on their interest:

Achievement Motivation[67]
>   **R**   Fear of Success[78]

It can be seen that such designations of terms and term relationships influenced the usages now found in LCSH. An example of an entry from this thesaurus is:

Communication Skills[73]
PN   2166   **SC** 10540
SN   Individual ability or competency in any type of communication. Limited to human populations.
>   **UF**   Communicative Competence
>   **B**   Ability [67]
>   **N**   Language Proficiency [88]
>   Rhetoric [91]
>   Writing Skills [85]
>   **R**   ↓ Communication [67]
>   ↓ Communication Disorders [82]
>   Communication Skills Training [82]
>   Pragmatics [85]
>   Social Cognition [94]
>   ↓ Verbal Communication [67]

(Use of a down arrow in front of any narrower or related term indicates that that term has narrower terms itself.)

Thesaurus of ERIC Descriptors

The *Thesaurus of ERIC Descriptors* uses the abbreviations for the relationships that were adopted by LCSH: UF—*Used for*; NT—*Narrower term*; BT—*Broader term*; RT—*Related term*.[8] "Use" is the mandatory reciprocal of UF, putting a non-postable term into place. Unlike LCSH, however, SN precedes a scope note. Under postable terms other kinds of information are also given. The date is the "add date" (date of first entry). Search strategies for materials entered into the database prior to that time should in most instances use different terminology. Posting counts (the number of citations available when the *ERIC Thesaurus* was published) are given for both the *Current Index to Journals in Education* (*CIJE*) and *Resources in Education* (*RIE*). A Group Code (GC) number is given to assist the user in identifying other Descriptors that are conceptually related to the term. Examples of *ERIC Thesaurus* entries are:

Dress Design
   USE   CLOTHING DESIGN

Drill Presses
   USE   MACHINE TOOLS

DRINKING   May 1974
            CIJE: 892   RIE: 696   GC: 210
   SN   Consumption of alcoholic beverages
   UF   Alcohol Consumption
          Alcohol Use
          Social Drinking
   NT   Alcohol Abuse
   BT   Behavior
   RT   Alcohol Education
          Alcoholic Beverages
          Drug Use
          Health Education
          Recreational Activities

INSPEC Thesaurus

A more complex example comes from the *INSPEC Thesaurus* of the Institution of Electrical Engineers (INSPEC stands for Information Services for the Physics and Engineering Communities).[9] It uses the following abbreviations:

UF:	*Used for*	indicates a 'lead-in' term from which reference is made
NT:	*Narrower Term(s)*	indicates one or more specific terms, one level lower in the hierarchy
BT:	*Broader Term(s)*	indicates one or more general terms, one level higher in the hierarchy
TT:	*Top Term(s)*	indicates the most general term(s) in the hierarchy
RT:	*Related Term(s)*	indicates conceptual relationships between terms, not related hierarchically
CC:	*Classification Code(s)*	one or more INSPEC classification codes used to indicate subjects related to that represented by the Thesaurus term
DI:	*Date of Input*	indicates the date the term was first used in the Thesaurus
PT:	*Prior Term(s)*	indicates terms used for the concept before establishment of the current preferred term.

Examples of *INSPEC Thesaurus* listings are:

dynamic braking
    USE   braking

dynamic nuclear polarisation
UF	dynamic nuclear polarization
	solid effect
NT	CIDNP
	Overhauser effect
BT	magnetic double resonance
TT	resonance
RT	nuclear polarisation
CC	A0758 A3335D A7670E
DI	January 1977
PT	magnetic double resonance

Art & Architecture Thesaurus (AAT)

A thesaurus that is truly arranged in hierarchical order is the *Art & Architecture Thesaurus (AAT)*. It is arranged in seven facets or categories: Associated Concepts, Physical Attributes, Styles and Periods, Agents, Activities, Materials, and Objects. Each facet is subdivided further. There are 33 subfacets, called "hierarchies." In the hierarchies the descriptors are displayed to show their broader term/narrower term relationships. For example, in the "furnishings hierarchy" one finds:[10]

. . .furnishings
. . . . . . <furnishings by form or function>
. . . . furniture
. . . . <furniture by location or context>
. . . . outdoor furniture

At any concept in the hierarchy, one can look at the term record to see synonyms and spelling variants, related concepts, and a scope note. For example, under "outdoor furniture" one finds:

Descriptor: outdoor furniture
Term ID: 165810
Hierarchy: Furnishings [TC]
Scope note - Term generally applied to a great variety of
         furniture specially designed for use outdoors.
Synonyms and spelling variants {UF}:
         furniture, garden
         furniture, outdoor
         furniture, patio
         furniture, porch
         garden furniture
         patio furniture
         porch furniture

You may also be interested in the following related
concepts {RT}
>   deck chairs
>   picnic tables
>   picnic benches
>   gliders (furniture)
>   Westport chairs
>   Adirondack chairs

The *AAT* has strict rules for the establishment of hierarchical relationships and related terms, which it calls "associative relationships." It has attempted to resolve much of the subjectivity that has plagued other thesauri.

Retrieval

The commands used to retrieve information from computer databases nearly all make use of the Boolean logic operators *and*, *or*, and *not*. With these machine-manipulated instructions, search commands that are highly sophisticated and very powerful examples of postcoordinate searching can be executed. For example, someone using the ERIC database might want to examine material on the consumption of alcohol in clubs, at social gatherings, and the like, but not have to wade through all those discussing related problems of health. Using the *ERIC Thesaurus*, he or she could construct the search command "(Drinking *or* Alcoholic Beverages) *and* ((Behavior *or* Recreational Activities) *not* (Health *or* Health Education))." Since the commands within parentheses are executed first, all documents indexed under the following rubrics would be retrieved:

Drinking *and* Behavior *but not* Health
Drinking *and* Behavior *but not* Health Education
Drinking *and* Recreational Activities *but not* Health
Drinking *and* Recreational Activities *but not* Health Education
Alcoholic Beverages *and* Behavior *but not* Health
Alcoholic Beverages *and* Behavior *but not* Health Education
Alcoholic Beverages *and* Recreational Activities *but not* Health
Alcoholic Beverages *and* Recreational Activities *but not* Health Education

The PREserved Context Indexing System (PRECIS)

From 1970 through 1990 a system was used for subject access to *The British National Bibliography (BNB)* that was neither a subject heading list nor a thesaurus. It was called *PRECIS (PREserved Context Indexing System)*. Derek Austin, one of the originators of the system and long-time director of the service, described it as follows:

> The system is firmly based upon the concept of an open-ended vocabulary, which means that terms can be admitted into the index at any time, as soon as they have been encountered in literature. Once a term has been admitted, its relationships with other terms are handled in two different

ways, distinguished as the syntactical and the semantic sides of the system.[11]

PRECIS indexers start by creating a phrase that describes what the item is about. From this phrase, index strings are established in which each term has a meaningful relationship with the preceding and following terms. For example, in the string "Training. Personnel. Cotton industries. India." each word relates to the next. But if a simple permutation placed Cotton industries first, followed by the rest of the string (i.e., "Cotton industries. India. Training. Personnel."), the concepts of personnel and cotton industry are separated. In *PRECIS*, a two-line printout is used so that each term in a permuted index can always remain in context, e.g.:

Cotton industries. India.
    Personnel. Training.

In this example, the concepts of cotton industries and personnel are still "next to" each other, and meaning is preserved.

The second main feature of *PRECIS* is the open-ended vocabulary which allows new terminology to be adopted as soon as it is used. Each term is semantically defined and syntactically related by *see* and *see also* references to synonyms and other associated words. The term is assigned a Reference Indicator Number (RIN) that identifies the semantic/syntactic package. When an index string is created, a subject package consisting of the string itself, associated classification numbers, and pertinent RINs is created and assigned a Subject Indicator Number (SIN). In this way, whenever the SIN is assigned to an information package the terms controlled by the RINs will be displayed in the bibliographic record. The terms can be updated without having to update every occurrence of the term in every record in the system.

The widespread availability of online keyword searching and the time-consuming nature of syntactic analysis and coding of *PRECIS* concept strings led the BNB to discontinue use of *PRECIS* at the end of 1990.[12] When a subject string is retrieved via keyword in an online system, it need not be displayed with the keyword in the lead position. It can always be displayed with the keyword in its context as it was placed in the original string.

AUTOMATIC INDEXING METHODS

Indexers, like other human beings, are fallible, often are inconsistent, are subject to extraneous influences on their work, operate at a slow pace, and are therefore the most expensive component of an indexing operation. The idea of replacing human indexers by feeding part or all of a text into a machine that would assign index terms automatically, impartially, and with unfailing consistency and accuracy arose, therefore, quite early in the computer age. Success has, however, largely eluded the best efforts of many investigators and inventors.

KWIC and KWOC Indexing

The earliest automatic indexing method relying on the power of computers to perform repetitive tasks at high speed was invented by Hans Peter Luhn, an IBM engineer, who in 1958 produced what became known as KWIC (Key Word In Context) indexing. Luhn reported his system in 1960.[13] On the assumption that titles of scientific and technical articles generally include words indicating the most significant concepts dealt with, he wrote a program that printed strings of title words, each word appearing once in alphabetical order in the center of a page, with all other words to the left or right of the center word printed in the order in which they appeared in the title; when the right-hand margin was reached, the rest of the title (if any) was "wrapped around" to the left-hand margin and continued inward. A user had only to scan the left-justified middle column for a desired keyword and could, when the word was found, read the rest of the title "in context." The method worked indeed fully automatically (i.e., without any human intervention other than the keyboarding) and resulted in a quickly and inexpensively produced display of potentially sought terms. Most KWIC programs also employ so-called stop lists to eliminate common words such as articles, prepositions, and conjunctions from the middle column where they presumably would not be sought. A specimen of a typical KWIC index is shown in figure 17.1. This earlier and rather crude form of automatic indexing has, ironically, remained the only one that has proven itself to be practical and is still being used.

Fig. 17.1. Sample from a KWIC index.

```
ORMATION AT THE NUCLEAR  SAFETY INFORMATION CENTER.      & INF  AINPBX-0005-0346A
UNCEMENT MEDIA ON CFSTI  SALES.=              & OF VARIOUS ANNO  AINPBX-0005-0327
          IMPACT OF A LARGE  SCALE COMPUTERIZED SDI SYSTEM ON A  AINPBX-0005-0223
WITH NASA/SCAN, A LARGE  SCALE SELECTIVE ANNOUNCEMENT SERVI  AINPBX-0005-0217
     OF INFORMATION-SMALL  SCALE. DISSEMINATION - CHOOSE IT  AINPBX-0005-0239
     OF INFORMATION-SMALL  SCALE. EXPERIMENTAL TRIAL OF SELEC  AINPBX-0005-0243
     OF INFORMATION-LARGE  SCALE. IMPACT OF A LARGE SCALE  AINPBX-0005-0223
  OF INFORMATION.  LARGE  SCALE. KWOC INDEX AS AN AUTOMATIC  AINPBX-0005-0211
     OF INFORMATION-SMALL  SCALE. MANAGEMENT OF SMALL, SPECIA  AINPBX-0005-0233
     OF INFORMATION-LARGE  SCALE. OP⌐ ⌐TING EXPERIENCE WITH  AINPBX-0005-0217
ON OF INFORMATION-LARGE  SCALE. PO⌐? MAN/S SDI.&DISSEMINATI  AINPBX-0005-0227
     EXPERIENCE WITH NASA/  SCAN, A LARGE SCALE SELECTIVE  AINPBX-0005-0217
TO THE DISSEMINATION OF  SCIENTIFIC AND EDUCATIONAL INFORMA  AINPBX-0005-0350A
           FOR FEDERAL  SCIENTIFIC AND TECHNICAL INFORMATI  AINPBX-0005-0311
  FORUM FOR SPECIALIZED  SCIENTIFIC COMMUNICATION.=  AINPBX-0005-0031
ATION.  LARGE SCALE. &  SCIENTIFIC DISSEMINATION OF INFORM  AINPBX-0005-0211
ATION-LARGE SCALE. &  SCIENTIFIC DISSEMINATION OF INFORM  AINPBX-0005-0217
ATION-LARGE SCALE. &  SCIENTIFIC DISSEMINATION OF INFORM  AINPBX-0005-0223
ATION-LARGE SCALE. &  SCIENTIFIC DISSEMINATION OF INFORM  AINPBX-0005-0227
```

An adaptation of the KWIC method, known as KWOC (Key Word Out Of Context), simply prints the sought words in the left-hand margin instead of in the middle of the page, the rest of the title (or the entire title, including the keyword itself) being printed to the right or beneath the keyword (*see* figure 17.2, page 410).

KWIC and KWOC indexing have, however, some severe limitations. For example, only words that appear in titles can be sought, while the article itself may deal with many other concepts not mentioned in the title. Since there is absolutely no vocabulary control (other than the elimination of stop-list words), synonymous terms are not available to users as potential access points for searching (i.e., there are no *see* references, say, from AGRICULTURE to FARMING or from SODIUM CHLORIDE to SALT). Also, many titles are not representative of the subject dealt with or are on purpose written to catch the attention of prospective readers without indicating the subject at all, e.g., "On the care and construction of white elephants" (on cataloging) or "The money-eating machines" (on computer management).

Fig. 17.2. Sample from a KWOC index.

CHEMICUS	Index Chemicus 4377.400 Q
CHEMISTRY	Abstracts of Bulgarian Scientific Literature; Chemistry 0554.515 X
	Berichte: Physiologie Physiologische Chemie und Pharmakologie (Chemistry) 1936.870
	Bibliographic Series: Institute of Paper Chemistry 1967.700
	Bibliography on the High Temperature Chemistry and Physics of Materials 2002.870
	Current Abstracts of Chemistry and Index Chemicus 3494.030 Q
	Current Titles in Electro Chemistry 3504.860 X
	Key to Turkish Science Chemistry 5091.830
	Papers and Patents from Olin Research (Chemistry) 6394.700
	Selected Bibliography of Pure Chemistry 8233.005
	Selected Bibliography of Applied Chemistry 8233.006
	USSR and East Europe Scientific Abstracts: Chemistry 9135.1014 X
CHEMISTS	Bibliographies of Chemists 1993.120
CHEMOTHERAPY	Cancer Chemotherapy Abstracts 3046.465
CHEST	Journal of Specialist Medicine: Heart and Chest including Tuberculosis 5066.130
CHEST DISEASES	Excerpta Medica: Chest Diseases Thoracic Surgery and Tuberculosis 3835.824 X
CHILD DEVELOPMENT	Child Development Abstracts and Bibliography 3172.942
CHILD EDUCATION	Exceptional Child Education Abstracts 3835.200
CHILDREN'S	'Courrier' of the International Children's Centre 3482.600
CHINA	Index to People's Republic of China Press etc. 4385.100

In addition, lengthy KWIC indexes are tiresome to scan, especially when they are printed in small type and in all capitals, as is often the case. Thus, contrary to the pun intended by the acronym KWIC, such indexes are neither quick for the user nor really indexes to concepts dealt with in texts but rather are listings of words that authors happened to put into titles. On the other hand, since the introduction of KWIC indexes, titles of scientific and technical articles have become more indicative of their contents because authors and editors became aware of the fact that inexpressive titles would be overlooked in KWIC and similar indexing techniques.[14] In the social sciences and humanities, however, the custom of authors to give catchy and uninformative titles to their papers is continuing unabated.

Extraction of Words

KWIC indexing was only the first of the so-called derivative indexing methods, all of which are based on the principle of extracting words from machine-readable text—a title, an abstract, or even the full text of a document. Automatic extraction of words is generally coupled with *truncation* in searching, that is, the possibility of searching for a word stem without regard to its prefixes or suffixes, in order to retrieve a maximum of potentially useful occurrences of that word. Thus, a physicist looking for the presence of the concept "pressure" may search for *PRESS* (the asterisks indicating that prefixes and suffixes are also to be searched), which may give:

COMPRESS
COMPRESSION
IMPRESSION
SUPPRESSION
PRESS
PRESSER
PRESSES
PRESSURE
PRESSURIZE
PRESSURIZATION
PRESSWORK

While truncation (or "stemming") does increase recall, it lowers precision because it may result in unwanted and irrelevant items being retrieved (the latter known as "false drops"). At least two phenomena dictate this. First, homonyms cannot be detected by mere extraction methods—that is, in the example just cited, IMPRESSION, SUPPRESSION, and PRESSWORK do not pertain to "pressure" in the physical sense, while PRESS may pertain both to mechanical equipment and to newspapers, the latter being of no interest to a physicist. Second, the elimination of "common" words by a stop list may also result in false drops whenever relationships are of importance, e.g., a Boolean search for TEACHERS *and* STUDENTS *and* EVALUATION will retrieve both teachers' evaluation of students and students' evaluation of teachers, because the elimination of the crucial words "of " and "by" makes it impossible to know who does what to whom.

For a time it was tried to correct the lack of indicators of relationships in derivative indexing by so-called *links* and *roles*, the former making explicit which words were linked to each other in a relationship, while the latter indicated functions (e.g., acting "as" or "for" something). These devices led indeed to higher precision, but they had to be assigned at the input stage by human beings. As that greatly diminished any gains made by automatic extraction of terms, the method was soon abandoned.

Term Frequency Methods

On the assumption that terms (other than common words) to be indexed are those occurring either very frequently in a text (and therefore indicating concepts dealt with) or very seldom (indicating a topic mentioned expressly only once or twice in the title or first paragraph but then being referred to by "it" or "this" and the like), methods were designed to perform automatic indexing on the basis of frequency of occurrence and co-occurrence of terms, using probabilistic models. Some investigators tried to couple such methods of determining how often a term is used (term frequency methods) with term weighting, i.e., assigning different degrees of importance to terms on the basis of what terms are used in a search request or on the basis of where and how terms appear (e.g., in the title, in an abstract, or in the first or last paragraph of a text, and whether they are italicized or capitalized), all of which can to some extent be determined automatically. While these methods are of interest to statisticians and mathematicians, and some have produced acceptable results under tightly controlled laboratory conditions when applied to very limited subject fields, they have as yet not found any practical large-scale application.

Linguistic Methods

A quite different approach to automatic indexing is by syntactic and semantic analysis. The former is concerned with the automatic recognition of significant word order in a phrase or sentence and with inflections, prefixes, and suffixes that indicate grammatical relationships, while the latter approach seeks to analyze noun phrases automatically with the aid of stored dictionaries and other linguistic aids. The two methods are also often used in conjunction. Research in the field of Natural Language Processing (NLP) has proliferated in recent years, and progress has been made; although the dream of information retrieval systems that can respond to a user's need through use only of natural language queries in full text databases analyzed only by computer has not been realized.

Ontologies

Linguistic ontologies are used in NLP to assist in the analysis of natural language text. Ontologies in the field of Artificial Intelligence are formal representations of what, to a human, is common sense. Linguistic ontologies must formalize the reality of using language for communication, and include the realities of grammar, semantics, and syntax. Ontologies are similar to subject heading lists and thesauri in that they organize words into sets of synonyms, and then use relationships like broader, narrower, and related terms to organize the synonym sets. They are unlike subject lists and thesauri in their analysis of categories such as nouns, verbs, adjectives, and adverbs. They also do not necessarily designate preferred terms in the synonym sets. For more information on NLP and ontologies, the reader is referred to Taylor's *The Organization of Information*.[15]

Computer-Aided Indexing

As indicated above, except for KWIC and KWOC indexing, none of the other automatic indexing methods have been applied on a large scale. For the time being, the large access services and databases still use human indexers and abstractors, even though their work is far from perfect or consistent, because none of the methods of automatic indexing invented so far has shown itself to be able to compete in terms of indexing quality or economic viability. According to Lancaster,[16] automatic indexing methods are now no longer the focus of interest of researchers, but computers will increasingly aid information retrieval in various other ways. Microcomputers are now widely used by indexers in *computer-aided* indexing, relying on stored dictionaries of synonyms and homonyms, lists of authors' names for automatic verification, lists of trade names and names of chemical compounds, plants and animals, etc. They are also used to take the drudgery out of indexing by automatically arranging entries in alphabetical order or subordinating subheadings and cross references in exact sequence under a heading, and by performing many other functions that previously had to be done manually and therefore were quite expensive and often subject to errors.

SWITCHING LANGUAGES

We have made a cursory examination of a number of subject access systems available for use in modern library cataloging. Most are self-contained, providing their own categories and terminology, with syntactical rules designed to express complex or multi-faceted concepts. Each exhibits both strengths and weaknesses. Not one has yet proved sufficient to meet all needs nor is demonstrably better than all others in every situation.

The information explosion, together with rapid developments in automation, has made intercommunication among subject disciplines, libraries, and nations both a possibility and a growing necessity. Several possible solutions to this problem have been proposed. One has been a movement toward "switching languages." With a multilateral translation program, materials already indexed would be more readily available, while libraries and information centers could avoid future duplication by joining systems of shared cataloging without discarding or revamping their own catalogs and indexes.

A number of attempts, such as umbrella (i.e., broad) classifications, have been tried and failed. A somewhat different approach is that of the BRS/TERM database, which was created to enhance online searching.[17] The vocabularies of six thesauri were organized into concept records that included hierarchical information and free-text searching suggestions. This kind of approach has an inherent linguistic interest that has led researchers to reexamine the structure and properties of indexing languages.

Another such project is the Unified Medical Language System (UMLS).[18] Begun in 1986 by the National Library of Medicine (NLM), the UMLS project aims to aid the development of systems to help health professionals and researchers in the retrieval of biomedical information from a variety of sources. Relevant information is scattered across many databases that use very different controlled vocabularies and/or classifications. The UMLS project brings together in a uniform format about 50 different vocabularies and links different terminology used for the same concepts. It does not attempt to make judgements about the "best" terminology to use—the usages in the source vocabularies are preserved; but it does establish new relationships among terms from different vocabularies.

There are three parts to the system: the UMLS Metathesaurus, the Specialist Lexicon, and the UMLS Semantic Network. The Metathesaurus is used in a variety of applications: information retrieval; linking patient records to related information in bibliographic or factual databases; NLP and automated indexing research; and structured data entry.[19] The Specialist Lexicon includes syntactic, morphological, and orthographic information for each term. The Semantic Network contains information about the categories to which Metathesaurus concepts have been assigned and the permissible relationships among these categories (e.g., bacteria cause disease). The three parts together are being used in research for natural language processing and information retrieval, among other research projects.

Projects in specialized subject areas like the UMLS project hold great promise. With these, the ideal of long-sought "switching languages" may finally be realized.

NOTES

1. John Rothman, "Index, Indexer, Indexing," in *Encyclopedia of Library and Information Science*, Vol. 11 (New York: Marcel Dekker, 1974), p. 289.

2. Mortimer Taube and Associates, *Studies in Coordinate Indexing* (Washington, D.C.: Documentation, Incorporated, 1953).

3. Marcia J. Bates, "Rethinking Subject Cataloging in the Online Environment," *Library Resources & Technical Services* 33, no. 4 (October 1989): 401.

4. International Organization for Standardization, *Documentation: Guidelines for the Establishment and Development of Monolingual Thesauri*, 2nd ed. ISO 2788 (Geneva: ISO, 1986, first edition published in 1974); British Standards Institution, *British Standard Guide to Establishment and Development of Monolingual Thesauri*, BS 5723 [Rev. ed.] (London: BSI, 1987); American National Standards Institute, *American National Standard Guidelines for Thesaurus Structure, Construction, and Use*, ANSI Z39.19–1980 (New York: ANSI, 1980).

5.   Mary Dykstra, "LC Subject Headings Disguised as a Thesaurus," *Library Journal* 113 (March 1, 1988): 42–46.

6.   Dykstra, "LC Subject Headings Disguised," p. 43.

7.   *Thesaurus of Psychological Index Terms*, 8th ed. (Washington, D.C.: American Psychological Association, 1997).

8.   *Thesaurus of ERIC Descriptors*, 13th ed. (Phoenix, Ariz.: Oryx Press, 1995).

9.   *INSPEC Thesaurus*, 1999 [ed.] (London: Institution of Electrical Engineers, 1999).

10.   *Art & Architecture Thesaurus Browser* (available: http://shiva.pub.getty.edu/aat_browser [accessed 08/15/99]).

11.   Derek Austin, "Progress in Documentation: The Development of PRECIS: A Theoretical and Technical History," *Journal of Documentation* 30 (March 1974): 47. In addition to this excellent article, the serious student is referred to: Derek Austin, *PRECIS: A Manual of Concept Analysis and Subject Indexing*, 2nd ed. (London: British Library, 1984); *The PRECIS Index System: Principles, Applications, and Prospects*, Proceedings of the International PRECIS Workshop, ed. by Hans H. Wellisch (New York: H. W. Wilson, 1977); and M. Mahapatra and S. C. Biswas, "PRECIS: Its Theory and Application—An Extended State-of-the-Art Review from the Beginning up to 1982," *Libri* 33 (December 1983): 316–330.

12.   National Bibliographic Service, *Newsletter* no. 1 (June/July 1990): 3–4.

13.   Hans Peter Luhn, "Keyword in Context Index for Technical Literature (KWIC Index)," *American Documentation* 11 (1960): 288–295.

14.   J. J. Tocatlian, "Are Titles of Chemical Papers Becoming More Informative?" *Journal of the American Society for Information Science* 21 (1970): 345–350.

15.   Arlene G. Taylor, *The Organization of Information* (Englewood, Colo.: Libraries Unlimited, 1999), pp. 158–166.

16.   F. W. Lancaster, "Trends in Subject Indexing from 1957 to 2000," in *New Trends in Documentation and Information: Proceedings of the 39th FID Congress, 1978* (London: Aslib, 1980), pp. 223–233.

17.   Sara D. Knapp, "Creating BRS/TERM, a Vocabulary Database for Searchers," *Database* 7, no. 4 (December 1984): 70–75.

18.   National Library of Medicine, "Unified Medical Language System (UMLS)" (available: http://www.nlm.nih.gov/research/umls/ [accessed 3/12/00]).

19.   National Library of Medicine, "UMLS Metathesaurus: Fact Sheet" (available: http://www.nlm.nih.gov/pubs/factsheets/umlsmeta.html [accessed 3/12/00]).

SUGGESTED READING

Bates, Marcia J. "Rethinking Subject Cataloging in the Online Environment." *Library Resources & Technical Services* 33, no. 4 (October 1989): 400–419.

Dykstra, Mary. *PRECIS: A Primer*. London: British Library, 1985.

Foskett, A. C. *The Subject Approach to Information*. 5th ed. London: Library Association Publishing, 1996. Part IV (Chapters 25–27): Post-coordinate Indexing Languages.

Lancaster, F. W. *Indexing and Abstracting in Theory and Practice*. 2nd ed. London: Library Association Publishing, 1998.

Mann, Thomas. *Library Research Models: A Guide to Classification, Cataloging, and Computers*. New York: Oxford University Press, 1993. Chapter 5: The Traditional Library Science Model. Part Three: Published Bibliographies and Indexes.

McKiernan, Gerry. *Beyond Bookmarks: Schemes for Organizing the Web*. Online, Ames, Iowa: G. McKiernan. Available: http://www.public.iastate.edu/~CYBERSTACKS/CTW.htm (accessed 3/5/00).

Soergel, Dagobert. *Organizing Information: Principles of Data Base and Retrieval Systems*. Orlando, Fla.: Academic Press, 1985. Chapters 12–15.

Part V
AUTHORITY CONTROL

18 Authority Control

INTRODUCTION

Authority control, as currently practiced, is the process of maintaining consistency in the verbal form used to represent an access point in a catalog and the further process of showing the relationships among names, works, and subjects. The goal is to make possible the identifying and collocating functions of the catalog.

As mentioned in several earlier chapters, authority control is becoming known as *access control* as we move into the international arena. This is true because of the need to allow the creators of catalogs in various countries using various languages to designate their own "authorized" forms of names. Everyone should not be required to use English language "authorized" forms, but we all should be able to use the same authority or access control records. In the text below the term *authority control* is used most often because that is the terminology still used in current practice by most catalogers and authority system vendors.

IDENTIFYING FUNCTION

Authority control enhances the identifying, or finding, function of the catalog through the use of consistent forms of access points with references from forms not used. In a system under authority control, a user can assume that all works relating to a name or a concept will be found together or will at least be connected with references. Once one determines, for example, that records are found under Cochrane, Pauline A., and not under Atherton, Pauline, one can assume that everything by this person will be found at this heading. It is not necessary to look under Cochrane, P. A., or the alternate spelling, Cochran, P., or to try to think of other possible spellings or forms.

It is also possible to identify titles through use of a consistent heading for works that have different titles. A particular edition of the Bible, for example, can be found under "Bible." One does not have to remember an exact title such as *Holy Bible*, or *Good News for Modern Man*, although they can also be found under these titles if one remembers them.

Likewise, once one determines that works about psychological help for families are found under "Family therapy" and not under "Family counseling," one can assume that everything on that topic will be found there. Identification of works on a particular subject is made easier by using only one of two synonyms or by always using the words of a phrase in the same order—e.g., "Serials control systems," not "Control systems (Serials)."

COLLOCATING FUNCTION

Authority control enhances the collocating, or gathering, function of the catalog through the linking of consistent headings in a syndetic structure. *Syndetic* is an adjective meaning "connective, connecting." It is used to characterize the nature of a catalog under authority control because of the connecting that is brought about by using consistent headings and by providing references to and among those headings.

Names are collocated by bringing everything by and about a person or corporate body together under the same form of name; or in some cases where a person or body actually has used two or more different *names* (not just different forms), collocation may be accomplished by connecting the names with references. Examples of the latter are:

> University of North Carolina at Chapel Hill.   School of Information and Library Science
>> For works issued by this body under its earlier name see:
> University of North Carolina at Chapel Hill.   School of Library Science.

> Dodgson, Charles Lutwidge, 1832–1898
>> For works written under this author's pseudonym see:
> Carroll, Lewis, 1832–1898.

Works are collocated by creating a uniform title for every work that has appeared under more than one title and by providing references from titles not chosen for the heading. In this way all manifestations of the Bible can be found together; and Dickens's *Life and Adventures of Nicholas Nickleby* can be found with his *Nicholas Nickleby*. Uniform titles also aid in showing relationships among works. Bibliographic records for the musical stage play and the film version of *Nicholas Nickleby* contain added entries for the uniform title for Dickens's original work, and can be found collocated with it. References also can help to show relationships among works. An example of this is:

> Tolkien, J.R.R. (John Ronald Reuel), 1892–1973.   Lord of the rings. 2. Two towers
>> see
> Tolkien, J.R.R. (John Ronald Reuel), 1892–1973.   Two towers.

The heading chosen for the work in this example collocates the bibliographic records for the work under the title of the part, but the reference collocates with the title of the whole larger work, letting the user know that parts of the whole work are available in addition to the whole work.

Authority control assures that subjects are collocated by providing consistent headings for discrete concepts, by assuring that there are references to those headings from terms not used, and by providing a network of references to and among broader terms, narrower terms, and related terms. For example, let us suppose that someone is using a catalog in which the subjects are from the *Library of Congress*

Subject Headings (*LCSH*) and in which appropriate references have been provided. If this person looks up "Heart attack," a reference will show that this term is not used, but that "Myocardial infarction," is used instead. At "Myocardial infarction," in addition to finding bibliographic records representing works on the subject, the user will find a reference to the narrower term "Cardiogenic shock." In an ideal world there would also be a reference to the broader term "Coronary heart disease," although, traditionally, library catalogs have referred only to narrower and related terms because it was felt that to refer to broader terms made an impossibly complicated network. (This was true in manual systems. Most libraries even gave up providing related and narrower term references in manual catalogs.) If the broader term reference *were* made, however, the user could follow up with a search under "Coronary heart disease" and would be referred to the related term "Type A behavior" and two other narrower terms besides the one that led to this term: "Angina pectoris" and "Coronary artery stenosis." There could also be a reference to the broader term "Heart—Diseases."

SYSTEM DESIGN

It should be emphasized that authority control of the terminology does not ensure that everything on a subject will be found together. The latter depends upon the subject analysis that has been done, as discussed in chapter 8, and upon the design of the system in which the subject headings will be displayed. Only if an item were determined to be about "heart attacks" as a result of the process of subject analysis, would it be found under "Myocardial infarction." In library catalogs, even that would be true only if the whole item, or at least 20 percent of it, were on the subject.

It should also be pointed out that not all terms thought of by a user will match a reference if they do not match a heading. For example, a user of an authority-controlled online catalog with references who searches for "heart attacks" will be told there are no matches, because the reference is from "heart attack" in the singular. This can be a problem in searching for names and titles as well as for subjects. For example, a person may search for a name spelled as it sounds (e.g., "Kirshenbaum, Baruch" instead of "Kirschenbaum, Baruch"). Systems can be designed with enhanced search capabilities to supplement authority control in such situations. An excellent discussion of how system design can supplement and enhance authority control can be found in Yee and Layne's *Improving Online Public Access Catalogs.*[1]

LACK OF AUTHORITY CONTROL

In systems without authority control, it is up to the user to try to think of all possible ways that a name, work, or subject could be verbally represented, while at the same time eliminating all possible representations that will not satisfy the need. For example, a user wanting material on "Mercury" as a metal must eliminate that which concerns the planet or the Roman god; and a user wishing to consult works by John F. Murphy on cash management (*see* figure 18.1, p. 422) must sort out these from works by other John F. Murphys who write about Christian education, law, parenting, and other subjects, and who do not always use titles that are descriptive of their contents.

Fig. 18.1. Partial authority records for five authors who use the name "John F. Murphy".

```
>   1  010    n 83175165 <
>   2  040    DLC $c DLC $d DLC <
>   3  005    19940301102149.4 <
>   4  100  1  Murphy, John F. <
>   5  670    Murphy, A. M. Successful parenting, c1983 (a.e.) $b CIP
t.p. (John F. Murphy, Ed. M.) <
```

```
>   1  010    n 83016187 <
>   2  040    DGPO $c DLC <
>   3  005    19840322000000.0 <
>   4  100  1  Murphy, John F. $q (John Francis), $d 1913- <
>   5  670    His Sound cash management and borrowing, 1981: $b t.p.
(John F. Murphy, retired bank exec. and member Manasota SCORE Chapter,
Sarasota, Fla.) <
```

```
>   1  010    no 90025472 <
>   2  040    DGPO $c DGPO <
>   3  005    19901127094724.7 <
>   4  100  1  Murphy, John F. $q (John Francis), $d 1922- <
>   5  670    Richmond, G.M. Preliminary quaternary geologic map of the
Dinwoody Lake area, Fremont County, Wyoming [MI], 1989?: $b t.p. (John
F. Murphy; U.S. Geological Survey) <
```

```
>   1  010    n 78011669 <
>   2  040    DLC $c DLC <
>   3  005    19840322000000.0 <
>   4  100  1  Murphy, John Francis, $d 1937- <
>   5  400  1  Murphy, John F. $q (John Francis), $d 1937- <
>   6  670    American Society of International Law. Legal aspects ...
1978 (a.e.) $b t.p. (John F. Murphy) <
```

```
>   1  010    n 80072584 <
>   2  040    DLC $c DLC <
>   3  005    19840322000000.0 <
>   4  100  1  Murphy, John F., $d 1922- <
>   5  400  1  Murphy, Jack, $d 1922- <
>   6  670    His Mary's immaculate heart, 1951. <
```

In fact, in many of today's supposedly authority-controlled online catalogs, users must do this same sorting because works by all John F. Murphys, regardless of variant qualifiers or birth dates, are interfiled and subarranged alphabetically by the titles of their various works, and there is no reference to the John F. Murphy who is entered as "Murphy, John Francis, 1937–   ". (*See* figure 18.2.) This is a step backward from card catalogs where all works by the person whose heading is "Murphy, John F. (John Francis), 1913–   " are filed together before works by the person whose heading is "Murphy, John F. (John Francis), 1922–   ".

Fig. 18.2. Partial alphabetical listing of titles in OCLC of at least five different authors named "John F. Murphy".

OLUC	dp murp,joh,f	G1: 1-92 bks 1883-1984		Records: 138
Rec#	Name	Title	Publisher	Date L
> 1<	Murphy, John F.	Across the western ocean : Fr		1982
> 2<	Murphy, John F.	An appraisal and abstract of	National Occup	1937
> 3<	Murphy, John F.,	The catechetical experience	Herder and Her	1968 D
> 4<	Murphy, John F.,	Catechetics from A to Z /	Ave Maria Pres	1982 D
> 5<	Murphy, John F.	The condensation of aliphatic		1940
> 6<	Murphy, John F.	Countdown to communication :	Distributors,	1973
> 7<	Murphy, John F.	Countdown to communication :	Sullivan Broth	1973
> 8<	Murphy, John F.	Developing language with youn	Educators Pub.	1973
> 9<	Murphy, John F.	Developing oral language with	Educators Pub.	1974
> 10<	Murphy, John F.	Developing oral language with	Educators Pub.	1975
> 11<	Murphy, John F.,	Doing, dance & drama /	Ave Maria Pres	1980 D
> 12<	Murphy, John F.	Eighty photographic views-- o	John F. Murphy	1890
> 13<	Murphy, John F.	Fifty photographic views of P	John F. Murphy	1900
> 14<	Murphy, John F.	Implications of the Irish pas		1983
> 15<	Murphy, John F.	In the Supreme Court of the s		1909
> 16<	Murphy, John F.	Knowledge is power: foreign p		1975
> 17<	Murphy, John F.	Listening, language & learnin	Educators Pub.	1970
> 18<	Murphy, John F.,	Mary's Immaculate Heart; the	Bruce	1951 D
> 19<	Murphy, John F.	The mathematical fundamental	s s.n.],	1972

It has been argued by some that users have for some time now been finding material in uncontrolled online databases that index papers and articles. This is true, but the process is not without some frustration. And the free text searching in search engines on the Internet can yield hundreds of "hits," many of which are unrelated to the desired search. A series of articles in 1985 and 1986 in *DATABASE* and *ONLINE* addressed the problem of searching for names in such databases.[2] Upon reading these articles the reader may be struck by the immense number of complications waiting to sabotoge the uninitiated, and may wonder how any searcher could possibly remember all the tricks necessary for a complete name search. These articles are mini-lessons in performing authority work, except that it is up to the user, not the cataloger, to do the work over and over as searches are performed.

AUTHORITY WORK

Authority control, of course, cannot be achieved automatically. It requires authority work to be done by catalogers. First, it is necessary to discover all available evidence relative to the naming of a person, body, work, topic, etc., and then to choose the form to use as the heading and the forms to use as references according to some rule. Then there must be creation of authority records. A carefully prepared authority record contains the form chosen for use as the heading, a list of variant forms or terms that may be used as references, and a list of sources consulted in the process of deciding upon the heading.

Name and Title Authority Work

The process followed for names, uniform titles, and series is somewhat different from that used for subjects. The first step in the process used for names, uniform titles, and series is verification, which means determining the existence of an author or other entity and the accepted form of heading to use. The name or title is first recorded as it appears in the work being cataloged. The next step usually is to check the library's catalog and authority files to determine if the heading already has been established for the library. If it has, the authorized form is noted and used in the cataloging in hand. If the heading is not already established, the cataloger checks the LC name authority file (LCNAF) either online through the utility in which the library holds membership or in the microfiche version. If the name or title is in the LCNAF and is coded as being in *Anglo-American Cataloguing Rules, Second Edition* (*AACR2*) form, the record is copied for the local file. This may be accomplished by downloading the authority record from the bibliographic utility to the local system, if the library has an online catalog. Another method, if the library relies on cards, is to download the authority record from the bibliographic utility onto a personal computer. Then the record can be printed on card stock from the machine-readable record. There are several programs available for this operation.

If the name or title is not in the LCNAF or is not coded as being in *AACR2* form, then *Anglo-American Cataloguing Rules, Second Edition, 1998 Revision* (*AACR2R98*) is consulted for the appropriate rules for form. If verification problems emerge, such as the existence of different names or different forms of the same name, further sources of information must be consulted. Such sources that might be consulted include other works by the same author or issued by the same body, publisher sites on the Internet, reliable directories or biographical dictionaries, or other reference sources. An authority record must then be made. The one or more sources used as authoritative may be cited on the authority record. Pertinent references are listed. References also should be made, as well as a revised authority record, for any conflicting heading that had to be changed in the process of creating the authority heading for the name or title in hand.

If a library is a NACO participant the cataloger submits the authority record to the international database through the NACO program. NACO is the name authorities program of the Program for Cooperative Cataloging (PCC), an international program operating out of LC, but consisting of a cooperative group of more than 200 institutions. NACO participants receive special training upon joining NACO.[3]

Following training, participants submit newly created or modified authority records to a liaison at LC who provides feedback for three to six months, after which the participants become independent. Independent catalogers enter the records directly into either OCLC or RLIN.

Many authority records are created in the MARC 21 (MAchine-Readable Cataloging format for the U.S. and Canada) by the Library of Congress (LC) and by NACO libraries, and most libraries try to use these as much as possible in order to reduce their local authority work. Figure 18.3 shows a name authority record coded according to the MARC 21 authorities format and formatted as is done in the OCLC system. In the MARC 21 format the authorized heading is given in a field beginning with 1 (100, 110, 111, 150, 151, etc). *See from* references are given in fields beginning with 4 (400, 410, etc.). *See also from* references are given in fields beginning with 5 (500, 510, etc.). Notes are given in fields beginning with 6 (667, 670, 675, 678, 680, 681, 682, 688). Special kinds of references are given in fields 663 through 666. MARC records, of course, can be displayed in any fashion that a system programmer chooses.

Fig. 18.3. MARC name authority record.

```
    ARN: 256371
    Rec stat: n      Entered:     19790314
>   Type:     z      Upd status: a    Enc lvl:   n      Source:
    Roman:    _      Ref status: a    Mod rec:          Name use: a
    Govt agn: _      Auth status: a   Subj:      a      Subj use: a
    Series:   n      Auth/ref:   a    Geo subd:  n      Ser use:  b
    Ser num:  n      Name:       a    Subdiv tp: n      Rules:    c <
>    1 010       n 79022593 <
>    2 040       DLC $c DLC <
>    3 005       19840322000000.0 <
>    4 100 1     Van Buren, Ariane. <
>    5 400 1     Buren, Ariane van <
>    6 400 1     Van Buren, E. Ariane <
>    7 670       Nuclear or not? 1978 (a.e.) $b t.p. (Ariane van Buren)
jkt. (E. Ariane van Buren, research assoc., International Inst. of
Environment & Development) <
```

A few libraries continue to use card authority files. Figure 18.4 shows one format that a manual name authority card might take. In this format the rules used are indicated in the upper right corner, the heading is given on the top line at the left margin, sources are given next, and references follow. A single *x* means that there will be a *see* reference from that form to the heading. A double *xx* would be used to mean that a *see also* reference would be made from that form, in cases where headings have been created for two or more names for the same person or body, e.g.:

Carroll, Lewis, 1832–1898.

xx   Dodgson, Charles Lutwidge, 1832–1898

Fig. 18.4. Sample name authority record in card format.

```
                                    AACR2
        Van Buren, Ariane.

        LCAF:   n    79022593

        Work cat:   Nuclear or not?   1978 (a.e.): t.p. (Ariane
        van Buren) jkt. (E. Ariane van Buren, research assoc.,
        International Inst. of Environment & Development)

        x    Buren, Ariane van
        x    Van Buren, E. Ariane


                           O
```

Subject Authority Work

Subject authority work is almost always done by verifying a heading as being the latest terminology used in the official list used by the library. In the case of *LCSH*, the online version of the Library of Congress Subject Authority File (LCSAF) can be searched through a bibliographic utility, through the *Cataloger's Desktop/Classification Plus*, or in the latest microfiche or book version. In a manual system it is then necessary to determine which of the headings following the codes for *see also from* references are already represented in the catalog. The cataloger must also choose from the list of recommended terms those from which *see* references should be made.

If a subject string is being constructed for original cataloging, and one is using *LCSH*, it is necessary also to consult the *Subject Cataloging Manual: Subject Headings* and *Free-Floating Subdivisions: An Alphabetical Index.* SACO participants may submit proposals to LC for either new subject headings not found in *LCSH*, or proposals to change headings that are found in *LCSH* but are deemed to be outdated, incomplete, or exhibit other such deficiencies.[4] SACO is the subject authorities program of the PCC. Unlike NACO, SACO is not institution based. Any individual cataloger at any institution who needs a subject heading not available may send a proposal to SACO. It is expected that a cataloger making a proposal is using the latest versions of *LCSH* and the manuals. It is also expected that research be performed to assure that the proposed heading is not a duplicate and that the necessary sources be cited to demonstrate that the term is used in writing and is needed. It is also possible to propose a new classification number. Persons making classification proposals should be using the latest available LC classification schedules and the *Subject Cataloging Manual: Classification.*

Figure 18.5 shows a subject authority record in the MARC format as displayed in OCLC. Terms coded 450 are "used for" terms from which *see* or *use* references should be made. Terms coded 550 can be either related terms or broader terms. The difference is made known through use of "$w g" following the broader terms. Both related and broader terms should have references made from them to *see also* the term in the 150 field. MARC 21 authority records do not show narrower terms, working on the assumption that the narrower terms are automatically taken care of when the system is programmed to display all the references from broader terms on every record.

Fig. 18.5. Sample MARC subject authority record.

```
  ARN: 2060424
  Rec stat: n        Entered:     19860211
> Type:      z        Upd status: a       Enc lvl:   n       Source:
  Roman:     _        Ref status: b       Mod rec:           Name use: b
  Govt agn: _         Auth status: a      Subj:      a       Subj use: a
  Series:    n        Auth/ref:   a       Geo subd:  i       Ser use:  b
  Ser num:   n        Name:       n       Subdiv tp: n       Rules:    n <
>   1 010    sh 85077571 <
>   2 040    DLC $c DLC <
>   3 005    19860211000000.0 <
>   4 053    PN55 $c General <
>   5 053    PR149.S4 $c English literature <
>   6 150    Literature and science <
>   7 450    Poetry and science <
>   8 450    Science and literature <
>   9 450    Science and poetry <
>  10 550    Science and the humanities $w g <
```

Although very few libraries use card subject authority files, some do use them. Figure 18.6 is an example of one format for a subject authority card, indicating the source of the information. In manual subject authority records, the initials NT (narrower term), UF (used for), RT (related term), and BT (broader term) are often used, although *x* and *xx* may be used as in name authority records.

Fig. 18.6. Sample subject authority record in card format.

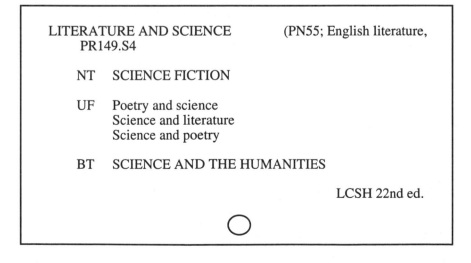

```
LITERATURE AND SCIENCE          (PN55; English literature,
    PR149.S4

    NT    SCIENCE FICTION

    UF    Poetry and science
          Science and literature
          Science and poetry

    BT    SCIENCE AND THE HUMANITIES

                                    LCSH 22nd ed.
```

CREATION OF AUTHORITY FILES

Following creation of authority records, the next step in authority work is the addition of the records into an authority file, either manual or machine-readable. In order for the authority file to serve its purpose it must be linked in some way to the bibliographic file. In card or paper systems the link is implicit. That is, the link is in the mind of a human who perceives the presence of an identical form on both the authority record and the catalog record and also perceives the presence in both files of the appropriate reference(s).

In many machine systems, also, the authority system linkage is implicit. In those systems, such as OCLC and RLIN, the authority file, although automated, is a completely separate file from the bibliographic file, and authority control of new records is dependent upon the cataloger finding the correct form of a heading in the authority file and then entering it correctly into the bibliographic record. There are no references in these files, although the authority files may be searched under the forms from which references are authorized. In such systems changes in headings mean that unless there are strict procedures for checking headings already in a file against every new heading entered, two or more forms of a heading may appear simultaneously with different bibliographic records displayed at each heading. A recent catalog search by the author returned the following headings with numbers of bibliographic records to the left of the heading:

    1   Williams, Tennessee, 1911– 1983.
  156   Williams, Tennessee, 1911–1983.
    1   Williams, Tennessee, 1914–1983.

The first heading has a space after the hyphen before the death date. The third heading has an incorrect birth date. A sophisticated automated linked authority control system should "catch" the first and third headings as being one-of-a-kind (and perhaps either new to the system or in error) and would identify them so that a catalog manager could check their validity.

Subject headings also can cause display problems when authority control is only implicit. Changes are made to *LCSH* headings with some frequency. In June 1999, for example, "Trade-unions" was changed to "Labor unions." In an authority file with only implicit authority control the cataloger first using the new heading must notice the change and take steps to have the records with the former heading changed to the current one. In such situations it is possible occasionally to run the bibliographic file against the authority file to check for headings that match references and to change any matches found to the new form; but it is not feasible to do this often, and in the meantime multiple forms exist unless someone notices and changes them individually. At this writing most catalogs still display "Trade-unions" as the authorized heading.

In more sophisticated systems the linkage between authority file and bibliographic file is explicit. That is, a direct internal linkage exists between a heading stored in the authority file and the same heading stored in the bibliographic file. In such systems the headings for every new record are checked against the authority file, and new or changed headings are flagged for review. In these systems also, references are displayed from unused terms to used ones and from used terms to narrower terms and sometimes also to related terms. References to broader terms are often not displayed, however (as discussed in earlier subject heading chapters 14–16).

In the most sophisticated systems there is a linkage that uses relational file techniques to link a bibliographic record with only identification numbers as headings to a system of authority records that store all the headings linked to identification number for each. The advantage here is that each heading is stored only once, and thus matching of bibliographic and authority headings is unnecessary. In addition when a heading has to be changed, the change is made only in the authority record. What the user sees in such a system is no different from what is seen in the previously described linked systems.

CATALOG AS AUTHORITY FILE

While it is possible to do authority work without making separate authority records, this is done less and less often. In manual card catalogs, libraries formerly would let the catalog itself serve as the authority file. That is, the heading used in the catalog was assumed to have been verified, and necessary references were kept track of on the back of one of the main entry cards for the heading in question. This method became difficult when notes were needed to resolve conflicting headings or when the set of cards on which the references were recorded were withdrawn from the catalog.

In online catalogs, too, the bibliographic record may be considered to contain the authoritative heading in situations where no notes or references are required. In some systems authority work is done for every heading, but authority records are made only when references or notes are required. In these latter systems the heading index is created from authority file headings and references combined with headings from bibliographic records that have no associated authority records.

When storage space was an issue, the advantage of this system was the saving of disk space necessary to store MARC authority records that contained no information that was not already available in bibliographic records. This advantage was offset in systems using relational file techniques, because in the latter, much space was/is saved by storing each heading only once instead of in every associated bibliographic record. Storage space is no longer an issue in most systems, and authority records are now often made for every heading so that a search for a heading can place the searcher in the authority file, where a particular heading can be chosen before the user is given a list of bibliographic records.

MAINTENANCE OF AUTHORITY SYSTEMS

In order to maintain an authority system, it is necessary to have routine error checking between authority and bibliographic files. There must also be routine error checking among authority records for consistency. For example, if a changed heading authority record does not replace the older heading record properly, it would be possible to have a response to a search for one term refer to another term only to have a reference at that term referring back to the first (e.g., "Trade-unions *see* Labor unions" and "Labor unions *see* Trade-unions" in the same catalog).

Updating is necessary when a library is using LC authority data as the basis of its authority system. Names are changed to reflect new usages by some authors; subjects are constantly changed to update terminology, add references, etc.; and new headings are added. There must be procedures for replacing the changed records and adding the new ones. Changed records are particularly difficult because there is not yet a mechanism for notifying a library that has used a bibliographic record in the past that its terminology or name form has now been changed. For example, the authority record for "Cochrane, Pauline Atherton, 1929–   " was changed in 1990 to "Cochrane, Pauline A. (Pauline Atherton), 1929–   " because 80 percent of her works as represented in OCLC's database were found to use the form with the initial "A." Records that appeared in LC's MARC file at the time were changed and reissued, but many records in the utilities and in local online catalogs remained in the old form for a number of years. One problem in such a case is that the titles of such authors appear in two or more separate alphabetical subsets—the same problem that can result when no authority work was done in the first place. Later, at OCLC and in other systems, special projects ran the authority file against the bibliographic file to check for and correct such discrepancies. Some systems (e.g., OCLC) now routinely run new authority records from LC against the bibliographic file on a regular basis, although it is not difficult to find catalogs where this has not been done and in which old forms of names and subjects abound.

CONCLUSION

There is great potential for use of authority control that has not yet been realized. One is the idea mentioned earlier of providing access to broader subject terms. Another is the potential for controlling elements of records not now even given as access points (e.g., names of publishers). A third potential lies in further control of works. Editions of works, for example, are now related only by either the fact of their having identical author and title access points or the provision of notes on bibliographic records giving earlier titles or authors. If authority control of works, which is only in its infancy, were extended to such relationships as editions and other derivative works, identifying works in fields such as music and literature would be greatly enhanced.

NOTES

1.   Martha M. Yee and Sara Shatford Layne, *Improving Online Public Access Catalogs* (Chicago: American Library Association, 1998). For additional discussion of how system design can supplement authority control, *see*: Marcia Bates, "Subject Access in Online Catalogs: A Design Model," *Journal of the American Society for Information Science* 37, no. 6 (November 1986): 357–376; Christine L. Borgman, "Why Are Online Catalogs *Still* Hard to Use?" *Journal of the American Society for Information Science* 47, no. 7 (July 1996): 493–503; Arlene G. Taylor, "Authority Control and System Design," in *Policy and Practice in the Bibliographic Control of Nonbook Media*, edited by Sheila S. Intner and Richard P. Smiraglia (Chicago: American Library Association, 1987), pp. 64–81; Arlene G. Taylor, *The Organization of Information* (Englewood, Colo.: Libraries Unlimited, 1999), pp. 211–226.

2.   Catherine E. Pasterczyk, "Russian Transliteration Variations for Searchers," *DATABASE* 8 (February 1985): 68–75; Anne B. Piternick, "What's in a Name? Use of Names and Titles in Subject Searching," *DATABASE* 8 (December 1985): 22–28; David M. Pilachowski and David Everett, "What's in a Name? Looking for People Online—Social Sciences," *DATABASE* 8 (August 1985): 47–65; David M. Pilachowski and David Everett, "What's in a Name? Looking for People Online—Current Events," *DATABASE* 9 (April

1986): 43–50; David Everett and David M. Pilachowski, "What's in a Name? Looking for People Online—Humanities," *DATABASE* 9 (October 1986): 26–34; Bonnie Snow, "Caduceus: People in Medicine: Searching Names Online," *ONLINE* 10 (September 1986): 122–127.

3.   "NACO: Program for Cooperative Cataloging" (available: http://lcweb.loc.gov/catdir/pcc/naco.html [accessed 3/12/00]).

4.   "SACO Program Description: Program for Cooperative Cataloging" (available: http://lcweb.loc.gov/catdir/pcc/sacopara.html [accessed 3/12/00]).

SUGGESTED READING

Authority Control in the 21st Century: An Invitational Conference, March 31–April 1, 1996. Online, Dublin, Ohio: OCLC Online Computer Library Center. Available: http://www.oclc.org/oclc/man/authconf/confhome.htm (accessed 3/12/00).

Burger, Robert H. *Authority Work: The Creation, Use, Maintenance, and Evaluation of Authority Records and Files.* Littleton, Colo.: Libraries Unlimited, 1985.

Clack, Doris Hargrett. *Authority Control: Principles, Applications, and Instructions.* Chicago: American Library Association, 1990.

The Future Is Now: Reconciling Change and Continuity in Authority Control: Proceedings of the OCLC Symposium, ALA Annual Conference, June 23, 1995. Dublin, Ohio: OCLC Online Computer Library Center, 1995.

Talmacs, Kerrie. "Authority Control." In *Technical Services Today and Tomorrow.* 2nd ed., edited by Michael Gorman. Englewood, Colo.: Libraries Unlimited, 1998, pp. 129–139.

Taylor, Arlene G. "Authority Control: Where It's Been and Where It's Going," and other papers from the conference "Authority Control: Why It Matters," sponsored by NELINET, November 1, 1999, Worcester, Mass. Available: http://www.nelinet.net/conf/cts/cts99/cts99.htm (accessed 3/12/00).

Tillett, Barbara B. "International Shared Resource Records for Controlled Access." *ALCTS Newsletter Online* 10, no. 1 (December 1998). Available: http://www.ala.org/alcts/alcts_news/v10n1/gateway.html (accessed 3/12/00).

Part VI
ADMINISTRATIVE ISSUES

19

Processing Centers, Networking, and Cooperative Programs

INTRODUCTION

With the continued growth in volume of published materials and increased use of computers and telecommunications to transmit bibliographic information and documents from producer to consumer, the resultant need is for more and better library service. The impact of computerization has significantly changed the traditional patterns of cataloging and processing of library materials. Most libraries and library systems have either centralized their technical services or entered into cooperative arrangements with other libraries through various levels of networking. Some libraries purchase their processing from commercial vendors. Thus we have centralized processing, cooperative processing, and commercial processing, most of which are automated.

For nearly all American libraries, the Library of Congress (LC) has been the primary source of bibliographic data for decades. With the advent of automation, LC's bibliographic products have been repackaged or reformatted by vendors, networks, and individual libraries. The result has been the development of large databases with LC records as the core. These databases are used directly by some libraries for their cataloging operations, are accessed by other libraries through a bibliographic utility, and are also used by commercial vendors who provide processing for still other libraries.

Major cataloging operations usually have two production lines: copy cataloging and original cataloging. The copy cataloging operation is usually the larger unit, staffed by well-trained technicians called "copy catalogers," who edit existing bibliographic records either found in machine-readable form, on printed cards or proofslips, in the *National Union Catalog* (*NUC*), or in other bibliographic tools. The original cataloging operation is usually staffed by a handful of professionally trained "original catalogers" who prepare bibliographic records when no cataloging "copy" has been found for the work in hand.

---

*This chapter has been edited, rewritten, and new material added by Barbara B. Tillett.

435

Cataloging operations are now an integral part of automated processing. The development of networking using telecommunications and computers has enhanced cooperation for processing services and systems. Automation has virtually eliminated the isolated individual library doing its own ordering, cataloging, and physical preparation of materials.

BIBLIOGRAPHIC SERVICES
OF THE LIBRARY OF CONGRESS

LC's bibliographic records offer complete coverage for materials, both foreign and domestic, cataloged by the Library. LC is, of course, the copyright depository for domestic works. Two federal legislative acts significantly increased LC's coverage of foreign materials starting in the early 1960s. One authorized certain foreign countries to pay some of their debts to the United States by sending printed materials. The other authorized LC to acquire, catalog, and distribute bibliographic records for all materials of research value published in foreign countries. The thrust of the legislation benefited not only LC, but also all American research libraries.

Cataloging Distribution Service (CDS)

In 1975 the Card Division of LC changed its name to the Cataloging Distribution Service (CDS).[1] The change reflected a trend from print to machine-readable format in its distribution of bibliographic records. The distribution of print formats includes the sale of *LC Rule Interpretations*, LC's *Subject Cataloging Manuals*, the *Library of Congress Classification* schedules, *Library of Congress Subject Headings,* etc. (CDS discontinued the production and sale of printed cards in 1997.) Most of these cataloging tools are available in *Cataloger's Desktop* and *Classification Plus* on CD-ROM with quarterly updates. LC's authority records for names and subjects and also LC's bibliographic records are available through the MARC Distribution Services of the CDS.

Cataloging in Publication (CIP)

Most current American books carry a partial bibliographic description, namely author, title, series statement, notes, subject and added entries, LC call number, *Dewey Decimal Classification* (*DDC*) number, and LC control number (LCCN), on the verso of the title page. The program responsible for providing this bibliographic information is known as Cataloging in Publication (CIP). This program was initiated in 1971. Publishers cooperate by sending paper or electronic data sheets and front matter for books nearing publication to LC for preliminary cataloging prior to publication of their books. CIP records are available on MAchine-Readable Cataloging (MARC) tapes, being later supplanted when the full record becomes machine-readable. CIP records are useful as a ready source of LCCNs. They can also be used to assist in the establishment of name headings. Some libraries use the CIP records for preliminary cataloging and later enhance the record when full LC records appear. Other libraries may use the brief CIP record instead of full cataloging, satisfied with the minimal-level record it provides. The illustration below shows the format and appearance of CIP data:

Library of Congress Cataloging-in-Publication Data

Anglo-American cataloguing rules / prepared under the direction of the Joint
    Steering Committee for Revision of AACR, a committee of the American
    Library Association, the Australian Committee on Cataloguing, the British
    Library, the Canadian Committee on Cataloguing, the Library Association,
    the Library of Congress. — 2nd ed., 1998 revision.
        p. cm.
    Includes index.
    ISBN 0-8389-3486-2. — ISBN 0-8389-3485-4 (pbk.)
        1. Descriptive cataloging—Rules. I. Joint Steering Committee
    for Revision of AACR. II. American Library Association.
    Z694.15.A56A53 1998
    025.3´2-dc21   98-8479

MARC Distribution Service /
MAchine-Readable Cataloging (MARC)

The importance of LC for setting catalog practice became even more evident
with the introduction of the MARC Distribution Service.[2] The initial study began in
1964; since that time, extensive experimentation proceeded in the MARC I and
MARC II, the Retrospective Conversion (RECON), the Cooperative MAchine-
Readable Cataloging (COMARC), the British UK/MARC pilot projects, MARC
format integration in 1995, and the harmonization of USMARC and CAN/MARC to
MARC 21 in 1999.

At first, records were available only for English-language monographs, but
now there are formats available for archival materials, audiovisual materials, computer files, films, manuscripts, maps, music, and serials as well as for books. In addition, the Library of Congress does cataloging in over 400 languages. MARC records
for materials in several non-roman-alphabet languages (Arabic, Hebrew, Chinese,
Japanese, Korean, Persian, and Yiddish) are entered with those character sets. Other
non-roman-alphabet languages are transliterated as the MARC records are created.

The Conversion of Serials (CONSER) automated database was sponsored by
the Council on Library Resources (CLR), using the online facilities of OCLC, and
distributed through the MARC Distribution Service—Serials. Starting in mid-1976
with nearly 30,000 LC/MARC serial records, and accepting input from 14 North
American libraries, it amassed over 200,000 records in its initial two years. Only
one-third of them were authenticated by LC and the National Library of Canada (the
Designated Centers of Responsibility), but the number of verifications increased
each year. Original plans were for LC to take over full support at the close of the
two-year pilot program, but when it ran into difficulties in expanding its automation
capacity, OCLC agreed to retain the master database, assuming managerial responsibility as well. LC continues to coordinate the project and maintain the CONSER
records through the Program for Cooperative Cataloging (PCC).

Another project to add machine-readable bibliographic records for materials
previously cataloged on cards was the REMARC project, a retrospective conversion
project. The REMARK database was created by Carrollton Press starting in 1980.
The goal was to convert to MARC format nearly five million titles cataloged by LC
between 1897 and 1968 (the year that most English-language LC cataloging of
monographs became available in MARC format). Carrollton also converted some
items cataloged by LC since 1968 that were not input into the MARC database by

LC (e.g., foreign-language items that were phased into the MARC program throughout the 1970s). These records are available through AutoGraphics, the current owner of REMARC. Users of LC's online catalog will see these records identified as "PREMARC," but they are not included in LC's MARC Distribution Service.

Other projects to add to the LC MARC database began as experiments in cooperative cataloging. In the early 1980s the University of Chicago and Harvard University joined with LC to create cataloging records in MARC format. Library staff at both Harvard and Chicago directly input bibliographic records into the LC database, which were then distributed along with LC records to MARC subscribers. This project expanded to become the National Cooperative Cataloging Project (NCCP), and in 1995 became the PCC.

The growth and nearly universal acceptance of the MARC formats, and even more, the publication of *Anglo-American Cataloguing Rules, Second Edition* (*AACR2*), highlighted the need for machine-readable authority records. A MARC format for name authority records was developed in the late 1970s, and LC began inputting name authority records in 1978. Later the MARC format for authorities was expanded to accommodate subjects, series, and uniform titles. All new names, series, uniform titles, and subjects are currently entered into the LC database in the MARC authorities format, and many records have been retrospectively converted.

It is possible to obtain a subscription to one or more of the MARC Distribution Services. One can receive only books, visual materials, music, computer files, maps, or CONSER serials, or all of these. Also available are Name Authorities and Subject Authorities. A product catalog describes this service.[3] All of the major bibliographic utilities subscribe to the MARC Distribution Services. Manuals on the MARC 21 formats are available.

In addition to the MARC 21 records created by LC and the National Library of Canada, other countries have accepted the MARC format with slight variations for creating machine-readable cataloging records, such as UKMARC used in parts of the United Kingdom. Some other countries utilize the variations of the UNIMARC format established through the International Federation of Library Associations and Institutions (IFLA), or have their own national format, such as MAB in Germany. Mapping across these formats enables sharing of records internationally.

CENTRALIZED PROCESSING

In library systems serving an entire region, county, municipality, university, public school district, commercial enterprise, or government agency, a central processing office normally handles the acquisition and preparation of materials for all public service branches. Subunits may do a final checking of records and file those records in their branch catalogs, but if any significant revision of the work is needed, it usually goes back to the central office. This type of organization received strong emphasis with the rapid growth of library systems after World War II.

The term *centralized processing* may be broadly defined as any consolidated effort to bring under one control the technical operations necessary to prepare library materials for access and use at different service points. In the ensuing discussion several comments are made that apply equally well—perhaps with some slight modification—to cooperative efforts and even to commercial sources of cataloging. The reader can carry over such observations into those discussions where they have a bearing.

Processing centers take a variety of forms, but can generally be grouped into broad categories according to one or more notable characteristics. Grouping by type of services rendered gives:

- Centers responsible for acquisition and complete technical processing, down to the physical marking and/or jacketing
- Centers that order, catalog, and classify
- Centers that only catalog and classify

There are, of course, advantages to setting up a processing center for a group of libraries or branches. They include:

- Increased efficiency in handling more material at less cost
- Higher quality cataloging
- Centralization and simplification of business routines
- Better deployment of staff through specialization
- Use of more sophisticated equipment
- Opportunities to create union catalogs

There are problems as well. Local variations in practice have to be identified and coordinated, or, if necessary, eliminated. Economic justification must be carefully determined, both before and after decision-making, to ensure that it is real, not imaginary. Many descriptive reports of individual centers lack critical self-appraisal and follow-up studies, especially in their cost analyses. Efficiency of operation is often the function of size. The "optimum" volume of processing in a given center should be determined. Combining several different types of libraries (e.g., school and public) within one system may lead to problems that even a highly structured organization cannot solve. We often learn as much from our failures as from our more successful attempts at consolidation.

COOPERATIVE SYSTEMS

The chief trait differentiating cooperative from centralized processing is that the cooperative approach involves several independent libraries or systems. Each member usually continues to perform some of its own technical service work, depending on exchange of data to achieve broader coverage or leaving a sizeable portion of its processing to be performed as a group project. Again, better use of resources, personnel, and equipment, as well as higher discounts on bulk purchases, are anticipated. The need for more standardization in ordering, cataloging, and processing may become either an advantage or a disruptive factor.

There are a number of cooperative arrangements in which several libraries share a single terminal connected to a bibliographic utility. Several libraries with small budgets and small staffs can pool resources to share one membership in a utility. Some such libraries may use the terminal only a few hours a month; others may use it one day a week. The librarians must commute to the location of the terminal and must schedule terminal time carefully.

UNION CATALOGS

Union catalog projects are not, strictly speaking, a type of processing arrangement, but they are essential to a successful processing center and can be a *sine qua non* of a cooperative system. For example, the Bibliographical Center for Research (BCR) in Denver started in 1936 with a WPA grant to develop a union catalog based on a depository set of Library of Congress cards marked to show the holdings of member libraries in the Rocky Mountain area. The catalog was designed chiefly to serve BCR as a clearinghouse for regional interlibrary loans. In 1975, after a period of waning membership and reduced revenues, new objectives were announced, including the brokerage of OCLC services, with aid to members in other, related fields of communication, systems study, and network stimulation. The union catalog and interlibrary loan (ILL) services continued, but were deemphasized in favor of newer forms of cooperation. As at BCR, most union catalog projects in printed card form are now valued primarily for having fostered early efforts at library cooperation in many kinds of consortia and networks.

Some of those consortia and networks have produced online union catalogs at various levels:

- International online union catalogs of the major bibliographic utilities

- Multi-institutional regional or state networks, such as the union catalog for libraries in Illinois or Wisconsin

- Single institution union catalogs, ranging from the statewide nine-campus online union catalog of the University of California to the union catalog for the branches of an individual public library

There are also specialized union catalogs for types of materials such as the Union Catalog of Newspapers on OCLC and numerous union lists of serials, including those available through the bibliographic utilities.

PROGRAM FOR
COOPERATIVE CATALOGING (PCC)

Initiated in February 1995, the PCC grew out of cooperative activities of the previous 20 years. LC began NACO in the late 1970s and expanded the cooperative projects for contributing full bibliographic records in NCCP. In November 1992 various participants from cooperative library programs met and formed the Cooperative Cataloging Council (CCC) that conducted studies to determine a strategic direction for future cooperative projects. The result was the PCC that incorporated the CONSER program in October 1997. PCC now has four components:

NACO (name authority program)
SACO (subject authority program)
BIBCO (bibliographic record program)
CONSER (cooperative online serials program)

According to its brochure, PCC is "an international cooperative effort aimed at expanding access to library collections by providing useful, timely, and cost-effective cataloging which meets mutually accepted standards of libraries around the world."[4] Participants contribute records through RLIN or OCLC and LC distributes those records through the MARC Distribution Service.

One of the major initiatives of PCC has been the promotion of a standard for what PCC calls the "core" record, a bibliographic record containing all essential bibliographic data elements. The purpose is to produce bibliographic records that can be created in a timely way and used by others with little or no editing, thus reducing the overall cost of cataloging.

ONLINE BIBLIOGRAPHIC UTILITIES

Various definitions of networking spell out theoretical criteria or conditions. In practice, however, the term covers any systematic interchange of materials, bibliographic data, services, information, or occasionally, the transfer of such resources from a central office to a number of libraries. *Network* has been used to describe multi-library organizations designed to facilitate interlibrary loan, reference, duplicate exchange, processing, and the like. Our concern in this section is with the last named activity.

There are at present two major online bibliographic utilities in the United States: OCLC Online Computer Library Center (OCLC),[5] which recently merged with and absorbed the former Western Library Network (WLN), and Research Libraries Information Network (RLIN).[6] A third utility, A-G Canada Ltd., also serves some libraries in the United States, although the majority of its members are in Canada.[7] The Network Development Office of LC coined the term *bibliographic utility* for these online processing systems, which is what they are commonly called today.[8] This term refers to providers of computerized cataloging records as distinguished from bibliographic service centers or regional networks, e.g., the Southeastern Library Network (SOLINET), which serve as regional brokers, providing intermediate communication, training, and service for participating libraries.

Bibliographic utilities seek to make catalog data widely and conveniently available, to foster processing speed and efficiency, to reduce the staff and cost of technical operations, and to facilitate resource sharing. Emphasis varies with the types of library a utility is designed to serve. RLIN, for example, caters to the needs of major research libraries, while OCLC appeals to a wider spectrum. As most bibliographic utilities evolved, their goals broadened to include support for different library functions.

Although the objectives of the two major bibliographic utilities are similar, their services, costs, and operating procedures differ considerably. Each offers unique features that involve advantages and disadvantages for different members. The library that has potential access to more than one utility must consider carefully such factors as cost, size of database, adaptation to its needs, types of service contracts, training and support arrangements, and the membership among neighboring libraries.

OCLC Online Computer Library Center (OCLC)

This oldest and largest of the bibliographic networks was incorporated in 1967 as the Ohio College Library Center, establishing an online, shared cataloging system with an online union catalog to the 54 academic libraries of Ohio. Online operations began in 1971 and expanded rapidly. By 1999 there were over 33,700 participating libraries throughout the world, cataloging most of their incoming materials through use of the existing online records, and inputting their original catalog records for cooperative use by other members. In 1978 it changed its name to the acronym OCLC, Inc., downplaying the former regional connotation. At the same time, the governing structure was altered to allow libraries outside Ohio equal participation in its governance.

In 1981 the official name was changed to OCLC Online Computer Library Center, Inc., in response to the fact that many people thought "OCLC" should stand for something. A Users' Council, elected from participants grouped in the regional service networks, chooses from among its members six of the 15 who serve on the Board of Trustees. The Users' Council also advises the Board, which is the corporation's governing body. Additionally, there are several Advisory Committees, including the Advisory Committees on College and University Libraries (ACCUL), on Public Libraries (ACPL), on Special Libraries (ACSL), the Higher Education Policy Advisory Committee, and the Research Libraries Advisory Committee (RLAC) made up of 12 directors of research libraries. RLAC meets three times a year to articulate the special needs and concerns of research libraries that are members of OCLC. There are also advisory committees on Collections and Technical Services, Resource Sharing, Reference Services, and Research.

OCLC serves individual libraries for the most part through 16 broker networks such as AMIGOS, FEDLINK, NELINET, OHIONET, SOLINET, and BCR. The western states, Europe, the Middle East and Africa, Latin America and the Carribean, Asia Pacific, and Canada each have a regional service center maintained by OCLC itself, and there are a few scattered independent members. The brokers negotiate group contracts on behalf of their affiliates, perform profiling and staff training according to each one's specific needs, handle billing and other business procedures, and offer general assistance in effective utilization of OCLC services. Most regional networks are financed through membership fees plus surcharges on OCLC's charges.

The primary OCLC service has always been the online cataloging subsystem creating a database called WorldCat (the OCLC Online Union Catalog). Because of its widespread use, it is described briefly here, but this overview is not intended to be a full introduction to its operation.[9] A library using the subsystem has access to a database that numbers over 38 million bibliographic records, for which there are over 685 million locations listed. LC MARC tapes and additional cataloging by affiliates are constantly expanding the database at the rate of about one record every 15 seconds. An authorized library staff member at any one of the terminals connected to the system via dedicated line, dial access, or Web access may access any record, then edit the data to agree with the item being processed, and add holdings statements, locations, or other in-house data. For those libraries with card catalogs, cards are produced offline at OCLC headquarters in Dublin, Ohio, and shipped daily. They come arranged in packs according to member specifications, ready for immediate filing in local catalogs. Other libraries receive their records on magnetic tapes, while still others download bibliographic and authority records directly into their local automated systems.

In 1990 OCLC began operation of a new online service, PRISM. It uses the same database that was created in the first online system, but there is a new computer system architecture that results in enhanced capabilities. WorldCat may be searched by personal, corporate, or conference name; a combination of name and title; title; LCCN; ISBN; ISSN; CODEN; or OCLC control number through use of special search keys. Any of these searches except the OCLC control number may be modified by type of material or by date of publication. A major feature of PRISM allows any two of these search keys (except OCLC control number) to be combined using the Boolean operator *AND*. PRISM also has a title browsing capability in which users enter as much or as little of a title as they know. In response the appropriate place in the title index appears and users can scroll up or down the list to find the desired title.

In addition to WorldCat, NACO and SACO authority files from LC are available. These are also searched with search keys. When found, an authority record may be placed in "Copy Display," and the user may then toggle between it and a bibliographic record in "Main Display." This feature may also be used to toggle between two authority records or between two bibliographic records. And, using this feature in the editing process, one may "cut and paste" blocks of text into bibliographic records from either authority records or other bibliographic records. There is also a capability to have a basic authority record generated automatically from a heading in a bibliographic record, which is a help to NACO participants.

Another service available through OCLC is their CJK system for cataloging materials in Chinese, Japanese, and Korean. Special terminals and a printer are used to create catalog cards and machine-readable records with fields in the vernacular characters. Also, a copy of WorldCat is used for the First Search service. First Search, begun in 1991, offers end user searching of WorldCat.

Records are held in WorldCat and in the authority databases in the MARC formats, although responses to searches may first be displayed in truncated or brief formats. New cataloging is entered in a MARC format. There are, of course, standard protocols for cataloging at the OCLC terminals. For one, member libraries are obliged to follow the latest version of *AACR2*. They are also requested, when inputting original cataloging, to check all name, uniform title, and series headings in the LC MARC authority file. Headings found in the authority file that are coded as being *AACR2* are to be input in that form into original cataloging. The system is highly flexible, allowing members to adapt local records to meet local practices and conventions.

Quality control exists in published standards to which participating libraries are expected to adhere. Participants are encouraged to report any errors they find in the database. OCLC staff members check and correct the master records from these reports. Certain authorized libraries have been able to correct errors directly since 1984.

Consultation of training manuals and, above all, hands-on use are needed to gain skill in tagging, searching, and operating the terminals. Most people who have been properly trained find the techniques simple to master. Suggested sources for further information include OCLC's "Documentation" site[10] and texts produced by participating networks. It must be remembered, however, that the online catalog subsystem is constantly developing and changing. Only recent tools should be used. In fact, it is often necessary to supplement published manuals with the serial *OCLC Technical Bulletin* to learn the latest instructions for using the system.[11]

OCLC also offers many other cataloging services including retrospective conversion services, authority control services, TechPro service cataloging, Site Search, InterCat, and related projects, such as Cooperative Online Resource Catalog (CORC) for cataloging Internet resources.[12]

OCLC also has a very active research operation that has in-house research staff and sponsors other library and cataloging research projects. They publish an annual report on OCLC research.

Research Libraries Information Network (RLIN)

RLIN resulted from adoption of Stanford University's Bibliographic Automation of Large Library Operations (BALLOTS) by the Research Libraries Group (RLG). RLG, Inc., was originally formed in 1974 by Columbia, Harvard, and Yale universities and the New York Public Library. Harvard withdrew at the time RLIN was formed, to be replaced by Stanford University. Membership exceeded 160 in 1999. Several hundred other institutions purchase RLG's services (e.g., "search only" access to RLIN).

The corporate objective is to foster interinstitutional support of scholarly communication and instruction in a rapidly changing climate of increasing costs and shrinking resources. Voting officers are elected annually by the member institutions to a 19-member Board of Directors. Together with the President—RLG's executive officer who serves on the Board as a voting member—they establish policies, programs, budgets, and fee structures and appoint committees.

The primary programs of RLG are bibliographic control and access, shared resources, collection management and cooperative development, preservation of research materials, CitaDel Article Citation File, Ariel document delivery, Eureka information discovery and delivery, Zephyr Z39.50 access, and RLG's subject programs. The bibliographic component, called RLIN, consists of a computerized set of data files and data manipulation programs. RLIN provides catalog worksheets, printed cards, magnetic tapes, and online bibliographic and authority records in the MARC 21 communications format; a variety of other acquisitions and in-process forms; and interlibrary loan capabilities.

Unlike OCLC, RLIN preserves bibliographic records in clusters with a separate bibliographic record for every title cataloged by each library. Each library has online access to its own records showing whatever local changes may have been made. Local holdings, etc., are available to each local library, and selected data are available from records of other institutions. This facilitates interlibrary loan.

All entries are in the MARC 21 format, including added copy cataloging and record maintenance. One of RLIN's strengths is its powerful query potential. Eureka is their easy to use search service that allows users to browse by author, title, and subject; to retrieve by keyword or exact heading; to limit a search by such qualifiers as date; to send results to a disk, a printer, or an email account, exporting in many formats. Search terms can be used singly or in any sequence. They include LC control numbers, all or part of call numbers, and LC subject headings. Truncation searching on main and added entry words includes personal surnames and names of corporate bodies and geographic entities. The Boolean logic operators *AND*, *OR*, and *NOT* help tailor search strategies. All searches are interactive and can be negotiated or changed as searching progresses. Searching is also available on authority records.

In 1999 RLIN introduced automatic generation of authority records from headings in bibliographic records. If a library has reason to believe an item will be cataloged by a national agency, brief bibliographic information can be keyed in once. It then is automatically searched against all new records entering the system.

The RLIN database had over 30 million titles as of March 1998, including all of the LC MARC bibliographic and authority records. RLIN has an excellent system to support the "JACKPHY" languages (Japanese, Arabic, Chinese, Korean, Persian, Hebrew, Yiddish) as well as Cyrillic. RLIN also provides access to the *English Short Title Catalogue* (*ESTC*), a research tool for scholars of British literature and culture. RLIN reflects the collections of major research, academic, and national libraries, law libraries, archives and museums, art and music libraries, theological libraries, medical libraries, area studies collections, public and corporate libraries, historical societies and book clubs.

RLG and RetroLink offer "Marcadia," a division of Ameritech Library Services. This service matches records that have been transmitted via FTP against the RLIN database to return records that follow a desired profile, including the insertion of standard local data. RLG offers tools and training. The cost for cataloging is comparable to that of OCLC. A free bimonthly newsletter, *RLIN Focus*, updates users on enhancements, searching tips, and general information about the system, databases, and services.

A-G Canada Ltd.

Canadian efforts toward computer-based network cataloging were sparked largely by the University of Toronto Library Automation Systems (UTLAS), which became a separate corporation in 1983 and changed its name in 1988 to Utlas International. In 1963 the Ontario New Universities Library Project started work on computer-produced book catalogs representing the initial library collections for five new campuses in the province. The project was to facilitate selection, acquisition, and cataloging, while remaining flexible in its record format, access, and products. Implementation in 1965 led to the University's participation in the LC MARC project. By 1970 it was producing cards from MARC tapes for sale to clients, including in 1971 the College Bibliocentre, a processing center for 19 colleges of applied technology. It started supplying computer-based systems and services to libraries in 1973.

The UTLAS system was purchased in the early 1990s and became ISM Information Systems Management Manitoba Corporation. In June 1999 A-G Canada purchased ISM and continues the cataloging products and services primarily to Canadian libraries.

A-G Canada *Impact*/ONLINE is a family of products for networked services for union catalogs, using the Internet. The products include WebPAC, ILL, and CAT for online cataloging, that provides original, derived, and shared cataloging in all formats. Like the other utilities, A-G Canada provides online interactive editing with generation of various offline products: cards, book and computer output microform (COM) catalogs, lists, and forms. Like RLIN, A-G Canada maintains online separate copies of every record produced by every user. These are kept in separate files, which can be searched, but not altered, by other users.

Searching of A-G Canada includes keyword capabilities along with the ability to "browse" personal, corporate, and conference names; titles; series; and subjects. One can also search LCCNs, ISBNs, and other control numbers. Boolean capabilities assist in narrowing keyword searches. The *Impact*/ONLINE database consists of over 30 million titles.

Cooperation

The obvious duplication of resources and effort among the utilities has been of concern for some time. It has been felt that there should be some means for exchanging data across utilities. However, there are political, technical, and economic factors that must be taken into account. In 1980 a study of this subject was completed by Battelle Institute under a grant from the Council on Library Resources. The study recommended either batch processing of search requests to be exchanged among the utilities or allowing a user of one utility direct online access to the others. The recommendations were not implemented, but the report drew attention to the need for cooperation.

As a result there were policy changes, and cooperative projects were initiated. In 1982, for example, OCLC began allowing partial membership and tapeload membership status. At reduced cost over full membership, this allows members of other networks (particularly RLIN) to have access to the OCLC database. Partial members may use noncataloging subsystems or search the database without entering their cataloging. For tapeload members, the location identifier is added to the OCLC master record for records on the library's archive tapes, which are run against the OCLC database. Most of RLG's full members have become tapeload members of OCLC. Similarly, RLIN has loaded some OCLC tapes. OCLC and RLIN exchange CJK records to keep their databases synchronized for Chinese, Japanese, and Korean records. A number of RLG members that were formerly OCLC members desired access to the records they had created on OCLC. By loading their archive tapes into RLIN, they were allowed that access.

FUTURE PROSPECTS

Trends in computer technology and progress in developing bibliographic standards are encouraging. For several years libraries have used minicomputers to operate local online catalogs and other processing functions, such as acquisitions and serials control, at reasonable cost in integrated library systems. Most of these systems, whether developed in-house or purchased from a commercial vendor, have access to the bibliographic utilities and to Internet resources as well as Z39.50 protocol access to the online catalogs of other libraries worldwide. Advances in telecommunication make possible distributed networks, consisting of a series of separate individual library catalogs interconnected by telecommunications links or Web access. Such a configuration is especially attractive in areas where many libraries engage in extensive resource sharing and coordinated collection development.

Even with local online catalogs, libraries still find the large network databases valuable as sources for extended record searching. It appears that cataloging will continue in much the same way as today, transferring the edited machine-readable record into the local online database. Closing of card catalogs, at least in some libraries, was a major step in the evolution of materials processing toward quality improvement and control in standardized entry, descriptive detail, filing, physical preparation, and economical production of records.

Networking and cooperative efforts expanded during the late 1990s to projects for bibliographic control of electronic resources and digital objects. OCLC's Intercat database continues to grow as a source for bibliographic records for Internet resources. The OCLC-sponsored CORC project provides a cooperative means to provide Extensible Markup Language (XML) records with metadata and links to full MARC records for electronic resources. These experiments provide links to search engines for retrieval of these resources in local catalogs.

The professional cataloger's contribution to an exclusively online situation is sometimes questioned. It is possible that many libraries that acquire only standard trade books and accept existing cataloging without modification will no longer need professional processing staff. On the other hand, there will likely be greater coordination of the national cataloging effort. LC cannot maintain timely coverage of the world's entire publication output. Other libraries at home and abroad have taken responsibility for cataloging in specific languages or subject categories. Consistently high standards will be kept in relatively few cataloging centers throughout the world. The number of professional catalogers may well be reduced, but the highly skilled cataloger with special language or subject competency will be in greater demand than ever. Moreover, public service librarians are finding that in-depth knowledge of catalog codes and conventions, machine search strategies, and MARC or other machine-readable formats immeasurably increases their effectiveness in reference work, information exchange, bibliographic problem solving, and implementation of online public-access catalogs.

NOTES

1. *Cataloging Service*, bulletin 113 (Spring 1975): 7–8.

2. Henriette D. Avram, *MARC: Its History and Implications* (Washington, D.C.: Library of Congress, 1975).

3. Library of Congress, Cataloging Distribution Service. "Bibliographic Products & Services" (available: http://lcweb.loc.gov/cds/ [accessed 3/5/00]).

4. "Program for Cooperative Cataloging" (available: http://lcweb.loc.gov/catdir/pcc/ [accessed 3/12/00]).

5. "OCLC Online Computer Library Center" (available: http://www.oclc.org/oclc/menu/home1.htm [accessed 3/12/00]).

6. "Research Libraries Group" (available: http://www.rlg.org/ [accessed 3/12/00]).

7. "A-G Canada, Ltd." (available: http://www.ag-canada.com/ [accessed 3/5/00]).

8. Library of Congress, Network Development Office, "A Glossary for Library Networking," *Network Planning Paper*, no. 2 (Washington, D.C.: Library of Congress, 1978): 7.

9. For general descriptions and comparisons of the major utilities *see* William Saffady, "The Bibliographic Utilities in 1993: A Survey of Cataloging Support and Other Services," Chicago: American Library Association, 1993, in *Library Technology Reports* 29, no. 1 (January/February 1993).

10.   OCLC. "Documentation" (available: http://www.oclc.org/oclc/menu/doc.htm [accessed 3/5/00]).

11.   OCLC. "Technical Bulletins" (available: http://www.oclc.org/oclc/menu/tb.htm [accessed 3/5/00]).

12.   OCLC. "Cooperative Online Resource Catalog" (available: http://www.oclc.org/oclc/corc/index.htm [accessed 3/12/00]).

SUGGESTED READING

Oddy, Pat. "Bibliographic Standards and the Globalization of Bibliographic Control." In *Technical Services Today and Tomorrow*. 2nd ed., edited by Michael Gorman. Englewood, Colo.: Libraries Unlimited, 1998, pp. 67–78.

Reynolds, Dennis. *Library Automation: Issues and Applications*. New York: R. R. Bowker, 1985. Chapters 2–4, pp. 10–14.

Rohrbach, Peter T. *Find: Automation at the Library of Congress: The First Twenty-five Years and Beyond*. Washington, D.C.: Library of Congress, 1985.

Saffady, William. "The Bibliographic Utilities in 1993: A Survey of Cataloging Support and other Services." Chicago: American Library Association, 1993. In *Library Technology Reports* 29, no. 1 (January/February 1993): 1–144.

———. "Commercial Sources of Cataloging Data: Bibliographic Utilities and Other Vendors." Chicago: American Library Association, 1998. In *Library Technology Reports* 34, no. 3 (May/June 1998): 281–432.

20 ⟩ Catalog Management

INTRODUCTION

Efficiency of bibliographic retrieval, and the quality of bibliographic description, are affected not only by the care and standards used to catalog each item, but also by several other important factors:

- The recording of local decisions and practices

- The currency of department files and records

- The organization and routines facilitating each phase of the process

- The continuing maintenance and editing of the catalog

- The oversight of any commercial processing for which the library has contracts

- The involvement with the integrated library system (ILS) with which most libraries function

Each of these factors should be carefully evaluated and efficiently administered. Here we will consider briefly the major responsibilities, summarizing those features for which patterns of implementation may vary from library to library. Organizational structure, including the specification of staff duties, is not within the scope of this text.[1]

CATALOGING RECORDS AND FILES

A catalog department maintains files essential for accuracy, efficiency, standardization, and record keeping. In the past such files were nearly always formatted on cards or slips. Technology now offers new formats, which are successfully used in many libraries.

---

*This chapter has been edited, rewritten, and new material added by Susan Hayes. The section on outsourcing was written by Katherine Ryner.

Catalog Formats

The historical development and present uses of various catalog formats were reviewed briefly in chapter 1, "Cataloging in Context." Although the dictionary catalog on 3" by 5" cards still exists in some libraries, active vendor merchandising of proprietary computer databases now brings alternative catalogs increasingly within the reach of smaller public and school libraries or systems. In some cases the existing card catalog remains in use, while another format is adopted to supplement and continue it.

At the initial conversion stage, machine-readable records may be stored in a large network database, in commercial automated service facilities, on archival tapes, or in the in-house computers of individual libraries. Machine-readable records can be used to generate a book, computer output microform (COM), or compact disk-read only memory (CD-ROM) catalog. CD-ROM catalogs have the same drawbacks as book and COM catalogs, in that they are static—a snapshot of the library's database at a certain point in time. However, the searching capabilities in CD-ROM catalogs are usually enhanced over the author, title, and subject listings in book and COM catalogs, often allowing searching by keyword using Boolean operators in addition to more traditional modes of access.

The number of online computer catalogs (online public access catalogs [OPACs]) in libraries has grown so rapidly that they are now the predominant form. Even in libraries that do not yet have them, most administrators feel that it will be ultimately more satisfactory to wait until they can put their bibliographic records directly online, rather than adopting interim solutions in the forms of book or COM catalogs. The online catalog retains the continuous expansion features of the card catalog, along with the compactness, speed, and ease of access characteristic of book and COM catalogs. Cost is still prohibitive for many smaller libraries but will continue to go down, rather than up, as computer services are expanded and refined. One popular refinement is the OPAC that has evolved from a catalog of the holdings of a particular collection into a "gateway" that provides Internet access as well as access to "virtual" collections.

All of the files discussed in the remainder of this section can and do exist in card, COM, CD-ROM, or online formats. (The only one likely to appear in book format is the catalog department manual, which is now often also found online.)

The Shelflist

The shelflist is a complete record of all titles in a collection, arranged by call number as the library materials are found on the shelves. Its primary purpose is to provide an official inventory record of the collection. Its classified arrangement shows what titles have been placed in a specific class notation. It serves, then, as an important classification aid, for catalogers consult it to verify their library's past use of each notation. The shelflist also displays, within certain limitations, related materials more general and more specific on either side of the notation referred to. In addition, it furnishes the matrix on which unique cutter numbers and workmarks are assigned, to differentiate titles collocated in the same class.

If the library has an online system searchable by call number, this can serve as the shelflist. This is more likely to occur in situations where there is an integrated system that is used for acquisition functions as well as for cataloging. In such a system a record is initiated with the order of an item. Dates, costs, etc., are part of the record and can be maintained for as long as the item is part of the system or even after the item is withdrawn or reported missing. Some libraries, however, maintain a card form shelflist as a backup to the online system. Other libraries, following the current trend away from paper-based records, have jettisoned their traditional shelflists altogether. This decision has been notably deplored by Nicholson Baker in an influential *New Yorker* article,[2] and opinion remains divided about the value and cost-effectiveness of maintaining a shelflist in card format in addition to an online catalog. Today many libraries, in deciding that accurate online records are their first priority, have made the decision not to maintain their shelflists; others, citing space considerations, have discarded theirs.

If a library has a shelflist in card format, and if the decision has been made to maintain it, decisions need to be made about what information is to be kept there. A full description of the card shelflist and a sample shelflist card may be found in the eighth edition of this text.[3]

Authority Files

The purpose of an authority file, or files, is to standardize and control a library's use of name, title, and subject headings and their respective references. (*See also* chapter 18.) Until recently (as discussed in chapter 18) it was thought necessary to have one "authorized" form for every name, title, and subject known by variant forms. Today, in the "global" information world, it is recognized that multiple language forms can be "authorized" forms for access purposes, and that authority records, sometimes called access control records, can contain all variant forms for an entity, without designating one as the "correct" one. Since the international "access control record" has yet to be widely implemented, current practice still dictates the use of an established "heading," or, the exact string of characters of the authorized form for each name, title, or subject that is to be an access point in a library's catalog.

Due to staffing and budget constraints some libraries do not maintain an authority file, and in many smaller libraries its upkeep has often been more honored in the breach than in the observance. Such libraries obviously depend on their prime cataloging sources (e.g., the Library of Congress [LC]) to suggest references and to keep the use of heading forms in standard order. The inconsistencies that inadvertently creep in, through rule changes, error, and the like, are remedied if and when found. In a limited operation there may be some economic justification for this *ad hoc* approach. In larger libraries, where inconsistent and erroneous entries cause misfiling, result in loss of entries in online catalogs, and otherwise obscure valuable entries in extensive files, the interest in authority files continues to escalate as more libraries join the name authorities program of the Program for Cooperative Cataloging (NACO) (*see* chapter 18).

Some libraries use the public catalog as their authority list, but some information that should be available to the acquisitions or catalog librarian does not lend itself to inclusion in a public file. Such information may include the series treatment or the locations of catalogs where the heading and its references were used. Moreover, the introduction of changes in cataloging rules leads to total review of how to integrate old and new forms of headings into the library's catalog.

As noted in chapter 18, there is a difference between the existence of an authority file and the processes of creating and using an authority file. *Authority work* is "the process of determining the form of a name, title, or subject concept that will be used as a heading on a bibliographic record; determining cross references needed to that form; and determining relationships of this heading to other authoritative headings."[4] The record of that work is given in a printed or machine-readable unit, called an *authority record*, that is entered into the *authority file*. The file is then used for the process of *authority control*—i.e., for maintaining the consistency of headings in a bibliographic file and for showing relationships among names, works, and subjects. In increasing numbers of online systems, the process of authority control is becoming at least partially automated, but the process of authority work remains highly tied to human endeavor.

A-G Canada (formerly Information Systems Management/Library Information Services [ISM/LIS]), a number of commercial suppliers of online systems, and some locally developed in-house systems have well-developed authority control programs. Some commercial suppliers of bibliographic services, such as Gaylord and Marcive, provide magnetic tape processing in which a library's archive tapes from a bibliographic utility may be edited to change older forms of headings to new forms. Online Computer Library Center (OCLC) and Research Libraries Information Network (RLIN)) provide their members with LC's authority file online but give no control over headings in their databases. In the systems that provide automated authority control, incoming headings on bibliographic records are automatically checked against the computer authority file. For systems where the bibliographic and authority records are linked, a heading on a new bibliographic record that matches one in the authority file automatically links the bibliographic record to the authority record. When a heading does not match, it is either referred to the cataloger for checking or the system creates a mini-authority record for it.[5] For systems where the bibliographic and authority records are unlinked, a match of an incoming heading with a reference will generate an invalid heading report, and a non-match will generate a new heading report.

Some libraries that maintain authority files still do so in card form; however, most libraries with online catalogs are moving to online authority files. Many authority files, whether online or manual are divided into separate files for names, subjects, and titles. Name authority files bring together in an alphabetic list all name headings, personal, corporate, conference, or geographic, that are used in a given catalog as main, added, analytic, or subject entries. Authority records for series, uniform titles, and topical subjects may be added, creating a general authority file, or they may be handled in separate files.

In-Process Files

Certain areas of acquisitions and cataloging overlap. Each library's requirements must be studied to avoid duplication of record keeping, verification, etc. This is a continuous administrative responsibility. Some file, whether maintained by the catalog manager or by the order librarian, must show "items in process." Its records continuously trace the status of each item from the time it is received in the library until it goes to the shelf, with its permanent catalog record available to the public. Libraries with card files that use multiple order forms can reserve one copy of the form for the in-process record. Some use the original requisition slip, once the book has been invoiced. Others with online systems may be able to use the order record as the in-process record and later enhance that record for the catalog record. Since the correct main entry may not be established until the item is cataloged, some libraries arrange their paper in-process files by title rather than by author. Other libraries capture full-level bibliographic records from the bibliographic utilities and display these in their online catalogs attached to item records displaying "In Processing" statuses. Library patrons interested in obtaining an "In Processing" item, may request, often through their library's circulation department, that it be rush cataloged. A library's interlibrary loan (ILL) department may also request the rush cataloging of an "In Processing" item to fill an ILL request from another institution.

Catalog Department Manuals

The purpose of a department manual is to codify all pertinent decisions and procedures. The manual should be readily available to every member of the library staff, and it should contribute to the in-service training of every new cataloging employee. Even public service staff should be able and willing to consult it on problems of local catalog interpretation and use. Until recently, most departmental manuals were in looseleaf format, so the various tagged and indexed sections could be withdrawn and replaced by updated material as needed. Today, many libraries mark up their manuals in HTML and mount them on their Web sites.

Foster recommends that a departmental manual give complete coverage of responsibilities and practices and that it be easy to use, to read, and to revise. He gives the following points to remember during its preparation:

1. Arrange material in logical order so that related information is found together.

2. Use precise and concrete words, not abstract words. And illustrate whenever possible.

3. Be alert to details. Write the manual so that there is no question about procedures and so that the newcomer can easily understand and follow each routine.

4. But do not over-detail. Too much detail provides no room for individual variation and will not allow for minor changes without complete rewriting.

5. Anticipate future revisions and additions.

6. Before adding a new procedure into the manual, test it out to discover and correct unforeseen problems.

7. Take advantage of auxiliary sources, particularly publications from LC and, if the library is part of a network, publications distributed by network headquarters.[6]

On the first and last points, both related information and LC publications can be hyperlinked in manuals that appear on Web sites. On the last point, the department manual may contain guidelines for input standards for automated systems or refer to those input standards of the bibliographic utility or network to which the library belongs.

Some catalog department manuals also contain expectations for cataloging staff job performance with specific guidelines for performance standards. Such guidelines are very useful for a clear understanding of expectations when it is time for performance evaluations.

CATALOGING ROUTINES

Copy Cataloging

We know that much cataloging performed in the United States today is derived from LC copy in machine-readable form.[7] Another large amount of cataloging is derived from copy created by other members of a bibliographic utility. Since LC uses International Standard Bibliographic Description (ISBD) and *Anglo-American Cataloguing Rules, Second Edition, 1998 Revision (AACR2R98)*, most present-day descriptive cataloging embodies the precepts of these two compatible and internationally recognized paradigms. (A particular usage of the ISBD, ISBD(ER) for electronic resources, is currently under consideration by the cataloging community.) Local catalogers may use a description, as found on LC or other copy, as it stands or may alter it to reflect differences in a copy of an item received locally, to correct occasional errors made on outside copy, to adjust headings to fit the local authority file, or to add name, title, or subject added entries.

In the area of subject analysis, LC provides in many of its records a suggested *Dewey Decimal Classification (DDC)* class number, as well as its own full call number, and sometimes provides possible alternative LC and DDC class numbers for such materials as bibliographies, biographies, and the separate parts of a monographic series. It also shows the subject headings it has chosen for the work. Local copy catalogers may use LC decisions as they stand, or may modify them to reflect variations in edition, impression, or format; to complete the DDC class numbers; to adjust official LC call numbers to their local shelflists; to substitute *Sears List of Subject Headings (Sears)* or other subject list terms for the LC subject headings; and to omit, add, or change other tracings. Searching for full-level bibliographic records that match the item in hand is a large part of the routine copy cataloging workflow: records are obtained through pre-searching by a library's acquisitions department, further searching by copy catalogers, or through a programmed searching service such as Research Library Group's (RLG) Marcadia. If no record is available from LC or some other reliable bibliographic agency, original cataloging is usually necessary.

It is more convenient to edit copy to local standards with online cataloging than when using printed cards from LC or other sources. Still, a high degree of local variation from standard LC practice tends to slow workflow, due largely to the need to consult local authority files and shelflist records.

To profit most from online cataloging, it is a good idea to review all local variations from standard practice at the time a library joins a bibliographic utility or network. This is not to suggest that all variations are misguided. Many local prerogatives are necessary because of inconsistent precedents over the years on the part of LC itself. Others may be justified by special local conditions. Librarians should review all such variations in the light of their costs and their effects on processing efficiency. Any decision will affect online cataloging in areas such as terminal staffing, policies on the use of other libraries' records, and the organization of authority (integration) procedures.

Original Cataloging

There are two phases in original cataloging: descriptive cataloging and subject cataloging. While most catalogers do both, there are separate mental processes to be followed in conducting the two phases.

Descriptive Cataloging

Most libraries follow LC, conforming to ISBD and *AACR2R* requirements, or some modification thereof. Bibliographic description requires transcription from the chief sources of information according to prescribed guidelines in *AACR2R* and *Library of Congress Rule Interpretations* as modified in local practice. Although professionals are often needed to catalog electronic resources using *AACR2R* or one of the recently developed encoding standards for metadata (e.g., the Dublin Core), much of descriptive cataloging is straightforward and is a task assigned to paraprofessional staff in many libraries.

Original descriptive cataloging is described briefly as follows. *AACR2R* outlines three levels of description, with increasing detail included at each of the two higher levels. It also offers options throughout, which frequently have to do with adding further details to the record. Main and added (non-subject) entries are determined in accordance with *AACR2R*, or perhaps with some adjustments for established practice. Any changes from LC practice, or *AACR2R* options exercised, should be described in the catalog department manual. All new headings should be recorded in the local authority list, along with references as indicated. Authority control takes place as discussed earlier.

Subject Cataloging

In original subject cataloging the cataloger must examine the information package in order to determine what it is about. With the "aboutness" concept in mind, the subject heading list and subject authority file used by the library must be consulted for consistent selection and recording of accepted headings and references. Obsolete terminology may be caught and changed at once, although it is usually better to postpone major overhauls until a designated time, in order to expedite new cataloging in progress.

For original cataloging, classifying an information package requires judgment. The task requires the selection of an appropriate classification number that fits the existing collection in subject emphasis and then requires adjusting the resulting call number to fit uniquely into the existing collection. Although research on the automatic classification of electronic resources is being conducted by OCLC in its Scorpion project,[8] it is not yet possible to rely on automatic classification. Most information packages still need to be classified by humans for original cataloging, and when no classification is provided on cataloging copy as well. After examining the information package to be cataloged in the light of the classification schedules used by the library, the cataloger usually consults the shelflist to see if the class notation chosen, or its possible alternative, has been previously used for similar or different materials. When the appropriate class notation is selected, the distinguishing cutter number, with any necessary additions, such as workmark, edition date, or location symbol, is added. The full call number may be recorded in the shelflist, on the information package proper (with volume and copy number if needed), and on a work form. If the shelflist is in card form, a temporary slip may be inserted in the shelflist pending arrival of permanent cards. Libraries using COM or book catalogs, and even OPACs, frequently maintain card shelflists for recent additions.

Use of Work Forms

Work forms are useful to make procedures routine and to ensure full coverage of essential points. In print format they may be sheets, cards, or slips pre-printed to exhibit the standard categories of information that catalogers must consider. If the cataloging is based primarily on a large union file of machine-readable records and is done at a terminal, the operator usually can call up prepared work forms. These are completed in substantive detail directly at the keyboard. Where the MAchine-Readable Cataloging (MARC) format is used, the online work form is customized to describe a "typical" information package, using preselected fields and tags which are then changed or expanded as needed. On the other hand, the cataloger may prefer to start in longhand on a printed form (*see* figure 20.1, page 457), handing the completed sheet to a terminal operator for inputting. Figure 20.2 (*see* page 458) shows the OCLC monographs work form as it looks when called up online.

Following the completion of work forms, the item is generally ready for final preparation. In some libraries the work form is manually translated by a typist onto pockets and labels before the item can have its final processing. Other libraries rely on a feature of their online catalogs which allows the call number from the holdings record to be mapped into a labeling program, enabling the labeler to complete the information package's final processing. Still other libraries have this step performed by commercial suppliers, by a network central office, or by in-house automated printers.

Catalog Maintenance

Like any ongoing function a catalog is subject to obsolescence, inadvertent clerical and professional errors, inconsistency, and a variety of related ills. It therefore requires continual editing and maintaining, although libraries, being continually shorthanded, often neglect or postpone the responsibility, to the detriment of effective service. As collections grow, the efforts needed to keep a catalog in satisfactory condition tend to increase exponentially. Call number changes, location changes, treatment changes, and blind references (i.e., references to or from headings once used but incompletely or inaccurately withdrawn) are among the major maintenance problems encountered in every kind of catalog. Other problems are specific to a particular catalog type. Online catalogs frequently contain data entry errors, invalid uniform resource locators (URLs), incomplete or defective records due to faulty migration from a previous online system, and problems stemming from the reindexing of the database following implementation of a new release of catalog software. Book, COM, CD-ROM, and online catalogs are particularly vulnerable to typographical errors. Such errors cause major retrieval problems.

Fig. 20.1. An OCLC participant's paper work form.

Type: a	ELvl: I	Srce: d	Audn:	Ctrl:	Lang:
BLvl: m	Form:	Conf:	Biog:	MRec:	Ctry:
	Cont:	GPub:	Fict:	Indx:	
Desc: a	Ills:	Fest:	DtSt:	Dates:	

010	041
040	043
020	090

1 ___ ___	Main entry
24 ___ ___	Uniform title
245 ___	Title
250	Edition
260	Publication info.
300	Phys. desc.
4 ___ ___	Series
5 ___	Note
5 ___	Note
5 ___	Note
6 ___ ___	Subject
6 ___ ___	Subject
6 ___ ___	Subject
7 ___ ___	Added entry
7 ___ ___	Added entry
8 ___ ___	Series traced differently
9 ___ ___	Local option

Fig. 20.2. OCLC work form for monographs.

```
OCLC:   NEW                    Rec stat:    n
  Entered:   19990820           Replaced:   19990820      Used:      19990820
> Type: a        ELvl: _        Srce:    _   Audn:        Ctrl:        Lang: ____
  BLvl: m        Form:          Conf:    0   Biog:        MRec:        Ctry: ____
                 Cont:          GPub:        Fict: 0      Indx:  0
  Desc: _        Ills:          Fest:    0   DtSt: _      Dates: ____,      <
>    1 010          <
>    2 040          $c DD0 <
>    3 020          <
>    4 041 _        $h $b  <
>    5 050 _        $b  <
>    6 090          $b  <
>    7 049          DD0A <
>    8 1__ _        <
>    9 245 __       $b $c  <
>   10 246 __       <
>   11 250          <
>   12 260          $b $c  <
>   13 300          $b $c  <
>   14 4__ __       $v  <
>   15 5__ _        <
>   16 6__ __       <
>   17 6__ __       <
>   18 7__ _        <
>   19 8__ __       <
```

Maintenance of every catalog is necessary to guard against obsolescence of terminology and to remedy the inconsistencies resulting from different rules for headings, especially in online catalogs lacking a global update capability. References must be maintained, and old name and title entries must sometimes be changed when there are conflicts with new entries to the catalog. In addition there must be concern for maintenance of the equipment necessary for use. Equipment maintenance, however, usually is not performed by catalog department staff.

Card catalogs are an even higher maintenance catalog type. Because they are subject to physical wear and tear, repair of damaged drawers or replacement of worn and soiled cards is important. Tray labels, guide cards, and instructions for use inside and outside the file should be altered whenever improvements are possible. Expansion inevitably requires occasional shifting of cards. Catalog editing is needed to eliminate unnecessary entries, to suggest improvements, and to plan for future development. Old entries may not have been removed during cancellation of a title. Inconsistent headings, misleading or blind references, filing errors, missing cards, wrong call numbers, etc., all cause perplexity and ill will.

Arrangement and Filing

Before the advent of online catalogs, some people thought that filing would become a nonissue in online catalogs. However, we have now learned that when more than ten or so entries are retrieved in response to a search, they need to appear on the screen in some logical order. Catalog users are not happy with responses in which the entries appear in the order in which the items happened to be acquired by the library. Filing order is somewhat less of a problem in online, book, and microform catalogs than it is in card catalogs. It is easier to scan one or more columns of entries and to discern their order than it is to determine the order of cards. In online catalogs it is often difficult to guess how many screens "in" one has to go or how far down one has to scroll, to find a desired bibliographic record in a retrieval set of 20 or more.

Neophyte catalogers are surprised to discover many alternative filing codes. They learn that choice of catalog arrangement (dictionary or divided) not only affects arrangement issues, but also affects cataloging decisions to some extent. Filing problems resulting from entry conflicts between the old *ALA Cataloging Rules* and the *Anglo-American Cataloging Rules* (*AACR*) were a major impetus to the closing of such large card catalogs as those of the New York Public Library and LC. Some libraries have attempted to interfile old and new forms of the same entry in card catalogs. In online catalogs all forms are arranged exactly as they appear. In either case, ample use of references is necessary.

Research libraries with card catalogs in the past often maintained one or another of various kinds of "categorical filing," particularly in those parts of their catalogs where relatively large numbers of highly formalized entries were concentrated. Categorical filing was based on the assumption that the user knows enough about a subject to prefer a partially classified arrangement over straight adherence to the alphabet. For instance, LC used to arrange its entries for individual books and groups of books of the Bible in canonical order, rather than alphabetically, as part of an intricate categorical arrangement.[9] Less scholarly libraries generally preferred a simpler and therefore more readily grasped alpha-arrangement. The large academic and research collections gradually succumbed to popular demand, and to the requirements of computer filing.

There is currently very little control over the arrangement of catalog displays. When one purchases an integrated library system (ILS) with its OPAC, one accepts the arrangement that has been programmed into that system. An understanding of certain filing dilemmas can be useful in making decisions about catalog maintenance of heading forms and references. An introduction to some filing/display dilemmas may be found in Taylor's *The Organization of Information*.[10] In addition the Appendix to this text includes a discussion of filing dilemmas, an introduction to the *ALA Filing Rules*,[11] and a discussion of shelflist filing. Many libraries continue to maintain card shelflists as supplements to their OPACs, making understanding of notational arrangement an important part of catalog maintenance.

Reproducing Catalog Cards

Catalog cards can be produced by typing each one individually. More often they are purchased in sets. One source of such sets is the bibliographic utility of which the library may be a member. In addition to the card sets mailed from the bibliographic utility, card sets may be produced from the utility's online records by downloading to a printer or by downloading to the library's own computer or personal computer. Cards are then printed using special card production software. It is also possible to photocopy a set from one master unit card by adapting information from Cataloging in Publication (CIP) or the *National Union Catalog* (*NUC*), or typing one copy of one's original cataloging.[12] There are also several computer programs on the market that will produce a catalog card set when main entry information is typed into the screen form.

Reclassification and Recataloging

There is inevitably a certain amount of recataloging to be performed in any library. Recataloging may be either a mass production affair or an individualized, single item performance. During the 1960s and early 1970s many medium-sized and larger libraries, especially academic ones, mounted full reclassification projects from *DDC* to *Library of Congress Classification (LCC)*. Large-scale reclassification was sometimes undertaken on special collections or a selected part of a collection. In the course of most such efforts, brief, inaccurate, or obsolete cataloging could be caught and redone. Many collections were at the same time weeded and surveyed for needed new materials.

More commonly, however, recataloging is performed on individual items for which the former records prove unsatisfactory. Classification notations within a given classification scheme (e.g., *DDC* or *LCC*) may need changing because the schedules have been revised or because of new interpretations and needs within the collection. Recataloging on a greater or lesser scale may also be the consequence of adopting a new or revised descriptive cataloging code. For instance, *Anglo-American Cataloguing Rules, Second Edition (AACR2)* called for many more corporate names to be entered directly under the body's own name. Previously, the rules called for entering most such names subordinately under a higher body (e.g., "Library of Congress" was "United States. Library of Congress"). Catalogers whose libraries were not yet ready to close their card files and start new ones based strictly on the changed rules had to decide what to do about superseded usages, particularly changed headings for already used entries that were likely to be used again.

Today some library catalogs still contain headings constructed under old rules. As more online systems provide linked authority control, the problem can be fixed in OPACs. However, in libraries with card catalogs, some attempt to solve this dilemma with full sets of *See also* references linking old and new forms of headings in unified or split files without actually recataloging the older works. Others refile old headings under guide-cards carrying the new heading forms, leaving *See* references at the old positions to assist users who still search under those outdated forms. Still other libraries recatalog under the new forms, particularly if there are only a limited number of entries under the obsolete forms. Old and new forms are often identified and corrected during preprocessing for an online catalog's database or in subsequent cleanup of the database. As mentioned previously, ongoing maintenance of changed forms of headings in online catalogs can be simplified through a "global update" capability.

Closing Card Catalogs

In 1965 studies were made at the New York Public Library that confirmed that a staggering number of the cards (actually 29 percent) in the public catalog of the Research Libraries Division were illegible, damaged, dirty, badly worn, or otherwise unfit to remain. The problem was aggravated by the fact that some entries had been there for over 100 years. It was a dramatic instance of a malaise that was reaching epidemic proportions in many long-established research libraries. Besides the deterioration problem, upkeep and maintenance were expensive and unsatisfactory. Space, lighting, and furniture posed real logistics problems in files of over 10 million cards. Labor costs for filing were also rising.

Libraries began to look to technology to solve the card problem. Book or COM catalogs could be made from machine-readable records. As the 1970s progressed, it began to be apparent that the machine-readable records could be accessed directly online. LC made plans to "freeze" its existing card files on January 1, 1980, in conjunction with the appearance of *AACR2*. At that time they planned to abandon their practice of "superimposition," by which they had retained most established headings regardless of rule changes, following *AACR* dictates only for those headings being established for the first time. Superimposition had been an attempt to avoid the Herculean task of updating all forms rendered obsolete by the new rules. Even with liberal use of references, it confounded catalogers and catalog users alike, with its legacy of inconsistent access forms in a single file.

Because most other libraries, even large ones, were not yet ready to go online, LC was convinced by other large libraries to postpone this action for a year. Starting in 1981, with all obsolete headings officially frozen in a searchable but defunct catalog, headings for new materials were established according to *AACR2* regardless of whether a given entry was identified differently in the old catalog. In situations where libraries closed old catalogs, complete bibliographic access to all the records in *both* catalogs under many personal, corporate, and geographic headings required that the search be conducted under heading forms that differed from one catalog to the other. The kind and number of references to be used in one or both catalogs occasioned much discussion.

Not all librarians in 1981 were convinced that a step as radical as closing one catalog and starting afresh on another was the best solution to problems of catalog lag. For the most part, only large research collections tried it. Most libraries maintained one catalog, using combinations of interfiling, split files, references, and revising old headings.

The advent of online catalogs during the following decades precipitated more card catalog closings than did *AACR2*. Most online catalogs did not have a distinct "opening" date. Several years' worth of entries appeared in both the closed card catalog and the online catalog. Eventually most libraries converted virtually everything in the card catalogs to machine-readable form through a process called "retrospective conversion," and many libraries have thrown out their card catalogs.

Retrospective conversion for an online catalog may involve four steps:

1. retrospective conversion to transform every record in the card shelflist into machine-readable form

2. preprocessing of archival tapes and retrospective conversion tapes by a commercial service on contract

3. systematic database cleanup projects using global update capabilities of the online system

4. ongoing database maintenance

During retrospective conversion and preprocessing operations, outdated headings may be changed to current forms. Retrospective conversion can be done through a bibliographic utility by searching for the records in the database and, when a match is found, adding that record to the library's archive tape. Retrospective conversion can also be done by a commercial service on contract (*see* the "Outsourcing" section in this chapter).[13]

COMMERCIAL PROCESSING

In the mid-1800s, Charles C. Jewett, librarian of the Smithsonian Institution, proposed "A Plan for Stereotyping Catalogues by Separate Titles...."[14] The Smithsonian was at that time a copyright depository. As it produced bibliographic records, they could, he suggested, be preserved on stereotype plates for a variety of applications, including the printing of cards for sale to other libraries on demand. While Jewett's proposal did not itself endure, it presaged the marketing of printed cards undertaken by LC in 1901. Neither venture was "commercial" in the strict sense, although they were later imitated by a host of business concerns. Barbara Westby defines *commercial cataloging* as "centralized cataloging performed and sold by a non-library agency operating for profit."[15] In some cases it has been a by-product of other commercial interests, e.g., the Standard Catalog compilations of H. W. Wilson, the vending emphasis of a book jobber such as Baker & Taylor, or the promotional activities of a corporation like the Society for Visual Education.

The Wilson Printed Catalog Card Service supplied many school and public libraries with simple but adequate card copy at nominal cost for widely read books from 1938 to 1975. During that period over 100 other distributors and publishers followed the Wilson example of supplying a packet of cards with each book sold. In 1976 the first edition of *Cataloging with Copy* listed 15 commercial processing services and 5 additional commercial sources of card sets.[16] Technological advances have caused considerable changes in the scene since then. Some of the services are no longer in business. Most of the others have radically changed their character. They have supplemented their print services with microform, CD-ROM, and/or online data retrieval systems. In recent years commercial processors have added catalogers to their staffs and provide cataloging services on a contract basis (*see* the discussion in the "Outsourcing" section of this chapter). Although changes occur rapidly, some recent publications attempt to identify current services.[17]

Outsourcing

One of the more controversial library issues of the past decade has been outsourcing. Outsourcing can be defined as the purchase from an outside vendor of specific services or functions that would otherwise be provided by in-house staff. Libraries have been contracting out services for years, but a more recent trend has been the outsourcing of entire library departments, or even entire libraries. Services that have been outsourced in libraries recently include collection development, cataloging, and processing.

Libraries have been purchasing catalog cards from LC and catalog records from OCLC for decades. Catalog departments often seek outside help for projects such as the cataloging of backlogs, special collections, and foreign language materials. The difference these days is that libraries are downsizing cataloging staff and are paying for-profit vendors for regular cataloging services.

Why would a library want an outside vendor to fulfill its cataloging needs? When a vendor can provide better quality catalog records at a faster pace and at a cheaper rate than in-house staff can provide, the library benefits. Cost savings can be realized because of reduced overhead costs such as equipment, supplies, and bibliographic utility connect time. Physical space can be saved, and staff can be moved into what some might consider to be more critical areas. Some libraries have outsourced cataloging in response to problems with personnel and productivity.

Some proponents of the outsourcing of cataloging services claim that cataloging is not a core function of libraries, and that those personnel resources formerly spent in cataloging should be geared towards such core functions as customer service. That organizing information is a core library service, and that the catalog is the key to the library, is not something that all library administrators agree upon.

Many librarians, though, feel that outsourcing is anathema to the obligations of professional librarianship. Outsourcing cataloging can mean that lower-skilled, lower-paid personnel replace highly-trained (and presumably higher-paid) catalogers. Catalog records that are inaccurate and incomplete can be produced. This results in long-term problems with the catalog database; patron access to collections can be hindered rather than helped by outsourcing.

More arguments against outsourcing include the library's dependency on the vendor. If a library commits to a vendor to perform a function such as cataloging, problems can arise if the vendor changes its core service, no longer supports certain technology, or goes out of business. When cataloging staff members are replaced by outside vendors, local knowledge of collections and user needs is lost, as is loyalty to the institution. Human costs are high: jobs can be lost. If cataloging staff remain employed by the institution, they can lose promotional opportunities and benefits. If displaced staff members are moved to other departments, those other departments are affected. Morale throughout the library can be damaged, and resentment can be fostered. One research study found that it was more cost effective to keep cataloging in-house.[18]

Whether the widespread outsourcing of library services is a wave of the future or just a temporary trend in management theory remains to be seen. The success of outsourced cataloging depends on how the vendor contract is negotiated and on how library administration manages the change. Poorly planned and/or managed outsourcing projects can be very detrimental to staff, to the catalog, and to the bottom line. When outsourcing cataloging, there must be a way to measure in-house performance and costs in order to compare them to outsourced performance and costs. Experienced catalogers must become contract managers, oversee quality control of the vendor's product, and constantly monitor costs and the value of the contract.

INTEGRATED LIBRARY SYSTEMS (ILS)

Most catalog managers are currently dealing with integrated library systems (ILS). When library automation began in the 1970s, most systems were based on a hierarchical model, involving a host mainframe computer and one or more "dumb" terminals. Eventually, minicomputers replaced mainframes, but the basic model, featuring text-based, command or menu-driven OPACs with terminal emulation software, did not change. As microcomputer technology advanced into the 1990s, tasks became distributed between the host, or server, and the requestor, or client, with standard communication methods such as Transmission Control Protocol/Internet Protocol (TCP/IP) and Z39.50 facilitating the sharing of information between client and server. According to Beheshti, the client/server model is "based on modular programming in which a large piece of software is divided into smaller, manageable modules. Each module can then be implemented in an appropriate hardware/software environment."[19]

Today, most library networks use the client/server model, in which the online public-access catalog, or OPAC, is supported by a range of other automated services, which function to heighten its effectiveness as a retrieval tool. As the most visible part of an ILS, the OPAC will display not only location information, but also circulation/reserve status and acquisitions information in the form of "on order/in processing" records.[20] Some OPACs provide serials check-in and bindery information, enabling users to initiate interlibrary loan and/or document delivery requests. Almost all include circulation functions. Other desirable state-of-the-art functions of an ILS include: commercial database access, flexible printing options, electronic reserves, vernacular display of languages, generation of statistics, security and user authentication, and the ability to handle special enhancements, such as interfaces with acquisitions and serials jobbers or a table-of-contents service.[21]

A library's online system may be integrated by using single sets of hardware or software, or it may be "functionally integrated" by linking automated modules supplied by a range of vendors. Shared library standards, such as *MARC 21*, and analogous standards in the computing and networking industries, make integrated library automation possible.[22]

Within the cataloging module, catalogers may create or edit bibliographic records and update holdings information. They may retrieve bibliographic records downloaded or transmitted via FTP from a cataloging resource file, not accessible to the public, for use in copy cataloging. They can copy a record in their own database, and use it as the basis for a new bibliographic record. They can also access, with greater or lesser degrees of interaction, functions located in other modules within the integrated system, such as circulation, acquisitions and reserve. Most online cataloging modules accommodate the creation of templates, usually called workforms, that allow catalogers to call up blank MARC records that have been customized to describe a "typical" information package of a given format. In the authority file, catalogers may create authority records, or edit records that have been generated from headings in bibliographic records.

Online Public Access Catalogs (OPACs)

Although experimentation with (OPACs) began in the 1960s, they did not become really functional until the 1980s. In spite of the fact that they are now the predominant form of catalog in American libraries, OPAC hardware and software is still at the stage of development at which card catalogs were at the beginning of the twentieth century, when there was little agreement on size of cards, amount and order of data to be included, etc. OPACs were developed locally in libraries and also commercially. Some expanded out of circulation systems that developed in the 1970s. Others were designed solely to serve as OPACs. Still others grew up as one component of integrated online systems that incorporate acquisitions and serials control functions as well as circulation and catalog functions.

Most OPACs are configured or customized according to a purchasing library's needs: all differ in the way in which data are displayed, the amount of data displayed, and the manner in which a user must interact with them, some being command-based, and others being menu-driven. Some allow users to limit a search by language, publication date, location or format. There are varying amounts of authority control from none at all to a complete authority record for every heading fully linked to the bibliographic records. OPACs also provide for very different kinds of access ranging from those that essentially duplicate the access points available in a card catalog to those that offer sophisticated levels of searching.

Today, many OPACs are "Webbed" OPACs or WebCats, which replace telnet sessions, and their accompanying logon/logoff protocol, with Web access. Through hypertext links, users can access other catalogs remotely, while Z39.50 technology offers the capacity to search different databases located in different servers. Catalogers as well as users benefit from the increased functionality of OPACs with "Webbed" interfaces: using Windows-based workstations, catalogers can locate bibliographic records from the catalogs of other institutions, extract summary or other notes, and cut-and-paste them into records in their own online catalog.[23]

Future developments in OPAC automation are already on the horizon and promise multilingual systems that permit advanced query processing, probabilistic ranked searching, and relevance feedback, as well as the integration of images, full texts with their associated metadata, and even sound and video clips. Borgman predicts that there will be a shift "from bibliographic data exchange between local integrated systems and between local systems and shared cataloging utilities to interoperability between digital libraries."[24]

IFLA Guidelines for OPAC Displays

In 1997 at the meeting of the International Federation of Library Associations and Institutions (IFLA) in Copenhagen, members from the sections on Bibliography, Cataloguing, Classification and Indexing from the Division of Bibliographic Control, and from the section on Information Technology formed a Task Force "to bring together in the form of guidelines or recommendations a corpus of good practice to assist libraries to design or redesign their OPACs."[25] The focus of the guidelines is on the display of cataloging, rather than circulation, serials check-in, fund accounting, acquisitions or bindery information, and they are intended to apply to all types of catalogs, including graphical user interface- (GUI-) based catalogs and Z39.50-Web interfaces. The intent of the guidelines is "to recommend a standard set of display defaults, defined as features that should be provided for users who have not selected other options, including users who want to begin searching right away without much instruction."[26] The guidelines are divided into principles and recommendations, the recommendations being an expansion of the principles into actual practice, with the principles providing "a context and rationale for the recommendations."[27]

One of the major frustrations for catalog managers in the era of online catalogs has been the loss of control over the display of the cataloging records that they produce. In the card catalog, it was possible to use guide cards, "filing titles," and other such mechanisms in order to place cards where they would be the most useful. The programming of OPACs has often been done by persons with little understanding of the cataloging process. Arrangement and display of headings has too often made catalogs look as if little thought had gone into creation of headings (e.g., when headings are displayed in all capital letters with no punctuation as, for example, "LA FONTAINE JEAN DE 16211695" or "CHICAGO ILL ETHNIC RELATIONS"). The IFLA guidelines are designed to help librarians in customizing OPAC software, and to inform and educate vendors and producers of this software.

Workstations

The origins of the technical services workstation (TSW) go back to the introduction of the personal computer (PC) in the early 1980's. TSWs were first utilized in cataloging departments to facilitate inventory control and timely processing of library materials. The TSW's design and development has varied from institution to institution, depending on the networking environment, system capabilities, and customization by staff.[28] However, according to Brisson and McCue, some features of the TSW have become standard, and form the conceptual model for the TSW used today in many cataloging departments:

> The emergent TSW is based on microcomputer technology. The platform can be an IBM-compatible PC, a Macintosh, a UNIX workstation, or the newly released Power PC, although it should be noted that the majority of libraries use IBM-compatible computers. Regardless of the platform, the microcomputer must have enough computing power to run multiple applications (ideally it should be multitasking). It must also possess local storage capabilities of sufficient size, and it must support graphic-based operations with high resolution monitors that are large enough to display multiple windows.
>
> Workstations are networked—to a LAN, to a TCP/IP ethernet link, and to the Internet. Networking supports access to resources and allows for the sharing of these resources among a work group. . . .
>
> Workstations provide access to a variety of resources through a uniform user interface. . . .
>
> Workstations support enhanced editing and inputting capabilities. For example, workstations possess a cut-and-paste feature so that information can be quickly moved from application to application. . . .
>
> Workstations provide electronic access to cataloging and acquisitions support tools. These tools include locally developed documentation, standards or manuals specific to cataloging or acquisitions (an example being the Cataloger's Desktop of the Library of Congress (LC), or reference resources such as dictionaries, encyclopedias, or language translators. . . .[29]

In the future, as more and more library online systems switch from a mainframe to a client-server environment, it is likely that most library TSW's will be client-based modular platforms that use vendor or local system-supplied software packages that feature update and Z39.50 search/retrieval capabilities.[30]

CATALOGING SUPPORT

As cataloging becomes increasingly automated, a range of electronic and Internet-based products, services, and resources has evolved to support the cataloging process. One of the most widespread is the previously mentioned *Cataloger's*

Desktop, a CD-ROM product of LC, which features the following LC publications: *Library of Congress Rule Interpretations,* Subject Cataloging Manuals for Classification, Shelflisting and Subject Headings, MARC 21 Formats for Bibliographic, Authority, Holdings, and Classification Data and Community Information, as well as the latest editions of all five MARC 21 Code Lists and *AACR2-e.*

OCLC, like LC, has developed several services that provide cataloging support. These include the OCLC Passport for Windows NACO macro, which creates completed authority workforms from bibliographic headings, and CatME for Windows, which allows a cataloger to upload, in real time, records created in a local system to WorldCat, the OCLC Online Union Catalog.

In addition to its Marcadia searching program mentioned previously, RLG offers the Authority Assistant for NACO contributors, which allows NACO catalogers using RLG's RLIN library processing system to select a heading in a bibliographic record and generate an authority record in the RLG Name Authority File.

The following Web sites of use to catalogers were selected from an AUTOCAT file, "Cataloging Tools on the Internet," compiled by Julie Crowley:[31]

ACADEMIC CATALOGING SITES:

Pennsylvania State University Libraries. Cataloging Reference Tools:
   http://www.libraries.psu.edu/iasweb/catsweb/index.htm

University of Missouri Cataloging Tools:
   http://cctr.umkc.edu/~wsistrunk/links.htm#Cataloging

University of Massachusetts at Amherst. Barbara Stewart's "Top 200 Technical Services Benefits of Home Page Development":
   http://tpot.ucsd.edu/Cataloging/Misc/top200.html

Cataloging Tools at Brigham Young University Library:
   http://www.lib.byu.edu/~catalog/hypertechs/

Stanford University Libraries Cataloging Reference Shelf:
   http://www-sul.stanford.edu/depts/catdept/refshelf/refshelf.html

Bridgewater State College. Cataloging Online Tools:
   http://www.bridgew.edu/DEPTS/MAXWELL/cattools.htm

Georgetown University. Online Tools and Resources:
   http://gulib.lausun.georgetown.edu/dept/catalog/tools/

Northwestern University Library. Networked Resources:
   http://www.library.nwu.edu/resources/

Queen Elizabeth II Library at Memorial University of Newfoundland. Charley Pennell's "Cataloguer's Toolbox":
   http://www.mun.ca/library/cat/

Queen's University in Kingston, Ontario. Tech Web. Choose "Cataloguing Tools":
   http://stauffer.queensu.ca/techserv/qtechweb.html

LIBRARY OF CONGRESS SITES:

Library of Congress MARC Standards:
http://lcweb.loc.gov/marc/

Library of Congress Cataloging:
http://lcweb.loc.gov/catdir/catdir.html

Library of Congress Catalog:
http://lcweb.loc.gov/catalog/

Library of Congress. The Experimental Search System:
http://lcweb2.loc.gov/resdev/ess/

Library of Congress's Z39.50 Gateway to Search Other Catalogs:
http://lcweb.loc.gov/z3950/gateway.html#other

Library of Congress Cataloging:
http://lcweb.loc.gov/catdir/catdir.html

NACO Home Page:
http://lcweb.loc.gov/catdir/pcc/naco.html

Library of Congress Cataloging Newsline (LCCN):
http://lcweb.loc.gov/catdir/lccn/

Cataloging Policy & Support Office (CPSO) Home Page:
http://lcweb.loc.gov/catdir/cpso/

Search Library of Congress Catalogs:
http://lcweb.loc.gov/z3950/gateway.html

LCSH Weekly Updates:
http://lcweb.loc.gov/catdir/cpso/wls.html

SACO Homepage:
http://lcweb.loc.gov/catdir/pcc/saco.html

Subject Authority Proposal Form:
http://lcweb.loc.gov/catdir/pcc/sacopropform.html

LCSH Change Proposal Form:
http://lcweb.loc.gov/catdir/pcc/sacochgform.html

OCLC INTERNET SITES:

OCLC Bibliographic Formats and Standards Manual:
http://www.oclc.org/oclc/bib/toc.htm

OCLC-MARC Code Lists:
http://www.oclc.org/oclc/man/code/codetoc.htm

OCLC Cataloging Internet Resources:
http://www.oclc.org/oclc/man/9256cat/toc.htm

Solinet Useful Library Links:
http://www.solinet.net/oclcserv/fourth.htm

Dewey Decimal Classification. Forest Press/OCLC:
http://www.oclc.org/oclc/fp/index.htm

SELECTED CATALOGING RESOURCES:

American Library Association reports from cataloging, etc.,
meetings—prepared by Sherman Clarke:
http://www.geocities.com/WestHollywood/9783/alagen.html

AUTOCAT:
http://ublib.buffalo.edu/libraries/units/cts/autocat/

Cataloger's Reference Shelf—from *The Library Companion*:
http://www.tlcdelivers.com/tlc/crs/CRS0000.htm

Cataloging & Classification Quarterly:
http://ccq.libraries.psu.edu

IFLA Functional Requirements for Bibliographic Records:
http://www.ifla.org/VII/s13/frbr/frbr.pdf

International Conference on the Principles and Future
Development of AACR:
http://www.nlc-bnc.ca/jsc/index.htm

MARBI (Machine-Readable Bibliographic Information),
ALCTS/LITA/RUSA:
http://www.ala.org/alcts/organization/div/marbi/marbi.html

Program for Cooperative Cataloging (PCC) Participants Group
Meeting—from *LC Web*
http://lcweb.loc.gov/catdir/pcc/

CONCLUSION

The catalog manager has responsibility for a major operating tool of the library. As can be seen in this chapter, the person(s) responsible for this area must be knowledgeable in several areas: cataloging, supervising, policies and procedures, managing contracts, and interfacing with ILS vendors. The constant growth of the database and the evolution of functionality of systems requires continuous re-evaluation in order to keep the operation moving smoothly and the database operating effectively.

NOTES

1.   Other reliable texts are available for this purpose. *See*, for example, Marty Bloomberg and G. Edward Evans, *Introduction to Technical Services for Library Technicians*, 5th ed. (Littleton, Colo.: Libraries Unlimited, 1985); and Donald L. Foster, *Managing the Catalog Department*, 3rd ed. (Metuchen, N.J.: Scarecrow, 1987).

2.   Nicholson Baker, "Discards," *The New Yorker* 70, no. 7 (April 4, 1994): 64–86.

3.   Bohdan S. Wynar, *Introduction to Cataloging and Classification*, 8th ed. by Arlene G. Taylor (Englewood, Colo.: Libraries Unlimited, 1992), pp. 518–519. For additional examples of shelflist cards and explanations, *see* Bloomberg and Evans, *Technical Services*.

4.   Arlene G. Taylor, "Authority Files in Online Catalogs: An Investigation of Their Value," *Cataloging & Classification Quarterly* 4 (Spring 1984): 1.

5.   For more detailed information on automated authority control *see* Arlene G. Taylor, "Authority Control: Where It's Been and Where It's Going," and other papers from the conference "Authority Control: Why It Matters," sponsored by NELINET, November 1, 1999, Worcester, Mass. (available: http://www.nelinet.net/conf/cts/cts99/cts99.htm [accessed 3/12/00]).

6.   Foster, *Managing the Catalog Department*, pp. 225–226.

7.   For discussion of adapting copy in the cataloging process, *see* Arlene G. Taylor, *Cataloging with Copy: A Decision-Maker's Handbook*, 2nd ed. (Englewood, Colo.: Libraries Unlimited, 1988).

8.   OCLC Office of Research, "The Scorpion Project" (available: http://orc.rsch.oclc.org:6109/ [accessed 3/12/00]).

9.   *A Catalog of Books Represented by Library of Congress Printed Cards Issued to July 31, 1942* (Ann Arbor, Mich.: Edwards Brothers, 1943); vol. 14, 3–13, gives full explanation of the arrangement.

10.   Arlene G. Taylor, *The Organization of Information* (Englewood, Colo.: Libraries Unlimited, 1999), chapter 9.

11.   *ALA Filing Rules* (Chicago: American Library Association, 1980).

12.   Taylor, *Cataloging with Copy*, 5–7.

13.   For in-depth discussions of retrospective conversion, *see* Ruth C. Carter and Scott Bruntjen, *Data Conversion* (White Plains, N.Y.: Knowledge Industry Publications, 1983); and Dennis Reynolds, *Library Automation: Issues and Applications* (New York: R. R. Bowker, 1985), pp. 280–324.

14.   Charles Coffin Jewett, *On the Construction of Catalogues of Libraries, and Their Publication by Means of Separate, Stereotyped Titles*, 2nd ed. (Washington, D.C.: Smithsonian Institution, 1853).

15.   Barbara M. Westby, "Commercial Services," *Library Trends* 16 (July 1967): 46.

16.   Arlene Taylor Dowell, *Cataloging with Copy: A Decision-Maker's Handbook* (Littleton, Colo.: Libraries Unlimited, 1976), pp. 248–257.

17.   Karen A. Wilson and Marylou Colver, "Outsourcing Library Technical Services Operations: Practices in Public, Academic, and Special Libraries" (Chicago: American Library Association, 1997); Karen Wilson, "Outsourcing Issues: Cons." The American Library Association Web page, July 1997 (available: http://www.ala.org/alcts/now/outsourcing-cons.html [accessed 3/12/00]) and "Outsourcing Issues: Pros." The American Library Association Web page, July 1997 (available: http://www.ala.org/alcts/now/outsourcing-pros.html [accessed 3/12/00]); Clare B. Dunkle, "Outsourcing the Catalog Department: A Meditation Inspired by the Business and Library Literature," *Journal of Academic Librarianship* 22, no. 1 (January 1996): 33–43.

18.   Dilys E. Morris and Gregory Wool, "Cataloging: Librarianship's Best Bargain," *Library Journal* 124, no. 11 (June 15, 1999): 44–46.

19.   Jamshid Beheshti, "The Evolving OPAC," *Cataloging & Classification Quarterly* 24, no. 1–2, (1997): 165.

20.   Walt Crawford, *The Online Catalog Book: Essays and Examples* (New York: G. K. Hall, 1992), p. 41.

21.   George Machovec, "ILS System Selection: Second Time Around," *Colorado Libraries* 23, no. 4 (Winter 1997): 6.

22.   L. W. Gassie, "What Do We Expect from the Next Generation of Library Systems?" *LLA Bulletin* 60, no.2 (Fall 1997): 97.

23.   Chris Evin Long, "The Internet's Value to Catalogers: Results of a Survey," *Cataloging & Classification Quarterly* 23, no. 3–4 (1997): 69.

24.   Christine L. Borgman, "From Acting Locally to Thinking Globally: A Brief History of Library Automation," *Library Quarterly* 67, no. 3 (July 1997): 230.

25.   Martha Yee, "Guidelines for OPAC Displays," prepared for the IFLA Task on Guidelines for OPAC Displays, November 24, 1998 (PDF file) (available: http://www.ifla.org/ifla/VII/s13/guide/opac.htm [accessed 3/5/00]).

26.   Ibid.

27.   Ibid.

28.   Roger Brisson and Janet McCue, "Retooling Technical Services," in *Encyclopedia of Library and Information Science*, vol. 58, suppl. 21 (New York: Marcel Dekker, 1996): 281.

29.   Brisson and McCue, 284–285.

30.   Michael Kaplan, "Introduction," in *Planning and Implementing Technical Services Workstations* (Chicago: American Library Association, 1997): xvii.

31.   Julie Crowley, (June 1999), "Cataloging tools on the Internet," AUTOCAT. Online (available E-mail: listserv@listserv.acsu.buffalo.edu, with command: get catalog.tools [accessed 8/23/99]).

SUGGESTED READING

Claire-Lise Bénaud, and Sever Bordeianu. *Outsourcing Library Operations in Academic Libraries: An Overview of Issues and Outcomes*. Englewood, Colo.: Libraries Unlimited, 1998.

Evans, G. Edward, and Sandra M. Heft. *Introduction to Technical Services for Library Technicians*. 6th ed. Englewood, Colo.: Libraries Unlimited, 1994.

Foster, Donald L. *Managing the Catalog Department*. 3rd ed. Metuchen, N.J.: Scarecrow, 1987.

Potter, William Gray. "The Online Catalogue in Academic Libraries." In *Technical Services Today and Tomorrow*. 2nd ed., edited by Michael Gorman. Englewood, Colo.: Libraries Unlimited, 1998, pp. 141–155.

Sellberg, Roxanne. "Cataloguing Management: Managing the Bibliographic Control Process." In *Technical Services Today and Tomorrow*. 2nd ed., edited by Michael Gorman. Englewood, Colo.: Libraries Unlimited, 1998, pp. 111–127.

Taylor, Arlene G. *Cataloging with Copy: A Decision-Maker's Handbook*. 2nd ed., with the assistance of Rosanna M. O'Neil. Englewood, Colo.: Libraries Unlimited, 1988. Chapters 1, 9.

Appendix:
Arrangement Dilemmas
and Filing Rules

As mentioned in chapter 20, "Catalog Management," there is currently very little control over the arrangement of online public access catalog (OPAC) displays. When one purchases an Integrated Library System (ILS) with its OPAC, one accepts the arrangement that has been programmed into that system. However, an understanding of certain filing dilemmas can be useful in making decisions about catalog maintenance of heading forms and references. In addition, many libraries continue to maintain card shelflists as supplements to their OPACs, making understanding of notational arrangement an important part of catalog maintenance. For those who are still maintaining card catalogs, the rules for filing are essential for good catalog construction.

FILING DILEMMAS

There is a significant difference between alphabetizing straight through to the end of a phrase entry and observing the breaks in the string that occur at the end of each word. Most filers know the admonition "nothing before something," or "blank to Z." It means that library catalogs are generally arranged letter-by-letter to the end of each word and then word-by-word to the end of the heading. However, not all files in libraries are based on this premise. Reference librarians have to remember that the *American Peoples Encyclopedia*, the *Americana*, and the *World Book* are arranged word-by-word, while *Britannica*, *Collier's*, and *Compton's* prefer uninterrupted letter-by-letter filing to the close of the entry phrase. The differences are in some areas important, e.g.:

Word-by-word	Letter-by-letter
New Hampshire	Newark (N.J.)
New Haven (Conn.)	Newcastle (N.S.W.)
New York (N.Y.)	Newfoundland
New York (State)	New Hampshire
New Zealand	New Haven (Conn.)
Newark (N.J.)	Newman, Arthur
Newcastle (N.S.W.)	Newport (Isle of Wight)
Newfoundland	NEWSPAPERS
Newman, Arthur	New York (N.Y.)
Newport (Isle of Wight)	New York (State)
NEWSPAPERS	New Zealand

473

In entries containing dates, early historical periods usually precede later ones. However, codes differ on whether longer periods should precede or follow shorter ones starting with the same year. The American Library Association's (ALA's) *ALA Filing Rules*[1] and the Library of Congress's (LC's) *Library of Congress Filing Rules*[2] both say to arrange periods of time beginning with the same year in chronological order. They give examples from which the following selection was made:

UNITED STATES—HISTORY—CONFEDERATION, 1783-1789
UNITED STATES—HISTORY—1783-1865
UNITED STATES—HISTORY—CONSTITUTIONAL PERIOD,
    1789-1809
UNITED STATES—HISTORY—1865-
UNITED STATES—HISTORY—1865-1898
UNITED STATES—HISTORY—WAR OF 1898
UNITED STATES—HISTORY—1898-
UNITED STATES—HISTORY—20TH CENTURY

The *ALA Rules for Filing Catalog Cards*, second edition,[3] called for arranging periods of time beginning with the same year so that the longest period would file first, e.g.,

UNITED STATES—HISTORY—1783-1865
UNITED STATES—HISTORY—CONFEDERATION, 1783-1789
UNITED STATES—HISTORY—1898-
UNITED STATES—HISTORY—WAR OF 1898

If there are two or more editions or impressions of a work, edition dates or numbers may be added to the entry line, solely as filing elements. Again, codes differ on whether the earliest or latest should file first. The *ALA Filing Rules* say to arrange editions in straight chronological order, with earliest date first, e.g.,

Schwartz, Seymour I.
        Principles of surgery. 1969.
        Principles of surgery. 2nd ed. 1974.
        Principles of surgery. 3rd ed. 1979.
        Principles of surgery. 4th ed. 1984.
        Principles of surgery. 5th ed. 1989.

In the list below, the latest ones come first, on the assumption that they are the ones the user is most likely to want:

Sackheim, George I.
        Introduction to chemistry for biology students. 3rd ed. 1983.
        Introduction to chemistry for biology students. 2nd ed. 1977.
        Introduction to chemistry for biology students. 1966.

Numbers or digits in catalog entries give further challenges. Under current sets of rules, character strings beginning with numerals (whether Arabic or non-Arabic) are arranged before character strings beginning with letters, e.g.,

The 24th Congress of the CPSU and its contribution to Marxism-Leninism.

XXIVth International Congress of Pure and Applied Chemistry, main section lectures presented at . . . .

Twenty-four dramatic cases of the International Academy of Trial Lawyers.

The twenty-fourth session of the International Labour Conference . . . .

According to the *ALA Filing Rules*, numerals precede character strings, and all such character string/numeral combinations are interfiled regardless of the type of entry, e.g.,

HENRY I, KING OF ENGLAND, 1068-1135
HENRY V, KING OF ENGLAND, 1367-1413
Henry VIII and his wives.
HENRY VIII, KING OF ENGLAND, 1491-1547
Henry VIII's fifth wife.
Henry the Eighth and his court.
Henry the Fifth of England.

However, under *LC Filing Rules* fields with identical leading elements are sub-grouped in the order of person, place, thing, title. Thus, while numerals precede character strings, the person entries are all grouped before the title entries, e.g.,

HENRY I, KING OF ENGLAND, 1068-1135
HENRY V, KING OF ENGLAND, 1367-1413
HENRY VIII, KING OF ENGLAND, 1491-1547
Henry VIII and his wives.
Henry VIII's fifth wife.
Henry the Eighth and his court.
Henry the Fifth of England.

In prior rules, however, numerals were most often filed as spelled, and spelled "as spoken," in whatever language the entry appeared. Many card catalogs and other sources still file numerals in this way. Interpretation becomes most critical when the primary filing element of a title is expressed on the chief source of information in numerals. In a catalog where numerals are filed as spoken, it is possible that the two books (one by Walter Sellar, the other by Reginald Arkell) entitled *1066 and All That* are lost forever to the patron who cannot pronounce "1066" appropriately. However, filing numerals first can also cause problems for users, regardless of kind of catalog. How would a user who has heard a title spoken (e.g., 100 classical studies for flute) know whether to look in the numerical section or the alphabetical section? References and/or added entries are required, regardless of the method of filing.

Extensive use of acronyms and initialisms has in recent years aggravated the familiar problem of how to file abbreviations. Computerized filing throws new light on the difficulties encountered in traditional approaches. In the past, initials were most often treated as one-letter words, regardless of whether spaces or punctuation intervened. For machine-readable databases it is easier to file strings of letters, or letters-and-numbers, lacking spacing or punctuation as multicharacter words. It is immaterial whether they consist entirely of capitals (e.g., FORTRAN) or of a combination of upper- and lowercase (e.g., MeSH or Unesco). Nor does pronounceability affect the filing, as it did under previous sets of filing rules that required that one determine whether or not an acronym or initialism was pronounced as a word in order to decide where to file it.

Abbreviated titles of respect or position (e.g., Mr., Dr., St.) formerly were filed as if spelled out in full. But social pressures, as well as the computer, have effected changes. For example, *Webster's New International Dictionary* (second edition) defined "Mrs." as "the form of Mistress when used as a title."[4] The problems ensuing from that edict were impressive. Fortunately, *Webster's* third edition substituted a more contemporary (and considerably more round-about) explanation that in effect recognizes the abbreviation at its face value. Meanwhile, many libraries had already decided to file "Mrs." and "Ms." as written. Under both of the 1980 sets of filing rules (ALA and LC) abbreviations are arranged exactly as they are written.

Initial articles are usually suppressed as filing words, especially in titles. The practice extends to all languages using articles, since even in inflected languages the number of articles is relatively limited. They can be tabulated for manual filing or programmed out of machine filing. But homonyms (e.g., the French article *la*, as in *la belle epoque*, and the British interjection, as in "La! she was a lady") must be differentiated. Also, articles that initiate proper names (e.g., "La Crosse, Herman Thomas" and "Los Angeles (Calif.)") are always filed as written for American or English names, and for other languages as well where usage so dictates.

In dictionary catalogs the order of entries with identical wording, which may or may not be punctuated differently, must be decided. The conventional arrangement is: author, subject, title. In practice, it is highly unusual to find an author entry, a subject entry, and a title entry, all with exactly the same wording; the question bears more often on different kinds of entries that start with the same word. Application of the "authors first" guideline leaves unanswered the ordering of surnames and given name entries that start alike (e.g., "Thomas . . ."). The *LC Filing Rules* file given name entries (e.g., "Francis, of Assisi, Saint" and "Francis Xavier, Saint") ahead of the same word used as a surname (e.g., "Francis, Connie"). The *ALA Filing Rules* undo that preference, interfiling all entries, regardless of type, word-by-word to the end of the character string. However, some older card catalogs are still filed according to the 1968 *ALA Rules*, according to which all surname entries come first, followed by all other entries that begin with the same word.

Many libraries, particularly large ones with comprehensive collections by and about certain versatile writers, have separated out main and added entries for those persons into at least two categories. However, the original edition of the *ALA Rules* discouraged the practice:

> Arrange in one file all the entries, both main and secondary, for a person as author, joint author, compiler, editor, illustrator, translator and general added entry. Subarrange alphabetically by the title of the book. *Note:* An earlier practice, still followed in some libraries, is to arrange the secondary author entries in a separate alphabet after the main author entries. This practice is not recommended because users of the catalog overlook entries so filed.[5]

It was observed in chapter 1 that divided catalogs permit a simpler filing scheme than do dictionary catalogs. The simplifications, though, depend on the way in which the division is made. Often, subject entries are alphabetized separately from author and title entries. Persons (e.g., "Shakespeare, William") who are both authors and subjects of books have entries in each catalog, rather than having all the entries about them collocated immediately behind all the entries by them. Titles that happen to be identical with a subject heading (e.g., *Freedom of the Press*) are similarly often located in a separate file. There is perhaps less danger of the title entries' being mis-filed or overlooked, but closely related titles and subjects are separated from each other.

In either divided or dictionary catalogs there is seldom any doubt about where to file a *see* reference, but there are definitely two schools of thought on the location of *see also* references. Most catalogers place them immediately after those entries from which they lead, on the theory that the user will have exhausted a search at that point and be most ready for new suggestions. However, both sets of 1980 filing rules (ALA and LC) say categorically to file *see also* references before the first entry under the same word or words.

THE 1980 FILING RULES

The first edition of the *A.L.A. Rules for Filing Catalog Cards* was published in 1942. A Subcommittee of the American Library Association's Editorial Committee was established twenty years later to prepare a revision that would correlate with the 1967 publication of the *Anglo-American Cataloging Rules (AACR)*. The second edition of filing rules, like the first, was primarily designed for a dictionary catalog.[6] Except for the surname-first groupings in cases of identical entry words, single-alphabet arrangements were preferred over categorical considerations in nearly all cases. Machine filing experiments undoubtedly influenced the trend toward straight alphabetization. Yet the *ALA Rules* were designed for the manually filed catalogs that would continue to predominate for at least another two decades.

The Filing Committee of the Resources and Technical Services Division was appointed in the early 1970s to look into rules for computer filing. However, contact was maintained with the committee that was developing *Anglo-American Cataloguing Rules, Second Edition (AACR2)* so that the new rules would be applicable for *AACR2* entries. The new *ALA Filing Rules* were thought to be so different from the earlier two sets of ALA rules that they were considered to be a new work, not another edition.[7] The introduction states that they are applicable to any bibliographic displays, not just card formats, and that they can be used to arrange records formulated according to any cataloging rules.[8]

The brief summary of the *ALA Filing Rules* that follows is designed to show the rules that a filer in a modest collection would be most likely to use. In cases where the LC *Filing Rules* vary significantly, this is brought to the reader's attention.

General Rules

As already mentioned, filing is character by character to the end of each word and word by word to the end of the filing element. This is a result of applying the "nothing files before something" principle, with spaces, dashes, hyphens, diagonal slashes, and periods all considered to be "nothing." Also, as already mentioned, numerals precede letters. In addition, letters of the English alphabet precede letters of nonroman alphabets.

Modified letters (e.g., ç or ñ) are filed as if they were the plain English equivalent, and diacritical marks are ignored. Punctuation and nonalphabetic signs and symbols (except those noted above as equivalent to "nothing," ampersands, and certain such marks in numeric character strings) are also ignored.

Examples of the Basic ALA Rules

10 ans de politique social en Pologne	"Life after death"
20 a week	LIFE (BIOLOGY)
150 science experiments step-by-step	Muellen, Abraham
1918, the last act	Mullen, Allen
130,000 kilowatt power station	Müllen, Gustav
A.A.	New York
A.B.C. programs	Newark
Aabel, Marie	% of gain
$$$ and sense	One hundred best books
Camp-fire and cotton-field	Parenting guidebook
Camp Fire Girls	Rolston, Brown
Campbell, Thomas J.	Rølyat, Jane
Campfire adventure stories	Zookeeper's handbook
LIFE	πΣA: A history
Life—a bowl of rice	

The *LC Filing Rules* differ on the treatment of nonroman alphabet letters: these are to be romanized for filing.

Note that under previous rules, hyphenated prefixes and compound words written both as separate words (or hyphenated) and as single words (e.g., *campfire, camp-fire*) were interfiled as the single word. Under the new rules a hyphen is regarded as a space.

Ampersands

Ampersands may be ignored or, optionally, may be spelled out in their language equivalents, e.g.,

Without option	**With option**
Art and beauty	Art and beauty
ART AND INDUSTRY	Art & commonsense
Art & commonsense	ART AND INDUSTRY

Under *LC Filing Rules* the ampersand has the lowest filing value in alphanumeric order, e.g.,

Art & commonsense
Art and beauty
ART AND INDUSTRY

Treatment of Access Points

If access points are not identical they are filed character by character and word by word according to the general rules. The major exceptions are for initial articles, certain kinds of numerals, and certain additions to names (e.g., relators and terms of honor and address). For explanation of these exceptions, *see* below.

When access points consist of a name and a title, they are filed as two separate elements. The title portion files with all other titles under the same name heading.

Identical Access Points

When arranging identical access points, the filer should first consider the functions of the access point. As mentioned earlier, *see* and *see also* references precede the entries of their type. In addition, main and added entries are interfiled but precede subject references and subject entries, e.g.,

Philadelphia.   Free Library.   [corporate name entry]
   Annual report . . .

Philadelphia Free Library   [title added entry]
Wagner, Robert L.
   The Philadelphia Free Library . . .

   PHILADELPHIA. FREE LIBRARY   [subject entry]
Bruns, Suzanne.
   A history of the Philadelphia Free Public Library . . .

As mentioned earlier, *LC Filing Rules* call for arranging entries with identical leading elements in the order: person, place, thing, title. "Thing" includes corporate body entries. Thus in the example above the title added entry would follow the subject entry.

Subarrangement of identical access points *with equivalent functions* in the *ALA Filing Rules* is determined by consideration of secondary data elements. For records with author or uniform title main entry, the next element considered is the title, followed by the date of publication, distribution, etc. For records with title main entry (not uniform title) the next element considered is the date. If the access point is a personal or corporate name added entry, the next element considered is the title, followed by the date. If the access point is a title added entry, the next element considered is the author or uniform title main entry, if there is one, followed by the date. If the access point is a series or subject added entry, the next element considered is the author or uniform title main entry, if there is one, followed by the title, followed by the date.

Examples Arranged by *ALA Filing Rules*
(examples are invented)

Love.
James, Samuel.
  Love . . .

Love and beauty.
Adams, Harriet.
  Love and beauty . . .

Love and beauty.
Hansen, Sigurd.
  Love and beauty . . .

LØVE (DENMARK)
Friis Møller, Jens.
  Life in a Danish town . . .

Love, Harold G., 1878-1926.
  The chemical industry . . .

Love, Harold G., 1911-
Symposium on the Social Organization of Anthropoid
      Apes (1st : 1954 : Berkeley, Calif.)
  Anthropoid apes and their society . . .

Love, Harold G., 1911-
  Behavior of nocturnal primates . . .

Love, Harold G., 1911-
  The primates of Africa . . .

Love, Harold G., 1911-
Atkins, Francis Harrison.
  Psychological studies of the great apes . . .

LOVE, HAROLD G., 1911-
Coffin, Lyle Warner.
  Harold Love . . .

LOVE, HAROLD G., 1911-
Driscoll, Maynard.
  Cousins, once removed . . .

LOVE, HAROLD G., 1911-   BIBLIOGRAPHY
Hennesey, Judy.
  Books by and about Harold Love . . .

LOVE (THEOLOGY)
Adam, Karl.
  Love and belief . . .

The above entries would have a somewhat different order under the *LC Filing Rules* because of the arrangement of fields with identical leading elements in the order of person (forename, then surname), place, thing (corporate body, then topical subject heading), title.

Examples Arranged by *LC Filing Rules*
(examples are invented)

Love, Harold G., 1878-1926.
   The chemical industry . . .

Love, Harold G., 1911-
Symposium on the Social Organization of Anthropoid
     Apes (1st : 1954 : Berkeley, Calif.)
   Anthropoid apes and their society . . .

Love, Harold G., 1911-
   Behavior of nocturnal primates . . .

Love, Harold G., 1911-
   The primates of Africa . . .

Love, Harold G., 1911-
Atkins, Francis Harrison.
   Psychological studies of the great apes . . .

LOVE, HAROLD G., 1911-
Coffin, Lyle Warner.
   Harold Love . . .

LOVE, HAROLD G., 1911-
Driscoll, Maynard.
   Cousins, once removed . . .

LOVE, HAROLD G., 1911-   BIBLIOGRAPHY
Hennesey, Judy.
   Books by and about Harold Love . . .

LØVE (DENMARK)
Friis Møller, Jens.
   Life in a Danish town . . .

LOVE (THEOLOGY)
Adam, Karl.
   Love and belief . . .

Love.
James, Samuel.
   Love . . .

Love and beauty.
Adams, Harriet.
   Love and beauty . . .

Love and beauty.
Hansen, Sigurd.
Love and beauty . . .

Special Rules

Abbreviations

As mentioned earlier, abbreviations are arranged as written.

Examples

Concord (Mass.)
The Concord saunterer
Concord (Va.)
CONCORD (VT.)

Doctor come quickly
Doktor Brents Wandlung
Dr. Christian's office
Dr. Mabuse der Spieler

Initial Articles

Initial articles that form integral parts of place names and personal names are filed as written. Initial articles at the beginning of corporate names, title, and subject headings are ignored unless they begin with a personal name or place name.

Examples

Las cartas largas.
El chico.
The Club.
Der Club.
Club 21 (New York)
Club accounts.
The Club (London)
El-Abiad, Ahmed H., 1926-
El Campo (Tex.)
The El Dorado Trail.
The John Crerar Library today.
La Fontaine, Jean de, 1621-1695.
Las Hurdes (Spain)
Laš, Michal.
Lasa, Jose Maria de.

Initials, Initialisms, and Acronyms

The filing of initials, initialisms, and acronyms depends upon the spacing and punctuation between the characters. If they are separated by spaces, dashes, hyphens, diagonal slashes, or periods, they are filed as if each character were a separate word. If they are separated by other marks or symbols or are not separated, the group of characters is filed as a single word.

Examples

A.A.
A., A.J.G.
A apple pie
A.B.C. programs
Aabel, Marie
AAUN news
The ABC about collecting
U.N.E.S.C.O.   See UNESCO and Unesco.
Under the old apple tree
Unesco
UNESCO bibliographical handbooks
Unesco fellowship handbook

Names and Prefixes

A prefix that forms part of the name of a person or place is filed as a separate word unless it is joined to the rest of the name without a space or is separated from it only by an apostrophe.

Examples

De Alberti, Amelia
De la Roche, Mazo
De Marco, Clara
De senectute
Defoe, Daniel
Del Mar, Eugene

El Dorado (Ark.)
El-Wakil, Mohamed Mohamed
Elagin, Ivan
Eldorado (Neb.)

MacAlister, James
Mach, Ernst
MACHINERY
MacHugh, Angus
Maclaren, Ian
MacLaren, J.
Maclaren, James
M'Bengue, Mamadou Seyni
McHenry, Lawson
McLaren, Jack
Mead, Edwin Doak
M'Laren, J. Wilson

Under previous ALA filing rules names beginning with the prefixes *M'* and *Mc* were filed as if written *Mac*, and card catalogs may still be filed that way.

Numerals

Numerals are arranged according to their value from lowest to highest, but there are some difficulties in reading numbers with punctuation, decimals, fractions, and non-Arabic notation and superscript/subscript numerals. If punctuation is for readability, it is treated as if it did not exist. Other punctuation is treated as a space. Decimals are arranged digit-by-digit, and if they are not combined with a whole integer, they precede the numeral 1. Fractions are arranged as if they are characters in the order numerator, line (treated as space), denominator (e.g., $2\frac{1}{2}$ is filed: 2 space 1 space 2). Non-Arabic numerals are interfiled with their Arabic equivalents. Superscript/subscript numerals are filed as if on the line and as if preceded by a space.

Examples

.300 Vickers machine gun mechanism
1:0 für Dich
$1\frac{3}{4}$ yards of silk
1.3 acres
1^3 is one
$\frac{1}{3}$ of an inch
2 x 2 = 5
3.2 beer for all
3:10 to Yuma
3 point 2 and what goes with it
$20 a week
XX Century cyclopaedia and atlas
20 humorous stories
XXth century citizen's atlas of the world
200 years of architectural drawing
2000 A.D., a documentary

Dates

Dates in titles are filed as numerals. Dates in a chronological file, such as subdivisions of subjects or personal names with dates, are arranged chronologically, with B.C. dates preceding A.D. dates. Historic time periods that are generalized or expressed only in words are filed with the full range of dates for the period (e.g., *18th century* is equivalent to 1800–1899). Subject period subdivisions are filed chronologically even when words (e.g., the name of a war) precede the dates. Geologic time periods are arranged alphabetically.

Examples

UNITED STATES—HISTORY
UNITED STATES—HISTORY—COLONIAL PERIOD, CA.1600-1775
UNITED STATES—HISTORY—REVOLUTION, 1775-1783
UNITED STATES—HISTORY—CONFEDERATION, 1783-1789
UNITED STATES—HISTORY—1783-1865
UNITED STATES—HISTORY—1865-

UNITED STATES—HISTORY—1865-1898
UNITED STATES—HISTORY—WAR OF 1898
UNITED STATES—HISTORY—1898-
UNITED STATES—HISTORY—20TH CENTURY
UNITED STATES—HISTORY—1933-1945
UNITED STATES—HISTORY—BIO-BIBLIOGRAPHY
UNITED STATES—HISTORY   DICTIONARIES

Under the *ALA Filing Rules*, subjects with subdivisions and those with qualifiers are interfiled ignoring punctuation.

Examples Arranged by *ALA Filing Rules*

COOKERY
COOKERY, AMERICAN
COOKERY, AMERICAN—BIBLIOGRAPHY
COOKERY (APPLES)
COOKERY, CHINESE
COOKERY—DICTIONARIES
COOKERY FOR DIABETICS
COOKERY, INTERNATIONAL
COOKERY—YEARBOOKS

The *LC Filing Rules*, however, are more inclined to categorize entries. Topical subject headings are grouped so that the leading element alone is first, followed by entries in the form: leading element—subject subdivision. These are followed by entries in the form: leading element, comma, additional word(s). Following these are entries in which the leading element is followed by a parenthetical qualifier. Finally, there come entries in which the word that has been the leading element in the preceding entries is the first word of a phrase.

Examples Arranged by *LC Filing Rules*

COOKERY
COOKERY—DICTIONARIES
COOKERY—YEARBOOKS
COOKERY, AMERICAN
COOKERY, AMERICAN—BIBLIOGRAPHY
COOKERY, CHINESE
COOKERY, INTERNATIONAL
COOKERY (APPLES)
COOKERY FOR DIABETICS

Subordinate elements that follow a dash are also grouped according to the *LC Filing Rules*. The order is period subdivision, form and topical subdivisions, and geographical subdivisions. This is the order in which printed versions of *Library of Congress Subject Headings* (*LCSH*) are arranged, and it is further discussed with examples in chapter 15.

SHELFLIST FILING

The notation of most modern classifications, whether pure or mixed, includes Arabic numerals (both integers and decimals) that are filed in normal mathematical sequence. A typical series of class numbers from the *Dewey Decimal Classification* (*DDC*) schedules, which use a pure decimal notation, could appear as follows:

DDC Class Number Order

001	- Knowledge
010	- Bibliography
016	- Subject bibliographies
070.01	- Theory of journalism
070.1	- News media
070.17	- Print media
070.172	- Newspapers
070.19	- Broadcast media
070.4	- Journalism
070.41	- Editing
070.509	- History of publishing
070.59	- Kinds of publishers
078	- Journalism in Scandinavia
	[etc.]

Class number notation for the LC system is mixed. In its simplest form it consists of one to three roman alphabet letters followed by one to four integers. However, decimals both in pure numeric form and in alphanumeric form may be introduced at various points. A typical sequence might be:

LC Class Number Order

T20	- History of technology in the 20th century
T26.G3	- History of technology in Germany
T26.G5B5	- History of technology in Berlin
TP572	- Directories of brewing and malting
TP573.A1	- General histories of brewing and malting
TP573.5	- Biography of brewers and malters
TP573.5A1	- Collective biography of brewers and malters
TP574	- Schools of brewing and malting
TP1107	- Exhibitions of plastics and plastics manufacture
TP1130	- Handbooks, manuals, tables, etc., of plastics
TP1135	- Plastics plants and equipment
	[etc.]

Cutter number notation also varies with the system. Libraries that use *DDC* may use cutter numbers assigned through use of the Cutter two- or three-figure alphanumeric tables or the Cutter-Sanborn tables. Two-figure Cutter and Cutter-Sanborn numbers can be filed in straight integer sequence, but those from the three-figure Cutter table must be arranged decimally, as shown:

DDC Call Numbers with Three-Figure Cutter Book Numbers

333 F189 - A work on land economics by an author surnamed Falkinson
333 F19 - A similar work by an author surnamed Fallaby
333 F191 - A similar work by an author surnamed Fallentz
333 F21   - A similar work by an author surnamed Famareus
333 F218 - A similar work by an author surnamed Fantine

Workmarks consisting of lowercase letters, and most often corresponding to the first significant word of the item's title, may be added to the cutter number as follows:

DDC Call Numbers with Workmarks

515.33 R4li   - Introduction to Differential Calculus, by an author surnamed
                Richmond
515.33 R41m - Mean Value Theorems, by the same author
515.33 R4lt   - Total and Directional Derivatives, by the same author

Many smaller libraries using *DDC* bypass the Cutter tables in favor of adding one to three or more capital letters from the main entry word of the item to the *DDC* class number. These book symbols are, of course, arranged alphabetically as follows. In such libraries congested files are rare, so that lowercase workmarks are not often needed:

DDC Call Numbers with Alphabetic Book Numbers

799.1 ROB   - A book on fishing by an author surnamed Robb
799.1 ROBE - A similar book by an author surnamed Robertson
799.1 ROBI - A similar book by an author surnamed Robinson

LC assigns its own unique cutter numbers to materials, as discussed in chapters 11 and 12. Many LC call numbers include two cutter numbers, of which only the final one is, or incorporates, the number for the particular item. A typical sequence might be:

HC59.7.B7	- Broekmeijer, M.W.J.M. *Fiction and truth about the decade of development.*
HC59.7.C28	- Caiden, Naomi. *Planning and budgeting in poor countries.*
HC59.7.C6	- Committee for Economic Development. *How low income countries can advance their growth.*
HN438.C5G2	- Galpern, A.N. *The religions of the people in sixteenth-century Champagne.*
HN438.P3R8	- Rudé, George F.E. *Paris and London in the eighteenth century.*
HN438.P6H52	- Higonnet, Patrice L.R. *Pont-de-Montvert; social structure and politics in a French village, 1700-1914.*

What needs to be remembered when filing LC call numbers is that the classification part of the notation up to the period files as integers, but any cutter numbers after the period file as decimals.

HN4	*but*	HN438.C15
HN5		HN438.C23
HN15		HN438.C4
HN23		HN438.C43
HN43		HN438.C5
HN59		HN438.C59

Dates or edition numbers may be added as a third element to either *DDC* or *LCC* call numbers to distinguish among different issues of the same title. These might be filed in either chronological or retrospective order, just as in catalog filing, but the majority of libraries prefer chronological shelflist filing. Location symbols of various kinds may also accompany call numbers of some materials. The shelflist filing of such additions is purely a matter of local preference.

NOTES

1.   *ALA Filing Rules* (Chicago: American Library Association, 1980).

2.   *Library of Congress Filing Rules* (Washington, D.C.: Library of Congress, 1980).

3.   *ALA Rules for Filing Catalog Cards*, 2nd ed. (Chicago: American Library Association, 1968).

4.   *Webster's New International Dictionary of the English Language*, 2nd ed., unabr. (Springfield, Mass.: G. & C. Merriam, 1959), p. 1605.

5.   *A.L.A. Rules for Filing Catalog Cards* (Chicago: American Library Association, 1942), p. 25.

6.   *See* Pauline Seely, "ALA Filing Rules—New Edition," *Library Resources & Technical Services* 11 (Summer 1967): 377–379; and Pauline Seely, "ALA Rules for Filing Catalog Cards: Differences between 2d and 1st Editions (Arranged by 2d Rule Numbers)," *Library Resources & Technical Services* 13 (Spring 1969): 291–294.

7.   For a critique of the *ALA Filing Rules*, *see* Hans W. Wellisch, "The *ALA Filing Rules*: Flowcharts Illustrating Their Application, with a Critique and Suggestions for Improvement," *Journal of the American Society for Information Science* 34 (September 1983): 313–330.

8.   *ALA Filing Rules*, pp. 1–2.

Glossary of Selected Terms and Abbreviations

Defined in this glossary are selected basic terms for students of cataloging, including a number of terms and identifiers used in bibliographic control, descriptive cataloging, classification, subject heading work, filing, document indexing, networking, and other topics treated in this text. Readers may wish to consult other sources for other terms used in the library profession.

AACR2 (Anglo-American Cataloguing Rules, Second Edition). A set of rules, published in 1978, for producing the descriptive and name-and-title access points part of a surrogate record for an information package; the creation of these rules was the result of collaboration among representatives from Canada, Great Britain, and the United States.

AACR2R (Anglo-American Cataloguing Rules, Second Edition, 1988 Revision). The first revision of *AACR2*. The abbreviation *AACR2R* is also used to indicate a collection of all of the additions and changes to *AACR2* in whatever physical manifestation they appear.

AACR2R98 (Anglo-American Cataloguing Rules, Second Edition, 1998 Revision). A printed-form revision of *AACR2*; rules are monitored by the Joint Steering Committee (JSC) for AACR, which is made up of representatives from Australia, Canada, Great Britain, and the United States.

AACR2-e. The computer file version of *AACR2R*.

Aboutness. The subject of an information package. *See also* **Subject analysis**.

Abstract. A condensed narrative description of an information package, which may serve as a surrogate for the document in a retrieval system.

Abstracting. The process of creating abstracts. *See also* **Cataloging**; **Indexing**.

Access. That portion of the descriptive cataloging that provides access points that have been selected and formulated by a cataloger or indexer. *See also* **Description**; **Descriptive cataloging**.

Access control. The results of the process of doing authority work, but without the necessity of choosing one form of name or title and one subject term to be the "authorized" selection. In access control every variant name, title, or term is given equal status, with one form chosen for default display; however, a searcher may use any of the forms to gain access to information packages related to the name, title, or subject. *See also* **Authority control**; **Authority work**.

Access point. Any term (i.e., word, heading, etc.) in a bibliographic record that may be used to locate that record. *See also* **Choice of access points; Entry; Heading**.

Accession number. A number assigned to each item as it is received in the library. Accession numbers may be assigned through continuous numbering (e.g., 30291, 30292) or a coded system (1999–201, 1999–202, etc.).

Accompanying materials. Dependent materials, such as answer books, teacher's manuals, atlases, portfolios of plates, slides, sound recordings, or computer disks.

Add instructions. Notes in classification schedules that specify what digits to add to a base number; they replace divide-like notes in *DDC*.

Added entry. A secondary access point; i.e., any other than the main entry or primary access point. In COM, book, or card catalogs an added entry record often duplicates the main entry record except that it has an additional heading to represent in the catalog a subject, joint author, illustrator, editor, compiler, translator, collaborator, series, etc.

A-G Canada. A computer-based bibliographic network offering its database and services to a variety of Canadian and northeastern United States libraries; formerly Utlas International. *See also* **Bibliographic utility**.

Alphabetical catalog. A catalog with entries arranged in alphabetical order, rather than according to the symbolic notation of a classification. *See also* **Classified catalog; Dictionary catalog; Divided catalog**.

Alphabetico-classed catalog. A catalog in which subject categories are used for arrangement of surrogate records; broad categories are subdivided by narrower categories which are placed alphabetically within each broad category.

Alternative title. The second title of a work, which is joined to the first title with *or* or its equivalent (e.g., *Maria, or, The Wrongs of Woman*). Both titles together are considered to constitute the title proper of the work. *See also* **Title proper**.

Analytical entry. An entry for a part of a work or for a whole work contained in a series or a collection for which a comprehensive entry is made. A name-title analytic, one kind of analytical entry, may be made in the form of an added entry. *See also* **Name-title added entry**.

Anonymous work. One in which the author's name does not appear anywhere in the information package; a work of unknown authorship.

Area. A major section of an ISBD bibliographic description; e.g., edition area or physical description area.

Artifact. *See* **Realia**.

Asynchronous responsibility. The situation in which the persons or corporate bodies involved in the creation of an information package have made different kinds of contributions to the creation of a work (e.g., author and illustrator; performer, conductor, choreographer, and producer; etc.). *See also* **Mixed responsibility; Synchronous responsibility**.

Author. The person chiefly responsible for the intellectual or artistic content of a work; e.g., writer of a book, compiler of a bibliography, composer of a musical work, artist, photographer, etc. *See also* **Compiler; Creator; Editor**.

Author entry. The place in a retrieval tool where a surrogate record containing the name of the creator of an information package may be found.

Author number. *See* **Cutter number**.

Authority control. The process of maintaining consistency in the verbal form used to represent an access point and the further process of showing the relationships among names, works, and subjects. *See also* **Access control**.

Authority file. A grouping of authority records.

Authority record. A printed or machine-readable unit that registers the decisions made during the course of authority work. It contains all the forms used for a particular name, title, or subject, and usually designates one of the forms as the "authorized" one to use in catalog records.

Authority work. The process of determining the form of a name, title, or subject concept that will be used as a heading on a bibliographic record; of determining references needed to that form; and of determining relationships of the name, title, or subject to other names, titles, or subjects.

Auxiliary table. A generalized subdivision table appended to a classification schedule for use in building specific class numbers where indicated in the schedule proper.

Bibliographic control. The process of creating, arranging, and maintaining systems for bibliographic information retrieval.

Bibliographic data. Information gathered in the process of creating bibliographic records.

Bibliographic databases. Computerized databases (such as A-G Canada, OCLC, RLIN, etc.) for retrieval of bibliographic records.

Bibliographic entity. *See* **Information package**.

Bibliographic file. A grouping of bibliographic records. In a catalog or bibliographic database, a bibliographic file is distinct from, but might be linked to, one or more authority files and a holdings file.

Bibliographic record. A catalog entry in card, microtext, machine-readable, or other form carrying full cataloging information for an information package. *See also* **Metadata**; **Surrogate record**.

Bibliographic service center. A regional broker, providing intermediate communication, training, and service for libraries participating in an online bibliographic network.

Bibliographic tools. Devices such as catalogs, indexes, bibliographies, etc., created for use as bibliographic retrieval systems. *See also* **Bibliographic databases**; **Bibliography**; **Catalog**; **Index**; **Retrieval tools**.

Bibliographic universe. The concept encompassing all instances of recorded knowledge.

Bibliographic utility. An online processing center based on a machine-readable database of catalog records; members of the utility can contribute new records and download existing ones.

Bibliography. A list of information packages on a given subject, by a given author, from a particular time period or place, or the like.

Book catalog. A catalog in which surrogate records are printed on pages and bound in book form.

Book number. *See* **Cutter number**.

Books in sets. *See* **Monographs in collected sets**.

Boolean operators. The terms *and*, *or*, and *not* as used to construct search topics through post-coordinate indexing.

Broad classification. A scheme that omits detailed subdivision of its main classes or that facilitates the use in smaller libraries of only its main classes and subdivisions. *See also* **Close classification**.

Broader term (BT). A term one level up from the term being examined in a listing where terms for subject concepts have been conceived in relationships that are hierarchical.

BSO. Broad System of Ordering, a classification developed for a proposed worldwide information network covering the whole field of knowledge.

Call number. The notation used to identify and locate a particular item on the shelves; it often consists of a classification notation and a cutter number, and it may also include a workmark and/or a date. *See also* **Cutter number**; **Workmark**.

Card catalog. A catalog in which every entry is printed or typed on a card (usually 3″ x 5″) and placed in a file drawer in a particular order (usually alphabetical or classified order).

Catalog. An organized set of surrogate records that represent the holdings of a particular collection and/or information packages to which access may be gained. It may be arranged by alphabet, by classification notation, or by subject. It may be in the form of online records, cards, books, or computer output microform (COM).

Catalog record. *See* **Bibliographic record**; **Surrogate record**.

Cataloger. Person in an archive, a library, or other such organization who creates surrogate records for the information packages collected by the organization and who works to maintain the system through which those surrogate records are made available to users; the person may also be an independent contractor.

Cataloging. The process of describing an information package, choosing name and title access points, conducting subject analysis, and assigning subject headings and a classification number. *See also* **Copy cataloging**; **Descriptive cataloging**; **Original cataloging**; **Subject cataloging**.

Cataloging in Publication. *See* **CIP**.

Categorical filing. The preference in some areas of a filing system for partially classified arrangements over a straight alphabetical sequence.

CD-ROM. Compact Disk-Read Only Memory; a computer storage medium that is "read" with a laser beam and can store 680 megabytes of data on a single disk.

CD-ROM catalog. *See* **Online catalog**.

Centralized processing. Any cooperative effort that results in the centralization of one or more of the technical processes involved in getting material ready for use in a library.

Chain index. A direct and specific index based on the extracted vocabulary of a classification system. It retains all necessary context but deletes unnecessary context.

Chief source of information. The source in an information package that is prescribed by the rules as the major source of data for use in preparing a bibliographic description. *See also* **Title page**.

Choice of access points. The process of selecting the main entry and any added entries under which an information package is to be listed in the catalog.

CIP. Cataloging-in-Publication, a program sponsored by the Library of Congress and cooperating publishers; a partial bibliographic description is provided on the verso of the title page of a book.

Class. The first order of structure in a hierarchical classification, at which level major disciplines are represented. A class may incorporate one or more divisions, which in turn may incorporate one or more subdivisions. *See also* **Division**; **Hierarchical classification**; **Subdivision**.

Classification. The placing of subjects into categories; in organization of information, classification is the process of determining where an information package fits into a given hierarchy and then assigning the notation associated with the appropriate level of the hierarchy to the information package and to its surrogate record.

Classification notation. The set of numbers, letters, symbols, or combinations of these assigned to an information package to show its subject area.

Classification schedule. The printed scheme of a particular classification system.

Classification scheme. A scheme for the systematic organization of knowledge, usually by subject.

Classification table. Supplementary part of a classification scheme in which a hierarchy is developed and notations are assigned for concepts that can be applied in conjunction with many different topical subjects. Tables commonly exist for geographic locations; time periods; standard subdivisions (e.g., dictionaries, theory, serial publications, historical treatment, etc.); racial, ethnic, and national groups; etc.

Classified catalog. A catalog arranged in the order of symbols, numbers, or other notations that represent the various subjects or aspects of subjects covered by the information packages owned by the library. *See also* **Shelflist**.

Close classification. The use of minute subdivisions for arranging materials by highly specific topics. *See also* **Broad classification**.

Closed stacks. Library collections not open to public access or limited to only a small group of users. *See also* **Open stacks**.

Code (as a noun). (1) A set of rules. (2) A specific designation in an encoding standard that defines and limits the kinds of data that can be stored at that point.

Code (as a verb). The process of assigning the appropriate specified designations of an encoding standard.

CODEN. A system of unique letters assigned for ready identification of periodicals and serials, now administered by Chemical Abstracts Service (CAS).

Coextensive subject entry. A principle of subject entry, by which a term, phrase, or set of terms defines precisely the complete contents, but no more than the contents, of an information package.

Collation. *See* **Physical description area**.

Collection. Three or more works or parts of works by one author published together, or two or more works or parts of works by more than one author published together. Each work in a collection was originally written independently or as part of an independent publication.

Collocating function. The function of bibliographic control that relates bibliographic entities through the process of collocation.

Collocation. The process of bringing together in a catalog records for names, titles, or subjects that are bibliographically related to one another.

Colon Classification. Classification scheme devised by S. R. Ranganathan in the early 1930s; it was the first fully faceted classification scheme.

COM. Computer Output Microform.

COM catalog. A catalog produced on COM and requiring a microform reader for its use.

Compiler. One who brings together matter from the works of various authors or the works of a single author. *See also* **Author; Editor**.

Computer file. A body of encoded information (either data or program) that can be read only by a computer.

Computer-produced catalog. *See* **COM; Online catalog**.

CONSER. Conversion of Serials project, a shared national database of serial records from selected libraries, now maintained on OCLC's database.

Content designation. The act of making a bibliographic or authority record machine-readable by encoding its various elements according to a specified scheme. *See also* **MARC; Code (as a verb)**.

Continuation. (1) A work issued as a supplement to an earlier one. (2) A part issued in continuance of a book, a serial, or a series.

Contract cataloging. An institution's use of a contractual relationship with a person or agency to provide surrogate records that represent the institution's acquisitions for its collection.

Control field. A field in the MARC format (0xx) that includes numeric or other encoded data for retrieval. *See also* **Field; Fixed field; Variable field**.

Controlled vocabulary. Language, usually in the form of a thesaurus or subject heading list, that is carefully systematized for use in retrieval systems. *See also* **Subject heading list; Thesaurus**.

Cooperative cataloging. *See* **Copy cataloging**.

Coordinate indexing. The enabling of information retrieval through the use of related terms in a catalog or database to identify concepts. *See also* **Postcoordinate indexing; Precoordinate indexing**.

Copy cataloging. Adapting for use in a catalog a copy of the original cataloging created by another library. *See also* **Original cataloging**.

Core record. Standard set by the Program for Cooperative Cataloging (PCC) that presents the minimum requirements for elements to be included in a nationally acceptable *AACR2* record.

Corporate body. An organization or group of persons who are identified by a name and who act as an entity.

Creator. Person who is responsible for the intellectual content of an information package. *See also* **Author**.

Cross reference. *See* **Reference**.

Cutter number. The symbols, usually a combination of letters and numbers, used to distinguish items with the same classification number in order to maintain the alphabetical order (by author, title, or other entry) of items on the shelves; sometimes called author number or book number. The word *cutter* is derived from the widespread use of the Tables first devised by Charles A. Cutter for use in such alphabetical arrangement. *See also* **Call number**; **Work mark**.

Dash. A symbol of punctuation and separation that in printing is referred to as "em" and consists of a single line, but in keyboarding is made by striking the hyphen key twice in succession. In descriptive cataloging the dash usually appears with one space on either side; for subject subdivisions no spaces are used.

Database. A set of records that are all constructed in the same way and are often connected by relationship links; the structure underlying retrieval tools.

DDC. *See* **Dewey Decimal Classification**.

Depth indexing. Assignment of subject terms to represent all of the main concepts in a document. *See also* **Exhaustivity**; **Summarization**.

Description. That portion of the descriptive cataloging process in which elements that identify an information package are transcribed into a bibliographic record; also, the portion of the bibliographic record (i.e., descriptive data) that results from this process. *See also* **Access**; **Descriptive cataloging**; **Descriptive data**.

Descriptive cataloging. That phase of the cataloging process that is concerned with the identification and description of an information package, the recording of this information in a bibliographic record, and the selection and formation of access points—with the exception of subject access points. *See also* **Access**; **Description**.

Descriptive data. Data that describes an information package, such as its title, its associated names, its edition, its date of publication, its extent, and notes identifying pertinent features.

Descriptor. Subject concept term, representing a single concept, usually found in thesauri and used in indexes. *See also* **Subject heading**.

Dewey Decimal Classification (DDC). Classification devised by Melvil Dewey in 1876; it divides the world of knowledge hierarchically into ten divisions, which are in turn divided into ten sections, and so on, using the ten digits of the Arabic numeral system. DDC is enumerative but with many faceting capabilities, especially in its later editions.

Diacritics. Modifying marks over, under, or through characters to indicate that pronunciation is different from that of the characters without the diacritics.

Dictionary catalog. A catalog arranged in alphabetical order with entries for names, titles, and subjects all interfiled.

Direct entry. A principle of formulation of subject headings that stipulates the entry of a concept directly under the term that names it, rather than as a subdivision of a broader concept. *See also* **Specific entry**.

Divide-like note. A place in a classification schedule referring the user to another location where similar sequencing and notation set a pattern.

Divided catalog. A catalog in which different types of entries are separated into different sections. Usually the subject entries are separated from other entries. Order is usually alphabetical in each section, but the subject section may be in classified order.

Division. In hierarchical classification, the second structural level at which major components of a discipline are represented. A division is a subset of a class and may incorporate one or more subdivisions. *See also* **Class**; **Hierarchical classification**; **Subdivision**.

Document. An information package; often associated in people's minds with text and illustrations having been produced on paper, but increasingly associated with a video, a music CD, a computer file, or other such manifestation.

Edition. Specific version of the intellectual content (work) found in an information package. In the case of books, an edition refers to all the impressions of a work printed at any time or times from one setting of type. In the case of nonbook materials, an edition is all the copies of an information package made from one master copy.

Edition area. The second area of an ISBD bibliographic description, which includes the following elements: named and/or numbered edition statement and statement of responsibility relating to a particular edition, if any.

Editor. One who prepares for publication or supervises the publication of a work or collection of works or articles that are authored by others. Responsibility may extend to revising, providing commentaries and introductory matter, etc. *See also* **Author**; **Compiler**.

Electronic resources. Materials that require the use of a computer to access the intellectual contents.

Element. A subsection of an area in the catalog record; for example, the alternative title is an element of the title and statement of responsibility area.

Entry. A representation of a bibliographic record at a particular point in a retrieval tool. There can be one or more entries for any one heading. *See also* **Access point**; **Bibliographic record**; **Heading**.

Entry word. The word by which the entry is arranged in the catalog, usually the first word (other than an article) of the heading. Also called "filing word."

Enumerative classification. A classification that attempts to assign a designation for every subject concept required in the system.

Evaluating function. The function of bibliographic control that allows a patron to make an informed choice of materials from a bibliographic tool.

Exhaustivity. The number of concepts covered in a document that will be represented in subject analysis. *See also* **Depth indexing; Summarization**.

Expansive classification. A scheme in which a set of coordinated schedules gives successive development possibilities from very simple (broad) to very detailed (close) subdivision.

Explanatory reference. A reference that gives the detailed guidance necessary for effective use of the headings involved.

Faceted classification. A classification constructed from the combination, usually in prescribed sequence, of clearly defined, mutually exclusive, and collectively exhaustive aspects, properties, or characteristics of a class or specific subject.

FID. Fédération Internationale de Documentation (International Federation for Documentation).

Field. A separately designated element of a MARC record. A field may contain one or more subfields. *See also* **Control field; Fixed field; Subfield; Variable field**.

File characteristics area. The third area of an ISBD bibliographic description for a computer file, which identifies whether the file contains data or program information and stipulates the extent of the file. *See also* **Computer file; Material specific details area**.

Filing. The process of placing paper records (e.g., catalog cards, acquisition forms, etc.) in order, usually in drawers.

Filing word. *See* **Entry word**.

Finding function. *See* **Identifying function**.

Fixed field. A field in a computer record that is of a set length. There are three major "fixed fields" in a standard MARC 21 record, 008 (fixed length data elements), 007 (physical characteristics), and 006 (special aspects). *See also* **Control field; Field; Subfield; Variable field**.

Fixed location. The assignment of each item in a collection to a definite position on a certain shelf.

Form division. *See* **Standard subdivision**.

Form heading. A subject list term that refers to the literary or artistic form or the publication format of a work rather than to its topical content.

Form of entry. The specific spelling and wording used to record an access point on a catalog record. *See also* **Heading**.

Free-floating subdivision. A term that can be added to a subject heading in a published list, as needed, whether or not it is written in the published list following that heading. In the LCSH system, however, terms called "free-floating" have scope notes that express limitations on the use of some such terms.

Full entry. *See* **Main entry (record)**.

Gathering function. *See* **Collocating function**.

Geographic name. The place name usually used in reference to a geographic area. It is not necessarily the political name. *See also* **Political name**.

GMD. General Material Designation, a term that is given in a catalog record to indicate the class of material to which an information package belongs (e.g., motion picture).

Guide card. A labeled card with a noticeable projection that distinguishes it from other cards. It is inserted in a card catalog to help the user find a desired place or heading in the catalog.

Hanging indention. The form of indention used in traditional print bibliographic record format when the main entry is under title; the title begins at the first indention and succeeding lines of the body of the record begin at the second indention.

Heading. (1) The character string provided at the beginning of a record entry in a printed bibliographic tool that provides means for finding that entry. A heading can represent the name of a person, corporate body, geographic area, title of a work, or a subject. Headings are also provided at the top of a column, page, or screen on which several entries for the heading may appear. (2) The exact string of characters of the authorized form of an access point as it appears in the authority record. *See also* **Access point**; **Entry**; **Form of entry**; **Term**.

Hierarchical classification. A classification that attempts to arrange subjects according to a "natural" order—proceeding from classes to divisions to subdivisions.

Hierarchical notation. In classification, the use of symbol groups of varying combinations and lengths to reflect a hierarchy of topics and subdivisions.

Holdings. Bibliographic items (volumes, parts, issues, etc.) contained in a library collection.

Holdings file. A group of holdings records. In an OPAC or a bibliographic database, a holdings file is usually distinct from, but might be linked to, a bibliographic file.

Holdings note. One note in the bibliographic record for a serial that tells which parts of the serial are held by the library. *See also* **Numeric and/or alphabetic, chronological, or other designation area**.

Holdings record. A record in a holdings file that gives complete holdings for an information package.

Identifying function. The function of bibliographic control that allows a user to recognize and locate a specific information package.

IFLA. International Federation of Library Associations and Institutions; formerly International Federation of Library Associations.

ILL. Interlibrary loan; the process of acquiring a physical information package or a copy of it from a library that owns it by a library that does not own it.

Imprint. *See* **Publication, distribution, etc., area**.

Indentions. Designated spaces or margins at which parts of a traditional catalog record begin; used especially in typing cards.

Index. A tool that exhibits the analyzed contents of an information package or a group of such packages, as contrasted with a library catalog, which traditionally lists and describes the holdings of a particular collection.

Indexer. A person who determines access points (usually subject terms, but may be authors or titles) that are needed in order to make surrogate records available to searchers; an indexer also may create surrogate records.

Indexing. The process of analyzing an information package and creating a surrogate record for it, especially subject access points, in an index.

Indexing vocabulary. *See* **Controlled vocabulary.**

Indicators. In the MARC encoding standards, indicators for a field contain coded information that is needed for interpreting or supplementing data in the field.

Information package. An instance of recorded information (e.g., book, article, video, Internet document or set of "pages," sound recording, electronic journal, etc.). *See also* **Item; Work.**

Information retrieval. The process of gaining access to stored data for the purpose of becoming informed.

ISBD. International Standard Bibliographic Description, an internationally accepted format for the representation of descriptive information in bibliographic records. ISBDs developed so far include: ISBD(A), ISBD for Older Monographic Publications (Antiquarian); ISBD(ER), ISBD for Electronic Resources; ISBD(CM), ISBD for Cartographic Materials; ISBD(G), General; ISBD(M), ISBD for Monographic Materials; ISBD(NBM), ISBD for Nonbook Materials; ISBD(PM), ISBD for Printed Music; ISBD(S), ISBD for Serials.

ISBN. International Standard Book Number, a distinctive and unique number assigned to a book. ISBNs are used internationally; the U.S. agency for ISBNs is R. R. Bowker Company.

ISDS. International Serials Data System, a network of national and international centers sponsored by UNESCO. The centers develop and maintain registers of serial publications; this includes the assignment of ISSNs and key title.

ISSN. International Standard Serial Number, a distinctive number assigned by ISDS.

Item. A manifestation of a work, focusing on the physical object, such as a book, a map, or a sound recording, as distinct from its intellectual content (i.e., the work it contains). *See also* **Information package; Work.**

Joint author. A person who collaborates with one or more associates to produce a work in which the individual contributions of the authors cannot be distinguished. *See also* **Shared responsibility; Synchronous responsibility.**

Key heading. *See* **Pattern heading.**

Keyword. A term that is chosen, either from actual text or from a searcher's head, that is considered to be a "key" to finding certain information.

Keyword indexing. Use of significant words from a title or a text as index entries. *See also* **Coordinate indexing.**

Keyword searching. The use of one or more keywords as the intellectual content of a search command.

KWIC indexing. Key Word In Context, a format for showing index entries within the context in which they occur.

KWOC indexing. Key Word Out of Context, the use of significant words from titles for subject index entries, each followed by the whole title from which the word was taken.

LC. Library of Congress.

LCC. *See* **Library of Congress Classification**.

LC-MARC. *See* **MARC 21**.

LCSH. *See* **Library of Congress Subject Headings**.

Leaf. A single thickness of paper; i.e., two pages, but usually printed only on one side.

Letter-by-letter filing. Arrangement of entries in a retrieval tool in which spaces and some punctuation marks are ignored so that the entry files as if it is all run together into one word (e.g., New York is treated as Newyork and follows Newark). *See also* **Word-by-word filing**.

Library of Congress Classification (LCC). Classification scheme created by the Library of Congress beginning in the late 1890s; it divides the world of knowledge hierarchically into categories using letters of the English alphabet and then using Arabic numerals for further subdivisions. LCC is basically an enumerative scheme, allowing only a limited amount of faceting.

Library of Congress Subject Headings (LCSH). List of terms to be used as controlled vocabulary for subject headings by the Library of Congress and any other agency that wishes to provide such controlled subject access to surrogate records.

Linkage. A relationship between or among headings or records that is manifested implicitly or explicitly in a bibliographic retrieval system.

Literary warrant. The concept that new notations are created for a classification scheme and new terms are added to a controlled vocabulary only when information packages actually exist about a new concept.

Locating function. *See* **Identifying function**.

Location device. A number or other designation on an item to tell where it is physically located.

MAchine-Readable Cataloging. *See* **MARC**.

Machine-readable data file. *See* **Computer file**; **Electronic resources**.

Main class. *See* **Class**.

Main entry (access point). The major access point chosen; the other access points are added entries.

Main entry (record). A full catalog record headed by the access point chosen as main entry, which gives all the information necessary for the complete identification of a work. This record also bears the tracing of all the other headings under which the work is entered. This is an obsolete concept in online catalogs.

Manufacturer. The agency that has made the item being cataloged (e.g., printer of a book).

Manuscripts. Papers created by an individual (not organizational papers); original hand-written or typed documents that usually exist in single copies (unless they have been copied).

Map series. A group of map sheets having the same scale and cartographic specifications, identified collectively by the producing agency. When the series is completed, it covers a given geographic area.

MARC. MAchine-Readable Cataloging. *See also* **MARC 21**; **UK/MARC**; **UNIMARC**.

MARC 21. A standard agreed upon by Canadian and United States representatives that pre-scribes a method for encoding surrogate records so that they can be read by computer. ("21" stands for the 21st century.)

MARC record. A computerized bibliographic record that has been content designated ac-cording to MARC conventions.

MARC tag. A number that designates the kind of field in a MARC record.

Material specific details area. The third area of an ISBD bibliographic description for cer-tain special materials. *See also* **File characteristics area**; **Mathematical data area**; **Musical presentation statement area**; **Numeric and/or alphabetic, chronological, or other designation area**.

Mathematical data area. The third area of an ISBD bibliographic description for a carto-graphic information package, which includes the following elements: scale, projection, and, optionally, coordinates and equinox.

Medical Subject Headings (MeSH). List of terms to be used as controlled vocabulary for subject headings by the National Library of Medicine and any other agency that wishes to provide controlled subject access to surrogate records in the field of medicine.

Metadata. An encoded description of an information package (e.g., an *AACR2* record en-coded with MARC, a Dublin Core record, etc.); the purpose of metadata is to provide a level of data at which choices can be made as to which packages one wishes to view or search, without having to search massive amounts of irrelevant full text.

Microfiche. A flat sheet of photographic film designed for storage of complete texts in multi-ple micro-images and having an index entry visible to the naked eye displayed at the top.

Microfilm. A length of photographic film containing sequences of micro-images of texts, title pages, bibliographic records, etc.

Microform. Usually a reproduction photographically reduced to a size difficult or impossi-ble to read with the naked eye; some microforms are not reproductions but original edi-tions. Microforms include microfilm, microfiche, microopaques, and aperture cards.

Mixed notation. A notation that combines two or more kinds of symbols, such as a combina-tion of letters and numbers.

Mixed responsibility. The combination of more than one category of intellectual responsi-bility for a work. *See also* **Asynchronous responsibility**; **Shared responsibility**.

Mnemonic devices. Devices intended to aid or assist the memory.

Monograph. A complete bibliographic unit or information package; it may be issued in successive parts at regular or irregular intervals, but it is not intended to continue indefinitely. It may be a single work or a collection that is not a serial.

Monographic series. A series of monographs with a collective title.

Monographs in collected sets. Collections or compilations by one or more authors issued in two or more volumes.

MRDF (Machine readable data file). *See* **Computer file; Electronic resources**.

Musical presentation statement. A statement in a chief source of information for music that indicates its physical form.

Musical presentation statement area. The third area of an ISBD bibliographic description for a music information package, in which a musical presentation statement (e.g., "playing score") is transcribed. *See also* **Material specific details area**.

NAL. National Agricultural Library, Washington, D.C.

Name authority file. A file of the name headings used in a given catalog with the references made to them from various forms of the names.

Name-title added entry. An added entry that includes the name of a person or corporate body and the title of a work (often a uniform title). It serves to identify a work that is included in the larger work that is being cataloged, to identify a work that is the subject of the work being cataloged, to identify a larger work of which the work being cataloged is part, or to identify another work to which the work being cataloged is closely related (e.g., an index).

Narrower term (NT). A term one level down from the term being considered in a listing where terms for subject concepts have been conceived in relationships that are hierarchical.

NLA. The National Library of Australia, Canberra.

NLM. The National Library of Medicine, Washington, D.C.

Nonbook materials. Term used to designate collectively maps, globes, motion pictures, filmstrips, videorecordings, sound recordings, and other information packages that do not consist of text in book form.

Notation. A system of numbers and/or letters used to represent a classification scheme.

Note area. The seventh area of an ISBD bibliographic description, reserved for recording catalog data that cannot be incorporated in the preceding parts of the record. Each note is usually recorded in a separate paragraph or separately encoded field.

NUC. The *National Union Catalog*, a publication in the Library of Congress Catalogs series that cumulates cataloging records from many libraries and indicates libraries that own a particular information package.

Numeric and/or alphabetic, chronological, or other designation area. The third area of an ISBD bibliographic description for a serial. It indicates volumes or parts of the serial, but not necessarily those held by a particular library. *See also* **Holdings note; Material specific details area**.

OCLC Online Computer Library Center. A computer-based bibliographic network that is the largest and most comprehensive utility in the world. *See also* **Bibliographic utility**.

Online catalog. A catalog based on and giving direct access to machine-readable cataloging records.

Online Computer Library Center. *See* **OCLC Online Computer Library Center**.

Online public access catalog. An online catalog that is available for use by the general public; also referred to as an OPAC. *See also* **Public access catalog**.

Online retrieval. Direct use of a computer to access stored data. *See also* **Information retrieval**.

Ontology. In the field of artificial intelligence, a formal representation of what, to a human, is common sense; in natural language processing, a formal representation of language, including realities of such things as grammar, semantics, and syntax.

OPAC. *See* **Online public access catalog**.

Open entry. A part of the descriptive cataloging not completed at the time of cataloging. Used for noncompleted works such as serials, series, etc.

Open stacks. A library collection where all users are admitted directly to the shelves. *See also* **Closed stacks.**

Original cataloging. The process of creating a bibliographic record for the first time, especially without reference to other records for the same information package. Also, the cataloging created by this process. *See also* **Copy cataloging**.

OSI. Open System Interconnection. An international system for linking computer networks.

Other title information. Words or phrases (e.g., a subtitle) that appear in conjunction with the title of an information package other than the title proper, parallel title, or alternative title. *See also* **Alternative title**; **Parallel title**; **Title proper**.

Outsourcing. A management technique whereby some activities, formerly conducted in house, are contracted out for completion by a contracting agency; technical services operations are sometimes outsourced.

Parallel title. The title proper written in another language or in another script. *See also* **Title proper**.

Paris Principles. The conventional name of the Statement of Principles agreed upon by attendees at the International Conference on Cataloging Principles in Paris, October 9–18, 1961.

Pattern heading. A representative heading from a category of terms that would normally be excluded from a subject heading list (e.g., names of individuals), included as an example of normal subdivision practice within that category.

PCC (Program for Cooperative Cataloging). An international cooperative program coordinated jointly by the Library of Congress and participants around the world; effort is aimed at expanding access to collections through useful, timely, cost-effective cataloging that meets internationally accepted standards.

Periodical. A publication with a distinctive title, which appears in successive numbers or parts at stated or regular intervals and which is intended to continue indefinitely. Usually each issue contains articles by several contributors. Newspapers and memoirs, proceedings, journals, etc., of corporate bodies primarily related to their internal affairs are not included in this definition. *See also* **Monograph**; **Serial**.

Phonograph records. *See* **Sound recordings**.

Physical description area. The fifth area of an ISBD bibliographic description, which includes a statement of the extent of an item, dimensions, and other physical details.

Place name. *See* **Geographic name**.

Plate. An illustrative leaf that is not included in the pagination of the text; it is not an integral part of a text gathering; it is often printed on paper different from that used for the text.

Plate number. A number used by a music publisher to identify a set of printing plates used to print a musical work.

Political name. The proper name of a geographical area according to the law. This name often changes with a change in government.

Postcoordinate indexing. Indexing that enters subject concepts as single concepts so that searchers can combine them to locate information packages on the compound and/or complex subjects in which they are interested.

PRECIS. Preserved Context Indexing System, a British-designed technique for subject retrieval in which an open-ended vocabulary can be organized according to a scheme of role-indicating operators, usually for computer manipulation.

Precoordinate indexing. The combination of subject terms at the time of indexing for use in the retrieval of information packages on compound and/or complex concepts.

Preliminaries (in a book). The title page or title pages, the verso of each title page, the cover, and any pages preceding the title page.

Primary access point. Access point that is chosen as the main or primary one; usually referred to as "main entry" in the library and archival worlds.

Processing center. A central office where the materials of more than one library are processed and distributed. Such a center may also handle the purchasing of materials for its constituents.

Producer. Person or agency responsible for financial and administrative production of a nonbook item, such as a motion picture or a computer file; also responsible for its commercial success.

Program (computer). *See* **Computer file**.

Pseudonym. An assumed name used by an author to conceal identity or to establish a separate bibliographic identity.

Pseudo-serial. A frequently reissued and revised publication which, upon first being published, is usually treated as a monographic work.

Public access catalog. The part of a catalog that is available for the use of library patrons. *See also* **Online public access catalog**.

Publication, distribution, etc., area. The fourth area of an ISBD bibliographic description, which includes the following elements: place of publication, distribution, etc.; name of publisher, distributor, etc.; date of publication, distribution, etc.; and sometimes place of manufacture, name of manufacturer, and date of manufacture.

Publisher. The person, corporate body, or firm responsible for issuing information packages to make them available for public use.

Pure notation. A notation that consistently uses only one kind of symbol (e.g., either letters or numbers, but not both).

Realia. Actual objects (artifacts, specimens, etc.).

Recon or RECON. *See* **Retrospective conversion**.

Record. *See* **Bibliographic record**; **Metadata**; **Surrogate record**.

Recto. In a book, the page on the right; the side of a leaf intended to be read first in cultures that read from left to right. *See also* **Verso**.

Reference (cross reference). An instruction in a catalog that directs a user to another catalog heading.

Related term (RT). A term at the same level of specificity or bearing a non-hierarchical relationship to another term in a listing where terms for subject concepts have been conceived in relationships that are hierarchical.

Relational database. A form of database architecture in which records are structured in such a way that information is not all stored in the same file; files for different kinds of information are created (e.g., a bibliographic file, a personal name file, a corporate name file, a subject file, a classification file, etc.); records in the bibliographic file contain pointers to records in the other files and vice versa. A relational database structure conserves storage space, allows for faster searching, and allows for easier modification of records. Pointers establish "relationships" among records.

Relative index. An index to a classification scheme that not only provides alphabetical references to the subjects and terms in the classification but also shows some of the relations between subjects and aspects of subjects.

Relative location. A classificatory arrangement of library materials, allowing the insertion of new material in its proper relation to that already on the shelves; thus, an item might be shelved in a different physical location each time it is reshelved. *See also* **Fixed location**.

Reprint. A new printing of an item either by photographic methods or by resetting substantially unchanged text.

Retrieval tools. Devices such as catalogs, indexes, search engines, etc., created for use as information retrieval systems.

Retrospective conversion. The process of changing information in eye-readable bibliographic records into machine-readable form; sometimes referred to as *recon* or *RECON*.

RLG. Research Libraries Group, a consortium formed originally by Columbia, Harvard, and Yale universities and the New York Public Library, now consisting of over 100 large research libraries.

RLIN. Research Libraries Information Network, a computer-based bibliographic network based at Stanford University under the aegis of RLG. *See also* **Bibliographic utility**.

Romanization. The representation of the characters of a nonroman alphabet by roman characters. *See also* **Transliteration**.

Scope note. A statement delimiting the meaning and associative relations of a subject heading, index term, or a classification notation.

Score. An arrangement of all of the parts of a piece of music one under another on different staves. A series of staves on which is written music composed originally for one instrument is not considered a score. Thus, "piano score" is used to designate, not music written originally for the piano, but music written originally for instrumental or vocal parts that has been arranged for the piano.

Search engine. A retrieval tool on the World Wide Web that, in general, matches keywords input by a user to words found at Web sites; the more sophisticated search engines may allow other than keyword searching.

Sears List of Subject Headings (Sears). A controlled vocabulary of terms and phrases that is used mostly in small libraries to provide subject access to information packages available in those libraries.

Secondary entry. *See* **Added entry**.

See also **reference.** A reference indicating related entries or headings.

See **reference.** A reference from a heading not used to a heading that is used.

Selecting function. *See* **Evaluating function**.

Serial. A publication issued in successive parts at regular or irregular intervals and intended to continue indefinitely. Included are periodicals, newspapers, proceedings, reports, memoirs, annuals, and numbered monographic series. *See also* **Monograph**; **Periodical**.

Series. A number of separate works, usually related in subject or form, that are issued successively. They are usually issued by the same publisher, distributor, etc., and in uniform style, with a collective title.

Series area. The sixth area of an ISBD bibliographic description, which includes series information.

Series authority file. A file of series headings used in a catalog with a record of references made to them from other forms, and a record of their treatment as to analysis, tracing, and classification.

Series title. The collective title given to volumes or parts issued in a series.

Shared authorship. *See* **Shared responsibility**.

Shared responsibility. More than one person is responsible for the creation of the intellectual content of a work. *See also* **Asynchronous responsibility**; **Mixed responsibility**; **Synchronous responsibility**.

Shelflist. Originally, a record of the items owned by a library with entries arranged in the order of the items on the shelves. In time the meaning has developed to indicate classification order of information packages, which now allows for intangible as well as physical information packages. *See also* **Classified catalog**.

S.l. (sino loco). Place of publication, distribution, etc., unknown.

s.n. (sine nomine). Name of publisher, distributor, etc., unknown.

Software. *See* **Computer file.**

Sound recordings. Aural recordings, including discs, cartridges, cassettes, cylinders, etc.

Specific entry. A principle observed in most library subject lists, by which an information package is listed under the most specific term available in the controlled vocabulary (or allowed to be created by the rules of the vocabulary), rather than under some broader heading. *See also* **Direct entry.**

Specificity. The level of subject analysis that is addressed by a particular controlled vocabulary (e.g., *LCSH* has greater specificity in its established headings than does *Sears*, as, for example, in the greater depth of subdivisions that are established under main headings by *LCSH*).

Standard number and terms of availability area. The eighth area of an ISBD bibliographic description, which includes ISBN or ISSN and, optionally, price or other terms on which the information package is available.

Standard subdivisions. Divisions used in DDC that apply to the form a work takes. Form may be physical (as in a periodical or a dictionary) or it may be philosophical (such as a philosophy or history of a subject). Formerly called form divisions.

Statement of responsibility. A statement in the information package being described that gives persons who are responsible for intellectual or artistic content, corporate bodies from which the content emanates, or persons or bodies who are responsible for performance.

Subdivision. The level of structure in a hierarchical classification, at which specific concepts are represented. *See also* **Class; Division; Hierarchical classification.**

Subfield. A separately content-designated segment of a field in a MARC record. *See also* **Field.**

Subject analysis. The process of discerning the concepts addressed in a document as a precursor to assigning subject headings, index terms, or classification; translating that conceptual analysis into a framework for a particular classification, subject heading, or indexing system; and then using the framework to assign specific notations or terminology to the information package and its surrogate record.

Subject authority file. A record of choices made in the development of a controlled vocabulary. The authority file contains such things as justification for the choice of one synonym over another; references from unused synonyms or near-synonyms; references for broader terms, narrower terms, and related terms; scope notes; citations for references used; etc. *See also* **Subject heading list; Thesaurus.**

Subject cataloging. The process of providing subject analysis, classification notation, and subject headings when creating catalog records.

Subject entry. The place in a catalog where a surrogate record containing a particular controlled vocabulary term is found.

Subject heading. A word or group of words indicating a subject. *See also* **Descriptor.**

Subject heading list. A list of authorized controlled vocabulary terms or phrases together with any references, scope notes, and subdivisions associated with each term or phrase. *See also* **Subject authority file; Thesaurus.**

Subject subdivision. A restrictive word or group of words added to a main subject heading to limit it to a more specific meaning or treatment.

Subtitle. A secondary title, often used to expand or limit the title proper; considered to be one kind of "other title information." *See also* **Alternative title; Other title information; Parallel title.**

Summarization. A form of subject analysis in which only the dominant or main theme of a document is recognized. *See also* **Depth indexing; Exhaustivity.**

Superimposition. A Library of Congress policy decision that only entries being established for the first time would follow *AACR* rules for form of entry and that only works new to LC would follow *AACR* rules for choice of entry. When LC adopted *AACR2*, the policy of superimposition was dropped.

Surrogate record. A presentation of the characteristics (e.g., title, creator, physical description if appropriate, date of creation, subject(s), etc.) of an information package.

Switching language. A mediating or communication indexing language used to establish subject equivalencies among various indexing languages or classification schemes.

Synchronous responsibility. The situation in which all persons or corporate bodies involved in the creation of an information package have made the same kind of contribution to the creation of the work. *See also* **Asynchronous responsibility; Joint author; Shared responsibility.**

Syndetic structure. An organizational framework in which related names, topics, etc., are linked to each other via connective terms such as *See* and *See also*.

Synthetic classification. A classification that assigns designations to single, unsubdivided concepts and gives the classifier generalized rules for combining these designations for composite subjects. *See also* **Faceted classification.**

Tag. *See* **MARC tag.**

Tagging. *See* **Content designation.**

Technical reading. The process of getting acquainted with an information package prior to cataloging, in which various internal sources of information are identified and examined.

Technical services. The group of activities in an institution that involves acquiring, organizing, housing, maintaining, and conserving collections and automating these activities. In some places circulating collections is also considered to be a technical service.

Term. A separately represented concept in a thesaurus. *See also* **Descriptor; Subject heading.**

Thesaurus. A specialized (usually restricted to a particular subject area) authority list of controlled vocabulary terms used with information retrieval systems; terms represent single concepts together with any references, scope notes, and subdivisions associated with each term; very similar to a list of subject headings. *See also* **Subject heading list.**

Title. The name of a work, usually identified from the chief source of information of an information package. *See also* **Alternative title**; **Other title information**; **Parallel title**; **Title proper**; **Uniform title**.

Title and statement of responsibility area. The first area of an ISBD bibliographic description, which includes the title of a work and information on its authorship.

Title entry. The place in a retrieval tool where a surrogate record containing the name of an information package may be found.

Title page. A page that occurs very near the beginning of a book and that contains the most complete bibliographic information about the book, such as the author's name, the fullest form of the book's title, the name and/or number of the book's edition, the name of the publisher, and the place and date of publication. *See also* **Chief source of information**.

Title proper. The title that is the chief name of an information package; excludes any parallel title or other title information. *See also* **Alternative title**; **Other title information**; **Parallel title**.

Tracing. The listing on a printed main entry record of all the additional entries under which the work is listed in the catalog; used to find (i.e., "trace") all copies of a record in a printed catalog.

Transliteration. A representation of the characters of one alphabet by those of another. *See also* **Romanization**.

UBC. Universal Bibliographic Control, the concept that it will someday be possible to have access to surrogate records for all the world's important information packages.

UDC. Universal Decimal Classification, a classification devised by Otlet and La Fontaine in the late 1890s. It was originally based on DDC, but has evolved into a much more faceted scheme than DDC.

UK/MARC. A machine-readable bibliographic record format developed by the British National Bibliography for use in the United Kingdom.

Uniform title. The title chosen for cataloging purposes when a work has appeared under varying titles or in more than one form; allows display of all manifestations of a work together. Uniform titles also are used to distinguish between and among different works that have the same title. *See also* **Title**; **Work**.

UNIMARC. Universal MARC format, first developed in 1977 by the Library of Congress to be an international communications format for the exchange of machine-readable cataloging records between national bibliographic agencies. A number of countries have adopted it as their national format.

Union catalog. A catalog that lists, completely or in part, the holdings of more than one library or collection.

Unit record. The basic catalog record, in the form of a main entry record, which when duplicated may be used as a unit for all other entries for that work in a printed catalog by the addition of appropriate headings.

USMARC. A machine-readable bibliographic record format developed by the Library of Congress and originally called LC-MARC. USMARC is being replaced by *MARC 21*.

USNAF. United States Name Authority File, a file housed at the Library of Congress (LC), containing not only the authority records created by LC and its cooperating United States contributors, but also records contributed from Australia, Canada, Great Britain, and others.

Utlas International. *See* **A-G Canada**.

Variable field. A field (1xx-9xx) in a MARC record that can be as long or as short as the data to be placed into that field. *See also* **Control field**; **Field**; **Fixed field**.

Verification. Determining the existence of an author and the form of name as well as the correct title of a particular work; in short, using bibliographic sources to verify (i.e., prove) the existence of an author and/or work. Alternatively, verification can refer to the process of determining whether a heading input in a record matches one in an authority file.

Vernacular name. A person's name in the form used in reference sources in his or her own country.

Verso. In a book, the page on the left; the side of a leaf intended to be read second in cultures that read from left to right. *See also* **Recto**.

Videorecording. A recording originally generated in the form of electronic impulses and designed primarily for television playback. The term includes videocassettes, videodiscs, and videotapes.

Vocabulary control. The process of creating and using a controlled vocabulary.

Volume. In the bibliographical sense, a major division of a work distinguished from the other major divisions of that work by having its own chief source of information.

WLN. Western Library Network, formerly a regional bibliographic network based at the State Library of Washington, that serviced libraries mainly in Alaska, Idaho, Oregon, and Washington; now absorbed by OCLC. *See also* **Bibliographic utility**; **OCLC**.

Word-by-word filing. Arrangement of terms in a retrieval tool in such a way that spaces between words take precedence over any letter that may follow (e.g. "New York" appears before "Newark"). *See also* **Letter-by-letter filing**.

Work. An intellectual entity; the informational content of an information package. *See also* **Information package**; **Item**.

Work form. A structured format into which information can be placed to create a catalog record; it can also include other information pertinent to the maintenance of a collection.

Work mark. A letter (or letters) placed after a cutter number; also called *work letter*. A work mark often is the first letter of the title of a work (exclusive of articles). *See also* **Call number**; **Cutter number**.

Worksheet. *See* **Work form**.

WWW. World Wide Web, a non-linear, multimedia, flexible system to provide information resources on the Internet and to gain access to such resources; based on hypertext and HyptertText Transfer Protocol (HTTP).

Z39.50. A national standard that provides for the exchange of information, such as surrogate records or full text, between otherwise noncompatible computer systems.

Bibliography

GENERAL WORKS

Berman, Sanford. *Joy of Cataloging*. Phoenix, Ariz.: Oryx Press, 1981.

Chan, Lois Mai. *Cataloging and Classification: An Introduction*. 2nd ed. New York: McGraw-Hill, 1994.

Dunkin, Paul S. *Cataloging U.S.A.* Chicago: American Library Association, 1969.

Hagler, Ronald. *The Bibliographic Record and Information Technology*. 3rd ed. Chicago: American Library Association, 1997.

Intner, Sheila S., and Jean Weihs. 2nd ed. *Standard Cataloging for School and Public Libraries*. Englewood, Colo.: Libraries Unlimited, 1996.

———. *Special Libraries: A Cataloging Guide*. Englewood, Colo.: Libraries Unlimited, 1998.

Levy, David M. "Cataloging the Digital Order." Available: http://www.csdl.tamu.edu/DL95/papers/levy/levy.html (accessed 3/12/00).

Oder, Norman. "Cataloging the Net: Can We Do It?" *Library Journal* 123, no. 16 (October 1, 1998): 47–51.

Saye, Jerry D. *Manheimer's Cataloging and Classification: A Workbook*. 4th ed., rev. and expanded. New York: Marcel Dekker, 1999.

Soergel, Dagobert. *Organizing Information: Principles of Data Base and Retrieval Systems*. Orlando, Fla.: Academic Press, 1985.

Svenonius, Elaine. "Directions for Research in Indexing, Classification, and Cataloging." *Library Resources & Technical Services* 25 (January/March 1981): 88–103.

Taylor, Arlene G., with the assistance of Rosanna M. O'Neil. *Cataloging with Copy: A Decision-Maker's Handbook*. 2nd ed. Englewood, Colo.: Libraries Unlimited, 1988.

———. "The Information Universe: Will We Have Chaos or Control?" *American Libraries* 25, no. 7 (July/August 1994): 629–632.

———. *The Organization of Information*. Englewood, Colo.: Libraries Unlimited, 1999.

Zyloff, Ellen. "Cataloging Is a Prime Number." *American Libraries* 27, no. 5 (May 1996): 47–48, 50.

SPECIALIZED WORKS

History

A.L.A. *Rules for Filing Catalog Cards*. Chicago: American Library Association, 1942.

Angell, Richard S. "Library of Congress Subject Headings—Review and Forecast." In *Subject Retrieval in the Seventies: New Directions*, edited by Hans Wellisch and Thomas D. Wilson. Westport, Conn.: Greenwood Publishing, 1972.

Baker, Nicholson. "Discards." *The New Yorker* 70, no. 7 (April 4, 1994): 64–86.

Cutter, Charles A. *Rules for a Dictionary Catalog*. 4th ed., rewritten. Washington, D.C.: GPO, 1904; republished, London: Library Association, 1972. The original version of this work was: Charles A. Cutter. "Rules for a Printed Dictionary Catalogue." In *Public Libraries in the United States of America: Their History, Condition, and Management*, U.S. Bureau of Education. Part II. Washington, D.C.: GPO, 1876.

Haykin, David Judson. *Subject Headings: A Practical Guide*. Washington, D.C.: GPO, 1951.

International Conference on Cataloguing Principles. Paris, 9th–18th October, 1961. *Report*. London: International Federation of Library Associations, 1963.

Jewett, Charles Coffin. *On the Construction of Catalogues of Libraries, and Their Publication by Means of Separate, Stereotyped Titles*. 2nd ed. Washington, D.C.: Smithsonian Institution, 1853.

LaMontagne, Leo E. "Historical Background of Classification," in *The Subject Analysis of Library Materials*. New York: Columbia University School of Library Service, 1953.

Lubetzky, Seymour. *Cataloging Rules and Principles: A Critique of the A.L.A. Rules for Entry and a Proposed Design for Their Revision*. Washington, D.C.: Processing Dept., Library of Congress, 1953.

———. *Code of Cataloging Rules, Author and Title: An Unfinished Draft . . . with an Explanatory Commentary by Paul Dunkin*. Chicago: American Library Association, 1960.

Martel, Charles, "Cataloging: 1876–1926," reprinted in *The Catalog and Cataloging*, edited by A. R. Rowland, 40–50. Hamden, Conn.: Shoe String Press, 1969.

Miksa, Francis. *The Subject in the Dictionary Catalog from Cutter to the Present*. Chicago: American Library Association, 1983.

Osborn, Andrew. "The Crisis in Cataloging." *Library Quarterly* 11 (October 1941): 393–411. [also reprinted in: Carpenter, Michael, and Elaine Svenonius, eds. *Foundations of Cataloging: A Sourcebook*. Littleton, Colo.: Libraries Unlimited, 1985, pp. 90–103]

Panizzi, Antonio. "Rules for the Compilation of the Catalogue." In *The Catalogue of Printed Books in the British Museum*. London: British Museum, 1841.

Pettee, Julia. *Subject Headings: The History and Theory of the Alphabetical Approach to Books*. New York: H. W. Wilson, 1946.

Reynolds, Dennis. *Library Automation: Issues and Applications*. New York: R. R. Bowker, 1985.

Russell, Beth M. "Hidden Wisdom and Unseen Treasure: Revisiting Cataloging in Medieval Libraries." *Cataloging & Classification Quarterly* 26, no. 3 (1998): 21–30.

Taube, Mortimer, and Associates, *Studies in Coordinate Indexing*. Washington, D.C.: Documentation, Inc., 1953.

Taylor, Arlene G. "Cataloguing." In *World Encyclopedia of Library and Information Services*, 3rd ed., 117–181. Chicago: American Library Association, 1993.

———. "Development of the Organization of Recorded Information in Western Civilization." Chapter 3 in *The Organization of Information*. Englewood, Colo.: Libraries Unlimited, 1999.

MARC Formats

Avram, Henriette D. *MARC, Its History and Implications*. Washington, D.C.: Library of Congress, 1975.

Byrne, Deborah J. *MARC Manual: Understanding and Using MARC Records*. 2nd ed. Englewood, Colo.: Libraries Unlimited, 1998.

Ferguson, Bobby. *MARC/AACR2/Authority Control Tagging: Blitz Cataloging Workbook*. Englewood, Colo.: Libraries Unlimited, 1998.

Fritz, Deborah A. *Cataloging with AACR2R and USMARC for Books, Computer Files, Serials, Sound Recordings, Videorecordings*. Chicago: American Library Association, 1998.

MARC 21 Format for Authority Data; Including Guidelines for Content Designation. Washington, D.C.: Cataloging Distribution Service, Library of Congress, 1999, 1v., looseleaf; *MARC 21 Concise Format for Authority Data*. Available: http://lcweb.loc.gov/marc/authority/ecadhome.html (accessed 5/12/00).

MARC 21 Format for Bibliographic Data: Including Guidelines for Content Designation Washington, D.C.: Cataloging Distribution Service, Library of Congress, 1999, 2 v.; *MARC 21 Concise Format for Bibliographic Data*. Available: http://lcweb.loc.gov/marc/bibliographic/ecbdhome.html (accessed 5/12/00).

MARC 21 Format for Holdings Data: Including Guidelines for Content Designation. Washington, D.C.: Cataloging Distribution Service, Library of Congress, 1999, 1v., looseleaf; *MARC 21 Concise Format for Holdings Data*. Available: http://lcweb.loc.gov/marc/holdings/echdhome.html (accessed 5/12/00).

MARC 21 Format for Classification Data: Including Guidelines for Content Designation. Washington, D.C.: Cataloging Distribution Service, Library of Congress, 1999, 1v., looseleaf; *MARC 21 Concise Format for Classification Data.* Available: http://lcweb. loc.gov/marc/classification/eccdhome.html (accessed 5/12/00).

MARC 21 Format for Community Information: Including Guidelines for Content Designation. Washington, D.C.: Cataloging Distribution Service, Library of Congress, 1999, 1v., looseleaf; *MARC 21 Concise Format for Community Information.* Available: http://lcweb.loc.gov/marc/community/eccihome.html (accessed 5/12/00).

"The MARC 21 Formats: Background and Principles." Prepared by MARBI in conjunction with Network Development and MARC Standards Office, Library of Congress. Washington, D.C.: Library of Congress, 1996. Available: http://lcweb.loc.gov/marc/96principl. html (accessed 3/11/00).

Understanding MARC: Bibliographic. Washington, D.C.: Library of Congress Cataloging Distribution Service, 1998. Also available: http://lcweb.loc.gov/marc/umb (accessed 3/11/00).

UNIMARC/Authorities: Universal Format for Authorities. London: IFLA Universal Bibliographic Control and International MARC Programme, 1989.

DESCRIPTION, ENTRY, AND HEADING

General

Anglo-American Cataloging Rules, Second Edition, 1998 Revisions. Prepared under the direction of the Joint Steering Committee for Revision of AACR. Chicago: American Library Association, 1998. Also available on CD-ROM: *AACR2-e, Anglo-American Cataloguing Rules, 2nd Edition, 1998 Revision.*

Baer, Eleanora A. *Titles in Series: A Handbook for Librarians and Students.* 3rd ed. Metuchen, N.J.: Scarecrow Press, 1978.

Books in Series. New York: Bowker, 1980–1989.

Books in Series in the United States. New York: Bowker, 1977–79.

Carpenter, Michael, and Elaine Svenonius, eds. *Foundations of Cataloging: A Sourcebook.* Littleton, Colo.: Libraries Unlimited, 1985.

Ferguson, Bobby. *Cataloging Nonprint Materials: Blitz Cataloging Workbook.* Englewood, Colo.: Libraries Unlimited, 1999.

———. *MARC/AACR2/Authority Control Tagging: Blitz Cataloging Workbook.* Englewood, Colo.: Libraries Unlimited, 1998.

Fritz, Deborah A. *Cataloging with AACR2R and USMARC for Books, Computer Files, Serials, Sound Recordings, Videorecordings.* Chicago: American Library Association, 1998.

Gorman, Michael. *The Concise AACR2, 1998 Revision*. Chicago: American Library Association, 1999.

———. "*AACR 2*: Main Themes." In International Conference on AACR 2, Florida State University, 1979, *The Making of a Code*, 45–46. Chicago: American Library Association, 1980.

International Conference on AACR 2, Florida State University, 1979. *The Making of a Code: The Issues Underlying AACR 2*. Chicago: American Library Association, 1980.

Intner, Sheila S., and Richard P. Smiraglia, eds. *Policy and Practice in Bibliographic Control of Nonbook Media*. Chicago: American Library Association, 1987.

Library of Congress Rule Interpretations. 2nd ed. Washington, D.C.: Cataloging Distribution Service, Library of Congress, 1990– , looseleaf, with updates.

Library of Congress Rule Interpretations for AACR 2, 1988 Revision: A Cumulation Through Cataloging Service Bulletin . . . , compiled with quarterly looseleaf supplements by Alan Boyd and Elaine Druesdow. Oberlin, Ohio: Oberlin College Library, 1989– .

Lubetzky, Seymour. "The Fundamentals of Bibliographic Cataloging and *AACR 2*." In International Conference on AACR 2, Florida State University, 1979, *The Making of a Code*, 18–23. Chicago: American Library Association, 1980.

Maxwell, Robert L., with Margaret F. Maxwell. *Maxwell's Handbook for AACR2R*. Chicago: American Library Association, 1997.

Mortimer, Mary. *Learn Descriptive Cataloging*. Lanham, Md.: Scarecrow, 2000.

Rogers, JoAnn V., with Jerry D. Saye. *Nonprint Cataloging for Multimedia Collections: A Guide Based on AACR2*. 2nd ed. Littleton, Colo.: Libraries Unlimited, 1987.

Saye, Jerry D., and Sherry L. Vellucci. *Notes in the Catalog Record Based on AACR2 and LC Rule Interpretations*. Chicago: American Library Association, 1989.

Smiraglia, Richard P. "Bibliographic Control Theory and Nonbook Materials." In *Policy and Practice in Bibliographic Control of Nonbook Media*, edited by Sheila S. Intner and Richard P. Smiraglia. Chicago: American Library Association, 1987.

Weihs, Jean, ed. *The Principles and Future of AACR: Proceedings of the International Conference on the Principles and Future Development of AACR*. Chicago: American Library Association, 1999.

Weihs, Jean, with Shirley Lewis. *Nonbook Materials: The Organization of Integrated Collections*. 3rd ed. Ottawa: Canadian Library Association, 1989.

Material-Specific AACR2 Cataloging

American Library Association, Interactive Multimedia Guidelines Review Task Force. *Guidelines for Bibliographic Description of Interactive Multimedia*. Chicago: American Library Association, 1994.

Cartographic Materials: A Manual of Interpretation for AACR 2. Chicago: American Library Association, 1982.

CONSER Editing Guide. Prepared by staff of the Serial Record Division under the direction of the CONSER operations coordinator. 1994 ed. Washington, D.C.: Cataloging Distribution Service, Library of Congress, 1994, 2v., looseleaf.

Fritz, Deborah A. *Cataloging with AACR2R and USMARC for Books, Computer Files, Serials, Sound Recordings, Videorecordings.* Chicago: American Library Association, 1998.

Frost, Carolyn O. *Media Access and Organization: A Cataloging and Reference Sources Guide for Nonbook Materials.* Englewood, Colo.: Libraries Unlimited, 1989.

Gamble, Betsy, ed. *Music Cataloging Decisions: As Issued by the Music Section, Special Materials Cataloging Division, Library of Congress in the Music Cataloging Bulletin, Through December 1991.* Canton, Mass.: Music Library Association, 1992.

Geer, Beverley, and Beatrice L. Caraway. *Notes for Serials Cataloging.* 2nd ed. Englewood, Colo.: Libraries Unlimited, 1998.

Gorman, Michael. "Cataloging and Classification of Film Study Material." In *Film Study Collections,* edited by Nancy Allen. New York: F. Ungar Publishing, 1979.

Graham, Crystal. "What's Wrong with AACR2: A Serials Perspective." In *The Future of the Cataloging Rules,* edited by Brian E. C. Schottlaender. Chicago: American Library Association, 1998.

Hensen, Steven L. *Archives, Personal Papers, and Manuscripts: A Cataloging Manual for Archival Repositories, Historical Societies, and Manuscript Libraries.* 2nd ed. Chicago: Society of American Archivists, 1990.

Hill, Janet Swan. "Descriptions of Reproductions of Previously Existing Works: Another View," *Microform Review* 11 (Winter 1982): 14–21.

Hirons, Jean L. "Revising AACR2 to Accommodate Seriality: Report to the Joint Steering Committee for Revision of AACR." 1999. Available: http://www.nlc-bnc.ca/jsc/ser-rep0.html (accessed 3/12/00).

Hirons, Jean L., ed. *CONSER Cataloging Manual.* Washington, D.C.: Serial Record Division, Library of Congress, 1993– .

International Standard Bibliographic Description.
    The following ISBDs have been published by the International Federation of Library Associations and Institutions:

> *ISBD(A): International Standard Bibliographic Description for Older Monographic Publications (Antiquarian).* 2nd rev. ed. 1991.
>
> *ISBD(CM): International Standard Bibliographic Description for Cartographic Materials.* 2nd ed. 1987.
>
> *ISBD(ER): International Standard Bibliographic Description for Electronic Resources.* 1997.
>
> *ISBD(G): General International Standard Bibliographic Description.* Rev. ed. 1992.
>
> *ISBD(M): International Standard Bibliographic Description for Monographic Publications.* Rev. ed. 1987.

ISBD(NBM): International Standard Bibliographic Description for Non-Book Materials. 2nd ed. 1987.

ISBD(PM): International Standard Bibliographic Description for Printed Music. 2nd rev. ed. 1991.

ISBD(S): International Standard Bibliographic Description for Serials. Rev. ed. 1988.

John, Nancy R. "Microforms," *Journal of Library Administration* 3 (Spring 1982): 3–8.

Liheng, Carol, and Winnie S. Chan. *Serials Cataloging Handbook: An Illustrative Guide to the Use of AACR2R and LC Rule Interpretations.* 2nd ed. Chicago: American Library Association, 1998.

Olson, Nancy B. *Cataloging Computer Files,* edited by Edward Swanson. Lake Crystal, Minn.: Soldier Creek Press, 1992.

———. *Cataloging Computer Files: 1996 Update,* edited by Edward Swanson. Lake Crystal, Minn.: Soldier Creek Press, 1996.

———. *Cataloging Motion Pictures and Videorecordings,* edited by Edward Swanson. Lake Crystal, Minn.: Soldier Creek Press, 1992.

———. *Cataloging Motion Pictures and Videorecordings: 1996 Update,* edited by Edward Swanson. Lake Crystal, Minn.: Soldier Creek Press, 1996.

———. *Cataloging of Audiovisual Materials and Other Special Materials: A Manual Based on AACR 2.* 4th ed. Edited by Sheila S. Intner and Edward Swanson. DeKalb, Ill.: Minnesota Scholarly Press, 1998.

Olson, Nancy B., ed. *Cataloging Internet Resources: A Manual and Practical Guide.* 2nd ed. Dublin, Ohio: OCLC Online Computer Library Center, Inc., 1997.

O'Neil, Rosanna M. "Analysis and 'In' Analytics," *Serials Review* 13, no. 2 (Summer 1987): 57–63.

Sandberg-Fox, Ann, and John D. Byrum. "From ISBD(CF) to ISBD(ER): Process, Policy, and Provisions." *Library Resources and Technical Services* 42 (April 1998): 89–101.

Smiraglia, Richard P. *Cataloging Music: A Manual for Use with AACR2.* 2nd ed. Lake Crystal, Minn.: Soldier Creek Press, 1986.

———. *Music Cataloging: The Bibliographic Control of Printed and Recorded Music in Libraries.* Englewood, Colo.: Libraries Unlimited, 1989.

Soper, Mary Ellen. "Description and Entry of Serials in *AACR2.*" *Serials Librarian* 4 (Winter 1979): 167–176.

Taylor, Arlene G. "Where Does AACR2 Fall Short for Internet Resources?" *Journal of Internet Cataloging* 2, no. 2 (1999): 43–50.

Tseng, Sally C. "Serials Cataloging and AACR2: An Introduction." *Journal of Educational Media Science,* 19 (Winter 1982): 177–216.

Entry and Heading

Carpenter, Michael. "Does Cataloging Theory Rest on a Mistake?" In *Origins, Content, and Future of AACR2 Revisited*, edited by Richard P. Smiraglia, 95–102. Chicago: American Library Association, 1992.

Dowell, Arlene Taylor. *AACR 2 Headings: A Five-Year Projection of Their Impact on Catalogs*. Littleton, Colo.: Libraries Unlimited, 1982.

Hagler, Ronald. "Access Points for Works." In *The Principles and Future of AACR2*, edited by Jean Weihs, 214–228. Chicago: American Library Association, 1998.

Smiraglia, Richard P. "Authority Control and the Extent of Derivative Bibliographic Relationships." Ph.D. dissertation, University of Chicago, 1992.

——. "Derivative Bibliographic Relationships: Linkages in the Bibliographic Universe." In *Navigating the Networks: Proceedings of the ASIS Mid-Year Meeting, Portland, Oregon, May 21–25, 1994*, 167–183. Medford, N.J.: Learned Information, 1994.

Tate, Elizabeth L. "Examining the 'Main' in Main Entry Headings." In International Conference on AACR 2, Florida State University, 1979, *The Making of a Code*, 109–140. Chicago: American Library Association, 1980.

Taylor, Arlene G. "Metadata: Access and Access Control." Chapter 6 in *The Organization of Information*. Englewood, Colo.: Libraries Unlimited, 1999.

Tillett, Barbara B. "Bibliographic Relationships: Toward a Conceptual Structure of Bibliographic Information Used in Cataloging." Ph.D. dissertation, University of California, Los Angeles, 1987.

——. "A Taxonomy of Bibliographic Relationships," *Library Resources and Technical Services* 35 (April 1991): 150–158.

——. "A Summary of the Treatment of Bibliographic Relationships in Cataloging Rules," *Library Resources and Technical Services* 35 (October 1991): 393–405.

——. "The History of Linking Devices," *Library Resources and Technical Services* 36 (January 1992): 23–36.

——. "Bibliographic Relationships: An Empirical Study of the LC Machine-Readable Records," *Library Resources and Technical Services* 36 (April 1992): 162–188.

Vellucci, Sherry L. "Bibliographic Relationships Among Musical Bibliographic Entities: A Conceptual Analysis of Music Represented in the Library Catalog with a Taxonomy of the Relationships Discovered." D.L.S. dissertation, Columbia University, 1995.

——. "Bibliographic Relationships." In *The Principles and Future of AACR2*, edited by Jean Weihs, 105–146. Chicago: American Library Association, 1998.

SUBJECT ANALYSIS

Aluri, Rao, D. Alasdair Kemp, and John J. Boll. *Subject Analysis in Online Catalogs*. Englewood, Colo.: Libraries Unlimited, 1991.

Bates, Marcia J. "Rethinking Subject Cataloging in the Online Environment." *Library Resources & Technical Services* 33, no. 4 (October 1989): 400–419.

Bates, Marcia. "Subject Access in Online Catalogs: A Design Model." *Journal of the American Society for Information Science* 37, no. 6 (November 1986): 360.

Chan, Lois Mai, Phyllis A. Richmond, and Elaine Svenonius. *Theory of Subject Analysis: A Sourcebook*. Littleton, Colo.: Libraries Unlimited, 1985.

Documentation: Methods for Examining Documents, Determining Their Subjects and Selecting Indexing Terms. Geneva, Switzerland: International Organization for Standardization, 1985.

Ferguson, Bobby. *Subject Analysis: Blitz Cataloging Workbook*. Englewood, Colo.: Libraries Unlimited, 1998.

Foskett, A. C. *The Subject Approach to Information*. 5th ed. London: Library Association Publishing, 1996.

Fugmann, Robert. *Subject Analysis and Indexing: Theoretical Foundation and Practical Advice*. Frankfurt am Main: Indeks Verlag, 1993.

Lakoff, George. *Women, Fire, and Dangerous Things: What Categories Reveal About the Mind*. Chicago: University of Chicago Press, 1987.

Mann, Thomas. *Doing Research at the Library of Congress: A Guide to Subject Searching in a Closed Stacks Library*. Washington, D.C.: Humanities and Social Sciences Division, Library of Congress, 1994.

———. *Library Research Models: A Guide to Classification, Cataloging, and Computers*. New York: Oxford University Press, 1993.

Markey, Karen. *Subject Searching in Library Catalogs: Before and After the Introduction of Online Catalogs*. Dublin, Ohio: OCLC, 1984.

McKiernan, Gerry. *Beyond Bookmarks: Schemes for Organizing the Web*. Available: http://www.public.iastate.edu/~CYBERSTACKS/CTW.htm (accessed 3/12/00).

Petersen, Toni, and Pat Molholt, eds. *Beyond the Book: Extending MARC for Subject Access*. Boston: G. K. Hall, 1990.

Subject Indexing: Principles and Practices in the 90's: Proceedings of the IFLA Satellite Meeting Held in Lisbon, Portugal, 17–18 August 1993. Munich: Saur, 1995.

Taylor, Arlene G. "On the Subject of Subjects." *Journal of Academic Librarianship* 21, no. 6 (November 1995): 484–491.

Wellish, Hans H. "Aboutness and Selection of Topics." *Key Words* 4, no. 2 (March/April 1996): 7–9.

Wilson, Patrick. "Subjects and the Sense of Position." In *Theory of Subject Analysis: A Sourcebook,* edited by Lois Mai Chan, Phyllis A. Richmond, and Elaine Svenonius, 253–268. Littleton, Colo.: Libraries Unlimited, 1985.

CLASSIFICATION

Bliss Classification Association. "Bliss Classification Association: homepage." Available: http://www.sid.cam.ac.uk/bca/bcahome.htm (accessed 3/12/00).

――――. "The Bliss Bibliographic Classification: Outline of Bliss Classification (2nd ed.)." Available: http://www.sid.cam.ac.uk/bca/bcoutline.htm (accessed 3/12/00).

British Standards Institution. *Universal Decimal Classification. International medium ed., English text, ed. 2.* Milton Keynes, England: BSI Standards, 1993. (BS 1000M)

British Standards Institution. *Universal Decimal Classification, Pocket Edition.* London: BSI, 1999.

Chan, Lois M. *A Guide to the Library of Congress Classification.* 5th ed. Englewood, Colo.: Libraries Unlimited, 1999.

Chan, Lois Mai, John P. Comaromi, Joan S. Mitchell, and Mohinder P. Satija. *Dewey Decimal Classification: A Practical Guide.* 2nd ed., revised for DDC21. Dublin, Ohio: OCLC Forest Press, 1996.

Dewey Decimal Classification Additions, Notes and Decisions, vol. 5, no. 1– . Albany, N.Y.: Forest Press, 1990– .

Dittmann, Helena, and Jane Hardy. *Learn Library of Congress Classification.* Lanham, Md.: Scarecrow Press, 2000.

Extensions and Corrections to the UDC. The Hague: FID, 1951– . Annual.

The Gale Group. [Publisher of *SUPERLCCS*™ . . .: *Library of Congress Classification Schedules Combined with Additions and Changes.*] Available: http://www.galegroup.com/ (accessed 3/12/00).

Herdman, M. M. *Classification: An Introductory Manual.* 3rd ed., revised by Jeanne Osborn. Chicago: American Library Association, 1978.

Koch, Traugott, and Michael Day. *The Role of Classification Schemes in Internet Resource Description and Discovery.* Available: http://www.ukoln.ac.uk/metadata/desire/classification/ (accessed 3/12/00).

Library of Congress Classification: Classes A-Z. Var. eds. Washington, D.C.: Cataloging Distribution Service, Library of Congress, 1976-2000.

Marcella, Rita, and Robert Newton. *A New Manual of Classification.* Aldershot, England; Brookfield, Vt.: Gower, 1994.

Markey, Karen, and Anh Demeyer. *Dewey Decimal Classification Online Project: Evaluation of a Library Schedule and Index Integrated into the Subject Searching Capabilities of an Online Catalog: Final Report to the Council on Library Resources*. Dublin, Ohio: OCLC, 1986.

McIlwaine, I. C. *Guide to the Use of the Universal Decimal Classification*. FID Occasional Paper No. 5, FID Publication No. 703. The Hague: FID on behalf of the UCC Consortium, 1995.

Miksa, Francis L. *The DDC, the Universe of Knowledge, and the Post-Modern Library*. Paper presented at the Fourth International ISKO Conference, July 15–18, 1996, Washington D.C. Albany, N.Y.: OCLC Forest Press, 1998.

Mitchell, Joan S., et al. *Abridged Dewey Decimal Classification and Relative Index*. 13th ed. Albany, N.Y.: Forest Press, 1997.

Mitchell, Joan S., Julianne Beall, Winton E. Matthews, Jr., Gregory R. New. *Dewey Decimal Classification and Relative Index*. 21st ed. Albany, N.Y.: Forest Press, a division of OCLC Online Computer Library Center, 1996. [also available in electronic form].

Mortimer, Mary. *Learn Dewey Decimal Classification (Edition 21)*. Lanham, Md.: Scarecrow, 2000.

National Library of Medicine Classification: A Scheme for the Shelf Arrangement of Books in the Field of Medicine and Its Related Sciences, 5th ed., revised. Bethesda, Md.: NLM, 1994.

OCLC Forest Press. *DC&: Changes and Corrections for DDC21 and Abridged Edition 13*. Available: http://www.oclc.org/fp/dcand/dc_toc.htm (accessed 3/12/00).

OCLC Office of Research. "The Scorpion Project." Available: http://orc.rsch.oclc.org:6109/ (accessed 3/12/00).

Ranganathan, S. R. *Colon Classification: Basic Classification*. 6th ed., completely revised. Bombay; New York: Asia Publishing House, 1960.

Rayward, W. Boyd. "The UDC and FID: A Historical Perspective." *Library Quarterly* 37 (July 1967): 259–278.

Rigby, Malcolm. *Automation and the UDC, 1948–1980*. 2nd ed. The Hague: FID, 1981.

Scott, Mona L. *Conversion Tables: LC–Dewey, Dewey–LC, and LC Subject Headings–LC and Dewey*. 2nd ed. Englewood, Colo.: Libraries Unlimited, 1999.

———. *Dewey Decimal Classification, 21st Edition: A Study Manual and Number Building Guide*. Englewood, Colo.: Libraries Unlimited, 1998.

Subject Cataloging Manual: Classification. 1st ed. Washington, D.C.: Cataloging Distribution Service, Library of Congress, 1992. Update, 1995. [Also available in *Cataloger's Desktop*.]

Thomas, Pat. "Implementing *DDC20*." *DC&* 5, no. 1 (March 1990): 7–8.

Vickery, B. C. *Faceted Classification: A Guide to the Construction and Use of Special Schemes*. London: Aslib, 1960.

Vizine-Goetz, Diane. "Online Classification: Implications for Classifying and Document[-like Object] Retrieval." Available: http://orc.rsch.oclc.org:6109/dvgisko.htm (accessed 3/12/00).

———. "Using Library Classification Schemes for Internet Resources." Available: http://www.oclc.org/oclc/man/colloq/v-g.htm [Table 1: http://www.oclc.org/oclc/man/colloq/v-g.htm#mcdl] (accessed 3/12/00).

Williamson, Nancy. "Classification in the Millennium." *Online & CDROM Review* 21, no. 5 (October 1997): 298–301.

VERBAL SUBJECT ACCESS

American Library Association. *List of Subject Headings for Use in Dictionary Catalogs.* Boston: Library Bureau, 1895.

———. Subject Analysis Committee. (1993) "Definition of Form Data." Available: http://www.pitt.edu/~agtaylor/ala/form-def.htm (accessed 3/12/00).

———. Subject Analysis Committee. Subcommittee on Subject Access to Individual Works of Fiction, Drama, etc. *Guidelines on Subject Access to Individual Works of Fiction, Drama, Etc.* Chicago: American Library Association, 1990 (new edition to be published in 2000).

American National Standards Institute. *American National Standard Guidelines for Thesaurus Structure, Construction, and Use,* ANSI Z39.19-1980. New York: ANSI, 1980.

Austin, Derek. *PRECIS: A Manual of Concept Analysis and Subject Indexing.* 2nd ed. London: British Library, 1984.

———. "Progress in Documentation: The Development of PRECIS: A Theoretical and Technical History." *Journal of Documentation* 30 (March 1974): 47.

Berman, Sanford. *Prejudices and Antipathies: A Tract on the LC Subject Heads Concerning People.* Metuchen, N.J.: Scarecrow, 1971.

———. *Prejudices and Antipathies: A Tract on the LC Subject Heads Concerning People.* Jefferson, N.C.: McFarland, 1993.

British Standards Institution. *British Standard Guide to Establishment and Development of Monolingual Thesauri,* BS 5723 [Rev. ed.] London: BSI, 1987.

Brown, A. G., in collaboration with D. W. Langridge, and J. Mills. *An Introduction to Subject Indexing.* 2nd ed. London: Bingley, 1982. [programmed text]

Chan, Lois Mai. *Library of Congress Subject Headings: Principles and Application.* 3rd ed. Englewood, Colo.: Libraries Unlimited, 1995.

Clack, Doris H. *Black Literature Resources: Analysis and Organization.* New York: Marcel Dekker, 1975.

Coates, E. J. *Subject Catalogues: Heading and Structure.* London: Library Association, 1960.

Dykstra, Mary. "LC Subject Headings Disguised as a Thesaurus." *Library Journal* 113 (March 1, 1988): 42–46.

———. *PRECIS: A Primer.* London: British Library, 1985.

Free-Floating Subdivisions: An Alphabetical Index. 1st ed.– . Washington, D.C.: Library of Congress, 1989– .

Ganendran, Jacki. *Learn LC Subject Access.* Lanham, Md.: Scarecrow, 2000.

Getty Information Institute. *Art & Architecture Thesaurus Browser.* Available: http://shiva.pub.getty.edu/aat_browser (accessed 3/12/00).

Hanson, J. C. M. "The Subject Catalogs of the Library of Congress." *Bulletin of the American Library Association* 3 (September 1909): 385–397.

Haykin, David Judson. *Subject Headings: A Practical Guide.* Washington, D.C.: GPO, 1951.

Hemmasi, Harriette, David Miller, and Mary Charles Lasater; edited by Arlene G. Taylor. "Access to Form Data in Online Catalogs." In "From Catalog to Gateway: Briefings from the CFFC," Paper no. 13. *ALCTS Newsletter Online* 10, no. 4 (July 1999). Available: http://www.ala.org/alcts/alcts_news/v10n4/formdat2.html (accessed 3/12/00).

INSPEC Thesaurus. 1999 [ed.] London: Institution of Electrical Engineers, 1999.

International Organization for Standardization. *Documentation: Guidelines for the Establishment and Development of Monolingual Thesauri.* 2nd ed. ISO 2788. Geneva: ISO, 1986.

Knapp, Sara D. "Creating BRS/TERM, a Vocabulary Database for Searchers." *Database* 7, no. 4 (December 1984): 70–75.

Lancaster, F. W. *Indexing and Abstracting in Theory and Practice.* 2nd ed. Champaign, Ill.: University of Illinois, Graduate School of Library and Information Science, 1998. [Also published: London: Library Association Publishing, 1998.]

———. "Trends in Subject Indexing from 1957 to 2000." In *New Trends in Documentation and Information: Proceedings of the 39th FID Congress, 1978*, 223–233. London: Aslib, 1980.

Library of Congress Subject Headings. "Introduction" in *Cataloger's Desktop/Classification Plus,* latest issue.

Library of Congress Subject Headings. 13th– eds. Washington, D.C.: Office for Subject Cataloging Policy, Library of Congress, 1990– . (Also available in *Classification Plus.* Washington, D.C.: Cataloging Distribution Service, Library of Congress, current issue supersedes all previous issues.)

Library of Congress Subject Headings in Microform. Washington, D.C.: Cataloging Distribution Service, Library of Congress, current issue supersedes all previous issues.

Library of Congress Subject Headings Weekly Lists. Washington, D.C.: Cataloging Policy and Support Office, Library of Congress, January 1984– . 1997, no. 1-date. Available: http://lcweb.loc.gov/catdir/cpso/cpso.html (accessed 3/12/00).

Lighthall, Lynne Isberg, ed. *Sears List of Subject Headings: Canadian Companion*. 4th ed. New York: H. W. Wilson, 1992.

Luhn, Hans Peter. "Keyword in Context Index for Technical Literature (KWIC Index)." *American Documentation* 11 (1960): 288–295.

Mahapatra, M., and S. C. Biswas. "PRECIS: Its Theory and Application—An Extended State-of-the-Art Review from the Beginning up to 1982." *Libri* 33 (December 1983): 316–330.

Markey, Karen. *Subject Searching in Library Catalogs: Before and After the Introduction of Online Catalogs*. Dublin, Ohio: OCLC Online Computer Library Center, 1984, pp. 75–87.

Marshall, Joan K. *On Equal Terms: A Thesaurus for Nonsexist Indexing and Cataloging*. Santa Barbara, Calif.: American Bibliographical Center– Clio Press, 1977.

Miller, Joseph, ed. *Sears List of Subject Headings*. 17th ed. New York: H. W. Wilson, 2000.

National Library of Medicine. "Free MEDLINE: PubMed and Internet Grateful Med." Available: http://www.nlm.nih.gov/databases/freemedl.html (accessed 3/12/00).

———. "UMLS Metathesaurus: Fact Sheet." Available: http://www.nlm.nih.gov/pubs/factsheets/umlsmeta.html (accessed 3/12/00).

———. "Unified Medical Language System (UMLS)." Available: http://www.nlm.nih.gov/research/umls/ (accessed 3/12/00).

Petersen, Toni. "The AAT: A Model for the Restructuring of LCSH." *Journal of Academic Librarianship* 9 (September 1983): 207–210.

"Principles of the Sears List of Subject Headings." In *Sears List of Subject Headings*. 16th ed., edited by Joseph Miller, xv–xxxviii. New York: H. W. Wilson, 1997.

Sears—Lista de Encabezamientos de Materia: Traducción y Adaptación de la 12a. Edición en Inglés, ed. por Barbara M. Westby; trans. por Carmen Rovira. New York: H. W. Wilson, 1984. [Spanish translation now out-of-print.]

Subject Cataloging Manual: Subject Headings. 5th ed. Washington, D.C.: Cataloging Distribution Service, Library of Congress, 1996. Updates, 1997– . [Also available in *Cataloger's Desktop*.]

Subject Headings Used in the Dictionary Catalogues of the Library of Congress, [1st]–3rd eds. Washington, D.C.: Catalog Division, Library of Congress, 1910–1928; *Subject Headings Used in the Dictionary Catalogs of the Library of Congress*, 4th–7th eds. Washington, D.C.: Subject Cataloging Division, Library of Congress, 1943–1966; *Library of Congress Subject Headings*, 8th–12th eds. Washington, D.C.: Subject Cataloging Division, Library of Congress, 1975–1989.

Thesaurus of ERIC Descriptors. 13th ed. Phoenix, Ariz.: Oryx Press, 1995.

Thesaurus of Psychological Index Terms. 8th ed. Washington, D.C.: American Psychological Association, 1997.

Wellisch, Hans H., ed. *The PRECIS Index System: Principles, Applications, and Prospects. Proceedings of the International PRECIS Workshop.* New York: H. W. Wilson, 1977.

AUTHORITY CONTROL

Authority Control in the 21st Century: An Invitational Conference, March 31 – April 1, 1996. Online. Dublin, Ohio: OCLC Online Computer Library Center. Available: http://www.oclc.org/oclc/man/authconf/confhome.htm (accessed 3/12/00).

Barnhart, Linda. "Access Control Records: Prospects and Challenges." In *Authority Control in the 21st Century, Invitational Conference, March 31–April 1, 1996.* Available: http://www.oclc.org/oclc/man/authconf/barnhart.htm (accessed 3/12/00).

Burger, Robert H. *Authority Work: The Creation, Use, Maintenance, and Evaluation of Authority Records and Files.* Littleton, Colo.: Libraries Unlimited, 1985.

Clack, Doris Hargrett. *Authority Control: Principles, Applications, and Instructions.* Chicago: American Library Association, 1990.

Everett, David, and David M. Pilachowski. "What's in a Name? Looking for People Online—Humanities." *DATABASE* 9 (October 1986): 26–34.

The Future Is Now: Reconciling Change and Continuity in Authority Control: Proceedings of the OCLC Symposium, ALA Annual Conference, June 23, 1995. Dublin, Ohio: OCLC Online Computer Library Center, 1995.

"NACO: Program for Cooperative Cataloging" Available: http://lcweb.loc.gov/catdir/pcc/naco.html (accessed 3/12/00).

Pasterczyk, Catherine E. "Russian Transliteration Variations for Searchers." *DATABASE* 8 (February 1985): 68–75.

Pilachowski, David M., and David Everett. "What's in a Name? Looking for People Online—Social Sciences." *DATABASE* 8 (August 1985): 47-65.

———. "What's in a Name? Looking for People Online—Current Events." *DATABASE* 9 (April 1986): 43–50.

Piternick, Anne B. "What's in a Name? Use of Names and Titles in Subject Searching." *DATABASE* 8 (December 1985): 22–28.

"SACO Program Description: Program for Cooperative Cataloging." Available: http://lcweb.loc.gov/catdir/pcc/sacopara.html (accessed 3/12/00).

Snow, Bonnie. "Caduceus: People in Medicine: Searching Names Online." *ONLINE* 10 (September 1986): 122–127.

Talmacs, Kerrie. "Authority Control." In *Technical Services Today and Tomorrow.* 2nd ed., edited by Michael Gorman, 129–139. Englewood, Colo.: Libraries Unlimited, 1998.

Taylor, Arlene G. "Authority Control and System Design." In *Policy and Practice in the Bibliographic Control of Nonbook Media*, edited by Sheila S. Intner and Richard P. Smiraglia, 64–81. Chicago: American Library Association, 1987.

———. "Authority Control: Where It's Been and Where It's Going," and other papers from the conference: "Authority Control: Why It Matters," sponsored by NELINET, November 1, 1999, Worcester, MA. Available: http://www.nelinet.net/conf/cts/cts99/cts99.htm (accessed 3/12/00).

———. "Authority Files in Online Catalogs: An Investigation of Their Value." *Cataloging & Classification Quarterly* 4 (Spring 1984): 1–17.

———. "Research and Theoretical Considerations in Authority Control." *Cataloging & Classification Quarterly* 9, no. 3 (1989): 29–56.

Tillett, Barbara B. "International Shared Resource Records for Controlled Access." *ALCTS Newsletter Online* 10, no. 1 (December 1998). Available: http://www.ala.org/alcts/alcts_news/v10n1/gateway.html (accessed 3/12/00).

ARRANGEMENT (Including Filing)

ALA Filing Rules. Chicago: American Library Association, 1980.

ALA Rules for Filing Catalog Cards. 2nd ed. Chicago: American Library Association, 1968.

Buckland, Michael K., Barbara A. Norgard, and Christian Plaunt. "Filing, Filtering and the First Few Found." *Information Technology and Libraries* 12, no. 3 (September 1993): 311–319.

Comaromi, John P. *Book Numbers: A Historical Study and Practical Guide to Their Use.* Littleton, Colo.: Libraries Unlimited, 1981.

Cutter, Charles A. *Cutter-Sanborn Three-Figure Author Table*, Swanson-Swift revision, 1969. Distributed by Libraries Unlimited, Inc., Englewood, Colo.

———. *Two-Figure Author Table*, Swanson-Swift revision, 1969. Distributed by Libraries Unlimited, Inc., Englewood, Colo.

———. *Three-Figure Author Table*, Swanson-Swift revision, 1969. Distributed by Libraries Unlimited, Inc., Englewood, Colo.

Lehnus, Donald J. *Book Numbers: History, Principles, and Application.* Chicago: American Library Association, 1980.

Library of Congress Filing Rules. Washington, D.C.: Library of Congress, 1980.

Subject Cataloging Manual: Shelflisting. 2nd ed. Washington, D.C.: Cataloging Distribution Service, Library of Congress, 1995. [Also available on *Cataloger's Desktop.*]

Taylor Arlene G. "Arrangement and Display." Chapter 9 in *The Organization of Information.* Englewood, Colo.: Libraries Unlimited, 1999.

ADMINISTRATIVE ISSUES

A-G Canada, Ltd. "A-G Canada, Ltd." Available: http://www.ag-canada.com/ (accessed 3/12/00).

Beheshti, Jamshid. "The Evolving OPAC." *Cataloging & Classification Quarterly* 24, nos. 1–2, (1997): 165.

Benaud, Claire Lise, and Sever Bordeianu. *Outsourcing Library Operations in Academic Libraries: An Overview of Issues and Outcomes.* Englewood, Colo.: Libraries Unlimited, 1998.

Borgman, Christine L. "From Acting Locally to Thinking Globally: A Brief History of Library Automation." *Library Quarterly* 67, no. 3 (July 1997): 215–249.

———. "Why Are Online Catalogs *Still* Hard to Use?" *Journal of the American Society for Information Science* 47, no. 7 (July 1996): 493–503.

Brisson, Roger, and Janet McCue. "Retooling Technical Services." In *Encyclopedia of Library and Information Science*, vol. 58, suppl. 21, 281–301. New York: Marcel Dekker, 1996.

Carter, Ruth C., and Scott Bruntjen. *Data Conversion.* White Plains, N.Y.: Knowledge Industry Publications, 1983.

Colver, Marylou, and Karen Wilson, eds. *Outsourcing Technical Services Operations.* Chicago: American Library Association, 1997.

Crawford, Walt. "The Card Catalog and Other Digital Controversies: What's Obsolete and What's Not in the Age of Information." *American Libraries* 30, no. 1 (January 1999): 52–58.

———. *The Online Catalog Book: Essays and Examples.* New York: G. K. Hall, 1992.

Crowley, Julie. (June 1999), "Cataloging Tools on the Internet." AUTOCAT [Online]. Available E-mail: listserv@listserv.acsu.buffalo.edu/getcatalog.tools (accessed 8/23/99).

Dunkle, Clare B. "Outsourcing the Catalog Department: A Meditation Inspired by the Business and Library Literature." *Journal of Academic Librarianship* 22, no. 1 (January 1996).

Evans, G. Edward, and Sandra M. Heft. *Introduction to Technical Services for Library Technicians.* 6th ed. Englewood, Colo.: Libraries Unlimited, 1994.

Foster, Donald L. *Managing the Catalog Department.* 3rd ed. Metuchen, N.J.: Scarecrow, 1987.

The Future Is Now: The Changing Face of Technical Services: Proceedings of the OCLC Symposium, ALA Midwinter Conference, February 4, 1994. Dublin, Ohio: OCLC Online Computer Library Center, 1994.

Gassie, L. W. "What Do We Expect from the Next Generation of Library Systems?" *LLA Bulletin* 60, no. 2 (Fall 1997): 97.

Hirshon, Arnold, and Barbara Winters. *Outsourcing Library Technical Services: A How-to-Do-It Manual for Librarians.* New York: Neal-Schuman, 1996.

Kaplan, Michael, ed. *Planning and Implementing Technical Services Workstations.* Chicago: American Library Association, 1997.

Long, Chris Evin. "The Internet's Value to Catalogers: Results of a Survey." *Cataloging & Classification Quarterly* 23, nos. 3–4 (1997): 65–74.

Machovec, George. "ILS System Selection: Second Time Around." *Colorado Libraries* 23, no. 4 (Winter 1997): 6.

Matthews, Joseph R., Gary S. Lawrence, and Douglas K. Ferguson, eds. Sponsored by the Council on Library Resources. *Using Online Catalogs: A Nationwide Survey.* New York: Neal-Schuman, 1983.

Meghabghab, Dania Bilal. *Automating Media Centers and Small Libraries: A Microcomputer-Based Approach.* Englewood, Colo.: Libraries Unlimited, 1997.

Morris, Dilys E., and Gregory Wool. "Cataloging: Librarianship's Best Bargain." *Library Journal* 124, no. 11 (June 15, 1999): 44–46.

OCLC. "Cooperative Online Resource Catalog." Available: http://www.oclc.org/oclc/corc/index.htm (accessed 3/12/00).

———. "OCLC Online Computer Library Center, Inc." Available: http://www.oclc.org/oclc/menu/home1.htm (accessed 3/12/00).

Oddy, Pat. "Bibliographic Standards and the Globalization of Bibliographic Control." In *Technical Services Today and Tomorrow.* 2nd ed., edited by Michael Gorman, 67–78. Englewood, Colo.: Libraries Unlimited, 1998.

Potter, William Gray. "The Online Catalogue in Academic Libraries." In *Technical Services Today and Tomorrow.* 2nd ed., edited by Michael Gorman, 141–155. Englewood, Colo., Libraries Unlimited, 1998.

"Program for Cooperative Cataloging [PCC]." Available: http://lcweb.loc.gov/catdir/pcc/ (accessed 3/12/00).

RLG. "Research Libraries Group." Available: http://www.rlg.org/ (accessed 3/12/00).

Rohrbach, Peter T. *Find: Automation at the Library of Congress: The First Twenty-five Years and Beyond.* Washington, D.C.: Library of Congress, 1985.

Rushoff, Carlen. "Cataloging's Prospects: Responding to Austerity with Innovation." *Journal of Academic Librarianship* 21, no. 1 (January 1995): 51–57.

Saffady, William. "The Bibliographic Utilities in 1993: A Survey of Cataloging Support and Other Services." *Library Technology Reports* 29, no. 1 (January/February 1993): 1–144.

———. "Commercial Sources of Cataloging Data: Bibliographic Utilities and Other Vendors." *Library Technology Reports* 34, no. 3 (May/June 1998): 281–432.

Sellberg, Roxanne. "Cataloguing Management: Managing the Bibliographic Control Process." In *Technical Services Today and Tomorrow*. 2nd ed., edited by Michael Gorman, 111–127. Englewood, Colo.: Libraries Unlimited, 1998.

Taylor, Arlene G., with the assistance of Rosanna M. O'Neil. *Cataloging with Copy: A Decision-Maker's Handbook*. 2nd ed. Englewood, Colo.: Libraries Unlimited, 1988. Chapters 1, 9.

Wilson, Karen. "Outsourcing Issues: Cons." American Library Association Web page, July 1997. Available: http://www.ala.org/alcts/now/outsourcingcons.html (accessed 3/12/00) and "Outsourcing Issues: Pros." American Library Association Web page, July 1997. Available: http://www.ala.org/alcts/now/outsourcingpros.html (accessed 3/12/00).

Yee, Martha. "Guidelines for OPAC Displays." In "From Catalog to Gateway: Briefings from the CFFC," Paper no. 14. *ALCTS Newsletter Online* 10, no. 6 (December 1999). Available: http://www.ala.org/alcts/alcts_news/v10n4/formdat2.html (accessed 3/12/00).

———. "Guidelines for OPAC Displays." Prepared for the 65th IFLA Council and General Conference, Bangkok, Thailand, August 20–August 28, 1999. Available: http://www.ifla.org/IV/ifla65/papers/098-131e.htm (accessed 3/12/00).

———. "Guidelines for OPAC Displays." Prepared for the IFLA Task on Guidelines for OPAC Displays, November 24, 1998. [PDF file]. Available: http://www.ifla.org/VII/s13/guide/opac.htm (accessed 3/12/00).

Yee, Martha M., and Sara Shatford Layne. *Improving Online Public Access Catalogs*. Chicago: American Library Association, 1998.

CURRENT INFORMATION AND UPDATING

Cataloger's Desktop. Washington, D.C.: Cataloging Distribution Service, Library of Congress, current issue supersedes all previous issues.

Cataloging & Classification Quarterly. Binghamton, N.Y.: Haworth Press, 1979– . Quarterly.

Cataloging Service Bulletin, no. 1– . Washington, D.C.: Processing Services, Library of Congress, 1978– .

Classification Plus. Washington, D.C.: Cataloging Distribution Service, Library of Congress, current issue supersedes all previous issues.

Hennepin County Library, Cataloging Section. *Cataloging Bulletin*, May 1973– .

Library of Congress, Cataloging Distribution Service. "Bibliographic Products & Services." Available: http://lcweb.loc.gov/cds/ (accessed 3/12/00).

The Library of Congress Cataloging Policy & Support Office. Available: http://lcweb.loc.gov/catdir/cpso/ (accessed 3/12/00).

Library Resources & Technical Services. Chicago: American Library Association, 1957– . Quarterly.

OCLC. "Documentation." Available: http://www.oclc.org/oclc/menu/doc.htm (accessed 3/12/00).

OCLC. "Technical Bulletins." Available: http://www.oclc.org/oclc/menu/tb.htm (accessed 3/12/00).

Author/Title/Subject Index